The Neuroscience of Attention

To our families

THE NEUROSCIENCE OF ATTENTION

Attentional Control and Selection

EDITED BY GEORGE R. MANGUN

OXFORD

UNIVERSITY PRESS

OXFORD
UNIVERSITY PRESS

Oxford University Press, Inc., publishes works that further
Oxford University's objective of excellence
in research, scholarship, and education.

Oxford New York
Auckland   Cape Town   Dar es Salaam   Hong Kong   Karachi
Kuala Lumpur   Madrid   Melbourne   Mexico City   Nairobi
New Delhi   Shanghai   Taipei   Toronto

With offices in
Argentina   Austria   Brazil   Chile   Czech Republic   France   Greece
Guatemala   Hungary   Italy   Japan   Poland   Portugal   Singapore
South Korea   Switzerland   Thailand   Turkey   Ukraine   Vietnam

Published by Oxford University Press, Inc.
198 Madison Avenue, New York, New York 10016
www.oup.com

Oxford is a registered trademark of Oxford University Press

Library of Congress Cataloging-in-Publication Data

The neuroscience of attention : attentional control and selection /
edited by George R. Mangun.
p. cm.
Includes bibliographical references and index.
ISBN 978-0-19-533436-4
1. Attention. 2. Selectivity (Psychology) 3. Cognitive neuroscience.
4. Visual perception. I. Mangun, G. R. (George Ronald), 1956-
BF321.A832 2011
153.7'33—dc23   2011024886

9 8 7 6 5 4 3 2 1

Printed in China
on acid-free paper

Acknowledgments

I am grateful to the following for their support, without which this first volume could not have been accomplished: My wife Tamara Swaab and our boys Alexander and Nicholas for their loving encouragement of this project; Joan Bossert, Catharine Carlin, Tracy O'Hara, Susan Lee and their colleagues at Oxford University Press for their enthusiastic backing and wise guidance; My students, staff and scientific colleagues who have contributed directly and indirectly to the research contained herein; and the National Institute of Mental Health, National Science Foundation, Fetzer Institute and the University of California, Davis, for their support.

Preface

Selective attention is an essential cognitive ability that permits us to effectively process and act upon relevant information while ignoring distracting events. The human capacity to focus attention is at the core of mental functioning. Elucidating the neural bases of human selective attention remains a key challenge for neuroscience and represents an essential aim in translational efforts to ameliorate attentional deficits in a wide variety of neurological and psychiatric disorders including autism, attention deficit disorder, dementia, Alzheimer's disease, spatial neglect and schizophrenia.

This volume "Attentional Control and Selection" is the first in the series "The Neuroscience of Attention". As the title reflects, the focus is on the basic neuroscience of attentional control and the influence of this control on sensory and motor processes. The work included herein was selected to cover a range of topics, but is not intended to be an encyclopedic review of attention research. Rather, the aim of this volume is to provide the reader with a selection of the models, mechanisms and findings in the neuroscience of attentional control and selection.

Chapters 1 through 4 focus on attentional selection, primarily using evidence from studies in vision. Chapter 1 begins with an introduction to models of attention and findings that have impacted theories of attention, and then goes on to review and provide new information about voluntary attention to locations, features and objects. Chapters 2 and 3 describe involuntary (reflexive) attention mechanisms (Chapter 2) and subcortical mechanisms of attentional selection (Chapter 3). Chapter 4 ties the discussion on attentional selection together by describing computational challenges to attentional selection and describing a model of attention.

Attentional control is the focus of Chapters 5 through 8. In these chapters, the networks for top-down control are described. Chapter 5 describes the dorsal and ventral cortical attention networks involved in control and orienting. Chapter 6 looks at cortical and subcortical networks for attentional control, providing information on midbrain systems. The role of the frontal eye fields in top-down attentional control is discussed in Chapter 7, and Chapter 8 provides a cogent analysis of parietal cortex in attentional control.

Higher aspects of attention are considered in Chapters 9 through 12. Chapter 9 integrates perceptual attention and action. Chapter 10 investigates the role of attention mechanisms in visual short-term memory, and Chapter 11 broadens the discussion to capture the role of top-done control systems in modulating ongoing behavior.

Lastly, Chapter 12 brings emotion into the equation, describing how brain affective systems modulate attention.

What emerges from these careful reviews and analyses is a description of brain attention systems for control and selection that involve widespread networks, networks which are nonetheless highly circumscribed to enable organisms to function in the face of a flurry of incoming signals and internal goals, all vying for control over behavior.

George R. Mangun
Davis, California
2011

Contents

Contributors

Katherine M. Armstrong
Department of Neurobiology
Stanford University School of Medicine
Stanford, CA, USA

James W. Bisley
Department of Neurobiology
Jules Stein Eye Institute
David Geffen School of Medicine
and
Department of Psychology
The Brain Research Institute
University of California, Los Angeles,
Los Angeles, CA, USA

Carsten N. Boehler
Otto-von-Guericke University Magdeburg
Leibniz Institute for Neurobiology
Magdeburg, Germany

Cameron S. Carter
Center for Neuroscience
Imaging Research Center
Department of Psychiatry and Behavioral Sciences
University of California, Davis
Davis, CA, USA

Mindy H. Chang
Department of Neurobiology
Stanford University School of Medicine
Stanford, CA, USA

Maurizio Corbetta
Washington University School of Medicine
Saint Louis, MO, USA
Institute of Technology and Advanced
    Bioimaging (ITAB)
Universita' Gabriele D'Annunzio
Chieti, Italy

Harlan M. Fichtenholtz
Department of Psychiatry
Yale University School of Medicine
New Haven, CT, USA

Angela Gee
Mahoney Center for Brain and Behavior
Center for Neurobiology and Kavli Institute
Columbia University College of Physicians
    and Surgeons
New York State Psychiatric Institute
New York, NY, USA
and
Department of Biology
LaGuardia Community College
Queens, NY, USA

Michael E. Goldberg
Departments of Neuroscience, Neurology,
    Psychiatry, and Opthalmology
The Mahoney-Keck Center for Brain and
    Behavior Research
and
The Kavli Institute for Neuroscience
Columbia University College of Physicians and
    Surgeons
New York State Psychiatric Institute
New York, NY, USA

Jacqueline Gottlieb
Department of Neuroscience
Mahoney-Keck Center for Brain and Behavior
    Research
Columbia University College of Physicians and
    Surgeons
New York State Psychiatric Institute
New York, NY, USA

Jens-Max Hopf
Otto-von-Guericke University Magdeburg
Leibniz Institute for Neurobiology
Magdeburg, Germany

Joseph B. Hopfinger
Department of Psychology
Biomedical Research Imaging Center
University of North Carolina at Chapel Hill
Chapel Hill, NC, USA

Hans-Jochen Heinze
Otto-von-Guericke University Magdeburg
Leibniz Institute for Neurobiology
Magdeburg, Germany

Anna Ipata
Mahoney Center for Brain and Behavior
Center for Neurobiology and Kavli Institute
Department of Neuroscience
Columbia University College of Physicians and
    Surgeons
New York State Psychiatric Institute
New York, NY, USA

Sabine Kastner
Princeton Neuroscience Institute
Department of Psychology
Princeton University, NJ, USA

Eric I. Knudsen
Department of Neurobiology
Stanford University
Stanford, CA, USA

Marie K. Krug
Imaging Research Center
Department of Psychiatry and Behavioral
    Sciences
University of California, Davis
Davis, CA, USA

Kevin S. LaBar
Center for Cognitive Neuroscience
Duke University
Durham, NC, USA

George R. Mangun
Center for Mind and Brain
Departments of Psychology and Neurology
University of California, Davis
Davis, CA, USA

Tirin Moore
Department of Neurobiology
Howard Hughes Medical Institute
Stanford University School of Medicine
Stanford, CA, USA

Anna C. Nobre
Department of Experimental Psychology
Oxford University
Oxford, UK

Emily L. Parks
Department of Psychology
University of North Carolina at Chapel Hill
Chapel Hill, NC, USA

Albert L. Rothenstein
Dept. of Computer Science & Engineering, and
    Centre for Vision Research
York University
Toronto, Canada

Yuri B. Saalmann
Princeton Neuroscience Institute
Department of Psychology
Princeton University
Princeton, NJ, USA

Robert J. Schafer
Department of Neurobiology
Stanford University School of Medicine
Stanford, CA, USA

Jeffrey D. Schall
Center for Integrative and Cognitive
    Neuroscience
Vanderbilt Vision Research Center
Department of Psychology
Vanderbilt University
Nashville, TN, USA

Keith A. Schneider
Department of Psychological Sciences
University of Missouri–Columbia
Columbia, MO, USA

Mircea A. Schoenfeld
Otto-von-Guericke University Magdeburg
Leibniz Institute for Neurobiology
Magdeburg, Germany

Carlo Sestieri
Washington University School of Medicine
Saint Louis, MO, USA
Institute of Technology and Advanced
    Bioimaging (ITAB)
Universita' Gabriele D'Annunzio
Chieti, Italy

Gordon L. Shulman
Washington University School of Medicine
Saint Louis, MO, USA

Evgueni Simine
Dept. of Computer Science & Engineering, and
    Centre for Vision Research
York University
Toronto, Canada

Mark Stokes
Department of Experimental Psychology
Oxford University
Oxford, UK

John K. Tsotsos
Dept. of Computer Science & Engineering, and
    Centre for Vision Research
York University
Toronto, Canada

Geoffrey F. Woodman
Center for Integrative and Cognitive
    Neuroscience
Vanderbilt Vision Research Center
Department of Psychology
Vanderbilt University
Nashville, TN, USA

Andrei Zaharescu
Dept. of Computer Science & Engineering, and
    Centre for Vision Research
York University
Toronto, Canada

The Neuroscience of Attention

1

Attentional Selection for Locations, Features, and Objects in Vision

JENS-MAX HOPF, CARSTEN N. BOEHLER, MIRCEA A. SCHOENFELD,
GEORGE R. MANGUN, AND HANS-JOCHEN HEINZE

VISUAL SELECTIVE attention is a powerful cognitive ability that aids us in our perceptions and action in the world around us (e.g., Posner, 1980; Treisman, 1988). Although behavioral characterizations of attentional processes have provided a solid understanding of the phenomena of selective attention, enabling the development of a theoretical framework for understanding attention, the neural mechanisms of selective attention remain incompletely understood. Nonetheless, we now understand that attention mechanisms involve the interactions of discrete brain attention systems that have been shaped during evolution to provide the organism with a highly refined ability to control information processing and action. When these brain systems are impaired by developmental disorders, disease, or damage, the results can be profound for individuals and society. Consequently, elucidating the neural bases of human selective attention remains a key challenge for neuroscience and represents an essential aim

in translational efforts to ameliorate attentional deficits in a wide variety of neurological and psychiatric disorders, including autism, attention deficit disorder, dementia, spatial neglect, and schizophrenia.

Far from being a unitary concept, visual attention has been proposed to operate on different visual representations, the most prominent being location-, feature-, and object-based representations (see Chapter 4, this volume). In this lead chapter, we describe neurophysiological research in humans that provides insights into the neural mechanisms mediating those different modes of attentional function. The first sections of this chapter will address mechanisms of location selection, with a particular focus on the neural operations that determine the spatial profile of the focus of attention. We discuss data indicating that the latter is not fixed, but varies depending on top-down (voluntary or goal-directed) requirements on target selection of a given task. The evidence reviewed here is pertinent to resolving a long-standing debate about the nature of what has been metaphorically referred to as the *spotlight* of attention. We will then review signatures of feature-based selection and focus on mechanisms and conditions underlying its operation in a spatially global way. Finally, we will consider findings that have documented the operation of object-based attention and discuss mechanisms that grant priority over feature selection. In general, we will argue that attentional selection based on locations, features, or objects is not subserved by a single neural process, but that different neural mechanisms are coordinated to operate on a tight spatiotemporal scale, to enable the organism to perceive and act in a complex and rapidly changing environment.

LOCATION SELECTION IN CUED ORIENTING

Seminal work by Posner and others (Bashinski & Bacharach, 1980; Posner, 1980; Downing, 1988; Hawkins et al., 1990; Handy et al., 1996) revealed that attention can be oriented to locations in space in a covert manner. Evidence for this was the observation that perceptual processing is significantly facilitated at attended, as compared to unattended locations. A central goal of research into visual attention has been to pinpoint the neural mechanisms responsible for the performance benefits and costs brought about by focal attention. The underlying neural mechanisms of selective attention, as described in this volume, have been investigated using electrophysiological recordings in humans and animals, and using electromagnetic recording and functional brain imaging in humans, as well as through consideration of the results of experimentally induced lesion in animal models, and of neurological disease and damage in human patients.

In humans, in the late 1960s and 1970s, signal averaging of the scalp-recorded electroencephalogram (EEG) to extract stimulus evoked event-related potentials (ERPs) provided compelling evidence regarding the neural mechanisms of selective attention. For example, ERP research provided the first evidence for an early sensory locus of selective attention in carefully controlled experiments by showing that attended stimuli elicit larger early sensory ERPs compared to the same stimuli when ignored (i.e., while attending elsewhere); this is true for auditory (Picton et al., 1971), somatosensory (Desmedt & Robertson, 1971) and visual processing (Van Voorhis & Hillyard, 1977; Eason, 1981; see Mangun, 1995; Hillyard & Anllo-Vento, 1998 for comprehensive reviews). Combining Posner's influential location cuing paradigm with recordings of ERPs (Figure 1.1A) showed that directing attention to a particular location prior to the actual stimulus presentation was associated with amplitude modulations of early stimulus evoked responses generated in visual cortex. The positive (P1 component) and negative (N1 component) deflections in the sensory evoked response at post-stimulus latencies between 70 and 200 ms are greater for cued-location targets (attended) than for uncued-location targets (Figure 1.1B) (Mangun & Hillyard, 1991; see also Harter, Anllo-Vento, & Wood, 1989).

Such modulations in the visual responses appeared without significant changes in latency or scalp topography. Moreover, amplitude enhancements (or reductions) of the P1/N1 due to attention are typically found to be graded, such that the increase or reduction of the amount of attentional resources devoted to a location is mirrored by a gradual enhancement or reduction of amplitudes, respectively (Van Voorhis & Hillyard, 1977; Mangun & Hillyard, 1990). Combined ERP or magnetoencephalogram (MEG) and functional brain imaging work (positron emission tomography [PET] or functional magnetic resonance imaging [fMRI]) have helped to confirm that the short latency effects of attention reflected in electromagnetic recordings reflect processing at least as early as the first stages of extrastriate cortex (Heinze et al., 1994b; Mangun et al., 1998; Hopf et al., 2002b; Noesselt et al., 2002). Such effects are organized retinotopically, and are consistent with attention effects focused at the attended location in a visual scene (Woldorff et al., 1997; Martinez et al., 1999; see also Tootell et al., 1998). Event-related potential effects of spatial attention were also observed at earlier stages of visual cortical processing, including the primary visual cortex (Martinez et al., 1999; Noesselt et al., 2002; Di Russo et al., 2003; see also Proverbio,

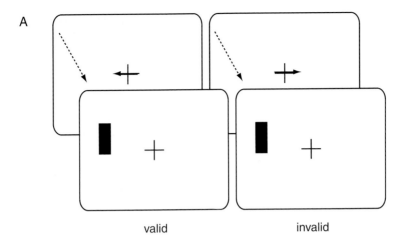

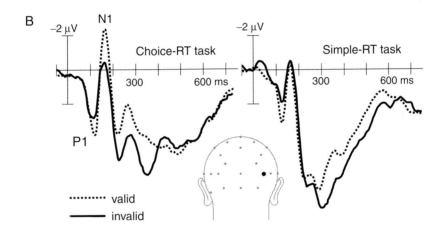

FIGURE 1.1 (**A**) Typical version of Posner's influential paradigm designed to investigate covert orienting of spatial attention upon a symbolic location cue. While fixating the center cross, subjects are cued (*arrow*) to covertly attend to one side of the visual field (VF) and expect an upcoming target (*the bar*) that needs to be detected or discriminated. The target may appear at the cued side (valid trial) or at the uncued side (invalid trial). A comparison of validly and invalidly cued targets at the same side permits researchers to identify the specific effects of attention onto target processing. (**B**) Enhancements of early sensory components of the event-related potential (ERP) response due to spatial attention. Shown are waveforms from an experiment reported in Mangun and Hillyard (1991), who used the experimental setup as illustrated in (**A**). Subjects were asked to either detect the occurrence of the target bar (Simple-RT task) or to discriminate its length (Choice-RT task). Validly cued targets were associated with a substantial amplitude enhancement of the first positive deflection (P1). This effect was seen under both experimental conditions, the subsequent enhancement of the N1 component appeared only in the Choice-RT task. Shown waveforms represent responses to left VF targets recorded from a right hemisphere occipital electrode, as illustrated by the insert.

Del Zotto, & Zani, 2007). Those effects were typically seen to arise later (around 150–250 ms) than the P1/N1 modulations, consistent with the possibility that attention-related activity in primary visual cortex reflects feedback-driven modulations that originate in higher-level extrastriate and frontal areas. Several observations from cell recordings in the macaque visual cortex appear to support this conclusion (Roelfsema et al., 1998; Mehta et al., 2000; Roelfsema et al., 2007). Nevertheless, recent research suggested that spatial attention may also modulate the C1 component of the ERP response (Kelly et al., 2008; Poghosyan & Ioannides, 2008; see also Karns & Knight, 2009). The C1 represents an early sensory component of the ERP that appears prior to the P1/N1 (around 75 ms), and at least initial portions of the C1 are known to index the initial feedforward sweep of processing in V1 (e.g., Foxe & Simpson, 2002). Such early onset in V1 would align with the observation that spatial attention modulates activity in lateral geniculate nucleus (LGN) (O'Connor et al., 2002) and that enhancements of cell firing due to attention in macaque LGN were found to arise as early as 26 ms after stimulus onset (McAlonan et al., 2008). In fact, attention effects in V1 are suggested to trace back to modulations in LGN, with the latter likely arising from subcortical modulatory influences (e.g., from the thalamic reticular nucleus) (McAlonan et al., 2008). This would account for why ERP effects of spatial attention appear already during the initial feedforward sweep of processing in V1; that is, before top-down modulatory influences from extrastriate areas could have an effect. So far, evidence for attention effects on the C1 component is limited and more research is needed to clarify the underlying operations.

Evidence for an early sensory locus of selection was also provided with steady-state visual evoked potentials (SSVEP) (Morgan et al., 1996; Hillyard et al., 1997; Muller et al., 1997; Muller et al., 1998b; Muller et al., 1998a). For example, Morgan et al. (1996) presented bilateral streams of alphanumeric characters, each superimposed onto a square background flickering with different frequencies in the left (12 Hz) and right (8.6 Hz) visual field (VF). Subjects were cued to attend to the stream in one VF (and ignore the one in the other VF) and detect occasional occurrences of a target item. They observed that the frequency-tagged SSVEP amplitude of the task-irrelevant flicker was enhanced when it was colocated with the task-relevant stream. Analogous location-selective SSVEP enhancements were observed with different versions of this paradigm (Hillyard et al., 1997; Muller et al., 1997; Muller et al., 1998b; Muller et al., 1998a). Source localization analyses of SSVEP enhancements revealed current sources in ventral-lateral extrastriate cortex consistent with the cortical locus of P1/N1 modulations

in the conventional ERP response. The time course and cortical localization of P1/N1 amplitude modulations, as well as the SSVEP modulations, provided evidence for the idea that spatial attention operates by controlling the gain of sensory processing in extrastriate cortex areas (Eimer, 1993; Hillyard et al., 1998). This notion paralleled conclusions independently drawn from single unit recordings in the monkey (Moran & Desimone, 1985; Luck et al., 1997a; McAdams & Maunsell, 2000; Lee et al., 2007).

Although P1 and N1 amplitude variations both index attention-driven gain modulations in extrastriate visual cortex (Hillyard et al., 1998), they do reflect different aspects of spatial selection (Mangun, 1995; Mangun & Buck, 1998). P1 modulations turned out to be more closely tied to the actual selection of information from the target location, whereas modulations of the N1 component were rather found to relate to the discrimination of stimulus properties within the focus of attention (see below). P1 amplitude changes were found to index the priority or efficiency of location selection during attentional focusing, regardless of whether the stimuli at the attended location were task relevant or irrelevant (Heinze et al., 1990; Handy et al., 2001b). P1 amplitude effects were also observed with "reflexive" or "involuntary" orienting (see Chapter 2, this volume). That is, P1 amplitude increases were observed for stimuli appearing at the location of a spatially nonpredictive exogenous cue, suggesting that voluntary and reflexive orienting involve at least partially similar operations of spatial selection. However, the typical enhancement of the P1 was only found for short cue-target stimulus onset asynchronies (SOAs; <100 ms); longer SOAs produced an attenuated P1 response consistent with the reduced priority of the cued location. Notably, the latter turns out to be closely paralleled by analogous decrements of behavioral performance (slower response times), commonly known as *inhibition of return* (IOR) (Hopfinger & Mangun, 1998; McDonald et al., 1999; Hopfinger & Mangun, 2001).

Finally, that the P1 amplitude reflects the relative priority of selected locations was also suggested by experimental protocols other than location cuing (Luck et al., 1993; Luck & Hillyard, 1995).

Luck and Hillyard (1995) investigated location selection in visual search by presenting irrelevant probe stimuli at target or distractor locations shortly after search frame onset (250 ms delay). They found that on target-present trials, the P1 amplitude to a probe presented at a distractor location (in the VF opposite to a target) was reduced relative to the same probe presented on target-absent trials; that is, when attention was not consistently focused onto a particular location. This P1 reduction was taken to index the suppression of input from distractor locations during consistent focusing. An analogous reduction of the P1 response was observed for an irrelevant probe stimulus presented at and shortly after an invalidly cued target (Luck et al., 1994). Likewise, raising the priority of selecting a particular location by increasing perceptual load of discrimination led to a reduction of the P1 amplitude elicited by stimuli presented at other locations (Handy et al., 2001a). Hence, different lines of experimental observations indicate that the P1 amplitude preferentially indexes a priority bias for location selection.

As already mentioned, modulations of the N1 component could be functionally dissociated from P1 effects (Hillyard et al., 1985; Mangun & Hillyard, 1991; Luck et al., 1993; Luck et al., 1994). With trial-by-trial cuing, Mangun and Hillyard (1991) observed that a simple detection of a target bar produced the typical P1 enhancement when cued validly but without an enhancement of the N1 component (Figure 1.1B, *right*). In contrast, when subjects were asked to discriminate the length of the target bar (choice reaction time task), both the P1 and N1 showed enhancements for validly versus invalidly cued locations (Figure 1.1B, *left*). Moreover, Luck et al. (1994) reported reductions of the P1 response to passive probe stimuli at unattended locations; modulations of the N1 amplitude, however, were only seen for stimuli presented at the attended location (Luck et al., 1994). It was concluded that modulations of the N1 component do not reflect the selection of relevant locations per se, but rather the discrimination of attributes of the target within the spatial focus of attention. Subsequent research has deepened this notion by revealing that modulations of the N1 component reflect

a signature of a general purpose discriminatory process (Vogel & Luck, 2000) that operates in ventral extrastriate cortex (Hopf et al., 2002b).

LOCATION SELECTION IN VISUAL SEARCH

Location selection in visual search deserves separate consideration, as it is generally different from location selection in spatial cuing experiments. In contrast to precuing experiments, cues about the spatial location of the target are not available before target presentation. Typical search tasks require the decoding of some object attribute(s) to guide focusing prior to target identification. Hence, electrophysiological signatures of location selection are expected to appear contingent on signatures of attribute selection—a prediction recently confirmed with electromagnetic recordings (Hopf et al., 2004). Furthermore, location selection in visual search involves multiple focusing steps (serial search) in many situations, in particular when attribute-based selection provides insufficient information about the target's location (Treisman, 1991; Wolfe, 1994). One may therefore expect that ERP correlates of location selection appear repeatedly during focusing, a prediction that has also been confirmed (see below).

The earliest electromagnetic effects of location selection in visual search have been observed roughly 100 ms later than the earliest effects of location selection in cuing experiments. Luck and coworkers were the first to describe respective modulations in the ERP response (Luck & Hillyard, 1994a,b, 1995; Luck et al., 1997b). In a typical version of their experiments, the ERP was recorded while subjects searched for a lateralized target item (appearing either in the left or right VF) among distractors. They observed that the selection of a target in one VF was associated with an enhanced negativity over the posterior scalp contralateral to the VF containing the target. This modulation, referred to as N2pc (N2 posterior contralateral) was found to appear in the N2 time range around 180–400 ms after search frame onset. Subsequent research revealed that the N2pc reflects an attentional selection mechanism that is not specific to the type of feature searched for (Girelli & Luck, 1997), and that it arises under a variety of search conditions (Eimer, 1996; Hopf et al., 2002a; Woodman & Luck, 2003b; Jolicoeur et al., 2006; Eimer & Kiss, 2007; Kiss et al., 2008; Tollner et al., 2008; Hickey et al., 2009). Importantly, the N2pc was demonstrated to permit rapid tracking of attentional location selection in visual search. To demonstrate this, Woodman and Luck (1999, 2003a) constructed search displays to bias the search order in a controlled way by rendering items with a certain feature value (e.g., a particular color) more or less likely to be the target. For example, as illustrated in Figure 1.2, the target could be a red or a green C with the gap oriented to the left and appearing on 50% of the trials. But when it appeared, the probability of the target being a red C was three times higher (75% of the trials, C75) than being a green C (25% of the trials, C25). Under those conditions, subjects would first focus onto the red item, and upon realizing that it is not the target, switch their focus onto the green item. Importantly, each focusing step should produce its own N2pc response that would be separable between hemispheres when the C75 and the C25 are presented opposite VFs (Figure 1.2A). This was indeed observed. The N2pc response appeared contralateral to the C75 item first (highlighted in red), and subsequently contralateral to the C25 item (highlighted in green), clearly in line with a serial deployment of attention. When the C75 and C25 item appeared in the same VF (Figure 1.2B), switching the focus of attention from C75 to C25 did not involve shifts between VFs, and hence the N2pc was not expected to show the contra-to-ipsi pattern shown in Figure 1.2A. This was indeed the case. As detailed in Woodman and Luck (2003a), there was a remaining possibility that this pattern arose from a limited capacity parallel search in which information about potential target items is accumulated simultaneously but with different temporal dynamics simply mimicking serial focusing. This possibility was addressed with a modification of the paradigm, permitting the analysis of the N2pc response to the first and the second focusing operation independently (Woodman & Luck, 2003a). For example, the initial focus item was presented at the vertical meridian, which eliminated the lateralized N2pc response to that

item, and the remaining N2pc effect was then solely attributable to the focusing onto the secondary (target) item. This allowed the assessment of whether effects of focusing onto the secondary target were already present in the time range of the first focusing operation; that is, appeared in parallel with the focusing onto the primarily selected item. It was found that this is not the case. No N2pc modulation appeared in this early time range, indicating that focusing onto the secondary item was completely delayed, strictly following the focusing onto the initial nontarget item. This and the previous observations together were taken to speak strongly in favor of a serial spatial sequence of focusing operations in visual search.

Beyond indexing spatial selection, as just reviewed, the N2pc was found to reflect the amount of interference from distractors in visual search. The N2pc was only observed for targets that were accompanied by distractors (Luck & Hillyard, 1994b), its amplitude was found to increase with increasing the number of distractors, and the search for a conjunctively defined target (e.g., color/orientation) gave rise to a bigger N2pc than popout search (Luck et al., 1997b). Increasing the number of feature dimensions on which the distractors overlap with the target increased the amplitude of the N2pc (Hopf et al., 2002a). More generally, situations causing ambiguities of feature/ location coding of the target were associated with the largest N2pc responses—an observation giving rise to the hypothesis that the neural operations underlying the N2pc reflect "ambiguity resolution" by means of filtering out distractor information (Luck et al., 1997b, Boehler et al., 2011). This notion was particularly strengthened by the observation that the N2pc shows striking parallels to attention-driven cell firing suppression in extrastriate cortex of monkeys performing visual search (Chelazzi et al., 1993; Chelazzi & Desimone, 1994; Chelazzi et al., 1998; Chelazzi et al., 2001) leading to the suggestion that the N2pc reflects a population-level analog of distractor attenuation (Luck et al., 1997b). In fact, current source localization of the N2pc response based on neuromagnetic recordings in humans revealed that a substantial portion of underlying source activity indeed originates in

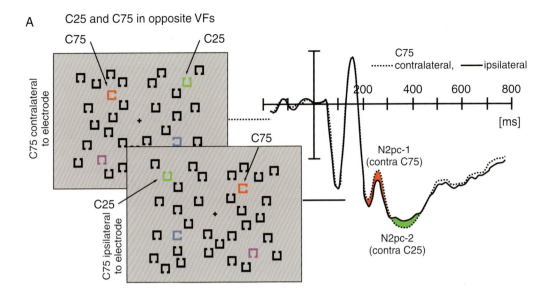

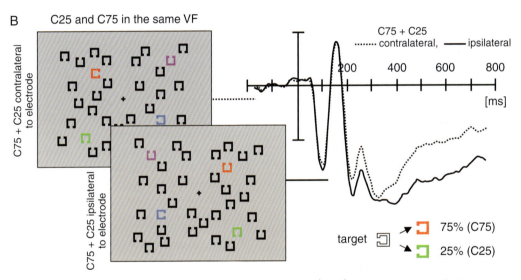

FIGURE 1.2   Key findings of experiments by Woodman and Luck (1999) demonstrating that the N2pc component can serve to track the serial allocation of attention in visual search. Subjects searched for a target item with the gap oriented to the left. To force sequential focusing, the target was more likely to be a red item (75% of the cases, C75) than a green item (25%, C25). (**A**) A situation in which the target is absent, but likely and unlikely potential target locations appear in opposite visual fields (VFs). The waveforms show event-related potential (ERP) responses when the C75 appeared in the VF contralateral (*dashed traces*) versus ipsilateral (*solid traces*) to an occipital electrode that the ERP was recorded from. The N2pc appeared first contralateral to the likely target location (*waveform difference highlighted in red*) and then contralateral to the unlikely target location (*green*), suggesting a serial allocation of spatial attention. The N2pc represents a relative negativity over the occipital scalp contralateral to the target item. Accordingly, the sequence of N2pc responses seen in **A** were not observed when the likely and unlikely target location both appeared in the same VF as illustrated in **B**.

ventral occipitotemporal cortex regions (Hopf et al., 2000), which is consistent with the recording sites in monkey extrastriate cortex. More importantly, and in direct support of the ambiguity resolution theory, the increase in source activity due to larger interference from distractors was found to coincide with ventral extrastriate current source maximum reflecting the N2pc (Hopf et al., 2002a, Boehler et al., 2011). Notably, ERP recordings in the macaque have recently confirmed the existence of an N2pc homologue (Woodman et al., 2007). Finally, the N2pc does not represent a unitary modulatory effect. Source localization based on neuromagnetic data revealed spatiotemporally separable contributions from parietal cortex followed by activity in ventral extrastriate cortex (Hopf et al., 2000). Furthermore, recent observations have raised the possibility that the N2pc, typically observed with bilaterally balanced search arrays, is in fact, a combination of opposite polarity components; that is, an ipsilateral positive and contralateral negative deflection, with the former reflecting distractor attenuation at nontarget locations, and the latter reflecting the actual discrimination of the target (Hickey et al., 2009).

In sum, converging evidence from different methodologies suggests that the neural operations underlying the N2pc index shifts of the spatial focus of attention as well as distractor attenuation processes in visual search. These are seemingly different functional descriptions, but it should be noted that they need not be disjunct. The link may become clear from a closer consideration of the actual mechanisms assumed to underlie distractor filtering in attentive vision. As reviewed above, the N2pc is believed to represent a population-level analog of attention-related cell firing modulations in monkey extrastriate cortex. Those firing modulations were suggested to reflect filtering based on a characteristic observation: firing changes due to attention were maximal when multiple items appeared in a neuron's receptive field (RF) (Moran & Desimone, 1985; Motter, 1993; Luck et al., 1997a), and the actual effect of attention was to change (bias) the response of the neuron toward its response to the attended item when presented in isolation. An influential interpretation of this finding in terms of spatial selection has been that the RF region effectively

responding to the input is reduced (shrunk) to only encompass the region of the attended input. In line with experimental evidence (Mehta et al., 2000; Tolias et al., 2001; Moore et al., 2003; Hopf et al., 2006b) and theoretical considerations (Tsotsos, 2005; Boehler et al., 2011; and Chapter 4, this volume) this likely arises from a top-down mediated attenuation of irrelevant information flow in the massively convergent visual processing hierarchy. Exactly this top-down attenuation of irrelevant information flow may provide the link between distractor attenuation and location selection as reflected by the N2pc. Figure 1.3A-B provides a principal illustration with a simplified visual system spanning just two hierarchical levels. The lower level encompasses seven units with small RFs, one representing input from the target (T) and the remaining representing distractor locations (D). The upper level consists of one large unit that represents all input because the projections of all lower-level RFs converge on that unit. The operation of attention as reflected by the N2pc consists in eliminating the input from distractor locations from further processing in the upward (forward) direction (see next paragraph for a detailed discussion). This is achieved by a top-down mediated attenuation of RFs representing distractor locations (grayed units in Figure 1.3B). However, this simultaneously accomplishes directing attention to the location of the target, as the subregion of the top-level unit receiving input is now identical with the target's location. Hence, location selection and distractor attenuation may be just two consequences of the same underlying operation indexed by the N2pc. A prediction of this interpretation would be that modulatory effects underlying the N2pc arise at hierarchical levels in the visual hierarchy, in which RF size corresponds to the spatial extent of the attended location. This has been supported recently with combined MEG and fMRI recordings (Hopf et al., 2006b; Boehler et al., 2011). Narrowing the spatial focus of attention in visual search was associated with N2pc source activity in progressively lower hierarchical levels of the ventral processing stream. Specifically, a wider focus produced a source activity maximum in a mid-level area, the lateral occipital complex (LOC), whereas a narrower focus produced activity maxima in LOC

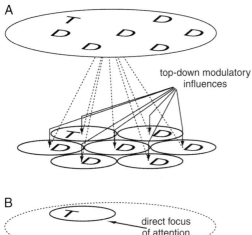

A

B

FIGURE 1.3 Illustration of the possible link between distractor attenuation and location selection, both reflected by the N2pc component. Shown is a forward convergent system of visual units with two hierarchical layers. (**A**) All units at the lower level project to the one upper unit, with all input (the target, T, and distractors, D) "seen" by the lower units also projected to the upper unit. (See Chapter 4 in this book for a full implementation in the framework of the selective tuning model.) (**B**) The operation believed to be reflected by the N2pc consists in a top-down attenuation of distractor input to bias the representation of the target. This operation eliminates distractor information from forward processing, and thereby directs the spatial focus of attention onto the target.

and in the lower-level area V4. This was taken to indicate that attention-driven modulations in extrastriate cortex adapt flexibly to the perceptual scale of discrimination, and also suggested that respective modulations arise in a coarse-to-fine manner in extrastriate cortex (see also Hopf et al., 2002a, for additional evidence), consistent with the proposal of several theories of visual selection and attention (Desimone & Duncan, 1995;

Hochstein & Ahissar, 2002; Ahissar & Hochstein, 2004; Tsotsos, 2005).

TOP-DOWN SELECTION AND THE SPATIAL PROFILE OF THE FOCUS OF ATTENTION

In fact, top-down coarse-to-fine selection as revealed by recent neuromagnetic/fMRI recordings turns out to be highly relevant for settling a long-lasting debate about the nature of the spotlight of attention. "Spotlight" or "zoom-lens" have been terms of metaphorical theorizing about the spatial focus of attention, suggesting a homogenous "illumination" of the attended region, in which intensity or resolution trades with extension of sensory enhancement (Posner, 1980; Eriksen & Yeh, 1985). Indeed, functional brain imaging revealed that spatial attention is associated with blood oxygen level–dependent (BOLD) enhancements in visual cortex areas retinotopically corresponding with attended locations, broadly consistent with those notions (Tootell et al., 1998; Brefczynski & DeYoe, 1999; Muller et al., 2003b). Psychophysical research addressing the actual activity profile representing the spotlight frequently observed activity distributions resembling a simple monotonic gradient (Downing & Pinker, 1985; Henderson & Macquistan, 1993; Handy et al., 1996), with peak and extension adjustable in a flexible way (LaBerge et al., 1997). However, other research has mounted evidence suggesting a more complex profile than a simple gradient. A frequent observation has been that perceptual processing at locations in the vicinity of an attended item is reduced relative to more distant locations, suggesting that the focus of attention has a center–surround structure, in which a circumscribed zone of attenuation surrounds a center of enhancement (Steinman et al., 1995; Cave & Zimmerman, 1997; Caputo & Guerra, 1998; Bahcall & Kowler, 1999; Mounts, 2000a,b; Cutzu & Tsotsos, 2003; McCarley & Mounts, 2007). In fact, neurophysiological studies in humans and monkeys have provided data suggesting such a profile (Vanduffel et al., 2000; Slotnick et al., 2002; Slotnick et al., 2003; Muller & Kleinschmidt, 2004; Schwartz et al., 2005; Hopf et al., 2006a; Boehler et al., 2009; Hopf et al., 2010; Boehler et al., 2011).

For example Hopf and coworkers (Hopf et al., 2006a; Boehler et al., 2009) used MEG recordings to characterize the spatial profile of the focus of attention in visual search. The general rationale of the experiments was to record the magnetic brain response to a task-irrelevant probe stimulus flashed at various distances to the search target and take this measure as an index of the profile of cortical responsivity at and around the focus of attention. Figure 1.4A shows the principal

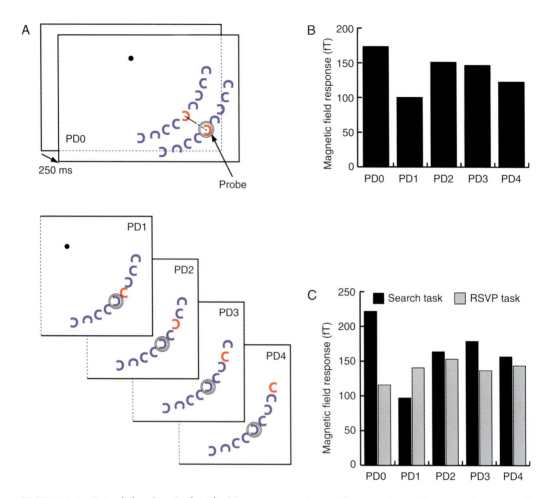

FIGURE 1.4   Setup (**A**) and results (**B, C**) of the neuromagnetic recording experiments demonstrating surround attenuation in visual search (Hopf et al., 2006a). (**A**) The general approach of the experiments was to assess the neuromagnetic response to a task-irrelevant probe (a white ring) flashed (50 ms) at a fixed item location 250 ms after search frame onset. The search frame always contained nine items (a red target and eight blue distractors) arrayed at an isoeccentric distance to the fixation point in the right lower visual quadrant. The target appeared randomly at any of the nine item locations, and therefore either at the probe's location (PD0) or at a location one to four items away from the probe (PD1–PD4). As the probe appeared only on 50% of the trials, the neuromagnetic response to the probe could be isolated by subtracting the response to a search frame without a probe from that of a search frame followed by a probe. (**B**) Bar graph showing the mean size of the probe response (average response between 130 and 150 ms after probe onset) as a function of distance to the focus of attention. Apparently, the response at PD1 is attenuated relative to PD0 and larger distances (PD2–4), suggesting that the passive responsiveness of the cortex is attenuated in a circumscribed region around the focus of attention. (**C**) Results of a control experiment showing that surround attenuation is absent when attention is drawn away from the search items by a demanding RSVP task at fixation (*gray bars*) versus when subjects did the original search task (*black bars*).

stimulus setup of the experiments. Subjects covertly searched and discriminated (gap orientation) a color popout target (a red C in Figure 1.4A) among distractors (blue Cs in Figure 1.4A) arrayed at an isoeccentric distance to fixation in the right lower visual quadrant. On 50% of the search trials, a small white ring (the probe) was flashed 250 ms after search frame onset, always around the center item's position. As the target appeared randomly at one of the possible item positions, the probe's distance (PD) to the focus of attention varied accordingly from zero to four items away from the probe (PD0 to PD4). The magnetic response to the probe could then be analyzed as a function of this distance. This was done by subtracting the MEG response to a search frame without a probe from the response to the same search frame (same target location) with a probe, separately for the five different target-to-probe distances. Figure 1.4B shows those differences collapsed over corresponding probe distances extending clockwise and counterclockwise from the center position. Obviously, the response was slightly enhanced when the target appeared at the probe's location (PD0); however, the response was significantly reduced when the position next to the probe was attended (PD1). Importantly, the response next to the probe was also reduced relative to attended positions farther away from the probe (PD2–PD4), suggesting that the focus of attention was, in fact, surrounded by a circumscribed region of neural attenuation. To confirm that this profile was indeed due to attentional focusing and not a simple consequence of low-level stimulus interactions between the target and the probe, an additional experiment was performed. In this experiment (Hopf et al., 2006a), subjects were presented the same search arrays, and on half of the trial blocks, subjects performed the search task as before (search task). But on the other half, probes and the search items were irrelevant, and attention was continuously drawn to a demanding rapid serial visual presentation (RSVP) task at fixation (RSVP task), which guaranteed that subjects did not attend to the peripheral search items. As illustrated in Figure 1.4C, under those conditions, no surround attenuation appeared (*gray bars*). However, when subjects performed the search task as in the previous

experiment while ignoring the RSVP stream at fixation (*black bars*), the probe response was again significantly attenuated at PD1 (*black bars*). This clearly confirmed that surround attenuation represents a true consequence of attentional focusing.

Although those observations from neuromagnetic brain responses are clearly in line with psychophysical data suggesting a center–surround structure of the attentional focus, they apparently conflict with behavioral and neurophysiological of studies that have rather found evidence in favor of a simple gradient. This discrepancy was recently addressed based on a key rationale of the selective tuning model (STM) of Tsotsos et al. (2005); namely, that surround attenuation arises as consequence of top-down attentional selection in the visual processing hierarchy. In other words, the question of whether the focus of attention takes a simple gradient or a more complex center–surround shape may in fact be a question of the degree to which recurrent top-down processing is required during focusing. As detailed in the selective tuning model (Tsotsos et al., 1995; Tsotsos, 2005; Tsotsos et al., 2008) (see Chapter 4, this volume), surround attenuation is proposed to arise as an inherent consequence of a top-down directed pruning of forward-projecting units, not representing relevant input in the visual processing hierarchy. Importantly, this top-down process is suggested to be the cortical operation that mediates the narrowing of the focus of attention when enhanced spatial resolution is required for input discrimination (see Figures 4.1 and 4.3 in Chapter 4, this volume). According to the model, decisions about the target are made as soon as task-relevant information is available at a given hierarchical level. In other words, if the coarse resolution of the feedforward processing suffices for target discrimination, the top-down directed pruning process would not be involved. Hence, a critical prediction would be that surround attenuation is less prominent or even absent when spatial resolution is not mandatory for discriminating the attended input. This was recently confirmed behaviorally (McCarley & Mounts, 2007) and with MEG recordings in human observers (Boehler et al., 2009). Boehler et al. (2009) used a similar experimental setup to that shown in Figure 1.4A

(Hopf et al., 2006a), but with the modification that the color popout target could be one of two colors (red or green) among blue distractors. In different experimental blocks, subjects were instructed to discriminate either the gap orientation (orientation task) or simply the color of the popout target (color task). The orientation task required narrowly focusing onto the target, the color task did not. In fact, successful performance on the color task did not even necessitate the spatially precise localization of the target. Therefore, the color task could be performed only based on color information provided with the feedforward sweep of processing, and would therefore be expected to not, or much less depend on recurrent processing than would the orientation task. Directly in line with this prediction, the orientation task was found to produce surround attenuation, whereas the color task was associated with a simple gradient. This clearly supported the notion that surround attenuation arises as a consequence of recurrent top-down processing in the visual system. More generally, it indicates that the spatial profile of the focus of attention is flexible and changes depending on the specific demands on target discrimination. Furthermore, the profile of the focus of attention was found to change even during the time course of discrimination. Boehler et al. (2009) used the gap orientation task with probes presented at different time points after search frame onset (100, 175, 250, 325, and 400 ms). Confirming previous observations (Hopf et al., 2006a), surround attenuation appeared around 250 ms, but thereafter the profile changed into one dominated by a center enhancement without significant attenuation in the surround. Hence, during the time course of attentional focusing, the spatial profile of attention is subject to dynamic changes, with the center–surround profile simply representing a transient consequence of attentional selection in visual search. To conclude, the debate about the spatial profile of the focus of attention may be (at least partially) resolvable by acknowledging that the profile can take the shape of a simple gradient or a more complex center–surround profile. Whether one or the other is observed depends on the time course and the demands required for the discrimination, with respect to the spatial resolution.

SPLITTING THE SPATIAL FOCUS OF ATTENTION

The spatial profile of the focus of attention continues to be a debated issue also with respect to other distributional aspects, such as whether it is inherently a unitary focus or can be divided between separated locations, or whether it can occupy space only contiguously or in a more flexible topological way. Depending on methodology and experimental approaches, neurophysiological research has arrived at different, partially conflicting conclusions. Event-related potential recordings, in which attention was focused onto briefly presented items, suggested a unitary focus that may be changed, contracted, or extended flexibly but may not be divided between noncontiguous regions of space (Heinze et al., 1994a). Heinze et al. asked subjects to attend to two of four horizontally arrayed item locations simultaneously, in order to detect short occurrences of matching symbols at those locations. The two attended locations could be adjacent or separated by one item position, and the ERP response to a single task-irrelevant probe sometimes presented at one of the four locations was analyzed. The key observation was that the P1 response elicited by a probe presented at an unattended position between attended positions was as large as the P1 response to the probe when that position was attended. In contrast, when the same position was unattended but not located between two attended positions, the P1 response was significantly reduced, suggesting that the focus of attention could not be divided. A different conclusion was drawn by (Muller et al., 2003a) based on SSVEP recordings. Mueller et al. used RSVP flicker stimulation in a stimulus configuration similar to that used by Heinze et al. (1994a). The SSVEP response to spatially separated, continuously attended flicker streams elicited an enhanced response, but the SSVEP corresponding to an item position between attended locations did not, suggesting that the spatial focus of attention could be split between separate locations. Recent fMRI studies addressing the possibility of sustained focusing onto spatially separated RSVP streams have come to a similar conclusion (McMains & Somers, 2004, 2005). Furthermore, SSVEP recordings even revealed evidence in favor of a topologically complex, ring-shaped assignment of spatial attention (Muller & Hubner, 2002). Again, those observations were made under continuous flicker presentation and sustained focusing. Notably, conventional ERP recordings using trial-by-trial focusing onto ring-shaped regions at different eccentricities failed to obtain correlates of early sensory selection (P1/N1 modulations); only indexes of post-perceptual selection (N2) were observed (Eimer, 1999). Although it may be premature to provide a definitive conclusion, it appears that continuous stimulation, such as RSVP or flicker presentation, is critical for obtaining more complex spatial distributions of attention, such as split focusing of attention. Attention to discontinuous and briefly presented items appears to involve attentional selection that is spatially inseparable, suggesting that demonstrations of unitary and divided foci of attention refer to different underlying neural operations.

FEATURE-BASED ATTENTION

Attentional selection can be based on stimulus features other than location (Maunsell & Treue, 2006). Analogous to the modulatory effects of attention to locations, attention to features turns out to operate by enhancing neural responses in visual cortex. Cell recordings in monkeys revealed that modulatory effects due to location- and feature-based attention appear in the same cells of area V4 (Treue & Martinez Trujillo, 1999; McAdams & Maunsell, 2000), indicating that both types of attention are closely linked. Moreover, it turns out that even minute spatial cues provided within a cell's receptive field can change feature-based effects substantially (Patzwahl & Treue, 2009). Hence, for a clean demonstration of feature-based attention, it is important to control spatial cues that potentially bias the selection. One approach to avoid such confounds is to use spatially superimposed stimulation as, for example, done by Muller and coworkers (Muller et al., 2006). Muller et al. (2006) presented superimposed, colored, randomly moving dot fields. Both dot fields flickered at different frequencies, which permitted researchers to record color-specific frequency-tagged SSVEP responses. Subjects attended one color in

order to detect occasional periods of coherent motion. The subjects' impression was a mix of irregularly moving colored dots, which preempted the possibility to use location cues for the selection of color. Under those conditions, the SSVEP response to the attended color was enhanced relative to the unattended color in early visual cortex areas, demonstrating that attention to color enhances neural responses even when location cannot serve as a reference frame for selection.

A typical observation from functional brain imaging studies has been that attention to features is particularly associated with activity changes in corresponding specialized cortical regions (Corbetta et al., 1990, 1991; Beauchamp et al., 1997). For example, attention to color produces enhanced responses in area V4, a region known to prefer the processing of color (McKeefry & Zeki, 1997; Wade et al., 2002), whereas attention to motion leads to enhancements in the motion-specific area MT (O'Craven et al., 1997; Liu et al., 2003; Schoenfeld et al., 2007). Such module-selective changes have been observed even upon the mere anticipation of feature-specific stimulation without physical input (Chawla et al., 1999). Recent combined ERP/MEG/fMRI recordings addressed the time course of modulatory effects in feature-specialized regions (Schoenfeld et al., 2007). In Schoenfeld et al. (2007), subjects viewed a group of stationary gray dots at fixation that either changed color (to red or orange) or started to move in one direction (with high or low speed). Subjects were cued to attend to color in order to detect occasional color changes (to orange), or alternatively, to attend to motion and detect occasional onsets of fast motion. Current source reconstruction of the attention-related activity in conjunction with fMRI localization of color- and motion-specific areas revealed that modulation maxima reflecting feature attention in fact arose from corresponding specialized cortex areas. Moreover, modulatory effects in those regions appeared rather rapidly, around 90–120 ms after change onset; that is, earlier than the typical onset of neural activity indexing the attentional selection of feature values within a dimension (e.g., red versus green). Event-related potential effects of within-dimension selection of color, motion, orientation, or spatial frequency (referred to as selection negativities or positivities) were regularly found to arise later, typically between 150–400 ms after stimulus onset (Harter & Guido, 1980; Hillyard & Münte, 1984; Wijers et al., 1989; Kenemans et al., 1993; Anllo-Vento & Hillyard, 1996; Karayanidis & Michie, 1996).

The mechanisms of within-dimension feature selection have been extensively investigated using cell recordings in feature-selective areas of the monkey extrastriate cortex. The general observation of those studies has been that attention to a particular feature value of color, orientation, or motion direction caused enhanced firing in cells particularly tuned to the attended feature value (Motter, 1994; McAdams & Maunsell, 1999; Treue & Martinez Trujillo, 1999; Martinez-Trujillo & Treue, 2004; Mirabella et al., 2007; Wannig et al., 2007). Most influential was the finding that attention enhanced firing in a multiplicative way, such that the enhancement was scaled to the degree to which the input matched the tuning of the cell (McAdams & Maunsell, 1999; Treue & Martinez Trujillo, 1999; Wannig et al., 2007). This led to the proposal that feature attention operates by a mechanism referred to as "feature similarity gain enhancement" (feature similarity gain model) (Treue & Martinez Trujillo, 1999). Importantly, feature similarity–dependent enhancements of firing were regularly demonstrated in cells with RFs situated outside the spatial focus of attention, suggesting that feature attention is a spatially global operation (Bichot et al., 2005). The spatially global nature of feature attention has also been demonstrated at the neural population level with fMRI, MEG, and ERP recordings in humans (Saenz et al., 2002, 2003; Hopf et al., 2004; Stoppel et al., 2007; Zhang & Luck, 2009) and was shown to arise even without physical stimulation (Serences & Boynton, 2007). Saenz et al. (2002), for example, had subjects attend to the direction of motion of one of two overlaid oppositely moving dot-fields presented to the side of fixation in one VF. The BOLD response to an unattended unidirectional dot motion field in the opposite VF was analyzed as a function of whether the motion direction in the unattended VF matched the attended motion direction or not. When the unattended motion matched the attended motion in direction, the BOLD response was enhanced relative to when motion directions did not match, indicating that feature attention also operates outside the focus of attention. A similar demonstration has been recently provided with ERPs (Zhang & Luck, 2009). In Zhang and Luck's experiment (2009), subjects attended two continuous superimposed streams of red and green dots in one VF, with either the red or green stream being the target. The ERP response to irrelevant red or green dot groups (probes) flashed in the opposite VF was analyzed. They observed a larger P1 response to the unattended probe when its color matched that of the attended stream. Beyond demonstrating that attention to color modulates neural activity at unattended locations, the data revealed that respective modulatory effects on feature processing arise very early, presumably during the initial feedforward sweep of processing in visual cortex. Furthermore, this modulation in the P1 range turned out to depend on the concurrent presentation of the target and the distractor stream at the target location. Alternating target and distractor stream eliminated the effect, indicating that the simultaneous competition between target and distractor color values is a critical condition for the attention effect to arise. In fact, a seminal ERP study (Hillyard & Münte, 1984) on the relation of feature- and location-based attention revealed no effects of color selection outside the spatial focus of attention (see also Anllo-Vento & Hillyard, 1996, for similar observations), which is in apparent contrast to the notion that feature attention operates in a spatially global manner. Hillyard and Münte (1984) used a stream-type task with blue and red bars simultaneously flashed in rapid succession to the left and right of fixation. Bar color was assigned randomly, with either the red or the blue bars in one VF being task relevant. In line with previous observations of feature-selective negativities (Harter & Previc, 1978; Harter & Guido, 1980; Harter et al., 1982), the attended color elicited an enhanced negativity between 150 and 350 ms (referred to as *selection negativity*) within the focus of attention. Outside, in contrast, the modulation of the ERP response was negligible, leading to the conclusion that the attentional selection of nonspatial features is not global, but hierarchically dependent upon prior location selection. In view of recent evidence by Zhang and Luck (2009), an alternative possibility may be considered; namely, that feature-based effects outside the focus of attention were not observed by Hillyard and Münte (1984) because target and distractor color were not competing at the attended location (only the target or the distractor color appeared in a given trial). Notably, this interpretation lines up with the general observation that effects of attention are typically maximal under stimulus competition (Motter, 1993; Luck et al., 1997a; Kastner & Ungerleider, 2000).

FEATURE-BASED ATTENTION IN VISUAL SEARCH

Further evidence for feature attention to operate in a spatially global manner has been provided with visual search. In visual search, the target is defined by (a set of) features, but its location among distractors is unknown. This situation is often complicated by fact that distractors share features with the target, and localizing the target not only requires the subject to identify the presence of relevant features but also to verify their correct combination (conjunction search). Influential theories on visual search proposed that feature decoding in conjunction search proceeds item-by-item in a strictly serial fashion under the control of spatial attention (Treisman & Gelade, 1980). However, under various conditions, conjunction search turned out to be more efficient than strictly sequential item-by-item feature decoding predicts (Egeth et al., 1984; Nakayama & Silverman, 1986; Wolfe et al., 1989; Treisman & Sato, 1990; Wolfe et al., 1990). To accommodate those conflicting findings, it was proposed that some form of parallel and global feature-based selection increases the efficiency of the search process. Specifically, global feature-based selection was suggested to collectively enhance the priority of target-defining features in all items carrying those features in parallel. This operation would eventually label only a subset of items as being potential targets, with only this subset then requiring serial search (see Treisman & Sato, 1990, for an equivalent solution based on the collective selection/rejection of distractors bearing a distinct nontarget feature). Either scenario above

would require that (a) the selection of relevant (irrelevant) features is spatially global in order to be collectively effective, (b) that it arises prior to the spatial selection of the target, and (c) that the selection of all relevant (irrelevant) features is parallel. In fact, those predictions were recently addressed and confirmed with EEG/MEG recordings in human observers. Hopf et al. (2004) used a simple search task in which subjects were required to search for and discriminate the gap orientation (e.g., left–right) of a colored C among differently colored Cs in the left and right VF. The distractor Cs differed in color from the target, but the orientation of their gap could be the same as the target (e.g., left–right, distractors with relevant orientation values, in short: relevant distractors, RD) or different from the target (up–down, distractors with irrelevant orientation values, irrelevant distractors, ID). The critical manipulation of the experiments was to vary the location of the relevant distractors relative to the target's location. Figure 1.5 shows examples of the different RD distributions (A–C) and control conditions that were used in the experiment. Specifically, RDs appeared in the target VF while IDs appeared in the nontarget VF (A), RDs were presented in the non-target VF and IDs in the target VF (B), RDs appeared in both VFs (C), or IDs appeared in both VFs (control). This distributional variation permitted researchers to assess whether the processing of the relevant orientation feature in distractors depends on the localization of the target or not. If yes, RDs should modulate the ERP/MEG response relative to the control condition only when they appear in the target VF. If not, the RD effects should appear no matter where the target is actually located. As visible in the ERP waveforms and distributions in Figure 1.5A-C, RDs elicited a negativity amplitude enhancement over the scalp strictly contralateral to the location of the RDs (see open arrows). Importantly, this modulation was independent of where the target item was located, indicating that the processing of the relevant orientation feature is, in fact, spatially global. Moreover, as shown in Figure 1.5D, this modulation due to the relevant orientation feature appeared between 140 and 300 ms after search frame onset (*solid line*), that is, it started approximately 40 ms earlier than the onset of the

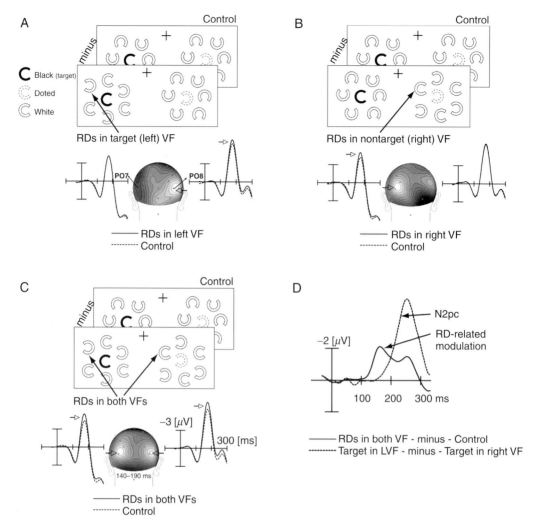

FIGURE 1.5 Stimuli and results of an experiment demonstrating that the selection of task-relevant features is spatially global and occurs prior to target selection in visual search (Hopf et al., 2004). The logic of the experiment was to vary the location of distractors sharing a task-relevant feature value (gap orientation left–right) with the target item (relevant distractors, RDs) independent of the target's location. The target was always a uniquely colored C (e.g., a red C, here shown as the black item in **A–C**) surrounded by distractors and combined with distractors in the opposite visual field (VF). The RDs either appeared only at the target's side (**A**), only at the side opposite to the target (**B**), or at both sides (**C**). As a reference condition, no RDs were presented (Control). The waveforms and topographical maps in **A–C** show the event-related potential (ERP) response to the different distributions of RDs (*solid lines*) in comparison to the control condition (*dashed lines*). The occurrence of RDs was associated with an enhanced negativity between 140 and 300 ms at electrode sites contralateral to the side of presentation (*arrows*), and regardless of where the target was located, suggesting that the selection of the relevant orientation feature was spatially global. (**D**)The RD-related modulation of the bilateral RD condition (difference of waveforms shown in **C**, collapsed over left and right hemisphere electrodes) together with the corresponding N2pc effect (difference of waveforms elicited by targets contralateral versus ipsilateral to recording electrode). The RD-related modulation appears ~40 ms earlier than the N2pc component indexing spatial focusing onto the target.

N2pc (~180 ms, *dashed line*). As outlined above, the N2pc reflects spatial focusing onto the target item. Hence, search involved a short phase prior to focusing onto the target, during which relevant features were highlighted globally at any location in the visual scene.

Finally, using SSVEPs, Anderson et al. (2008) recently provided evidence suggesting that the selection of different feature dimensions (color, orientation) can in fact be parallel in visual cortex. Subjects viewed a circular aperture of randomly distributed vertical and horizontal, red and blue bars. Each feature combination (red–horizontal, red–vertical, blue–horizontal, blue–vertical) flickered at a different frequency, permitting researchers to obtain frequency-tagged SSVEP responses. When subjects attended to a certain feature combination (e.g., blue–horizontal), the corresponding SSVEP response was enhanced. The SSVEP response to the attended features in combinations with unattended features (blue–vertical, red–horizontal) was also enhanced. Importantly, the SSVEP enhancement to the attended features individually added up to approximately match the enhancement to the attended feature conjunction, suggesting that attention to color and orientation acts independently and in parallel in visual cortex. In sum, recent EEG/MEG research on the mechanisms of feature attention has made a number of observations directly compatible with current accounts of visual search proposing that spatially global and parallel feature selection can guide the search for feature conjunctions.

ON THE PRIORITY OF OBJECT-BASED ATTENTIONAL SELECTION

The previous paragraph reviewed some evidence from visual search indicating that feature selection has temporal priority relative to the operation of focusing attention onto the target object. This is expected, given that target identification depends on the correct decoding of features in visual search. However, there are many conditions in which this dependency is reversed; that is, in which the encoding of object features requires the prior identification of an object. This situation is commonly referred to as *object-based attentional*

selection. A hallmark of object-based attention has been that attention to an object entails the selection of all of its features, even those that are irrelevant for the task. The best-known expression of this fact is the so-called *same-object advantage*: the discrimination of multiple object features is better when those features pertain to the same, rather than to different objects (Duncan, 1984; Baylis & Driver, 1993; Behrmann et al., 1998). According to an influential account, the *integrated competition model* (Duncan et al., 1997), the dominance of object features arises because the object biases competition in all sensory-motor systems that code its properties. Evidence in support of this notion has been provided with ERPs and fMRI (Muller & Kleinschmidt, 2003; He et al., 2004; Martinez et al., 2007b; Martinez et al., 2007a) based on a popular experimental approach developed by Egly et al. (1994). The general idea is to compare performance at a cued/uncued location when that same location is part of an attended or unattended object. In their ERP study, Martinez and colleagues used a typical version of the experiment with two parallel bars, either both oriented horizontally (one in the upper and one in the lower VF, spanning from mirror image locations in the left and right VF) or vertically (one in the left and one in the right VF, spanning from corresponding locations in the upper and lower VFs) (Martinez et al., 2006). The corner of the bars always occupied the same spatial region in each visual quadrant, no matter whether the bars were oriented horizontally or vertically. On each trial, parts of a corner in a random quadrant were briefly offset, while subjects covertly attended to one quadrant (e.g., the right upper) to detect the brief corner offsets there. The critical comparison for showing object-based attention was to compare the ERP response elicited by offsets at an unattended corner (e.g., the left upper corner) as a function of whether that corner was part of the cued (horizontal configuration) or the uncued bar (vertical configuration). Martinez et al. (2006) found that uncued offsets elicited a larger N1 response when they pertained to the attended object than to the unattended object, consistent with an object-based attention effect. Importantly, the P1 component was not changed under this comparison, suggesting that location-based selection did not play a confounding role.

Despite the abundance of demonstrations of same-object advantage effects with different experimental approaches and methodologies, a truly confound-free demonstration of object-based selection turned out to be challenging. For example, the critical demonstration of object-based effects in the paradigm by Egly et al. (1994) involves spatially changing stimulus configurations. Also, the uncued corner offset in the just-reviewed study by Martinez et al. (2006) may capture spatial attention to some degree, and it may simply be easier to shift the focus of attention involuntarily within an object, as compared to between separate objects. In fact, it has been shown with fMRI that location- and object-based components jointly contribute to the attention effects in this type of paradigm (Muller & Kleinschmidt, 2003). Although those problems may not apply in all cases (note that the P1 was uninfluenced by object-based comparisons in Martinez et al. [2006], suggesting that location selection was unlikely an issue), explanations in terms of spatial selection cannot be entirely ruled out.

For a satisfying demonstration of attention to operate in an object-based reference frame, it would be indispensable to eliminate the possibility of relying on spatial cues. A first convincing paradigmatic solution was provided by Valdes-Sosa and coworkers (Valdes-Sosa et al., 1998b; Valdes-Sosa et al., 2000; Pinilla et al., 2001). Valdes-Sosa et al. asked subjects to attend to one of two superimposed rotating dot groups. Those dot groups differed in color but filled the same circular region in space while rotating coherently in opposite directions. As this formed mutually transparent surfaces (objects) occupying the same location, confounds in terms of location selection were almost perfectly eliminated. The general experimental approach was to assess the behavioral performance (Valdes-Sosa et al., 2000) or the ERP response (Valdes-Sosa et al., 1998a) to feature changes (sudden changes of motion direction) as a function of whether they appeared in the attended or the unattended surface. Valdes-Sosa (1998b) observed that the P1/N1 response elicited by the changes in motion direction were smaller in the unattended as compared to the

attended surface, suggesting—in line with the integrated competition model—that attention biased competition between surface objects by attenuating the object representation of the unattended surface. Analogous effects were also observed at the behavioral level, where subjects were impaired in judging motion changes in the unattended versus the attended surface (Valdes-Sosa et al., 2000; Rodriguez et al., 2002). One issue with the study by Valdez-Sosa (1998b) was that the superimposed surface objects differed in color, leaving open the possibility that color-based biasing could account for the effects attributed to object based selection. This was addressed by Mitchell et al. (2003), who modified the experiment to eliminate color as a cue to the target surface. They used the fact that a short translation of one surface is sufficient to attract attention effectively to that surface (Reynolds et al., 2003). A subsequent translation in the attended or unattended surface could then be used as a performance index of object-based selection. Indeed, the reduced performance for the unattended object persisted after eliminating the color differences between surfaces, thus confirming that the performance difference is truly object-mediated. With a subsequent ERP study, Khoe et al. (2005) investigated the neural underpinnings of the exogenous cuing effects reported by Mitchell et al. (2003). They observed that the posterior C1 and N1 component of the response elicited by translations of the cued surface were larger relative to the uncued surface. Importantly, this exogenous cuing effect on the C1 and N1 components was independent of whether the superimposed surfaces differed in color or not, indicating that color-based selection cannot account for the observed effects. Notably, although a reduction of the N1 represents a typical observation of previous studies, Khoe et al. (2005) were the first to report an effect on the C1 component between 75 and 110 ms. Initial portions of the C1 component are known to reflect visual processing in primary visual cortex (Di Russo et al., 2001; Foxe & Simpson, 2002), suggesting that competitive biasing of neural processing due to object-based selection (at least for motion-defined objects) appears at rather early stages of visual processing.

BINOCULAR RIVALRY

Further intriguing evidence for object-based attention was the recent demonstration that attentional biasing of binocular rivalry is object-dominated (Mitchell et al., 2004). Mitchell et al. (2004) used short motion translations to direct attention to one of two superimposed motion-defined surfaces analogous to the paradigm of (Reynolds et al., 2003). Short translations of one surface served as exogenous cues to attract attention to one or the other surface. After 150 ms, however, the presentation was changed to dichoptic viewing (by removing one surface from each eye, in that each eye saw a different surface). This resulted in interocular rivalry, which always resumed toward the dominance of the previously cued surface. As this was seen regardless of whether the previously cued surface was presented to the left or the right eye, surface-based selection must have been the critical determinant and not the interocular rivalry. A recent study (Khoe et al., 2008) provided converging evidence from ERPs. Khoe et al. used a slightly modified paradigm in which a second motion translation appeared during the binocular viewing phase, in which it served as a probe to elicit an ERP response. A monocular viewing condition was included as a control. They observed that under both the binocular and the monocular viewing conditions, the N1 (160–220 ms) and P2 (250–300 ms) components elicited by translations of the cued surface were enhanced relative to the uncued surface. Most notably, the earlier latency P1 (110–160 ms) component was enhanced under binocular rivalry, but not during monocular viewing. Hence, surface-based attentional modulations influence visual processing earlier under conditions of binocular competition, compatible with the relative priority of object-based over interocular selection, and hence in line with the behavioral observations of Mitchell et al. (2004).

We have reviewed experimental data strongly suggesting that object-based selection dominates the selection of features like color/motion or the resolution of binocular rivalry, consistent with the integrated competition account. An important question, so far unaddressed, regards the actual time it takes for the visual system to establish that dominance. In other words, it would be important to know whether the object-mediated bias of feature processing is in fact rapid enough to build a temporally coherent, integrated representation of an attended object. This issue was addressed explicitly with ERP/MEG and fMRI in human observers (Schoenfeld et al., 2003). Schoenfeld et al. cued subjects to attend to one of two superimposed dot groups that moved coherently in opposite horizontal directions for 300 ms on a given trial, leading to the perception of separate surface objects (Figure 1.6A). The motion in each direction could be fast or slow, and subjects were required to detect infrequent fast motion (25% of the trials) in the attended direction. Between trials, the dots did not move and were all uniformly colored (white). Each trial started with dot motion sometimes accompanied by a color change (to red) in the attended or the unattended surface; sometimes no color change appeared at all. The color changes were completely irrelevant to the task, which was confirmed by behavioral measures. With this stimulation setup, the object-mediated effect on irrelevant color processing could be assessed by comparing color changes when they occurred in the attended versus the unattended surface object (dashed trace in Figure 1.6B). In addition, the "sensory" effect of color presentation could be analyzed by comparing the response to motion onsets in the unattended surface with and without color change (solid trace in Figure 1.6B). The latter revealed BOLD maxima in color-specific regions of the fusiform gyrus (V4v), and current source localization of the corresponding ERP/MEG response yielded generators coinciding with those localizations (Figure 1.6C left). When comparing the effect of color change in the attended versus the unattended surface, an enhanced amplitude of the ERP/MEG response was observed at 220–240 ms after stimulus, with the corresponding current source maxima and fMRI activations again found in area V4v (Figure 1.6C, *right*). Importantly, the object-based enhancement of color processing occurred with a delay of 40–50 ms relative to the onset of the color-specific sensory response in V4v, indicating that the binding of irrelevant features into an attended object indeed arises very rapidly and in line with the integrated competition model (Duncan et al., 1997).

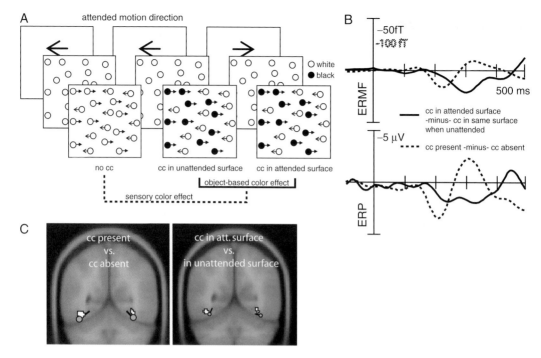

FIGURE 1.6   Design and key results of a study by Schoenfeld et al. (2003) addressing the temporal dynamics of object-based feature integration. Subjects viewed superimposed white dot groups that started moving in opposite directions on a given trial. The subjects' impression was to view two superimposed surfaces, and they were cued to attend to just one of them for detecting occasional onsets of fast motion. As illustrated in **A**, with motion-onset, the color of the dots in the attended or the unattended surface could change to red (*shown in black*), or no color change appeared (all color changes were task-irrelevant). A comparison of the event-related potential (ERP)/event-related magnetic field (ERMF) response to motion onsets with versus without color change (*cc*) served to assess the sensory effect of color, shown as dashed lines in **B**. A comparison of the color change in the attended versus unattended surface was taken to assess the object-based selection of the irrelevant color feature (*solid lines*). The object-based color enhancement was observed to arise with a delay of 30–50 ms relative to the sensory color effect, indicating that irrelevant features are rapidly integrated into the attended object. **C** summarizes that source activity underlying both the sensory (*left*) and the object-based color enhancement (*right*) localized to the color selective region V4v. This localization was further confirmed with a functional magnetic resonance imaging (fMRI) study that applied the same experimental design.

CONCLUSION

We have seen that, under many experimental conditions, object-based mechanisms govern feature selection for building coherent representations. Those integration processes operate on a rapid temporal schedule, permitting subjects to integrate features within a few tens of milliseconds. However, feature selection may gain temporal priority over location and object selection in other situations like visual search, where relevant target-defining features were observed to be globally selected approximately 40 ms prior to the selection of the

target object (Hopf et al., 2004). Yet other experimental conditions cause feature selection to depend upon the prior selection of locations, in that location selection preempts the subsequent processing of features at unattended locations or objects (Hillyard & Münte, 1984). Hence, the relations among location-, feature-, and object-based attentional mechanisms are not rigid. Instead, the different mechanisms operate rather flexibly to coordinate their priority of operation, such that attentional processing is optimized for the momentary goals and demands of the organism in its environment.

ACKNOWLEDGMENTS

This work was supported in part by grants from the DFG, NSF (0727115) and NIMH (MH55714).

References

Ahissar, M., & Hochstein, S. (2004). The reverse hierarchy theory of visual perceptual learning. *Trends in Cognitive Sciences, 8,* 457–464.

Anderson, S. K., Hillyard, S. A., & Mueller, M. M. (2008). Attention facilitates multiple stimulus features in parallel in human visual cortex. *Current Biology, 18,* 1006–1009.

Anllo-Vento, L., & Hillyard, S. A. (1996). Selective attention to the color and direction of moving stimuli: electrophysiological correlates of hierarchical feature selection. *Perception & Psychophysics, 58,* 191–206.

Bahcall, D. O., & Kowler, E. (1999). Attentional interference at small spatial separations. *Vision Research, 39,* 71–86.

Bashinski, H. S., & Bacharach, V. R. (1980). Enhancement of perceptual sensitivity as the result of selectively attending to spatial locations. *Perception & Psychophysics, 28,* 241–248.

Baylis, G. C., & Driver, J. (1993). Visual attention and objects: evidence for hierarchical coding of location. *Journal of Experimental Psychology. Human Perception and Performance, 19,* 451–470.

Beauchamp, M. S., Cox, R. W., & DeYoe, E. A. (1997). Graded effects of spatial and featural attention on human area MT and associated motion processing areas. *Journal of Neurophysiology, 78,* 516–520.

Behrmann, M., Zemel, R. S., & Mozer, M. C. (1998). Object-based attention and occlusion: Evidence from normal participants and a computational model. *Journal of Experimental Psychology. Human Perception and Performance, 24,* 1011–1036.

Bichot, N. P., Rossi, A. F., & Desimone, R. (2005). Parallel and serial neural mechanisms for visual search in macaque area V4. *Science, 308,* 529–534.

Boehler, C. N., Tsotsos, J. K., Schoenfeld, A., Heinze, H.-J., & Hopf, J. M. (2009). The center-surround profile of the focus of attention arises from recurrent processing in visual cortex. *Cerebral Cortex, 19,* 982–991.

Boehler, C. N., Tsotsos, J. K., Schoenfeld, A., Heinze, H.-J., & Hopf, J. M. (2011). Neural mechanisms of surround attenuation and distractor competition in visual search. *Journal of Neuroscience, 31,* 5213–5224.

Brefczynski, J. A., & DeYoe, E. A. (1999). A physiological correlate of the "spotlight" of visual attention. *Nature Neuroscience, 2,* 370–374.

Caputo, G., & Guerra, S. (1998). Attentional selection by distractor suppression. *Vision Research, 38,* 669–689.

Cave, K. R., & Zimmerman, J. M. (1997). Flexibility in spatial attention before and after practice. *Psychological Science, 8,* 399–403.

Chawla, D., Rees, G., & Friston, K. J. (1999). The physiological basis of attentional modulation in extrastriate visual areas. *Nature Neuroscience, 2,* 671–676.

Chelazzi, L., & Desimone, R. (1994). Responses of V4 neurons during visual search. *Society for Neuroscience Abstracts, 20,* 1054.

Chelazzi, L., Duncan, J., Miller, E. K., & Desimone, R. (1998). Response of neurons in inferior temporal cortex during memory-guided visual search. *Journal of Neurophysiology, 80,* 2918–2940.

Chelazzi, L., Miller, E. K., Duncan, J., & Desimone, R. (1993). A neural basis for visual search in inferior temporal cortex. *Nature, 363,* 345–347.

Chelazzi, L., Miller, E. K., Duncan, J., & Desimone, R. (2001). Responses of neurons in macaque area V4 during memory-guided visual search. *Cerebral Cortex, 11,* 761–772.

Corbetta, M., Miezin, F. M., Dobmeyer, S., Shulman, G. L., & Petersen, S. E. (1990). Attentional modulation of neural processing of shape, color, and velocity in humans. *Science, 248,* 1556–1559.

Corbetta, M., Miezin, F. M., Dobmeyer, S., Shulman, G. L., & Petersen, S. E. (1991). Selective and divided attention during visual discriminations of shape, color, and speed: Functional anatomy by positron emission tomography. *Journal of Neuroscience, 11,* 2383–2402.

Cutzu, F., & Tsotsos, J. K. (2003). The selective tuning model of attention: Psychophysical evidence for a suppressive annulus around an attended item. *Vision Research, 43,* 205–219.

Desimone, R., & Duncan, J. (1995). Neural mechanisms of selective visual attention. *Annual Review of Neurosciences, 18,* 193–222.

Desmedt, J. E. & Robertson, D. (1977). Differential enhancement of early and late components of the cerebral somatosensory evoked potentials during forced-paced cognitive tasks in man. *Journal of Physiology, 271,* 761–782.

Di Russo, F., Martinez, A., & Hillyard, S. A. (2003). Source analysis of event-related cortical activity during visuo-spatial attention. *Cerebral Cortex, 13,* 486–499.

Di Russo, F., Martinez, A., Sereno, M. I., Pitzalis, S., & Hillyard, S. A. (2001). Cortical sources of the early components of the visual evoked potential. *Human Brain Mapping, 15*, 95–111.

Downing, P. E. (1988). Expectancy and visual-spatial attention: effects on perceptual quality. *Journal of Experimental Psychology. Human Perception and Performance, 14*, 188–202.

Downing, P. E., & Pinker, S. (1985). The spatial structure of visual attention. In M. I. Posner, & O. S. Marin (Eds.), *Attention and performance XI* (pp. 171–188). Hillsdale, NJ: Erlbaum.

Duncan, J. (1984). Selective attention and the organization of visual information. *Journal of Experimental Psychology: General, 113*, 501–517.

Duncan, J., Humphreys, G. W., & Ward, R. M. (1997). Competitive brain activity in visual attention. *Current Opinion in Neurobiology, 7*, 255–261.

Eason, R. G. (1981). Visual evoked potential correlates of early neural filtering during selective attention. *Bulletin of the Psychonomic Society, 18*, 203–206.

Egeth, H. E., Virzi, R. A., & Garbat, H. (1984). Searching for conjunctively defined targets. *Journal of Experimental Psychology. Human Perception and Performance, 10*, 32–39.

Egly, R., Driver, J., & Rafal, R. D. (1994). Shifting visual attention between objects and locations: Evidence from normal and parietal lesion subjects. *Journal of Experimental Psychology: General, 123*, 161–177.

Eimer, M. (1993). Spatial cueing, sensory gating and selective response preparation: An ERP study on visuo-spatial orienting. *Electroencephalography and Clinical Neurophysiology, 88*, 408–420.

Eimer, M. (1996). The N2pc component as an indicator of attentional selectivity. *Electroencephalography and Clinical Neurophysiology, 99*, 225–234.

Eimer, M. (1999). Attending to quadrants and ring-shaped regions: ERP effects of visual attention in different spatial selection tasks. *Psychophysiology, 36*, 491–503.

Eimer, M., & Kiss, M. (2007). Attentional capture by task-irrelevant fearful faces is revealed by the N2pc component. *Biological Psychology, 74*, 108–112.

Eriksen, C. W, & Yeh, Y.-Y. (1985). Allocation of attention in the visual field. *Journal of Experimental Psychology: Human Perception and Performance, 11*, 583–597.

Foxe, J. J., & Simpson, G. V. (2002). Flow of activation from V1 to frontal cortex in humans. A framework for defining "early" visual processing. *Experimental Brain Research, 142*, 139–150.

Girelli, M., & Luck, S. J. (1997). Are the same attentional mechanisms used to detect visual search targets defined by color, orientation, and motion? *Journal of Cognitive Neuroscience, 9*, 238–253.

Handy, T. C., Kingstone, A., & Mangun, G. R. (1996). Spatial distribution of visual attention: Perceptual sensitivity and response latency. *Perception and Psychophysics, 58*, 613–627.

Handy, T. C., Soltani, M., & Mangun, G. R. (2001a). Perceptual load and visuocortical processing: Event-related potentials reveal sensory-level selection. *Psychological Science, 12*, 213–218.

Handy, T. C., Green, V., Klein, R. M., & Mangun, G. R. (2001b). Combined expectancies: Event-related potentials reveal the early benefits of spatial attention that are obscured by reaction time measures. *Journal of Experimental Psychology. Human Perception and Performance, 27*, 303–317.

Harter, M. R., Aine, C., & Schroeder, C. (1982). Hemispheric differences in the neural processing of stimulus location and type: Effects of selective attention on visual evoked potentials. *Neuropsychologia, 20*, 421–438.

Harter, M. R., Anllo-Vento, L., & Wood, F. B. (1989). Event-related potentials, spatial orienting, and reading disabilities. *Psychophysiology, 26*(4)., 404–421.

Harter, M. R., & Guido, W. (1980). Attention to pattern orientation: Negative cortical potentials, reaction time, and the selection process. *Electroencephalography and Clinical Neurophysiology, 49*, 461–475.

Harter, M. R., & Previc, F. H. (1978). Size-specific information channels and selective attention: Visual evoked potential and behavioral measures. *Electroencephalography and Clinical Neurophysiology, 45*, 628–640.

Hawkins, H. L., Hillyard, S. A., Luck, S. J., Mouloua, M., Downing, C., & Woodward, D. P. (1990). Visual attention modulates signal detectability. *Journal of Experimental Psychology. Human Perception and Performance, 16*, 802–811.

He, X., Fan, S., Zhou, K., & Chen, L. (2004). Cue validity and object-based attention. *Journal of Cognitive Neuroscience, 16*, 1085–1097.

Heinze, H. J., Luck, S. J., Mangun, G. R., & Hillyard, S. A. (1990). Visual event-related potentials index focused attention within bilateral stimulus arrays. I. Evidence for early selection. *Electroencephalography and Clinical Neurophysiology, 75*, 511–527.

Heinze, H. J., Luck, S. J., Münte, T. F., Gös, A., Mangun, G. R., & Hillyard, S. A. (1994a). Attention to adjacent and separate positions in space: An electrophysiological analysis. *Perception & Psychophysics, 56*, 42–52.

Heinze, H. J., Mangun, G. R., Burchert, W., Hinrichs, H., Scholz, M., Münte, T. F., et al. (1994b). Combined spatial and temporal imaging of brain activity during visual selective attention in humans. *Nature, 372,* 543–546.

Henderson, J. M., & Macquistan, A. D. (1993). The spatial distribution of attention following an exogenous cue. *Perception and Psychophysics, 53,* 221–230.

Hickey, C., Di Lollo, V., & McDonald, J. J. (2009). Electrophysiological indices of target and distractor processing in visual search. *Journal of Cognitive Neuroscience, 21,* 760–775.

Hillyard, S. A., & Anllo-Vento, L. (1998). Event-related brain potentials in the study of visual selective attention. *Proceedings of the National Academy of Sciences of the United States of America, 95,* 781–787.

Hillyard, S. A., Hinrichs, H., Tempelmann, C., Morgan, S. T., Hansen, J. C., Scheich, H., & Heinze, H.-J. (1997). Combining steady-state visual evoked potentials and fMRI to localize brain activity during selective attention. *Human Brain Mapping, 5,* 287–292.

Hillyard, S. A., & Münte, T. F. (1984). Selective attention to color and location: An analysis with event-related brain potentials. *Perception & Psychophysics, 36,* 185–198.

Hillyard, S. A., Münte, T. F., & Neville, H. J. (1985). Visual-spatial attention, orienting and brain physiology. In M. I. Posner, & O. S. Marin (Eds.), *Mechanisms of attention: Attention and performance XI* (pp. 63–84). Hillsdale, NJ: Erlbaum.

Hillyard, S. A., Vogel, E. K., & Luck, S. J. (1998). Sensory gain control (amplification) as a mechanism of selective attention: electrophysiological and neuroimaging evidence. *Philosophical Transactions of the Royal Society of London. Series B, Biological Sciences, 353,* 1257–1270.

Hochstein, S., & Ahissar, M. (2002). View from the top: Hierarchies and reverse hierarchies in the visual system. *Neuron, 36,* 791–804.

Hopf, J.-M., Luck, S. J., Girelli, M., Hagner, T., Mangun, G. R., Scheich, H., & Heinze, H.-J. (2000). Neural sources of focused attention in visual search. *Cerebral Cortex, 10,* 1233–1241.

Hopf, J. M., Boelmans, K., Schoenfeld, A. M., Heinze, H.-J., & Luck, S. J. (2002a). How does attention attenuate target-distractor interference in vision? Evidence from magnetoencephalographic recordings. *Cognitive Brain Research, 15,* 17–29.

Hopf, J. M., Vogel, E., Woodman, G., Heinze, H. J., & Luck, S. J. (2002b). Localizing visual discrimination processes in time and space. *Journal of Neurophysiology, 88,* 2088–2095.

Hopf, J. M., Boelmans, K., Schoenfeld, A., Luck, S. J., & Heinze, H.-J. (2004). Attention to features precedes attention to locations in visual search: Evidence from electromagnetic brain responses in humans. *Journal of Neuroscience, 24,* 1822–1832.

Hopf, J. M., Boehler, C. N., Schoenfeld, M. A., Heinze, H.-J., & Tsotsos, J. K. (2010). The spatial profile of the focus of attention in visual search: Insights from MEG recordings. *Vision Research, 50,* 1312–1320.

Hopf, J. M., Boehler, N., Luck, S. J., Tsotsos, J. K., Heinze, H.-J., & Schoenfeld, M. A. (2006a). Direct neurophysiological evidence for spatial suppression surrounding the focus of attention in vision. *Proceedings of The National Academy of Sciences of the United States of America, 103,* 1053–1058.

Hopf, J. M., Luck, S. J., Boelmans, K., Schoenfeld, A., Boehler, N., Rieger, J. W., & Heinze, H.-J. (2006b). The neural site of attention matches the spatial scale of perception. *Journal of Neuroscience, 26,* 3532–3540.

Hopfinger, J. B., & Mangun, G. R. (1998). Reflexive attention modulates processing of visual stimuli in human extrastriate cortex. *Psychological Science, 9,* 441–447.

Hopfinger, J. B., & Mangun, G. R. (2001). Tracking the influence of reflexive attention on sensory and cognitive processing. *Cognitive, Affective, & Behavioral Neuroscience, 1,* 56–65.

Jolicoeur, P., Sessa, P., Dell'acqua, R., & Robitaille, N. (2006). On the control of visual spatial attention: Evidence from human electrophysiology. *Psychological Research, 70,* 414–424.

Karayanidis, F., & Michie, P. T. (1996). Frontal processing negativity in a visual attention task. *Electroencephalography and Clinical Neurophysiology, 99,* 38–56.

Karns, C. M., & Knight, R. T. (2009). Intermodal auditory, visual, and tactile attention modulates early stages of neural processing. *Journal of Cognitive Neuroscience, 21,* 669–683.

Kastner, S., & Ungerleider, L. G. (2000). Mechanisms of visual attention in the human cortex. *Annual Review of Neuroscience, 23,* 315–341.

Kelly, S. P., Gomez-Ramirez, M., & Foxe, J. J. (2008). Spatial attention modulates initial afferent activity in human primary visual cortex. *Cerebral Cortex, 18,* 2629–2636.

Kenemans, J. L., Kok, A., & Smulders, F. T. (1993). Event-related potentials to conjunctions of spatial frequency and orientation as a function of stimulus parameters and response requirements. *Electroencephalography and Clinical Neurophysiology, 88,* 51–63.

Khoe, W., Mitchell, J. F., Reynolds, J. H., & Hillyard, S. A. (2005). Exogenous attentional selection of transparent superimposed surfaces modulates early event-related potentials. *Vision Research, 45,* 3004–3014.

Khoe, W., Mitchell, J. F., Reynolds, J. H., & Hillyard, S. A. (2008). ERP evidence that surface-based attention biases interocular competition during rivalry. *Journal of Vision, 8,* 1–11.

Kiss, M., Van Velzen, J., & Eimer, M. (2008). The N2pc component and its links to attention shifts and spatially selective visual processing. *Psychophysiology, 45,* 240–249.

LaBerge, D., Carlson, R. L., Williams, J. K., & Bunney, B. G. (1997). Shifting attention in visual space: Tests of moving-spotlight models versus an activity-distribution model. *Journal of Experimental Psychology. Human Perception and Performance, 23,* 1380–1392.

Lee, J., Williford, T., & Maunsell, J. H. (2007). Spatial attention and the latency of neuronal responses in macaque area V4. *Journal of Neuroscience, 27,* 9632–9637.

Liu, T., Slotnick, S. D., Serences, J. T., & Yantis, S. (2003). Cortical mechanisms of feature-based attentional control. *Cerebral Cortex, 13,* 1334–1343.

Luck, S. J., Fan, S., & Hillyard, S. (1993). Attention-related modulation of sensory-evoked brain activity in a visual search task. *Journal of Cognitive Neuroscience, 5,* 188–195.

Luck, S. J., Chelazzi, L., Hillyard, S. A., & Desimone, R. (1997a). Neural mechanisms of spatial selective attention in areas V1, V2, and V4 of macaque visual cortex. *Journal of Neurophysiology, 77,* 24–42.

Luck, S. J., Girelli, M., McDermott, M. T., & Ford, M. A. (1997b). Bridging the gap between monkey neurophysiology and human perception: An ambiguity resolution theory of visual selective attention. *Cognitive Psychology, 33,* 64–87.

Luck, S. J., & Hillyard, S. A. (1994a). Electrophysiological correlates of feature analysis during visual search. *Psychophysiology, 31,* 291–308.

Luck, S. J., & Hillyard, S. A. (1994b). Spatial filtering during visual search: Evidence from human electrophysiology. *Journal of Experimental Psychology. Human Perception and Performance, 20,* 1000–1014.

Luck, S. J., & Hillyard, S. A. (1995). The role of attention in feature detection and conjunction discrimination: An electrophysiological analysis. *International Journal of Neuroscience, 80,* 281–297.

Luck, S. J., Hillyard, S. A., Mouloua, M., Woldorff, M. G., Clark, V. P., & Hawkins, H. L. (1994). Effects of spatial cueing on luminance detectability: Psychophysical and electrophysical evidence for early selection. *Journal of Experimental Psychology. Human Perception and Performance, 20,* 887–904.

Mangun, G. R. (1995). Neural mechanisms of visual selective attention. *Psychophysiology, 32,* 4–18.

Mangun, G. R., & Buck, L. A. (1998). Sustained visual-spatial attention produces costs and benefits in response time and evoked neural activity. *Neuropsychologia, 36,* 189–200.

Mangun, G. R., Buonocore, M., Girelli, M., & Jha, A. (1998). ERP and fMRI measures of visual spatial selective attention. *Human Brain Mapping, 6,* 383–389.

Mangun, G. R., & Hillyard, S. A. (1990). Allocation of visual attention to spatial locations: Tradeoff functions for event-related brain potentials and detection performance. *Perception & Psychophysics, 47,* 532–550.

Mangun, G. R., & Hillyard, S. A. (1991). Modulations of sensory-evoked potentials indicate changes in perceptual processing during visual-spatial priming. *Journal of Experimental Psychology. Human Perception and Performance, 17,* 1057–1074.

Martinez, A., Ramanathan, D. S., Foxe, J. J., Javitt, D. C., & Hillyard, S. A. (2007b). The role of spatial attention in the selection of real and illusory objects. *Journal of Neuroscience, 27,* 7963–7973.

Martinez, A., Teder-Salejarvi, W., & Hillyard, S. A. (2007a). Spatial attention facilitates selection of illusory objects: Evidence from event-related brain potentials. *Brain Research, 1139,* 143–152.

Martinez, A., Teder-Salejarvi, W., Vazquez, M., Molholm, S., Foxe, J. J., Javitt, D. C., et al. (2006). Objects are highlighted by spatial attention. *Journal of Cognitive Neuroscience, 18,* 298–310.

Martinez, A., Anllo-Vento, L., Sereno, M. I., Frank, L. R., Buxton, R. B., Dubowitz, D. J., et al. (1999). Involvement of striate and extrastriate visual cortical areas in spatial attention. *Nature Neuroscience, 2,* 364–369.

Martinez-Trujillo, J. C., & Treue, S. (2004). Feature-based attention increases the selectivity of population responses in primate visual cortex. *Current Biology, 14,* 744–751.

Maunsell, J. H., & Treue, S. (2006). Feature-based attention in visual cortex. *Trends in Neurosciences, 29,* 317–322.

McAdams, C. J., & Maunsell, J. H. R. (1999). Effects of attention on orientation-tuning functions of single neurons in macaque cortical area V4. *Journal of Neuroscience, 19,* 431–441.

McAdams, C. J., & Maunsell, J. H. (2000). Attention to both space and feature modulates neuronal responses in macaque area V4. *Journal of Neurophysiology, 83,* 1751–1755.

McAlonan, K., Cavanaugh, J., & Wurtz, R. H. (2008). Guarding the gateway to cortex with attention in visual thalamus. *Nature, 456,* 391–394.

McCarley, J. S., & Mounts, J. R. (2007). Localized attentional interference affects object individuation, not feature detection. *Perception, 36,* 17–32.

McDonald, J. J., Ward, L. M., & Kiehl, K. A. (1999). An event-related brain potential study of inhibition of return. *Perception and Psychophysics, 61,* 1411–1423.

McKeefry, D. J., & Zeki, S. (1997). The position and topography of the human colour centre as revealed by functional magnetic resonance imaging. *Brain, 120,* 2229–2242.

McMains, S. A., & Somers, D. C. (2004). Multiple spotlights of attentional selection in human visual cortex. *Neuron, 42,* 677–686.

McMains, S. A., & Somers, D. C. (2005). Processing efficiency of divided spatial attention mechanisms in human visual cortex. *Journal of Neuroscience, 25,* 9444–9448.

Mehta, A. D., Ulbert, I., & Schroeder, C. E. (2000). Intermodal selective attention in monkeys. I: Distribution and timing of effects across visual areas. *Cerebral Cortex, 10,* 343–358.

Mirabella, G., Bertini, G., Samengo, I., Kilavik, B. E., Frilli, D., Della Libera, C., & Chelazzi, L. (2007). Neurons in area V4 of the macaque translate attended visual features into behaviorally relevant categories. *Neuron, 54,* 303–318.

Mitchell, J. F., Stoner, G. R., & Reynolds, J. H. (2004). Object-based attention determines dominance in binocular rivalry. *Nature, 429,* 410–413.

Mitchell, J. F., Stoner, G. R., Fallah, M., & Reynolds, J. H. (2003). Attentional selection of superimposed surfaces cannot be explained by modulation of the gain of color channels. *Vision Research, 43,* 1323–1328.

Moore, T., Armstrong, K. M., & Fallah, M. (2003). Visuomotor origins of covert spatial attention. *Neuron, 40,* 671–683.

Moran, J., & Desimone, R. (1985). Selective attention gates visual processing in the extrastriate cortex. *Science, 229,* 782–784.

Morgan, S. T., Hansen, J. C., & Hillyard, S. A. (1996). Selective attention to stimulus location modulates the steady-state visual evoked potential. *Proceedings of the National Academy of Sciences of the United States of America, 93,* 4770–4774.

Motter, B. (1993). Focal attention produces spatially selective processing in visual cortical areas V1, V2, and V4 in the presence of competing stimuli. *Journal of Neurophysiology, 70,* 909–919.

Motter, B. C. (1994). Neural correlates of attentive selection for color or luminance in extrastriate area V4. *Journal of Neuroscience, 14,* 2178–2189.

Mounts, J. R. (2000a). Attentional capture by abrupt onsets and feature singletons produces inhibitory surrounds. *Perception and Psychophysics, 62,* 1485–1493.

Mounts, J. R. (2000b). Evidence for suppressive mechanisms in attentional selection: Feature singletons produce inhibitory surrounds. *Perception and Psychophysics, 62,* 969–983.

Muller, M. M., Andersen, S., Trujillo, N. J., Valdes-Sosa, P., Malinowski, P., & Hillyard, S. A. (2006). Feature-selective attention enhances color signals in early visual areas of the human brain. *Proceedings of the National Academy of Sciences of the United States of America, 103,* 14250–14254.

Muller, N. G., Bartelt, O. A., Donner, T. H., Villringer, A., & Brandt, S. A. (2003b). A physiological correlate of the "zoom lens" of visual attention. *Journal of Neuroscience, 23,* 3561–3565.

Muller, M. M., & Hubner, R. (2002). Can the spotlight of attention be shaped like a doughnut? Evidence from steady-state visual evoked potentials. *Psychological Science, 13,* 119–124.

Muller, N. G., & Kleinschmidt, A. (2003). Dynamic interaction of object- and space-based attention in retinotopic visual areas. *Journal of Neuroscience, 23,* 9812–9816.

Muller, N. G., & Kleinschmidt, A. (2004). The attentional "spotlight's" penumbra: Center-surround modulation in striate cortex. *Neuroreport, 15,* 977–980.

Muller, M. M., Malinowski, P., Gruber, T., & Hillyard, S. A. (2003a). Sustained division of the attentional spotlight. *Nature, 424,* 309–312.

Muller, M. M., Picton, T. W., Valdes-Sosa, P., Riera, J., Teder-Salejarvi, W. A., & Hillyard, S. A. (1998b). Effects of spatial selective attention on the steady-state visual evoked potential in the 20–28 Hz range. *Brain Research. Cognitive Brain Research, 6,* 249–261.

Muller, M. M., Teder, W., & Hillyard, S. A. (1997). Magnetoencephalographic recording of steady-state visual evoked cortical activity. *Brain Topography, 9,* 163–168.

Muller, M. M., Teder-Sälejärvi, W., & Hillyard, S. A. (1998a). The time course of cortical facilitation during cued shifts of spatial attention. *Nature Neuroscience, 1,* 631–634.

Nakayama, K., & Silverman, G. H. (1986). Serial and parallel processing of visual feature conjunctions. *Nature, 320*, 264–265.

Noesselt, T., Hillyard, S., Woldorff, M., Schoenfeld, A., Hagner, T., Jancke, L., et al. (2002). Delayed striate cortical activation during spatial attention. *Neuron, 35*, 575–587.

O'Connor, D. H., Fukui, M. M., Pinsk, M. A., & Kastner, S. (2002). Attention modulates responses in the human lateral geniculate nucleus. *Nature Neuroscience, 5*, 1203–1209.

O'Craven, K. M., Rosen, B. R., Kwong, K. K., Treisman, A., & Savoy, R. L. (1997). Voluntary attention modulates fMRI activity in human MT-MST. *Neuron, 18*, 591–598.

Patzwahl, D. R., & Treue, S. (2009). Combining spatial and feature-based attention within the receptive field of MT neurons. *Vision Research, 49*, 1188–1193.

Picton, T. W., Hillyard, S. A., Galambos, R., & Schiff, M. (1971). Human auditory attention: A central or peripheral process? *Science, 173*(994), 351–353.

Pinilla, T., Cobo, A., Torres, K., & Valdes-Sosa, M. (2001). Attentional shifts between surfaces: Effects on detection and early brain potentials. *Vision Research, 41*, 1619–1630.

Poghosyan, V., & Ioannides, A. A. (2008). Attention modulates earliest responses in the primary auditory and visual cortices. *Neuron, 58*, 802–813.

Posner, M. I. (1980). Orienting of attention. *Quarterly Journal of Experimental Psychology, 32*, 3–25.

Proverbio, A. M., Del Zotto, M., & Zani, A. (2007). Inter-individual differences in the polarity of early visual responses and attention effects. *Neuroscience Letters, 419*, 131–136.

Reynolds, J. H., Alborzian, S., & Stoner, G. R. (2003). Exogenously cued attention triggers competitive selection of surfaces. *Vision Research, 43*, 59–66.

Rodriguez, V., Valdes-Sosa, M., & Freiwald, W. (2002). Dividing attention between form and motion during transparent surface perception. *Brain Research. Cognitive Brain Research, 13*, 187–193.

Roelfsema, P. R., Lamme, V. A. F., & Spekreijse, H. (1998). Object-based attention in the primary visual cortex of macaque monkey. *Nature, 395*, 376–381.

Roelfsema, P. R., Tolboom, M., & Khayat, P. S. (2007). Different processing phases for features, figures, and selective attention in the primary visual cortex. *Neuron, 56*, 785–792.

Saenz, M., Buracas, G. T., & Boynton, G. M. (2002). Global effects of feature-based attention in human visual cortex. *Nature Neuroscience, 5*, 631–632.

Saenz, M., Buracas, G. T., & Boynton, G. M. (2003). Global feature-based attention for motion and color. *Vision Research, 43*, 629–637.

Schoenfeld, M., Hopf, J. M., Martinez, A., Mai, H., Sattler, C., Gasde, A., et al. (2007). Spatio-temporal analysis of feature-based attention. *Cerebral Cortex, 17*, 2468–2477.

Schoenfeld, M. A., Tempelmann, C., Martinez, A., Hopf, J. M., Sattler, C., Heinze, H. J., & Hillyard, S. A. (2003). Dynamics of feature binding during object-selective attention. *Proceedings of the National Academy of Sciences of the United States of America, 100*, 11806–11811.

Schwartz, S., Vuilleumier, P., Hutton, C., Maravita, A., Dolan, R. J., & Driver, J. (2005). Attentional load and sensory competition in human vision: Modulation of fMRI responses by load at fixation during task-irrelevant stimulation in the peripheral visual field. *Cerebral Cortex, 15*, 770–786.

Serences, J. T., & Boynton, G. M. (2007). Feature-based attentional modulations in the absence of direct visual stimulation. *Neuron, 55*, 301–312.

Slotnick, S. D., Hopfinger, J. B., Klein, S. A., & Sutter, E. E. (2002). Darkness beyond the light: Attentional inhibition surrounding the classic spotlight. *Neuroreport, 13*, 773–778.

Slotnick, S. D., Schwarzbach, J., & Yantis, S. (2003). Attentional inhibition of visual processing in human striate and extrastriate cortex. *Neuroimage, 19*, 1602–1611.

Steinman, B. A., Steinman, S. B., & Lehmkuhle, S. (1995). Visual attention mechanisms show a center-surround organization. *Vision Research, 35*, 1859–1869.

Stoppel, C. M., Boehler, C. N., Sabelhaus, C., Heinze, H. J., Hopf, J. M., & Schoenfeld, M. A. (2007). Neural mechanisms of spatial- and feature-based attention: A quantitative analysis. *Brain Research, 1181*, 51–60.

Tolias, A. S., Moore, T., Smirnakis, S. M., Tehovnik, E. J., Siapas, A. G., & Schiller, P. H. (2001). Eye movements modulate visual receptive fields of V4 neurons. *Neuron, 29*, 757–767.

Tollner, T., Gramann, K., Muller, H. J., Kiss, M., & Eimer, M. (2008). Electrophysiological markers of visual dimension changes and response changes. *Journal of Experimental Psychology. Human Perception and Performance, 34*, 531–542.

Tootell, R. B. H., Hadjikhani, N., Hall, E. K., Marrett, S., Vanduffel, W., Vaughan, J. T., & Dale, A. M. (1998). The retinotopy of visual spatial attention. *Neuron, 21*, 1409–1422.

Treisman, A. (1991). Search, similarity, and integration of features between and within dimensions. *Journal of Experimental Psychology. Human Perception and Performance, 17*, 652–676.

Treisman, A., & Gelade, G. (1980). A feature-integration theory of attention. *Cognitive Psychology, 12,* 97–136.

Treisman, A., & Sato, S. (1990). Conjunction search revisited. *Journal of Experimental Psychology. Human Perception and Performance, 16,* 459–478.

Treue, S., & Martinez Trujillo, J. C. (1999). Feature-based attention influences motion processing gain in macaque visual cortex. *Nature, 399,* 575–579.

Tsotsos, J. K. (2005). The selective tuning model for visual attention. In L. Itti, G. Rees, & J. K. Tsotsos (Eds.), *Neurobiology of attention* (pp. 562–569). San Diego: Elsevier.

Tsotsos, J. K., Culhane, S. M., Wai, W. Y. K., Lai, Y., Davis, N., & Nuflo, F. (1995). Modeling visual attention via selective tuning. *Artificial Intelligence, 78,* 507–545.

Tsotsos, J. K., Rodriguez-Sanchez, A. J., Rothenstein, A. L., & Simine, E. (2008). The different stages of visual recognition need different attentional binding strategies. *Brain Research, 1225,* 119–132.

Valdes-Sosa, M., Bobes, M. A., Rodriguez, V., & Pinilla, T. (1998b). Switching attention without shifting the spotlight object-based attentional modulation of brain potentials. *Journal of Cognitive Neuroscience, 10,* 137–151.

Valdes-Sosa, M., Cobo, A., & Pinilla, T. (1998a). Transparent motion and object-based attention. *Cognition, 66,* B13–B23.

Valdes-Sosa, M., Cobo, A., & Pinilla, T. (2000). Attention to object files defined by transparent motion. *Journal of Experimental Psychology. Human Perception and Performance, 26,* 488–505.

Van Voorhis, S., & Hillyard, S. A. (1977). Visual evoked potentials and selective attention to points in space. *Perception & Psychophysics, 22,* 54–62.

Vanduffel, W., Tootell, R. B. H., & Orban, G. A. (2000). Attention-dependent suppression of metabolic activity in early stages of the macaque visual system. *Cerebral Cortex, 10,* 109–126.

Vogel, E. K., & Luck, S. (2000). The visual N1 component as an index of a discrimination process. *Psychophysiology, 37,* 190–203.

Wade, A. R., Brewer, A. A., Rieger, J. W., & Wandell, B. A. (2002). Functional measurements of human ventral occipital cortex: Retinotopy and colour. *Philosophical Transactions of the Royal Society of London. Series B, Biological Sciences, 357,* 963–973.

Wannig, A., Rodriguez, V., & Freiwald, W. A. (2007). Attention to surfaces modulates motion processing in extrastriate area MT. *Neuron, 54,* 639–651.

Wijers, A. A., Lamain, W., Slopsema, J. S., Mulder, G., & Mulder, L. J. (1989). An electrophysiological investigation of the spatial distribution of attention to colored stimuli in focused and divided attention conditions. *Biological Psychology, 29,* 213–245.

Woldorff, M. G., Fox, P. T., Matzke, M., Lancaster, J. L., Veeraswamy, S., Zamarripa, F., et al. (1997). Retinotopic organization of early visual spatial attention effects as revealed by PET and ERSs. *Human Brain Mapping, 5,* 280–286.

Wolfe, J. (1994). Guided search 2.0 A revised model of visual search. *Psychonomic Bulletin & Review, 1,* 202–238.

Wolfe, J. M., Cave, K. R., & Franzel, S. L. (1989). Guided search: An alternative to the feature integration model for visual search. *Journal of Experimental Psychology. Human Perception and Performance, 15,* 419–433.

Wolfe, J. M., Yu, K. P., Steward, M. I., Shorter, A. D., Friedman-Hill, S. R., & Cave, K. R. (1990). Limitations on the parallel guidance of visual search: Color x color and orientation x orientation conjunctions. *Journal of Experimental Psychology. Human Perception and Performance, 16,* 879–892.

Woodman, G. F., & Luck, S. J. (1999). Electrophysiological measurement of rapid shifts of attention during visual search. *Nature, 400,* 867–869.

Woodman, G. F., & Luck, S. J. (2003a). Serial deployment of attention during visual search. *Journal of Experimental Psychology. Human Perception and Performance, 29,* 121–138.

Woodman, G. F., & Luck, S. J. (2003b). Dissociations among attention, perception, and awareness during object-substitution masking. *Psychological Science, 14,* 605–611.

Woodman, G. F., Kang, M. S., Rossi, A. F., & Schall, J. D. (2007). Nonhuman primate event-related potentials indexing covert shifts of attention. *Proceedings of the National Academy of Sciences of the United States of America, 104,* 15111–15116.

Zhang, W., & Luck, S. J. (2009). Feature-based attention modulates feedforward visual processing. *Nature Neuroscience, 12,* 24–25.

2

Involuntary Attention

JOSEPH B. HOPFINGER AND EMILY L. PARKS

THE CAPACITY of human cognitive systems is limited, and thus, mechanisms of attention are critical in the selection of relevant information. Of particular interest for the present chapter are the neural mechanisms underlying the type of attention described in the following quote from Titchener.

> There is, in the first place, an attention that we are compelled to give and are powerless to prevent. . . . there are impressions that we cannot help attending to . . . they force their way to the focus of consciousness, whatever the obstacles that they have to overcome. (Titchener, 1916)

This type of involuntary attention has been labeled in a variety of ways, and descriptions of it date back to Augustine of Hippo (354–430 AD), who contrasted it with voluntary control (reviewed in Hatfield, 1998). William James referred to it as "passive attention" and contrasted it with "active attention," reflecting the difference in effort between these forms of attention (James, 1890). Others have used the terms "exogenous" and "endogenous" to reflect the locus of the triggering event (exogenous, meaning outside the person; endogenous, meaning within the person). Similarly, "reflexive attention" and "attentional capture" have been contrasted with "controlled attention" or "voluntary attention" (see, for example, Chapter 1 of this volume). Although the terms may have slightly different connotations, in this chapter, we will use the term *involuntary attention* to refer to the attention that we are "powerless to prevent." Elsewhere in this volume, the terms *reflexive attention* and *bottom-up attention* are employed, and should be understood to refer, except as otherwise noted, to the processes described in this chapter.

The powerful effects of involuntary attention can be appreciated simply by reflecting on daily events. A flash of lightning across a moonless night or the crash of broken glass at a quiet restaurant grabs attention quickly and without effort or volition. The ease of appreciation of this process contributed to descriptions of involuntary attention predating even the earliest psychology textbooks; however, this may also have led to it not being investigated as intensely by early psychologists. Much of the initial research into attention concerned the voluntary type of attention. In one of the earliest studies of attention, Helmholtz demonstrated that attention was not restricted to the direction of gaze, but rather could move without movement of the head or eyes ("covert attention") (1867/1925). Although his experiments investigated voluntary attention, the establishment of attention as being distinct from the center of eye gaze is important for understanding involuntary attention as well, and most of the research reviewed in this chapter relies on paradigms of covert attention. The effects of involuntary attention were not as intensely studied by early psychologists, perhaps because these effects may have seemed less in need of explanation, in that sometimes a stimulus "simply" captures attention. However, as this chapter will try to make clear, powerful mechanisms of involuntary attention are not always readily apparent to introspection, and the distinction between voluntary and involuntary attention is not simply a difference in the control of a single mental spotlight.

Following the insights of the turn-of-the-century psychologists, cognitive psychologists in the late 1970s began using chronometric methods to more precisely define the effects of involuntary attention. These studies of attention, which often used visual stimuli, showed that a nonpredictive luminance change ("cue" in Figure 2.1) captured attention and sped reaction times (RTs) to subsequent target stimuli at that same location (the cued location) versus targets at other locations (the uncued locations) (Posner et al., 1987; Jonides, 1981; Müller & Rabbitt, 1989). These data provided empirical support for intuitive descriptions of this type of attention as acting quickly and reflexively, without effort, and in a way that enhances perception. In addition, these studies provided new details about the time course of attention, showing that involuntary attention affected processing very shortly after the capturing effect (even within 50 ms), in contrast to voluntary attention, which took much longer to exert its strongest effects (earliest robust effects at ~300 ms; Cheal & Lyon, 1991). This research also provided foundational experimental paradigms that could be adapted to investigate the underlying brain mechanisms, the neuroscience of attention.

Although the initial involuntary capture to a salient stimulus is easily perceived and appreciated through introspection, this facilitation of processing has been shown to be fleeting, lasting only a few hundred milliseconds (if voluntary attention is not subsequently engaged to hold attention at that location). In the absence of voluntary attention, the initial reflexive facilitation at the cued location is quickly followed by another involuntary inhibitory effect, and this latter effect is much less accessible to conscious awareness. Indeed, whereas description of the capture of attention dates back to antiquity (reviewed in Hatfield, 1998), there is little evidence that philosophers or early psychologists imagined the existence of this later inhibitory mechanism that follows the initial capture of attention. In fact, this inhibitory effect was not revealed until the 1980s, when behavioral studies demonstrated that, when attention is not kept at the captured location through voluntary effort, manual responses to stimuli at that location are significantly slowed compared to other locations in the visual field (Figure 2.1, *bottom*). In other words, the captured location quickly goes from being given preferential treatment to being shunned. Posner and Cohen (1984) first described this slowing, and labeled it *inhibition of return* (IOR), suggesting that attention was inhibited from returning to the location where it had recently been captured. Whereas IOR has been shown to be a robust effect of involuntary attention (reviewed in Klein, 2000), covert voluntary attention does not show this effect, as it can remain focused on a location for prolonged periods of time. In fact, the facilitatory effects of voluntary covert attention are usually only beginning to reach maximum levels at approximately the same time that the involuntary facilitation is being replaced by IOR (Cheal & Lyon, 1991).

The finding of this automatic inhibitory mechanism highlights a general feature of involuntary processes that has spurred (and continues to

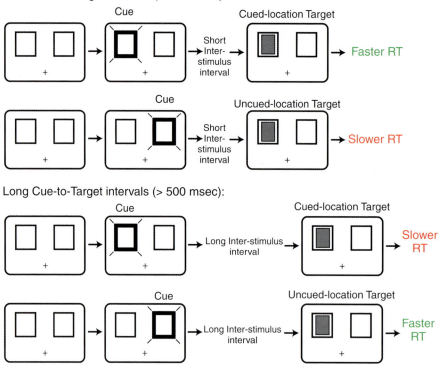

FIGURE 2.1 Typical trial sequence for studies of involuntary attention. *Top*: At short cue-to-target intervals, a nonpredictive cue (shown here as thicker outline of one of the two standing background boxes) captures attention and speeds reaction times to subsequent target stimuli at the cued location versus targets at the uncued location. *Bottom*: At long cue-to-target intervals, cued location targets are responded to significantly slower then uncued location targets, an effect referred to as *inhibition of return*. Note that the cued location target display and the uncued location target display are physically identical, but are preceded by cues at different locations. It is critical when investigating attention effects with event-related potentials to ensure the physical stimulus is the same in both the attended and unattended conditions.

spur) interest and research into involuntary attention. Specifically, as with IOR, neural mechanisms that are "reflexive" or even "automatic" can be shown to significantly affect our behavior despite our lack of conscious awareness of the processes. Whereas the initial capture of attention is readily apparent and easily appreciated, the subsequent inhibition at this location affects our perceptions and behavior without bothering to rise into our consciousness. This raises the question of what other effects involuntary attention has on neural processing that are beyond our power to consciously perceive. Such questions drive ongoing research into elucidating the mechanisms of involuntary attention and understanding how

these processes affect our perceptions, cognition, and behavior.

In this chapter, we will focus predominately on research using the event-related potential (ERP) method to investigate the mechanisms of involuntary attention. Given the very rapid time course of reflexive attention, and given its rapid switch from facilitating to inhibiting target processing, methods that directly measure neural activity are important for understanding the rapid dynamics of involuntary attention. The critical issues being reviewed in the present chapter revolve around the following questions: What stage or stages of processing, from initial sensation through response execution, are modulated by mechanisms of involuntary attention? Do involuntary and voluntary attention affect neural processing in the same way? How do voluntary and involuntary attention interact when pitted against each other? Is the capture of attention automatic, or is it contingent on top-down goals? What distinguishes the ability of some subjects to avoid distraction better than others? Beyond the initial reflexive orienting toward a salient stimulus, what involuntarily *holds* attention?

NEURAL EFFECTS OF INVOLUNTARY ATTENTION

Event-related Potential Methodology

Before describing the experimental results that have answered some of these questions about involuntary attention, a brief introduction on the primary method used in these studies may be helpful. The event-related potential (ERP) method provides a measure of neural activity at a time scale very well suited to investigate the fast-acting effects of involuntary attention. The ERP waveform is obtained by averaging sections of the ongoing electroencephalogram (EEG) over many instances of the same stimulus or cognitive event. In a typical experiment, the ongoing EEG is sampled at rates of 250–1000 times/sec from electrodes placed on the scalp. The EEG contains electrical activity due to a large variety of sources (e.g., muscle activity, homeostatic processes) in addition to the activity related to specific cognitive or sensory events. By repeating the event of interest, the stimulus-locked EEG can be extracted and averaged, allowing the consistent neural activity ("signal") related to the event to remain in the ERP waveform, whereas other electrical activity (neural or other) unrelated to the event of interest (the "noise") is averaged out.

Although the specific shape of the ERP waveforms differ across sensory modalities, consistent features of ERPs make them very useful for studying cognitive processing. Specifically, the early peaks and troughs ("components") of the waveform are usually related to activity in early sensory processing regions, whereas later components reflect higher-order cognitive processes and response preparation. Since most of the ERP results presented in this chapter will be visually evoked waveforms, it is useful to highlight key components of the canonical ERP generated by visual stimuli (Figure 2.2A). For ease of presentation, all the components in this cartoon are shown on a single waveform, but note that in real data, different components are observed at different locations across the scalp. The first major component of the visual-evoked ERP is the C1, with the "C" referring to its central location (over central posterior scalp sites), and the "1" referring to it being the first major component of the visual ERP. The C1 peaks around 70–100 ms and is generated in striate visual cortex ("V1"); therefore, it is a marker of the earliest visual processing within the cortex (that can be observed with this method). The polarity (positive or negative) of the C1 depends on the location of the physical stimulus because the striate cortex curves along the calcarine sulcus. Therefore, upper visual field stimuli evoke a negative C1, and lower field stimuli evoke a positive C1. Following the C1, the components are generally named by their polarity as these later components do not change polarity with visual field location. The first component after the C1 is the P1: the first ("1") exclusively positive ("P") visual evoked component. The P1 peaks at about 100–130 ms and is thought to be generated from extrastriate regions (Heinze et al., 1994; Mangun et al., 1997), with the earliest portion of this component arising from middle occipital gyrus and a later portion from fusiform gyrus (Di Russo et al., 2001). Following the P1 are the anterior and posterior N1 components. In this chapter, we are most interested in the posterior N1, which peaks at about 170–200 ms and is thought to have multiple generators, including parietal and lateral occipital regions (Di Russo et al., 2001). In general, the neural sources of the longer-latency components are not as well understood, as each is probably composed of multiple generators. Following these early sensory-evoked components, there are other components that are not automatically evoked by the presence of a stimulus, but rather are related to cognitive processing. For example, a longer-latency component that is relevant to the present review is the P3, sometimes referred to as the P300, in reference to the latency (300 ms) at which this component

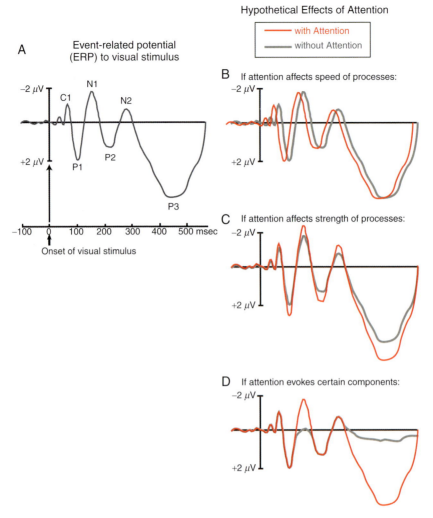

FIGURE 2.2   (**A**) Canonical event-related potential components evoked by a visual stimulus. All the components are shown on a single waveform, but note that in real data, different components are observed at different locations across the scalp. (**B**) Depiction of the hypothetical effect of attention on the speed of processes. (**C**) Depiction of the hypothetical effect of attention on the strength of processes. (**D**) Depiction of hypothetical effects if attention causes specific processes to be evoked.

sometimes occurs (although latency of this component can vary substantially). Multiple P3 components have been identified, and each is thought to reflect different processes and have multiple neural sources. For the present chapter, the relevant P3 is that related to making decisions about a stimulus. It is thought to reflect a process of "context updating," in which the new stimulus information is integrated into one's ongoing perceptual representation of the environment (Donchin, 1981). It is important to note, however, that the

P3 is not simply a motor preparation component, as it can be observed even if no overt response is required, as long as the stimulus is relevant and is processed to a semantic level. In contrast, other ERP components (not shown in Figure 2.2, but explained in sections below where relevant) are specifically linked to overt manual responses, such as the lateralized readiness potential (LRP). Of note, the entire ERP waveform shown in Figure 2.2 represents processes that all happen within approximately half of a second following the stimulus onset. Thus, ERPs have the millisecond temporal resolution necessary to track the fast-acting involuntary attention system. Furthermore, ERPs provide measures of processing from the earliest cortical processing through to response preparation and generation processes, permitting the effects of involuntary attention to be precisely tracked.

Before turning to the results of ERP studies of reflexive attention, it may be helpful to review specific examples of the possible effects of attention on neural processing and how those effects would be observed with ERPs. One possible effect of attention may be to speed processing at one or multiple stages of analysis, in which case the ERPs would reveal a latency shift of the waveform for attended versus unattended stimuli (Figure 2.2B). Another possibility is that attention may affect the strength of processing, in which case the components would be larger for attended versus unattended stimuli (Figure 2.2C). In the illustrations for these two examples, the effects are drawn as present at all stages of processing; however, it is also possible that only some components would be affected, and it could be a mix of these effects (speeding some components, enhancing others). Furthermore, some components could be entirely dependent on attention, being generated only to attended stimuli, and not being generated to unattended stimuli (Figure 2.2D). Any of these possibilities could account for the behavioral effects of attention mentioned above. Therefore, it is necessary to directly examine neural processing to understand the mechanisms of involuntary attention.

Neural Effects of Attentional Capture at Short Cue–Target Intervals

As described above, behavioral studies have shown that a noninformative peripheral "cue" stimulus captures attention and speeds processing of targets at the cued location, relative to the uncued location. The facilitation of manual response times, however, could be due to changes at any one of many stages of processing from the earliest subcortical levels of sensory processing through to response generation. We (Hopfinger & Mangun, 1998) investigated this issue using ERPs in a cuing paradigm, in which the peripheral cue stimulus was nonpredictive of target location (targets occurred equally often at the cued location and the uncued location). In this study, there were two location markers, similar to the paradigm shown in Figure 2.1, and the task was to discriminate whether the target bar was short or tall. In this study, we used two ranges of cue–target intervals: a short interval (68–268 ms) to investigate the initial facilitation at the cued location, and a longer cue–target interval (600–800 ms) to investigate IOR. The long ISI results are reviewed in a later section; here, we focus on the short ISI results.[1]

By analyzing the ERPs evoked by the targets, it was possible to determine the stages of processing that were affected by involuntary capture (i.e., that show a difference between cued versus uncued location targets) as well as those stages that involuntary attention can't change (i.e., that show no difference between cued and uncued location targets). In this and subsequent studies, we found that the earliest level of cortical processing, the C1, was immune to involuntary attention. This suggests that processing up to this stage, including the subcortical visual processing leading up to this stage, is not changed by involuntary attentional orienting. However, the P1 component was significantly changed by involuntary attention (Figure 2.3A). The latency of the P1 component did not change, suggesting that involuntary attention was not speeding up the process, but the size of the component was significantly greater for the cued versus uncued location targets. These results provide evidence that the facilitation of RTs by attentional capture is associated with an enhancement in early sensory processing. It is important to note that changes in processing at one stage do not necessarily propagate to every subsequent stage of processing. For instance, we have found no evidence that the N1, the component that follows the P1 and which is considered to index a discrimination process (Vogel & Luck, 2000), is similarly enhanced by involuntary attention. This provides evidence for the specificity of the involuntary mechanism, as it is not simply increasing the strength of the response at all levels, but selectively acts at the stage of the P1. These results, an enhanced P1 without an enhancement of the N1,

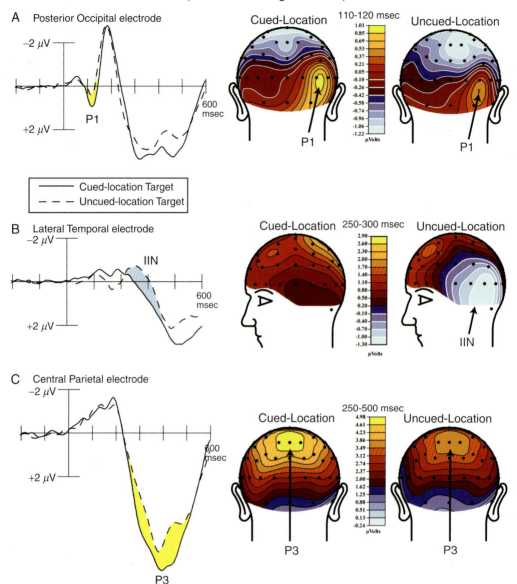

Effects of Involuntary Attention
(short cue-to-target interval)

FIGURE 2.3   Effects of involuntary attention at a *short* cue-to-target interval (data from Hopfinger & Mangun, 1998). Event-related potential results time-locked to target stimulus, as a function of location of preceding cue stimulus. "Cued location" targets refer to targets that occurred at the same location as the preceding cue stimulus. "Uncued location" targets refer to targets that were preceded by a cue at a different location. (**A**) The amplitude of the P1 component was found to be significantly greater for the cued versus uncued location targets, reflecting an enhancement in early sensory-processing by involuntary attention. (**B**) The ipsilateral invalid negativity (IIN) was produced only when involuntary attention had been captured to the wrong location (uncued location target). (**C**) The P3 was significantly enhanced for cued location targets relative to uncued location targets. Figure adapted from Hopfinger, J. B., & Mangun, G. R. (1998). Reflexive attention modulates processing of visual stimuli in human extrastriate cortex. *Psychological Science, 9,* 441–447, with permission from Wiley-Blackwell.

have now been shown across multiple tasks and levels of difficulty, specifically: a difficult discrimination task (Hopfinger & Mangun, 1998), a simple detection task (Hopfinger & Mangun, 2001), and a task in which the evoking stimulus could be ignored (passive viewing condition; Hopfinger & Maxwell, 2005). Thus, this enhancement of the P1 appears to be truly involuntary and task independent.

Along with the effect on early sensory-evoked processing, later processing is also affected by involuntary attention. We identified a component that appears to be uniquely evoked only when involuntary attention has been captured to one location and must be rapidly disengaged and reoriented to a different location. We labeled this component the *ipsilateral invalid negativity* (IIN) (Hopfinger & Mangun, 2001) because it occurs only on invalid trials, and it is a negativity (negative-going component) ipsilateral to the target (and therefore contralateral to the cue that captured attention to the wrong location). "Invalid" here simply refers to uncued location targets; "valid" refers to cued location targets. We suggested that no IIN is generated on valid trials because attention has already been captured to that location by the cue, and therefore, attention doesn't need to be reoriented to the target. As shown in Figure 2.3B (and from the experiment described above; Hopfinger & Mangun, 1998) the IIN peaks around 200–250 ms latency, and it is distributed over temporoparietal scalp sites, potentially consistent with a generator in the temporoparietal junction (TPJ). The TPJ has been found to be active in functional magnetic resonance imaging (fMRI) studies when attention must be disengaged and reoriented (Corbetta et al., 2000). The timing of the IIN also coincides with transcranial magnetic stimulation (TMS) results showing that disabling parietal cortex during this latency range impairs the ability to reorient attention (Chambers et al., 2004).

In addition to the P1 and IIN effects, our results revealed a third major effect of involuntary attention. As shown in Figure 2.3C, the central posterior P3 was significantly enhanced for cued location targets relative to uncued location targets. The posterior P3 can be affected by stimulus probability, with unexpected (or more improbable)

stimuli eliciting larger P3s than expected stimuli (Duncan-Johnson & Donchin, 1982). In our studies of involuntary attention, however, the cued location and uncued location stimuli were exactly equal in terms of likelihood and probability. Nevertheless the cued location targets evoked a larger P3, highlighting the influence of involuntary attention apart from stimulus probability. Previous studies have suggested that the P3 is also sensitive to stimulus relevance (Squires et al., 1977); therefore, the enhanced P3 in our studies of involuntary attention may be due to the tagging of the cued location as being, for a brief period, more important than other locations. This enhancement of the P3 has been found during both difficult discrimination tasks (Hopfinger & Mangun, 1998) and simple discrimination tasks (Hopfinger & Mangun, 2001), suggesting that it doesn't depend on task difficulty. However, this P3 effect does depend on the evoking stimulus being task-relevant. During conditions in which the evoking stimulus is completely task-irrelevant and ignored, no P3 component is generated and no differences are observed during this time window (Hopfinger & Maxwell, 2005). Taken together, the above studies have identified three stages of processing (the P1, IIN, and P3) that are affected by involuntary attention. These three indices can thus be used to further investigate the neural underpinning of other involuntary mechanisms, such as IOR, as well as the interactions between voluntary and involuntary attention, as will be described in the following sections.

Neural Effects at Long Cue–Target Intervals

As described earlier, the facilitatory effects of reflexive attention are fleeting and are quickly replaced by inhibition of return (IOR) at the same location. Event-related potential studies of involuntary attention have revealed both similarities and differences between the neural effects at longer cue–target intervals and the effects at shorter intervals described above. A critical debate regarding IOR has been whether it is a mechanism that affects perceptual-level processes or is rather simply a motor bias, affecting response-level processes while leaving early sensory processes intact. In our initial study of involuntary orienting, we found that at long cue–target intervals (600–800 ms), the P1 was significantly reduced for cued location targets relative to uncued location targets (Figure 2.4; Hopfinger & Mangun, 1998). Thus, at a long cue–target interval, perceptual processing is diminished for cued location targets at the same stage at which involuntary attention enhances processing at short cue–target intervals. The P3, however, showed no effect of involuntary attention at long cue–target intervals, in contrast to the robust effect on the P3 at short cue–target intervals. In addition, the IIN was not generated in this long interval condition. Thus, effects on the IIN and P3 appear to be transient and unique to the initial facilitative stage of involuntary attention, whereas the stage of processing indexed by the P1 is modulated by involuntary attention at both short and long intervals.

Although we found a significant reduction in the P1 at long SOAs in that initial study, we did not find a significant IOR in behavior in that study (Hopfinger & Mangun, 1998). Indeed, the link between inhibited sensory processing and IOR, measured behaviorally, hasn't always been clear. In a subsequent study, we found significant IOR

in behavior, but not a significant effect on the P1 (although there was a trend in the same direction; Hopfinger & Mangun, 2001). McDonald and colleagues (1999) were able to show a significant reduction in the P1 along with significant IOR in behavior, providing support for the view that IOR reflects an inhibition of perceptual processing. However, even in that study, the largest behavioral IOR effects (across conditions) were not associated with the largest early sensory-level ERP effects. Therefore, although a reduction in early visual processing appears to be an involuntary effect, it remained somewhat unclear if the early perceptual-level effect (P1) was underlying IOR, or if IOR was more strongly linked to an inhibition of motor-related processes (reviewed in Klein, 2000). Prime and Ward (2004) provided a direct test of this issue by analyzing both perceptual and motor-related ERP components. In addition to the P1 (perceptual) effect described above, they also analyzed the lateralized readiness potential (LRP), a motor-related component. Specifically, the LRP is a component that can be used to index overt response preparation. The LRP is calculated by comparing scalp sites overlying motor regions and subtracting the activity from sites ipsilateral

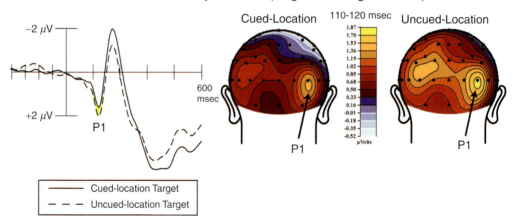

FIGURE 2.4   Effects of involuntary attention at a *long* cue-to-target interval (data from Hopfinger & Mangun, 1998). Event-related potential results time-locked to target stimulus, as a function of location of preceding cue stimulus. At long cue-to-target intervals, the P1 was significantly *reduced* for cued location targets relative to uncued location targets. Figure adapted from Hopfinger, J. B., & Mangun, G. R. (1998). Reflexive attention modulates processing of visual stimuli in human extrastriate cortex. *Psychological Science, 9,* 441–447, with permission from Wiley-Blackwell.

to the hand of response from activity contralateral to the responding hand, followed by averaging the resulting difference waves from each hand of response (Coles, 1989). The LRP can be time-locked to the manual response, in which case it reflects the timing of motor planning and execution. In their study of IOR, Prime and Ward (2004) found that early perceptual processing showed robust and consistent inhibition as indexed by reduced P1 and N1 amplitudes, along with behavioral IOR. In contrast, the response-locked LRP showed no latency difference, suggesting that IOR is not associated with changes in motor preparation processes. Together, these studies provide evidence that IOR is associated with processes that precede motor preparation, and that involuntary attention produces an inhibition of perceptual level processing at long cue–target intervals.

Capture Across Sensory Modalities

Much of the research on involuntary attention has, thus far, focused on the visual modality alone. Recent research has begun to investigate how these attention mechanisms function across sensory modalities. Behavioral results have shown attentional capture effects between visual, auditory, and tactile modalities, with cues in one modality improving perceptual judgments in another modality (e.g., McDonald & Ward, 1999; Ward, 1994; Schmitt et al., 2000; Spence et al., 1998; Kennett, Spence, & Driver, 2002). Using ERPs, McDonald and Ward (2000) found that involuntary attention to a non-predictive auditory cue affected visual processing. However, this cross-modal effect occurred at a slightly later stage of processing than is found following a visual cue. Specifically, whereas visual cues affect visual processing as early as the P1 (i.e., at ~100 ms latency), auditory cues modulated visual processing later, as indexed through an effect referred to as a "negative difference" (Nd) (latency 200–400 ms in this study, maximal at frontocentral electrodes). The Nd is measured by subtracting the ERP triggered by an unattended item from that triggered by the same item when attended. Looking at the reverse relationship, McDonald and colleagues (2001) found a visual cue modulated processing of

an auditory target at roughly the same stage of processing as they previously found for auditory cues affecting visual targets. In addition, an Nd effect is also found in tactile--visual cross-modal capture (Kennett, Eimer, Spence, & Driver, 2001). There has been debate about whether the Nd is a unique component (or even set of components) or simply part of the N1 (Näätänen, 1992; Nelson, Luciana, & Collins, 2001; Woldorff & Hillyard, 1991). Regardless, it has been effectively used to index attention effects across modalities and provides evidence for a relatively early effect of involuntary capture (although later than unimodal visual capture effects). Of note, all of the cross-modality capture effects described above were found at relatively short cue–target intervals (<350 ms). To our knowledge, no IOR-like ERP effects have yet been found in cross-modal studies at long cue–target intervals, although cross-modal IOR has been demonstrated behaviorally (Spence et al., 2000). Further work is required to fully understand the relation between unimodal and cross-modal studies of attentional capture. In the remainder of this chapter, we return to involuntary visual attention, and we discuss how this particular bottom-up system interacts with top-down attention mechanisms.

INTERACTIONS BETWEEN VOLUNTARY AND INVOLUNTARY ATTENTION

The previous sections focused on isolating involuntary attention and describing its unique contribution to perceptions and actions. In many everyday situations, however, voluntary and involuntary attention are both active, and thus understanding our perception and cognition requires understanding how these types of attention interact. Having gained a better understanding of the effects of involuntary attention alone through the studies described earlier in this chapter, it is possible to examine how these effects may change when combined with voluntary attention. Before addressing the interactions between voluntary and involuntary attention, however, it's appropriate to discuss an underlying assumption that may have delayed research into these interactions. Specifically, descriptions of the differences between voluntary and involuntary attention often focused on the means by which orienting took place (voluntarily pushed there or involuntarily captured there), but often assumed that the same "spotlight" of attention was being moved. It was thought that once attention is focused on a location, it has the same effects regardless of how it arrived there. Thus, the only interaction of interest would be how one system wins control of the orienting mechanism. However, a number of recent findings suggest that voluntary and involuntary attention may actually be orienting two different "spotlights." Briand and colleagues (Briand, 1998; Briand & Klein, 1987) have shown that voluntary orienting and involuntary orienting have qualitatively distinct behavioral effects, depending on the type of task being performed. When comparing performance on feature search tasks (e.g., detecting a letter "O" among "T" and "X" distracters) with performance on conjunction search tasks (e.g., finding the blue "O" among green "O" distracters and "T" and "X" distracters that could be green or blue), they find an interaction between attention type (voluntary vs. involuntary) and search type (conjunction vs. feature). Specifically, only involuntary attention produces a significant difference in performance between these types of search tasks. Berger, Henik, and Rafal (2005) also provide evidence for the separation of these types of attention, showing that when both types of attention are engaged on the same trials, they can have independent effects on RTs. Prinzmetal and colleagues (2005) provide additional evidence that voluntary and involuntary orienting do not produce the same attentional effects, finding that involuntary attention affects RTs, but not accuracy, whereas voluntary attention significantly affects both RT and accuracy. These findings do not yet converge on a simple explanation for the differences between voluntary and involuntary attention; however, they do provide evidence that voluntary and involuntary attention involve different mechanisms. Therefore, there are many possibilities for how these systems may interact, and the interactions may be different across levels of processing.

Event-related potential studies have provided evidence for similarities, as well as distinctions, between voluntary and involuntary attention.

Neither type of spatial attention, when tested in isolation, has been found to consistently affect the C1 component—the earliest stage of cortical visual processing (but see Khoe et al., 2005 for a C1 effect of object-based selection). Both voluntary and involuntary attention have been shown to modulate the P1 and P3 components, but only voluntary attention has been found to enhance the N1 component (e.g., Mangun & Hillyard, 1991; Vogel & Luck, 2000). Furthermore, the effects of voluntary attention on the P1 and N1 have been shown to be dependent on the type of task (Vogel & Luck, 2000) and on perceptual load/difficulty (Handy & Mangun, 2000), whereas the effects of involuntary attention are the same regardless of task or difficulty (Hopfinger & Mangun, 1998, 2001; Hopfinger & Maxwell, 2005). Although these similarities and differences across attention type are informative, these comparisons have been across subjects, across experiments, and often across labs.

Recently, we have directly compared and contrasted the neural effects of voluntary and involuntary attention, using a within-subject design (Hopfinger & West, 2006). In one experiment, we replicated previous results of the effects of each type of attention when tested in isolation. Specifically, a voluntary cue produced enhanced processing at early sensory stages (i.e., the P1 and N1 components) and later higher-order stages (P3) of target processing, and an involuntary cue produced significant enhancements of the P1 and P3, but not the N1 (Figure 2.5, top). To highlight the effects of attention, Figure 2.5 (middle) presents difference waves, created by subtracting uncued location target ERPs from cued location target ERPs. In this experiment, we confirmed, in a within-subject design and using identical target stimuli, that voluntary and involuntary attention both affect early stages of sensory processing but have unique effects, as well. Having indexed these similarities and differences, we were able to then investigate the interactions between these attention systems. Would one type of attention dominate all the stages of processing? Would there be modulations of size or latency of the effects when voluntary and involuntary attention converge versus compete? Given that these attention systems are often engaged at the same time in real-world situations,

Involuntary and Voluntary Attention in Isolation

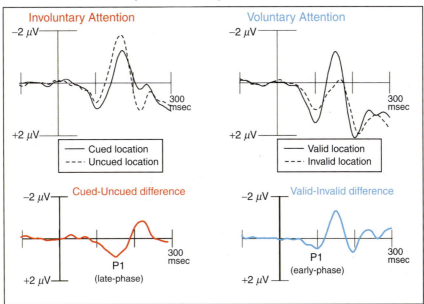

Interaction of Involuntary and Voluntary Attention

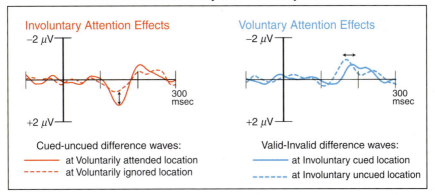

FIGURE 2.5   Comparison of involuntary and voluntary attention effects on early visual processing (data from Hopfinger & West, 2006). Event-related potential waveforms are from the same lateral posterior occipital electrode site shown for the P1 in Figures 2.3 and 2.4. *Top*: Involuntary and voluntary attention in isolation. An involuntary cue (*upper left plot*) significantly enhanced the P1, but not the N1, whereas a voluntary cue (*upper right plot*) significantly enhanced both the P1 and the N1. Difference waves (*middle left and middle right plots*) highlight the attention effects and were calculated by subtracting the uncued location stimuli from the cued location stimuli. *Bottom*: Difference waves plots from the experiment in which voluntary and involuntary attention were both engaged on each trial. Left plot shows the involuntary cuing effect (cued location minus uncued location) as a function of where voluntary attention was allocated on that trial. Involuntary attention enhanced the P1 in both conditions, but this effect was significantly larger at the voluntarily attended location. Right plot shows the voluntary cuing effect (valid location minus invalid location) as a function of where involuntary attention had been captured. Contrary to when voluntary attention was engaged in isolation, voluntary attention here no longer enhanced the P1. Voluntary attention still enhanced the N1, and involuntary attention modulated the latency of this voluntary attention effect. Figure adapted Hopfinger, J. B., & West, V. M. (2006). Interactions between endogenous and exogenous attention on cortical visual processing. *NeuroImage, 31*, 774–789, with permission from Elsevier.

understanding the interactions between voluntary and involuntary attention is at least equally important, and potentially more critical, than understanding their effects in isolation.

In another experiment in that study, we investigated the interactions between these types of attention by utilizing a paradigm in which both a voluntary and an involuntary cue were presented (Hopfinger & West, 2006). On each trial, a voluntary cue presented at central fixation first instructed subjects where to expect a target. A noninformative involuntary cue (brief luminance change of one of the boxes surrounding potential target locations) then appeared briefly, followed shortly thereafter by a target stimulus. The timing was arranged so that the interval between the voluntary cue and the target should produce robust voluntary attention effects, and the interval between the involuntary cue and target was set at a shorter interval at which we had previously found robust involuntary attention effects. In other words, the interval between each cue and target was set to produce strong attentional effects for both cues types (and thus, for both types of attention). These intervals were also used in the experiment above that replicated previous studies of voluntary and involuntary attention in isolation. These intervals allowed for robust effects of each type of attention, and the critical question here was what the interaction between these systems would reveal. Figure 2.5 (*bottom*) presents the difference waves from the combined cuing experiment, to highlight the effects of attention. We found that when both types of attention were concurrently engaged, voluntary and involuntary attention had separable, yet interacting effects at multiple levels. Voluntary attention no longer directly modulated the P1, but involuntary attention still significantly enhanced this level of processing. However, the size of the involuntary P1 attention effect was modulated by voluntary attention: The largest involuntary P1 effect occurred when voluntary attention was focused on the same location, whereas the smallest (yet still significant) involuntary enhancement of the P1 occurred when voluntary attention was focused on the opposite location (Figure 2.5, *bottom left*). Although involuntary attention dominated the earliest stage of processing typically modulated by attention, voluntary attention

modulated intermediate and late stages of processing. Voluntary attention enhanced the N1 component, although the latency of this effect was modulated by involuntary attention (Figure 2.5, *bottom right*). Finally, the P3 (which can be affected by both voluntary and involuntary attention) was completely dominated by voluntary attention, showing enhanced activity for voluntary valid versus invalid trials and no interaction between voluntary and involuntary attention (not shown here). These results suggest that voluntary and involuntary attention are separable systems and that the interactions between these types of attention are complex and variable across stages of processing. Further research is necessary to understand whether these interactions are stable or whether they vary, depending on the relative degrees of engagement of voluntary and involuntary attention. Overall, these results have provided further evidence that involuntary and voluntary attention reflect two distinct, yet interacting "spotlights." This finding thus generates additional questions regarding the nature of the interactions between voluntary and involuntary attention and specifically, the automaticity of these attention systems and their interacting effects. Recent work focusing on this issue of automaticity is discussed below.

Contingent Capture

Although involuntary attention is often characterized as being reflexive, there is debate about how automatic this process is. As described above, there are situations in which voluntary attention can be directly opposed to involuntary attention, as each is focused on a different spatial location. However, in the situation in which voluntary attention is not focused on a spatial location, it had often been assumed that salient physical stimuli automatically control attentional focus through the involuntary mechanisms described above. Folk and colleagues challenged this view and suggested that top-down control settings determine whether or not a stimulus will capture attention (Folk, Remington, & Johnston, 1992; Folk, Remington, & Wright, 1994). Their "contingent capture" theory suggests that attentional capture is not wholly dependent on bottom-up attributes, but instead is *contingent* upon top-down task sets. Their behavioral studies found that a nonpredictive cue speeded manual RTs to subsequent targets at the cued location, but only when the cue shared key features with the expected target. When the cue didn't share key features with the expected target, cuing had no effect on RT. For example, a "color cue" (i.e., a single uniquely colored item within a multi-element cue display) captured attention when the target was also defined by being a unique color item in a multielement target display, but this same color cue did not capture attention when the target was known to be a single item presented in isolation (Folk et al., 1992). Although overt response times are often found to be consistent with the contingent capture theory, other evidence suggests that highly salient stimuli still capture attention in an automatic manner. The automatic capture hypothesis holds that attentional capture is wholly dependent on the salience of stimuli, and thus, occurs in a bottom-up fashion regardless of top-down influences (Theeuwes, 1991, 1992, 1994, 2004). It is proposed that the initial orienting toward the salient stimuli is automatic, but that congruence with top-down settings may affect how long attention remains on that stimulus (with attentional hold increased for task-relevant distractors; Theeuwes, Atchley, & Kramer, 2000). Therefore, although the cue may capture attention equally well in both conditions, attention remains at the cued location longer in the congruent versus the incongruent condition. Thus, when tested at certain intervals, attention has been reoriented back from the distractor in the incongruent condition but not the congruent condition, giving the false impression that attention was never captured in the incongruent condition.

It is important to note that "capture" in the above studies is defined as a significant effect on manual RTs. However, behavioral RTs may not always be sensitive to effects at earlier stages of processing that precede motor preparation and execution. Handy and colleagues (2001) provided a clear example of this in an ERP study of combined expectancies, in which informative cues provided information about both the location and type of upcoming stimulus. Although manual RTs indicated that spatial attention had no effect on processing, their ERP results revealed that spatial attention was significantly modulating early sensory processing levels. As this study demonstrates, ERPs can sometimes provide details of neural mechanisms that may be obscured or masked in behavioral measures. Thus, to further address whether "involuntary" attention mechanisms are triggered in a purely automatic stimulus-driven manner or whether they are contingent upon top-down control settings, we utilized ERPs to investigate the interaction of involuntary attention and top-down control settings at multiple stages of processing (Hopfinger & Ries, 2005).

In a series of experiments, we dissociated two types of processing occurring during the capture of attention: sensory-driven mechanisms that automatically bias early stages of visual processing (and thus reflect automatic capture) and later mechanisms that are contingent on top-down expectations (Hopfinger & Ries, 2005). In the first experiment, the cue was the abrupt onset of new objects (four dots surrounding one of the standing background boxes), and there were two target conditions: in the Congruent condition, the target was also the abrupt onset of a single stimulus (a checkerboard-patterned bar requiring a discrimination response); in the Incongruent condition, the target was defined by color (i.e., a red-black checkerboard target was presented simultaneously with a black-white checkerboard at another location). In this experiment, manual RTs confirmed the results of Folk et al. (1992)— the cue affected RTs only in the congruent condition. Although these behavioral results supported contingent capture, the ERPs revealed that the cue was triggering involuntary effects automatically. Specifically, the P1 component was enhanced for cued location targets relative to uncued location targets, regardless of top-down settings (Figure 2.6). Although the P1 effect was therefore automatically triggered by the new object cue, the *duration* of the P1 effect was significantly affected by top-down settings. Specifically, the enhancement of the P1 was for a briefer period of time in the incongruent condition (Figure 2.6, *bottom,* highlights this effect by plotting the difference waves). Overall, our results are in line with Theeuwes and colleagues' (2000) view that the initial orienting of attention is automatic and that top-down

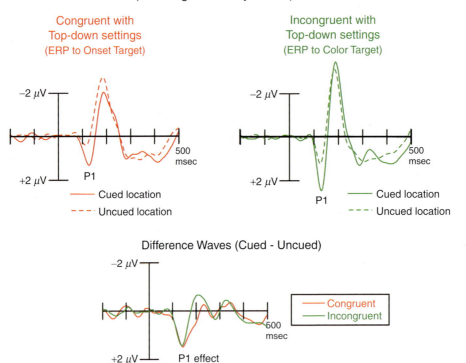

Automaticty of Involuntary P1 Attention Effect
(following a new object cue)

Congruent with
Top-down settings
(ERP to Onset Target)

-2 μV

P1

500
msec

+2 μV

— Cued location
- - - Uncued location

Incongruent with
Top-down settings
(ERP to Color Target)

-2 μV

500
msec

+2 μV

P1

— Cued location
- - - Uncued location

Difference Waves (Cued - Uncued)

-2 μV

500
msec

+2 μV   P1 effect

— Congruent
— Incongruent

FIGURE 2.6   Automatic versus contingent capture following a new object cue (data from Experiment 1 of Hopfinger & Ries, 2005). Event-related potentials to target stimuli at lateral posterior occipital site. Congruent condition (*left*) refers to condition in which the target was the abrupt appearance of a single object, and thus matched the single new object cue. Incongruent condition (*right*) refers to the condition in which the target was a red item in a display with a red item and a white item, and therefore the new object cue did not match the top-down set for this color-defined target. *Top*: The P1 was enhanced regardless of whether or not top-down settings matched cue stimulus. *Bottom*: Difference waves were calculated by subtracting the uncued location targets from the cued location targets. The peak of the P1 enhancement is the same for both conditions, but this enhanced processing lasts longer in the congruent condition than in the incongruent condition. Figure adapted from Hopfinger, J. B., & Ries, A. J. (2005). Automatic versus contingent mechanisms of sensory-driven neural biasing and reflexive attention. *Journal of Cognitive Neuroscience, 17*, 1341–1352, with permission from MIT Press.

settings affect how long attention dwells at the captured location, at least in the case of luminance increment, new-object cues. These cues also automatically triggered an IIN and a robust enhancement of the P3, regardless of top-down settings (not shown here). Thus, a new object with a luminance increment automatically triggers involuntary mechanisms that affect at least these three stages of processing, regardless of top-down control settings.

In addition to investigating the attention effects triggered by a new object cue, we also investigated

the effects of a different type of cue–a color popout. In this experiment (Hopfinger & Ries, 2005, Experiment 3), the targets were again either a single new object or a uniquely colored object in a multielement (four items total, all of equiluminance) target display. However, the cue in all conditions of this experiment was a color popout; specifically, a set of yellow dots at one location appearing simultaneously with three sets of equiluminant cyan dots, each at one of the other possible target locations. Thus, the congruent condition in this experiment was when the target was also a color popout, and the incongruent condition was now when the target was a single new object display. Our behavioral effects again showed the standard "contingent capture" pattern of a significant RT effect only in the congruent condition. However, there was no significant modulation of early sensory ERP components. Unlike the effects from the first experiment (with a new object cue), equiluminant cues did not trigger a P1

enhancement, regardless of condition (Figure 2.7, *top*). Thus, together with the experiment described above, these results suggest that the earliest involuntary attention effect (the P1) is triggered automatically by the abrupt appearance of a new object (with its associated luminance change), but that other salient features, such as equiluminant color popout, do not affect this early stage of processing. Of note, however, top-down settings

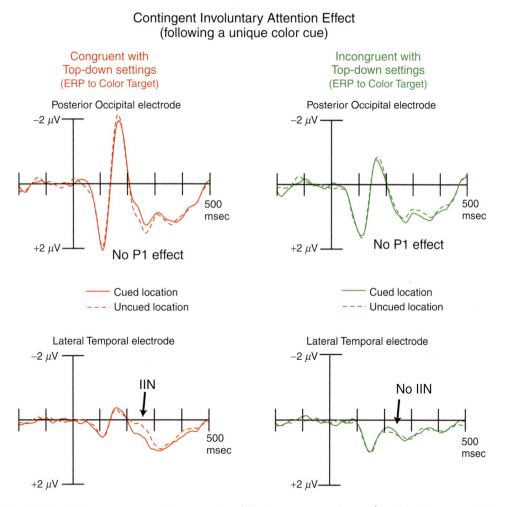

FIGURE 2.7   Automatic versus contingent capture following a unique color cue (data from Experiment 3 of Hopfinger & Ries, 2005). *Top*: Event-related potentials to the target stimuli at the lateral posterior occipital site where the P1 is maximal. No P1 enhancement was found regardless of whether or not top-down settings matched cue stimulus, as shown at lateral occipital electrodes. *Bottom*: Event-related potentials to the target stimuli at the lateral temporal site where the ipsilateral invalid negativity (IIN) is typically observed. The IIN was generated only following a congruent cue stimulus (*left column*). Figure adapted from Hopfinger, J. B., & Ries, A. J. (2005). Automatic versus contingent mechanisms of sensory-driven neural biasing and reflexive attention. *Journal of Cognitive Neuroscience, 17,* 1341–1352, with permission from MIT Press.

had a significant effect, on later stages of processing in the color cue experiment. Specifically, an *ipsilateral invalid negativity* (IIN; 220–260 ms latency) was generated in this experiment, but only in the congruent condition; there was no evidence of an IIN in the incongruent condition (Figure 2.7, *bottom*). Whereas a new object cue automatically triggered an IIN regardless of top-down control, the color cue experiment shows that this level of processing can be contingent upon top-down settings when it isn't automatically triggered by a new object cue. Overall, these experiments demonstrate that the effects of involuntary attention at early sensory processing stages occur in an automatic bottom-up manner, whereas the effects on later higher-order processing can be contingent on top-down control settings.

Recently, other studies have investigated the contingent versus automatic capture debate by measuring a different ERP feature, that has been labeled the N2pc. The N2pc is a negativity over posterior ("p") scalp sites contralateral ("c") to attended stimuli within the latency range typically seen for the N2 components (~175–300 ms post stimulus onset). The N2pc is a derived component, calculated by taking the difference in amplitude between electrodes contralateral versus ipsilateral to the visual field of the target. The N2pc is considered to reflect the focusing of visuospatial attention (Luck et al., 1997; Woodman & Luck, 1999) and more specifically, it has been proposed to represent a filtering stage that weakens distractor input (Hopf et al., 2002; Hopf et al., 2006; Luck et al., 1997). Recently, it has been used to investigate the role of top-down control settings in attentional capture, although the results have been mixed. Hickey et al. (2006) used a visual search paradigm to determine if highly salient, but task-irrelevant distracters would capture attention in the presence of less perceptually salient targets. They found that a distractor-elicited N2pc occurred prior to a target-elicited N2pc, in line with the hypothesis that attention is initially automatically captured to highly salient stimuli and only later is attention shifted to target stimuli. However, Eimer and Kiss (2008) found evidence in support of contingent capture. Using a spatial cuing paradigm, they found that the cue elicited an N2pc only when it contained a task-relevant feature, specifically color. Leblanc et al. (2008) also found that the presence of a distractor-elicited N2pc was dependent on the distractor sharing target-defining features. Experimental design differences may account for some of these mixed results, as different tasks highlight different aspects of attentional processing. Of note, however, in all the N2pc experiments investigating the contingent capture hypothesis, the potential capture was to a unique feature (color or shape) within a multielement array; none of these studies utilized a display consisting of only the abrupt appearance of a solitary new object. This was likely due in part to the previous findings that the N2pc is not generated unless competing stimuli are present in the display (Luck & Hillyard, 1994). In addition, however, the appearance of a new object may hold a privileged place in capturing attention, and therefore may not be under the control of top-down settings. Yantis and colleagues initially suggested that new objects capture attention automatically (Hillstrom & Yantis, 1994), and Folk and colleagues have suggested that there may be a "default top-down setting" for new objects, in which new objects represent a special class of stimuli that seem to elicit the most automatic form of capture (Folk et al., 1992). Overall, then, the ability of some features of stimuli to capture attention may be contingent on top-down settings in some situations, but the abrupt appearance of a new object seems to trigger involuntary attentional orienting in an automatic fashion. Therefore, this particular stimulus attribute—the abrupt appearance of a new object—is very useful for investigating the neural basis of distraction and understanding what separates those who are good at avoiding distraction from those who are not, as we describe below.

DISTRACTION

Certain stimulus attributes, such as the onset of a new object, seem to reflexively capture attention, and yet there are wide differences between individuals in the degree of distraction that ensues following this involuntary orienting. Whereas distraction from irrelevant information can become frequent and debilitating to some individuals, others (e.g., trained meditators) have been found to have especially efficient attention mechanisms that allow them to greatly reduce distraction (Slagter et al., 2007; Tang et al., 2007). Recently, we (Kim & Hopfinger, 2010) investigated the neural basis of distraction in healthy subjects, and we compared those who were effective at resisting distraction with those who were more highly distractible. In that fMRI study, subjects performed a challenging orientation discrimination task at fixation, while irrelevant distractor stimuli occurred in the periphery at random intervals. Although the distractors were known to be completely irrelevant and always occurred at the same location, subjects exhibited distraction (as measured by reduced accuracy and slower RTs to judging the orientation of the central target stimuli) in the condition wherein the distractor was the abrupt appearance of a new object. At the neural level, we demonstrated that the appearance of a new object not only evoked strong activity in distractor processing regions of visual cortex, but also significantly reduced activity in target processing regions. These effects occurred even though the distractor did not match the attentional set for the target stimulus. Beyond visual processing regions, our analyses also revealed that regions in the parietal and temporal lobe (i.e., intraparietal sulcus [IPS] and TPJ) showed increased activity related to the appearance of the new object distractor. Having identified this network of regions involved in distraction, we then investigated differences between more versus less distractible subjects.

Theoretically, differences in distractibility could be caused by at least two distinct possibilities. It could be the case that highly distractible individuals, compared to those who are better at resisting distraction, exhibit hyperactive reflexive orienting toward the irrelevant stimulus. Alternatively, or in addition, highly distractible subjects may have deficient control mechanisms to counteract the initial orienting. In our study, we found that behavioral measures of distraction did not correlate strongly with activity in either of the early visual processing regions (target or distractor), suggesting that the strength of sensory-level processing of the distractor stimulus was not the critical

factor in determining the degree of distraction. However, behavioral measures of distraction were associated with the level of activity in the IPS and TPJ, suggesting that distractibility relates more to deficient control rather than hyperactive orienting. Critically, we found that participants who were less distractible engaged the IPS and TPJ regardless of the type of distractor (e.g., new object or simple luminance decrement), whereas the more distractible participants had activity in these regions only when the distractor was a highly salient new object (summarized in Figure 2.8). This pattern suggests that participants who consistently engage these regions, across all events, decrease distraction overall. In contrast, highly distractible subjects engage these regions only when urgently needed (in the case of an especially strong distractor) and, therefore, are less efficient and effective at using these control systems to minimize distraction. As indicated in Figure 2.8, bottom-up processing of the distractor did not differ significantly between groups. This provides evidence against the view that more distractible individuals simply have enhanced sensory processing that leads to capture and distraction. Instead, our results suggest that the processes supported by the IPS and TPJ (registering the distractor event, disengaging attention from it, shifting and reorienting attention) are the more critical elements in determining the degree of distraction suffered by individuals.

Recent studies on meditation may provide additional insight into the differences in distractibility that we observed. After extensive meditation training, activity in attentional control regions was found to be reduced below the level observed in control subjects (Brefczynski-Lewis et al., 2007; Pagnoni, Cekic, & Guo, 2008; Slagter et al., 2007; Tang et al., 2007). This result has been interpreted as improved efficiency of these attention networks. Importantly, this may fit with our finding that less distractible participants show less activity in the IPS and TPJ than do more distractible participants, in the critical case when a new object distractor appears. In other words, our less distractible participants may show better efficiency because they engage this attention network (e.g., TPJ and IPS) more consistently, activating these regions even when the distractor isn't especially

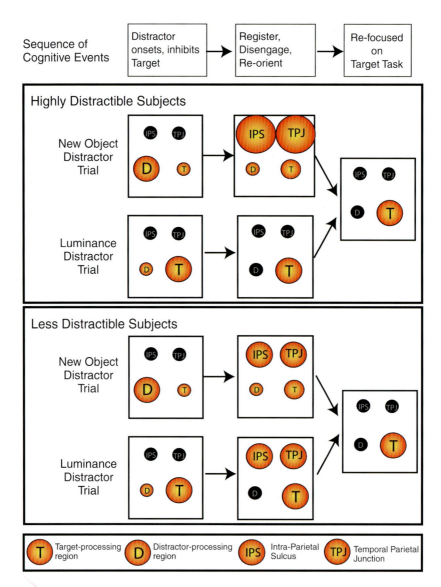

FIGURE 2.8 Differences in high versus low distractibility subjects. Each circle represents the level of activity associated with the labeled region (see bottom legend). Activity in the distractor processing region of visual cortex and the target processing region of visual cortex did not differ significantly between groups for either the highly salient new object distractor or the less salient luminance decrement distractor. However, activity in the intraparietal sulcus (IPS) and temporoparietal junction (TPJ) did show a different pattern between the two groups of participants. Highly distractible participants had activity in the IPS and TPJ only when the distractor was a highly salient new object, whereas less distractible participants engaged these regions regardless of the type of distractor (e.g., new object onset or offset). Figure adapted from Kim, S. & Hopfinger, J. B. (2010). Neural basis of distraction. *Journal of Cognitive Neuroscience, 22,* 1794–1807, with permission from MIT Press.

salient, in order to register the distractor, disengage from it, and reorient back to the target task. This is in contrast to the hypothesis that less distractible subjects simply block out all incoming distraction. Indeed, meditation training may not instruct individuals to completely block out irrelevant stimuli or thoughts, but rather to register and acknowledge the sensation or thought and then disengage from that distraction and return to the focus of the meditation. By putting effort into processing the less salient distractors, the attentional control regions become more efficient and therefore, these individuals have a better ability to avoid distraction when the distractor is highly salient (i.e., new object onset). More distractible participants, on the other hand, engage these attention systems only when it is most critical (i.e., new object onset), and thus must work harder (greater IPS and TPJ activity) and are less effective at utilizing these processes. Therefore, consistent and efficient engagement of these attentional control regions may be critical for reducing distraction. In addition to considering *what* causes increasing levels of distraction (i.e., capture by a new object onset vs. an object offset), it is also critical to evaluate *how long* attention is held by a stimulus. As discussed in the following section, this should allow for a more complete understanding of attentional capture and distraction, from the initial orienting to the eventual disengagement of attention.

THE "HOLDING" OF ATTENTION

What holds attention determines action.
– William James (1892/2001)

A final issue to consider regarding the involuntary capture of attention is the holding of attention. As succinctly expressed in the above quote from William James, this holding of attention may be the most critical mechanism underlying the relationship between attention and behavior. Indeed, although reflexive orienting toward salient stimuli is a powerful process, the ultimate effect of this reflex may be trivial if attention isn't also held on that salient stimulus. Without any hold, the effect of reflexive orienting may be minor and fleeting; in contrast, if attention is held, the capture is complete. Below, we describe a particular property of stimuli that has been shown to affect the involuntary holding of attention.

Recent work has investigated the effect of higher-order factors on attention, and one such factor, item memory, has been found to affect not only the initial capture of attention, but also the length of attentional hold. Specifically, previous studies investigating the effects of item memory

on attention have produced somewhat mixed results, with some studies finding that novel items capture attention (Johnston et al., 1993; Wang et al., 1994) and others finding that familiar items capture attention (Christie & Klein, 1995). Although these findings suggest that item memory can affect attention, there is inconsistency regarding whether the novel or the familiar items capture attention. Furthermore, these studies sought only to investigate one aspect of attention—the initial orienting of attention. Those studies were not designed to measure another critical aspect of attentional allocation: how long attention dwells on an item. This aspect of attention has not been investigated as thoroughly as the initial orienting of attention, yet the holding of attention may ultimately be even more important in influencing cognition and actions.

To more thoroughly investigate the possible effects of memory on attention, we turned to eye tracking, because this method allows measurement of dwell time as well as orienting. We (Chanon & Hopfinger, 2008) found that the dominant effect of memory is not to capture attention and cause an involuntary orienting to the object, but rather to prolong attentional dwell time when the item is attended (i.e., fixated). In this experiment, participants first completed three blocks of deep encoding, making semantic judgments about a set of isolated objects. Participants then viewed scenes in preparation for a later memory test (item memory test or scene memory test, counterbalanced across subjects). Two items within each scene were designated as objects of interest (with the studied item counterbalanced across subjects). The duration of the first set of fixations on the critical item (i.e., the time spent on the item before looking elsewhere) revealed that attention dwelled on old objects significantly longer than on new objects. Old items were also fixated a significantly greater number of times throughout the viewing period, and the average duration of fixations on old objects lasted longer than fixations on novel comparison items. Voluntary intention did not affect the dwell time, as there were no significant differences between participants who, according to self-report surveys, intended to dwell longer on the new item, longer on the old, or equally long on both. All groups spent more time looking at the old objects. Overall, these results provided new evidence that memory, in an involuntary manner, affects how long attention dwells on an item.

Based on these results, we suggested that the major effect of item memory on attention is to prolong attentional dwell time. To further investigate this hypothesis, and to explore whether it is due to memory per se or to memorial context (as the hold of attention described above was found for *old* items within a *novel* scene), we utilized the *attentional blink* (AB) paradigm. In the typical AB task, subjects are required to report the identity of two targets in a series of stimuli presented in a rapid serial visual presentation (RSVP) stream. The AB refers to the decrement in the ability to report the identity of the second target ("T2") when it occurs shortly after the first target ("T1"). In a series of experiments, we provided new evidence that memory significantly affects attentional dwell time, and that it is the memory context as well as the item memory itself, that is critical in lengthening the AB (Parks & Hopfinger, 2008). In each of the four experiments in that article, participants first completed a "deep encoding phase," to ensure that these items had a strong, recollective memory trace. Participants then performed an AB task, in which half of the T1 pictures had been studied during the encoding phase ("old items") and the other half had never been viewed ("new items"). To test whether it was the individual item memory per se or the memorial uniqueness that caused the protracted AB, we manipulated the memory context across experiments, by altering the memory status of the distractors ("old" vs. "new" items). The critical result was that the AB (deficit in accurately reporting the second target) was extended for a longer period when the memory status of T1 was different from the memory context. These data provided new evidence that the memory status of an item (old or new) interacts with the ongoing memorial context to exert a powerful effect on the allocation of attention. Critically, this effect is demonstrated not when examining the initial capture of attention, but instead when examining the hold of attention. As suggested by James, elucidating the mechanisms by which attention is held allows for a greater understanding of the relation between attention and behavior. This recent evidence does just that, suggesting that item memory and memory context play a key role in the involuntary hold of attention.

CONCLUSION

The power of salient stimuli to automatically capture our attention has been appreciated for centuries, but only relatively recently have the mechanisms and neural substrates of this involuntary attention begun to be understood. In this chapter, we reviewed ERP studies that have revealed that involuntary attention affects multiple levels of stimulus processing, from early sensory analysis (i.e., P1 component) through to context updating (i.e., P3). These studies have also revealed an effect linked to the reorienting of attention (i.e., IIN). These three effects have been shown to be reflexive and involuntary, occurring across multiple tasks and regardless of top-down control settings, at least when the capturing stimulus is the appearance of a new object. Although highly focused voluntary spatial attention can disrupt the effects of involuntary attention on late stages of processing, the early stage of visual processing (i.e., the P1) is dominated by involuntary attention, even when voluntary and involuntary attention directly compete. The interactions between voluntary and involuntary attention vary across levels and affect both the strength and timing of the attention effects triggered by each type of attention. In regards to how to diminish the distraction that can result from these powerful effects of involuntary capture, recent studies suggest that trying to completely ignore these stimuli may not be the most effective strategy. Instead, enhancing the efficiency of attentional control, through a more consistent and moderate response to all levels of distractor, may allow for a quicker disengagement and reorienting from even the most highly salient distractors. Finally, recent work has shown that item memory has an involuntarily effect on the temporal allocation of attention, affecting how long attention is held by an item. The studies reviewed here highlight how recent work on the capture and holding of attention are advancing our understanding of the neural mechanisms of involuntary attention, mechanisms that can subtly but profoundly affect our perceptions, cognitions and actions.

ACKNOWLEDGMENTS

This research was supported by funding from the NIH (R01MH066034). We would like to thank Jeff Maxwell, Anthony Ries, Vicki West Chanon, and So-Yeon Kim for assistance with the experiments described here.

References

Berger, A., Henik, A., & Rafal, R. (2005). Competition between endogenous and exogenous orienting of visual attention. *Journal of Experimental Psychology. General, 134*, 207–221.

Brefczynski-Lewis, J. A., Lutz, A., Schaefer, H. S., Levinson, D. B., & Davidson, R. J. (2007). Neural correlates of attentional expertise in long-term meditation practitioners. *Proceedings of the National Academy of Sciences of the United States of America, 104*, 11483–11488.

Briand, K. A. (1998). Feature integration and spatial attention: More evidence of a dissociation between endogenous and exogenous orienting. *Journal of Experimental Psychology. Human Perception and Performance, 24*, 1243–1256.

Briand, K. A., & Klein, R. M. (1987). Is Posner's "beam" the same as Treisman's "glue"?: On the relation between visual orienting and feature integration theory. *Journal of Experimental Psychology: Human Perception and Performance, 13*, 228–241.

Chambers, C. D., Payne, J. M., Stokes, M. G., & Mattingley, J. B. (2004). Fast and slow parietal pathways mediate spatial attention. *Nature Neuroscience, 7*, 217–218.

Chanon, V. W., & Hopfinger, J. B. (2008). Memory's grip on attention: The influence of item memory on the allocation of attention. *Visual Cognition, 16*, 325–340.

Cheal, M. L., & Lyon, D. R. (1991). Central and peripheral precuing of forced-choice discrimination. *Quarterly Journal of Experimental Psychology, 43A*, 859–880.

Christie, J., & Klein, R. (1995). Familiarity and attention: Does what we know affect what we notice? *Memory & Cognition, 2*, 547–550.

Coles, M. G. (1989). Modern mind-brain reading: Psychophysiology, physiology, and cognition. *Psychophysiology, 26*(3), 251–269.

Corbetta, M., Kincade, M. J., Ollinger, J. M., McAvoy, M. P., & Shulman, G. L. (2000). Voluntary orienting is dissociated from target detection in human posterior parietal cortex. *Nature Neuroscience, 3*, 292–297.

Di Russo, F., Martinez, A., Sereno, M. I., Pitzalis, S., & Hillyard, S. A. (2001). Cortical sources of the early components of the visual evoked potential. *Human Brain Mapping, 15*(2), 95–111.

Donchin, E. (1981). Surprise!. . . Surprise? *Psychophysiology, 18*, 493–513.

Duncan-Johnson, C., & Donchin, E. (1982). The P300 component of the event-related potential as an index of information processing. *Biological Psychology, 14*, 1–52.

Eimer, M., & Kiss, M. (2008). Involuntary attentional capture is determined by task set: Evidence from event-related brain potentials. *Journal of Cognitive Neuroscience, 20*(8), 1423–1433.

Folk, C. L., Remington, R. W., & Johnston, J. C. (1992). Involuntary covert orienting is contingent on attentional control settings. *Journal of Experimental Psychology. Human Perception and Performance, 18*, 1030–1044.

Folk, C. L., Remington, R. W., & Wright, J. H. (1994). The structure of attentional control: Contingent attentional capture by apparent motion, abrupt onset, and color. *Journal of Experimental Psychology. Human Perception and Performance, 20*, 317–329.

Handy, T. C., Green, V., Klein, R., & Mangun, G. R. (2001). Combined expectancies: ERPs reveal the early benefits of spatial attention that are obscured by reaction time measures. *Journal of Experimental Psychology. Human Perception and Performance, 27*, 303–317.

Handy, T. C., & Mangun, G. R. (2000). Attention and spatial selection: Electrophysiological evidence for modulation by perceptual load. *Perception & Psychophysics, 62*, 175–186.

Hatfield, G. (1998). Attention in early scientific psychology. In R. D. Wright (Ed.), *Visual Attention* (pp. 3–25). New York: Oxford University Press.

Heinze, H. J., Mangun, G. R., Burchert, W., Hinrichs, H., Scholz, M., Munte, T. F., et al. (1994). Combined spatial and temporal imaging of brain activity during visual selective attention in humans. *Nature, 372*, 543–546.

Hickey, C., McDonald, J. J., & Theeuwes, J. (2006). Electrophysiological evidence of the capture of visual attention. *Journal of Cognitive Neuroscience, 18*, 604–613.

Hillstrom, A., & Yantis, S. (1994). Visual motion and attentional capture. *Perception & Psychophysics, 55*, 399–411.

Hopf, J. M., Boelmans, K., Schoenfeld, A. M., Heinze, H. J., & Luck, S. J. (2002). How does attention attenuate target-distractor interference in vision? Evidence from magnetoencephalographic

recordings. *Cognitive Brain Research, 15*(1), 17–29.

Hopf, J. M., Luck, S. J., Boelmans, K., Schoenfeld, M. A., Boehler, C. N., Rieger, J., & Heinze, H. J. (2006). The neural site of attention matches the spatial scale of perception. *Journal of Neuroscience, 26*(13), 3532–3540.

Hopfinger, J. B., & Mangun, G. R. (1998). Reflexive attention modulates processing of visual stimuli in human extrastriate cortex. *Psychological Science, 9*, 441–447.

Hopfinger, J. B., & Mangun, G. R. (2001). Tracking the influence of reflexive attention on sensory and cognitive processing. *Cognitive, Affective, & Behavioral Neuroscience, 1*, 56–65.

Hopfinger, J. B., & Maxwell, J. (2005). Appearing and disappearing stimuli trigger a reflexive modulation of visual cortical activity. *Cognitive Brain Research, 25*, 48–56.

Hopfinger, J. B., & Ries, A. J. (2005). Automatic versus contingent mechanisms of sensory-driven neural biasing and reflexive attention. *Journal of Cognitive Neuroscience, 17*, 1341–1352.

Hopfinger, J. B., & West, V. M. (2006). Interactions between endogenous and exogenous attention on cortical visual processing. *NeuroImage, 31*, 774–789.

James, W. (1890). *The principles of psychology*. New York: Henry Holt and Company.

James, W. (1892/2001). *Psychology: Briefer course*. Toronto, Canada: General Publishing Company, Ltd. (Original work published 1892).

Johnston, W. A., Hawley, K. J., & Farnham, J. (1993). Novel popout: Empirical boundaries and tentative theory. *Journal of Experimental Psychology. Human Perception & Performance, 19*, 140–153.

Jonides, J. (1981). Voluntary versus automatic control over the mind's eye movement. In J. B. Long, & A. D. Baddeley (Eds.), *Attention and performance* (Vol. IX, pp. 187–203). Hillsdale, NJ: Erlbaum Associates.

Kennett, S., Eimer, M., Spence, C., & Driver, J. (2001). Tactile-visual links in exogenous spatial attention under different postures: Convergent evidence from psychophysics and ERPs. *Journal of Cognitive Neuroscience, 13*, 462–478.

Kennett, S., Spence, C., & Driver, J. (2002). Visuo-tactile links in covert exogenous spatial attention remap across changes in unseen hand posture. *Perception & Psychophysics, 64*(7), 1083–1094.

Khoe, W., Mitchell, J. F., Reynolds, J. H., & Hillyard, S. A. (2005). Exogenous attentional selection of transparent superimposed surfaces modulates early event-related potentials. *Vision Research, 45*, 3004–3014.

Kim, S., & Hopfinger, J. B. (2010). Neural basis of distraction. *Journal of Cognitive Neuroscience, 22*(8), 1794–1807.

Klein, R. M. (2000). Inhibition of return. *Trends in Cognitive Sciences, 4*(4), 138–147.

Leblanc, E., Prime, D. J., & Jolicoeur, P. (2008). Tracking the location of visuospatial attention in a contingent capture paradigm. *Journal of Cognitive Neuroscience, 20*(4), 657–671.

Luck, S. J., Girelli, M., McDermott, M. T., & Ford, M. A. (1997). Bridging the gap between monkey neurophysiology and human perception: An ambiguity resolution theory of visual selective attention. *Cognitive Psychology, 33*, 64–87.

Luck, S. J. & Hillyard, S. A. (1994). Spatial filtering during visual search: Evidence from human electrophysiology. *Journal of Experimental Psychology. Human Perception and Performance, 20*, 1000–1014.

Mangun, G. R., & Hillyard, S. A. (1991). Modulations of sensory-evoked brain potentials indicate changes in perceptual processing during visual-spatial priming. *Journal of Experimental Psychology. Human Perception and Performance, 17*, 1057–1074.

Mangun, G. R., Hopfinger, J. B., Kussmaul, C. L., Fletcher, E., & Heinze, H. J. (1997). Covariations in ERP and PET measures of spatial selective attention in human extrastriate visual cortex. *Human Brain Mapping, 5*, 273–279.

McDonald, J. J., Teder-Sälejärvi, W. A., Heraldez, D., & Hillyard, S. A. (2001). Electrophysiological evidence for the "missing link" in crossmodal attention. *Canadian Journal of Experimental Psychology, 55*(2), 141–149.

McDonald, J. J., & Ward, L. M. (1999). Spatial relevance determines facilitatory and inhibitory effects of auditory covert spatial orienting. *Journal of Experimental Psychology: Human Perception and Performance, 25*(5), 1234–1252.

McDonald, J. J., Ward, L. M., & Kiehl, K. A. (1999). An event-related brain potential study of inhibition of return. *Perception & Psychophysics, 61*, 1411–1423.

Müller, H. J., & Rabbitt, P. M. (1989). Reflexive and voluntary orienting of attention: Time course of activation and resistance to interruption. *Journal of Experimental Psychology. Human Perception and Performance, 15*, 315–330.

Näätänen, R. (1992). *Attention and brain function*. Hillsdale, NJ: Erlbaum.

Nelson, C. A., Luciana, M., & Collins, M. L. (2001). *Handbook of developmental cognitive neuroscience*. Cambridge, MA: The MIT Press.

Pagnoni, G., Cekic, M., & Guo, Y. (2008). "Thinking about not-thinking": Neural correlates of conceptual processing during zen meditation. *PLoS One, 3*(9), e3083. Available at: http://www.plosone.org/article/info%3Adoi%2F10.1371%2Fjournal.pone.0003083

Parks, E. L., & Hopfinger, J. B. (2008). Hold it! Memory affects attentional dwell time. *Psychonomic Bulletin & Review, 15,* 1128–1134.

Posner, M. I., & Cohen, Y. (1984). Components of visual orienting. In H. Bouma, & D. Bouwhis (Eds.), *Attention and Performance* (Vol. X, pp. 531–56). Hillsdale, NJ: Erlbaum Associates.

Posner, M. I., Inhoff, A., Friedrich, F. J., Cohen, A. (1987). Isolating attentional systems: A cognitive-anatomical analysis. *Psychobiology, 15,* 107–121.

Prime, D. J., & Ward, L. M. (2004). Inhibition of return from stimulus to response. *Psychological Science, 15,* 272–276.

Prinzmetal, W., McCool, C., & Park, S. (2005). Attention: Reaction time and accuracy reveal different mechanisms. *Journal of Experimental Psychology. General, 134,* 73–92.

Schmitt, M., Postma, A., & De Haan, E. (2000). Interactions between exogenous auditory and visual spatial attention. *The Quarterly Journal of Experimental Psychology. A, Human Experimental Psychology, 53*(1), 105–130.

Slagter, H. A., Lutz, A., Greischar, L. L., Francis, A. D., Nieuwenhuis, S., Davis, J. M., & Davidson, R. J. (2007). Mental training affects distribution of limited brain resources. *PLoS Biology, 5*(6), e138. Available at: http://www.plosbiology.org/article/info%3Adoi%2F10.1371%2Fjournal.pbio.0050138

Spence, C., Lloyd, D., McGlone, F., Nicholls, M. E., & Driver, J. (2000). Inhibition of return is supramodal: A demonstration between all possible pairings of vision, touch, and audition. *Experimental Brain Research, 134*(1), 42–48.

Spence, C., Nicholls, M. R., Gillespie, N., & Driver, J. (1998). Crossmodal links in exogenous covert spatial orienting between touch, audition, and vision. *Perception & Psychophysics, 60,* 544–557.

Squires, K. C., Donchin, E., Herning, R. I., & McCarthy, G. (1977). Influence of task relevance and stimulus probability on event-related-potential components, *Electroencephalography and Clinical Neurophysiology, 42,* 1–14.

Tang, Y. Y., Ma, Y., Wang, J., Fan, Y., Feng, S., Lu, Q., et al. (2007). Short-term meditation training improves attention and self-regulation. *Proceedings of the National Academy of Sciences of the United States of America, 104*(43), 17152–17156.

Theeuwes, J. (1991). Exogenous and endogenous control of attention: The effect of visual onsets and offsets. *Perception & Psychophysics, 49*(1), 83–90.

Theeuwes, J. (1992). Perceptual selectivity for color and form. *Perception & Psychophysics, 51*(6), 599–606.

Theeuwes, J. (1994). Stimulus-driven capture and attentional set: Selective search for color and visual abrupt onsets. *Journal of Experimental Psychology. Human Perception and Performance, 20,* 799–799.

Theeuwes, J. (2004). Top-down search strategies cannot override attentional capture. *Psychonomic Bulletin and Review, 11*(1), 65–70.

Theeuwes, J., Atchley, P., & Kramer, A. F. (2000). On the time course of top-down and bottom-up control of visual attention. *Control of cognitive processes: Attention and performance* (Vol. XVIII, pp. 105–124). Cambridge, MA: MIT Press.

Titchener, E. B. (1916). *A text-book of psychology* New York: MacMillan.

Vogel, E. K., & Luck, S. J. (2000). The visual N1 component as an index of a discrimination process. *Psychophysiology, 37,* 190–203.

Wang, Q., Cavanaugh, P., & Green, M. (1994). Familiarity and pop-out in visual search. *Perception & Psychophysics, 56*(5), 495–500.

Ward, L. M. (1994). Supramodal and modality-specific mechanisms for stimulus-driven shifts of auditory and visual attention. *Canadian Journal of Experimental Psychology, 48*(2), 242–257.

Woldorff, M. G. (1993). Distortion of ERP averages due to overlap from temporally adjacent ERPs: Analysis and correction. *Psychophysiology, 30,* 98–119.

Woldorff, M. G., & Hillyard, S. A. (1991). Modulation of early auditory processing during selective listening to rapidly presented tones. *Electroencephalography and Clinical Neurophysiology, 79*(3), 170–191.

Woodman, G. F., & Luck, S. J. (1999). Electrophysiological measurement of rapid shifts of attention during visual search. *Nature, 400*(6747), 867–868.

3

Thalamic Control of Visual Attention

SABINE KASTNER, YURI B. SAALMANN, AND KEITH A. SCHNEIDER

IN 1932, Le Gros Clark wrote about the thalamus: "Not only does the thalamus . . . determine a spatial location in the cortex, but it is possible for sensory impulses on their way through the thalamus to undergo modification and selection as the result of being brought into relation with the activities of intrinsic thalamic mechanisms. In other words, the [cortex] must depend entirely on the thalamus for the precise nature of the sensory material which it receives indirectly from peripheral receptors. It is true that there is evidence to indicate that cortical mechanisms can modify thalamic activities by inhibitory influences, but the fact remains that . . . the [cortex] from the developmental and functional point of view is to be regarded as a dependency of the thalamus and not *vice versa*." (Le Gros Clark, 1932). The notion that cortical processing cannot be understood without a profound understanding of thalamic processing and thalamocortical interactions is as timely as ever. Indeed, we will argue in

this chapter that understanding thalamocortical interactions is central to our understanding of perception and cognition.

Even though the anatomical organization, functional connectivity, and basic response properties of the thalamus have been well established (Jones, 2007; Sherman & Guillery, 2001), its role in controlling perception and cognition has remained poorly understood. Studies in awake, behaving monkeys during the last decades have focused almost exclusively on defining the roles of cortical areas in cognitive tasks related to attention, memory, decision making, and others. Similarly, human neuroimaging studies have heavily emphasized the functions of cortical rather than subcortical networks, partially due to technical difficulties such as the small sizes of thalamic nuclei in relation to the typical spatial resolution of neuroimaging techniques. This has changed only recently with the development of functional magnetic resonance imaging (fMRI) at high resolution that permitted for the first time the study of the human thalamus in some detail (see Saalmann & Kastner, 2009, for review) and was followed by a renewed interest of physiologists in thalamic function in awake, behaving monkeys (e.g., McAlonan et al., 2006, 2008). We will focus this chapter on the visual thalamus and its role in controlling selective attention, which refers to our ability to select behaviorally relevant visual information from the cluttered natural environments that we live in.

The visual thalamus consists of three main nuclei: the lateral geniculate nucleus (LGN), the thalamic reticular nucleus (TRN), and the pulvinar. The LGN is the thalamic station in the retinocortical projection and has traditionally been viewed as the gateway to the visual cortex. In addition to retinal afferents that form only a minority of the input to the LGN, it receives projections from multiple sources including striate cortex, the TRN, and the brainstem. Thus, the LGN represents the first stage in the visual pathway at which cortical top-down feedback signals could affect information processing. However, the LGN has traditionally been viewed as a relay that transmits information faithfully from the retina to the cortex without much modulation. The TRN forms a thin shell of neurons surrounding the thalamus and providing an interface between the thalamus and cortex in that thalamo-cortical and (layer 6) corticothalamic projections also have collateral branches to the TRN (Guillery et al., 1998). This connectivity has led to a notion that the TRN may be the guardian of the thalamic gateway (Crick, 1984). The pulvinar is a large nucleus located in the dorsal thalamus. It contains several visual maps that are reciprocally connected to striate and extrastriate cortex, in addition to being substantially interconnected with frontal and parietal cortex. This connectivity suggests that the pulvinar serves in aiding corticocortical transmission through thalamic loops. Thus, from an anatomical perspective, the visual thalamus is ideally positioned to regulate the transmission of information to the cortex and between cortical areas, as was originally proposed more than 20 years ago (Singer, 1977; Crick, 1984; Sherman & Koch, 1986). Only during the last few years has experimental evidence emerged that

suggests a role for the thalamus in controlling visual attention, integration and awareness.

THE LATERAL GENICULATE NUCLEUS: AN EARLY "GATEKEEPER"

At the cortical level, converging evidence from physiological studies in monkeys and functional brain mapping studies in humans indicates that selective attention modulates neural activity in the visual system (see Chapters 1 and 2 of this volume). In nonhuman primates, visual attentional response modulation was originally demonstrated in extrastriate cortex (e.g., Moran & Desimone, 1985) and has also been shown in striate cortex, where the modulation appears to depend more on task-related factors, such as the attentional demands of the task at hand or the need to integrate contextual information from areas beyond the classical receptive field (RF) (Motter, 1993; Watanabe et al., 1998; Gandhi et al., 1999; Ito & Gilbert, 1999; Martinez et al., 1999; Somers et al., 1999). These findings, in combination with negative results failing to demonstrate attentional modulation at the thalamic stage of the retinocortical projection, the LGN, led to a notion that selective attention affects neural processing only at the cortical level (Mehta et al., 2000; Bender & Youakim, 2001). This notion has been revised during the last few years based on reports of attentional modulation in the human and macaque LGN (O'Connor et al., 2002; McAlonan et al., 2008; Schneider & Kastner, 2009). Outside of the visual system, a large-scale network of areas in frontal and parietal cortex is activated during the selection of behaviorally relevant information and may play a critical role in controlling modulatory influences on sensory systems (see Corbetta & Shulman, 2000, and Yantis & Serences, 2003, for review). The overall view that emerges from these studies is that neural mechanisms of selective attention operate at multiple cortical and subcortical stages in the visual system (Kastner & Pinsk, 2004). It is a major goal of the field of cognitive neuroscience to characterize the functional role that each processing stage plays during the attentional selection process and to reveal the neural mechanisms underlying the computations performed at each stage. In this section, we will focus on the role of the LGN and also the TRN in the control of selective attention.

ANATOMICAL AND FUNCTIONAL ORGANIZATION

The LGN is the thalamic station in the projection of the visual pathway from retina to primary visual cortex. Its topographic organization and the response properties of its neurons have been extensively studied in nonhuman primates (e.g., Polyak, 1953; Kaas et al., 1972; Malpeli & Baker, 1975; Connolly & Van Essen, 1984). The LGN is typically organized into six main layers, each of which receives input from either the contra- or ipsilateral eye and contains a retinotopic map of the contralateral hemifield. The four dorsal layers contain small (parvocellular) neurons character-ized by sustained discharge patterns and low con-trast gain, and the two ventral layers contain large (magnocellular) neurons characterized by tran-sient discharge patterns and high contrast gain (Wiesel & Hubel, 1966; Dreher et al., 1976; Creutzfeldt et al., 1979; Shapley et al., 1981; Derrington & Lennie, 1984; Merigan & Maunsell, 1993). There are also six thin LGN layers, one ventral to each parvo- and magnocellular layer. These thin layers contain very small (koniocellular) neurons, some of which carry signals from short wavelength–sensitive, or blue, cones (Casagrande, 1994; Martin et al., 1997; Hendry & Reid, 2000; Xu et al., 2001; Roy et al., 2009). Unfortunately, because there is currently little data relating to attention effects on the koniocellular pathway, only limited discussion of this pathway will follow in this chapter.

The contralateral visual hemifield is repre-sented in the LGN with the horizontal meridian dividing the structure into a superior and medial half, representing the lower visual field (VF) and an inferior and lateral half, representing the upper VF. The fovea is represented medially in the posterior pole of the nucleus, whereas more peripheral VF representations are located more anteriorly and laterally (Malpeli & Baker, 1975). In the LGN, as in other visual areas, more neurons are devoted to the representation of the fovea than to an equivalent area of the visual periphery.

In the human LGN, anatomical studies have revealed a similar organization compared to the macaque LGN in terms of laminar patterns of parvo- and magnocellular subdivisions. The layout of the representation of the VF had been initially studied using postmortem anatomical analyses of degeneration patterns following reti-nal or cortical lesions (Rönne, 1910; Juba & Szatmári, 1937; Kupfer, 1962; Hickey & Guillery, 1979). Only recently, it has been characterized in detail with the help of high-resolution fMRI techniques that revealed a close correspondence in the topographic organization of the macaque and human LGNs (Schneider et al., 2004). Similar to the macaque, in the human, the horizontal meridian divides the lower VF representation, located in the medial superior section of the nucleus, and the upper VF representation, located in the lateral-inferior section (Figure 3.1, *near left and right columns*). The central parts of the VF are represented mainly in its posterior and superior portions, whereas more peripheral field represen-tations are systematically represented in anterior and inferior regions of the nucleus (Figure 3.1, *far left and right columns*).

Current neuroimaging techniques are insuffi-cient to resolve single lamina within the human LGN. However, magno- and parvocellular regions of the LGN can be identified based on their differ-ences in sensitivity to stimulus contrast. Monkey physiology studies have shown that magnocellu-lar cells have much higher contrast sensitivity than do parvocellular cells (Derrington & Lennie, 1984; Sclar et al., 1990). In accordance with these physiology studies, a nonuniform distribution of contrast responses has been found throughout the human LGN, with one class of voxels that respond strongly to low contrast stimuli and exhibit only a small modulation in response amplitude evoked by a low- and a high-contrast stimulus (these are likely to be dominated by magnocellular inputs), and other voxels that respond little or not at all to low-contrast stimuli and exhibit large differences in response to low- and high-contrast stimuli (these are likely to be dominated by parvocellular inputs) (Schneider et al., 2004). Hence, it is

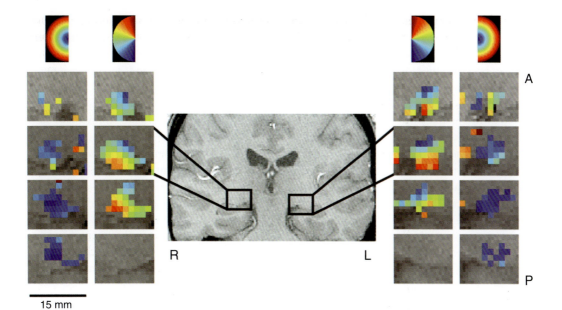

15 mm

FIGURE 3.1   Retinotopic maps in the human lateral geniculate nucleus (LGN). Polar angle and eccentricity maps are shown for one representative subject. The central panel shows an anatomical image in the coronal plane through the posterior thalamus. The boxes indicate the locations of the panels to the left and right. Details of the polar angle maps in the right (R) and left (L) LGNs are shown in the near left and right columns, arranged in several sequential slices from anterior (A) to posterior (P). The eccentricity maps are shown in the far left and right columns and have been spatially registered with the polar angle maps. The color code (shown for voxels whose responses were correlated with the fundamental frequency of the stimulus, $r \geq .25$) indicates the phase of the response and labels the portion of the visual field (VF) to which the voxel is most responsive, as depicted in the VF color legend at the top of each column. From Schneider et al. (2004), in modified form.

possible to segregate the magno- and parvocellular subdivisions of the human LGN on the basis of functional criteria. This is a useful approach when probing visual functions of the two processing streams in relation to human behavior and cognition, since the LGN is the only location in the visual system where the magno- and parvocellular channels are spatially segregated.

As mentioned earlier, the LGN receives input from multiple sources including striate cortex, the TRN, and the brainstem and is therefore the first stage in the visual pathway at which cortical top-down feedback signals could affect information processing. In the following sections, we will review a series of recent neuroimaging and physiology studies that have probed modulatory effects of spatial attention on the neural activity in the human and macaque LGN.

ATTENTIONAL MODULATION IN THE HUMAN LATERAL GENICULATE NUCLEUS

Three Modulatory Effects of Attention

At the cortical level, selective attention has been shown to affect visual processing in at least three different ways. First, neural responses to attended visual stimuli are enhanced relative to the same stimuli when unattended (attentional enhancement; e.g., Moran & Desimone, 1985; Corbetta et al., 1990). Second, neural responses to unattended stimuli are attenuated depending on the load of attentional resources engaged elsewhere (attentional suppression; e.g., Rees et al., 1997). And third, directing attention to a location in the absence of visual stimulation and in anticipation of the stimulus onset increases neural baseline activity (attention-related baseline increases; e.g., Luck et al., 1997; Kastner et al., 1999). These effects of selective attention were investigated in a series of three experiments that were designed to establish attentional response modulation, if existent, in the human LGN. In these studies, neural activity in the LGN as measured by fMRI signals was monitored across the entire structure, that is, averaging across both magno- and parvocellular subdivisions. Subsequent studies reviewed later investigated modulatory attention effects separately in the two subdivisions.

In the initial studies that investigated the LGN as a whole, flickering checkerboard stimuli of high or low contrast were used, which activated the LGN optimally (Chen et al., 1999) and also areas in visual cortex, including V1, V2, ventral and dorsal V3, V4, TEO (that, is part of the VO-complex; see Arcaro et al., 2009), V3A, and MT/MST (referred to as MT), as determined on the basis of retinotopic mapping (Sereno et al., 1995; Kastner et al., 2001).

To investigate attentional response enhancement in the LGN, checkerboard stimuli were presented to the left or right hemifield while subjects directed attention to the stimulus (attended condition) or away from the stimulus (unattended condition). In the unattended condition, attention was directed away from the stimulus by having subjects count letters at fixation. The letter counting task ensured proper fixation and prevented subjects from covertly attending to the checkerboard stimuli (Kastner et al., 1998). In the attended condition, subjects were instructed to covertly direct attention to the checkerboard stimulus and to detect luminance changes that occurred randomly in time at 10 degrees eccentricity. In the statistical model, stimulation of the left visual hemifield was contrasted with stimulation of the right visual hemifield. Thereby, the analysis was restricted to voxels activated by the peripheral checkerboard stimuli and excluded foveal stimulus representations. Relative to the unattended condition, the neural activity evoked by both the high-contrast stimulus and the low-contrast stimulus increased significantly in the attended condition (Figure 3.2A). The attentional response enhancement was shown to be spatially

specific in a variation of the experimental design, in which checkerboard stimuli were presented to both the right and left visual hemifield, and subjects directed attention to either stimulus while the other one was ignored. These results suggest that attention facilitates visual processing in the LGN by enhancing neural responses to an attended stimulus relative to those evoked by the same stimulus when ignored.

To investigate attentional load-dependent suppression in the LGN, high- and low-contrast checkerboard stimuli were presented to the left or right hemifield while subjects performed either an easy attention task or a hard attention task at fixation and ignored the peripheral checkerboard stimuli. During the easy attention task, subjects counted infrequent, brief color changes of the fixation cross. During the hard attention task, subjects counted letters at fixation. Behavioral performance was 99% correct on average in the easy attention task and 54% in the hard attention task, thus indicating the differences in attentional demands. Relative to the easy task condition, neural activity evoked by the high- and the low-contrast stimuli decreased significantly in the hard task condition (Figure 3.2B). This finding suggests that neural activity evoked by ignored stimuli was attenuated in the LGN depending on the load of attentional resources engaged elsewhere.

To investigate attention-related baseline increases in the LGN, subjects were cued to covertly direct attention to the periphery of the left or right visual hemifield and to expect the onset of the stimulus. The expectation period was followed by attended presentations of a high-contrast checkerboard stimulus during which subjects counted the occurrence of luminance changes. During the expectation period, fMRI signals increased significantly relative to the preceding blank period in which subjects were fixating but not directing attention to the periphery. Because the visual input, a gray blank screen, was identical in both conditions, the increase in baseline activity appeared to be related to directed attention and may be interpreted as a bias in favor of the attended location. The baseline increase was followed by a further response increase evoked by the visual stimuli (Figure 3.2C). It is important to note that, because of the statistical

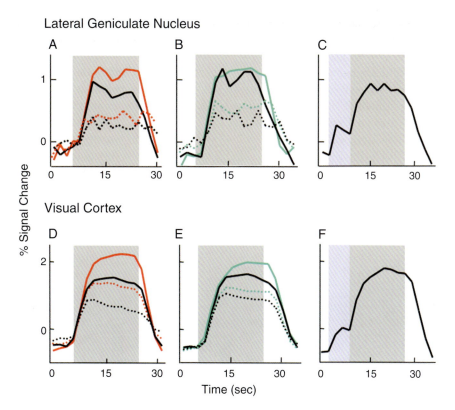

Lateral Geniculate Nucleus

Visual Cortex

% Signal Change (y-axis)

Time (sec) (x-axis)

FIGURE 3.2   Time series of functional magnetic resonance imaging (fMRI) signals in the lateral geniculate nucleus (LGN) and in visual cortex. Group analysis ($n = 4$). Data from the LGN and visual cortex were combined across left and right hemispheres. Activity in visual cortex was pooled across areas V1, V2, V3/VP, V4, TEO, V3A, and MT/MST. (**A, D**) Attentional enhancement. During directed attention to the stimuli (*gray curves*), responses to both the high-contrast stimulus (100%, *solid curves*) and low-contrast stimulus (5%, *dashed curves*) were enhanced relative to an unattended condition (*black curves*). (**B, E**) Attentional suppression. During an attentionally demanding "hard" fixation task (*black curves*), responses evoked by both the high-contrast stimulus (100%, *solid curves*) and low-contrast stimulus (10%, *dashed curves*) were attenuated relative to an easy attention task at fixation (*gray curves*). (**C, F**) Baseline increases. Baseline activity was elevated during directed attention to the periphery of the visual hemifield in expectation of the stimulus onset; the beginning of the expectation period is indicated by the dashed vertical line. Gray vertical lines indicate the beginning of checkerboard presentation periods. From O'Connor et al. (2002).

model used to analyze the experiment that "subtracted out" the foveal representations, the increase in baseline activity was not related to the cue, which was presented at fixation. This finding suggests that neural activity in the LGN can be affected by attention-related top-down signals even in the absence of any visual stimulation whatsoever.

Together, these studies were the first to demonstrate that selective attention modulates neural activity in the LGN by enhancing neural responses to attended stimuli, by attenuating those to

ignored stimuli, and by increasing baseline activity in the absence of visual stimulation.

COMPARISON OF ATTENTION EFFECTS IN THE LATERAL GENICULATE NUCLEUS AND VISUAL CORTEX

At the cortical level, qualitatively similar effects of attention were found, as shown in the time series of fMRI signals averaged across all activated areas in visual cortex, that is, areas V1, V2, V3, V4, TEO, V3A, and MT (Figure 3.2D–F). The attention effects found at the thalamic and at the cortical level were compared by normalizing the mean fMRI signals evoked in the LGN and in each activated cortical area and by computing index values for each attention effect and each area, which are measures of the magnitude of a given attention effect. This analysis is shown in Figure 3.3; larger index values indicate larger effects of attention. It should be noted that index values cannot be easily compared across attention effects due to differences in index definitions and attention tasks.

In accordance with previous findings (Kastner et al., 1998; Martinez et al., 1999; Mehta et al., 2000; Cook & Maunsell, 2002), the magnitude of all attention effects increased from early to more advanced processing levels along both the ventral and dorsal pathways of visual cortex (Figure 3.3A–C). This is consistent with the idea that attention operates through top-down signals that are transmitted via corticocortical feedback connections in a hierarchical fashion. Thereby, areas at advanced levels of visual cortical processing are

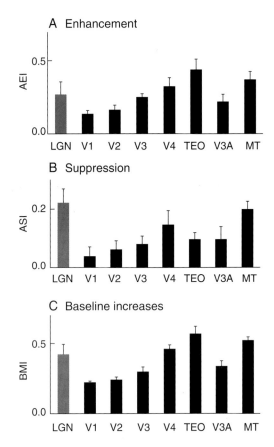

FIGURE 3.3 Attentional response modulation in the lateral geniculate nucleus (LGN) and in visual cortex. Attention effects that were obtained in the experiments presented in Figure 3.2 were quantified by defining several indices: (**A**) attentional enhancement index (AEI), (**B**) attentional suppression index (ASI), (**C**) baseline modulation index (BMI). For all indices, larger values indicate larger effects of attention. Index values were computed for each subject based on normalized and averaged signals obtained in the different attention conditions and are presented as averaged index values from four subjects (for index definitions, see O'Connor et al., 2002). In visual cortex, attention effects increased from early to later processing stages. Attention effects in the LGN were larger than in V1. Vertical bars indicate standard errors of the mean across subjects. From O'Connor et al. (2002).

more strongly controlled by attention mechanisms than are early processing levels. This idea is supported by single-cell recording studies, which have shown that attention effects in area TE of inferior temporal cortex have a latency of approximately 150 ms (Chelazzi et al., 1998), whereas attention effects in V1 have a longer latency of approximately 230 ms (Roelfsema et al., 1998). According to this account, one would predict smaller attention effects in the LGN than in striate cortex. Surprisingly, it was found that all attention effects tended to be larger in the LGN than in striate cortex (Figure 3.3A–C). This finding suggests that attentional response modulation in the LGN is unlikely to be due solely to corticothalamic feedback from striate cortex, but may be further influenced by additional sources of input such as the TRN (see later sections for further discussion).

To gain a better understanding of why there may be a difference between attention effects in the LGN and visual cortex measured using fMRI, it is useful to consider the neural basis of the blood oxygen level–dependent (BOLD) signal that is measured with fMRI. BOLD activity has been shown to better correlate with local field potentials than action potentials (Logothetis & Wandell, 2004; Niessing et al., 2005; Viswanathan & Freeman, 2007). Local field potentials reflect synaptic potentials, subthreshold membrane potential oscillations, and afterpotentials. Consequently, it is likely that BOLD responses, including the attentional influences determined with the index values shown in Figure 3.3, represent inputs to a brain area as well as local processing. The fact that the LGN receives substantial modulatory input, seemingly greater than V1, may thus explain the larger effects of attention in the LGN measured using fMRI. Interestingly, it has recently been reported that local field potentials recorded in the LGN and V1 differ in their utility as predictors of spiking activity (Rasch et al., 2008). This result suggests differences in local field potential characteristics between the LGN and V1 that may underlie the different magnitude of attention effects in each area. However, other possibilities that may explain the differences in magnitude of the modulation between the LGN and V1 need to be considered, including regional disparities underlying the BOLD signal or nonlinearities in thalamocortical signal transmission.

ATTENTION EFFECTS IN MAGNO- AND PARVOCELLULAR LATERAL GENICULATE NUCLEUS SUBDIVISIONS

Thus far, we have reviewed evidence of attentional modulation of neural responses in the human LGN in comparison to effects on visual cortex. However, the LGN is the only structure in which the parvo- and magnocellular systems that originate in the retina are entirely separated and therefore can be investigated in isolation with respect to their functional organization and response properties (e.g., Merigan & Maunsell, 1993). Subsequent studies using high-resolution fMRI were therefore conducted to investigate the effects of spatially selective attention on the magno- and parvocellular parts of the human LGN (Schneider & Kastner, 2009). These studies were motivated by accounts of a "magnocellular theory of selective attention" that has been based on behavioral studies and suggests a critical role for the magnocellular system in attentional processes (Steinman et al., 1997; Cheng et al., 2004). Such a magnocellular attention account has been corroborated by deoxyglucose studies in monkeys, in which attention suppressed the metabolic activity in regions encoding the VF outside the focus of attention in the magnocellular, but not parvocellular LGN layers (Vanduffel et al., 2000).

Attention effects on the magno- and parvocellular LGN were investigated using a visual tracking paradigm. Visual stimuli consisted of two opposing angular segments that formed a bow tie-shaped pattern rotating slowly about the fixation point. The segments were either filled with moving dots or with colorful shapes. Subjects were instructed to covertly direct attention to one segment and to detect a change in motion direction with the motion stimulus or a unique color–shape combination with the color–shape stimulus, while the other segment of the bow tie stimulus was ignored. The magno- and parvocellular subdivisions of the LGN were defined functionally based on the contrast sensitivity profile of single voxels, as described earlier.

As the bow-tie stimuli traveled periodically through the VF, they evoked periodic responses in the LGN, with the hemodynamic response increasing as each segment of the stimulus passed through the portion of the VF represented by each voxel, and decreasing in response to a blank VF. Data from two typical voxels are shown in Figure 3.4A. With the voxel shown in the upper panel, the first response was evoked by the attended segment of the motion stimulus, whereas the second response was evoked when the unattended segment passed through the same part of the VF represented by this voxel. In this case, the resulting response amplitudes for the attended and unattended segments of the stimulus were approximately equal, and there was little attentional modulation. In contrast, the voxel in the lower panel exhibited strong attentional modulation, and the response evoked by the attended segment of the stimulus was more than twice the amplitude of the response evoked by the unattended segment.

To evaluate the effects of attention on neural signals in the LGN quantitatively, the mean response amplitudes evoked by the attended and unattended segments of the two types of stimuli were calculated and collapsed across stimulus type. Stimulus type was an important variable to demonstrate the generality of any attention effects. However, it turned out not to be a significant factor, and the attention effects were very similar regardless of stimulus type. Across the entire LGN, the responses evoked by the attended segment of the stimulus were about 10% larger than the responses evoked by the unattended segment (Figure 3.4B, *subject mean*), thereby confirming the earlier LGN attention studies that had used coarser spatial resolution (O'Connor et al., 2002). More interestingly, this main effect of attentional enhancement was found in both the magno- and the parvocellular LGN. A contrast modulation index (CMI) was computed to characterize differences in contrast sensitivity for each voxel. Voxels with small contrast response differences

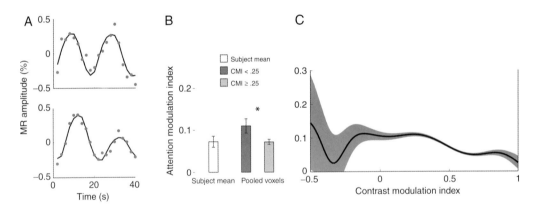

FIGURE 3.4 Attentional response modulation in the magno- and parvocellular lateral geniculate nucleus (LGN). (**A**) Functional magnetic resonance imaging (fMRI) time series of two typical individual voxels are shown in response to rotating bow-tie stimulus, half of which was attended. The peaks in the response occur when the segments of the stimulus rotate through the receptive fields of the voxels. For each voxel, the response to the attended segment occurs first, followed by the second response to the unattended segment. The voxel in the upper panel shows little attentional modulation between the attended and unattended segments of the stimulus. The voxel in the lower panel exhibits a large attentional modulation, as seen in the different amplitudes of the two responses. The difference in response on the attended and unattended segment reflects the strength of the attention effect, as measured with the attention modulation index (AMI). (**B**) AMIs are shown averaged over subject (*white bars*) and over voxels grouped by contrast modulation index (CMI) (*shaded bars*; * indicates $p < .05$). Voxels with CMI < .25 are assumed to be dominated by magnocellular inputs, those with CMI > .25 by parvocellular inputs. (**C**) The mean AMI as a function of CMI is shown for the LGN. The shaded area represents the standard error of the mean From Schneider & Kastner (2009) in modified form.

were grouped together (CMI <0.25), and it was assumed that they were dominated by magnocellular inputs. In contrast, voxels with larger contrast response differences (CMI >0.25) were grouped under the assumption that they were more strongly dominated by parvocellular inputs. After normalizing the attention effects for each subdivision with the help of an index value (Attentional Modulation Index, AMI), it turned out that, although both subdivisions were modulated by selective attention, the effects were significantly larger on the magnocellular LGN (Figure 3.4B). Thus, the LGN voxels that were less modulated in contrast exhibited stronger attentional enhancement, independent of whether the attended stimulus was composed of moving dots or shapes of different color (Figure 3.4C). This result suggests that the magnocellular layers are more strongly enhanced by sustained spatial attention than are the parvocellular layers, thereby corroborating accounts of selective attention suggesting that the magnocellular neurons are essential for the allocation of attentional resources (Cheng et al., 2004). However, these findings also show that, although the attentional modulation was stronger in LGN voxels likely to be dominated by magnocellular input, they were not confined to these portions of the LGN. This differential response modulation of the magno- and parvocellular LGN may be key in understanding the nature of attentional control exerted at the level of the LGN, as will be discussed later.

Spatial Distribution and Specificity of Attention Effects

As described earlier, the LGN contains a retinotopic map of the VF that can be resolved in humans using high-resolution fMRI (Schneider et al., 2004; Schneider & Kastner, 2005). By examining the attentional effects in individual voxels in relation to the voxels' locations within the retinotopic map of the LGN, it is possible to determine the effects of spatial attention throughout the VF, and, thereby, to obtain a detailed measure of the spatial specificity of the attentional effects in the LGN. For that purpose, the data obtained with the attentional tracking paradigm described in the previous section were analyzed in relation to the retinotopic LGN maps of the

same subjects. This is illustrated in Figure 3.5A, in which the mean AMIs averaged across both types of stimuli used in the attentional tracking paradigm are plotted for each voxel of one subject's LGN; the retinotopic organization of that subject's LGN is shown in comparison (Figure 3.5B; see also Figure 3.1). In Figure 3.5A, attentional response enhancement with AMI of greater than 0 is indicated by reddish colors, whereas attentional suppression with AMI of less than 0 is indicated by the bluish colors. In Figure 3.5B, the color code labels the part of the VF to which the voxel is most responsive, as depicted in the circular VF color legend. Interestingly, both attention effects were found in the LGN, suggesting that there appears to be some internal structure within the LGN, with localized regions of relatively strong attentional enhancement, mixed among relatively weak but more expansive regions of attentional suppression. A systematic analysis of attentional response enhancement and suppression effects relative to features in the retinotopic organization of the LGN revealed that the distribution of AMIs was relatively uniform across the VF, with each location in the VF being represented by some voxels exhibiting attentional enhancement and others exhibiting suppression (Figure 3.5C). The suppressive regions within the LGN are different from the zones of suppression that might surround a "spotlight" of attentional enhancement or from the suppression that has been observed in the unattended regions of the VF (e.g., Tootell et al., 1998; Brefczynski & DeYoe, 1999); rather, the suppressive regions in the LGN are those in which the response to the attended half of the stimulus was weaker than the response to the unattended half that was located in the opposite hemifield. The functional and structural significance of the suppressive regions within the LGN is unclear and deserves further investigation.

SOURCES OF MODULATORY INFLUENCES ON LATERAL GENICULATE NUCLEUS: ROLE OF THE THALAMIC RETICULAR NUCLEUS, CORTEX, AND BRAINSTEM

The findings reviewed thus far challenge the classical notion that attention effects are confined to cortical processing and suggest the need to revise

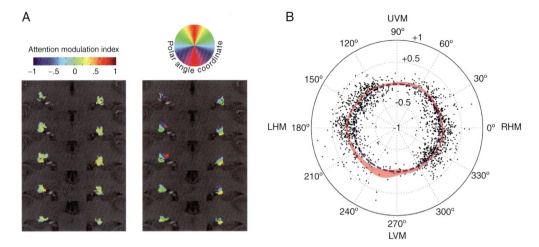

FIGURE 3.5 Spatial specificity of attention effects in the lateral geniculate nucleus (LGN). (**A**) In the left panel, the attention modulation index (AMI) is plotted for each voxel in the LGN of one subject. The AMI is indicated by color, as shown on the color bar. In the right panel, the polar angle coordinate of the retinotopic representation of each voxel in the LGN is shown for the same subject. The colored disc indicates the position of the VF that the voxels in the LGN map are most responsive to, with yellowish colors representing the upper hemifield and bluish colors the lower hemifield. (**B**) For each voxel and each subject, the AMIs are plotted against the polar angle coordinate. Each dot represents a single voxel, with dots in the right side of the graph representing voxels in the left LGN, and dots on the left, the right LGN. The dashed blue line indicates AMI = 0, i.e., no attentional modulation. AMI = −1, which is the maximum possible attentional suppression, is plotted in the center, and AMI = +1, the maximum attentional enhancement, is plotted at the perimeter. The red shaded area indicates the 95% confidence interval of the mean smoothed AMI at that polar angle coordinate. From Schneider & Kastner (2009) in modified form.

the traditional view of the LGN as a mere gateway to the visual cortex. In fact, due to its afferent input, the LGN may be in an ideal strategic position to serve as an early "gatekeeper" in attentional gain control. In addition to corticothalamic feedback projections from V1, which comprise about 30% of its modulatory input, the LGN receives another 30% of modulatory inputs from the TRN (Sherman & Guillery, 2002). The TRN forms a thin shell of neurons surrounding the thalamus and only projects to other thalamic nuclei. Francis Crick (1984) defined a functional role for the TRN in spatial attention in his "searchlight hypothesis": "The dorsal thalamus and the reticular complex . . . control and express the internal attentional searchlight. . . . An important function of the reticular complex may be to limit the number of subjects the thalamus can pay attention to at any one time." Although we do not embrace the idea of selective attention operating

as a moving spotlight, the notion that the dorsal thalamus (i.e., the LGN) in concert with the TRN plays a functional role in filtering information by controlling the gain of cortical neurons is an important one, as we will further discuss later. There are a number of reasons why the TRN has long been implicated in theoretical accounts of selective attention. First, feedforward projections from the thalamus to the cortex, as well as corticothalamic feedback projections (generally from cortical layer 6), send collaterals to the TRN (Guillery, 1995; Sherman & Guillery, 2002). Second, the TRN receives not only inputs from the LGN and V1, but also from the prefrontal cortex, extrastriate areas, superior colliculus, and the pulvinar (Guillery & Harting, 2003; Zikopoulos & Barbas, 2006). Therefore, it may serve as a node with a "switchboard function," in which several cortical areas and thalamic nuclei of the visual system can interact to modulate thalamocortical transmission through inhibitory connections to LGN neurons (Guillery et al., 1998). And third, the TRN contains topographically organized representations of the VF and can therefore modulate thalamocortical or corticothalamic transmission in spatially specific ways. Similarly, all corticofugal projections are organized in topographic order. However, a recent study reported that there are three classes of corticothalamic neurons, each class selectively targeting parvo-, magno-, or koniocellular neurons in the LGN (Briggs & Usrey, 2009). This finding suggests that corticothalamic feedback may differentially modulate information processing in parvo-, magno-, and koniocellular afferent pathways according to behavioral requirements, and thus be more selective than the TRN input to the LGN. Other modulatory influences on the LGN stem from the parabrachial nucleus of the brainstem. These cholinergic projections, another 30% of the modulatory input to the LGN, are more diffusely organized (Erişir et al., 1997), which makes a possible role in spatially selective attention more difficult to account for. The superior colliculus also projects to the LGN, primarily to the koniocellular layers (Harting et al., 1991) and may provide information about saccadic eye movements and their possible targets. Recent physiologic studies in the macaque have shed further light on the role of the TRN in modulating LGN responses during the allocation of attention.

Attentional Modulation in the Macaque Lateral Geniculate Nucleus and Thalamic Reticular Nucleus

There are currently only a few examples of attentional modulation of the macaque LGN. In a recent electrophysiology study (McAlonan et al., 2008), macaque monkeys were cued to attend to one of two peripheral visual stimuli. Attention increased the median stimulus-evoked response of magnocellular and parvocellular neurons by 11% and 9%, respectively. However, attention did not significantly change baseline activity, in contrast with the human fMRI results (a discrepancy that we will address later in this section). Preliminary data showing similar attention effects on LGN responses have been reported by another

laboratory (Casagrande et al., 2005). These effects of attention on LGN responses may occur during two different epochs. There appears to be a rapid effect within the first 100 ms after the onset of an attended stimulus and a later effect that manifests after 200 ms of the stimulus onset (McAlonan et al., 2008). We will now briefly discuss the evidence for different sources of modulatory input to the LGN contributing during these different time periods.

Thalamic reticular nucleus responses have been shown to be modulated by attention (McAlonan et al., 2006, 2008). In the McAlonan et al. (2008) study, recordings were made from the TRN and LGN on alternate days, during performance of the same task. Effects in the TRN and LGN were of opposite directions; that is, TRN responses decreased and LGN responses increased with attention. Such an inverse correlation has also been reported between simultaneously recorded neurons in the perigeniculate nucleus (displaced portion of the visual sector of the cat TRN) and LGN in anesthetized cats (Funke & Eysel, 1998). These anticorrelation patterns are consistent with attention reducing the reticular inhibition of the LGN, thereby enhancing LGN output. The TRN neurons have short response latencies and this presumably allows the TRN to modulate the early effects of attention on the LGN. However, the TRN responses quickly return to baseline, which means that later attention effects in the LGN may have a different source, for instance, V1 feedback.

A remaining issue is that there have been reports of little or no attentional modulation of LGN responses in other physiology studies (Mehta et al., 2000; Bender & Youakim, 2001). It is possible that these negative findings might reflect differences in attention tasks and task difficulty among the studies. However, it appears that findings from single-cell physiology regarding attentional modulation of LGN responses have been less consistent than the human fMRI studies. Further, the size of attentional modulation in the LGN as measured with fMRI tended to be quite substantial and comparable to typical effect sizes in extrastriate cortex. Therefore, there may indeed exist a difference in the findings between fMRI and electrophysiology, which may be related to the different neural signals that are measured with fMRI and single-neuron recordings. As mentioned earlier, fMRI has been shown to better correlate with local field potentials than with action potential output (Logothetis & Wandell, 2004; Niessing et al., 2005; Viswanathan & Freeman, 2007). Local field potentials reflect postsynaptic potentials, oscillatory potentials, and after-potentials. In contrast, recordings from the macaque LGN have primarily measured action potential rate (Bender & Youakim, 2001; McAlonan et al., 2008). Therefore, it should not be surprising that the human and macaque data are not entirely consistent as they have measured different types of neural activity. As previously mentioned, attention-related baseline increases in the LGN have been demonstrated using fMRI (O'Connor et al., 2002), but single-neuron recordings from the LGN to date have not shown significant change in baseline action potential rate (Casagrande et al., 2005; McAlonan et al., 2008). However, neural synchrony and oscillatory activity can increase when no stimuli are present, as has been shown during the delay period of match-to-sample and memory-saccade tasks (e.g., Pesaran et al., 2002; Saalmann, et al., 2007). Such modulation of neural synchrony and oscillations is important for gain control and may underlie the attention-related baseline changes measured with BOLD signals.

RESPONSE AND CONTRAST GAIN CONTROL BY ATTENTION

What may be the nature of the attentional gain effect that is controlled by attention at the level of the LGN? One possibility is that selective attention increases simply the responsiveness of LGN neurons in a multiplicative fashion, thereby increasing neural signals evoked by visual stimuli relative to background noise (spontaneous activity). Evidence in support of multiplicative attentional gain control has been found in monkey and human extrastriate cortex (McAdams & Maunsell, 1999; Murray & Woijciulik, 2004). It was shown in physiology studies that responses evoked by an attended preferred stimulus (e.g., an optimally oriented bar) were enhanced more strongly than were those evoked by an attended nonpreferred stimulus. A second possibility is that selective

attention increases neural gain, dependent on stimulus contrast. Attention has been shown to increase contrast sensitivity in V4 neurons by enhancing neural responses evoked by low-contrast stimuli more strongly relative to those evoked by high-contrast stimuli (Reynolds et al., 2000). This result can be interpreted as an increase in effective stimulus contrast by attention. Consistent with these neurophysiological findings, it has been shown in behavioral studies that attention decreases contrast thresholds and changes the perceived salience of a stimulus, thereby altering its appearance (Cameron et al., 2002; Carrasco et al., 2004). Response and contrast gain control are not mutually exclusive and may depend on experimental conditions and subjects' strategies in allocating attention, as recently proposed by Reynolds and Heeger (2009) in their normalization model of attention (see also Boynton, 2009; Lee & Maunsell, 2009). The attentional effects on neural gain that have thus far been only demonstrated at cortical processing stages may well be controlled by the thalamus. As reviewed above, it has been shown with neuroimaging that spatial attention differentially influences the magnocellular and parvocellular neural systems at the level of the LGN (Schneider & Kastner, 2009; see also Vanduffel et al., 2000). Importantly, due to the sensitivity of the magnocellular system to stimulus contrast, which is ten times higher than that of the parvocellular system, and the saturation of magnocellular responses at higher contrasts, a stronger modulation of the magnocellular system may account for some of the attention effects on contrast gain found at the cortical level.

NEURAL MECHANISMS OF GAIN CONTROL

We have largely discussed how attention changes the magnitude of LGN neuronal responses and how this modulation of LGN output affects visual cortical processing. However, the timing of neural activity in the LGN may also have a large impact on cortical processing, by changing the efficacy of thalamocortical transmission. There are a number of ways that response timing can control neuronal gain, and here we present two important mechanisms. First, synchronizing inputs can have a greater effect on postsynaptic neurons. Second, inputs arriving at depolarizing phases of postsynaptic neurons can increase action potential probability. In these cases, oscillatory processes are useful in shaping membrane potential fluctuations and action potential timing (Singer & Gray, 1995). There is growing evidence that adjusting oscillations (phase, amplitude, and/or frequency) can modulate neuronal gain (Sejnowski & Paulsen, 2006; Saalmann et al., 2007; Womelsdorf et al., 2007; Lakatos et al., 2008). Cortical areas show changes in oscillatory behavior and synchrony under a variety of conditions, including perception, attention, and memory (e.g., Fries et al., 2001; Pesaran et al., 2002). Importantly, thalamocortical circuits (e.g., circuits incorporating the TRN, LGN, or pulvinar, and the cortex) give rise to and support oscillations (Steriade et al., 1996; Huguenard & McCormick, 2007). What is the contribution of these oscillations and, more generally, the timing of LGN activity to attention?

BOLD responses have been reported to strongly correlate with subthreshold oscillatory activity, especially in the γ frequency band (Leopold et al., 2003; Logothetis & Wandell, 2004; Niessing et al., 2005; Viswanathan & Freeman, 2007). Therefore, it is possible that the modulatory effects on the human LGN discussed above may involve changes in oscillatory processes and, consequently, changes in action potential timing. Physiology studies in awake, behaving animals have primarily measured response magnitude (e.g., McAlonan et al., 2008), and for this reason there is limited data on the temporal structure of LGN activity during cognitive manipulations. However, there is already some support for the idea that task demands modulate the timing of LGN responses. For example, visual attention has been shown to increase (β) oscillatory activity in the cat LGN and V1 (Bekisz & Wróbel, 1993; Wróbel et al., 1994) and corticothalamic feedback appears to potentiate the LGN responses (Lindstrom & Wróobel, 1990; Bekisz & Wróbel, 1993). Using in vitro and anesthetized animal preparations, it has been shown that corticothalamic feedback regulates oscillations and action potential timing (Deschênes & Hu, 1990; Bal et al., 2000; Blumenfeld & McCormick, 2000), thereby helping to synchronize activity in the LGN and between the LGN and visual cortex

(Castelo-Branco et al., 1998). Importantly, correlated firing of LGN cells is more effective in eliciting V1 responses than uncorrelated inputs (Alonso et al., 1996). Thus, oscillations and neuronal synchrony are able to modify the efficacy of retinocortical transmission.

SUMMARY

Converging evidence from recent neuroimaging and physiology studies demonstrate that the LGN is the first stage in the visual processing hierarchy at which selective attention modulates neural activity. Remarkably, the same principal modulatory effects of response enhancement, load-dependent response suppression, and increases of baseline activity that have previously been established for cortical processing were found at the thalamic processing stage using fMRI. Attentional modulation of LGN responses has recently also been established using single-cell physiology. Importantly, attentional response modulation is not confined to the magnocellular LGN, but affects both parvo- and magnocellular layers. These findings suggest the need to revise the traditional view of the LGN as a relay nucleus that transmits visual information more or less faithfully from the retina to the cortex. Instead, they suggest a fundamental role of the LGN in the attentional selection process that involves controlling neural gain. Even though the exact nature of the gain control mechanism exerted by the LGN in conjunction with its feedback sources needs to be examined, the LGN appears to be in a unique position to play such a functional role due to its feedback input from visual cortex and, through the TRN, also from large parts of higher-order cortex.

THE PULVINAR: AN INTEGRATOR OF VISUAL INFORMATION?

Several lines of evidence indicate that the pulvinar, located in the dorsal thalamus, is also part of the distributed network that subserves visuospatial attention (Robinson & Petersen, 1992; Shipp, 2004). First, when the pulvinar is inactivated by muscimol, a γ-aminobutyric acid (GABA) agonist, monkeys show impairments in filtering out irrelevant information from distracter stimuli (Desimone et al., 1990). A similar role of the pulvinar in filtering unwanted information has also been suggested by neuroimaging studies in humans (LaBerge & Buchsbaum, 1990). And second, both patients with lesions in the pulvinar and monkeys with an inactivated pulvinar exhibit attentional deficits, such as impairments in directing attention to the contralateral hemifield (Petersen et al., 1987; Rafal & Posner, 1987; Karnath et al., 2002). A similar role of the pulvinar in mediating shifts of attention has also been suggested by neuroimaging studies in normal human subjects (Yantis et al., 2002). As we will review in this section, based on its anatomical connectivity and functional organization, it is possible that the pulvinar may operate by integrating visual information and coordinating attentional function in concert with the frontoparietal attention network, a distributed system of brain regions in frontal and parietal cortex that generate modulatory attention signals fed back to sensory cortex (Kastner et al., 1999; Mesulam, 1999; Corbetta & Shulman, 2002; Moore & Armstrong, 2003; Buschman & Miller, 2007; Saalmann et al., 2007; Gregoriou et al., 2009). However, since the functions of the pulvinar are generally not well understood, future research will be needed to support the ideas about a possible role of the pulvinar as a thalamic integrator of visual information and coordinator of attentional function.

Anatomical and Functional Organization

In the macaque monkey, the pulvinar has classically been partitioned into inferior, lateral, and medial subdivisions based on cytoarchitectonic criteria (cell density and fiber locations; Stepniewska, 2003; Kaas & Lyon, 2007). However, these cytoarchitectonically defined subdivisions show poor correspondence with areas defined according to their connections (Maunsell & van Essen, 1983; Standage & Benevento, 1983; Ungerleider et al., 1983; Ungerleider et al., 1984; Shipp, 2003) or functional properties using neurochemical (e.g., calcium-binding proteins and acetylcholinesterase; Gutierrez et al., 1995; Stepniewska & Kaas, 1997; Gutierrez et al., 2000; Stepniewska, 2003) and electrophysiological techniques (Bender, 1981; Petersen et al., 1985). At least four visual areas can be distinguished on the basis of their visuotopic organization and connectivity with striate, extrastriate, parietal, and frontal cortical areas (Figure 3.6). Two of these areas are located in the

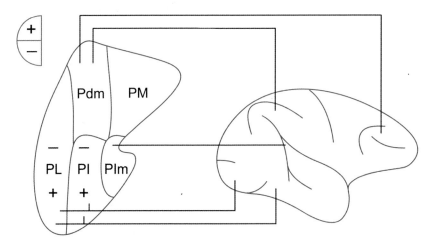

FIGURE 3.6 Pulvinar organization and cortical connections. Schematized coronal section of the macaque pulvinar (*left*) showing pulvinar subdivisions and representation of the contralateral upper (+) and lower (−) visual hemifields (*top left*, schematized visual hemifield). The inferior (*PI*) and lateral (*PL*) parts of the pulvinar are connected with striate and extrastriate cortical areas (*right*); the medial portion of inferior pulvinar is connected with MT, MST, and FST; and the dorsomedial portion of the lateral pulvinar (Pdm) is connected with parietal and frontal cortex. See text for more details. PM, medial pulvinar.

inferior and lateral part of the pulvinar. These areas contain clearly organized retinotopic maps and are reciprocally connected with cortical areas V1, V2, V4, and MT. Both areas also receive inputs from the superficial layers of the superior colliculus (SC), the SC layers innervated by retinal afferents (Harting et al., 1980; Benevento & Standage, 1983). This connectivity gives rise to a retino-colliculo-pulvinar pathway, which provides a route for transmitting visual information to the pulvinar independent of the geniculocortical pathway. A third area, described on the basis of its connections with dorsal extrastriate areas MT, MST, and FST, is located in the medial portion of the inferior subdivision and does not appear to have a well-defined retinotopic map (Ungerleider et al., 1983, 1984). A fourth area has been identified dorsal to these areas, in the dorsomedial portion of the lateral subdivision (referred to as Pdm by Petersen et al., 1985), and it shows poor visuotopic organization (Petersen et al., 1985). The Pdm area receives input from the deeper layers of the SC that have visuomotor and polysensory properties (Benevento & Standage, 1983); Pdm appears to be connected with the dorsal visual pathway, including the posterior parietal cortex (Shipp, 2003; Kaas & Lyon, 2007).

Very little is known about the anatomical and functional organization of the human pulvinar. Possible candidates for areas with topographic organization have been identified using complex motion dot patterns (Cotton & Smith, 2007; Smith et al., 2009). One area was identified in the inferior pulvinar, located medial and anterior to the LGN, and a second area in the dorsal pulvinar. Both of these areas showed a bias toward contralateral relative to ipsilateral visual stimulation. A third area, also located in the dorsal pulvinar and possibly functionally similar to Pdm, had been found earlier (Kastner et al., 2004) and will be described in greater detail in a later section. The clearest evidence for an organization of the human pulvinar into more detailed retinotopic maps has emerged from the patient literature. Patient T.N., who suffered from unilateral damage to the rostral part of the pulvinar, shows impairments in localizing stimuli in the inferior VF contralateral to the lesion, suggesting a retinotopic organization that dissociates at least visual

quadrants within the inferior pulvinar (Ward et al., 2002).

Most pulvinar neurons show a phasic response to the onset of visual stimuli; nonetheless, a number of pulvinar neurons show more tonic responses (Petersen et al., 1985). Mean response latency appears to be longer in Pdm (e.g., 84 ms in Petersen et al., 1985) than in the retinotopically organized areas in the inferior (e.g., 67 ms) and lateral (e.g., 64 ms) pulvinar subdivisions, although there is greater variability in Pdm. Pulvinar neurons have been reported to show broad orientation tuning (Bender, 1982; Petersen et al., 1985) and weak directional preference to moving stimuli (Petersen et al., 1985). A number of pulvinar neurons show color sensitivity, including color-opponent responses (Felsten et al., 1983). The receptive field size of many cells in the inferior pulvinar falls within the range of 1 to 5 degrees and, in the retinotopic lateral pulvinar, tends to be slightly larger at the same eccentricity; in comparison, receptive fields are often quite large in Pdm (Bender, 1982; Petersen et al., 1985). Neural responses in these areas can also be influenced by eye movements and eye position (Robinson et al., 1986, 1990), which is likely related to the frontoparietal and SC inputs to the pulvinar and suggests a functional role in the network for the control of eye movements.

In addition to the functional evidence described thus far, a role for the pulvinar as a thalamic integrator and coordinator of attentional function has been suggested on the basis of its unique anatomical connectivity (e.g., Shipp, 2004). First, the visual maps in areas of the pulvinar are organized such that neurons representing corresponding parts of the VF in cortical visual areas project to similar parts of the pulvinar maps (Adams et al., 2000; Shipp, 2001, 2003). Therefore, visual information from different cortical areas could be integrated in pulvinar areas. Indeed, striate and extrastriate areas might use the pulvinar maps for indirect transcortical communication that may complement and extend local corticocortical circuits. Evidence in support of such an idea has been found in single-cell physiology studies (Benevento & Port, 1995; Merabet et al., 1998). Benevento and Port (1995) demonstrated that pulvinar neurons in the macaque integrate both object and spatial properties of visual stimuli that are represented in separate cortical areas. Moreover, Merabet et al. (1998) showed that the lateral-posterior pulvinar complex in the cat contains neurons that respond selectively to the global motion of plaid patterns (two superimposed moving gratings of different orientation) rather than the individual grating components (Merabet et al., 1998). It appears that the anterior ectosylvian visual cortex may be the only cortical region in the cat that has a large number of cells that respond to pattern motion. When the anterior ectosylvian cortex was deactivated, some neurons in the lateral-posterior pulvinar complex still responded selectively to the plaid pattern motion (Merabet et al., 1998). This result suggests that different motion elements may be integrated in the pulvinar itself. Consistent with these physiology studies, fMRI studies have reported that the human pulvinar responds to global motion in plaid (Villeneuve et al., 2005) and random dot patterns (Cotton & Smith, 2007; Smith et al., 2009). Second, areas of the frontoparietal attention network, namely the frontal eye field (FEF) and the lateral intraparietal area (LIP), have reciprocal connections with the dorsal pulvinar and with the SC, which also projects to visual areas of the pulvinar (Harting et al., 1980; Benevento & Standage, 1983). Hence, the cortico-colliculo-pulvinar pathway provides a link between the frontoparietal attention network and the ventral pulvinar, thus providing a route for influencing cortical areas in the ventral visual stream. In addition, the direct frontoparietal cortico-dorsal pulvinar route could play an important role in coordinating attentional control functions (Shipp, 2004), which may be exerted in concert by cortical and subcortical networks. This hypothesis will be further discussed below.

Attentional Modulation in the Monkey Pulvinar

A specific role in selective visual attention has been proposed for Pdm. In this area, neural responses were enhanced when an animal attended to a visual stimulus compared to when the same stimulus was ignored (Petersen et al., 1985). Importantly, the enhancement effects were only seen when the

monkey attended to a stimulus in the RF, but not when it attended to a simultaneously presented stimulus elsewhere in the VF, indicating the spatial selectivity of the attention effects. At the behavioral level, inactivation of Pdm by injecting a GABA agonist led to impairments in directing attention to the contralateral hemifield, whereas injections of a GABA antagonist induced a facilitation of the allocation of attention (Petersen et al., 1987). Attention effects have also been demonstrated for pulvinar subdivisions other than Pdm. In an attentive fixation task, Bender and Youakim (2001) reported that one-quarter of cells in the retinotopic areas of the inferior and lateral pulvinar, as well as in Pdm, were influenced by attention. Responses of these cells were modulated by up to 25% or more and, in some cases, spontaneous activity was also affected. In addition to response magnitude, the timing and variability of responses are also important for neural coding. Petersen et al. (1985) showed modulation of the response variability of pulvinar cells and, during a peripheral attention or saccade task, response variability could be reduced. The implications of this effect of attention on response timing and variability for gain control are discussed further below.

Attentional Modulation in the Human Pulvinar

In fMRI studies, a series of experiments was performed aimed at identifying a homologue for area Pdm in the human pulvinar (Kastner et al., 2004). Flickering checkerboard stimuli were presented simultaneously to both hemifields interleaved with blank periods or unilaterally in alternation to the right or left hemifield. In one set of studies, subjects were instructed by an arrow presented at fixation to covertly direct attention either to the left or right checkerboard and to detect luminance changes that occurred at random times and at 10 degrees eccentricity. In another set of studies, subjects were instructed to maintain fixation and to passively view the stimuli without performing any specific task.

During bilateral attended presentations of the checkerboard stimuli, two regions within the pulvinar were consistently activated across subjects and were found to be located superior and medial to the human LGN. The region in the right pulvinar is depicted for an individual subject in Figure 3.7A. Given the individual variability of the locations of activated regions within the pulvinar, it is not clear whether the regions in the left and right pulvinar represent corresponding visual areas. Importantly, the attention-related activity in dorsomedial regions of the human pulvinar was located in the same region as the lesion site in some neglect patients (Karnath et al., 2002). When subjects directed attention to checkerboard stimuli presented unilaterally in alternation to the right and left hemifield, no activations in the pulvinar were found (Figure 3.7B). Because our statistical analyses contrasted presentations to one hemifield with presentations to the other

hemifield, it is possible that similar regions in the pulvinar were activated in both cases and therefore "subtracted out" in the analysis. This finding may therefore indicate that visually responsive neurons in the activated region of the pulvinar had large RFs extending over the entire VF. To test the possibility that the visually evoked pulvinar activity was driven by selective attention rather than by sensory input, the same experiments were performed while subjects did not direct attention to the checkerboard stimuli, but rather passively viewed the stimuli while maintaining fixation. No activation in the pulvinar was found under these conditions, as illustrated in Figure 3.7C for the bilateral presentations and in Figure 3.7D for the unilateral presentations. Thus, as in areas of the frontoparietal network,

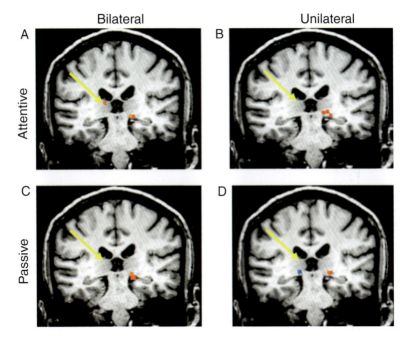

FIGURE 3.7 Functional activation of the pulvinar during directed attention and passive viewing. Results from one subject tested in four different experiments. (**A**) Bilateral attentive: The arrow indicates functional activation of the right pulvinar. The subject directed attention to a checkerboard stimulus presented simultaneously to the right and left visual hemifield. (**B**) Unilateral attentive: No functional activation was found in the pulvinar when the stimuli were presented unilaterally and in alternation to the right and left hemifield while subjects directed attention to the checkerboards. (**C**) Bilateral passive: No functional activation was obtained in the pulvinar when the stimuli were presented bilaterally and passively viewed by the subjects while maintaining fixation. (**D**) Unilateral passive: No functional activation was found in the pulvinar when the stimuli were presented in alternation to the right or left hemifield and passively viewed by the subjects while maintaining fixation. From Kastner et al. (2004).

the pulvinar activity appeared to be driven by the attentional operations themselves rather than by sensory input.

Several of these findings support the idea that the activated regions in the left and right dorsomedial pulvinar may be homologous to area Pdm of the macaque pulvinar. First, the human pulvinar areas were strongly modulated by visuospatial attention, as has been described for Pdm (Petersen et al., 1985). Second, the human pulvinar areas appeared to have a coarse visuotopic organization with large receptive fields (RFs) extending over the entire VF. Neurons with large RFs of greater than 30 degrees extending across the vertical meridian have been found in macaque Pdm, but not in other pulvinar areas (Petersen et al., 1985). And third, it is unlikely that the human pulvinar activations occurred in retinotopically organized pulvinar areas because they were not evoked by alternating hemifield stimuli. It is not clear why retinotopically organized areas of the human pulvinar were not activated in our studies. However, given the small size of the activated volumes within the pulvinar, this may reflect a lack of sensitivity and spatial resolution of the fMRI methods used in these studies.

Attentional effects have also been found in areas of the human pulvinar that show a contralateral response bias and may be topographically organized. These areas are different from the Pdm-like region found by Kastner et al. (2004) in that they appear to have smaller RFs. In these regions, the attentional response enhancement was found to be on the order of 20% (Smith et al., 2009). Other neuroimaging studies have demonstrated pulvinar activations in selective attention tasks that emphasized the filtering of unwanted information (LaBerge & Buchsbaum, 1990; Buchsbaum et al., 2006) and shifts of attention across the VF (Yantis et al., 2002). Taken together, these findings support the notion of a functional role of the pulvinar in visuospatial attention in accordance with findings from physiology studies in nonhuman primates.

Effects of Pulvinar Lesions

The arguably most compelling evidence for an important role of the pulvinar in controlling the selection of behaviorally relevant information comes from studies in patients with circumscribed brain lesions. Thalamic lesions that include the pulvinar may lead to profound attentional deficits such as visuospatial hemineglect (Karnath et al., 2002). *Neglect* is a syndrome associated with a failure to direct attention to contralesional space. In the most severe cases, the patients behave as if the contralesional visual space did not exist, such as eating from only one half of their plate or applying make-up to only one half of their face. Neglect is not only associated with thalamic lesions, but rather typically occurs after lesions of inferior parietal cortex, the superior temporal gyrus, or frontal cortex, most frequently with right- rather than left-hemispheric lesions. Even though thalamic neglect is rare and severe attentional deficits that occur as a consequence of pulvinar lesions typically do not persist, a milder deficit that may be a residual form of thalamic neglect is the slowing of orienting responses to contralesional space. If a patient with a unilateral pulvinar lesion is asked to detect a target stimulus in contralesional space (i.e., the left hemifield with a right pulvinar lesion), the patient's response in detecting the stimulus will be slower than the response to the same target stimulus in ipsilesional space (Rafal & Posner, 1987; Danziger et al., 2001/2002).

More generally, patients with pulvinar lesions appear to have deficits in coding spatial information in the contralesional VF. For example, they have difficulty localizing stimuli in the affected visual space (Ward et al., 2002). These difficulties extend to the binding of visual features based on spatial information, which is one of the most fundamental operations that the visual system has to perform to integrate visual information across various feature dimensions. For example, these patients will have difficulties binding the appropriate color to each of multiple shapes that are presented simultaneously. A red square and a blue circle may be mistaken to be a blue square or red circle. Such errors in binding information from different feature dimensions that require accurate spatial coding had been classically associated with lesions of posterior parietal cortex (PPC) (Friedman-Hill et al., 1995), but appear to be also typical for patients with pulvinar lesions (Ward et al., 2002; Arend et al., 2008). Interestingly, and in an additional analogy to PPC function, the spatial coding deficits can be observed in a retinotopic as well as an object-based spatial reference frame, thereby underlining the close functional relationship of the pulvinar and PPC (Ward & Arend, 2007).

Finally, in agreement with findings from human neuroimaging and monkey physiology that have emphasized a role for the pulvinar in filtering unwanted information (LaBerge & Buchsbaum, 1990; Desimone et al., 1990), patients with pulvinar lesions show deficits in filtering distracter information. The patients show similar performance in a target discrimination task (e.g., discriminating an orientation of a grating stimulus) as compared to healthy subjects when the target is shown alone, or in the absence of distracters. However, once distracters of high salience are present to compete with the target for attentional resources, the discrimination performance of the patients is impaired, suggesting a difficulty in filtering out the unwanted information present in the visual display (Snow et al., 2009; see also Danziger et al., 2004). Similar filtering deficits have been observed after PPC lesions in humans (Friedman-Hill et al., 2003) and after extrastriate cortex lesions that include area V4 in humans (Gallant et al., 2000) and monkeys (De Weerd et al., 1999) suggesting that any lesion to the distributed network of brain areas that subserves visuospatial attention may lead to such deficit.

Taken together, studies in patients with pulvinar lesions point to a number of fundamental attention functions that the pulvinar is critically involved with, including orienting responses and the exploration of visual space, spatial coding of visual information necessary for feature binding, and the filtering of unwanted information.

Mechanisms of Regulating Cortical Responses by the Pulvinar

The pulvinar is widely interconnected with the cerebral cortex. A putative feedforward cortico-pulvino-cortical pathway projects from cortical layer 5 to the pulvinar, which in turn projects to cortical layer 4 (Sherman & Guillery, 2001). There is also a putative feedback pathway projecting from cortical layer 6 to the pulvinar, which then projects to superficial cortical layers (Sherman

& Guillery, 2001). Generally, two directly connected cortical areas will be indirectly connected via the pulvinar as well (Shipp, 2003). This means the pulvinar is well positioned to regulate corticocortical transmission. The pulvinar receives information about behavioral requirements from a number of areas that are associated with the attention network in the brain, including the frontoparietal cortex, superior colliculus, and TRN (Shipp, 2003). This information can be used by the pulvinar to regulate corticocortical transmission accordingly.

There are at least two ways that the pulvinar can regulate corticocortical transmission (Saalmann & Kastner, 2009). First, stimulus information can be sent to the pulvinar, which filters this information and only sends potentially important information back to the cortex for further processing. Second, the pulvinar can adjust the degree of synchrony between two or more cortical areas. That is, the pulvinar either sets up the rhythms in each cortical area, or manipulates the phase and amplitude of ongoing rhythms, in order to change the efficacy of cortical information transfer. The available evidence appears to be consistent with both ways. The activity of pulvinar neurons can either be enhanced or suppressed depending on the behavioral context (Petersen et al., 1985; Bender & Youakim, 2001), consistent with the idea that the pulvinar filters out irrelevant information at the level of the thalamus. In addition, Wróbel et al. (2007) have reported that activity in the cat pulvinar and cortex synchronizes during visual attention. Moreover, pulvinar lesions modulate cortical oscillations in anesthetized cats (Molotchnikoff & Shumikhina 1996; Shumikhina & Molotchnikoff, 1999), suggesting that the pulvinar may also adjust oscillatory processes in the cortex in the awake, behaving state as necessary. Clearly, further systems level work is required to clarify the role of the pulvinar in corticocortical transmission.

SUMMARY

Based on its anatomical connectivity, the pulvinar of the thalamus appears to be in a unique position to operate both as an integrator of visual information by virtue of the registered visual topographic maps of cortico-pulvino-cortical circuits and as a coordinator of attentional function by virtue of its link to the frontoparietal attention network directly or via a cortico-colliculo-pulvinar pathway. Studies aimed at elucidating particularly the functional connectivity of Pdm and cortical areas and probing more complex function using simultaneous recordings from multiple sites of the cortical and subcortical attention network in behaving monkeys will be needed to provide the experimental evidence in support of these ideas.

CONCLUSION

There is growing evidence for attentional modulation of visual thalamic responses from fMRI and electrophysiology studies. This modulation has a number of potential sources, including the frontoparietal attention network, which provides feedback via cortical and subcortical (i.e., via the TRN) pathways. The feedback may serve to alter the magnitude or timing of thalamic responses, which in turn influence cortical responsiveness. By this means, the LGN and pulvinar can respectively regulate the transmission of information along retinocortical and corticocortical pathways, according to attentional requirements. However, several key issues need to be explored to clarify the role of the visual thalamus in attentional processes. Possible future experimental directions include characterizing the temporal structure of thalamic activity during perceptual and cognitive tasks to shed light on how neuronal synchrony, oscillations, and spike timing influence gain control in thalamocortical circuits; distinguishing the contributions of magnocellular, parvocellular, and koniocellular neurons in the LGN during attentional allocations, for which no published data currently exists on koniocellular neurons; and resolving the functional attributes of pulvinar subdivisions and the different roles played by the retinotopic maps in the pulvinar. Although further work is necessary, current evidence suggests that attentional selection starts as early as the thalamus.

ACKNOWLEDGMENTS

We thank Ryan Smith and Tyler Clark for help with text editing. Some of the research reviewed in this chapter has been supported by grants of the National Science Foundation (BCS-0633281) and the National Institutes of Health (RO1 MH64043, RO1 EY017699, R21 EY021078).

References

Adams, M. M., Hof, P. R., Gattass, R., Webster, M. J., & Ungerleider, L. G. (2000). Visual cortical projections and chemoarchitecture of macaque monkey pulvinar. *Journal of Comparative Neurology, 419,* 377–393.

Alonso, J. M., Usrey, W. M., & Reid, R. C. (1996). Precisely correlated firing in cells of the lateral geniculate nucleus. *Nature, 383,* 815–819.

Arcaro, M. A., McMains, S. A., Singer, B., & Kastner, S. (2009). Retinotopic organization of the human ventral visual cortex. *Journal of Neuroscience.* In press.

Arend, I., Rafal, R., & Ward, R. (2008). Spatial and temporal deficits are regionally dissociable in patients with pulvinar lesions. *Brain, 131,* 2140–2152.

Bal, T., Debay, D., & Destexhe, A. (2000). Cortical feedback controls the frequency and synchrony of oscillations in the visual thalamus. *Journal of Neuroscience, 20,* 7478–7488.

Bekisz, M., & Wróbel, A. (1993). 20 Hz rhythm of activity in visual system of perceiving cat. *Acta Neurobiologiae Experimentalis, 53,* 175–182.

Bender, D. B. (1981). Retinotopic organization of macaque pulvinar. *Journal of Neurophysiology, 46,* 672–693.

Bender, D. B. (1982). Receptive-field properties of neurons in the macaque inferior pulvinar. *Journal of Neurophysiology, 48,* 1–17.

Bender, D. B., & Youakim, M. (2001). Effect of attentive fixation in macaque thalamus and cortex. *Journal of Neurophysiology, 85,* 219–234.

Benevento, L. A., & Port, J. D. (1995). Single neurons with both form/color differential responses and saccade-related responses in the nonretinotopic pulvinar of the behaving macaque monkey. *Visual Neuroscience, 12,* 523–544.

Benevento, L. A., & Standage, G. P. (1983). The organization of projections of the retinorecipient and nonretinorecipient nuclei of the pretectal complex and layers of the superior colliculus to the lateral pulvinar and medial pulvinar in the macaque monkey. *Journal of Comparative Neurology, 217,* 307–336.

Blumenfeld, H., & McCormick, D. A. (2000). Corticothalamic inputs control the pattern of activity generated in thalamocortical networks. *Journal of Neuroscience, 20,* 5153–62.

Boynton, G. M. (2009). A framework for describing the effects of attention on visual responses. *Vision Research, 49,* 119–143.

Brefczynski, J. A., & DeYoe, E. A. (1999). A physiological correlate of the "spotlight" of visual attention. *Nature Neuroscience, 2,* 370–374.

Briggs, F., & Usrey, W. M. (2009). Parallel processing in the corticogeniculate pathway of the macaque monkey. *Neuron, 62,* 135–146.

Buchsbaum, M. S., Buchsbaum, B. R., Chokron, S., Tang, C., Wei, T. C., & Byne, W. (2006). Thalamocortical circuits: FMRI assessment of the pulvinar and medial dorsal nucleus in normal volunteers. *Neuroscience Letters, 404,* 282–287.

Buschman, T. J., & Miller, E. K. (2007). Top-down versus bottom-up control of attention in the prefrontal and posterior parietal cortices. *Science, 315,* 1860–1862.

Cameron, E. L., Tai, J. C., & Carrasco, M. (2002). Covert attention affects the psychometric function of contrast sensitivity. *Vision Research, 42,* 949–967.

Carrasco, M., Ling, S., & Read, S. (2004). Attention alters appearance. *Nature Neuroscience, 7,* 308–313.

Casagrande, V. A. (1994). A Third parallel visual pathway to primate area V1. *Trends in Neurosciences, 17,* 305–310.

Casagrande, V. A., Sáry, G., Royal, D., & Ruiz, O. (2005). On the impact of attention and motor planning on the lateral geniculate nucleus. *Progress in Brain Research, 149,* 11–29.

Castelo-Branco, M., Neuenschwander, S., & Singer, W. (1998). Synchronization of visual responses between the cortex, lateral geniculate nucleus, and retina in the anesthetized cat. *Journal of Neuroscience, 18,* 6395–6410.

Chelazzi, L., Duncan, J., Miller, E. K., & Desimone, R. (1998). Responses of neurons in inferior temporal cortex during memory-guided visual search. *Journal of Neurophysiology, 80,* 2918–2940.

Chen, W., Zhu, X. H., Thulborn, K. R., & Ugurbil, K. (1999). Retinotopic mapping of lateral geniculate nucleus in humans using functional magnetic resonance imaging. *Proceedings of the National Academy of Sciences of the United States of America, 96,* 2430–2434.

Cheng, A., Eysel, U. T., & Vidyasagar, T. R. (2004). The role of the magnocellular pathway in serial deployment of visual attention. *European Journal of Neuroscience, 20,* 2188–2192.

Connolly, M., & Van Essen, D. (1984). The representation of the visual field in parvicellular and magnocellular layers of the lateral geniculate nucleus in the macaque monkey. *Journal of Comparative Neurology, 226,* 544–564.

Cook, E. P., & Maunsell, J. H. (2002). Attentional modulation of behavioral performance and neuronal responses in middle temporal and ventral intraparietal areas of macaque monkey. *Journal of Neuroscience, 22,* 1994–2004.

Corbetta, M., Miezin, F. M., Dobmeyer, S., Shulman, G. L., & Petersen, S. E. (1990). Attentional modulation of neural processing of shape, color, and velocity in humans. *Science, 248,* 1556–1559.

Corbetta, M., & Shulman, G. L. (2002). Control of goal-directed and stimulus-driven attention in the brain. *Nature Reviews. Neuroscience, 3,* 201–15.

Cotton, P. L., & Smith, A. T. (2007). Contralateral visual hemifield representations in the human pulvinar nucleus. *Journal of Neurophysiology, 98,* 1600–1609.

Creutzfeldt, O. D., Lee, B. B., & Elepfandt, A. (1979). A quantitative study of chromatic organisation and receptive fields of cells in the lateral geniculate body of the rhesus monkey. *Experimental Brain Research, 35,* 527–545.

Crick, F. (1984). Function of the thalamic reticular complex, the searchlight hypothesis. *Proceedings of the National Academy of Sciences of the United States of America, 81,* 4586–4590.

Danziger, S., Ward, R., Owen, V., & Rafal, R. (2001–2002). The effects of unilateral pulvinar damage in humans on reflexive orienting and filtering of irrelevant information. *Behavioural Neurology, 13,* 95–104.

Danziger, S., Ward, R., Owen, V., & Rafal, R. (2004). Contributions of the human pulvinar to linking vision and action. *Cognitive, Affective, and Behavioral Neuroscience, 4,* 89–99.

Derrington, A. M., & Lennie, P. (1984). Spatial and temporal contrast sensitivities of neurones in lateral geniculate nucleus of macaque. *Journal of Physiology, 357,* 219–240.

Deschênes, M., & Hu, B. (1990). Membrane resistance increase induced in thalamic neurons by stimulation of brainstem cholinergic afferents. *Brain Research, 513,* 339–342.

Desimone, R., Wessinger, M., Thomas, L., & Schneider, W. (1990). Attentional control of visual perception: cortical and subcortical mechanisms. *Cold Spring Harbor Symposia on Quantitative Biology, 55,* 963–971.

De Weerd, P., Peralta, M. R., 3rd, Desimone, R., & Ungerleider, L. G. (1999). Loss of attentional stimulus selection after extrastriate cortical lesions in macaques. *Nature Neuroscience, 1999 Aug; 2(8),* 753–758.

Dreher, B., Fukada, Y., & Rodieck, R. W. (1976). Identification, classification and anatomical segregation of cells with X-like and Y-like properties in the lateral geniculate nucleus of old-world primates. *Journal of Physiology, 258,* 433–452.

Erişir, A., Van Horn, S. C., Bickford, M. E., & Sherman, S. M. (1997). Immunocytochemistry and distribution of parabrachial terminals in the lateral geniculate nucleus of the cat: A comparison with corticogeniculate terminals. *Journal of Comparative Neurology, 377,* 535–549.

Felsten, G., Benevento, L. A., & Burman, D. (1983). Opponent-color responses in macaque extrageniculate visual pathways: The lateral pulvinar. *Brain Research, 288,* 363–367.

Friedman-Hill, S. R., Robertson, L. C., Desimone, R., & Ungerleider, L. G. (2003). Posterior parietal cortex and the filtering of distractors. *Proceedings of the National Academy of Sciences of the United States of America, 100,* 4263–4268.

Friedman-Hill, S. R., Robertson, L. C., & Treisman, A. (1995). Parietal contributions to visual feature binding: Evidence from a patient with bilateral lesions. *Science, 269,* 853–855.

Fries, P., Reynolds, J. H., Rorie, A. E., & Desimone, R. (2001). Modulation of oscillatory neuronal synchronization by selective visual attention. *Science, 291,* 1560–1563.

Funke, K., & Eysel, U. T. (1998). Inverse correlation of firing patterns of single topographically matched perigeniculate neurons and cat dorsal lateral geniculate relay cells. *Visual Neuroscience, 15,* 711–729.

Gallant, J. L., Shoup, R. E., & Mazer, J. A. (2000). A human extrastriate area functionally homologous to macaque V4. *Neuron, 27,* 227–235.

Gandhi, S. P., Heeger, D. J., & Boynton, G. M. (1999). Spatial attention affects brain activity in human primary visual cortex. *Proceedings of the National Academy of Sciences of the United States of America, 96,* 3314–3319.

Gregoriou, G. G., Gotts, S. J., Zhou, H., & Desimone, R. (2009). High-frequency, long-range coupling between prefrontal and visual cortex during attention. *Science, 324,* 1207–1210.

Guillery, R. W. (1995). Anatomical evidence concerning the role of the thalamus in corticocortical communication: A brief review. *Journal of Anatomy, 187,* 583–592.

Guillery, R. W., & Harting, J. K. (2003). Structure and connections of the thalamic reticular nucleus: Advancing views over half a century. *Journal of Comparative Neurology, 463,* 360–371.

Guillery, R. W., Feig, S. L., & Lozsádi, D. A. (1998). Paying attention to the thalamic reticular nucleus. *Trends in Neurosciences, 21,* 28–32.

Gutierrez, C., Cola, M. G., Seltzer, B., & Cusick, C. (2000). Neurochemical and connectional organization of the dorsal pulvinar complex in monkeys. *Journal of Comparative Neurology, 419,* 61–86.

Gutierrez, C., Yaun, A., & Cusick, C. G. (1995). Neurochemical subdivisions of the inferior pulvinar in macaque monkeys. *Journal of Comparative Neurology, 363,* 545–562.

Harting, J. K., Huerta, M. F., Frankfurter, A. J., Strominger, N. L., & Royce, G. J. (1980). Ascending pathways from the monkey superior colliculus: An autoradiographic analysis. *Journal of Comparative Neurology, 192,* 853–882.

Harting, J. K., Huerta, M. F., Hashikawa, T., & van Lieshout, D. P. (1991). Projection of the mammalian superior colliculus upon the dorsal lateral geniculate nucleus: Organization of tectogeniculate pathways in nineteen species. *Journal of Comparative Neurology, 304,* 275–306.

Hendry, S. H., & Reid, R. C. (2000). The koniocellular pathway in primate vision. *Annual Review of Neuroscience, 23,* 127–153.

Hickey, T. L., & Guillery, R. W. (1979). Variability of laminar patterns in the human lateral geniculate nucleus. *Journal of Comparative Neurology, 183,* 221–246.

Huguenard, J. R., & McCormick, D. A. (2007). Thalamic synchrony and dynamic regulation of global forebrain oscillations. *Trends in Neurosciences, 30,* 350–356.

Ito, M., & Gilbert, C. D. (1999). Attention modulates contextual influences in the primary visual cortex of alert monkeys. *Neuron, 22,* 593–604.

Jones, E. G. (2007). *The Thalamus.* Cambridge, UK: Cambridge University Press.

Juba, A., & Szatmári, A. (1937). Ueber seltene hirnanatomische befunde in fällen von einseitiger peripherer blindheit. *Klinische Monatsblätter für Augenheilkunde, 99,* 173–188.

Kaas, J. H., Guillery, R. W., & Allman, J. M. (1972). Some principles of organization in the dorsal lateral geniculate nucleus. *Brain, Behavior and Evolution, 6,* 253–299.

Kaas, J. H., & Lyon, D. C. (2007). Pulvinar contributions to the dorsal and ventral streams of visual processing in primates. *Brain Research, Rev 55,* 285–296.

Karnath, H. O., Himmelbach, M., & Rorden, C. (2002). The subcortical anatomy of human spatial neglect: Putamen, caudate nucleus and pulvinar. *Brain, 125,* 350–360.

Kastner, S., DeWeerd, P., Desimone, R., & Ungerleider, L. G. (1998). Mechanisms of directed attention in the human extrastriate cortex as revealed by functional MRI. *Science, 282,* 108–111.

Kastner, S., De Weerd, P., Pinsk, M. A., Elizondo, M. I., Desimone, R., & Ungerleider, L. G. (2001). Modulation of sensory suppression: Implications for receptive field sizes in the human visual cortex. *Journal of Neurophysiology, 86,* 1398–1411.

Kastner, S., O'Connor, D. H., Fukui, M. M., Fehd, H. M., Herwig, U., & Pinsk, M. A. (2004). Functional imaging of the human lateral geniculate nucleus and pulvinar. *Journal of Neurophysiology, 91,* 438–448.

Kastner, S., & Pinsk, M. A. (2004). Visual attention as a multilevel selection process. *Cognitive, Affective, and Behavioral Neuroscience, 4,* 483–500.

Kastner, S., Pinsk, M. A., De Weerd, P., Desimone, R., & Ungerleider, L. G. (1999). Increased activity in human visual cortex during directed attention in the absence of visual stimulation. *Neuron, 22,* 751–761.

Kupfer, C. (1962). The projection of the macula in the lateral geniculate nucleus of man. *American Journal of Ophthalmology, 54,* 597–609.

LaBerge, D., & Buchsbaum, M. S. (1990). Positron emission tomographic measurements of pulvinar activity during an attention task. *Journal of Neuroscience, 10,* 613–619.

Lakatos, P., Karmos, G., Mehta, A. D., Ulbert, I., & Schroeder, C. E. (2008). Entrainment of neuronal oscillations as a mechanism of attentional selection. *Science, 320,* 110–113.

Le Gros Clark, W. (1932). The structure and connections of the thalamus. *Brain, 55,* 406–470.

Lehky, S. R., & Maunsell, J. H. (1996). No binocular rivalry in the LGN of alert macaque monkeys. *Vision Research, 36,* 1225–1234.

Lee, J., & Maunsell, J. H. (2009). A normalization model of attentional modulation of single unit responses. *PLoS One, 4,* e4651. Available at: http://www.plosone.org/article/info%3Adoi%2F10.1371%2Fjournal.pone.0004651

Leopold, D. A., Murayama, Y., & Logothetis, N. K. (2003). Very slow activity fluctuations in monkey visual cortex: Implications for functional brain imaging. *Cerebral Cortex, 13,* 422–433.

Lindström, S., & Wróbel, A. (1990). Frequency dependent corticofugal excitation of principal cells in the cat's dorsal lateral geniculate nucleus. *Experimental Brain Research, 79,* 313–318.

Logothetis, N. K., & Wandell, B. A. (2004). Interpreting the BOLD signal. *Annual Review of Physiology, 66,* 735–769.

Luck, S. J., Chelazzi, L., Hillyard, S. A., & Desimone, R. (1997). Neural mechanisms of spatial selective attention in areas V1, V2, and V4 of macaque visual cortex. *Journal of Neurophysiology, 77,* 24–42.

Malpeli, J. G., & Baker, F. H. (1975). The representation of the visual field in the lateral

geniculate nucleus of Macaca mulatta. *Journal of Comparative Neurology, 161,* 569–594.

Martin, P. R., White, A. J., Goodchild, A. K., Wilder, H. D., & Sefton, A. E. (1997). Evidence that blue-on cells are part of the third geniculocortical pathway in primates. *European Journal of Neuroscience, 9,* 1536–1541.

Martínez, A., Anllo-Vento, L., Sereno, M. I., Frank, L. R., Buxton, R. B., Dubowitz, D. J., et al. (1999). Involvement of striate and extrastriate visual cortical areas in spatial attention. *Nature Neuroscience, 2,* 364–369.

Maunsell, J. H., & van Essen, D. C. (1983). The connections of the middle temporal visual area (MT) and their relationship to a cortical hierarchy in the macaque monkey. *Journal of Neuroscience, 3,* 2563–2586.

McAdams, C. J., & Maunsell, J. H. (1999). Effects of attention on orientation-tuning functions of single neurons in macaque cortical area V4. *Journal of Neuroscience, 19,* 431–41.

McAlonan, K., Cavanaugh, J., & Wurtz, R. H. (2006). Attentional modulation of thalamic reticular neurons. *Journal of Neuroscience, 26,* 4444–4450.

McAlonan, K., Cavanaugh, J., & Wurtz, R. H. (2008). Guarding the gateway to cortex with attention in visual thalamus. *Nature, 456,* 391–394.

Mehta, A. D., Ulbert, I., & Schroeder, C. E. (2000). Intermodal selective attention in monkeys. *I: distribution and timing of effects across visual areas. Cerebral Cortex, 10,* 343–358.

Merabet, L., Desautels, A., Minville, K., & Casanova, C. (1998). Motion integration in a thalamic visual nucleus. *Nature, 396,* 265–268.

Merigan, W. H., & Maunsell, J. H. (1993). How parallel are the primate visual pathways? *Annual Review of Neuroscience, 16,* 369–402.

Mesulam, M. M. (1999). Spatial attention and neglect, parietal, frontal and cingulate contributions to the mental representation and attentional targeting of salient extrapersonal events. *Philosophical Transactions of the Royal Society of London. Series B, Biological Sciences, 354,* 1325–1346.

Molotchnikoff, S., & Shumikhina, S. (1996). The lateral posterior-pulvinar complex modulation of stimulus-dependent oscillations in the cat visual cortex. *Vision Research, 36,* 2037–2046.

Moore, T., & Armstrong, K. M. (2003). Selective gating of visual signals by microstimulation of frontal cortex. *Nature, 421,* 370–373.

Moran, J., & Desimone, R. (1985). Selective attention gates visual processing in the extrastriate cortex. *Science, 229,* 782–784.

Motter, B. C. (1993). Focal attention produces spatially selective processing in visual cortical areas

V1, V2, and V4 in the presence of competing stimuli. *Journal of Neurophysiology, 70,* 909–919.

Murray, S. O., & Woijciulik, E. (2004). Attention increases neural selectivity in the human lateral occipital complex. *Nature Neuroscience, 7,* 70–74.

Niessing, J., Ebisch, B., Schmidt, K. E., Niessing, M., Singer, W., & Galuske, R. A. (2005). Hemodynamic signals correlate tightly with synchronized gamma oscillations. *Science, 309,* 948–951.

O'Connor, D. H., Fukui, M. M., Pinsk, M. A., & Kastner, S. (2002). Attention modulates responses in the human lateral geniculate nucleus. *Nature Neuroscience, 5,* 1203–1209.

Pesaran, B., Pezaris, J. S., Sahani, M., Mitra, P. P., & Andersen, R. A. (2002). Temporal structure in neuronal activity during working memory in macaque parietal cortex. *Nature Neuroscience, 5,* 805–811.

Petersen, S. E., Robinson, D. L., & Keys, W. (1985). Pulvinar nuclei of the behaving rhesus monkey, visual responses and their modulation. *Journal of Neurophysiology, 54,* 867–886.

Petersen, S. E., Robinson, D. L., & Morris, J. D. (1987). Contributions of the pulvinar to visual spatial attention. *Neuropsychologia, 25,* 97–105.

Polyak, S. (1953). Santiago Ramón y Cajal and his investigation of the nervous system. *Journal of Comparative Neurology, 98,* 3–8.

Rafal, R. D., & Posner, M. I. (1987). Deficits in human visual spatial attention following thalamic lesions. *Proceedings of the National Academy of Sciences of the United States of America, 84,* 7349–7353.

Rasch, M. J., Gretton, A., Murayama, Y., Maass, W., & Logothetis, N. K. (2008). Inferring spike trains from local field potentials. *Journal of Neurophysiology, 99,* 1461–1476.

Rees, G., Frackowiak, R., & Frith, C. (1997). Two modulatory effects of attention that mediate object categorization in human cortex. *Science, 275,* 835–838.

Reynolds, J. H., & Heeger, D. J. (2009). The normalization model of attention. *Neuron, 61,* 168–185.

Reynolds, J. H., Pasternak, T., & Desimone, R. (2000). Attention increases sensitivity of V4 neurons. *Neuron, 26,* 703–714.

Robinson, D. L., McClurkin, J. W., & Kertzman, C. (1990). Orbital position and eye movement influences on visual responses in the pulvinar nuclei of the behaving macaque. *Experimental Brain Research, 82,* 235–246.

Robinson, D. L., & Petersen, S. E. (1992). The pulvinar and visual salience. *Trends in Neurosciences, 15,* 127–132.

Robinson, D. L., Petersen, S. E., & Keys, W. (1986). Saccade-related and visual activities in the pulvinar nuclei of the behaving rhesus monkey. *Experimental Brain Research, 62,* 625–634.

Roelfsema, P. R., Lamme, V. A., & Spekreijse, H. (1998). Object-based attention in the primary visual cortex of the macaque monkey. *Nature, 395,* 376–381.

Rönne, H. (1910). Pathologisch-anatomische untersuchungen über alkoholische intoxikationsamblyopie. *Archives of Ophthalmology, 77,* 1–95.

Roy, S., Jayakumar, J., Martin, P. R., Dreher, B., Saalmann, Y. B., Hu, D., & Vidyasagar, T. R. (2009). Segregation of short-wavelength sensitive (S) cone signals in the macaque dorsal lateral geniculate nucleus. *European Journal of Neuroscience, 30,* 1517-1526.

Saalmann, Y. B., & Kastner, S. (2009). Gain control in the visual thalamus during perception and cognition. *Current Opinion in Neurobiology, 19*(4), 408–414.

Saalmann, Y. B., Pigarev, I. N., & Vidyasagar, T. R. (2007). Neural mechanisms of visual attention: How top-down feedback highlights relevant locations. *Science, 316,* 1612–1615.

Schneider, K. A., & Kastner, S. (2005). Visual responses of the human superior colliculus: A high-resolution fMRI study. *Journal of Neurophysiology, 94,* 2491–2503.

Schneider, K. A., & Kastner, S. (2009). Effects of sustained spatial attention in the human lateral geniculate nucleus and superior colliculus. *Journal of Neuroscience, 29,* 1784–1795.

Schneider, K. A., Richter, M. C., & Kastner, S. (2004). Retinotopic organization and functional subdivisions of the human lateral geniculate nucleus: A high-resolution functional magnetic resonance imaging study. *Journal of Neuroscience, 24,* 8975–8985.

Sclar, G., Maunsell, J. H., & Lennie, P. (1990). Coding of image contrast in central visual pathways of the macaque monkey. *Vision Research, 30,* 1–10.

Sejnowski, T. J., & Paulsen, O. (2006). Network oscillations: Emerging computational principles. *Journal of Neuroscience, 26,* 1673–1676.

Sereno, M. I., Dale, A. M., Reppas, J. B., Kwong, K. K., Belliveau, J. W., Brady, T. J., et al. (1995). Borders of multiple visual areas in humans revealed by functional magnetic resonance imaging. *Science, 268,* 889–893.

Shapley, R., Kaplan, E., & Soodak, R. (1981). Spatial summation and contrast sensitivity of X and Y cells in the lateral geniculate nucleus of the macaque. *Nature, 292,* 543–545.

Sherman, S. M., & Guillery, R. W. (2001). *Exploring the thalamus*. Cambridge, MA: MIT Press.

Sherman, S. M., & Guillery, R. W. (2002). The role of the thalamus in the flow of information to the cortex. *Philosophical Transactions of the Royal Society of London. Series B, Biological Sciences, 357*, 1695–1708.

Sherman, S. M., & Koch, C. (1986). The control of retinogeniculate transmission in the mammalian lateral geniculate nucleus. *Experimental Brain Research, 63*, 1–20.

Shipp, S. (2001). Corticopulvinar connections of areas V5, V4, and V3 in the macaque monkey: A dual model of retinal and cortical topographies. *Journal of Comparative Neurology, 439*, 469–490.

Shipp, S. (2003). The functional logic of cortico-pulvinar connections. *Philosophical Transactions of the Royal Society of London. Series B, Biological Sciences, 358*, 1605–1624.

Shipp, S. (2004). The brain circuitry of attention. *Trends in Cognitive Sciences, 8*, 223–230.

Shumikhina, S., & Molotchnikoff, S. (1999). Pulvinar participates in synchronizing neural assemblies in the visual cortex, in cats. *Neuroscience Letters, 272*, 135–139.

Singer, W. (1977). Control of thalamic transmission by corticofugal and ascending reticular pathways in the visual system. *Physiological Reviews, 57*, 386–420.

Singer, W., & Gray, C. M. (1995). Visual feature integration and the temporal correlation hypothesis. *Annual Review of Neuroscience, 18*, 555–586.

Smith, A. T., Cotton, P. L., Bruno, A., & Moutsiana, C. (2009). Dissociating vision and visual attention in the human pulvinar. *Journal of Neurophysiology, 101*, 917–925.

Snow, J. C., Allen, H. A., Rafal, R. D., & Humphreys, G. W. (2009). Impaired attentional selection following lesions to human pulvinar: Evidence for homology between human and monkey. *Proceedings of the National Academy of Sciences of the United States of America, 106*, 4054–4059.

Somers, D. C., Dale, A. M., Seiffert, A. E., & Tootell, R. B. (1999). Functional MRI reveals spatially specific attentional modulation in human primary visual cortex. *Proceedings of the National Academy of Sciences of the United States of America, 96*, 1663–1668.

Standage, G. P., & Benevento, L. A. (1983). The organization of connections between the pulvinar and visual area MT in the macaque monkey. *Brain Research, 262*, 288–294.

Steinman, B. A., Steinman, S. B., & Lehmkuhle, S. (1997). Transient visual attention is dominated by the magnocellular stream. *Vision Research, 37*, 17–23.

Stepniewska, I. (2003). The pulvinar complex. In J. C. Kaas, & C. E. Collins (Eds.), The primate visual system, (pp. 53–80). Boca Raton, FL: CRC Press.

Stepniewska, I., & Kaas, J. H. (1997). Architectonic subdivisions of the inferior pulvinar in New World and Old World monkeys. *Visual Neuroscience, 14*, 1043–1060.

Steriade, M., Contreras, D., Amzica, F., & Timofeev, I. (1996). Synchronization of fast (30–40 Hz) spontaneous oscillations in intrathalamic and thalamocortical networks. *Journal of Neuroscience, 16*, 2788–2808.

Tootell, R. B., Hadjikhani, N., Hall, E. K., Marrett, S., Vanduffel, W., Vaughan, J. T., & Dale, A. M. (1998). The retinotopy of visual spatial attention. *Neuron, 21*, 1409–1422.

Ungerleider, L. G., Desimone, R., Galkin, T. W., & Mishkin, M. (1984). Subcortical projections of area MT in the macaque. *Journal of Comparative Neurology, 223*, 368–386.

Ungerleider, L. G., Galkin, T. W., & Mishkin, M. (1983). Visuotopic organization of projections from striate cortex to inferior and lateral pulvinar in rhesus monkey. *Journal of Comparative Neurology, 217*, 137–157.

Vanduffel, W., Tootell, R. B., & Orban, G. A. (2000). Attention-dependent suppression of metabolic activity in the early stages of the macaque visual system. *Cerebral Cortex, 10*, 109–126.

Villeneuve, M. Y., Kupers, R., Gjedde, A., Ptito, M., & Casanova, C. (2005). Pattern-motion selectivity in the human pulvinar. *NeuroImage, 28*, 474–480.

Viswanathan, A., & Freeman, R. D. (2007). Neurometabolic coupling in cerebral cortex reflects synaptic more than spiking activity. *Nature Neuroscience, 10*, 1308–1312.

Ward, R., & Arend, I. (2007). An object-based frame of reference within the human pulvinar. *Brain, 130*, 2462–2469.

Ward, R., Danziger, S., Owen, V., & Rafal, R. (2002). Deficits in spatial coding and feature binding following damage to spatiotopic maps in the human pulvinar. *Nature Neuroscience, 5*, 99–100.

Watanabe, T., Harner, A. M., Miyauchi, S., Sasaki, Y., Nielsen, M., Palomo, D., & Mukai, I. (1998). Task-dependent influences of attention on the activation of human primary visual cortex. *Proceedings of the National Academy of Sciences of the United States of America, 95*, 11489–11492.

Wiesel, T. N., & Hubel, D. H. (1966). Spatial and chromatic interactions in the lateral geniculate body of the rhesus monkey. *Journal of Neurophysiology, 29*, 1115–1156.

Womelsdorf, T., Schoffelen, J. M., Oostenveld, R., Singer, W., Desimone, R., Engel, A. K., & Fries, P. (2007). Modulation of neuronal interactions through neuronal synchronization. *Science, 316,* 1609–1612.

Wróbel, A., Bekisz, M., Kublik, E., & Waleszczyk, W. (1994). 20 Hz bursting beta activity in the cortico-thalamic system of visually attending cats. *Acta Neurobiologiae Experimentalis, 54,* 95–107.

Wróbel, A., Ghazaryan, A., Bekisz, M., Bogdan, W., & Kamiński, J. (2007). Two streams of attention-dependent beta activity in the striate recipient zone of cat's lateral posterior-pulvinar complex. *Journal of Neuroscience, 27,* 2230–2240.

Xu, X., Ichida, J. M., Allison, J. D., Boyd, J. D., Bonds, A. B., & Casagrande, V. A. (2001). A comparison of koniocellular, magnocellular and parvocellular receptive field properties in the lateral geniculate nucleus of the owl monkey (*Aotus trivirgatus*). *Journal of Physiology, 531,* 203–218.

Yantis, S., Schwarzbach, J., Serences, J. T., Carlson, R. L., Steinmetz, M. A., Pekar, J. J., & Courtney, S. M. (2002). Transient neural activity in human parietal cortex during spatial attention shifts. *Nature Neuroscience, 5,* 995–1002.

Yantis, S., & Serences, J. T. (2003). Cortical mechanisms of space-based and object-based attentional control. *Current Opinion in Neurobiology, 13,* 187–193.

Zikopoulos, B., & Barbas, H. (2006). Prefrontal projections to the thalamic reticular nucleus form a unique circuit for attentional mechanisms. *Journal of Neuroscience, 26,* 7348–7361.

4

Visual Attention

Computational Problems, Strategies, and Mechanisms

JOHN K. TSOTSOS, ALBERT L. ROTHENSTEIN, EVGUENI SIMINE, AND
ANDREI ZAHARESCU

VISUAL ATTENTION seems to be a magnet for experiment and theory. Indeed, the quantity of experimental methods and data seems overwhelming and new theories appear with increasing frequency. Yet, somehow, progress seems slow, and instead of moving closer to a deep understanding of visual attention, the field seems to continually diverge. Why is this? This chapter suggests that there is too great an emphasis on finding explanations or models of the phenomenology rather than on seeking an explanation of the underlying causes of the phenomenon. With the belief that the language of computation—distinct from mathematics or equation simulation alone—can provide a theoretical foundation for such an investigation, we outline the computational problems that lead to the capacity to attend—in other words, the causal need for attention in vision. Then, possible strategies to deal with those problems will be described, followed by one particular set of mechanisms that solves those computational problems. In this way, we distinguish the computational, algorithmic

(strategies), and implementation (mechanistic) elements of visual attention (Marr, 1992).

COMPUTATIONAL PROBLEMS

The number of computational problems that play a role in a theory of the human brain's visual processes is no doubt larger than those presented here and far from being understood. The focus here is on those problems in which attention appears to be involved. Previously, Anderson and Van Essen (1987) described some problems of information flow in the visual cortex, while Tsotsos (1990) presented those arising from the computational complexity[1] of visual information processing. In both cases, attention is a suggested solution; these will be the main topics of this section.

Computational Complexity

If a vision system knows which subset of an image corresponds to an object and the object type (and its expected pose and illumination among other factors) is known, the task of matching image subset to object model is relatively straightforward. In fact, this is a subarea of computational vision for which somewhat successful algorithms exist. The trick is to quickly determine which is the image subset of interest and the corresponding object model. However, far too much computation is required to solve this problem in its general form with guarantees that the optimal solution is found in all cases, without making a priori assumptions. There are an exponential number of possible image subsets against which to match each potential object model appearance; whatever the details of the algorithm for accomplishing this, optimal solutions seem computationally intractable in any implementation, machine or neural. This conclusion can be proved formally using methods from theoretical computational complexity (see Tsotsos, 1988, 1989, 1990; Parodi et al., 1998). This also provides theoretical support for the prevailing argument for why the brain needs visual attention: Insufficient neural machinery is available to deal with all stimuli equally (for example, see Broadbent, 1971, p. 147). The problem with this common argument is that it is not useful in any way; it provides no constraint on what this means or how to deal with the problem. However, the nature of the proofs referred to can remedy this.

The problem is not one only of region-of-interest selection; rather, it is a combinatorial problem involving the combination of many locations with many features. The previously cited papers show that the number of possible combinations is an exponential function of the number of locations (P, pixels) multiplied by the number of measurements (F, features) computed at each location. This function has order 2^{PF}. Since P is a very large number whereas F is not huge, but not so small either, the overall value of this term is far greater than the number of connections in the brain and thus the overall problem seems intractable, as stated.

What form could visual processing take to eliminate this intractability? In other words, how can the problem be reshaped? Basically, the starting point would be to find ways of reducing or eliminating the exponents of the complexity function. A well-understood computational solution is that of pyramid representations (Uhr, 1972; Tsotsos, 1987; Anderson & Van Essen, 1987; Burt, 1988; Nakayama, 1991). Such representations lead to smaller sets of locations to examine at the higher layers of processing, and thus smaller P. Another is the incorporation of the observation that usually, objects and events in the real world are spatiotemporally localized and thus not all possible subsets of image locations need be considered (see Chapter 1 of this volume). This eliminates P from the exponent, transforming the function to order $P^{1.5}2^{F}$. Third, is the observation that not all objects or events involve all possible features at all points. If it were possible to know in advance which subset of features is relevant, the F exponent can be reduced. Further, a priori knowledge of a target and its location could also eliminate much computation, bringing the $P^{1.5}$ factor to a small integer or better. As a result, the vision problem, stated in its most general form earlier, is reshaped to a less general yet still useful form. Although these strategies (detailed in Tsotsos, 1988, 1990; see Tsotsos & Bruce, 2008, for an expanded treatment) help tremendously, they do not solve the full problem and in fact introduce new problems.

The Information Flow Problem

Pyramid representations solve part of the complexity problem by reducing the size of the representations to be processed, but in doing so, introduce another problem. By the nature of the computations that are performed—namely, combining inputs from several neurons at one level into a single neuron at the next level (also known as *neural convergence*)—they necessarily corrupt the signals flowing through the pyramid. For example, neurons in higher layers of visual processing have large receptive fields, large enough to include more than one stimulus element. Inputs from two stimuli are routed into one neuron, leading to a potential signal interference problem. Note that this corruption problem is common to all pyramid architectures, as well as to any other multilayer network scheme (Jolion & Rosenfeld, 1994). Such pyramid schemes are used by Uhr (1972), Burt (1988), Sandon

(1989), and Olshausen et al. (1993) and others, and are implied by Nakayama (1991). In fact, it is this specific issue that gave rise to the *shifter circuits* model of Anderson and Van Essen (1987). They suggested that a multiplexing circuit could shift input from a stimulus onto an appropriate pathway, so that it reaches the neurons of interest at higher layers without interference. The shifting, layer by layer, would be controlled by external attention signals (see Chapter 5, this volume). Olshausen et al. (1993) then provided a realization of this idea. Unfortunately, shifter circuits solve only one of the information flow problems.

Five information flow problems due to pyramidal processing will be described. The first problem is the most obvious one, namely that the visual field (VF) is represented by units that sample an increasing portion of the VF as one proceeds from bottom to top of the pyramid; this is the *sampling problem*. If the sampling is linked to spatial resolution in a straightforward manner, then we may say that the pyramid represents the VF at a coarse spatial scale at the top and at a fine spatial scale at the bottom. If the higher levels of processing are associated with more abstract computations, then those computations are represented at a coarse spatial resolution. A key paradox is posed as a result: The top layer is comprised of units with very large receptive fields, which therefore represent space coarsely and do not provide for the detail seemingly required for high-resolution vision (see Moran & Desimone, 1985, for the biological argument and Tsotsos, 1990, for the computational one).

The second problem with pyramids is the *context effect*. A single unit at the top of the pyramid receives input from a large subpyramid, and thus from a large portion of the VF (i.e., its receptive field, RF). Unless an object is alone in the VF, the response of neurons whose RFs contain the object will necessarily be affected not only by the object but also by any other image event in that RF. These other image events may be termed the *context* in which the object is found. Thus, the response of those neurons is confounded by the object's context.

The *blurring problem* is the third difficulty introduced by pyramid architectures. A single

event at the input will affect a subpyramid of units; that is, signals from it connect to a diverging pattern of neurons layer to layer. Thus, although a single event may be well localized at the input layer, location specificity is lost because a spatially large portion of the output layer is affected by it. How, then, can vision be precise and detailed?

The fourth problem with pyramids is the *crosstalk problem*. Two separate visual events in the VF will activate two subpyramids (diverging neural connectivity patterns) that overlap. The region of overlap will contain units whose activity is a function of both events. Thus, each event interferes with the interpretation of other events in the VF. The blurring and crosstalk problems negatively impact one another, creating greater interference than each alone.

The final problem is the *boundary problem*. Due to the nature of convolutions—the basic mathematical counterpart of the implementation of neural tuning—at each layer, a filter half-width at the edge of the field is left unprocessed. This is compounded layer by layer because the half-widths are additive. The result is that a sizeable annulus at the top layer contains responses that do not faithfully represent the input. Tsotsos et al. (1995) and van der Wal and Burt (1992) point out that this is an inherent issue with all pyramid representations.

Although pyramid processes are observed in primate visual cortex and commonly used in many models of vision, the problem they partially address (reduction of computational complexity) is joined by a new set of problems.

STRATEGIES

As may be inferred from the above discussion, the view that attention is some monolithic mechanism is not justifiable. Especially in computer vision and in many computational models, this seems to be the prevailing view, especially from authors who focus on saliency and fixation selection. Here, it is argued that attention is a *set* of mechanisms whose goal is to optimize the search processes inherent in perception and cognition and to do it in such a manner that the problems listed above are solved. The argument is not without its controversy (see Pastukhov et al., 2009). The motivations for these mechanisms were very briefly described in the previous section; additional discussion can be found in Tsotsos (1990) and Tsotsos et al. (1995, 2005, 2008). As mentioned in the introduction, the goal here is to search for the cause of attention and not focus on only its manifestations. At the first principles level, the cause is the mismatch between the computational complexity of vision and the brain's neural machinery. This has been formalized (Tsotsos, 1990), and no *single* solution exists save for the evolution of a much larger brain. The reason that no single solution exists has to do with the multivariate nature of the problem. Although, earlier, two variables of relevance were described (pixels and features), there are many more, ranging from neural packaging and heat management to nutrient and waste transport, to more computational issues such as memory, connectivity, transmission speed, and more. No single mechanism could possibly optimize all of this effectively. In any case, as is well-known in all engineering tasks, simultaneously optimizing many interrelated variables can only be dealt with by defining sufficient criteria for a solution. Optimizing one variable often leads to suboptimal values for another, and as a result, a globally satisfying solution is what is sought in practice. Even if we restrict consideration to visual processes, it is very difficult to be precise about the nature of the objective function for this optimization, although it is clear that minimizing processing time, minimizing neural cost, and maximizing correctness of perception are primary ingredients.

Three main classes of strategies are identified here, each including a number of more specific ones:

SELECTION

- Choose a spatiotemporal region of interest.
- Choose features of interest.
- Choose which world/task/object/event model is relevant for the current task.
- Select the best fixation point and best viewpoint from which to view a three-dimensional (3D) scene.
- Select the best interpretation/response.

RESTRICTION

- Restrict processing to the task relevant search space.
- Consider only the locations or features previously presented as cues.
- Limit the extent of search for task-specified results.

SUPPRESSION

- Suppress interference within RFs
- Suppress task-irrelevant computations (location, feature, feature range, etc.).
- Suppress previously seen locations or objects.

How each of these may have relevance in addressing the five problems outlined above should be clear. The next section will focus on possible mechanisms that realize these strategies.

MECHANISMS

The previous section outlines five selection, three restriction, and three suppression strategies. It is likely that this set is not complete and others may prove useful in addition. Selection occurs by some decision process over a set of possibilities, so that one element of that set is chosen. Winner-take-all (WTA; Feldman & Ballard, 1982) or soft-max (Yuille & Geiger, 1995) are two possible mechanisms. Restriction occurs by a decision process over a set of possibilities, so that a subset, with more than one element, is chosen. *Branch-and-bound* is a classic mechanism that is used for such a task in optimization problems (Lawler & Wood, 1966). Recursive pruning within the branch-and-bound strategy is especially useful for a hierarchical system. Suppression could occur by multiplicatively inhibiting (not necessarily complete suppression) a set of items within one or more representations. Apparent suppression can occur by enhancing selected items. Of course, to perceive any particular scene or stimulus configuration may require combinations of these mechanisms. It may be that the difficulties of the field of attention arise because any particular experiment taps into a subset of mechanisms to varying degrees, and it is difficult to tease the effects apart. The *selective tuning* (ST) model is one that combines most of these strategies into a coherent processing structure and is the focus of the balance of this chapter.

Selective Tuning: The Basic Model

The ST model was first described in Tsotsos (1990), with its theoretical foundations elaborated in Tsotsos (1987, 1988, 1989). The first papers to describe the mechanisms that realize ST appeared in Tsotsos (1991, 1993), and the first implementation was described in Culhane and Tsotsos (1992). A more detailed presentation can be found in Tsotsos et al. (1995), where the name "selective tuning" also first appeared. Extensions of the model can be found in Zaharescu et al. (2004), Tsotsos et al. (2005, 2008), Rodriguez-Sanchez et al. (2007), and Rothenstein et al. (2008). The general description of the model has appeared in several theoretical as well as experimental papers. Comparisons with other models have also appeared previously. As a result, repetitive exposition will not be included here. Selective tuning incorporates many but not all of the strategies described in the previous section and makes important predictions that, since their presentation, have been strongly supported experimentally (see Cutzu & Tsotsos, 2003; Hopf et al., 2006; Tombu & Tsotsos, 2008; Loach et al., 2008; Böhler et al., 2009, for example). Solutions to the sampling, context, blurring, crosstalk, and boundary problems are all introduced in Tsotsos et al. (1995). Of these, the boundary problem was the least developed and remained largely separate from the full model. The focus in this chapter will be on the introduction of a new extension to the model that deals with the boundary problem, parsimoniously combining fixation control with the ST framework. This was previously presented by Zaharescu et al. (2004), but in a manner separate from ST. An overview of the basic operation of ST follows, and the full model with fixation control will be presented in the following section.

Figure 4.1 shows the sequence of actions taken by ST in a simple task. The visual processing architecture is pyramidal in structure, with layers of neurons with decreasing spatial resolution but increasing abstraction and complexity of selection in higher layers. A hypothetical five-layer pyramid is caricatured in Figure 4.1A, with most of the connections removed for clarity. The connections shown are based on the same observations and conclusions that Salin and Bullier (1995), Lamme and Roelsfema (2000), and Bullier (2001) describe. There are both feedback (recurrent), feedforward, and lateral connections for each neuron, and the spatial extent of connectivity is reciprocal. Each neuron has diverging connections to the next highest layer and receives converging input from neurons in the previous layer. Similarly, each neuron provides diverging feedback signals to lower layers and receives converging feedback from higher layers. There is no assumption of only one "processing stream" (such as dorsal and ventral), and the model allows complex lattices of processing layers.

At the beginning of any task—say, for example, a visual search task—subjects are provided with information about the task: what the stimuli will be, where will they appear, what is the goal, how to respond, and so forth. Such task information affects processing, as has been shown in all experimental work since the Posner cue paradigm was first presented (Posner et al. 1978), if not earlier. In ST, such task information affects the processing pyramid by inhibition of irrelevant computations. Figure 4.1B shows this top-down pass through the pyramid and the subsequent coloring of the pyramid is meant to represent the fact that the whole pyramid is affected.

When a stimulus is presented to the input layer of the pyramid (Figure 4.1C), it activates in a feedforward manner all of the units within the pyramid with RFs that include the stimulus location; the result is a diverging cone of activity within the processing pyramid. It is assumed that response strength of units in the network is a measure of goodness-of-match of the stimulus within the RF to the model that determines the selectivity of that unit. We term the portion of each layer that is affected the neuron's *projective field*.

Decisions on the perceived stimulus occur at the level at which the information appropriate for the task is computed. This may be at the topmost layer if the task is a categorization one, for example. In ST decisions are made in a competitive manner, as first described in Tsotsos (1990), using the task-modulated (or biased) responses of neurons

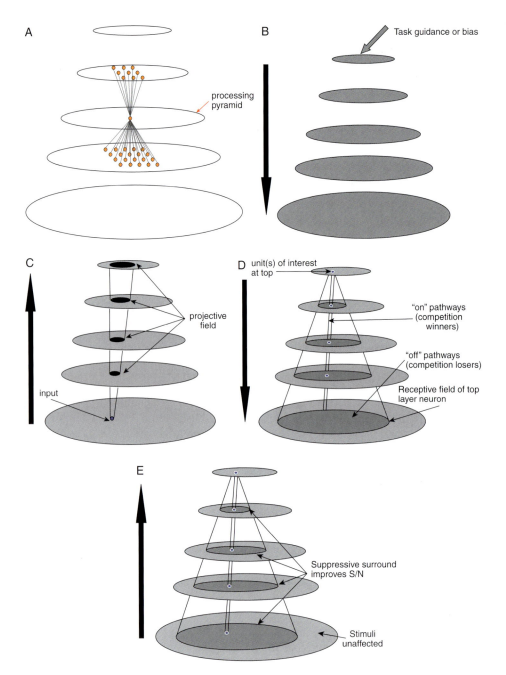

FIGURE 4.1 (**A**) A hypothetical five-layer pyramid representation. Each layer is a retinotopic set of neurons. Each neuron has feedforward, feedback, and lateral connections to and from adjoining layers as shown. There is no commitment or restriction on the type of neural selectivity represented. Lateral connectivity is not used for the examples that follow. (**B**) The pyramid representation after task information has primed the entire representation, the gray shading representing the fact that whole pyramid is affected. In ST, this action requires a top-down pass through the pyramid suppressing task-irrelevant neurons. (**C**) A visual stimulus appears in the lower (input) layer. It activates neurons in that layer for which it is in their receptive field, and this in turn then activates neurons in the next layer in a diverging activation pattern. This activation proceeds all the way to the highest layers of the pyramid. (**D**) The strongest response(s) at the top layer are selected and, in order to localize and segment the stimulus from its surround, a top-down (recurrent) pass is employed that selects the stimulus while pruning away or suppressing the background. (**E**) Once the surround has been suppressed, the stimulus can be reinterpreted as if it appeared on a blank (or significantly muted) background. This reinterpretation occurs simultaneously with the recurrent pruning process but can complete only after the recurrent phase completes.

throughout the processing network. Decisions rely on a hierarchy of WTA processes. Winner-take-all is a parallel algorithm for finding the maximum value in a set.[2] First, a WTA process operates across the entire VF at the top layer, where it computes the global winner; that is, those unit(s) with largest response (see Figure 4.1D). The global winner activates a WTA that operates only over its direct inputs to select the strongest responding region within its RF. Next, all of the feedforward connections in the visual pyramid that do not contribute to the winner are pruned (inhibited). As a result, the input to the higher-level unit changes and thus its output changes. The projective field shrinks in each layer as the pruning process proceeds down the pyramid. We suggest that this is the source of the well-observed attentional modulation of single neuron responses. This refinement of unit responses is important; it provides a solution to the signal interference problem described earlier. By the end of this refinement process, the output of the attended units at the top layer will be the same as if the attended stimulus appeared on a blank field. This strategy—a variant of the well-known branch-and-bound search method—of finding the winners within successively smaller RFs, layer by layer, in the pyramid and then pruning away irrelevant connections through inhibition is applied recursively through the pyramid. The end result is that, from a globally strongest response in the top layer projective field, the cause of that largest response is localized in the sensory field at the earliest levels. The paths remaining may be considered the pass zone of the attended stimulus, while the pruned paths form the inhibitory zone of an attentional beam (Figure 4.1D). A final feedforward pass permits reinterpretation of the stimulus by all neurons within the pass zone with context reduced or removed. However, this final pass is not strictly ordered, as shown in Figure 4.1E, and the feedforward changes arise while the recurrent pass is in progress.

Selective Tuning with Fixation Control

Previous solutions for the boundary problem described earlier have concentrated on extending the edges of the input images in a variety of ways (van der Wal & Burt, 1992) to enable convolutions at the edges to have full, albeit fake, input for their computation. However, a different and more biologically plausible solution exists if one simply remembers that the eyes can move. Suppose that instead of artificially altering the input layer size and contents, an independent mechanism is provided that could detect peripheral salient items separately and saccade to fixate them, thus bringing them to the central region and allowing veridical processing. To detect the most salient item in the input layer peripheral annulus, an independent selection mechanism is required whose inputs are representations of early layers before the boundary problem becomes significant. This idea first appeared in Tsotsos et al. (1995). A simple algorithm emerges:

1. Compute both the overall most salient item at the top (call this the *next central focus* [NCF]) and the *peripheral priority map* [PPM]).
2. Combine the two representations to create a full field representation.
3. Choose the most salient location. If a peripheral item is more salient than the central item, move the eye to fixate it; otherwise, the central item is the one attended covertly.

Saccades have been previously described that appear to have similar function (Hallett, 1978; Whittaker & Cummings, 1990). These saccades are elicited in response to a visual stimulus in the periphery (differences most apparent with ≥10 degrees of eccentricity), where the exact location of the stimulus is unpredictable. The saccade results in the approximate foveation of the stimulus. Those authors hypothesized that a separate mechanism must be present to drive these special saccades. In monkey, the parieto-occipital (PO) area seems to have the connectivity described earlier in addition to representing the peripheral 10 degrees of the VF, and may be a candidate region for this function (Colby et al. 1988). In ST, the central region is treated differently from the periphery, specifically to deal with the boundary problem; the two separate representations are clear in Figure 4.2. The central attentional field in the figure represents the central 10 degrees of the VF and all the responses of neurons of the top layer of the pyramid whose RFs are within this

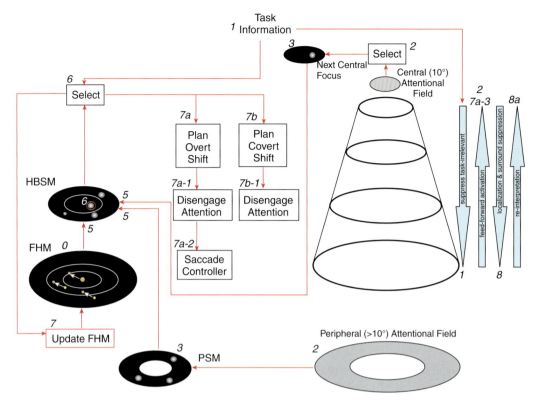

FIGURE 4.2   The full selective tuning control structure including fixation control. Following the arrows around the figure leads to the algorithm presented in the text. The way to view this is as follows. Imagine the eye has just changed gaze for some visual scene. The system may or may not have a task to perform; but if it does, that task bias had been previously applied and remains in place (the suppress task-irrelevant arrow). New input is passed from the eye to the layers of visual processing (the four-layer pyramid of ovals). This follows the feedforward activation arrow. The peripheral attentional field and the central attentional field produce their representations, both of which go into the decision to choose what to attend. If the decision is to attend the central item, then it is a covert shift and that central item is localized with a top-down pass (the localization and surround suppression arrow) followed by reinterpretation if the task demands it. If the decision was overt, then the eye would shift gaze to bring the peripheral item to the central attentional field. In both cases, the fixation history map must be updated to reflect what in the visual world has been seen.

central area. The peripheral attentional field in the figure represents the neural responses of early layers of the pyramid, say, V1, V2, and MT—areas early enough in the pyramid to not have been too strongly affected by the boundary problem, in the region outside the central 10-degree area. Saliency computations in ST are accomplished via the *attention by information maximization* (AIM) algorithm (Bruce & Tsotsos, 2005, 2009), a method based on the goal of information maximization. Using AIM, the representations in the peripheral attentional field are combined into the peripheral priority map.

The simple algorithm above hides a problem. Once the eyes move away from a fixation point, how does fixation not return to that point over and over (i.e., how does fixation not oscillate between strongest and second strongest locations)? In the original Koch and Ullman (1985) formulation, location inhibition was included after an item was attended, so that attention may shift to the next most salient item. In fact, the mathematics of the WTA selection process demands this by definition. All models seem to have reached the same conclusion on this point. If, however, the covert system is linked with the overt system, a new dimension is added to the inhibition. Not only must locations within an image be inhibited, but also locations outside the current image. When the eyes move to attend a peripheral item, previously attended items may not be present in the new image. Subsequent movement of fixation may bring those previously attended locations back into view; the result would be an oscillating system. This inhibition of return (IOR) (Posner et al. 1985) plays an important computational role, but not with the breadth of that suggested experimentally (Klein, 2000). Here, we include a *fixation history map* (FHM), a representation of two-dimensional (2D) visual space larger than the VF containing the sequence of recent fixations, and it provides the source of location information for IOR used in a subsequent computation. The size of the FHM is an open issue.

The FHM is centered at the current eye fixation and represents space in an eye-centered system. The FHM is constructed as a 2D map that encodes position in the world; previously fixated locations are marked as "on" and others "off." These are all reset to "off" at the end of the task. The FHM is updated on each fixation with an associated saccade history shift with direction and magnitude opposite to the trajectory of the eye movement, so that correct relative positions of fixation points are maintained (see Zaharescu et al., 2004). It is doubtful that this will suffice in the general case; this does not address specific object-based inhibition of return (IOR) nor task-related issues that may override IOR (see Klein, 2000). Consider it as a first step toward a solution of this problem.

The main fixation decision is made using the *history-biased priority map* (HBPM), a representation that is the closest in our model to the common saliency map (Koch & Ullman, 1985; Itti et al., 1998). The main difference is that the saliency map model always has eye movement as output, whereas our model permits both covert and overt fixations. A secondary difference is that, in the central area, only one location is represented, the NCF, and in the periphery, a full saliency map is present. Third, the particular computation of saliency differs; ST uses the AIM algorithm. A final difference is that this representation is always

modulated by task demands that inhibit task-irrelevant locations and feature contributions (because the feedforward computations on which both the NCF and the PPM are based are task-biased in advance). Like the saliency map model, previous fixations are inhibited using the FHM representation. In reality, our HBPM is more closely related to the priority map of Fecteau and Munoz (2006).

This solution is mapped out in Figure 4.2, and the following briefly describes the sequence of actions involved in one attentive cycle (bold font signifies elements that are components of the figure):

0. In advance of a new task, the **FHM** contains some set of previously viewed locations.

1. Prime the processing network with **task information** using a top-down traversal of the processing network to **suppress task-irrelevant computations**.

2. A stimulus is presented at input causing **feedforward activation** of neurons within the pyramid. During this feedforward activation, representations in the **peripheral attentional field** from the early layers of the pyramid are combined with the AIM algorithm to derive the **peripheral priority map**.

3. **Select** the **next central focus** from the **central attentional field**.

4. Combine **next central focus, peripheral priority map,** and **fixation history map** into **the history-biased priority map**. The fixation history negatively biases the final priority map.

5. **Select** the next fixation target, biased by **task information**.

6. **Update fixation history map** with new fixation point, shifting other remembered fixations appropriately in space.

7. Decide on appropriate action for winning fixation target:

7a. If target is a peripheral one, then **plan overt shift**.

7a-1. **Disengage attention**, releasing suppressive surround if present.

7a-2. Foveate target via **saccade-pursuit controller** using location from **HBPM**.

7a-3. Allow time for **feedforward activation** through pyramid.

7a-4. **Select** neurons to attend in top layer.

7b. If target is the central one, then **plan covert shift** (if attention is to be maintained on same item, skip 7b-1).

7b-1. **Disengage attention**, releasing suppressive surround if present.

7b-2. Attend **NCF** neurons in top layer.

8. If the task requires more than detection or categorization, then deploy the **localization/ surround suppression** process.

8a. **Reinterpret** the stimulus after surround suppression.

The level of resolution of the HBPM is an issue, since it is the source of location information for saccade planning; it is necessarily coarse, perhaps at best, at the level of the number of columns in V1. As a result, the precision of each saccade is limited. If the fixation misses the target by a little, so that the target falls within the suppressive surround of the resulting localization, then the target is not seen. It can only be seen when the suppression is released, and in the context of the algorithm, this occurs after a commitment to make an eye movement has been made. Sheinberg and Logothetis (2001) describe such "double-take" eye movements.

Selective Tuning Example

An example is included here to help clarify this overall process, although the FHM and HBPM are not shown. The visual representation on which ST is demonstrated is a representation of visual motion. Visual areas V1, MT, MST, and 7a are modeled. Although many motion models have been presented in the past, this one is unique because it is the only one that features such a broad set of neural tunings. Specifically, V1 represents direction and speed tuned translation motion, in 12 direction bands and three speed bands. The twelve directions can be seen in Figure 4.3, organized in a circle, each including three speed tunings (the thickness of each of the small squares represents the columns). In other words, V1 includes 36 differently tuned neuron types for each location. Area MT is split into two, shown in the figure as MT-t and MT-g. MT-t represents

pure translation, at 12 directions and also three speed tuning bands, but at lower resolution than V1 (it's a pyramid). MT-g represents gradient computations; that is, spatial derivatives of velocity (Martinez-Trujillo et al., 2005). Again, 12 directions of local motion and 12 gradient directions for each of the three speed tunings are represented. As a result, the columns in each of the MT-g squares are 36 units deep; overall, 432 tunings are included. Areas MST and 7a are similarly split, the left side of the figure representing pure translation at differing levels of spatial abstraction and the right side representing complex motion. MST-s represents spiral motion (Martinez-Trujillo et al., 2005), 12 different quanta around the approach, counterclockwise rotate, recede, clockwise rotate circle as in (Treue & Anderson, 1996), and again at three speed tunings. 7a-t and 7a-s represent coarser scale versions of MST-t and MST-s. A total of 684 different motion tunings are represented in this four-layer pyramid. By comparison, the well-known Heeger et al. (1996) model includes the left side of this figure only; it is blind to complex motion, such as approach or rotation, whereas this motion model captures them well, as will be seen in the following example. The mathematical details can be found in Tsotsos et al. (2005).

The input for this example is a video showing pure motion-defined form. There are two apertures and within them random noise is moving in a coherent manner on a background of the same random noise. One image of the video is depicted in Figure 4.4 with the background removed for clarity. There are two stimulus areas, the larger one contains counterclockwise rotation, the smaller one rightward translation. The smaller one is central and is thus attended first. The system then makes a fixation shift to the larger, bringing it centrally, and attends it.

The responses within the hierarchy after the first feedforward pass after stimulus onset are shown in Figure 4.5. White represents zero response, while maximum response is shown in black. Although it is not apparent here, several frames of video have elapsed because neural responses within the hierarchy are all time varying and require time to settle on the values shown here. The responses to

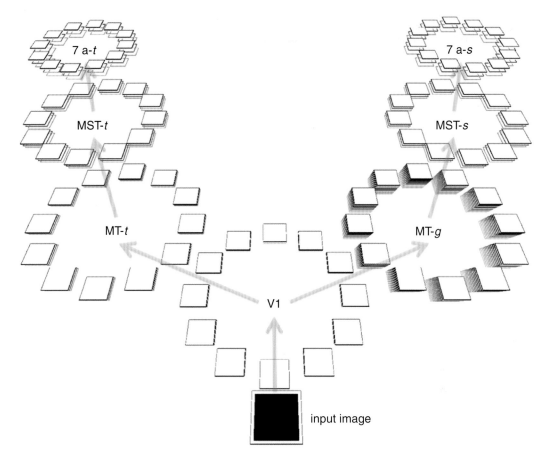

FIGURE 4.3   The motion processing hierarchy used to illustrate selective tuning. This is a pyramid representation for portions of visual areas V1, MT, MST, and 7a. The diagram separates the pyramid in two parts for ease of presentation only. The left part is for pure translation motion while the right part is for complex motion. Each rectangle represents the responses of neurons across the full visual field, at the resolution dictated by the pyramid level, for one kind of neural selectivity. This partitioning is solely for the purpose of exposition; actual neuroanatomy would likely include columnar components and perhaps even separate subregions of the visual areas for specific tunings. V1 represents direction and speed tuned translation motion (12 direction bands, three speed bands for each). The 12 directions can be seen organized in a circle. Area MT is split into MT-t and MT-g. MT-t represents pure translation (12 directions, two speed bands each). MT-g represents gradient computations, i.e., spatial derivatives of velocity. Again 12 directions of local motion and 12 gradient directions for each of the three speed tunings are represented. Areas MST and 7a are similarly split, the left side of the figure representing pure translation at differing levels of spatial abstraction and the right side representing complex motion. MST-s represents spiral motion at 12 different quanta around the approach, counterclockwise rotate, recede, clockwise rotate circle, and again at three speed tunings. 7a-t and 7a-s represent coarser scale versions of MST-t and MST-s.

the stimuli are easily seen in area V1; however, they blur as they move through the pyramid. It is clear that the strongest responses are for rightward translation. The red square in the representation in area 7a-t signifies the winner of the competition for attention.

Figure 4.6 shows the form of the attentional beam after the top-down localization and surround suppression process. The suppressed portion is shown in blue in the intermediate layers and black on the image; the pass zone of the beam is in green. Via the beam's pass zone, all the neurons

FIGURE 4.4 One image from the input video used in Figures 4.5, 4.6, 4.7, and 4.8. The video depicts pure motion defined form, moving stimuli made up of random noise on a background of the same random noise. Here, the background is removed to reveal the stimuli. There are two stimuli: the larger item is rotating and the smaller one in the center is translating to the right. This configuration is the initial one for the example.

that represent aspects of the attended stimulus are linked. Only the translational representations are part of the attended beam even though, as in Figure 4.5, parts of the complex motion pathway also respond to portions of the input.

In Figure 4.7, a fixation shift has occurred to bring the peripheral stimulus—the rotating one in the corner of Figure 4.4—to the center, and the responses within the hierarchy after the feedforward pass are shown. Now, the spiral side of the hierarchy is more strongly affected. The previously fixated item now is seen in the upper left corner of the representations and still causes responses throughout; however, they do not win the competition in this configuration. Again, the responses highlighted in red at the top of the complex motion hierarchy win the competition.

The last figure in the sequence, Figure 4.8, shows the attentional beam for the attended rotation. It has a very different structure than for the translating item. The translating item had uniform field of motion directions and magnitudes, and single neurons are present in the representation that are selective for the combination. Rotation— and this is the case for any of the complex motions that Treue and Anderson (1996) describe—cannot be so simply encoded. The pattern of motion

directions and magnitudes varies across the spatial extent of the stimulus. As argued in Tsotsos et al. (2005) and evidenced by the experiments in Martinez-Trujillo et al. (2005), the computation of the spatial gradient of velocity is key here. For each of these complex motions, the spatial derivative of the velocity vector is constant across the spatial extent of the stimulus. The MST-s level neurons are tuned for this homogeneity, whereas the MT-g neurons detect its value.

To summarize, this example—not a simulation but rather actual processing of the input video sequence—illustrates how ST both attends to complex stimuli and also deals with fixation shifts. Further, it shows the form of the attentional beam computed by the model; it correctly locates not only the attended item in the input but also all the neurons that contribute to its overall identification at each level of abstraction. Selective tuning's unique recurrent process for localization is the reason for this functionality. Additional examples can be found in previous papers; in particular, examples of fixation control in a large image visual search experiment are shown in Zaharescu et al. (2004), with comparisons to data from the same experiment in monkey. The motion representation presented points to a motion model that has the power to encode complex motion in a way that is significantly different from past models such as Heeger et al. (1996).

CONCLUSION

Differences with Other Models

First, ST does not rely on a single saliency map for all its attentional functionality. The view that attention is a set of mechanisms is the main distinguishing feature between this model and others, particularly those that are direct descendants of the original, 1985 model of Koch and Ullman, which itself was an attempt to realize feature integration theory (Treisman & Gelade, 1980). The original saliency map model dealt only with the selection of a single spatial point of interest, of maximum conspicuity. The first implementation and simulation of it was due to Sandon (1989). Later, Itti and colleagues developed a new and expanded implementation (Itti et al., 1998).

FIGURE 4.5   The responses within the hierarchy after the first feedforward pass after stimulus onset. White represents zero response, while maximum response is shown in black. Although it is not apparent here, several frames of video have elapsed because neural responses within the hierarchy are all time-varying and require time to settle on the values shown here. The stimuli are clearly seen in area V1; however, they blur as they move through the pyramid. It is clear that the strongest responses are for rightward motion. The red square in the representation in area 7a-t signifies the winner of the competition for attention.

He and his group have added task bias, motion, and other elements to it. Throughout this development, the original form of the saliency model has remained intact and does not deal with attentive effects in any other representation of visual processing. The ST view of attention includes (as predicted in Tsotsos, 1990; Figures 7 and 8, p. 440) effects due to attentive processing throughout the visual processing network. The statement there is even stronger; attention *controls* the subnetwork that feeds neurons at the top of the visual processing hierarchy. To quote the description of the attentional beam idea in that paper: "The output of a given unit at the top of the hierarchy is directly affected by the subhierarchy for which it is the root. Thus the beam must affect the branches and leaves of the selected sub-tree. The beam expands as it traverses the hierarchy, covering all portions of the processing mechanism that directly contribute to the output at its point of entry at the top. In other words, the effective receptive field of the output unit selected for attention is that entire sub-hierarchy, and the attentional beam must control that receptive field. The central portion of the beam allows the stimulus of interest to pass through unaffected, while the remainder of the beam selectively inhibits portions of the processing hierarchy that may give rise to interfering signals." Recently, Gilbert & Sigman (2007) have suggested exactly the same.

Selective tuning uses recurrent tracing of connections to achieve localization. The idea of tracing

FIGURE 4.6   The form of the attentional beam after the top-down localization and surround suppression process. The suppressed portion is shown in blue in the intermediate layers and black on the image; the pass zone of the beam is in green. Via the beam's pass zone, all the neurons that represent aspects of the attended stimulus are linked. Only the translational representations are part of the attended beam even though, as is seen in the previous figure, parts of the spiral pathway also respond to portions of the input.

back connections in a top-down fashion was present in part, in the neocognitron model of Fukushima (1986) and suggested even earlier by Milner (1974). It also appeared later in the reverse hierarchy model of Ahissar and Hochstein (1997). Within the selective tuning model, it was first described in Tsotsos (1991, 1993), with accompanying details and proofs in Tsotsos et al. (1995). Only neocognitron and selective tuning provide realizations; otherwise, the two differ in all details. Fukushima's model included a maximum detector at the top layer to select the highest responding cell, and all other cells were set to their rest state. Only afferent paths to this cell are facilitated by action from efferent signals from this cell. In contrast, neural inhibition is the only action of

ST, with no facilitation. The neocognitron competitive mechanism is lateral inhibition that finds strongest single neurons. By contrast, ST finds strongest regions of neurons. For ST, units losing the competition at the top are left alone and not affected at all. Selective tuning's inhibition is only within afferent sets to winning units. This now broadly supported prediction of a space-limited suppressive surround firmly distinguishes the two approaches.

Selective tuning employs surround suppression in the spatial and feature domains to improve signal/noise in neural response. Koch and Ullman's (1985) saliency map features a prediction that locations near the focus of attention are facilitated for next focus choice; the model includes a proximity

FIGURE 4.7   A fixation shift has occurred to bring the peripheral stimulus—the rotating one in the corner of Figure 4.4—to the center and the responses within the hierarchy after the feedforward pass are shown. Now, the spiral side of the hierarchy is more strongly affected.

effect, which would favor shifts to neighboring locations (see page 224 of their paper, the section titled "Proximity Preference"). In fact, Koch and Crick went to great pains to show how an attentive suppressive surround was not biologically feasible, going through the options of attentive enhancement, suppression, and their combination in the development and explicitly rejecting the suppressive penumbra idea (Crick & Koch, 1990, p. 959). In ST, this differs. Consider the following. Neurons have a preferred tuning; that is, they are selective for certain kinds of stimuli. A preferred stimulus within its RF is the "signal" it seeks, whereas whatever else may lie within the RF is not of interest; it can be considered "noise." The overall response of the neuron is clearly a function of both the signal and the noise. The response to the signal would be maximized if the noise were

suppressed; a Gaussian-shaped inhibition on the surround was described in (Tsotsos, 1990, pp. 439–440). This stood as a prediction for years but now enjoys a great deal of support (see Tsotsos et al., 2008, for extensive pointers). Also, this attentive suppression has an interesting side effect: an apparent enhancement of neural response, because the "noise" is removed (this later became the foundation of the biased competition model of attention Desimone & Duncan, 1995). Thus, ST predicts that there is no active process of neural enhancement.

Selective tuning also differs greatly from biased competition (BC). The BC model of visual attention has provided inspiration for many other studies and models (Desimone & Duncan, 1995; Reynolds et al., 1999). It is based on an equation that shows how an attentional bias may affect the

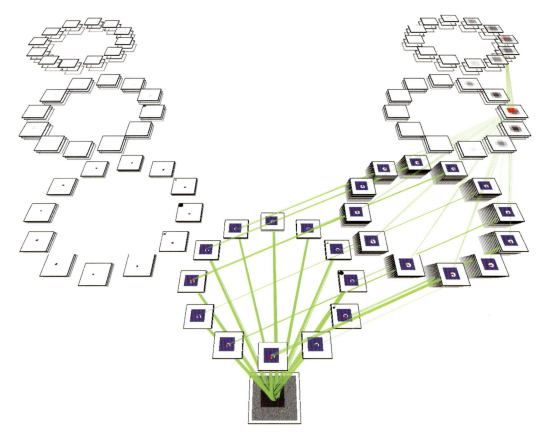

FIGURE 4.8   The form of the attentional beam after the second top-down localization and surround suppression process. The coding is as described for Figure 4.6. There are several noteworthy points here. First, the attentional beam is not unitary, rather it begins with a unitary region at the top of the pyramid, and then after moving past area MST-s splits into 12 sub-beams. The reason is that the neurons in MT-g compute the gradient of velocity with respect to local velocity. Thus, for a rotating object, although the local motion differs along the circumference, the gradient is always in the same direction. Each of the neural tunings here are specific for one direction and speed of local motion and respond to the direction of the gradient with respect to this local motion. As result, the overall motion is split—like slices of a pie—into 12 groups. This is clearly seen by inspecting the highlighted areas in the MT-g layer. V1 codes each of these local motions. These 12 "pie pieces" are then reassembled into the rotating object because they arise from spatially adjoining regions in the input image.

response of a neuron that receives input from excitatory and inhibitory neuron pools. As a result, it shows how an RF might shrink-wrap a stimulus when it is attended. It also provides a good fit to the firing patterns of V4 neurons in macaque. In contrast, ST is not a single neuron theory; BC is, as evidenced by the only formal description of it in Reynolds et al. (1999). Biased competition does not provide a method for how a particular neuron may be selected nor for how attentional influence might arrive there. The mathematics of the model makes the assumption

that the excitatory and inhibitory neuron pools are statistically independent—this is clearly untrue since they must arise from common input earlier in the hierarchy. Selective tuning provides a network-based mechanism, and shows how selection is accomplished and how the selection is communicated through the network. In BC, attention is simply a multiplier; in ST attention is a broad set of mechanisms, more closely connecting to the range of observations made by so many studies over the years. Moreover, the enhanced response effect due to attention in a single neuron that is the cornerstone of the BC model is described as part of the original ST model (Tsotsos, 1990, p. 441).

Significance

The relevance and significance of any theory is determined by the breadth and quality of experimental data that it explains and by its predictive power. There are many levels of abstraction and detail at which explanations can occur, and the same is true for predictions. Theories can be at a system level, at the level of a single visual area, at the neuronal level, or at synaptic and molecular levels. They may be quantitative or qualitative. Selective tuning provides explanations primarily at system levels and at neuronal levels in a mostly qualitative manner. Visual search performance, for example, can be shown for a wide variety of stimulus sets for covert fixations in humans (Rodriguez-Sanchez et al., 2007) and overt fixations in monkey (Zaharescu et al., 2004). Single neuron attentional modulation can be qualitatively characterized (Tsotsos et al., 2001) and explanations for how both enhancement and suppression of neural responses can be provided using only suppression (Tsotsos et al., 2001). Predictions that have been counterintuitive—notably those predicting an attentive suppressive surround and a top-down latency pattern of attentional modulation described in Tsotsos (1990)—have since received substantial experimental support. As Braun and Koch say (Overview, p. xv):

"[A] strong prediction of the model in chapter 14 (Tsotsos, Culhane and Cutzu) is that attentional latencies should *decrease* from lower to higher visual areas, in sharp contrast to stimulus latencies, which *increase* in this order. . . . In its most developed form, such a structural theory makes predictions at multiple levels, many of them unforeseen and counterintuitive (Chapter 14). Although all types of theories have their place, we feel that today the most promising approaches are those which combine the comprehensiveness of psychological theories with a general understanding of neural architecture and cortical circuits. (Braun et al., 2001)"

More recently, the model has made suggestions about the relationship between the ST strategy for attention and visual feature binding and visual recognition (Rothenstein et al., 2008; Tsotsos et al., 2008). In contrast, BC provides explanations at neuronal levels only but in a quantitative fashion. Although the cornerstones of BC—that representation in the visual system is competitive, that both top-down and bottom-up biasing mechanisms influence the ongoing competition, and that competition is integrated across brain systems (see Beck & Kastner, 2009)—were all present in the description of Tsotsos (1990), the quantitative explanation afforded by Reynolds et al. (1998) is important and points to a current limitation of ST. Nevertheless, a full understanding of this magnetic phenomenon of attention will remain elusive until we are able to find satisfactory qualitative and quantitative explanations at all levels, and in this we agree with Braun and Koch's last sentence above.

ACKNOWLEDGMENTS

JKT holds the Canada Research Chair in Computational Vision and acknowledges its support, as well as the support of the Natural Sciences and Engineering Research Council of Canada.

References

Ahissar, M., & Hochstein, S. (1997). Task difficulty and the specificity of perceptual learning. *Nature* 387, 401–406.

Anderson, C., & Van Essen, D. (1987). Shifter circuits: A computational strategy for dynamic aspects of visual processing. *Proceedings of the National Academy of Sciences of the United States of America, 84*(17), 6297–6301.

Böehler, C. N., Tsotsos, J. K., Schoenfeld, M., Heinze, H.-J., & Hopf, J.-M. (2009). The center-surround profile of the focus of attention arises from recurrent processing in visual cortex. *Cerebral Cortex, 19,* 982–991.

Beck, D. M., & Kastner, S. (2009). Top-down and bottom-up mechanisms in biasing competition in the human brain. *Vision Research, 49*(10), 1154–1165.

Braun, J., Koch, C., & Davis, J. (Eds.). (2001). *Visual attention and cortical circuits.* Cambridge MA: MIT Press.

Broadbent, D. (1971). *Decision and stress.* London: Academic Press.

Bruce, N. D. B., & Tsotsos, J. K. (2005). *Saliency based on information maximization.* Proceedings of

Neural Information Processing Systems (NIPS), Vancouver, BC.

Bruce, N. D. B., & Tsotsos, J. K. (2009). Saliency, attention and visual search: An information theoretic approach. *Journal of Vision, 9*(3), article 5. Retrieved from http://journalofvision.org/9/3/5/

Bullier, J. (2001). Integrated model of visual processing. *Brain Research Reviews, 36*, 96–107.

Burt, P. (1988). Attention mechanisms for vision in a dynamic world. *Proceedings of the International Conference on Pattern Recognition*, Vol. 2, pp. 977–987.

Colby, C., Gattass, R., Olson, C., & Gross, C. (1988). Topographical organization of cortical afferents to extrastriate visual area PO in the macaque: A dual tracer study. *Journal of Comparative Neurology, 269*(3), 392–413.

Crick, F., & Koch, C. (1990). Some reflections on visual awareness. *Cold Spring Harbor Symposia on Quantitative Biology, 55*, 953–962.

Culhane, S., & Tsotsos, J. K. (1992). An attentional prototype for early vision. In G. Sandini (Ed.), *Proceedings of the Second European Conference on Computer Vision, Santa Margherita Ligure, Italy* (LNCS-Series Vol. 588, pp. 551–560). Berlin: Springer Verlag.

Cutzu, F., & Tsotsos, J. K. (2003). The selective tuning model of visual attention: Testing the predictions arising from the inhibitory surround mechanism. *Vision Research, 43*, 205–219.

Desimone, R., & Duncan, J. (1995). Neural mechanisms of selective attention. *Annual Review of Neuroscience, 18*, 193–222.

Fecteau, J., & Munoz, D. (2006). Salience, *relevance*, and firing: A Priority map for target selection. *Trends in Cognitive Science, 10*(8), 382–390.

Feldman, J., & Ballard, D. (1982). Connectionist models and their properties. *Cognitive Science, 6*, 205–254.

Fukushima, K. (1986). A neural network model for selective attention in visual pattern recognition. *Biological Cybernetics, 55*(1), 5–15.

Gilbert, C. D., & Sigman, M. (2007). Brain states: Top-down influences in sensory processing. *Neuron, 54*, 677–696.

Hallett, P. (1978). Primary and secondary saccades to goals defined by instructions. *Vision Research, 18*, 1279–1296.

Heeger, D. J., Simoncelli, E. P., & Movshon, J. A. (1996). Computational models of cortical visual processing. *Proceedings of the National Academy of Sciences of the United States of America, 93*(2), 623–627.

Hopf, J.-M., Boehler C. N., Luck S. J., Tsotsos, J. K., Heinze, H.-J., & Schoenfeld, M. A. (2006). Direct neurophysiological evidence for spatial suppression surrounding the focus of attention in vision. *Proceedings of the National Academy of Sciences of the United States of America, 103*(4), 1053–1058.

Itti, L., Koch, C., & Niebur, E. (1998). A model of saliency-based visual attention for rapid scene analysis. *IEEE Transactions on Pattern Analysis and Machine Intelligence, 20*(11), 1254–1259.

Jolion, J. -M., & Rosenfeld, A. (1994). *A Pyramid framework for early vision.* Dordrecht: Kluwer.

Klein, R. (2000). Inhibition of return. *Trends in Cognitive Sciences, 4*, 138–1347.

Koch, C., & Ullman, S. (1985). Shifts in selective visual attention: Towards the underlying neural circuitry. *Human Neurobiology, 4*, 219–227.

Lamme, V., & Roelfsema, P. (2000). The distinct modes of vision offered by feedforward and recurrent processing. *Trends in Neuroscience, 23*, 571–579.

Lawler, E., & Wood, D. (1966). Branch-and-bound methods: A survey. *Operations Research, 14*(4), 699–719.

Loach, D., Frischen, A., Bruce, N., & Tsotsos, J. K. (2008). An attentional mechanism for selecting appropriate actions afforded by graspable objects. *Psychological Science, 19*(12), 1253–1257.

Marr, D. (1982). *Vision: A computational investigation into the human representation and processing of visual information.* New York: Henry Holt and Co.

Martinez-Trujillo, J. C., Tsotsos, J. K., Simine, E., Pomplun, M., Wildes, R., Treue, S., et al. (2005). Selectivity for speed gradients in human area MT/V5. *Neuroreport, 16*(5), 435–438.

Moran, J., & Desimone, R. (1985). Selective attention gates visual processing in the extrastriate cortex. *Science, 229*, 782–784.

Nakayama, K. (1991). The iconic bottleneck and the tenuous link between early visual processing and perception. In C. Blakemore (Ed.), *Vision: Coding and efficiency* (pp. 411–422). Cambridge University Press: Cambridge, UK.

Olshausen, B., Anderson, C., & Van Essen, D. (1993). A neurobiological model of visual attention and invariant pattern recognition based on dynamic routing of information. *Journal of Neuroscience, 13*(11), 4700–4719.

Parodi, P., Lanciwicki, R., Vijh, A., & Tsotsos, J. K. (1998). Empirically-derived estimates of the complexity of labeling line drawings of polyhedral scenes. *Artificial Intelligence, 105*, 47–75.

Pastukhov, A., Fischer, F., & Braun, J. (2009). Visual attention is a single, integrated resource. *Vision Research, 49*, 1166–1173.

Posner, M. I., Nissen, M., & Ogden, W. (1978). Attended and unattended processing modes: The role of set for spatial locations. In H. L. Pick & E. Saltzmann (Eds.), *Modes of perceiving and processing information* (pp. 137–158). Hillsdale, NJ: Erlbaum.

Posner, M. I., Rafal, R. D., Choate, L. S., & Vaughan, J. (1985). Inhibition of return: Neural basis and function. *Cognitive Neuropsychology, 2*(3), 211–228.

Reynolds, J., Chelazzi, L., & Desimone, R. (1999). Competitive mechanisms subserve attention in macaque areas V2 and V4. *Journal of Neuroscience, 19*(5), 1736–1753.

Rodriguez-Sanchez, A. J., Simine, E., & Tsotsos, J. K. (2007). Attention and visual search. *International Journal of Neural Systems, 17*(4), 275–288.

Rothenstein, A., Rodriguez-Sanchez, A., Simine, E., & Tsotsos, J. K. (2008). Visual feature binding within the selective tuning attention framework. Special Issue: Brain, vision and artificial intelligence. *International Journal of Pattern Recognition and Artificial Intelligence, 22*(5), 861–881.

Salin, P., & Bullier, J. (1995). Corticocortical connections in the visual system: Structure and function. *Physiological Reviews, 75,* 107–154.

Sandon, P. (1989). Simulating visual attention. *Journal of Cognitive Neuroscience, 2*(3), 213–231.

Sheinberg, D. L., & Logothetis, N. K. (2001). Noticing familiar objects in real world scenes: The role of temporal cortical neurons in natural vision. *Journal of Neuroscience, 21*(4), 1340–1350.

Tombu, M., & Tsotsos, J. K. (2008). Attending to orientation results in an inhibitory surround in orientation space. *Perception & Psychophysics, 70*(1), 30–35.

Treisman, A. M., & Gelade, G. (1980). A feature-integration theory of attention. *Cognitive Psychology, 12*(1), 97–136.

Treue, S., & Andersen, R. A. (1996). Neural responses to velocity gradients in macaque cortical area MT. *Visual Neuroscience, 13,* 797–804.

Tsotsos, J. K. (1987, June). *A 'complexity level' analysis of vision.* Proceedings of International Conference on Computer Vision: Human and Machine Vision Workshop, pp. 346–355, London, England.

Tsotsos, J. K. (1988). A "complexity level" analysis of immediate vision. *International Journal of Computer Vision, 2*(1), 303–320.

Tsotsos, J. K. (1989). The complexity of perceptual search tasks. In *Proceedings of the International Joint Conference on Artificial Intelligence* (pp. 1571–1577). Detroit.

Tsotsos, J. K. (1990). Analyzing vision at the complexity level. *Behavioral and Brain Sciences, 13*(3), 423–469.

Tsotsos, J. K. (1991). *Localizing stimuli in a sensory field using an inhibitory attentional beam* (RBCV-TR-91-37). Toronto, Canada: University of Toronto.

Tsotsos, J. K. (1993). An inhibitory beam for attentional selection. In L. Harris, & M. Jenkin (Eds.), *Spatial vision in humans and robots* (pp. 313–331). Cambridge University Press:Cambridge.

Tsotsos, J. K., & Bruce, N. D. B. (2008). Computational foundations for attentive processes. *Scholarpedia, 3*(12), 6545.

Tsotsos, J. K., Culhane, S., & Cutzu, F. (2001). From theoretical foundations to a hierarchical circuit for selective attention. In J. Braun, C. Koch, & J. Davis (Eds.), *Visual attention and cortical circuits* (pp. 285–306). Cambridge, MA: MIT Press.

Tsotsos, J. K., Culhane, S., Wai, W., Lai, Y., Davis, N., & Nuflo, F. (1995). Modeling visual attention via selective tuning. *Artificial Intelligence, 78*(1–2), 507–547.

Tsotsos, J. K., Liu, Y., Martinez-Trujillo, J., Pomplun, M., Simine, E., & Zhou, K. (2005). Attending to visual motion. *Computer Vision and Image Understanding, 100*(1–2), 3–40.

Tsotsos, J. K., Rodriguez-Sanchez, A., Rothenstein, A., & Simine, E. (2008). Different binding strategies for the different stages of visual recognition. *Brain Research, 1225,* 119–132.

Uhr, L. (1972). Layered "recognition cone" networks that preprocess, *classify and describe. IEEE Transactions on Computers, 21,* 758–768.

Van der Wal, G., & Burt, P. (1992). A VLSI pyramid chip for multiresolution image analysis. *International Journal of Computer Vision, 8*(3), 177–190.

Whittaker, S., & Cummings, R. (1990). Foveating saccades. *Vision Research, 30*(9), 1363–1366.

Yuille, A., & Geiger, D. (1995). Winner-take-all mechanisms. In M. Arbib (Ed.), *The Handbook of brain theory & neural networks* (pp. 1056–1060). Cambridge, MA: MIT Press.

Zaharescu, A., Rothenstein, A., & Tsotsos, J.K. (2004). Towards a biologically plausible active visual search model. In L. Paletta (Ed.), *Attention and performance in computational vision, LNCS* (Vol. 3368, pp. 133–147). Berlin: Springer.

5

Orienting to the Environment

Separate Contributions of Dorsal and Ventral Frontoparietal Attention Networks

CARLO SESTIERI, GORDON L. SHULMAN, AND MAURIZIO CORBETTA

ALTHOUGH CAPACITY limitations in processing of sensory stimuli are often invoked as the main reason for the development of attentional mechanisms, novel anatomical evidence indicates that the brain is connected to the environment through a tiny thread of sensory inputs (for instance, there are only about 10^6 retinal ganglion cells projecting to the brain, a meager 5% of the synapses present in area V1) (Douglas & Martin, 2007), and that most activity is intrinsic and not task-evoked (Raichle & Mintun, 2006). Hence, estimates of working memory access from visual processing on the order of 10 bits per second may not reflect only the filtering of massive amounts of sensory information, but also the coordination between internal endogenous activity and sparse sensory inputs.

The coordination of ongoing goals and expectations with incoming sensory inputs has long been recognized as one of the main functions of attention. The term "voluntary" or "endogenous"

attention underscores the idea that it is possible to modulate what we perceive through internal signals. More recently, psychological and neural models of attention have conceptualized this interaction as one between signals that control attention (sources of attention) and signals that bias sensory processing (sites at which attention operates). For instance, according to the influential model of Desimone and Duncan (1995), sensory stimuli compete for access to short-term memory, and this competition can be biased toward behaviorally relevant stimuli by means of top-down signals generated in the prefrontal cortex. The objects that win this competition, as described in formal models of attention (Bundesen, 1990), are remembered and selected for action.

The most important contribution of brain imaging in the last 20 years has been to directly show a separation between source signals and modulations of sensory processing, and to identify a set of dorsal frontoparietal regions, or *dorsal frontoparietal attention network (DAN)*, which are consistently involved in the selection of task-relevant stimuli and responses. Forecasted in a seminal article by Posner and Petersen (1990), the notion of attention networks has been strongly supported, with functional connectivity studies clearly demonstrating that control systems constitute brain networks that are separate from sensory and motor networks.

Although sensory input often matches internal expectations, unpredictable events sometimes occur in the environment that can dramatically affect an individual's well-being, such as alarms that signal unexpected and infrequent events (fires, storms, tornados, etc.). Under these conditions, ongoing expectations are violated and adaptive behavior requires a *reorienting* of attention to the novel source of information.

The impact of sensory stimuli on attention has been long recognized (see Chapter 2 of this volume). William James spoke of stimuli that attract attention either because of their impression on the senses as in "very intense, voluminous, sudden," or "their affinity for congenital impulses, in man: strange things, moving things, wild animals, bright things, pretty things, metallic things, blows, blood, etc. stimulus-driven," and contrasted "automatic or reflexive" attention to voluntary attention (James, 1890). Psychologists have continued to study these two forms of attention (Posner et al., 1982), although the degree to which they are completely independent is controversial (Folk & Remington, 2010; Theeuwes, 2010). Recent experiments have examined the degree to which sensory capture of attention is modulated by task relevance (Folk et al., 1992), and conversely how sensory salience facilitates the selection of task relevant information (Yantis & Egeth, 1999). We note that ecological descriptions corresponding to exogenous orienting typically involve highly salient stimuli that are presented very infrequently within a temporally unstructured context (e.g., orienting to an alarm), conditions in which those stimuli may well be automatically assigned behavioral significance. Instead, experimental studies of exogenous orienting typically involve regular presentations of salient stimuli within a temporally structured and predictable task setting (e.g., a "trial").

A second general contribution of neuroimaging has been to clearly show that both goal-driven and stimulus-driven forms of attention are mediated by a single neural system, the dorsal frontoparietal network and associated subcortical regions (e.g., superior colliculus and perhaps pulvinar), and that a more fundamental distinction at the neural level is between *orienting*, implemented by the DAN, and *reorienting*, jointly implemented by the DAN and a separate *ventral frontoparietal attention network* (VAN). The VAN is tuned to all those circumstances in which endogenous expectations do not match sensory inputs, and as such is of fundamental importance for survival. One of the most interesting aspects of this network is its right hemisphere lateralization, which has allowed researchers to formulate questions about hemispheric asymmetries of attention in the healthy and damaged brain.

THE DORSAL ATTENTION NETWORK

Definition

Early evidence for a frontoparietal DAN came from blocked design studies with positron emission tomography (PET) in which subjects covertly directed attention to peripheral visual locations compared to appropriate control conditions (Corbetta et al., 1993; Nobre et al., 1997). The core regions identified include, bilaterally, dorsal parietal cortex along the medial wall of the ventral and posterior intraparietal sulcus (IPS) and in the superior parietal lobule (SPL), and dorsal frontal cortex along the precentral sulcus, near or at the intersection with the superior frontal sulcus (frontal eye field [FEF]). Additional regions include the motion sensitive area MT+ in visual cortex and regions along the medial wall near/at the supplementary eye field (SEF). These regions were similarly driven by covert and overt (eye movements) attention shifts (Corbetta et al., 1998; Nobre, 2001), consistent with the notion that shifts of spatial attention are functionally related to eye movement plans (Rizzolatti et al., 1997; Corbetta, 1998).

However, those early studies confounded signals for shifting attention with other signals like target detection, motor responses, and possible feedback signals from motor responses (Jack et al., 2006). A more accurate functional anatomy of signals related to shifting or maintaining attention was determined using functional magnetic resonance imaging (fMRI), which offered superior temporal resolution to PET (Buckner et al., 1996; Ollinger et al., 2001a,b). Attention signals were isolated by distinguishing between activity triggered by a cue directing attention to a location (or stimulus feature) and activity triggered by the presentation and detection of a target. These studies confirmed the recruitment of a small number of regions including ventral and medial IPS, SPL, FEF, SEF during the cue period (Figure 5.1A), and showed that the response in these regions is sustained as subjects maintain attention to a peripheral location (Kastner et al., 1999; Shulman et al., 1999; Corbetta et al., 2000; Hopfinger et al., 2000). The response is typically bilateral, but some regions also show evidence of spatial selectivity (Sylvester et al., 2007), with greater activity contralateral to the locus of attention. When attention is directed to the features of an object, similar regions are recruited, although some regional specialization has been reported (Shulman et al., 2002a; Giesbrecht et al., 2003; Mangun & Fannon, 2007; Slagter et al., 2007; Mangun et al., 2009).

An important recent development has been the advent of functional connectivity magnetic resonance imaging (fcMRI). Although the original observations date back nearly 15 years, only recently has the importance of this signal been recognized. FcMRI measures the temporal correlation of the blood oxygen level-dependent (BOLD) signal across multiple regions (Biswal et al., 1995). "Functionally connected" regions show strong low-frequency (<0.1 Hz) temporal correlations even when the subject is lying at rest with no task or stimulation. The signal is thought to reflect slow-frequency fluctuations of neuronal activity between anatomically connected areas (Fox & Raichle, 2007; He et al., 2008; de Pasquale et al., 2010), but also functional factors such as the history of regional coactivation or prior experience (Fox & Raichle, 2007; Lewis et al., 2009) This technique is very appealing for mapping brain networks, as patterns of functional connectivity

can be evaluated irrespective of task activation or subject performance.

A surprising result is that fcMRI not only identifies separate sensory and motor networks, but also several associative networks that maintain an independent level of correlation in their spontaneous activity (Toro et al., 2008; Smith et al., 2009). For example, regions of the dorsal frontoparietal network (MT+, ventral and medial IPS, SPL, FEF, SEF) that are active during shifts or maintenance of attention remain strongly correlated at rest (Figure 5.1A) and separate from the sensory and motor regions with which they interact during tasks (Fox et al., 2005b; He et al., 2007). Other associative networks include the default mode network (DMN) (Greicius et al., 2003; Fox et al., 2005b) (Figure 5.1A), the VAN (Fox et al., 2006; Shulman et al., 2009) (Figure 5.1B), and the frontoparietal and cingulo-opercular control networks (Dosenbach et al., 2006; Seeley et al., 2007; Vincent et al., 2008). A network corresponding to the human DAN and DMN has also been identified using fcMRI in anesthetized monkeys (Vincent et al., 2007), thus supporting interspecies homologies.

Functions

ORIENTING

In our original review, we proposed that the DAN was important for generating attentional sets and linking relevant stimulus to response (Corbetta & Shulman, 2002). It is well known that performance in a perceptual task is enhanced when subjects know in advance some properties of the target stimulus (Eriksen & Hoffman, 1973; Ball & Sekuler, 1980; Posner et al., 1980; Egeth et al., 1984; Dosher & Lu, 2000) as well as when they know what type of response is required (Rosenbaum, 1980; Abrams & Jonides, 1988). This attentional facilitation relies on the capacity to use the available information to create a "set" to bias the processing of the incoming information. The attentional set may code for stimulus position (location-based or spatial attention); other features, such as its shape, color, or direction of motion (feature-based attention); whole objects; or relevant responses (see Chapter 1).

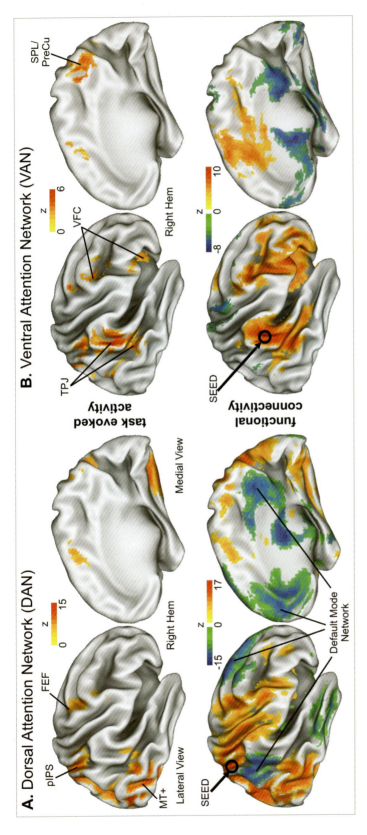

FIGURE 5.1 **(A)** Voxelwise statistical map (*upper row*) showing the key regions of the dorsal attention network (DAN). The map was obtained from a meta-analysis of several cueing experiments (Corbetta et al., 2000; Astafiev et al., 2003; Kincade et al., 2005), in which subjects were shown a cue instructing them to attend to a specific location in space prior to the onset of a target stimulus. The displayed activations reflect preparatory signals related to the cue, rather than signals related to target detection and the motor response. Activations are superimposed over a representation of the right hemisphere (fiducial surface, PALS Atlas, Caret 5.61; Van Essen, 2005). The color bar indicates the equivalent z-score from a voxelwise ANOVA testing for the presence of significant cue-related activity. The DAN is largely reproduced in the statistical map (*bottom row*) obtained using one of the key regions (pIPS) as a seed in a resting state functional connectivity analysis. The color scale reflects the equivalent z-score from a voxelwise random-effects one-sample t-test of whether the Fisher-z transformed correlation of the voxel with the seed region is different from zero. Positive and negative correlations with the seed region are represented by warm and cool colors, respectively. Regions that show significant negative correlations with the pIPS roughly reproduce the default mode network (DMN), possibly indicating a push-pull relationship between the two networks. **(B)** Voxelwise map (*upper row*) showing the key regions of the ventral attention network (VAN). These regions, obtained from the same metaanalysis as in **A**, are more activated by the detection of invalid compared to valid targets. The VAN is largely reproduced in the correlation map (*bottom row*) obtained using the right temporoparietal junction (TPJ) as a seed for functional magnetic resonance imaging (fcMRI). VFC, Ventral frontal cortex.

The role of the DAN in the implementation of attention sets and stimulus–response selection is based on the following observations. First, the DAN is focally recruited during purely endogenous allocation of spatial attention without confounding activity related to target analysis or detection (Kastner et al., 1999; Shulman et al., 1999; Corbetta et al., 2000). Second, similar DAN regions are recruited during the allocation of attention to features or objects (Shulman et al., 1999; Wojciulik & Kanwisher, 1999; Shulman et al., 2002a; Giesbrecht et al., 2003; Corbetta et al., 2005b; Slagter et al., 2007), although specialized subregions for specific features may exist (Mangun & Fannon, 2007). Third, these regions maintain a sustained response as attention is maintained over longer periods of time (tens of seconds) (Corbetta et al., 2002). Fourth, the level of preparatory activity in some DAN regions is predictive of performance to subsequent targets (Pessoa & Padmala, 2005; Sapir et al., 2005; Sylvester et al., 2007). Fifth, regions in IPS and FEF are recruited not only for covert spatial attention, but also when eye or hand movements are prepared (Corbetta et al., 1998; Nobre, 2001; Astafiev et al., 2003). Finally, neighboring medial and lateral parietal regions are recruited for other forms of control including shifts of stimulus-response mapping (medial) (Rushworth et al., 2001), and task sets (lateral) (Kimberg et al., 2000; Sohn et al., 2000).

The notion of a frontoparietal attention network has now been well accepted, not just in human cognitive neuroscience, but also in monkey primate neurophysiology. Although just 10 years ago the emphasis was on the dorsolateral prefrontal cortex (Desimone & Duncan, 1995; Miller & Cohen, 2001) as the main source of top-down signals in visual cortex, recent studies have focused on the DAN regions, including lateral intraparietal (LIP) and FEF (Moore & Armstrong, 2003; Buschman & Miller, 2009; Gregoriou et al., 2009; Herrington & Assad, 2009). In human cognitive neuroscience, there have been primarily four important developments over the last 5 years, reviewed below: the discovery of separate regions in frontoparietal cortex for shifting as opposed to maintaining attention; the discovery of retinotopic organization in regions of the DAN, which supports their role as saliency maps; the demonstration that these regions are the source of top-down biases onto visual cortex; and the separation of mechanisms for location versus feature or object coding.

EVIDENCE FOR SEPARATE DAN REGIONS FOR SHIFTING AND MAINTAINING ATTENTION

The precueing paradigms modeled after the Posner task that were used in early studies were ideal for separating cue from target activity (Kastner et al., 1999; Shulman et al., 1999; Corbetta et al., 2000), but they did not capture precisely the timing at which attention shifts between locations or stimulus features. In 2002, Steve Yantis and colleagues developed a procedure that time locks more precisely the fMRI signal to shifts of attention. Two streams of distracter stimuli are rapidly presented, one on each side of fixation. Cue stimuli embedded in the stream instruct subjects to either shift or stay on the same stream while their task is to detect a target, a specific object in the stream of distracters. Yantis and colleagues showed in a series of experiments that a similar region in medial parietal cortex is transiently active when attention is switched between locations (Yantis et al., 2002; Kelley et al., 2008), superimposed objects (Serences et al., 2004), modalities (Shomstein & Yantis, 2004), or between superimposed random dot arrays with different visual features (Liu et al., 2003). Interestingly, recent studies have also reported shift-related activity during switching between categorization or working memory rules (Chiu & Yantis, 2009; Rosenau et al., 2009). An early conclusion was that this region responded similarly irrespective of the domain, but a recent analysis using multivoxel pattern classifiers indicates that different neural populations respond within the same regions for shifting attention between different domains (Esterman et al., 2009). Serences and Yantis have proposed that this region may be important for enabling networks to "settle" into a state appropriate to the newly attended object (Serences & Yantis, 2006). This region, along with other prefrontal and parietal areas involved in switching between different categorization rules (Braver et al., 2003; Cools et al., 2004; Crone et al., 2006) may form a distinct frontoparietal network involved in cognitive control (Cole & Schneider, 2007; Dosenbach et al., 2008).

Shulman and colleagues recently used a modified version of the Yantis et al. paradigm to compare frontoparietal regions involved in maintaining lateralized spatial attention versus shifting attention from one to another location. In their experiment, salient color cues were embedded in one of two rapid visual presentation streams of natural objects (Shulman et al., 2009; Shulman et al., 2010) (Figure 5.2A), and subjects were instructed to pay attention to the stream indicated by the cue, which would contain infrequent target objects. By comparing images when attention was maintained or shifted to the left versus right stream of stimuli, they showed a clear dissociation between different frontoparietal regions. Regions along the medial bank of IPS, corresponding to those showing retinotopic maps (see below), and parts of FEF were more strongly modulated by attending to contralateral than ipsilateral stimuli, with sustained activations that were larger for shifting as compared to maintaining attention (Figure 5.2B). Regions in SPL and medial parietal cortex, including the region of Yantis et al., and other parts of FEF, instead showed strong but transient shift-related modulations (shift > > stay) that were less spatially selective (Figure 5.2C). These results, along with those of Yantis and colleagues (Yantis et al., 2002; Kelley et al., 2008) and retinotopic studies reviewed later, indicate a medial-to-lateral gradient, with nontopographic regions located more medially and topographic regions located more laterally in dorsal parietal cortex (see also similar gradient shown by Vandenberghe et al., 2001; Vandenberghe & Gillebert, 2009).

The functional segregation observed within the DAN makes sense since attention operates on spatially and non–spatially bound representations. Many forms of attention are object-based (e.g., shifts between overlapping objects, or between local and global scales of an object), and do not involve a change of location. Furthermore, neuronal representations originally used for sensory–motor transformations may have been co-opted to control shifts between higher-order cognitive categories, for example, semantic representations, based on learning-dependent mechanisms that have been shown in posterior parietal cortex (Stoet &

Snyder, 2004; Freedman & Assad, 2009). Important issues for the future will be to understand the flow of information between different control regions during a shift of attention, and how different subregions in the DAN control the flow of information in sensory and motor regions.

SALIENCY MAPS AND TOPOGRAPHIC ORGANIZATION OF DAN

Computational models of attention emphasize the importance of saliency maps, topographically organized representations coding for the behavioral relevance of objects (Koch & Ullman, 1985; Wolfe, 1994; Itti & Koch, 2001; Navalpakkam & Itti, 2005; see also Chapter 4 of this volume). These maps are thought to receive information from multiple sensory areas specialized for the analysis of different features and send back biasing signals to modulate their activity. In our original review, we proposed that regions in the DAN showed some of the physiological properties of a saliency map. Early studies by Schall and colleagues, and Gottlieb and colleagues had shown that neurons in FEF and LIP responded preferentially to behaviorally relevant stimuli, even when the sensory distinctiveness of objects was matched (Schall & Hanes, 1993; Gottlieb et al., 1998; Thompson & Schall, 1999). Brain imaging studies showed that regions in the DAN similar to the neurons in FEF and LIP responded preferentially to targets, and not to equally salient distracters (Shulman et al., 2001).

The formation of saliency maps requires mechanisms for coding stimulus location and stimulus relevance based on endogenous and exogenous information. Regions in the DAN seem to contain both sets of mechanisms.

Retinotopically organized responses in the DAN have been described by several groups (Sereno et al., 2001; Wandell et al., 2007; Silver & Kastner, 2009). Since the pioneering study by Sereno and colleagues (Sereno et al., 2001), who described a single topographic map of the contralateral hemifield in human medial IPS, several other groups have shown the presence of multiple maps along the IPS, near/at FEF, and additional maps in precuneus (PreCu), superior temporal

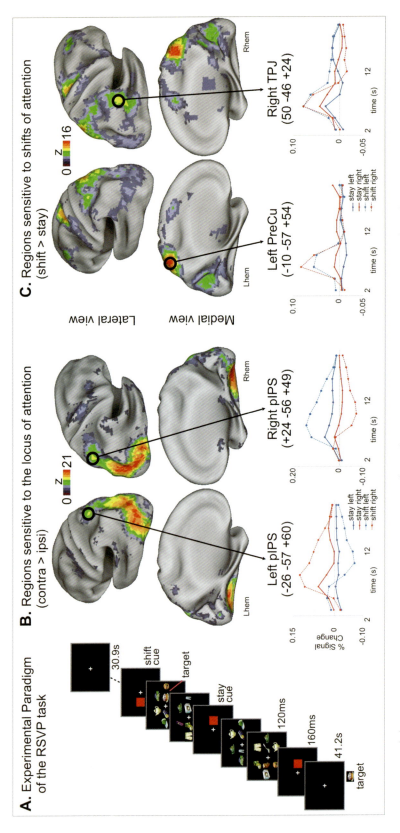

FIGURE 5.2 (A) Task structure of the rapid serial visual presentation (RSVP) paradigm used by Shulman and colleagues (2009). The target object to be detected was presented at the beginning of the scan. Following a fixation period (41.2 s), a red square (160 ms duration) cue indicated the RSVP stream in which targets would appear. Subsequent cues indicated targets would continue to appear in the currently attended stream (stay cues) or would appear in the opposite stream (shift cues). Successive cues were separated by 2.06, 4.12, or 6.18 s, while successive targets were separated on average by 10.5 s. The scan ended following a post-task fixation period (30.9 s). Adapted from Shulman, G. L., Astafiev, S. V., Franke, D, Pope, D. L., Snyder, A. Z., McAvoy, M. P., & Corbetta, M. (2009) Interaction of stimulus-driven reorienting and expectation in ventral and dorsal frontoparietal and basal ganglia-cortical networks. *Journal of Neuroscience, 29*, 4392–4407, with permission of the publisher. (B) Voxelwise map, obtained from a combined analysis of two RSVP experiments (Shulman et al., 2009); Tosoni et al., unpublished data) representing voxels more strongly modulated by attending to contralateral than ipsilateral stimuli. The map is superimposed on an inflated representation (PALS Atlas, Caret 5.61; Van Essen, 2005) of the left and right hemispheres. The color bar indicates the equivalent z-score for the p-value from a random-effects ANOVA testing for the effect of Cue Location on the time course

(*Continued on next page*)

FIGURE 5.2 (*Continued*)   of cue-evoked activity (Cue Location by Time). The graphs at the bottom represent time courses of blood oxygen level–dependent (BOLD) activity from specific regions of interest (ROIs; left and right posterior IPS [pIPS] regions) following stay (*full lines*) and shift cues (*broken lines*) to either the left (*blue*) or the right (*red*) hemifield. The contralateral preference is particularly strong following a shift of attention. (**C**) Voxelwise map representing voxels more strongly activated by shifting as compared to maintaining attention. The color bar indicates the equivalent z-score for the p-value from a random-effects ANOVA testing for a differential effect of cues that shift or maintain attention on the time course of cue-evoked activity (Attention [shift, stay] by Time.) The graphs at the bottom represent time courses of BOLD activity from a region of the left medial parietal cortex (PreCu) and a region of the right temporoparietal junction (TPG) showing strong but transient shift-related modulations (shift > > stay) that are less spatially selective compared to regions shown in **B**.

sulcus (STS), and at the junction of precentral and inferior frontal sulcus (IFJ) (Schluppeck et al., 2005; Silver et al., 2005; Hagler & Sereno, 2006; Hagler et al., 2007; Jack et al., 2007; Kastner et al., 2007; Swisher et al., 2007). A recent fMRI study reported a retinotopic map in monkey LIP, a likely homologue of one of the medial IPS regions (Patel et al., 2010).

However, the presence of retinotopic maps, albeit supportive of a role of these regions in location coding, does not necessarily explain how stimulus location is actually encoded. In contrast to visual cortex, where the majority of the signal is accounted for by a retinotopic organization, spatially selective signals represent only about 10% of the total signal within a map in posterior parietal cortex (Jack et al., 2007). There is a gradient moving from occipital to parietal cortex, whereby topographic signals (both retinotopy and contralateral selectivity) decrease in strength. Although this result may not be surprising given the general role of the DAN in selection, sorting out this issue will require painstaking analyses of response properties in different areas using different methods (retinotopy, eye position, multivoxel classifiers, etc.; see Konen & Kastner, 2008, for responses in IPS to location, motion, etc.).

The second mechanism that is required for a role of the DAN in saliency coding is the modulation of activity in these regions based on both cognitive expectations (see previous section) and the sensory distinctiveness of objects in the visual field (VF). Kincade et al. studied cue-related activity in dorsal (and ventral) frontoparietal regions following the presentation of different salient displays.

In one kind of display (exogenous orienting), a salient object marked a location of interest among other homogenous objects (e.g., a red square among green squares), whereas in a control display (neutral orienting) multiple objects of different colors were presented. In a control condition, locations were cued by symbolic instructions (endogenous orienting). Behaviorally, response times (RTs) to targets presented at exogenously cued locations were faster than to targets presented at control locations. fMRI scans showed stronger cue activity for endogenous attention in the DAN regions (IPS, FEF), but also stronger activity for exogenous than neutral cueing in FEF. These findings suggest that locations of interest can be selected either through endogenous or exogenous mechanisms implemented by DAN regions (Kincade et al., 2005). This result has been subsequently confirmed by other human studies (de Fockert et al., 2004; Serences et al., 2005; Indovina & Macaluso, 2007), and is consistent with similar findings in monkeys (Schall & Hanes, 1993; Gottlieb et al., 1998; Thompson & Schall, 1999).

TOP-DOWN INFLUENCE OF THE DAN ONTO SENSORY CORTICES

Although physiological recordings provide correlative evidence that frontoparietal regions in the DAN are the source of attention biases onto sensory cortex (Desimone & Duncan, 1995; Kastner & Ungerleider, 2000; Corbetta & Shulman, 2002; Reynolds & Chelazzi, 2004), more recent studies have provided direct causal evidence for this proposition. Moore and colleagues (see Chapter 7 of this volume) microstimulated FEF neurons and produced modulation of sensory activity in area V4 of the visual cortex in neurons with corresponding receptive fields (RFs) (Moore & Armstrong, 2003); FEF microstimulation also results in the modulation of the threshold for detection of a low-contrast stimulus (Moore & Fallah, 2001). Similar noninvasive studies have also been conducted in humans with combined transcranial magnetic stimulation (TMS) of IPS or FEF and simultaneous recordings of evoked patterns of fMRI activity in primary and extrastriate visual cortex (Ruff et al., 2006; Ruff et al., 2009). Notably, interference with parietal cortex produces changes in visual cortex during passive visual stimulation, whereas interference with the FEF produces endogenous changes that are stimulus independent. The functional significance of fMRI changes in visual cortex induced by TMS is supported by parallel changes in psychophysical sensitivity for stimuli presented at the same eccentricity (Ruff et al., 2006; Bestmann et al., 2007). More recently, TMS stimulation in FEF has been shown to increase the size of attention-dependent modulation in visual cortex for attended versus unattended locations (Blankenburg et al., 2010). A similar approach to Ruff et al. has been adopted by Vanduffel and colleagues in awake, behaving monkeys (Ekstrom et al., 2008; Ekstrom et al., 2009).

Although electrical or magnetic stimulation of cortical areas produces distant changes in cortical responses, this artificial stimulation may not be akin to a physiological top-down signal. An alternative approach has been to study patterns of physiological interaction between regions using statistical methods that inform about "causal" interactions. One such method is Granger causality, which estimates how much variance from one signal (e.g., time series recorded from FEF) explains the variance of another signal (e.g., a time series in visual cortex). Using this approach, Bressler and colleagues (Bressler et al., 2008) found that activity in the DAN during the cue period of a spatial attention task (Figure 5.3A) predicts activity in visual cortex (top-down influence) (Figure 5.3B-C). Overall, these studies make a powerful case for the DAN as a source of top-down control.

Future studies will need to concentrate on the actual neural mechanisms underlying this top-down interaction. This will require recordings of neural activity from both source and site regions simultaneously at high spatial and temporal resolution, as well as experiments in which physiological activity is disrupted at one site, at a moment at which that region is effectively communicating with another region.

One hypothesis that is gaining experimental traction is that neural activity in one group of neurons most strongly affects activity in a second group of neurons when their neural activity is synchronized or coherent (Fries, 2005). In the case of top-down biases, a control region may entrain oscillatory activity in visual neurons coding for an attended location, and not synchronize with visual neurons that code for an unattended location. This would facilitate the feedforward transmission of sensory responses at attended locations, as the excitability of visual neurons would be aligned with the excitability of higher-order regions. A number of studies have investigated local neuronal synchronization and demonstrated its relation to, for example, selective attention (Engel et al., 2001; Fries et al., 2001; Bichot et al., 2005; Taylor et al., 2005; Womelsdorf et al., 2006) and working-memory maintenance (Pesaran et al., 2002; Howard et al., 2003). There have been also a couple of studies that have shown γ synchronization between control regions (FEF, LIP) and visual sensory regions (V4, MT) (Gregoriou et al., 2009; Herrington & Assad, 2009), consistent with this hypothesis.

In humans, several MEG/EEG studies have shown large-scale synchronization of activity between frontoparietal and visual areas during top-down attention. Siegel et al. found synchronization both during the delay period between a cue and target, as well as during the stimulus interval (Siegel et al., 2008). The modulations were spatially and frequency specific, with a prominent drop of α/β synchronization during the delay in occipital cortex, followed by increased γ synchronization during stimulus processing. Interestingly, a recent combined TMS/EEG study provided evidence that interference with either posterior IPS or FEF during a cue–target delay (Figure 5.3D) abolished the physiological drop

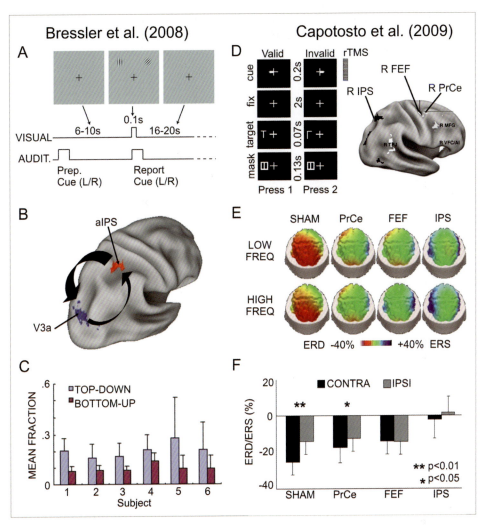

FIGURE 5.3 (**A**) Task structure of the study by Bressler and colleagues (2008), same as in Sylvester et al. (2007). Each trial began with an auditory preparatory cue indicating which of two peripheral locations subjects should covertly attend. After variable stimulus onset asynchronies (SOA), Gabor patches appeared briefly at both locations, coincident with an auditory cue indicating the target stimulus. Subjects reported the orientation of the Gabor at the target location with a button press. (**B**) The schematic diagram shows Granger causality represented as arrows in the two directions between a region of the DAN (aIPS) and a region of the visual cortex (V3A). Regions are illustrated on an inflated representation of the right hemisphere. Arrow thickness corresponds to the significant fraction representing Granger causality strength. (**C**) The mean fraction of significant F is significantly greater for top-down (*blue*) than for bottom-up (*red*) Granger causality when measured separately for each subject. (**D**) Task and rTMS localization in the study by Capotosto et al. (2009). The left panel illustrates task structure for valid and invalid trials. Subjects maintained central fixation. Every 5.9 + 1 seconds, a cue stimulus was presented for 200 ms duration, cueing randomly (50%) either a left or right visual field location. After 2 seconds, a target stimulus was briefly presented for 70 ms at one of two (left, right) target peripheral locations. The target stimulus was either the letter L (50%) or the letter T (50%) and could appear at either the cued (80%, valid) or the uncued (20%, invalid) location. Immediately after the target stimulus, a mask stimulus (130 ms duration) was presented to interrupt the visual processing of the target shape. The right panel illustrates the three rTMS sites over an inflated view of the right hemisphere with superimposed regions of dorsal and ventral attention networks as in the meta-analysis of He et al. (2007).

(*Continued on next page*)

FIGURE 5.3 (*Continued*)   (**E**) Topographic maps of anticipatory low- and high-α ERD/ERS during the cue period (+500–2,000 ms after the onset of the cue) as function of rTMS conditions. (F) Contralateral spatial selectivity of α power by rTMS condition. Group means (±SE) of the high-α ERD/ERS for the four conditions (Sham, Right PrCe, Right FEF, Right IPS) divided by hemisphere (contra or ipsi to cue stimulus). Adapted from Sylvester, C. M., Shulman, G. L., Jack, A. I., & Corbetta, M. (2007). Asymmetry of anticipatory activity in visual cortex predicts the locus of attention and perception. *Journal of Neuroscience, 27*, 14424–14433; Bressler, S. L., Tang, W., Sylvester, C. M., Shulman, G. L., & Corbetta, M. (2008). Top-down control of human visual cortex by frontal and parietal cortex in anticipatory visual spatial attention. *Journal of Neuroscience, 28*, 10056–10061; and Capotosto, P., Babiloni, C., Romani, G. L., & Corbetta, M. (2009). Frontoparietal cortex controls spatial attention through modulation of anticipatory alpha rhythms. *Journal of Neuroscience, 29*, 5863–5872, with permission of the publishers.

of α/β synchronization in occipital cortex (Figure 5.3E–F), which led to impaired detection of subsequently presented targets (Capotosto et al., 2009). This study is direct evidence that frontoparietal regions influence the synchronization of activity in visual cortex prior to stimulus presentation, and that interference with such synchronization has detrimental effects on perception.

SEPARATE MECHANISMS FOR THE SELECTION OF SPATIAL LOCATIONS AND OBJECT FEATURES IN VISUAL CORTEX

It is now well established that attention has a number of modulatory effects on the sensory evoked response to visual stimuli, including an increment of the response to attended stimuli, which, depending on task/stimuli, may appear as a gain increase or an additive modulation; an attenuation of the response to unattended stimuli; a synchronization of the oscillatory activity time-locked to the presentation of the attended stimulus; and a reduction in the correlation of low-frequency noise. One important advance of the last 5 years has been that of imaging anticipatory signals simultaneously in frontoparietal regions and visual cortex with the goal of understanding how spatial attention biases visual representations.

Early neurophysiological studies from extrastriate visual cortex showed that when an animal was covertly directing attention to a peripheral location, the baseline neuronal activity representing that location would increase (Luck et al., 1997). This led to the idea that attention provides a competitive advantage to to-be-attended objects among all the objects represented in visual cortex (Desimone & Duncan, 1995). Similar baseline increases were observed in posterior parietal cortex, one of the possible sources of the bias, during the tonic allocation of attention to a peripheral location (Colby et al., 1996). Next, we consider how these top-down modulations intervene on visual cortex. Human neuroimaging studies provided additional support for this idea, showing parallel prestimulus increases both in frontoparietal regions and attended locations in visual cortex (Kastner et al., 1999; Hopfinger et al., 2000; Muller et al., 2003; Serences et al., 2004; Sylvester et al., 2007; Sestieri et al., 2008; Sylvester et al., 2008). However, more recent studies have clearly shown that the situation is more complicated as the landscape of anticipatory signals in visual cortex is more widespread than previously appreciated (Silver et al., 2007; Sylvester et al., 2007; Sestieri et al., 2008; Sylvester et al., 2008). For instance the paper by Sylvester et al. (2007) shows that an area of relative increase at an attended location in one visual quadrant is bordered by a large region of deactivation in the fovea and by a shallower response in the other visual quadrant (Figure 5.4A–B). Furthermore, corresponding changes can be recorded in the ipsilateral visual cortex with a strong positive trial-to-trial correlation (Figure 5.4C) that is greater between homologous representations in visual cortex (e.g., fovea–fovea).

The presence of interhemispheric correlated noise on a trial-to-trial basis has never been reported in single-unit experiments because electrodes are typically not placed simultaneously on both sides

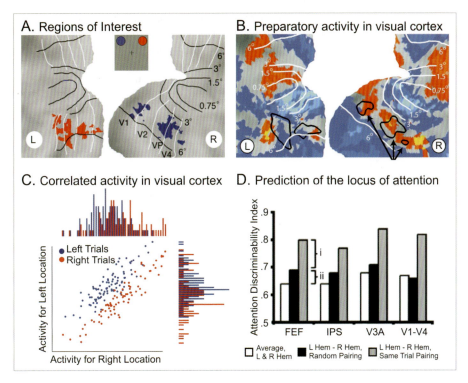

FIGURE 5.4 (**A**) Visual cortex contains a retinotopic map in which nearby portions of cortex represent nearby portions of space. Representations of the target locations in the experimental task (Sylvester et al., 2007), as well as unattended locations in the lower and central fields, are displayed on a flattened view of early visual cortex. These outlines are based on independent localizer scans. (**B**) Covert attention to a particular location, in the absence of visual stimulation, modulates activity representing all locations. Endogenous BOLD activity after cues to covertly attend to the top left target location (5-degree eccentricity) in the absence of visual stimulation. Note the swath of positive modulation corresponding to the attended location for each condition. BOLD activity in early visual cortex corresponding to the rest of the visual field is mostly negative. This pattern creates a sharp peak of activity at the portion of visual cortex representing the attended location. (**C**) Activity in portions of cortex representing the left and right target locations is positively correlated across trials. The plot represents trial-by-trial preparatory activity in the portion of visual cortex representing the right location (left hemisphere) versus preparatory activity in the portion representing the left location (right hemisphere). Each dot represents a single trial. The histograms on the x and y axes are projections of the trial data and display the distributions of preparatory activity for the left and right hemispheres, respectively. Although the signal related to the locus of spatial attention goes in opposite directions for regions from opposite hemispheres, preparatory activity is nevertheless positively correlated across trials. (**D**) Comparing activity between portions of cortex representing the two target locations dramatically improves decoding of the locus of attention compared with measuring activity for a single location. This improvement is mostly caused by removal of positively correlated activity. Bars in the graph indicate how well the activity in each region (dorsal attention network [DAN] regions: frontal eye field [FEF], intraparietal sulcus [IPS]; visual cortex: V3A, V1–V4) discriminates between leftward and rightward cued trials, according to different decoding schemes. White bars indicate sampling only one of the two target locations, gray bars indicate comparing cortical activity for left and right locations on the same trial, and black bars indicate comparing activity when the trial pairings are randomly assigned. The bracket (i) represents the increase in the Attention Discriminability Index (ADI) caused by the removal of positively correlated activity. The bracket (ii) shows the increase in the ADI caused by the constructive combination of signals related to the locus of attention that go in opposite directions. The subtractions (*black and gray bars*) are between homologous regions in opposite hemispheres. Adapted from Sylvester, C. M., Shulman, G. L., Jack, A. I., & Corbetta, M. (2007). Asymmetry of anticipatory activity in visual cortex predicts the locus of attention and perception. *Journal of Neuroscience, 27,* 14424–14433, with permission of the publisher.

of the brain, but it appears to be functionally important. Receiving Operator Characteristics (ROC) analysis predicting the locus of attention (left vs. right) based on cue-related activity at the attended location only shows modest prediction (~.60 prediction, with chance = .50), but a much stronger prediction (~.80 at a single trial level) is obtained when subtracting from activity at the attended location activity from the homologous location in the opposite visual cortex (Figure 5.4D). That a coding scheme based on the subtraction of two signals is more efficient depends on two different signals that work in opposite directions: a relative gradient with stronger contralateral than ipsilateral preparatory activity; and a trial-to-trial positive correlation between homologous loci in visual cortex that significantly decreases signal-to-noise at a single location. A similar scheme was also demonstrated in dorsal areas (IPS and FEF) known to be sources of attention and matches neurophysiological evidence from Bisley and Goldberg (2003), who found a similar mechanism at the level of single neurons in area LIP (see also Chapter 8 of this volume). However, a significant problem of this relative coding scheme is that downstream representations must integrate information from both visual cortices to obtain a good estimate of the locus of attention.

Very similar mapwise anticipatory modulations have been reported in human electroencephalogram/magnetoencephalogram (EEG/MEG) studies. Directing attention in anticipation of a visual stimulus is known to decrease α/β power in the occipital lobe; when the stimulus is lateralized the α/β suppression is also lateralized with stronger suppression contralaterally to the side of attention (Sauseng et al., 2005; Babiloni et al., 2006; Thut et al., 2006; Siegel et al., 2008). Trial-to-trial fluctuations of contra-ipsi bias in α/β power has been shown to correlate with the efficiency of attentional allocation as measured by faster reaction times to subsequent targets (Thut et al., 2006). Moreover, TMS interference with anticipatory activity in human IPS and FEF has been shown to interfere with the α/β power desynchronization and disrupt this lateralized bias in visual cortex (Capotosto et al., 2009) (Figure 5.3E–F). Taken together, both BOLD and EEG/MEG studies suggest the importance of the gradient of activity

across the hemispheres for the control of visual attention. Correspondingly, lesion data indicate that disruption of this gradient correlates with deficits of spatial attention (Corbetta et al., 2005a; He et al., 2007; Carter et al., 2010).

Attention can also be allocated to features and objects, even in the presence of complete spatial uncertainty (Wolfe, 1994). Features like color are important for the early segregation of a visual scene, and this operation occurs typically over the whole VF (Treisman & Gelade, 1980; Julesz, 1981; Nothdurft, 1993; Wolfe, 1994). Although it is possible to allocate attention to a single feature typically, attention operates at the object level, and multiple features of an object become available once one feature is selected (Duncan, 1984). Different objects compete in a visual scene, and attention biases the representation of the attended object at the expense of unattended objects (Desimone & Duncan, 1995).

At the neural level, early neuroimaging evidence suggested that attention could modulate feature-specific maps in visual cortex (Corbetta et al., 1990, 1991). Later studies suggested that this modulation occurs across the VF and is relatively independent of the locus of attention (Treue & Martinez Trujillo, 1999; Saenz et al., 2002; Martinez-Trujillo & Treue, 2004; Serences & Boynton, 2007). Selection of one feature of an object with a relative modulation in visual cortex leads to the automatic selection of another feature of that object (O'Craven et al., 1999). More recently, top-down object-related biases have been identified using multivoxel fMRI classifiers. One study (Reddy et al., 2009) showed that attention biases as a weighted average multivoxel classification for the attended object. Another study showed a category-specific biasing mechanism operating in parallel across the VF in object-selective cortex (Peelen et al., 2009).

A number of studies have concentrated on identifying sources of feature or object biases onto visual cortex (see Chapter 1 of this volume). In general, the dorsal frontoparietal network shows anticipatory signals both for feature and objects, although some regional specialization has been identified. Explicit comparisons between cues for location and color (Giesbrecht et al., 2003; Slagter et al., 2007) for motion and color

(Shulman et al., 2002a; Mangun & Fannon, 2007) and for location and motion (Mangun et al., 2009) indicate both the presence of common and specific regions of the DAN that are specialized for different kinds of attentional selection.

VENTRAL ATTENTION NETWORK

Definition

In contrast to the fairly focal pattern of activation observed in dorsal frontoparietal regions during the preparatory interval between an attention cue and a target, a much broader set of brain areas is activated by target detection (Shulman et al., 1999; Corbetta et al., 2000; Hopfinger et al., 2000). However, a more restricted subset of regions is modulated by the validity of the target; that is, whether a target appears at an unattended (invalidly cued) or attended (validly cued) location. These regions include, in addition to dorsal regions SPL/precuneus, IPS, and FEF, the posterior sector of the superior temporal sulcus (STS) and gyrus (STG) and the ventral part of the supramarginal gyrus (SMG) (what we call temporoparietal junction [TPJ]), and middle frontal gyrus (MFG), inferior frontal gyrus (IFG), frontal operculum, and anterior insula (what we call collectively the ventral frontal cortex [VFC]). All these regions respond more strongly to invalid than valid targets, and show lateralization to the right hemisphere (Figure 5.1B). In our review (Corbetta & Shulman, 2002), we proposed that ventral frontoparietal regions TPJ and VFC form a ventral frontoparietal network specialized in *stimulus-driven reorienting* that co-activates with the dorsal network when a novel behaviorally relevant event occurs in the environment (see functions in the following section).

The existence of this right hemisphere–dominant VAN has been confirmed by many studies from different labs around the world (Arrington et al., 2000; Corbetta et al., 2000; Downar et al., 2000; Macaluso et al., 2002; Shulman et al., 2009). A search on Google Scholar with keywords "ventral frontoparietal network AND attention" yields over 5,000 citations. Two especially important advances in the definition of the VAN have occurred in the last few years. First, the demonstration of the VAN as an independent functional network has been confirmed by studies of fcMRI. Second, the right hemisphere dominance of the VAN has been confirmed by quantitative studies of task-evoked activity as well as by fcMRI.

As reviewed in the previous section, studies of fMRI connectivity have recently confirmed that regions of the VAN maintain, even at rest, a high level of temporal correlation (Fox et al., 2006; He et al., 2007; Liu et al., 2009; Shulman et al., 2009) that is independent from that observed in the DAN (Figure 5.1B). However, a region in right lateral prefrontal cortex shares common variance with both networks and could represent a pivot point (Fox et al., 2006; He et al., 2007). A region at the junction of the inferior frontal sulcus with precentral sulcus (IFJ, inferior frontal junction) also shows task-evoked properties that are common to both networks (Asplund et al., 2010).

Notably, the VAN is one of the few networks in the brain that shows a strong hemispheric lateralization in the resting state (Liu et al., 2009). As a matter of fact, a very consistent finding in studies of functional connectivity is the prominent strong temporal correlation at rest between homologous regions in the two hemispheres. This correlation depends on the intactness of the corpus callosum (Johnston et al., 2008). However, activity in right SMG, the posterior core of the VAN, tends to correlate with other intrahemispheric regions in the inferior frontal gyrus, and shows relatively modest interhemispheric correlations. Because the SMG has undergone a large nonlinear expansion in the human brain as compared to macaque (Van Essen & Dierker, 2007), callosal connectivity in this region may be organized differently than in other brain regions.

The right hemisphere lateralization found at rest in the VAN is maintained during tasks, albeit not to the same extent in all paradigms. For instance, although the comparison between invalidly versus validly cued spatial targets shows robust right hemisphere dominance (Corbetta et al., 2000; Astafiev et al., 2006), task-driven deactivations of TPJ (see below) are more bilaterally organized (Shulman et al., 2003; Todd et al., 2005; Shulman et al., 2007). Conversely, right hemisphere lateralization during the detection of auditory oddballs is widespread but not centered within the VAN (Stevens et al., 2005).

In a recent study, Shulman and colleagues quantitatively compared left and right hemisphere activations during a paradigm in which spatial attention was shifted to salient visual cues. Shift signals were fairly symmetrical in the dorsal system, with equal strength activation in left or right IPS-FEF regions, but strong right lateralization was observed in the TPJ (Shulman et al., 2010). A recent study by Szczepansky and colleagues reported some asymmetrical activations in the dorsal network, but the direction of the asymmetry was not consistent over regions, and signals for shifting attention were not separated from sensory-evoked modulations (Szczepanski et al., 2010).

Functions

STIMULUS-DRIVEN CONTROL OF ATTENTION: EXOGENOUS VERSUS CONTINGENT ORIENTING

The enhancement observed in the ventral (and dorsal) network for unattended versus attended targets could be related to a number of different signals. One possibility is that unattended (typically low-frequency) stimuli trigger an exogenous orienting response (Posner & Cohen, 1984; Muller & Rabbitt, 1989). Another possibility is that the ventral network detects a stimulus-driven mismatch with ongoing task goals and provides a reorienting signal (or circuit-breaker) to the dorsal network. Although both hypotheses were clearly discussed in our review (Corbetta & Shulman, 2002) many studies in the literature have emphasized the first hypothesis, equating the VAN with an exogenous orienting network. Subsequent work, however, has unequivocally demonstrated that exogenous orienting does not involve the VAN when the sensory stimuli that orient attention are not behaviorally relevant (de Fockert et al., 2004; Kincade et al., 2005; Indovina & Macaluso, 2007). Under these conditions, dorsal regions thought to house saliency maps sensitive to both sensory and behavioral relevance are modulated (see previous section on sensory salience). However, the VAN (at least the TPJ) is highly sensitive to "contingent orienting"; that is, orienting to sensory stimuli that are behaviorally relevant or important for the current goal (Folk et al., 1992). For example, Serences and

colleagues showed that right TPJ responds to colored peripheral distracters only when the color matches that of a to-be-detected target in a foveal stream of stimuli (Serences et al., 2005; see also Natale et al., 2010). Recently, Shulman and colleagues have shown a physiological distinction between posterior and anterior nodes of the VAN. Although right TPJ always shows a response for stimulus-driven shifts of attention, VFC as well as anterior cingulate does so only when the stimuli occur infrequently. This result suggests that TPJ acts as a switch signal, whereas VFC is activated only when an ongoing task set is reconfigured.

NOT JUST SPATIAL REORIENTING

Although most studies on the VAN have been performed using spatial attention paradigms, ventral frontoparietal regions also are recruited during paradigms that do not require a spatial shift of attention. For example, both dorsal and ventral attention regions respond to target stimuli (oddballs) that appear infrequently in a stream of frequent stimuli (McCarthy et al., 1997; Linden et al., 1999; Marois et al., 2000; Braver et al., 2001; Bledowski et al., 2004; Stevens et al., 2005). Right TPJ and IFG are also observed under passive conditions when a stream of sensory stimuli changes unexpectedly, not just in the visual but also in the tactile and auditory modality (Downar et al., 2000).

More recent evidence supports the view that the ventral attention system exhibits a reorienting response in a much broader sense. For example, several studies suggest that the VAN responds to event transitions or event boundaries (Zacks et al., 2001), such as when an event or behavior is interrupted and a new one is initiated. Furthermore, the VAN, along with other cortical regions, is activated at the time of a task transition, when the paradigm switches between sustained periods of rest and task (Konishi et al., 2001; Fox et al., 2005a; Dosenbach et al., 2006). Also, in the course of a single trial, both the VAN and the DAN are co-activated at task offset, possibly signaling the end of a task set (Shulman et al., 2002b). Importantly, in most of these paradigms (with the exception of event boundaries in temporal segmentation experiments; Zacks et al., 2001) sensory stimuli clearly mark the event or task transitions, hence the notion that reorienting is driven by stimuli in the environment (or *stimulus-driven reorienting*).

A possible interpretation is that the ventral network provides a reset signal that helps the reorganization of behavior to new goals or tasks (see below for a possible physiological basis of this hypothesis). Importantly, the same response is not observed when task changes are frequent or expected or part of the overall task set, as in classic task-switching paradigms, which seem to activate more dorsal parietal and frontal regions.

SOURCES OF TASK RELEVANCE IN VAN, AND FILTERING OF IRRELEVANT SENSORY INFORMATION

The observations that the VAN responds to stimuli that are not only salient but also behaviorally relevant, and does not respond to equally salient distracters (Serences et al., 2005), suggest that VAN regions receive information about task relevance from elsewhere in the brain. As the dorsal network is one of the main sources of endogenous expectations during visual behavior, it would be logical to assume that the same dorsal regions are also the source of task relevance signals in the VAN. A few years ago, we reported a striking dissociation between profiles of activation in DAN and VAN regions during visual search that are consistent with this hypothesis. Shulman and colleagues (2003; 2007) had subjects search for infrequent targets (digits) among a rapid serial visual presentation (RSVP) stream of letters (Figure 5.5A). Although dorsal regions (IPS, FEF) showed a sustained activation during search, a sustained deactivation was observed in TPJ (Figure 5.5B) and in lateral and inferior prefrontal cortex, regions strongly overlapping with those involved in spatial reorienting. Our interpretation was that dorsal regions deactivated TPJ to suppress involuntary stimulus driven reorienting to distracting sensory information (Shulman et al., 2003). Consistent with this idea, the degree of deactivation correlates with higher performance on the visual search task (Shulman et al., 2007). Deactivations of right TPJ have also been also reported in studies of visual working memory load (Todd et al., 2005; Anticevic et al., 2010). In Todd et al. (2005),

greater working memory loads produced larger deactivations of the TPJ and greater impairments in target detection, supporting a unitary explanation for the TPJ activation during reorienting and TPJ deactivation during search.

RIGHT TPJ ACTIVITY DURING THEORY OF MIND

In addition to its well-characterized role in attention, right TPJ has been recently highlighted as one of the core regions of a network for social cognition and theory of mind (ToM), which refers to the ability to reason about other people's mental states (Fletcher et al., 1995; Gallagher & Frith, 2003). In typical ToM paradigms, subjects either watch scenes or read stories that involve people, and then judge the character's beliefs by answering questions. In a control condition, typically, subjects watch scenes or read stories that involve relationships between physical objects, and then answer questions about the objects. The ToM condition produces a larger activation or lesser deactivation in right TPJ compared to the control condition.

A strong interpretation of these findings is that right TPJ is a module for ToM that is uniquely developed in the human brain and that emerges at about 24 months in the developing brain (Saxe, 2006). However, this conclusion does not fit well with the attention literature reviewed above. Direct comparisons of the topography of attention-related versus ToM-related activity in right TPJ yield very similar regions, although there is controversy concerning whether the ToM region is nonetheless slightly different; e.g., slightly more posterior (Decety & Lamm, 2007; Mitchell, 2008; Scholz et al., 2009).

To the extent that the regions are the same, Occam's principle suggests that a unifying process may explain both sets of activations. We believe that an attention-related explanation remains more likely. First, the stimuli used in ToM experiments have been modified from developmental studies, and tend to be complex (stories, vignettes) and hence more difficult to control. In most experiments these stimuli are presented in a block design, which does not allow separation of the many different processes involved in stimulus and

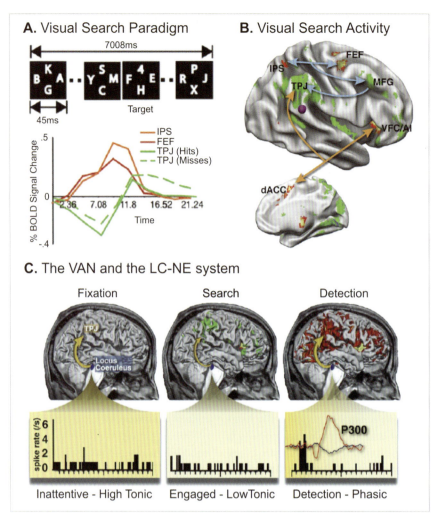

FIGURE 5.5   (**A**) Task structure of the visual search paradigm used by Shulman et al. (2003, 2007). Subjects searched a rapid serial visual presentation (RSVP) display for a target digit. The number of distracter frames containing only letters prior to the target frame containing the target was varied, determining a variable search duration across trials. The graph shows the time course of activity in dorsal regions frontal eye field (FEF) and intraparietal sulcus (IPS) and ventral region temporoparietal junction (TPJ) under conditions in which the target appeared near the end of the trial. In TPJ, a deactivation to the letter distracters was followed by an activation when the digit was presented or the trial was terminated. Interestingly, the deactivation to the letters was significantly greater when the subsequent digit was detected than when it was missed. Conversely, IPS and FEF showed sustained activations during search. (B) The filtering hypothesis. The statistical map shows regions with sustained activity as subjects searched through letter distracters in the RSVP experiment, including dorsal attention regions IPS and FEF (red/orange in surface-rendered brain) but also regions in anterior insula and anterior cingulate that form a putative task-control network (Dosenbach et al., 2006). These regions may send top-down signals (see arrows) to the ventral network, which showed sustained deactivations during search (blue/green in surface-rendered brain), restricting its input to task-relevant objects. (C) Relationship between activity in TPJ and locus coeruleus/noradrenergic system. The surface-rendered brains show fMRI BOLD activations and deactivations relative to when subjects are fixating in an otherwise blank field (i.e., the baseline, left panel), when searching through letter distracters of an RSVP display (same as in B) and when detecting the target. The bottom panel shows spiking activity in monkey locus coeruleus neurons during analogous periods: an inattentive period in which a task is poorly performed and tonic activity is high, an attentive period in

linguistic analysis, attention, working memory, and error detection. To date, no satisfactory analysis has been carried out of the comparability of ToM and control stimuli in terms of their linguistic complexity or dependence on working memory. All these factors may be important contributors to the ToM response in right TPJ. For example, we know from previous work that TPJ is more deactivated by stimuli or conditions that are also more demanding in terms of perceptual or working memory load. Theory of mind stories, as compared to physical stories, tend to be easier and lead to faster reaction times. Although a very limited set of stories has been used in most experiments, the sign of the response in TPJ during ToM experiments varies across papers (activation in some, e.g., Saxe & Kanwisher, 2003; deactivation in others, e.g., Mitchell, 2008) for reasons that are not clear. To the extent that deactivation is the true description, greater TPJ "activation" to ToM stories (minus physical stories) could simply reflect a weaker load on working memory.

Right TPJ activation during ToM may also reflect a simpler attention process broadly related to stimulus-driven reorienting. Theory of mind stories contain unexpected twists (Vogeley et al., 2001; Gallagher & Frith, 2003), which can generate breaches of expectation that, in turn, modulate TPJ (Arrington et al., 2000; Corbetta et al., 2000; Macaluso et al., 2002), although controls for this factor have been employed (Young et al., 2010). Theory of mind stories may contain information that drives lateral temporal regions involved in biological motion as during shifts, perception, or imagery of eye gaze (Allison et al., 2000; Pelphrey et al., 2003; Pelphrey et al., 2004), or during the perception of one's own body (Blanke & Arzy, 2005; Arzy et al., 2006). It is also possible, according to a broader view of the VAN as a network that

helps the reorganization of behavior to new goals or tasks, that reorienting processes in TPJ may be co-opted in the case of ToM processing to switching between internal, bodily, or self-perspective and external, environmental, or other's viewpoint, a key ingredient of ToM cognition.

Importantly, during ToM, right TPJ is typically co-activated with other regions, such as medial prefrontal cortex and posterior cingulate/precuneus, which belong to the default mode network (Shulman et al., 1997; Raichle et al., 2001; Greicius et al., 2003), a network distinct from the VAN. Yet, resting-state fcMRI studies have consistently shown that seeds placed in the right TPJ region involved in reorienting do not correlate with the default network (Fox et al., 2006; He et al., 2007; Shulman et al., 2009). It would be very useful to check the resting-state connectivity of right TPJ foci activated during ToM tasks.

THE VAN AND THE LC-NE SYSTEM

As reviewed earlier, the VAN is generally activated by the violation of expectations that indicates the need for an update of the current model. Along with other neuromodulators (Dayan & Yu, 2006), the norepinephrine system that originates from the locus coeruleus (LC-NE) has been strongly associated with shifts of attention to unexpected and behaviorally important stimuli. Locus coeruleus neurons exhibit both tonic and phasic activity modes (Figure 5.5C). The tonic activity is low during states of low arousal (Aston-Jones & Bloom, 1981; Rajkowski et al., 1994), moderate during the maintenance of the attentional set (Usher et al., 1999), and high during states of exploration and "unexpected uncertainty" (Aston-Jones et al., 1997). Decrease in tonic activity has been reported during the delay period between a warning

FIGURE 5.5 (*Continued*)   which the task is performed well and tonic activity is decreased, and target detection, which produces a phasic increase in activity (Usher et al., 1999). The inset trace shows event-related potentials recorded from the scalp of a human when a target is detected in a completely separate experiment, with the large positive deflection indicating the P300. Adapted from Corbetta, M., Patel, G., & Shulman, G. L. (2008). The reorienting system of the human brain: From environment to theory of mind. *Neuron, 58*, 306–324, with permission of the publisher.

temporal cue and a rewarded target stimulus (Bouret & Sara, 2005), and may reflect the higher utility associated with the detection of upcoming target stimuli (Aston-Jones & Cohen, 2005). The phasic activity is instead observed in response to target stimuli and is mainly generated during the moderate tonic mode. The phasic response may facilitate the output from the target-related network (Aston-Jones & Cohen, 2005), or instead represent an "interrupt" (Dayan & Yu, 2006) or "network reset" signal (Bouret & Sara, 2005). Interestingly, the reduced tonic LC activity observed during a task-focused state strongly resembles the sustained TPJ deactivation observed during RSVP and working memory paradigms. Furthermore, the phasic response in the LC is strikingly similar to the target-related response in the VAN and the P300 potentials, an electroencephalographic index of target detection in TPJ and VFC (Knight et al., 1989; Yamaguchi & Knight, 1991; Menon et al., 1997; Daffner et al., 2003; Bledowski et al., 2004). In fact, all of these responses share a similar multimodal property and an enhanced response to infrequent targets. Overall, there seems to be a strong functional parallel between the activity of the LC-NE system and the VAN that can further advance the understanding of the neural mechanism involved in attentional operations. Recent studies have attempted to image activity in the LC with fMRI (Minzenberg et al., 2008), but important technical challenges remain (Astafiev et al., 2010). Future investigations could involve parallel recordings of LC and TPJ activity to confirm this hypothesis.

INTERACTIONS BETWEEN DORSAL AND VENTRAL ATTENTION NETWORKS

INTERACTIONS BETWEEN VAN AND DAN DURING REORIENTING: TIMING

Although the ventral and the dorsal attention systems are both involved in stimulus-driven reorienting, a significant hole in our functional anatomical model is some understanding of the dynamics with which these networks interact. Earlier, we discussed the possibility that the ventral network receives suppressive modulation from the dorsal network during demanding perceptual or working memory tasks, but there is no information on how the two networks interact when a salient sensory stimulus grabs our attention. We originally hypothesized that the VAN acts as a "circuit breaker" that sends fast latency signal to dorsal regions that are eventually responsible for the actual reorienting (Corbetta & Shulman, 2002), since regions of the DAN, unlike the VAN (Corbetta & Shulman, 2002; Macaluso et al., 2002; Hagler & Sereno, 2006; Jack et al., 2007; Macaluso & Patria, 2007), show clear evidence of both spatial selectivity and oculomotor properties that are necessary for the overt and covert reorienting of attention. According to this hypothesis, activation of the VAN should precede that of the DAN, but the present experimental evidence, although not conclusive, suggests a different temporal relationship. Several EEG/MEG studies have reported a characteristic target-related potential (P300) whose properties are very similar to those of the VAN, and lesion studies indicated that TPJ is critical for the generation of the P300 (Knight et al., 1989; Yamaguchi & Knight, 1991; Menon et al., 1997; Daffner et al., 2003; Bledowski et al., 2004). This latency is considerably longer than visual response latency to targets for an eye movement in the dorsal network (130–170 ms; Evdokimidis et al., 2001; McDowell et al., 2005; Sestieri et al., 2007). Other event-related potential (ERP)/MEG studies during spatial reorienting do not provide clear results concerning the relative latency of dorsal and ventral parietal regions (Mangun & Hillyard, 1991; Luck et al., 1994). On the other hand, TMS studies support a key role for the VAN in reorienting attention and detecting targets in conjunction with dorsal frontoparietal regions (IPS, FEF). Virtual lesions of the inferior parietal lobule (TPJ, SMG, AG) negatively affect target detection and reorienting at latencies ranging from 90 to 120 ms (Chambers et al., 2004) to 200 to 300 ms following target onset (Chambers et al., 2004; Ellison et al., 2004; Meister et al., 2006). Overall, the available evidence suggests that, although reorienting is probably initiated in the DAN, in conjunction with subcortical structures, the VAN may be necessary for slower regulation involved in more complex operations such as shifts of task sets, expectations, reward contingencies, and arousal.

INTERACTIONS BETWEEN VAN AND DAN: SYNDROME OF SPATIAL NEGLECT

Hemispatial neglect is a spatial attention syndrome characterized by a deficit to attend, respond to, and even conceive stimuli in the contralesional hemifield (Mesulam, 1981; Heilman et al., 1987; Mesulam, 1999). Interestingly, neglect patients may exhibit both spatial (particularly affecting one side of the VF) and nonspatial (vigilance/ arousal and spatial/temporal capacity) deficits. This distinction is reminiscent of the functional properties of the two attention networks: The DAN contains spatially selective and eye movement signals, as well as maps of contralateral space, whereas the VAN responds to targets that are novel and behaviorally relevant, hence more arousing, in a spatially nonspecific way. However, neglect is typically associated with lesions that selectively involve regions of the VAN and underlying white matter (Vallar & Perani, 1987; Husain & Kennard, 1996; Mort et al., 2003; Karnath et al., 2004) (Figure 5.6A). Corbetta and colleagues have proposed a model of neglect according to which anatomical lesions of the ventral network cause abnormal functioning of the dorsal network due to defective interaction between networks (Corbetta et al., 2005a; He et al., 2007) (Figure 5.6B-E). In a longitudinal study of 11 patients with neglect, the authors found that, although the parietal nodes of the DAN were intact, they nonetheless exhibited an interhemispheric imbalance of task-evoked activity (Figure 5.6B) that correlated with the severity of the spatial deficits. Activity of the ventral network was instead correlated with the speed of detection of unattended targets irrespective of spatial location (Corbetta et al., 2005a).

In a follow-up study, they measured functional connectivity in the same patients and demonstrated that disrupted interhemispheric connectivity within the DAN (Figure 5.6C) correlated with the severity of spatial neglect at 2 weeks post-stroke, and that the functional connectivity was improved at 9 months, in parallel with the improvement of spatial neglect. In contrast, disrupted connectivity between nodes of the VAN correlated with poor performance in both fields, consistent with the nonspatial selectivity of the response of VAN

regions' to targets. Importantly, the degree of spatial neglect across subjects correlated with the presence of white matter damage in the superior longitudinal fascicle connecting anterior to posterior brain regions, which in turn negatively impacted the correlation between left and right DAN regions. Finally, the strength of the correlation between anterior and posterior nodes of the VAN correlated with the degree of interhemispheric DAN connectivity dysfunction, suggesting that intact communication in VAN regions corresponds to better communication in DAN regions. These results are consistent with a large body of behavioral literature that suggest an interaction between vigilance and spatial attention in healthy and brain-injured subjects (Robertson, 2001).

FUTURE DIRECTIONS

The notion of two attention networks for orienting and reorienting has been extremely helpful in guiding neuroscience research on attention in healthy humans and for studying the pathophysiology of attention deficits in neurologically impaired individuals.

Although the separation between voluntary or goal-driven, and automatic or stimulus-driven orienting traces back to William James, and has been embraced by nearly 50 years of psychological research emphasizing the differences between these forms of orienting, neuroimaging has shown us that these two forms of orienting are mediated at different time scales by the same neural system, the DAN. In contrast, stimulus-driven reorienting seems to rely uniquely on the co-activation of the dorsal network with the VAN. The implications for performance-based research of this neural separation are just being explored.

We have argued that it is unlikely that the dorsal network is the source of endogenous biases. Rather, we see this network as a middleman that receives bias signals from other neural systems (reward, long-term memory, working memory) and translates/integrates them for sensory systems (see also Chapter 10 of this volume). To understand this second-order interaction (i.e., how sensory systems via the DAN are influenced by memory or reward signals), recordings of neural activity at higher

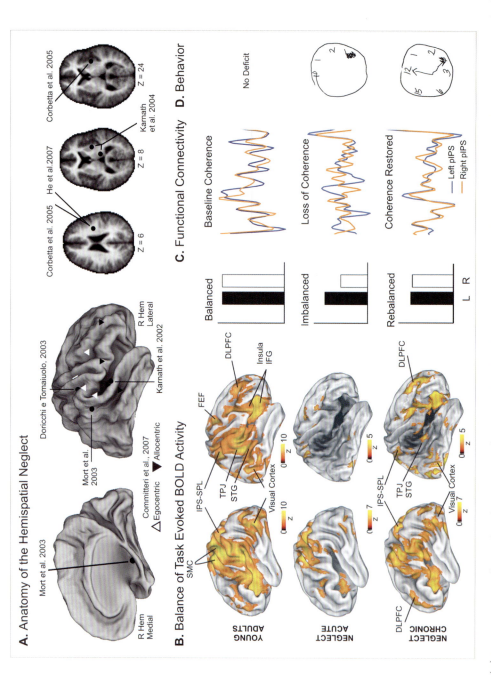

FIGURE 5.6 (A) Numerous sites of injury have been associated with spatial neglect. The medial and lateral representation of the right hemisphere (*left*) and the three transversal slices (*right*) illustrate cortical and subcortical gray matter lesions associated with spatial neglect from studies where Talairach coordinates could be obtained. *(Continued on next page)*

FIGURE 5.6 (*Continued*)   Coordinates from Committeri et al. (2007) were converted from Montreal Neurological Institute (MNI) to Talairach coordinates using the Nonlinear Yale MNI to Talairach conversion algorithm. (**B–D**) Acutely after stroke there is (**B**) a reduction of evoked BOLD activity in both hemispheres and a marked imbalance of evoked BOLD activity between the two hemispheres, (**C**) a loss of interhemispheric coherence of spontaneous BOLD activity between core regions of the DAN and (**D**) impaired spatial performance. In the chronic state, there is a reactivation of evoked BOLD activity, rebalancing of relative activity between left and right posterior parietal cortex, return of spontaneous BOLD coherence, and behavioral improvement. SMC: somatomotor eortex; DLFPC: dorsolateral prefrontal cortex. Adapted from Carter, A. R., Astafiev, S. V., Lang, C. E., Connor, L. T., Rengachary, J., Strube, M. J., et al. (2010). Resting interhemispheric functional magnetic resonance imaging connectivity predicts performance after stroke. *Annals of Neurology, 67*, 365–375; data from Corbetta, M., Kincade, M. J., Lewis, C., Snyder, A. Z., & Sapir, A. (2005a). Neural basis and recovery of spatial attention deficits in spatial neglect. *Nature Neuroscience, 8*, 1603–1610; and He, B. J., Snyder, A. Z., Vincent, J. L., Epstein, A., Shulman, G. L., & Corbetta, M. (2007). Breakdown of functional connectivity in frontoparietal networks underlies behavioral deficits in spatial neglect. *Neuron, 53*, 905–918, with permission of the publishers.

temporal resolution will likely be essential. Toward this exciting goal, we have recently combined BOLD-fMRI with electrocorticography (ECOG) to study the interactions between large-scale neural systems that are expressed in many different physiological signals (power, phase, coupling of power-to-phase).

A final important framework for future investigation is to consider attention as a system for controlling correlated noise rather than sensory-evoked activity. There is emerging evidence, not only from neuroimaging (Cohen & Maunsell, 2009; Mitchell et al., 2009), that correlated noise can be modulated by attention. This framework links research on attention to studies of spontaneous activity, an area of growing importance in neuroscience.

ACKNOWLEDGMENTS

This research was supported by NIH grants: MH71920–06, and HD061117–05A2.

References

Abrams, R. A., & Jonides, J. (1988). Programming saccadic eye movements. *Journal of Experimental Psychology, Journal of Experimental Psychology. Human Perception and Performance, 14*, 428–443.

Allison, T., Puce, A., & McCarthy, G. (2000). Social perception from visual cues: Role of the STS region. *Trends in Cognitive Sciences, 4*, 267–278.

Anticevic, A., Repovs, G., Shulman, G. L., & Barch, D. M. (2010). When less is more: TPJ and default network deactivation during encoding predicts working memory performance. *Neuroimage, 49*, 2638–2648.

Arrington, C. M., Carr, T. H., Mayer, A. R., & Rao, S. M. (2000). Neural mechanisms of visual attention: Object-based selection of a region in space. *Journal of Cognitive Neuroscience, 12*(Suppl 2), 106–117.

Arzy, S., Thut, G., Mohr, C., Michel, C. M., & Blanke, O. (2006). Neural basis of embodiment: Distinct contributions of temporoparietal junction and extrastriate body area. *Journal of Neuroscience, 26*, 8074–8081.

Asplund, C. L., Todd, J. J., Snyder, A. P., & Marois, R. (2010). A central role for the lateral prefrontal cortex in goal-directed and stimulus-driven attention. *Nature Neuroscience, 13*, 507–512.

Astafiev, S. V., Shulman, G. L., & Corbetta, M. (2006). Visuospatial reorienting signals in the human temporo-parietal junction are independent of response selection. *European Journal of Neuroscience, 23*, 591–596.

Astafiev, S. V., Shulman, G. L., Stanley, C. M., Snyder, A. Z., Van Essen, D. C., & Corbetta, M. (2003). Functional organization of human intraparietal and frontal cortex for attending, looking, and pointing. *Journal of Neuroscience, 23*, 4689–4699.

Astafiev, S. V., Snyder, A. Z., Shulman, G. L., & Corbetta, M. (2010). Comment on "Modafinil shifts human locus coeruleus to low-tonic, high-phasic activity during functional MRI" and "Homeostatic sleep pressure and responses to sustained attention in the suprachiasmatic area." *Science, 328*, 309; author reply 309.

Aston-Jones, G., & Bloom, F. E. (1981). Activity of norepinephrine-containing locus coeruleus neurons in behaving rats anticipates fluctuations in the sleep-waking cycle. *Journal of Neuroscience, 1,* 876–886.

Aston-Jones, G., & Cohen, J. D. (2005). An integrative theory of locus coeruleus-norepinephrine function: Adaptive gain and optimal performance. *Annual Review of Neuroscience, 28,* 403–450.

Aston-Jones, G., Rajkowski, J., & Kubiak, P. (1997). Conditioned responses of monkey locus coeruleus neurons anticipate acquisition of discriminative behavior in a vigilance task. *Neuroscience, 80,* 697–715.

Babiloni, C., Vecchio, F., Miriello, M., Romani, G. L., & Rossini, P. M. (2006). Visuo-spatial consciousness and parieto-occipital areas: a high-resolution EEG study. *Cerebral Cortex, 16,* 37–46.

Ball, K., & Sekuler, R. (1980). Models of stimulus uncertainty in motion perception. *Psychological Review, 87,* 435–469.

Bestmann, S., Ruff, C. C., Blakemore, C., Driver, J., & Thilo, K. V. (2007). Spatial attention changes excitability of human visual cortex to direct stimulation. *Current Biology: CB, 17,* 134–139.

Bichot, N. P., Rossi, A. F., & Desimone, R. (2005). Parallel and serial neural mechanisms for visual search in macaque area V4. *Science, 308,* 529–534.

Bisley, J. W., & Goldberg, M. E. (2003). Neuronal activity in the lateral intraparietal area and spatial attention. *Science, 299,* 81–86.

Biswal, B., Yetkin, F. Z., Haughton, V. M., & Hyde, J. S. (1995). Functional connectivity in the motor cortex of resting human brain using echo-planar MRI. *Magnetic Resonance in Medicine, 34,* 537–541.

Blanke, O., & Arzy, S. (2005). The out-of-body experience: Disturbed self-processing at the temporo-parietal junction. *Neuroscientist, 11,* 16–24.

Blankenburg, F., Ruff, C. C., Bestmann, S., Bjoertomt, O., Josephs, O., Deichmann, R., & Driver, J. (2010). Studying the Role of Human Parietal Cortex in Visuospatial Attention with Concurrent TMS-fMRI. *Cerebral Cortex 20,* 2702–2711.

Bledowski, C., Prvulovic, D., Goebel, R., Zanella, F. E., & Linden, D. E. (2004). Attentional systems in target and distractor processing: a combined ERP and fMRI study. *Neuroimage, 22,* 530–540.

Bouret, S., & Sara, S. J. (2005). Network reset: a simplified overarching theory of locus coeruleus noradrenaline function. *Trends in Neurosciences, 28,* 574–582.

Braver, T. S., Barch, D. M., Gray, J. R., Molfese, D. L., & Snyder, A. (2001). Anterior cingulate cortex and response conflict: Effects of frequency, inhibition and errors. *Cerebral Cortex, 11,* 825–836.

Braver, T. S., Reynolds, J. R., & Donaldson, D. I. (2003). Neural mechanisms of transient and sustained cognitive control during task switching. *Neuron, 39,* 713–726.

Bressler, S. L., Tang, W., Sylvester, C. M., Shulman, G. L., & Corbetta, M. (2008). Top-down control of human visual cortex by frontal and parietal cortex in anticipatory visual spatial attention. *Journal of Neuroscience, 28,* 10056–10061.

Buckner, R. L., Bandettini, P. A., O'Craven, K. M., Savoy, R. L., Petersen, S. E., Raichle, M. E., & Rosen, B R. (1996). Detection of cortical activation during averaged single trials of a cognitive task using functional magnetic resonance imaging. *Proceedings of the National Academy of Sciences of the United States of America, 93,* 14878–14883.

Bundesen, C. (1990). A theory of visual attention. *Psychological Review, 97,* 523–547.

Buschman, T. J., & Miller, E. K. (2009). Serial, covert shifts of attention during visual search are reflected by the frontal eye fields and correlated with population oscillations. *Neuron, 63,* 386–396.

Capotosto, P., Babiloni, C., Romani, G. L., & Corbetta, M. (2009). Frontoparietal cortex controls spatial attention through modulation of anticipatory alpha rhythms. *Journal of Neuroscience, 29,* 5863–5872.

Carter, A. R., Astafiev, S. V., Lang, C. E., Connor, L. T., Rengachary, J., Strube, M. J., et al. (2010). Resting interhemispheric functional magnetic resonance imaging connectivity predicts performance after stroke. *Annals of Neurology, 67,* 365–375.

Chambers, C. D., Payne, J. M., Stokes, M. G., & Mattingley, J. B. (2004). Fast and slow parietal pathways mediate spatial attention. *Nature Neuroscience, 7,* 217–218.

Chiu, Y. C., & Yantis, S. (2009). A domain-independent source of cognitive control for task sets: shifting spatial attention and switching categorization rules. *Journal of Neuroscience, 29,* 3930–3938.

Cohen, M. R., & Maunsell, J. H. (2009). Attention improves performance primarily by reducing interneuronal correlations. *Nature Neuroscience, 12,* 1594–1600.

Colby, C. L., Duhamel, J. R., & Goldberg, M. E. (1996). Visual, presaccadic, and cognitive activation of single neurons in monkey lateral intraparietal area. *Journal of Neurophysiology, 76,* 2841–2852.

Cole, M. W., & Schneider, W. (2007). The cognitive control network: Integrated cortical regions with dissociable functions. *NeuroImage, 37,* 343–360.

Committeri, G., Pitzalis, S., Galati, G., Patria, F., Pelle, G., Sabatini, U., et al. (2007). Neural bases of personal and extrapersonal neglect in humans. *Brain, 130,* 431–441.

Cools, R., Clark, L., & Robbins, T. W. (2004). Differential responses in human striatum and prefrontal cortex to changes in object and rule relevance. *Journal of Neuroscience, 24*, 1129–1135.

Corbetta, M. (1998). Frontoparietal cortical networks for directing attention and the eye to visual locations: Identical, independent, or overlapping neural systems? *Proceedings of the National Academy of Sciences of the United States of America, 95*, 831–838.

Corbetta, M., Akbudak, E., Conturo, T. E., Snyder, A. Z., Ollinger, J. M., Drury, H. A., et al. (1998). A common network of functional areas for attention and eye movements. *Neuron, 21*, 761–773.

Corbetta, M., Kincade, M. J., Lewis, C., Snyder, A. Z., & Sapir, A. (2005a). Neural basis and recovery of spatial attention deficits in spatial neglect. *Nature Neuroscience, 8*, 1603–1610.

Corbetta, M., Kincade, J. M., Ollinger, J. M., McAvoy, M. P., & Shulman, G. L. (2000). Voluntary orienting is dissociated from target detection in human posterior parietal cortex. *Nature Neuroscience, 3*, 292–297.

Corbetta, M., Kincade, J. M., & Shulman, G. L. (2002). Neural systems for visual orienting and their relationships to spatial working memory. *Journal of Cognitive Neuroscience, 14*, 508–523.

Corbetta, M., Miezin, F. M., Dobmeyer, S., Shulman, G. L., & Petersen, S. E. (1990). Attentional modulation of neural processing of shape, color, and velocity in humans. *Science, 248*, 1556–1559.

Corbetta, M., Miezin, F. M., Dobmeyer, S., Shulman, G. L., & Petersen, S. E. (1991). Selective and divided attention during visual discriminations of shape, color, and speed: Functional anatomy by positron emission tomography. *Journal of Neuroscience, 11*, 2383–2402.

Corbetta, M., Miezin, F. M., Shulman, G. L., & Petersen, S. E. (1993). A PET study of visuospatial attention. *Journal of Neuroscience, 13*, 1202–1226.

Corbetta, M., Patel, G., & Shulman, G. L. (2008). The reorienting system of the human brain: From environment to theory of mind. *Neuron, 58*, 306–324.

Corbetta, M., & Shulman, G. L. (2002). Control of goal-directed and stimulus-driven attention in the brain. *Nature Reviews. Neuroscience, 3*, 201–215.

Corbetta, M., Tansy, A. P., Stanley, C. M., Astafiev, S. V., Snyder, A. Z., & Shulman, G. L. (2005b). A functional MRI study of preparatory signals for spatial location and objects. *Neuropsychologia, 43*, 2041–2056.

Crone, E. A., Wendelken, C., Donohue, S. E., & Bunge, S. A. (2006). Neural evidence for dissociable components of task-switching. *Cerebral Cortex, 16*, 475–486.

Daffner, K. R., Scinto, L. F., Weitzman, A. M., Faust, R., Rentz, D. M., Budson, A. E., & Holcomb, P. J. (2003). Frontal and parietal components of a cerebral network mediating voluntary attention to novel events. *Journal of Cognitive Neuroscience, 15*, 294–313.

Dayan, P., & Yu, A. J. (2006). Phasic norepinephrine: A neural interrupt signal for unexpected events. *Network, 17*, 335–350.

de Fockert, J., Rees, G., Frith, C., & Lavie, N. (2004). Neural correlates of attentional capture in visual search. *Journal of Cognitive Neuroscience, 16*, 751–759.

de Pasquale, F., Della Penna, S., Snyder, A. Z., Lewis, C., Mantini, D., Marzetti, L., et al. (2010). Temporal dynamics of spontaneous MEG activity in brain networks. *Proceedings of the National Academy of Sciences of the United States of America, 107*, 6040–6045.

Decety, J., & Lamm, C. (2007). The role of the right temporoparietal junction in social interaction: How low-level computational processes contribute to meta-cognition. *Neuroscientist, 13*, 580–593.

Desimone, R., & Duncan, J. (1995). Neural mechanisms of selective visual attention. *Annual Review of Neuroscience, 18*, 193–222.

Dosenbach, N. U., Fair, D. A., Cohen, A. L., Schlaggar, B. L., & Petersen, S. E. (2008). A dual-networks architecture of top-down control. *Trends in Cognitive Sciences, 12*, 99–105.

Dosenbach, N. U., Visscher, K. M., Palmer, E. D., Miezin, F. M., Wenger, K. K., Kang, H. C., et al. (2006). A core system for the implementation of task sets. *Neuron, 50*, 799–812.

Dosher, B. A., & Lu, Z. L. (2000). Mechanisms of perceptual attention in precuing of location. *Vision Research, 40*, 1269–1292.

Douglas, R. J., & Martin, K. A. (2007). Mapping the matrix: The ways of neocortex. *Neuron, 56*, 226–238.

Downar, J., Crawley, A. P., Mikulis, D. J., & Davis, K. D. (2000). A multimodal cortical network for the detection of changes in the sensory environment. *Nature Neuroscience, 3*, 277–283.

Duncan, J. (1984). Selective attention and the organization of visual information. *Journal of Experimental Psychology. General, 113*, 501–517.

Egeth, H. E., Virzi, R. A., & Garbart, H. (1984). Searching for conjunctively defined targets. *Journal of Experimental Psychology. Human Perception and Performance, 10*, 32–39.

Ekstrom, L. B., Roelfsema, P. R., Arsenault, J. T., Bonmassar, G., & Vanduffel, W. (2008). Bottom-up dependent gating of frontal signals in early visual cortex. *Science, 321*, 414–417.

Ekstrom, L. B., Roelfsema, P. R., Arsenault, J. T., Kolster, H., & Vanduffel, W. (2009). Modulation of the contrast response function by electrical microstimulation of the macaque frontal eye field. *Journal of Neuroscience, 29*, 10683–10694.

Ellison, A., Schindler, I., Pattison, L. L., & Milner, A. D. (2004). An exploration of the role of the superior temporal gyrus in visual search and spatial perception using TMS. *Brain, 127*, 2307–2315.

Engel, A. K., Fries, P., & Singer, W. (2001). Dynamic predictions: oscillations and synchrony in top-down processing. *Nature Reviews. Neuroscience, 2*, 704–716.

Eriksen, C. W., & Hoffman, J. E. (1973). The extent of processing of noise elements during selective encoding from visual displays. *Perception & Psychophysics, 14*, 155–160.

Esterman, M., Chiu, Y. C., Tamber-Rosenau, B. J., & Yantis, S. (2009). Decoding cognitive control in human parietal cortex. *Proceedings of the National Academy of Sciences of the United States of America, 106*, 17974–17979.

Evdokimidis, I., Smyrnis, N., Constantinidis, T. S., Gourtzelidis, P., & Papageorgiou, C. (2001). Frontal-parietal activation differences observed before the execution of remembered saccades: An event-related potentials study. *Brain Research. Cognitive Brain Research, 12*, 89–99.

Fletcher, P. C., Happe, F., Frith, U., Baker, S. C., Dolan, R. J., Frackowiak, R. S., & Frith, C. D. (1995). Other minds in the brain: a functional imaging study of "theory of mind" in story comprehension. *Cognition, 57*, 109–128.

Folk, C. L., & Remington, R. (2010). A critical evaluation of the disengagement hypothesis. *Acta Psychologica*.

Folk, C. L., Remington, R. W., & Johnston, J. C. (1992). Involuntary covert orienting is contingent on attentional control settings. *Journal of Experimental Psychology. Human Perception and Performance, 18*, 1030–1044.

Fox, M. D., Corbetta, M., Snyder, A. Z., Vincent, J. L., & Raichle, M. E. (2006). Spontaneous neuronal activity distinguishes human dorsal and ventral attention systems. *Proceedings of the National Academy of Sciences of the United States of America, 103*, 10046–10051.

Fox, M. D., & Raichle, M. E. (2007). Spontaneous fluctuations in brain activity observed with functional magnetic resonance imaging. *Nature Reviews. Neuroscience, 8*, 700–711.

Fox, M. D., Snyder, A. Z., Barch, D. M., Gusnard, D. A., & Raichle, M. E. (2005a). Transient BOLD responses at block transitions. *NeuroImage, 28*, 956–966.

Fox, M. D., Snyder, A. Z., Vincent, J. L., Corbetta, M., Van Essen, D. C., & Raichle, M. E. (2005b). The human brain is intrinsically organized into dynamic, anticorrelated functional networks. *Proceedings of the National Academy of Sciences of the United States of America, 102*, 9673–9678.

Freedman, D. J., & Assad, J. A. (2009). Distinct encoding of spatial and nonspatial visual information in parietal cortex. *Journal of Neuroscience, 29*, 5671–5680.

Fries, P. (2005). A mechanism for cognitive dynamics: Neuronal communication through neuronal coherence. *Trends in Cognitive Sciences, 9*, 474–480.

Fries, P., Neuenschwander, S., Engel, A. K., Goebel, R., & Singer, W. (2001). Rapid feature selective neuronal synchronization through correlated latency shifting. *Nature Neuroscience, 4*, 194–200.

Gallagher, H. L., & Frith, C. D. (2003). Functional imaging of "theory of mind." *Trends in Cognitive Sciences, 7*, 77–83.

Giesbrecht, B., Woldorff, M. G., Song, A. W., & Mangun, G. R. (2003). Neural mechanisms of top-down control during spatial and feature attention. *NeuroImage, 19*, 496–512.

Gottlieb, J. P., Kusunoki, M., & Goldberg, M. E. (1998). The representation of visual salience in monkey parietal cortex. *Nature, 391*, 481–484.

Gregoriou, G. G., Gotts, S. J., Zhou, H., & Desimone, R. (2009). High-frequency, long-range coupling between prefrontal and visual cortex during attention. *Science, 324*, 1207–1210.

Greicius, M. D., Krasnow, B., Reiss, A. L., & Menon, V. (2003). Functional connectivity in the resting brain: A network analysis of the default mode hypothesis. *Proceedings of the National Academy of Sciences of the United States of America, 100*, 253–258.

Hagler, D. J., Jr., Riecke, L., & Sereno, M. I. (2007). Parietal and superior frontal visuospatial maps activated by pointing and saccades. *NeuroImage, 35*, 1562–1577.

Hagler, D. J., Jr., & Sereno, M. I. (2006). Spatial maps in frontal and prefrontal cortex. *NeuroImage, 29*, 567–577.

He, B. J., Snyder, A. Z., Vincent, J. L., Epstein, A., Shulman, G. L., & Corbetta, M. (2007). Breakdown of functional connectivity in frontoparietal networks underlies behavioral deficits in spatial neglect. *Neuron, 53*, 905–918.

He, B. J., Snyder, A. Z., Zempel, J. M., Smyth, M. D., & Raichle, M. E. (2008). Electrophysiological correlates of the brain's intrinsic large-scale functional architecture. *Proceedings of the National Academy of Sciences of the United States of America, 105*, 16039–16044.

Heilman, K. M., Bowers, D., Valenstein, E., & Watson, R. T. (Eds.). (1987). Hemispace and hemispatial neglect. Amsterdam: North-Holland Elsevier Science Publishers.

Herrington, T. M., & Assad, J. A. (2009). Neural activity in the middle temporal area and lateral intraparietal area during endogenously cued shifts of attention. *Journal of Neuroscience, 29,* 14160–14176.

Hopfinger, J. B., Buonocore, M. H., & Mangun, G. R. (2000). The neural mechanisms of top-down attentional control. *Nature Neuroscience, 3,* 284–291.

Howard, M. W., Rizzuto, D. S., Caplan, J. B., Madsen, J. R., Lisman, J., Aschenbrenner-Scheibe, R., et al. (2003). Gamma oscillations correlate with working memory load in humans. *Cerebral Cortex, 13,* 1369–1374.

Husain, M., & Kennard, C. (1996). Visual neglect associated with frontal lobe infarction. *Journal of Neurology, 243,* 652–657.

Indovina, I., & Macaluso, E. (2007). Dissociation of stimulus relevance and saliency factors during shifts of visuospatial attention. *Cerebral Cortex, 17,* 1701–1711.

Itti, L., & Koch, C. (2001). Computational modelling of visual attention. *Nature Reviews. Neuroscience, 2,* 194–203.

Jack, A. I., Patel, G. H., Astafiev, S. V., Snyder, A. Z., Akbudak, E., Shulman, G. L., & Corbetta, M. (2007). Changing human visual field organization from early visual to extra-occipital cortex. *PLoS One, 2,* e452. Available at: http://www.plosone.org/article/info:doi%2F10.1371%2Fjournal.pone.0000452

Jack, A. I., Shulman, G. L., Snyder, A. Z., McAvoy, M., & Corbetta, M. (2006). Separate modulations of human V1 associated with spatial attention and task structure. *Neuron, 51,* 135–147.

James, W. (1890). *Principles of psychology.* New York: Holt.

Johnston, J. M., Vaishnavi, S. N., Smyth, M. D., Zhang, D., He, B. J., Zempel, J. M., et al. (2008). Loss of resting interhemispheric functional connectivity after complete section of the corpus callosum. *Journal of Neuroscience, 28,* 6453–6458.

Julesz, B. (1981). Textons, the elements of texture perception, and their interactions. *Nature, 290,* 91–97.

Karnath, H. O., Fruhmann Berger, M., Kuker, W., & Rorden, C. (2004). The anatomy of spatial neglect based on voxelwise statistical analysis: A study of 140 patients. *Cerebral Cortex, 14,* 1164–1172.

Kastner, S., DeSimone, K., Konen, C. S., Szczepanski, S. M., Weiner, K. S., & Schneider, K. A. (2007). Topographic maps in human frontal cortex revealed in memory-guided saccade and spatial working-memory tasks. *Journal of Neurophysiology, 97,* 3494–3507.

Kastner, S., Pinsk, M. A., De Weerd, P., Desimone, R., & Ungerleider, L. G. (1999). Increased activity in human visual cortex during directed attention in the absence of visual stimulation. *Neuron, 22,* 751–761.

Kastner, S., & Ungerleider, L. G. (2000). Mechanisms of visual attention in the human cortex. *Annual Review of Neuroscience, 23,* 315–341.

Kelley, T. A., Serences, J. T., Giesbrecht, B., & Yantis, S. (2008). Cortical mechanisms for shifting and holding visuospatial attention. *Cerebral Cortex, 18,* 114–125.

Kimberg, D. Y., Aguirre, G. K., & D'Esposito, M. (2000). Modulation of task-related neural activity in task-switching: An fMRI study. *Brain Research. Cognitive Brain Research, 10,* 189–196.

Kincade, J. M., Abrams, R. A., Astafiev, S. V., Shulman, G. L., & Corbetta, M. (2005). An event-related functional magnetic resonance imaging study of voluntary and stimulus-driven orienting of attention. *Journal of Neuroscience, 25,* 4593–4604.

Knight, R. T., Scabini, D., Woods, D. L., & Clayworth, C. C. (1989). Contributions of temporal-parietal junction to the human auditory P3. *Brain Research, 502,* 109–116.

Koch, C., & Ullman, S. (1985). Shifts in selective visual attention: towards the underlying neural circuitry. *Human Neurobiology, 4,* 219–227.

Konen, C. S., & Kastner, S. (2008). Representation of eye movements and stimulus motion in topographically organized areas of human posterior parietal cortex. *Journal of Neuroscience, 28,* 8361–8375.

Konishi, S., Donaldson, D. I., & Buckner, R. L. (2001). Transient activation during block transition. *NeuroImage, 13,* 364–374.

Lewis, C. M., Baldassarre, A. Committeri, G. Romani, G. L. Corbetta, M. (2009) Learning sculpts the spontaneous activity of the resting human brain. *Proceedings of the National Academy of Sciences of the United States of America, 106,* 17558–17563.

Linden, D. E., Prvulovic, D., Formisano, E., Vollinger, M., Zanella, F. E., Goebel, R., & Dierks, T. (1999). The functional neuroanatomy of target detection: An fMRI study of visual and auditory oddball tasks. *Cerebral Cortex, 9,* 815–823.

Liu, H., Stufflebeam, S. M., Sepulcre, J., Hedden, T., & Buckner, R. L. (2009). Evidence from intrinsic activity that asymmetry of the human brain is controlled by multiple factors. *Proceedings of the National Academy of Sciences of the United States of America, 106,* 20499–20503.

Liu, T., Slotnick, S. D., Serences, J. T., & Yantis, S. (2003). Cortical mechanisms of feature-based attentional control. *Cerebral Cortex, 13,* 1334–1343.

Luck, S. J., Chelazzi, L., Hillyard, S. A., & Desimone, R. (1997). Neural mechanisms of spatial selective attention in areas V1, V2, and V4 of macaque visual cortex. *Journal of Neurophysiology, 77,* 24–42.

Luck, S. J., Hillyard, S. A., Mouloua, M., Woldorff, M. G., Clark, V. P., & Hawkins, H. L. (1994). Effects of spatial cuing on luminance detectability: psychophysical and electrophysiological evidence for early selection. *Journal of Experimental Psychology. Human Perception and Performance, 20,* 887–904.

Macaluso, E., Frith, C. D., & Driver, J. (2002). Supramodal effects of covert spatial orienting triggered by visual or tactile events. *Journal of Cognitive Neuroscience, 14,* 389–401.

Macaluso, E., & Patria, F. (2007). Spatial re-orienting of visual attention along the horizontal or the vertical axis. *Experimental Brain Research, 180,* 23–34.

Mangun, G. R., & Fannon, S. P. (2007). Networks for attentional control and selection in spatial vision. In F. Mast, & L. Jäncke (Eds.), *Spatial processing in navigation, imagery and perception* (pp. 411–32). Amsterdam: Springer.

Mangun, G. R., Fannon, S. P., Geng, J. J., & Saron, C. D. (2009). Imaging brain attention systems: Control and selection in vision. In M. Filippi (Ed.), *FMRI techniques and protocols* (pp. 353–78). New York, NY: Humana Press.

Mangun, G. R., & Hillyard, S. A. (1991). Modulations of sensory-evoked brain potentials indicate changes in perceptual processing during visual-spatial priming. *Journal of Experimental Psychology. Human Perception and Performance, 17,* 1057–1074.

Marois, R., Leung, H. C., & Gore, J. C. (2000). A stimulus-driven approach to object identity and location processing in the human brain. *Neuron, 25,* 717–728.

Martinez-Trujillo, J. C., & Treue, S. (2004). Feature-based attention increases the selectivity of population responses in primate visual cortex. *Current Biology: CB, 14,* 744–751.

McCarthy, G., Luby, M., Gore, J., & Goldman-Rakic, P. (1997). Infrequent events transiently activate human prefrontal and parietal cortex as measured by functional MRI. *Journal of Neurophysiology, 77,* 1630–1634.

McDowell, J. E., Kissler, J. M., Berg, P., Dyckman, K. A., Gao, Y., Rockstroh, B., & Clementz, B. A. (2005). Electroencephalography/magnetoencephalography study of cortical activities preceding prosaccades and antisaccades. *Neuroreport, 16,* 663–668.

Meister, I. G., Wienemann, M., Buelte, D., Grunewald, C., Sparing, R., Dambeck, N., & Boroojerdi, B. (2006). Hemiextinction induced by transcranial magnetic stimulation over the right temporo-parietal junction. *Neuroscience, 142,* 119–123.   ·

Menon, V., Ford, J. M., Lim, K. O., Glover, G. H., & Pfefferbaum, A. (1997). Combined event-related fMRI and EEG evidence for temporal-parietal cortex activation during target detection. *Neuroreport, 8,* 3029–3037.

Mesulam, M. M. (1981). A cortical network for directed attention and unilateral neglect. *Annals of Neurology, 10,* 309–325.

Mesulam, M. M. (1999). Spatial attention and neglect: Parietal, frontal and cingulate contributions to the mental representation and attentional targeting of salient extrapersonal events. *Philosophical Transactions of the Royal Society of London. Series B, Biological Sciences, 354,* 1325–1346.

Miller, E. K., & Cohen, J. D. (2001). An integrative theory of prefrontal cortex function. *Annual Review of Neuroscience, 24,* 167–202.

Minzenberg, M. J., Watrous, A. J., Yoon, J. H., Ursu, S., & Carter, C. S. (2008). Modafinil shifts human locus coeruleus to low-tonic, high-phasic activity during functional MRI. *Science, 322,* 1700–1702.

Mitchell, J. F., Sundberg, K. A., & Reynolds, J. H. (2009). Spatial attention decorrelates intrinsic activity fluctuations in macaque area V4. *Neuron, 63,* 879–888.

Mitchell, J. P. (2008). Activity in right temporo-parietal junction is not selective for theory-of-mind. *Cerebral Cortex, 18,* 262–271.

Moore, T., & Armstrong, K. M. (2003). Selective gating of visual signals by microstimulation of frontal cortex. *Nature, 421,* 370–373.

Moore, T., & Fallah, M. (2001). Control of eye movements and spatial attention. *Proceedings of the National Academy of Sciences of the United States of America, 98,* 1273–1276.

Mort, D. J., Malhotra, P., Mannan, S. K., Rorden, C., Pambakian, A., Kennard, C., & Husain, M. (2003). The anatomy of visual neglect. *Brain, 126,* 1986–1997.

Muller, H. J., & Rabbitt, P. M. (1989). Reflexive and voluntary orienting of visual attention: Time course of activation and resistance to interruption. *Journal of Experimental Psychology. Human Perception and Performance, 15,* 315–330.

Muller, N. G., Bartelt, O. A., Donner, T. H., Villringer, A., & Brandt, S. A. (2003). A physiological correlate of the "Zoom Lens" of visual attention. *Journal of Neuroscience, 23,* 3561–3565.

Natale, E., Marzi, C. A., & Macaluso, E. (2010). Right temporal-parietal junction engagement during spatial reorienting does not depend on strategic attention control. *Neuropsychologia, 48,* 1160–1164.

Navalpakkam, V., & Itti, L. (2005). Modeling the influence of task on attention. *Vision Research, 45,* 205–231.

Nobre, A. C. (2001). The attentive homunculus: Now you see it, now you don't. *Neuroscience and Biobehavioral Reviews, 25,* 477–496.

Nobre, A. C., Sebestyen, G. N., Gitelman, D. R., Mesulam, M. M., Frackowiak, R. S., & Frith, C. D. (1997). Functional localization of the system for visuospatial attention using positron emission tomography. *Brain, 120*(Pt 3), 515–533.

Nothdurft, H. C. (1993). The role of features in preattentive vision: Comparison of orientation, motion and color cues. *Vision Research, 33,* 1937–1958.

O'Craven, K. M., Downing, P. E., & Kanwisher, N. (1999). fMRI evidence for objects as the units of attentional selection. *Nature, 401,* 584–587.

Ollinger, J. M., Corbetta, M., & Shulman, G. L. (2001b). Separating processes within a trial in event-related functional MRI: II. Analysis. *NeuroImage, 13,* 218–229.

Ollinger, J. M., Shulman, G. L., & Corbetta, M. (2001a). Separating processes within a trial in event-related functional MRI: I. The Method. *NeuroImage, 13,* 210–217.

Patel, G. H., Shulman, G. L., Baker, J. T., Akbudak, E., Snyder, A. Z., Snyder, L. H., & Corbetta, M. (2010). Topographic organization of macaque area LIP. *Proceedings of the National Academy of Sciences of the United States of America, 107,* 4728–4733.

Peelen, M. V., Fei-Fei, L., & Kastner, S. (2009). Neural mechanisms of rapid natural scene categorization in human visual cortex. *Nature, 460,* 94–97.

Pelphrey, K. A., Mitchell, T. V., McKeown, M. J., Goldstein, J., Allison, T., & McCarthy, G. (2003). Brain activity evoked by the perception of human walking: Controlling for meaningful coherent motion. *Journal of Neuroscience, 23,* 6819–6825.

Pelphrey, K. A., Morris, J. P., & McCarthy, G. (2004). Grasping the intentions of others: The perceived intentionality of an action influences activity in the superior temporal sulcus during social perception. *Journal of Cognitive Neuroscience, 16,* 1706–1716.

Pesaran, B., Pezaris, J. S., Sahani, M., Mitra, P. P., & Andersen, R. A. (2002). Temporal structure in neuronal activity during working memory in macaque parietal cortex. *Nature Neuroscience, 5,* 805–811.

Pessoa, L., & Padmala, S. (2005). Quantitative prediction of perceptual decisions during near-threshold fear detection. *Proceedings of the National Academy of Sciences of the United States of America, 102,* 5612–5617.

Posner, M. I., & Cohen, Y. (1984). Components of visual attention. In H. Bouma, & D. G. Bouwhuis (Eds.), *Attention & performance* (Vol. 10, pp. 531–556). Hillsdale, NJ: Erlbaum.

Posner, M. I., Cohen, Y., & Rafal, R. D. (1982). Neural systems control of spatial orienting. *Philosophical Transactions of the Royal Society of London. Series B, Biological Sciences, 298,* 187–198.

Posner, M. I., & Petersen, S. E. (1990). The attention system of the human brain. *Annual Review of Neuroscience, 13,* 25–42.

Posner, M. I., Snyder, C. R., & Davidson, B. J. (1980). Attention and the detection of signals. *Journal of Experimental Psychology, 109,* 160–174.

Raichle, M. E., MacLeod, A. M., Snyder, A. Z., Powers, W. J., Gusnard, D. A., & Shulman, G. L. (2001). A default mode of brain function. *Proceedings of the National Academy of Sciences of the United States of America, 98,* 676–682.

Raichle, M. E., & Mintun, M. A. (2006). Brain work and brain imaging. *Annual Review of Neuroscience, 29,* 449–476.

Rajkowski, J., Kubiak, P., & Aston-Jones, G. (1994). Locus coeruleus activity in monkey: Phasic and tonic changes are associated with altered vigilance. *Brain Research Bulletin, 35,* 607–616.

Reddy, L., Kanwisher, N. G., & VanRullen, R. (2009). Attention and biased competition in multi-voxel object representations. *Proceedings of the National Academy of Sciences of the United States of America, 106,* 21447–21452.

Reynolds, J. H., & Chelazzi, L. (2004). Attentional modulation of visual processing. *Annual Review of Neuroscience, 27,* 611–647.

Rizzolatti, G., Fogassi, L., & Gallese, V. (1997). Parietal cortex: From sight to action. *Current Opinion in Neurobiology, 7,* 562–567.

Robertson, I. H. (2001). Do we need the "lateral" in unilateral neglect? Spatially nonselective attention deficits in unilateral neglect and their implications for rehabilitation. *NeuroImage, 14,* S85–90.

Rosenau, B. J., Esterman, M., Chiu, Y. C., & Yantis, S. (2009). A domain-independent source of cognitive control for shifting attention in vision and working memory. *Journal of Vision, 9,* 164.

Rosenbaum, D. A. (1980). Human movement initiation: specification of arm, direction, and extent. *Journal of Experimental Psychology. General, 109,* 444–474.

Ruff, C. C., Blankenburg, F., Bjoertomt, O., Bestmann, S., Weiskopf, N., & Driver, J. (2009). Hemispheric differences in frontal and parietal influences on human occipital cortex: Direct confirmation with concurrent TMS-fMRI. *Journal of Cognitive Neuroscience, 21*, 1146–11461.

Ruff, C. C., Blankenburg, F., Bjoertomt, O., Bestmann, S., Freeman, E., Haynes, J. D., et al. (2006). Concurrent TMS-fMRI and psychophysics reveal frontal influences on human retinotopic visual cortex. *Current Biology: CB, 16*, 1479–14788.

Rushworth, M. F., Paus, T., & Sipila, P. K. (2001). Attention systems and the organization of the human parietal cortex. *Journal of Neuroscience, 21*, 5262–5271.

Saenz, M., Buracas, G. T., & Boynton, G. M. (2002). Global effects of feature-based attention in human visual cortex. *Nature Neuroscience, 5*, 631–632.

Sapir, A., d'Avossa, G., McAvoy, M., Shulman, G. L., & Corbetta, M. (2005). Brain signals for spatial attention predict performance in a motion discrimination task. *Proceedings of the National Academy of Sciences of the United States of America, 102*, 17810–17815.

Sauseng, P., Klimesch, W., Stadler, W., Schabus, M., Doppelmayr, M., Hanslmayr, S., et al. (2005). A shift of visual spatial attention is selectively associated with human EEG alpha activity. *European Journal of Neuroscience, 22*, 2917–2926.

Saxe, R. (2006). Uniquely human social cognition. *Current Opinion in Neurobiology, 16*, 235–239.

Saxe, R., & Kanwisher, N. (2003). People thinking about thinking people. *The role of the temporo-parietal junction in "theory of mind." NeuroImage, 19*, 1835–1842.

Schall, J. D., & Hanes, D. P. (1993). Neural basis of saccade target selection in frontal eye field during visual search. *Nature, 366*, 467–469.

Schluppeck, D., Glimcher, P., & Heeger, D. J. (2005). Topographic organization for delayed saccades in human posterior parietal cortex. *Journal of Neurophysiology, 94*, 1372–1384.

Scholz, J., Triantafyllou, C., Whitfield-Gabrieli, S., Brown, E. N., & Saxe, R. (2009). Distinct regions of right temporo-parietal junction are selective for theory of mind and exogenous attention. *PLoS One, 4*, e4869. Available at: http://www.plosone.org/article/info%3Adoi%2F10.1371%2Fjournal.pone.0004869

Seeley, W. W., Menon, V., Schatzberg, A. F., Keller, J., Glover, G. H., Kenna, H., et al. (2007). Dissociable intrinsic connectivity networks for salience processing and executive control. *Journal of Neuroscience, 27*, 2349–2356.

Serences, J. T., & Boynton, G. M. (2007). Feature-based attentional modulations in the absence of direct visual stimulation. *Neuron, 55*, 301–312.

Serences, J. T., Schwarzbach, J., Courtney, S. M., Golay, X., & Yantis, S. (2004). Control of object-based attention in human cortex. *Cerebral Cortex, 14*, 1346–1357.

Serences, J. T., Shomstein, S., Leber, A. B., Golay, X., Egeth, H. E., & Yantis, S. (2005). Coordination of voluntary and stimulus-driven attentional control in human cortex. *Psychological Science, 16*, 114–122.

Serences, J. T., & Yantis, S. (2006). Selective visual attention and perceptual coherence. *Trends in Cognitive Sciences, 10*, 38–45.

Sereno, M. I., Pitzalis, S., & Martinez, A. (2001). Mapping of contralateral space in retinotopic coordinates by a parietal cortical area in humans. *Science, 294*, 1350–1354.

Sestieri, C., Pizzella, V., Cianflone, F., Luca Romani, G., & Corbetta, M. (2007). Sequential activation of human oculomotor centers during planning of visually-guided eye movements: A combined fMRI-MEG study. *Frontiers in Human Neuroscience, 1*, 1.

Sestieri, C., Sylvester, C. M., Jack, A. I., d'Avossa, G., Shulman, G. L., & Corbetta, M. (2008). Independence of anticipatory signals for spatial attention from number of nontarget stimuli in the visual field. *Journal of Neurophysiology, 100*, 829–838.

Shomstein, S., & Yantis, S. (2004). Control of attention shifts between vision and audition in human cortex. *Journal of Neuroscience, 24*, 10702–10706.

Shulman, G. L., d'Avossa, G., Tansy, A. P., & Corbetta, M. (2002a). Two attentional processes in the parietal lobe. *Cerebral Cortex, 12*, 1124–1131.

Shulman, G. L., Astafiev, S. V., Franke, D., Pope, D. L., Snyder, A. Z., McAvoy, M. P., & Corbetta, M. (2009). Interaction of stimulus-driven reorienting and expectation in ventral and dorsal frontoparietal and basal ganglia-cortical networks. *Journal of Neuroscience, 29*, 4392–4407.

Shulman, G. L., Astafiev, S. V., McAvoy, M. P., d'Avossa, G., & Corbetta, M. (2007). Right TPJ deactivation during visual search: Functional significance and support for a filter hypothesis. *Cerebral Cortex, 17*, 2625–2633.

Shulman, G. L., Fiez, J. A., Corbetta, M., Buckner, R. L., Miezin, F. M., Raichle, M. E., & Petersen, S. E. (1997). Common blood flow changes across visual tasks: II. *Decreases in cerebral cortex. Journal of Cognitive Neuroscience, 9*, 648–663.

Shulman, G. L., McAvoy, M. P., Cowan, M. C., Astafiev, S. V., Tansy, A. P., d'Avossa, G., & Corbetta, M. (2003). Quantitative analysis of attention and detection signals during visual search. *Journal of Neurophysiology, 90*, 3384–3397.

Shulman, G. L., Ollinger, J. M., Akbudak, E., Conturo, T. E., Snyder, A. Z., Petersen, S. E., & Corbetta, M. (1999). Areas involved in encoding and applying directional expectations to moving objects. *Journal of Neuroscience, 19*, 9480–9496.

Shulman, G. L., Ollinger, J. M., Linenweber, M., Petersen, S. E., & Corbetta, M. (2001). Multiple neural correlates of detection in the human brain. *Proceedings of the National Academy of Sciences of the United States of America, 98*, 313–318.

Shulman, G. L., Pope, D. L., Astafiev, S. V., McAvoy, M. P., Snyder, A. Z., & Corbetta, M. (2010). Right hemisphere dominance during spatial selective attention and target detection occurs outside the dorsal frontoparietal network. *Journal of Neuroscience, 30*, 3640–3651.

Shulman, G. L., Tansy, A. P., Kincade, M., Petersen, S. E., McAvoy, M. P., & Corbetta, M. (2002b). Reactivation of networks involved in preparatory states. *Cerebral Cortex, 12*, 590–600.

Siegel, M., Donner, T. H., Oostenveld, R., Fries, P., & Engel, A. K. (2008). Neuronal synchronization along the dorsal visual pathway reflects the focus of spatial attention. *Neuron, 60*, 709–719.

Silver, M. A., & Kastner, S. (2009). Topographic maps in human frontal and parietal cortex. *Trends in Cognitive Sciences, 13*, 488–495.

Silver, M. A., Ress, D., & Heeger, D. J. (2005). Topographic maps of visual spatial attention in human parietal cortex. *Journal of Neurophysiology, 94*, 1358–1371.

Silver, M. A., Ress, D., & Heeger, D. J. (2007). Neural correlates of sustained spatial attention in human early visual cortex. *Journal of Neurophysiology, 97*, 229–237.

Slagter, H. A., Giesbrecht, B., Kok, A., Weissman, D. H., Kenemans, J. L., Woldorff, M. G., & Mangun, G. R. (2007). fMRI evidence for both generalized and specialized components of attentional control. *Brain Research, 1177*, 90–102.

Smith, S. M., Fox, P. T., Miller, K. L., Glahn, D. C., Fox, P. M., Mackay, C. E., et al. (2009). Correspondence of the brain's functional architecture during activation and rest. *Proceedings of the National Academy of Sciences of the United States of America, 106*, 13040–13045.

Sohn, M. H., Ursu, S., Anderson, J. R., Stenger, V. A., & Carter, C. S. (2000). Inaugural article: The role of prefrontal cortex and posterior parietal cortex in task switching. *Proceedings of the National Academy of Sciences of the United States of America, 97*, 13448–13453.

Stevens, M. C., Calhoun, V. D., & Kiehl, K. A. (2005). Hemispheric differences in hemodynamics elicited by auditory oddball stimuli. *NeuroImage, 26*, 782–792.

Stoet, G., & Snyder, L. H. (2004). Single neurons in posterior parietal cortex of monkeys encode cognitive set. *Neuron, 42*, 1003–1012.

Swisher, J. D., Halko, M. A., Merabet, L. B., McMains, S. A., & Somers, D. C. (2007). Visual topography of human intraparietal sulcus. *Journal of Neuroscience, 27*, 5326–5337.

Sylvester, C. M., Jack, A. I., Corbetta, M., & Shulman, G. L. (2008). Anticipatory suppression of nonattended locations in visual cortex marks target location and predicts perception. *Journal of Neuroscience, 28*, 6549–6556.

Sylvester, C. M., Shulman, G. L., Jack, A. I., & Corbetta, M. (2007). Asymmetry of anticipatory activity in visual cortex predicts the locus of attention and perception. *Journal of Neuroscience, 27*, 14424–14433.

Szczepanski, S. M., Konen, C. S., & Kastner, S. (2010). Mechanisms of spatial attention control in frontal and parietal cortex. *Journal of Neuroscience, 30*, 148–160.

Taylor, K., Mandon, S., Freiwald, W. A., & Kreiter, A. K. (2005). Coherent oscillatory activity in monkey area v4 predicts successful allocation of attention. *Cerebral Cortex, 15*, 1424–1437.

Theeuwes, J. (2010). Top-down and bottom-up control of visual selection. *Acta Psychologica.*

Thompson, K. G., & Schall, J. D. (1999). The detection of visual signals by macaque frontal eye field during masking. *Nature Neuroscience, 2*, 283–288.

Thut, G., Nietzel, A., Brandt, S. A., & Pascual-Leone, A. (2006). Alpha-band electroencephalographic activity over occipital cortex indexes visuospatial attention bias and predicts visual target detection. *Journal of Neuroscience, 26*, 9494–9502.

Todd, J. J., Fougnie, D., & Marois, R. (2005). Visual short-term memory load suppresses temporo-parietal junction activity and induces inattentional blindness. *Psychological Science, 16*, 965–972.

Toro, R., Fox, P. T., & Paus, T. (2008). Functional coactivation map of the human brain. *Cerebral Cortex, 18*, 2553–2559.

Treisman, A. M., & Gelade, G. (1980). A feature-integration theory of attention. *Cognitive Psychology, 12*, 97–136.

Treue, S., & Martinez Trujillo, J. C. (1999). Feature-based attention influences motion processing gain in macaque visual cortex. *Nature, 399*, 575–579.

Usher, M., Cohen, J. D., Servan-Schreiber, D., Rajkowski, J., & Aston-Jones, G. (1999). The role of locus coeruleus in the regulation of cognitive performance. *Science, 283*, 549–554.

Vallar, G., & Perani, D. (Eds.). (1987). *The anatomy of spatial neglect in humans*. Amsterdam: Elsevier Science.

Van Essen, D. C. (2005). A Population-Average, Landmark- and Surface-based (PALS) atlas of human cerebral cortex. *Neuroimage, 28*, 635–662.

Van Essen, D. C., & Dierker, D. L. (2007). Surface-based and probabilistic atlases of primate cerebral cortex. *Neuron, 56*, 209–225.

Vandenberghe, R., Gitelman, D. R., Parrish, T. B., & Mesulam, M. M. (2001). Functional specificity of superior parietal mediation of spatial shifting. *NeuroImage, 14*, 661–673.

Vandenberghe, R., & Gillebert, C. R. (2009). Parcellation of parietal cortex: convergence between lesion-symptom mapping and mapping of the intact functioning brain. *Behavioral Brain Research, 199*, 171–182.

Vincent, J. L., Kahn, I., Snyder, A. Z., Raichle, M. E., & Buckner, R. L. (2008). Evidence for a frontoparietal control system revealed by intrinsic functional connectivity. *Journal of Neurophysiology, 100*, 3328–3342.

Vincent, J. L., Patel, G. H., Fox, M. D., Snyder, A. Z., Baker, J. T., Van Essen, D. C., et al. (2007). Intrinsic functional architecture in the anaesthetized monkey brain. *Nature, 447*, 83–86.

Vogeley, K., Bussfeld, P., Newen, A., Herrmann, S., Happe, F., Falkai, P., et al. (2001). Mind reading: Neural mechanisms of theory of mind and self-perspective. *NeuroImage, 14*, 170–181.

Wandell, B. A., Dumoulin, S. O., & Brewer, A. A. (2007). Visual field maps in human cortex. *Neuron, 56*, 366–383.

Wojciulik, E., & Kanwisher, N. (1999). The generality of parietal involvement in visual attention. *Neuron, 23*, 747–764.

Wolfe, J. M. (1994). Guided Search 2.0 A revised model of visual search. *Psychonomic Bulletin & Review, 1*, 202–238.

Womelsdorf, T., Fries, P., Mitra, P. P., & Desimone, R. (2006). Gamma-band synchronization in visual cortex predicts speed of change detection. *Nature, 439*, 733–736.

Yamaguchi, S., & Knight, R. T. (1991). Anterior and posterior association cortex contributions to the somatosensory P300. *Journal of Neuroscience, 11*, 2039–2054.

Yantis, S., & Egeth, H. E. (1999). On the distinction between visual salience and stimulus-driven attentional capture. *Journal of Experimental Psychology. Human Perception and Performance, 25*, 661–676.

Yantis, S., Schwarzbach, J., Serences, J. T., Carlson, R. L., Steinmetz, M. A., Pekar, J. J., & Courtney, S. M. (2002). Transient neural activity in human parietal cortex during spatial attention shifts. *Nature Neuroscience, 5*, 995–1002.

Young, L., Dodell-Feder, D., & Saxe, R. (2010). What gets the attention of the temporo-parietal junction? An fMRI investigation of attention and theory of mind. *Neuropsychologia, 48*, 2658–2664.

Zacks, J. M., Braver, T. S., Sheridan, M. A., Donaldson, D. I., Snyder, A. Z., Ollinger, J. M., et al. (2001). Human brain activity time-locked to perceptual event boundaries. *Nature Neuroscience, 4*, 651–655.

6

Midbrain and Forebrain Systems for Bottom-up Control of Spatial Attention

ERIC I. KNUDSEN

ANIMALS DEPEND on attention to behave adaptively in a complex world. Spatial attention enables the central nervous system to differentially process information from a limited region of space. A location may be selected for attention because of the physical distinctiveness, or salience, of an object at that location, referred to as bottom-up control of spatial attention (see Chapter 2 of this volume), or because of the relevance of a location to information being processed in working memory, referred to as top-down control of spatial attention (Egeth & Yantis, 1997; Itti & Koch, 2001; see Chapters 1 and 5 of this volume). Here, we will focus on the processes and mechanisms that underlie bottom-up control of attention.

Most studies of neural correlates of attention focus on forebrain systems (Goldberg et al., 2002; Constantinidis & Wang, 2004; Reynolds & Chelazzi, 2004; see Chapters 5 and 8 in this volume). However, recent research has documented the existence of a midbrain system that is capable of

bottom-up control of attention (Carello & Krauzlis, 2004; Ignashchenkova et al., 2004; McPeek & Keller, 2004; Muller et al., 2005; Fecteau & Munoz, 2006; Knudsen, 2011). Normally, the midbrain and forebrain systems operate together as a single integrated system (e.g., Sommer & Wurtz, 2000; Hanes & Wurtz, 2001). However, when the suddenness, motion, or contrast of a stimulus is sufficiently strong, the midbrain system can, itself, initiate orienting behavior and trigger shifts of attention (Sommer & Tehovnik, 1997; see Chapter 2 in this volume). The adaptive advantage of the midbrain system derives from the speed with which it reacts to potentially dangerous stimuli.

This chapter presents evidence that both forebrain and midbrain systems contribute to the bottom-up control of attention. The argument is made that these dual systems are linked with the well-studied forebrain and midbrain systems for controlling gaze direction (Schiller et al., 1987).

We will highlight similarities in the challenges that the midbrain and forebrain systems face in selecting targets for gaze and attention. Finally, we review recent studies of specialized neural circuits that have been discovered in the midbrain system that may underlie the competitive selection process, a process that is essential to both attention and gaze control.

FUNDAMENTAL COMPONENTS OF ATTENTION

Before we can appreciate the roles that the forebrain and midbrain systems play in the bottom-up control of attention, we must first analyze attention into its component processes (Figure 6.1). Attention involves the interaction of at least four component processes: filtering for stimulus salience, top-down regulation of neural sensitivity, competitive selection, and working memory (Knudsen, 2007).

Salience filters are essential to bottom-up control of attention (Itti & Koch, 2000; Fecteau & Munoz, 2006). Salience filters are neural circuits that respond differentially to features of stimuli that are likely to be biologically important. There are salience filters for features that are intrinsically distinctive, such as motion, contrast, or sudden changes, as detected by various sensory modalities. The salience of these features increases with the magnitude of the feature value. These features are encoded early in sensory pathways, and for the visual pathway they are encoded already in the retina (Olveczky et al., 2003; Munch et al., 2009; Gollisch & Meister, 2010). Other salience filters detect feature values that occur sparsely within groups of stimuli, such as a red stimulus in a field of green stimuli or a vertical bar in a field of horizontal bars (Cave & Wolfe, 1990; Joseph & Optican, 1996; Irwin et al., 2000; Itti & Koch, 2001). The responses of these filters cause the unusual stimulus to "popout" perceptually. Filters for popout stimuli require that the sensory information be processed first by filters tuned to different values of the feature, then by salience filters that detect rare occurrences of a given value. Because of the additional processing that popout salience requires, its evaluation takes longer and occurs later in sensory processing (Constantinidis

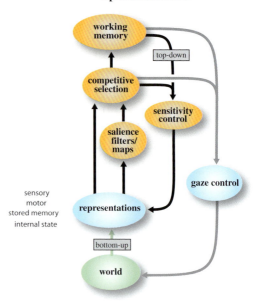

Spatial Attention

FIGURE 6.1   A schema for the fundamental components of attention. Black arrows highlight the bottom-up flow of information. Neural representations encode information about the world as well as information (not shown) about internal state, stored memories, motor plans, etc. Information from these representations is processed through salience filters, to signal the locations of salient stimuli in salience maps. Salience information competes with other information, and the highest-priority information gains access to working memory. During sustained attention, working memory maintains high responsiveness of relevant representations via top-down sensitivity control. When shifting the locus of attention, working memory shifts the locus of enhanced responsiveness via top-down sensitivity control or shifts both the locus of enhanced responsiveness and the direction of gaze. Modified from Knudsen, E. I. (2011). Control from below: The role of a midbrain network in spatial attention. *European Journal of Neuroscience, 33*(11), 1961–1972.

& Steinmetz, 2005; Ipata et al., 2006; Burrows & Moore, 2009). Finally, there are salience filters for complex stimuli that are of particular importance to the individual (Phelps et al., 2006; Peck et al., 2009) as a result of learning (the voice of a parent, for example) or natural selection over the course of evolution (the profile of a major predator, for example).

Maps of stimulus salience are a key component in computational models of bottom-up control of attention (Itti & Koch, 2001). A salience map is a representation of the salience of stimuli at all locations in space. The salience of a stimulus is encoded by the amount of neural activity, and the location of the stimulus is encoded by the location of the activity in the map. In this hypothetical map, neurons are tuned for stimulus location but are not tuned to different values of stimulus features (such as visual orientation or color or auditory frequency, for example). This is necessary so that the physical properties of stimuli do not confound the valuation of their salience in terms of spike rates. Salience maps for different features may be added together to form master salience maps that represent stimulus salience across many (or all) features.

Top-down sensitivity control is a process that is essential to the voluntary control of attention (Desimone & Duncan, 1995; Reynolds & Chelazzi, 2004). Areas of the brain that are involved in working memory and areas that control shifts of gaze (critical to the topic of this chapter) are able to alter the sensitivity of neurons encoding specific stimuli or specific locations based on the relevance of the stimulus or location to behavior. These top-down signals lower the thresholds, increase the gain, and improve the spatial resolution of neurons that represent the stimulus or location. At the same time, they can decrease the gain of neurons representing all other stimuli or locations (Winkowski & Knudsen, 2008; Han et al., 2009). In this way, top-down signals bias representations to favor stimuli or locations that are relevant to behavior.

A competitive selection process determines the most important information at any moment in time (Lee et al., 1999; Itti & Koch, 2001; Dehaene et al., 2003; Huang & Pashler, 2007). Competitive selection takes into account information from all representations, including salience maps (Figure 6.1). These representations combine information about the stimuli (bottom-up) with information about the relevance of a particular stimulus or location to behavior (top-down). This information competes ultimately for access to working memory and for access to gaze control or other relevant sensorimotor circuitry (Sumner et al., 2006).

A fourth component process of attention is working memory (Awh et al., 1998; Baddeley, 2003). Working memory holds, manipulates, and evaluates information over periods of seconds. It represents the information that animals use to make decisions. This form of memory is capable of analyzing and synthesizing an enormous range of information in uniquely powerful ways, but it is able to process only a limited number of different items at a time. The information that gains access to working memory is the information determined to be of the highest priority, based on the competitive selection process. Once information gains access to working memory, it then competes with information currently in working memory for representation (Baddeley, 2003; Koch & Tsuchiya, 2007).

A LINKAGE BETWEEN SPATIAL ATTENTION AND GAZE CONTROL

Spatial attention is linked closely with gaze control. This linkage makes sense intuitively for a number of reasons. First, for both shifts in the locus of spatial attention and shifts in gaze, the goal is a location in space. This location can be encoded topographically in neural maps of space. Moreover, once the position of the eyes in the orbits has been accounted for, the goals for these two functions can be encoded in the same maps, in either retinocentric or craniocentric frames of reference. Second, shifts of gaze and shifts of spatial attention serve a common purpose: They both improve the quality of the information being processed in working memory. Orienting the eyes toward a stimulus aligns the region of the retina capable of the highest spatial resolution with the stimulus of interest. Alternatively, top-down regulation of sensory networks improves their sensitivity to and encoding of the relevant information (Lee & Maunsell, 2009; Reynolds & Heeger, 2009). Thus, shifts in gaze and spatial attention act cooperatively and, when employed simultaneously, they maximize the quality of the sensory information being processed in working memory.

Psychophysical studies have demonstrated that a tight linkage exists between gaze control and spatial attention. Numerous experiments have shown that when we plan to move our eyes to a new location, our ability to detect and discriminate stimuli increases specifically at the target of the planned eye movement. For example, when humans are required to identify a letter (T or L) among distractors (Es and Fs) that appears just before they move the eyes, letter identification is most accurate when the location of the letter matches the location of the planned eye movement (Hoffman & Subramaniam, 1995). Moreover, superior letter identification occurs at the location of the planned eye movement even when subjects are instructed to attend voluntarily to a different location. Analogous results have been reported by others (Kowler et al., 1995; Deubel & Schneider, 1996). Such experiments indicate that planning a voluntary eye movement to a location necessarily causes spatial attention to shift, at least momentarily, to that location.

The converse is not true. Animals often direct spatial attention to a location without moving the eyes to that location, a phenomenon referred to as *covert attention* (Juan et al., 2004; Awh et al., 2006; Juan et al., 2008). Covert attention allows working memory to augment or improve the quality of information concerning different items without having to direct gaze at each item (Koch & Tsuchiya, 2007). Thus, although working memory can direct spatial attention to a location without directing an eye movement to that location, when an eye movement is indeed planned, spatial attention always shifts to that location.

TWO NEURAL SYSTEMS CONTROL SHIFTS OF GAZE

As described above, shifts of gaze engender shifts in the locus of attention. This suggests that neural circuits that command shifts of gaze also command shifts of attention. Two different brain structures directly command shifts of gaze. A structure in the forebrain that controls gaze is called the frontal eye field (FEF) in mammals and the archopallial gaze field (AGF) in birds (Bruce et al., 1985; Knudsen et al., 1995). The midbrain structure that can shift gaze is called the intermediate and deep layers of the superior colliculus (SCi-d) in mammals and the intermediate and deep layers of the optic tectum (OTi-d) in nonmammalian vertebrates (Wurtz & Albano, 1980; Stein &

Meredith, 1993). For simplicity, the mammalian nomenclature will be used in this chapter as the collective term, unless the results were obtained specifically from nonmammalian vertebrates.

Both the FEF and the SCi-d project directly to premotor nuclei in the brainstem tegmentum that generate the signals for saccadic shifts of gaze (Harting, 1977; Stanton et al., 1988; Masino & Knudsen, 1992; Stein & Meredith, 1993; Knudsen et al., 1995). The FEF also projects to the SCi-d and controls its excitability with tonic inhibition via the substantia nigra (Hikosaka & Wurtz, 1985b). When the FEF issues a command for an eye movement, it not only sends that command directly to the brainstem saccade generators, it also disinhibits the SCi-d and instructs it to command the movement as well. The converse is not true. The SCi-d can command eye movements without engaging the motor circuitry of the FEF (Bruce et al., 1985; Schall, 1991). Inactivation of either the FEF or the SCi-d alone leaves animals still capable of making saccadic eye movements to a visual target, whereas inactivation of both structures leaves animals apparently incapable of making goal-directed saccadic eye movements (Hikosaka & Wurtz, 1985a; Schiller et al., 1987; Knudsen & Knudsen, 1996a; Sommer & Tehovnik, 1997).

The two systems are not redundant. The FEF controls voluntary eye movements not only to sensory targets, but also to targets that are held in working memory, "remembered targets." Following inactivation of the FEF, orienting eye movements to visual and auditory stimuli that are present in the environment are only slightly affected, whereas orienting movements to remembered targets are severely impaired (Knudsen & Knudsen, 1996b; Sommer & Tehovnik, 1997; Dias & Segraves, 1999). On the other hand, following inactivation of the SCi-d, animals continue to make long-latency saccades (>120 ms) to existing and remembered targets, although the probability of making a saccade and the accuracy of the saccades tend to decrease; however, the animals no longer make short-latency (<120 ms) saccades, referred to as "express" saccades (Schiller et al., 1987; Knudsen & Knudsen, 1996a). The evidence indicates that the FEF plays an essential role in planning memory-based saccades, whereas the SCi-d is essential for planning and executing express saccades.

The behavioral advantage of being able to make short-latency saccades may have driven the co-evolution of forebrain and midbrain systems for controlling gaze and attention. Short-latency saccades provide an animal with a strong selective advantage in that they orient the eyes to potentially dangerous stimuli extremely rapidly, saving time that can make the difference between life and death under natural conditions. The ability to plan and execute short-latency saccades requires that the midbrain system, like the forebrain system, be able to evaluate and select appropriate stimuli as targets for gaze shifts.

FOREBRAIN GAZE CONTROL CIRCUITS ARE LINKED TO SPATIAL ATTENTION

Several lines of evidence indicate that the FEF, a structure in the forebrain system that plans and executes changes in gaze, also contributes to directing spatial attention (see Chapter 7 in this volume; Wardak et al., 2006).

Neurophysiological recordings in monkeys making voluntary eye movements demonstrate the role of the FEF in motor planning. Neurons in the FEF discharge in close association with voluntary eye movements to either existing (visual or auditory) or remembered targets (Bruce, 1990; Russo & Bruce, 1994). One class of FEF neurons, called *movement-related neurons*, discharge briskly only when eye movements are directed toward a limited region of space, referred to as the neuron's *motor field* (Hanes & Schall, 1996; Ray et al., 2009). Movement-related neurons in the FEF are organized according to the location of their motor fields to form a crude but topographic, motor map of space. In addition, electrical microstimulation applied to the FEF results in eye saccades of fixed direction and magnitude, and the endpoints of the evoked saccades correspond to the motor map of space.

A different class of FEF neurons responds to visual stimuli located within spatial receptive fields (RFs; Bruce, 1990). Unlike visual neurons in the visual cortex, visual neurons in the FEF are not tuned strongly to values of stimulus features, such as color or contour orientation. Instead, they respond to intrinsically salient or popout stimuli

and their responses are greatly enhanced when a stimulus is behaviorally relevant as the result of training (Schall, 2004; Thompson et al., 2005; Buschman & Miller, 2007; Zhou & Thompson, 2009). Thus, FEF visual responses appear to represent the priority of stimuli for either attention or gaze.

A third major class of FEF neurons responds to visual stimuli and is also active in association with voluntary eye movements (Bruce, 1990). The visual and movement related activities of these neurons are temporally separated when monkeys make delayed eye saccades to brief visual stimuli. The visual selectivities of these neurons are the same as those of visual FEF neurons. However, many visuo-movement neurons tend to remain active from the time they begin responding to a stimulus until the time that the animal executes an eye saccade to the stimulus. Thus, this class of neuron can encode the locations of remembered stimuli.

The representation of the visual field in the FEF, as expressed by visual neurons, aligns with the motor map of space, as expressed by movement-related neurons (Awh et al., 2006). This sensory–motor alignment of space representations suggests that the FEF could convert information about the location of a selected stimulus into plans for eye saccades within a retinocentric frame of reference.

Results from electrical microstimulation experiments indicate that activity in the FEF can also direct spatial attention (see Chapter 7 in this volume). Moore and Fallah applied low-level, focal microstimulation to the FEF while monkeys performed a detection task that required covert spatial attention (Moore & Fallah, 2001). The current strengths used for microstimulation were below those necessary to evoke an eye saccade. On interleaved trials with and without FEF microstimulation, Moore and Fallah measured the threshold sensitivity of a monkey in detecting the dimming of a peripheral visual target that was presented together with flashing distracting stimuli. They found that monkeys detected a smaller change in target luminance with FEF microstimulation, but only when the target was at the location corresponding to the motor field of the FEF stimulation site. The remarkable observation was that focal electrical microstimulation of the FEF actually improves a monkey's performance in a way that resembles the way in which voluntary spatial attention improves a monkey's performance in a stimulus detection task.

Subsequent experiments went on to show that low-level microstimulation of the FEF also results in the regulation of neuronal sensitivity in the extrastriate visual area V4 (Moore & Armstrong, 2003; Moore et al., 2003). They observed a micro-stimulation-induced increase in the response gain of V4 neurons that was specific for the region of space encoded by the FEF microstimulation site. The increase in response gain mimicked the increase in response gain exhibited by V4 neurons when monkeys attend to stimuli voluntarily.

The proposition that the FEF acts as a source of top-down signals for enhancing the sensitivity of sensory responses, as suggested by the micro-stimulation results, is supported by results from simultaneous recordings in the FEF and V4 of monkeys performing a covert attention task (Gregoriou et al., 2009). Those neurons in the FEF and V4 with overlapping visual RFs were recorded while a monkey either attended or ignored the stimulus in the visual RF. Differential responses to the attended stimulus appeared first in the FEF, followed about 50 ms later by differential activity in V4. Simultaneous recordings of local field potentials (LFPs) in the FEF and V4 indicated a causality to this order of activation. When monkeys attended to the stimulus in the shared visual RF, LFPs measured in the FEF and V4 exhibited a strong increase in power in the 40–60 Hz range (in the γ range), and a measure of causality (Granger causality) indicated that the γ activity in each area had a significant influence on the activity in the other area. Together, the results suggest that increased neuronal responses in the FEF lead to increased oscillatory coupling between the FEF and the V4, which in turn leads to increased neuronal responsiveness in the V4.

Accumulating evidence indicates that these two functions of the FEF—that is, shifting the direction of gaze and transmitting space-specific signals for regulating sensory gain and sensitivity—are mediated in parallel. Anatomical studies show that FEF neurons projecting to the SCi-d (involved in gaze control) originate in layer 5, whereas those projecting to visual areas V4 and TEO (involved

in sensory processing) originate predominantly in layers 2–3 (Pouget et al., 2009). In addition, neurophysiological studies show that when monkeys shift attention covertly, movement-related neurons are inhibited whereas visual and visuo-movement neurons exhibit enhanced visual responsiveness (Thompson et al., 2005).

These properties suggest that the FEF is positioned at the branch point from working memory to both gaze control and top-down sensitivity control (Figure 6.1). According to the schema, working memory signals, for example from the dorsolateral prefrontal cortex (PFC) (Buschman & Miller, 2009), can either shift the locus of attention or shift both the locus of attention and the direction of gaze, by activating the circuitry of the FEF. This role of the FEF in implementing spatial shifts of attention or shifts of both attention and gaze is consistent with results of pharmacological inactivation experiments in which FEF inactivation produced severe deficits in both visually guided saccades and covert search tasks (that did not involve eye movements), regardless of the difficulty of the search task (Wardak et al., 2006).

MIDBRAIN GAZE CONTROL CIRCUITS ARE ALSO LINKED TO SPATIAL ATTENTION

The other region of the brain that directly controls orienting eye movements is in the midbrain: the SCi-d (called the OTi-d in non-mammalian vertebrates). The SCi-d and the FEF are similar in their functional organization, and both project directly to saccade generating circuitry in the brainstem tegmentum (Harting, 1977; Stanton et al., 1988; Masino & Knudsen, 1992; Knudsen et al., 1995). Like the FEF, the SCi-d contains neurons that respond to visual as well as to auditory stimuli originating from a restricted, spatial RF (Knudsen, 1982; Jay & Sparks, 1984; Stein & Meredith, 1993). Neurons in the SCi-d have functional properties that are similar to those in the FEF. The SCi-d, like the FEF, contains multisensory neurons that respond to salient and behaviorally relevant stimuli (Stein & Meredith, 1993), visuo-movement neurons that encode the locations of remembered targets (Glimcher & Sparks, 1992; Kustov & Robinson, 1996; Ignashchenkova et al., 2004), and movement-related neurons that discharge in close association with the execution of eye saccades to particular locations (Munoz & Wurtz, 1995). Electrical microstimulation applied to the SCi-d evokes short-latency, saccadic eye movements with fixed directions and magnitudes, the endpoints of which vary with the site of stimulation according to the retinotopic map of space (Robinson, 1972; Stryker & Schiller, 1975; du Lac & Knudsen, 1990). Finally, visual responses in the SCi-d, like those in the FEF, are modulated by top-down signals when a stimulus is behaviorally relevant and the location of the stimulus is either expected or has been cued with a prior stimulus (Wurtz & Goldberg, 1972; Kustov & Robinson, 1996; McPeek & Keller, 2002; Ignashchenkova et al., 2004; Li & Basso, 2008).

When an animal makes voluntary eye saccades, movement-related activity in the SCi-d can be driven directly by descending input from the FEF (Segraves & Goldberg, 1987). However, the SCi-d is, itself, capable of generating commands

for shifting gaze and attention (Figure 6.2). The SCi-d generates commands for short-latency saccades and for saccades when the FEF is inactivated (Schiller et al., 1987; Knudsen & Knudsen, 1996a; Sommer & Tehovnik, 1997). More generally, Ignashchenkova et al. (2004) demonstrated, in a visual discrimination task, that the SCi-d generates signals for shifting spatial attention to the location of the stimulus to be judged when the cue to shift attention is at the location where the stimulus will appear, but not when the location to be attended is represented symbolically by the cue. These findings imply that the SCi-d contains the neural circuitry necessary to select stimuli for attention and to convert the locations of selected stimuli into commands for orienting eye movements (Figure 6.2).

Electrical microstimulation experiments show that the SCi-d can act as a source of signals that enhance behavioral performance in sensory decision and discrimination tasks. Like electrical microstimulation of the FEF, electrical microstimulation

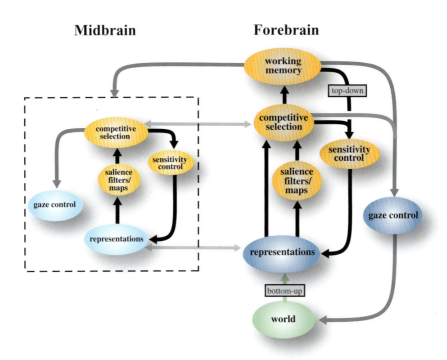

FIGURE 6.2   A schema for the midbrain and forebrain systems for bottom-up control of spatial attention. The symbols are the same as those in Figure 6.1.

of the SCi-d biases the selection of stimuli and improves the discrimination of stimuli at current strengths below those required to generate saccadic eye movements, and it has this effect specifically at the location encoded by the microstimulation site (Carello & Krauzlis, 2004; Cavanaugh & Wurtz, 2004). In one such experiment (Muller et al., 2005), monkeys were trained to report the direction of motion of random dots located in a restricted portion of the visual field as the proportion of coherently moving dots decreased. The monkeys performed this task with or without electrical microstimulation of the SCi-d on interleaved trials. The ability of the monkeys detect coherent dot motion improved when the moving dots were placed at the location encoded by the stimulation site in the SCi-d, but not when the dots were located at a control location. These kinds of experiments demonstrate that SCi-d activation can evoke, directly or indirectly, top-down signals that enhance behavioral sensitivity and stimulus discrimination in a space-specific manner (Figure 6.2), both effects being diagnostic of spatial attention.

A FOREBRAIN SALIENCE MAP FOR BOTTOM-UP STIMULUS SELECTION

The evidence cited above indicates that activation of either the midbrain or forebrain system can shift spatial attention. Does each system contain the requisite neural circuitry for analyzing the relative salience of stimuli and for selecting the highest-priority stimulus for attention and for a potential eye movement?

In the forebrain system, the FEF (discussed earlier) and the posterior parietal cortex both contain neurons that encode the relative salience of stimuli, and both areas have been proposed to contain salience maps that could contribute to stimulus selection (Fecteau & Munoz, 2006). However, three lines of evidence suggest that sensory responses in the FEF are downstream from the selection process. First, pharmacological inactivation of the FEF (Wardak et al., 2006) causes severe deficits in covert stimulus selection that are independent of the difficulty of the selection task (easy: color difference; difficult: conjunction of

features). This effect is most consistent with the FEF encoding the result of the selection process, rather than contributing to the analysis of relative salience. In contrast, the same kind of inactivation of the lateral intraparietal area (LIP) in the posterior parietal cortex (Wardak et al., 2004) causes selection deficits that increase with the difficulty of the task.

Second, simultaneous recordings in the FEF, LIP, and lateral PFC during a popout search task indicate that neuronal activity in the LIP begins encoding the location of the popout stimulus first, followed by activity in the PFC and the FEF (Buschman & Miller, 2007; but see comments of Schall et al., 2007). If true, this temporal sequence suggests that bottom-up stimulus selection under these conditions occurs in the LIP, and the selected information is subsequently transmitted to working memory and to gaze control circuitry.

Third, competitive selection in the forebrain system involves competition among representations that encode information in a variety of different coordinate frames, including retinocentric, egocentric, and various allocentric frames of reference (Knudsen, 2007). The FEF processes information only in a retinocentric frame of reference, whereas the posterior parietal cortex processes information in a variety of coordinate frames (Andersen et al., 1997; Colby & Goldberg, 1999; Mullette-Gillman et al., 2005).

Thus, in the forebrain system, the posterior parietal cortex is a prime candidate for analyzing stimulus salience (see Chapter 8 in this volume). It has been known for some time that damage to the posterior parietal cortex results in profound deficits in the ability of humans to attend to stimuli, particularly in the presence of distracting stimuli (Friedland & Weinstein, 1977; Friedman-Hill et al., 2003; Shomstein & Yantis, 2006; Husain & Nachev, 2007). Neurophysiological recordings in the LIP and in area 7a, two posterior parietal areas, reveal neurons with response properties consistent with those of master salience maps (Fecteau & Munoz, 2006; see also Chapter 8 in this volume). Neurons in these areas respond to all types of salient features, whether or not a stimulus is relevant to the immediate task (Gottlieb et al., 1998; Kusunoki et al., 2000; Bisley & Goldberg, 2003; Constantinidis & Steinmetz, 2005). Sensory responses exhibit little tuning for stimulus features, unless a feature is behaviorally relevant. For example, LIP neurons are not color selective unless a monkey has been rewarded for making a decision based on color (Toth & Assad, 2002). In addition, sensory responses in both the LIP and area 7a are modulated powerfully by top-down signals that represent the behavioral relevance of stimuli. The combined influences of these bottom-up and top-down effects create representations of the priority of stimuli for attention and shifts of gaze (Constantinidis & Steinmetz, 2005; Balan & Gottlieb, 2006; Fecteau & Munoz, 2006). Indeed, neurophysiological recordings from monkeys performing delayed saccade tasks, in which the monkey tries to ignore a salient distracting stimulus (a flashed dot), reveal that the relative levels of stimulus-related activity in the LIP correspond to the location and temporal dynamics of spatial attention measured behaviorally (Bisley & Goldberg, 2003).

The circuits in the forebrain system that perform the competitive selection of the highest-priority stimulus (Figure 6.2, *right side*) have not been identified. It is possible, however, that such a circuit resides in the posterior parietal cortex, since the information necessary to evaluate relative salience in different frames of reference is present in the LIP, and the posterior parietal cortex is essential for attending to stimuli in the presence of distractors.

A MIDBRAIN SALIENCE MAP FOR BOTTOM-UP STIMULUS SELECTION

The midbrain system also contains the requisite circuitry for analyzing the relative salience of stimuli and for selecting the highest-priority stimulus (Knudsen, 2011; Figure 6.2, *left side*). Sensory responses in the SCi-d, like those in the FEF and the posterior parietal cortex, exhibit properties consistent with those of a salience map (McPeek & Keller, 2002; Mysore et al., 2011a). Sensory neurons respond strongly to intrinsically salient stimulus features: the suddenness of stimuli, contrast, and movement in any direction (Wurtz & Goldberg, 1972; Stein & Meredith, 1993; Sparks, 2002). Unexpected stimuli are particularly effective in driving SCi-d responses. As stimuli become

predictable, responses adapt dramatically, usually to a baseline level, and some neurons stop responding altogether to repeated stimuli. At the same time, sensory neurons in the SCi-d show little or no selectivity for values of stimulus features. They respond to positive or negative contrasts, to spots or bars at all orientations, and to all visible colors (White et al., 2009). Some visual neurons exhibit a preference for direction of motion, but the preference is no stronger than the motion preferences of retinal ganglion cells (Olveczky et al., 2003; Gollisch & Meister, 2010). Many SCi-d neurons also respond to auditory and/or somatosensory stimuli, with little tuning for spectral or temporal properties of the stimulus (Knudsen, 1984; Jay & Sparks, 1987; Stein & Meredith, 1993). In summary, there is no evidence that the SCi-d processes sensory information in a way that would contribute to the analysis of stimulus identity, as is characteristic of sensory processing pathways in the forebrain. Instead, sensory responses in the SCi-d appear to represent primarily the strength of intrinsically salient features of a stimulus.

Sensory responses in the SCi-d are tuned for stimulus location, and those that respond to multiple sensory modalities have mutually aligned spatial RFs for the different modalities (Knudsen, 1982; Stein & Meredith, 1993). As mentioned previously, neurons are organized according to the location of their sensory RFs to form a multimodal map of space. Thus, consistent with the properties of the hypothetical salience map (Itti & Koch, 2001), SCi-d neurons are tuned to stimulus location and respond according to the strengths of intrinsically salient features, but are rarely tuned to particular values of stimulus features or even to a particular sensory modality.

Sensory responses in the SCi-d encode relative, rather than absolute, salience. When tested with multiple simultaneous stimuli, the responses of an SCi-d neuron to a visual stimulus within its classical receptive field (CRF) are suppressed by the presence of a second stimulus, even one that is located far away (>30 degrees) from the neuron's CRF (Rizzolatti et al., 1974; Mysore et al., 2010). The suppressive influence of the second stimulus depends on the intrinsic salience of the stimulus and not on the feature values of the stimulus. For example, responses to a moving dot in a neuron's

CRF can be suppressed by a distant dot moving rapidly in the same or in different directions, by a stationary dot of high contrast, or by an intense sound (Mysore et al., 2010). Moreover, the second stimulus can be located anywhere in the visual field (visual competitors) or throughout space (auditory competitors). As discussed in the next section, the global extent of this suppressive influence suggests the existence of a specialized circuit capable of exerting powerful inhibition across the entire map of space in the SCi-d.

For the majority of SCi-d neurons, global inhibition serves not only as a normalizing influence on responses (Carandini & Heeger, 1994; Pouille et al., 2009), it also dramatically enhances the representation of differences in the salience of stimuli, especially when the differences are small (Mysore et al., 2011b). A subpopulation of neurons in the OTi-d of owls responds differentially to the strongest stimulus among multiple stimuli (Figure 6.3): They respond vigorously when the stimulus in the CRF is the stronger stimulus and weakly when the same stimulus in the CRF is the weaker stimulus (Figure 6.3B). Among these neurons that exhibit switch-like response suppression in the presence of a strong competing stimulus, the strength of the competing stimulus that causes inhibition to switch from weak to strong is, on average, the strength of the stimulus in the neuron's CRF (S1). Moreover, when the strength of the CRF stimulus increases, the strength of the competitor stimulus necessary to suppress the responses of these neurons increases by an equivalent amount (Figure 6.3C). Any intrinsically salient property of a competing stimulus (motion strength, visual contrast, sound level or suddenness) contributes to its suppressive influence (Figure 6.3D). Thus, the activity of these neurons in the OTi-d provides a categorical signal that specifies the location of the strongest stimulus. These properties set the stage for a process that selects the next target for gaze or spatial attention (Itti & Koch, 2001).

As in the FEF and LIP (see previous sections), sensory responses in the OTi-d are modulated by top-down signals. Electrical microstimulation of the archopallial gaze field (AGF), the bird's equivalent of the FEF, leads to space-specific increases in the sensitivity and spatial resolution of sensory responses (both visual and auditory) of OTi-d neurons (Winkowski & Knudsen, 2007, 2008). The improved sensory resolution is specific for locations in the OTi-d space map that correspond to the location encoded at the site of microstimulation in the AGF. At the same time, AGF microstimulation decreases the response gain of neurons that encode all other locations in space. The data predict that when an owl plans to orient gaze voluntarily to a particular location in space, this top-down signal acts much like a "spotlight" of enhanced sensitivity, corresponding to the heightened behavioral relevance of this location in the midbrain salience map. This prediction remains to be tested in behaving owls. However, an effect of this kind has been observed in the SCi-d of behaving monkeys (Sommer & Wurtz, 2000; Li & Basso, 2005). Thus, the salience map in the midbrain, as in the forebrain, represents the combined effects of automatic, bottom-up processes and top-down influences (Knudsen, 2011).

SPECIALIZED CIRCUITRY MEDIATING STIMULUS SELECTION IN THE MIDBRAIN SYSTEM

The insight that the SCi-d is capable of selecting stimuli as targets for shifts of gaze has focused interest on candidate neural circuits that might perform the underlying, specialized functions. Two of the specialized functions are the capacity to regulate sensitivity and spatial resolution at specific locations in the map as a consequence of top-down signals (Winkowski & Knudsen, 2008), and the capacity to mediate competition among stimuli across the entirety of space (Mysore et al., 2010). Midbrain circuits that exhibit architectures and response properties that are suited to perform these functions have been identified in several classes of vertebrates (Knudsen, 2011). In birds, in which these circuits have been studied most thoroughly, they are referred to as the *isthmic nuclei* (Wang, 2003; Wang et al., 2006); in mammals, they are referred to as the *parabigeminal* and *lateral tegmental nuclei* (Graybiel, 1978; Wang et al., 2004). These nuclei comprise separate populations of cholinergic and γ-aminobutyric acid (GABA)ergic neurons, respectively.

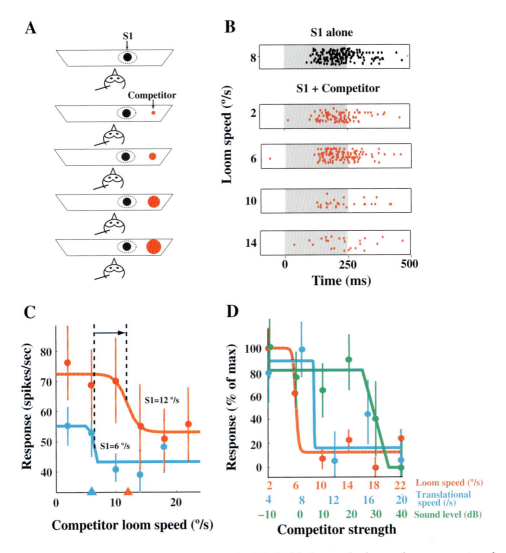

FIGURE 6.3   Switch-like response suppression in the OTi-d of the barn owl enhances the representation of the most salient stimulus. (**A**) Experimental paradigm. Top view of the owl, the projection screen, and the side of unit recording. The dotted circle represents the unit's classical receptive field (CRF). S1 (black dot): a looming stimulus centered in the CRF. Competitor (red dot): a looming stimulus located 30 degrees to the side of the CRF. The size of the dot symbolizes the speed of the looming stimuli. (**B**) Raster plots of switch-like response suppression by the stimuli shown in A. Each dot represents a spike. S1 = 8 degree/s loom speed. The gray interval (0–250 ms) is the duration of the stimulus. (**C**) Responses to S1 as a function of the changing strength of the competitor stimulus loom speed. These competitor-response profiles were measured as shown in B using two different S1 loom speeds. The data show mean, s. e. m., and sigmoidal fits to the data. Vertical dashed lines indicate the switch value: the strength of the competitor that caused a 50% reduction in the response to the S1 stimulus. Horizontal arrow: the shift in the switch value resulting from the increment in S1 loom speed. Upward triangles: speed of the S1 stimulus. (**D**) Competitor-response profiles using the same S1 stimulus (6 degree/s loom speed) and different competitor features: loom speed, translational speed, or sound level. Same conventions as in C. The data are from Mysore, S. P., Asadollahi, A., & Knudsen, E. I. (2011a). Signaling of the strongest stimulus in the owl optic tectum. *Journal of Neuroscience, 31,* 5186–5196.

The cholinergic neurons of the isthmic complex exhibit structural and functional properties that suggest that they mediate focal modulations of neuronal sensitivity in the OTi-d (Wang et al., 2006). The nuclei isthmi pars parvocellularis (Ipc) and semilunaris (SLu), analogous to the parabigeminal nucleus in mammals, contain cholinergic neurons that receive topographically precise input from a special class of OT neurons in layer 10, at the boundary between the superficial and intermediate layers (Figure 6.4). Ipc and SLu neurons send topographically precise feedback to the same location in the OT map that provides their input, and this feedback goes to both the retino-recipient superficial OT layers (predominantly from the Ipc), as well as to the OTi-d (predominantly from the SLu).

Neurophysiological recordings from the Ipc reveal neurons that are tuned to the location of stimuli (visual or auditory) and are organized into a map of space (Sherk, 1979; Maczko et al., 2006). They respond with increasing firing rates to increases in the strength of intrinsically salient features (motion and contrast), and they are not tuned to values of visual or auditory features (Asadollahi et al., 2010). Most importantly, approximately half of the neurons exhibit switch-like response suppression in the presence of a strong competing stimulus (Figure 6.5A): They respond vigorously when the stimulus in their CRF is the strongest stimulus, but weakly when the same stimulus is the weaker stimulus. Thus, Ipc neurons send a spatially precise, cholinergic signal to the OT that differentially favors the stronger stimulus.

Neurons in the Ipc and SLu contain acetylcholine (ACh), and ACh has been shown to enhance the sensitivity of OT neurons to retinal input as well as to activate local inhibitory networks in the OT (Binns & Salt, 2000; Lee et al., 2001; Endo et al., 2005). These simultaneous effects of ACh could simultaneously enhance the sensitivity and improve the spatial resolution of OTi-d neurons (Winkowski & Knudsen, 2007).

Another intriguing property of Ipc neurons is that they discharge in bursts of spikes and, in

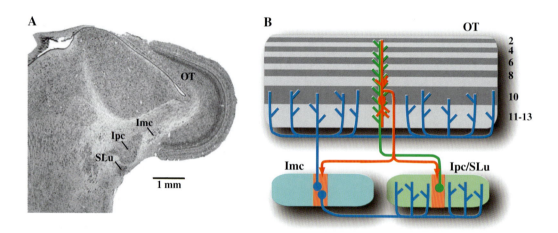

FIGURE 6.4 The midbrain network for competitive stimulus selection in birds. (**A**) Transverse Nissl-stained section from the barn owl (*Tyto alba*). OT, optic tectum; Ipc, nucleus isthmi pars parvocellularis; SLu, nucleus semilunaris; Imc, nucleus isthmi pars magnocellularis. Dorsal is up and lateral is to the right. (**B**) Schematic of cellular connections between the OT and the isthmic nuclei. OT layer 10 neurons (*red*), with bipolar dendrites radiating into the superficial layers (layers 1–9) and into the intermediate and deep layers (layers 11–13), send axons to cholinergic neurons (*green*) in the Ipc and SLu and to GABAegic neurons (*blue*) in the Imc. The pink zones indicate the termination zones for the layer 10 neuron. Ipc neurons project back topographically to the OT, preferentially to the superficial layers; SLu neurons project back topographically, preferentially to the OTi-d layers, as well as to the thalamus and pretectum (not shown). Imc neurons project broadly to the OTi-d, Ipc and SLu.

response to sensory stimulation, the bursts occur with a periodicity of 25–50 Hz (Figure 6.5B, C, D). As a result, stimulus conditions that drive Ipc neurons result in periodic drive to the OT that can be measured as γ-band oscillations in the OT LFP (Sridharan et al., 2011). Stimulus-driven activity from the Ipc to the OT—that is, periodic in this frequency band—has been shown to be exceptionally effective in gating ascending visual information from the OT to the thalamus, on the way to the forebrain (Marin et al., 2007). As mentioned previously, synchronized γ-band oscillations have been measured in the LIP, FEF, and PFC in monkeys involved in tasks in which attention is under bottom-up control (Buschman & Miller, 2007).

Neurons in another nucleus in the isthmic complex, the nucleus isthmi pars magnocellularis (Imc), exhibit structural properties that suggest that they mediate competition among stimuli represented anywhere in the entire OT space map (Wang et al., 2004). The Imc contains exclusively GABAergic neurons. Imc neurons, like the cholinergic Ipc and SLu neurons, receive topographically organized input from neurons in layer 10 of the OT (see Figure 6.4B). However, in contrast to the cholinergic neurons, Imc neurons project back to all locations in the OTi-d, except to the location that provides their input. In addition, a second population of Imc neurons projects with the same pattern to the cholinergic isthmic nuclei (Figure 6.4B).

The spatial pattern of the Imc projections to the OTi-d and Ipc corresponds with the spatial pattern of global inhibition that has been measured in these nuclei in the context of distant competing stimuli (Asadollahi et al., 2010; Mysore et al., 2010). As discussed earlier, global inhibition is apparent in the OTi-d when two or more stimuli compete for representation. This

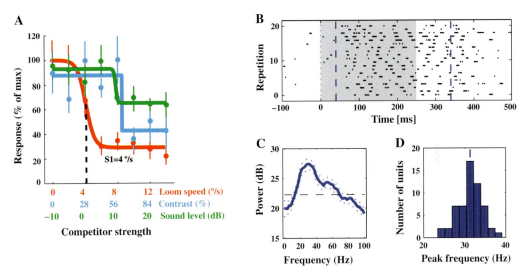

FIGURE 6.5   Unit responses to stimulus competition in the cholinergic Ipc of the barn owl. (**A**) Competitor-response profiles (measured as described in Figure 6.3) using different competitor features: loom speed, contrast, or sound level. In each case, the S1 stimulus, centered in the unit's classical receptive field (CRF), was a 4 degrees/s looming dot. Data show mean, s. e. m., and sigmoidal best fit. Competitors were located 30 degrees to the side of the CRF of the unit. *Vertical dashed line*: switch value measured with looming dot competitors. (**B**) Bursting unit responses to a 6 degrees/s looming dot centered in the CRF. Gray interval (0–250 ms): duration of the stimulus; *dashed lines*: period of analysis for C. (**C**) Power spectrum of the spike discharges shown in B. Dots indicate jackknife errors. The peak oscillation frequency was 30 Hz for this unit. (**D**) Distribution of peak oscillation frequencies of bursting responses measured across a population of Ipc units. Modified from Asadollahi, A., Mysore, S. P., & Knudsen, E. I. (2010). Stimulus-driven competition in a cholinergic midbrain nucleus. *Nature Neuroscience, 30*, 1727–1738.

global competitive inhibition could underlie both the mapwide normalization of salience representation and the enhancement of the signaling of relative stimulus salience that are expressed in the OTi-d (Mysore et al., 2011b). This proposition remains to be tested.

TWO SYSTEMS FOR BOTTOM-UP CONTROL OF ATTENTION

The schema for the bottom-up control of attention proposed in this chapter is summarized in Figure 6.2. According to this schema, two systems influence bottom-up control of competitive selection in the forebrain. The midbrain system receives direct visual input from the retinotectal pathway and processes multimodal information about the locations of salient stimuli, based primarily on the suddenness, motion, and contrast of stimuli. At the same time, the forebrain system receives direct visual input from the retinothalamic pathway and processes information about all aspects of sensory stimuli.

The schema proposes that the midbrain system evaluates information related to stimulus salience and sends this information to the competitive selection process in the forebrain (Figure 6.2). Experiments in which the SCi-d is either microstimulated or inactivated support this conclusion. As mentioned previously, electrical microstimulation of the SCi-d at current levels below those necessary to evoke an eye saccade improves the ability of monkeys to detect and discriminate stimuli positioned specifically at the location represented by the site of stimulation (Carello & Krauzlis, 2004; Cavanaugh & Wurtz, 2004; Muller et al., 2005). In addition, reversible inactivation of the SCi-d alters stimulus selection in monkeys trained to select targets in a visual search task (Figure 6.6). McPeek and Keller (2004) trained monkeys to make an eye saccade to a color (or contrast) singleton that was presented either alone or together with three other stimuli of a different color (or contrast). The stimuli were positioned so that one of the stimuli was located at the center of the region of the SCi-d space map that was to be inactivated (Figure 6.6A). The other stimuli were at equivalent eccentricities, but separated by 90 degrees in direction from the starting fixation point (Figure 6.6B). Before SCi-d inactivation, the monkey made eye saccades accurately and reliably to the target stimulus when it was presented either alone or as a singleton with distractors at any of the four locations (Figure 6.6B). After SCi-d inactivation, the monkey still made accurate eye saccades toward the target stimulus alone at all locations. However, when the target was presented as a singleton among distractors, and it was at the location inactivated by the SCi-d injection, the monkey no longer selected only the singleton stimulus. Instead, it selected any of the four stimuli (Figure 6.6C).

These results demonstrate that information from the SCi-d contributes to the representation and selection of stimuli for attention, even when an animal is not making express saccades toward stimuli. According to the schema in Figure 6.2, the results of this experiment are explained as follows: Before inactivation, the salience map in the SCi-d represents the locations of the four stimuli based primarily on their contrasts. After inactivation, when the portion of the SCi-d that is inactivated corresponds to the location of the color popout stimulus, the SCi-d signals only the locations of the three distractor stimuli. The SCi-d sends this information to the competitive selection process in the forebrain system (Shipp, 2004), which also receives input about the location of the popout stimulus via cortical representations (dorsal and ventral streams). The results suggest that the representations of the three distractor locations (signaled by the midbrain system) were added to that of the popout stimulus (from the forebrain system), when the target for an eye movement was selected (Figure 6.6C).

The property that distinguishes the input from the midbrain system from the many other sources of input to the competitive selection process in the forebrain is that the midbrain system can, itself, trigger shifts of gaze (Figure 6.2). In doing so, the midbrain system drives stimulus selection by the forebrain system and causes information about the signaled location to access working memory, at least momentarily. This special capacity of the midbrain system assures that potentially dangerous stimuli are indeed attended and analyzed in working memory.

One advantage of the midbrain system for bottom-up control of attention is its speed of action.

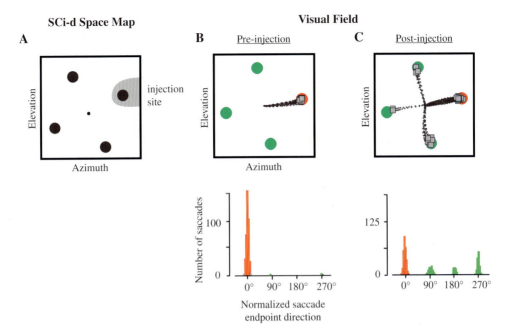

FIGURE 6.6 Effect of superior colliculus (SC) inactivation on target selection for gaze in a monkey. In this task, the monkey fixated on a central dot, then made an eye saccade to the location of the red dot either with or without three green distractor dots. (**A**) Schematic of the lidocaine injection site and the representations of the four stimuli and the fixation dot in the SC map of space. (**B**) Responses to the four dots before SC inactivation; 100% correct responses. (**C**) Responses after SC inactivation; responses were distributed among the four stimuli. Modified from McPeek, R. M., & Keller, E. L. (2004). Deficits in saccade target selection after inactivation of superior colliculus. *Nature Neuroscience, 7,* 757–763.

In nature, the difference between life and death depends on the ability to detect predators or prey quickly. Animals are often camouflaged in terms of shape, texture, brightness, and coloring. The most versatile and reliable feature for signaling the presence of another animal is motion. Unlike shape, texture, stereopsis, and color, which depend on forebrain circuits for evaluation, motion (along with contrast) is encoded rapidly and early in sensory processing (Rodieck, 1965; Olveczky et al., 2003; Gollisch & Meister, 2010). It is the motion and contrast of stimuli (including the motion and contrast of auditory and somatosensory stimuli) that are particularly effective in driving sensory activity in the midbrain system.

CONCLUSION

This chapter has presented evidence that the brain contains two systems capable of bottom-up control of the locus of attention; one system resides in the forebrain and the other in the midbrain (Figure 6.2). These two systems operate in a cooperative and coordinated fashion. Both systems evaluate the salience of stimuli in the environment. According to the schema, the midbrain system dominates bottom-up control of attention when sudden, high-contrast, or fast-moving stimuli are detected. Under these potentially dangerous conditions, the midbrain system can select the location of the salient stimulus and command an immediate shift of gaze toward the location, enhance the representations of sensory information for that location, and dictate stimulus selection in the forebrain system. Because the midbrain system is able to act with speed, which can make the difference between life and death, it confers a selective advantage to the animal.

Under all other conditions, the forebrain system dominates the selection of information that gains access to working memory (Koch & Tsuchiya, 2007). The forebrain system evaluates a far greater range of information from all systems, including information that is remembered as well as present in the environment, and information that is encoded in a variety of frames of reference. Under these conditions, the midbrain system still contributes to stimulus selection, but it does not dictate selection.

Although the midbrain system processes a far more restricted set of information than does the forebrain system, the computations required to select the highest priority information are similar in many ways. For both systems, the relative salience of stimuli is evaluated across all of space, top-down influences bias these evaluations based on behavioral relevance, and a categorization process determines the highest priority information for attention or a shift of gaze.

ACKNOWLEDGMENTS

I gratefully acknowledge funding from the NIH (R01 EY019179), and I thank Phyllis Knudsen for preparing the figures and Shreesh Mysore, Devarajan Sridharan, Ali Asadollahi and Alex Goddard for critically reviewing the manuscript.

References

Andersen, R. A., Snyder, L. H., Bradley, D. C., & Xing, J. (1997). Multimodal representation of space in the posterior parietal cortex and its use in planning movements. *Annual Review of Neuroscience, 20,* 303–330.

Asadollahi, A., Mysore, S. P., & Knudsen, E. I. (2010). Stimulus-driven competition in a cholinergic midbrain nucleus. *Nature Neuroscience, 13,* 889-895.

Awh, E., Armstrong, K. M., & Moore, T. (2006). Visual and oculomotor selection: Links, causes and implications for spatial attention. *Trends in Cognitive Sciences, 10,* 124–130.

Awh, E., Jonides, J., & Reuter-Lorenz, P. A. (1998). Rehearsal in spatial working memory. *Journal of Experimental Psychology. Human Perception and Performance, 24,* 780–790.

Baddeley, A. (2003). Working memory: Looking back and looking forward. *Nature Reviews. Neuroscience, 4,* 829–839.

Balan, P. F., & Gottlieb, J. (2006). Integration of exogenous input into a dynamic salience map revealed by perturbing attention. *Journal of Neuroscience, 26,* 9239–9249.

Binns, K. E., & Salt, T. E. (2000). The functional influence of nicotinic cholinergic receptors on the visual responses of neurones in the superficial superior colliculus. *Visual Neuroscience, 17,* 283–289.

Bisley, J. W., & Goldberg, M. E. (2003). Neuronal activity in the lateral intraparietal area and spatial attention. *Science, 299,* 81–86.

Bruce, C. J. (1990). Integration of sensory and motor signals in primate frontal eye fields. In G. M. Edelman, W. E. Gall, W. M. Cowan (Eds.), *From signal and sense: Local and global order in perceptual map* (pp. 261–314). New York: Wiley-Liss.

Bruce, C. J., Goldberg, M. E., Bushnell, M. C., & Stanton, G. B. (1985). Primate frontal eye fields. II. Physiological and anatomical correlates of electrically evoked eye movements. *Journal of Neurophysiology, 54,* 714–734.

Burrows, B. E., & Moore, T. (2009). Influence and limitations of popout in the selection of salient visual stimuli by area V4 neurons. *Journal of Neuroscience, 29,* 15169–15177.

Buschman, T. J., & Miller, E. K. (2007). Top-down versus bottom-up control of attention in the prefrontal and posterior parietal cortices. *Science, 315,* 1860–1862.

Buschman, T. J., & Miller, E. K. (2009). Serial, covert shifts of attention during visual search are reflected by the frontal eye fields and correlated with population oscillations. *Neuron, 63,* 386–396.

Carandini, M., & Heeger, D. J. (1994). Summation and division by neurons in primate visual cortex. *Science, 264,* 1333–1336.

Carello, C. D., & Krauzlis, R. J. (2004). Manipulating intent: Evidence for a causal role of the superior colliculus in target selection. *Neuron, 43,* 575–583.

Cavanaugh, J., & Wurtz, R. H. (2004). Subcortical modulation of attention counters change blindness. *Journal of Neuroscience, 24,* 11236–11243.

Cave, K. R., & Wolfe, J. M. (1990). Modeling the role of parallel processing in visual search. *Cognitive Psychology, 22,* 225–271.

Colby, C. L., & Goldberg, M. E. (1999). Space and attention in parietal cortex. *Annual Review of Neuroscience, 22,* 319–349.

Constantinidis, C., & Steinmetz, M. A. (2005). Posterior parietal cortex automatically encodes the location of salient stimuli. *Journal of Neuroscience, 25,* 233–238.

Constantinidis, C., & Wang, X. J. (2004). A neural circuit basis for spatial working memory. *Neuroscientist, 10,* 553–565.

Dehaene, S., Sergent, C., & Changeux, J. P. (2003). A neuronal network model linking subjective reports and objective physiological data during conscious perception. *Proceedings of the National Academy of Sciences of the United States of America, 100,* 8520–8525.

Desimone, R., & Duncan, J. (1995). Neural mechanisms of selective visual attention. *Annual Review of Neuroscience, 18,* 193–222.

Deubel, H., & Schneider, W. X. (1996). Saccade target selection and object recognition: evidence for a common attentional mechanism. *Vision Research, 36,* 1827–1837.

Dias, E. C., & Segraves, M. A. (1999). Muscimol-induced inactivation of monkey frontal eye field: Effects on visually and memory-guided saccades. *Journal of Neurophysiology, 81,* 2191–2214.

Du Lac, S., & Knudsen, E. I. (1990). Neural maps of head movement vector and speed in the optic tectum of the barn owl. *Journal of Neurophysiology, 63,* 131–146.

Egeth, H. E., & Yantis, S. (1997). Visual attention: Control, representation, and time course. *Annual Review of Psychology, 48,* 269–297.

Endo, T., Yanagawa, Y., Obata, K., & Isa, T. (2005). Nicotinic acetylcholine receptor subtypes involved in facilitation of GABAergic inhibition in mouse superficial superior colliculus. *Journal of Neurophysiology, 94,* 3893–3902.

Fecteau, J. H., & Munoz, D. P. (2006). Salience, relevance, and firing: A priority map for target selection. *Trends in Cognitive Sciences, 10,* 382–390.

Friedland, R. P., & Weinstein, E. A. (1977). Hemi-inattention and hemisphere specialization: Introduction and historical review. In E. A. Weinstein, & R. P. Friedland (Eds.), *Advances in neurology. Hemi-inattention and hemisphere specialization* (pp. 1–31). New York: Raven.

Friedman-Hill, S. R., Robertson, L. C., Desimone, R., & Ungerleider, L. G. (2003). Posterior parietal cortex and the filtering of distractors. *Proceedings of the National Academy of Sciences of the United States of America, 100,* 4263–4268.

Glimcher, P. W., & Sparks, D. L. (1992). Movement selection in advance of action in the superior colliculus. *Nature, 355,* 542–545.

Goldberg, M. E., Bisley, J., Powell, K. D., Gottlieb, J., & Kusunoki, M. (2002). The role of the lateral intraparietal area of the monkey in the generation of saccades and visuospatial attention. *Annals of the New York Academy of Sciences, 956,* 205–215.

Gollisch, T., & Meister, M. (2010). Eye smarter than scientists believed: Neural computations in circuits of the retina. *Neuron, 65,* 150–164.

Gottlieb, J. P., Kusunoki, M., & Goldberg, M. E. (1998). The representation of visual salience in monkey parietal cortex. *Nature, 391,* 481–484.

Graybiel, A. M. (1978). A satellite system of the superior colliculus: the parabigeminal nucleus and its projections to the superficial collicular layers. *Brain Research, 145,* 365–374.

Gregoriou, G. G., Gotts, S. J., Zhou, H., & Desimone, R. (2009). High-frequency, long-range coupling between prefrontal and visual cortex during attention. *Science, 324,* 1207–1210.

Han, X., Xian, S. X., & Moore, T. (2009). Dynamic sensitivity of area V4 neurons during saccade preparation. *Proceedings of the National Academy of Sciences of the United States of America, 106,* 13046–13051.

Hanes, D. P., & Schall, J. D. (1996). Neural control of voluntary movement initiation. *Science, 274,* 427–430.

Hanes, D. P., & Wurtz, R. H. (2001). Interaction of the frontal eye field and superior colliculus for saccade generation. *Journal of Neurophysiology, 85,* 804–815.

Harting, J. K. (1977). Descending pathways from the superior colliculus: An autoradiographic analysis in the rhesus monkey (Macaca mulatta). *Journal of Comparative Neurology, 173,* 583–612.

Hikosaka, O., & Wurtz, R. H. (1985a). Modification of saccadic eye movements by GABA-related substances. I. Effect of muscimol and bicuculline in monkey superior colliculus. *Journal of Neurophysiology, 53,* 266–291.

Hikosaka, O., & Wurtz, R. H. (1985b). Modification of saccadic eye movements by GABA-related substances. *II. Effects of muscimol in monkey substantia nigra pars reticulata. Journal of Neurophysiology, 53,* 292–308.

Hoffman, J. E., & Subramaniam, B. (1995). The role of visual attention in saccadic eye movements. *Perception & Psychophysics, 57,* 787–795.

Huang, L., & Pashler, H. (2007). A Boolean map theory of visual attention. *Psychological Review, 114,* 599–631.

Husain, M., & Nachev, P. (2007). Space and the parietal cortex. *Trends in Cognitive Sciences, 11,* 30–36.

Ignashchenkova, A., Dicke, P. W., Haarmeier, T., & Thier, P. (2004). Neuron-specific contribution of the superior colliculus to overt and covert shifts of attention. *Nature Neuroscience, 7,* 56–64.

Ipata, A. E., Gee, A. L., Goldberg, M. E., & Bisley, J. W. (2006). Activity in the lateral intraparietal area predicts the goal and latency of saccades in a free-viewing visual search task. *Journal of Neuroscience, 26,* 3656–3661.

Irwin, D. E., Colcombe, A. M., Kramer, A. F., & Hahn, S. (2000). Attentional and oculomotor capture by onset, luminance and color singletons. *Vision Research, 40,* 1443–58.

Itti, L., & Koch, C. (2000). A saliency-based search mechanism for overt and covert shifts of visual attention. *Vision Research, 40,* 1489–1506.

Itti, L., & Koch, C. (2001). Computational modelling of visual attention. *Nature Reviews. Neuroscience, 2,* 194–203.

Jay, M. F., & Sparks, D. L. (1984). Auditory receptive fields in primate superior colliculus shift with changes in eye position. *Nature, 309,* 345–347.

Jay, M. F., & Sparks, D. L. (1987). Sensorimotor integration in the primate superior colliculus. I. Motor convergence. *Journal of Neurophysiology, 57,* 22–34.

Joseph, J. S., & Optican, L. M. (1996). Involuntary attentional shifts due to orientation differences. *Perception & Psychophysics, 58,* 651–665.

Juan, C. H., Muggleton, N. G., Tzeng, O. J., Hung, D. L., Cowey, A., & Walsh, V. (2008). Segregation of visual selection and saccades in human frontal eye fields. *Cerebral Cortex, 18,* 2410–2415.

Juan, C. H., Shorter-Jacobi, S. M., & Schall, J. D. (2004). Dissociation of spatial attention and saccade preparation. *Proceedings of the National Academy of Sciences of the United States of America, 101,* 15541–15544.

Knudsen, E. I. (1982). Auditory and visual maps of space in the optic tectum of the owl. *Journal of Neuroscience, 2,* 1177–1194.

Knudsen, E. I. (1984). Auditory properties of space-tuned units in owl's optic tectum. *Journal of Neurophysiology, 52,* 709–723.

Knudsen, E. I. (2007). Fundamental components of attention. *Annual Review of Neuroscience, 30,* 57–78.

Knudsen, E. I., Cohen, Y. E., & Masino, T. (1995). Characterization of a forebrain gaze field in the archistriatum of the barn owl: Microstimulation and anatomical connections. *Journal of Neuroscience, 15,* 5139–5151.

Knudsen, E. I., & Knudsen, P. F. (1996a). Contribution of the forebrain archistriatal gaze fields to auditory orienting behavior in the barn owl. *Experimental Brain Research, 108,* 23–32.

Knudsen, E. I., & Knudsen, P. F. (1996b). Disruption of auditory spatial working memory by inactivation of the forebrain archistriatum in barn owls. *Nature, 383,* 428–431.

Knudsen, E. I. (2011). Control from below: The role of a midbrain network in spatial attention. *European Journal of Neuroscience, 33*(11), 1961–1972.

Koch, C., & Tsuchiya, N. (2007). Attention and consciousness: Two distinct brain processes. *Trends in Cognitive Sciences, 11,* 16–22.

Kowler, E., Anderson, E., Dosher, B., & Blaser, E. (1995). The role of attention in the programming of saccades. *Vision Research, 35,* 1897–1916.

Kustov, A. A., & Robinson, D. L. (1996). Shared neural control of attentional shifts and eye movements. *Nature, 384,* 74–77.

Kusunoki, M., Gottlieb, J., & Goldberg, M. E. (2000). The lateral intraparietal area as a salience map: The representation of abrupt onset, stimulus motion, and task relevance. *Vision Research, 40,* 1459–1468.

Lee, D. K., Itti, L., Koch, C., & Braun, J. (1999). Attention activates winner-take-all competition among visual filters. *Nature Neuroscience, 2,* 375–381.

Lee, J., & Maunsell, J. H. (2009). A normalization model of attentional modulation of single unit responses. *PLoS One, 4,* e4651.

Lee, P. H., Schmidt, M., & Hall, W. C. (2001). Excitatory and inhibitory circuitry in the superficial gray layer of the superior colliculus. *Journal of Neuroscience, 21,* 8145–8153.

Li, X., & Basso, M. A. (2005). Competitive stimulus interactions within single response fields of superior colliculus neurons. *Journal of Neuroscience, 25,* 11357–11373.

Li, X., & Basso, M. A. (2008). Preparing to move increases the sensitivity of superior colliculus neurons. *Journal of Neuroscience, 28,* 4561–4577.

Maczko, K. A., Knudsen, P. F., & Knudsen, E. I. (2006). Auditory and visual space maps in the cholinergic nucleus isthmi pars parvocellularis of the barn owl. *Journal of Neuroscience, 26,* 12799–12806.

Marin, G., Salas, C., Sentis, E., Rojas, X., Letelier, J. C., & Mpodozis, J. (2007). A cholinergic gating mechanism controlled by competitive interactions in the optic tectum of the pigeon. *Journal of Neuroscience, 27,* 8112–8121.

Masino, T., & Knudsen, E. I. (1992). Anatomical pathways from the optic tectum to the spinal cord subserving orienting movements in the barn owl. *Experimental Brain Research, 92,* 194–208.

McPeek, R. M., & Keller, E. L. (2002). Saccade target selection in the superior colliculus during a visual search task. *Journal of Neurophysiology, 88,* 2019–34.

McPeek, R. M., & Keller, E. L. (2004). Deficits in saccade target selection after inactivation of superior colliculus. *Nature Neuroscience, 7,* 757–763.

Moore, T., & Armstrong, K. M. (2003). Selective gating of visual signals by microstimulation of frontal cortex. *Nature, 421,* 370–373.

Moore, T., Armstrong, K. M., & Fallah, M. (2003). Visuomotor origins of covert spatial attention. *Neuron, 40,* 671–683.

Moore, T., & Fallah, M. (2001). Control of eye movements and spatial attention. *Proceedings of the*

National Academy of Sciences of the United States of America, 98, 1273–1276.

Muller, J. R., Philiastides, M. G., & Newsome, W. T. (2005). Microstimulation of the superior colliculus focuses attention without moving the eyes. *Proceedings of the National Academy of Sciences of the United States of America, 102*, 524–529.

Mullette-Gillman, O. A., Cohen, Y. E., & Groh, J. M. (2005). Eye-centered, head-centered, and complex coding of visual and auditory targets in the intraparietal sulcus. *Journal of Neurophysiology, 94*, 2331–2352.

Munch, T. A., da Silveira, R. A., Siegert, S., Viney, T. J., Awatramani, G. B., & Roska, B. (2009). Approach sensitivity in the retina processed by a multifunctional neural circuit. *Nature Neuroscience, 12*, 1308–1316.

Munoz, D. P., & Wurtz, R. H. (1995). Saccade-related activity in monkey superior colliculus. I. *Characteristics of burst and buildup cells. Journal of Neurophysiology, 73*, 2313–2333.

Mysore, S. P., Asadollahi, A., & Knudsen, E. I. (2010). Global inhibition and stimulus competition in the owl optic tectum. *Journal of Neuroscience, 30*, 1727–1738.

Mysore, S. P., Asadollahi, A., & Knudsen, E. I. (2011a). Signaling of the strongest stimulus in the owl optic tectum. *Journal of Neuroscience, 31*, 5186–5196.

Mysore, S. P., Asadollahi, A., & Knudsen, E. I. (2011b). Flexible categorization of relative stimulus strength by the optic tectum. *Journal of Neuroscience, 31*, 7745–7752.

Olveczky, B. P., Baccus, S. A., & Meister, M. (2003). Segregation of object and background motion in the retina. *Nature, 423*, 401–408.

Peck, C. J., Jangraw, D. C., Suzuki, M., Efem, R., & Gottlieb, J. (2009). Reward modulates attention independently of action value in posterior parietal cortex. *Journal of Neuroscience, 29*, 11182–11191.

Phelps, E. A., Ling, S., & Carrasco, M. (2006). Emotion facilitates perception and potentiates the perceptual benefits of attention. *Psychological Science, 17*, 292–299.

Pouget, P., Stepniewska, I., Crowder, E. A., Leslie, M. W., Emeric, E. E., Nelson, M. J., & Schall, J. D. (2009). Visual and motor connectivity and the distribution of calcium-binding proteins in macaque frontal eye field: implications for saccade target selection. *Frontiers in Neuroanatomy, 3*, 2.

Pouille, F., Marin-Burgin, A., Adesnik, H., Atallah, B. V., & Scanziani, M. (2009). Input normalization by global feedforward inhibition expands cortical dynamic range. *Nature Neuroscience, 12*, 1577–1585.

Ray, S., Pouget, P., & Schall, J. D. (2009). Functional distinction between visuomovement and movement neurons in macaque frontal eye field during saccade countermanding. *Journal of Neurophysiology, 102*, 3091–3100.

Reynolds, J. H., & Chelazzi, L. (2004). Attentional modulation of visual processing. *Annual Review of Neuroscience, 27*, 611–647.

Reynolds, J. H., & Heeger, D. J. (2009). The normalization model of attention. *Neuron, 61*, 168–185.

Rizzolatti, G., Camarda, R., Grupp, L. A., & Pisa, M. (1974). Inhibitory effect of remote visual stimuli on visual responses of cat superior colliculus: Spatial and temporal factors. *Journal of Neurophysiology, 37*, 1262–1275.

Robinson, D. A. (1972). Eye movements evoked by collicular stimulation in the alert monkey. *Vision Research, 12*, 1795–1808.

Rodieck, R. W. (1965). Quantitative analysis of cat retinal ganglion cell response to visual stimuli. *Vision Research, 5*, 583–601.

Russo, G. S., & Bruce, C. J. (1994). Frontal eye field activity preceding aurally guided saccades. *Journal of Neurophysiology, 71*, 1250–1253.

Schall, J. D. (1991). Neuronal activity related to visually guided saccadic eye movements in the supplementary motor area of rhesus monkeys. *Journal of Neurophysiology, 66*, 530–558.

Schall, J. D. (2004). On the role of frontal eye field in guiding attention and saccades. *Vision Research, 44*, 1453–1467.

Schall, J. D., Pare, M., & Woodman, G. F. (2007). Comment on "Top-down versus bottom-up control of attention in the prefrontal and posterior parietal cortices." *Science, 318*, 44; author reply 44.

Schiller, P. H., Sandell, J. H., & Maunsell, J. H. (1987). The effect of frontal eye field and superior colliculus lesions on saccadic latencies in the rhesus monkey. *Journal of Neurophysiology, 57*, 1033–1049.

Segraves, M. A., & Goldberg, M. E. (1987). Functional properties of corticotectal neurons in the monkey's frontal eye field. *Journal of Neurophysiology, 58*, 1387–1419.

Sherk, H. (1979). Connections and visual-field mapping in cat's tectoparabigeminal circuit. *Journal of Neurophysiology, 42*, 1656–1668.

Shipp, S. (2004). The brain circuitry of attention. *Trends in Cognitive Sciences, 8*, 223–230.

Shomstein, S., & Yantis, S. (2006). Parietal cortex mediates voluntary control of spatial and nonspatial auditory attention. *Journal of Neuroscience, 26*, 435–439.

Sommer, M. A., & Wurtz, R. H. (2000). Composition and topographic organization of signals sent from the frontal eye field to the superior colliculus. *Journal of Neurophysiology, 83*, 1979–2001.

Sommer, M. A., & Tehovnik, E. J. (1997). Reversible inactivation of macaque frontal eye field. *Experimental Brain Research, 116*, 229–249.

Sparks, D. L. (2002). The brainstem control of saccadic eye movements. *Nature Reviews. Neuroscience, 3*, 952–964.

Sridharan D., Boahen, B., & Knudsen, E. I. (2011). Space coding by gamma oscillations in the barn owl optic tectum. *Journal of Neurophysiology, 105*, 2005–2017.

Stanton, G. B., Goldberg, M. E., & Bruce, C. J. (1988). Frontal eye field efferents in the macaque monkey: I. *Subcortical pathways and topography of striatal and thalamic terminal fields. Journal of Comparative Neurology, 271*, 473–492.

Stein, B. E., & Meredith, M. A. (1993). *The merging of the senses.* Cambridge, MA: MIT Press.

Stryker, M. P., & Schiller, P. H. (1975). Eye and head movements evoked by electrical stimulation of monkey superior colliculus. *Experimental Brain Research, 23*, 103–112.

Sumner, P., Tsai, P. C., Yu, K., & Nachev, P. (2006). Attentional modulation of sensorimotor processes in the absence of perceptual awareness. *Proceedings of the National Academy of Sciences of the United States of America, 103*, 10520–10525.

Thompson, K. G., Biscoe, K. L., & Sato, T. R. (2005). Neuronal basis of covert spatial attention in the frontal eye field. *Journal of Neuroscience, 25*, 9479–9487.

Toth, L. J., & Assad, J. A. (2002). Dynamic coding of behaviourally relevant stimuli in parietal cortex. *Nature, 415*, 165–168.

Wang, S. R. (2003). The nucleus isthmi and dual modulation of the receptive field of tectal neurons in non-mammals. *Brain Research. Brain Research Reviews, 41*, 13–25.

Wang, Y., Major, D. E., & Karten, H. J. (2004). Morphology and connections of nucleus isthmi pars magnocellularis in chicks (*Gallus gallus*). *Journal of Comparative Neurology, 469*, 275–297.

Wang, Y., Luksch, H., Brecha, N. C., & Karten, H. J. (2006). Columnar projections from the cholinergic nucleus isthmi to the optic tectum in chicks (*Gallus gallus*): A possible substrate for synchronizing tectal channels. *Journal of Comparative Neurology, 494*, 7–35.

Wardak, C., Ibos, G., Duhamel, J. R., & Olivier, E. (2006). Contribution of the monkey frontal eye field to covert visual attention. *Journal of Neuroscience, 26*, 4228–4235.

Wardak, C., Olivier, E., & Duhamel, J. R. (2004). A deficit in covert attention after parietal cortex inactivation in the monkey. *Neuron, 42*, 501–508.

White, B. J., Boehnke, S. E., Marino, R. A., Itti, L., & Munoz, D. P. (2009). Color-related signals in the primate superior colliculus. *Journal of Neuroscience, 29*, 12159–12166.

Winkowski, D. E., & Knudsen, E. I. (2007). Top-down control of multimodal sensitivity in the barn owl optic tectum. *Journal of Neuroscience, 27*, 13279–13291.

Winkowski, D. E., & Knudsen, E. I. (2008). Distinct mechanisms for top-down control of neural gain and sensitivity in the owl optic tectum. *Neuron, 60*, 698–708.

Wurtz, R. H., & Albano, J. E. (1980). Visual-motor function of the primate superior colliculus. *Annual Review of Neuroscience, 3*, 189–226.

Wurtz, R. H., & Goldberg, M. E. (1972). Activity of superior colliculus in behaving monkey. 3. Cells discharging before eye movements. *Journal of Neurophysiology, 35*, 575–586.

Zhou, H. H., & Thompson, K. G. (2009). Cognitively directed spatial selection in the frontal eye field in anticipation of visual stimuli to be discriminated. *Vision Research, 49*, 1205–1215.

7

Attention and Action in the Frontal Eye Field

KATHERINE M. ARMSTRONG, ROBERT J. SCHAFER, MINDY H. CHANG,
AND TIRIN MOORE

ATTENTION AND ITS NEURONAL CORRELATES IN VISUAL CORTEX

Despite the compelling impression that our eyes relay a complete image of the visual world, our perceptual abilities are more limited than we realize. As William James famously addressed the topic, "My experience is what I agree to attend to. Only those items which I notice shape my mind (James, 1890)." Since James' time, investigators have studied our ability to select signals for enhanced processing from among the continual flood of sensory input. In the visual domain, attention and gaze are typically in register, such that the stimuli lying at the center of gaze, and on the most acute region of the retina (the fovea), tend to be the focus of attention. However, what we see is not dictated solely by the stimuli at the center of gaze: Attention can also be deployed in the periphery and without overt shifts of gaze. Some tasks require that peripheral stimuli be monitored without overtly orienting gaze toward them. For example, while driving it is necessary to monitor cars and bicycles in adjacent lanes without taking your eyes off the road ahead. This capacity is referred to as *covert* attention.

The German physician and physicist Hermann von Helmholtz was among the first to examine covert attention empirically. In doing so, he laid the groundwork for the next century's psychophysical investigations. Helmholtz stumbled onto the phenomenon of covert attention inadvertently while he was examining other aspects of visual perception using a device for displaying stereoscopic images using the flash of a spark in an otherwise dark room to present stimuli briefly to each eye (James, 1890). Helmholtz noticed that when complicated photographs were presented for only a single flash, he could not perceive the entire image. However, while maintaining a steady gaze straight ahead, as was required to avoid seeing a double image in the stereoscopic display, he found he could willfully keep his attention fixed at a particular location so as to "receive an impression only from such parts of the picture as lie in this region," and noted thus that "our attention is quite independent of the position and accommodation of the eyes" (James, 1890). Nearly a century later, George Sperling formally studied covert attention using a strikingly similar paradigm to that of Helmholtz and confirmed that subjects could willfully select which part of a briefly flashed display entered their perception (Sperling, 1960). Since Sperling's time, the study of covert attention has emerged as a major area of psychological research. *Spatial* attention, the cognitive faculty studied and described by Helmholtz and Sperling, can be operationally defined as the enhanced processing of visual signals at a particular location in space, and has been shown to decrease behavioral response times (Posner, 1980), facilitate memory (Sperling, 1960), enhance visual discrimination (Lee et al., 1997), and even gate visual perception of stimuli that can otherwise go unnoticed for up to several minutes (Rensink, 2002).

Over the past 40 years, neuroscientists have demonstrated neural correlates of these effects in visual cortex (e.g., Reynolds & Chelazzi, 2004; see Chapter 1 for an overview). Many of these findings come from studies of nonhuman primates trained to perform tasks in which the monkey must maintain its gaze on a central point and covertly monitor visual stimuli appearing at one peripheral location while ignoring stimuli appearing at other locations (Figure 7.1). The responses of visual cortical neurons to physically identical stimuli are then compared between the different conditions. In general, neuronal responses to attended stimuli are enhanced compared to ignored stimuli, and these enhancements have been reported in many visual areas. For example, in area V4, a region of extrastriate visual cortex (see Figure 7.2), neurons are modulated by attention. As with all neurons in the visual system, V4 neurons have receptive fields (RFs); that is, they exhibit spiking responses only during stimulation of the region of the visual field (VF) from which they receive input. A V4 neuron responds with more spikes when an attended stimulus appears inside its RF compared to when the same stimulus

appears there but is ignored. In addition, area V4 neurons are tuned to stimulus features, responding preferentially, for example, to a stimulus of a particular orientation (e.g., 90 degrees), and exhibiting a weak response to a stimulus of other orientations (e.g., 0 degrees). During attention, V4 responses to stimuli of preferred orientations are more enhanced than responses to nonpreferred stimuli (Figure 7.1). Thus, the stimulus-selective attentional enhancement increases orientation tuning for attended stimuli compared to ignored stimuli (McAdams & Maunsell, 1999), which could contribute to the improvements in visual discrimination behavior that have been reported during attention (Lee et al., 1997).

Before it was known that the effects of covert attention are widespread within visual cortex, it had been observed that visual evoked neuronal responses in a number of brain regions are enhanced when an animal targets an RF stimulus with a saccadic eye movement (Figure 7.1). This effect was first observed by Wurtz and Goldberg (1972) among neurons within the superficial layers of the superior colliculus (SC) and subsequently by Mountcastle and colleagues (1975) in posterior parietal cortex. Later studies demonstrated that the presaccadic visual enhancement is also observed among neurons in area V4 (Fischer & Boch, 1981) and in inferior temporal cortex (Chelazzi et al., 1993). Moore and colleagues (1998; Moore & Chang, 2009) followed up on the studies of Fischer and Boch and found that, as is observed during covert attention, the presaccadic enhancement of V4 visual responses is selective for the features of the saccade target, just as is the initial response of the target in the RF. Again, as in covert attention, presaccadic enhancement is greatest prior to saccades to targets presented at a V4 neuron's preferred orientation (Figure 7.1). To address the significance of the presaccadic signals in V4, Moore (1999) examined the metrics of saccades made to targets of varying orientation and found that saccades on trials with more robust presaccadic activity were more influenced by the shape of the targets than were saccades on trials with weaker activity. Thus, in addition to their presumed role in representing stimulus shape, V4 neurons may also contribute to the visual guidance of saccades.

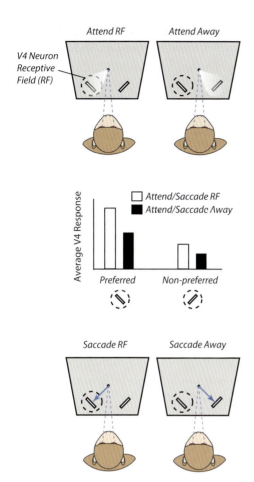

SACCADIC EYE MOVEMENTS AND ATTENTIONAL SELECTION

Although there is a striking parallel between the enhancements of visual cortical responses observed during covert attention and immediately before saccades targeting the RF stimulus, a causal connection between the two was far from obvious since attentional enhancement in some structures originally appeared to be contingent upon a saccade actually being made (e.g., Goldberg & Bushnell, 1981). However, other lines of evidence suggested that covert visual attention might indeed depend upon the same circuits that guide saccadic eye movements. The earliest evidence of an oculomotor involvement in attention comes from Sir David Ferrier, a Scottish physiologist working in the late 19th century. Ferrier performed a series of lesion experiments to localize functions within the brain. He found that after removing part of prefrontal cortex (PFC) in a single hemisphere of the brain, monkeys were unable to direct their gaze into the affected hemifield and that this movement deficit was accompanied by a "loss of the faculty of attention." He hypothesized that the "power of attention is intimately related to volitional movements of the head and eyes" (Ferrier, 1890).

Further hints of interdependence between saccades and attention came from a psychophysical study in which subjects made discriminations about peripherally flashed digits (Crovitz, 1962). This study reported a positive correlation between discrimination performance and the direction of the first saccade subjects made after the stimulus was presented, suggesting that eye movements might facilitate attention. Two decades later, psychologists performed experiments specifically designed to test whether saccade programming and attention are independent. The approach used most often was to examine the impact of performing a saccade task on visual discrimination and detection performance. The results of one such study suggested that planning and executing a saccade to a peripheral stimulus interfered with subjects' ability to detect visual targets at locations other than the saccade endpoint (Remington, 1980). Subsequent studies demonstrated that visual detection and discrimination were in fact

FIGURE 7.1   Neural correlates of covert and overt attention in visual cortex. *Top panel*: Monkeys are trained to perform a covert visual attention task in which they must maintain fixation on a central spot and are cued to monitor one of two stimuli presented in the periphery. On a given trial, the monkey monitors either the stimulus appearing inside the V4 neuron's receptive field (RF, *dotted circle, left*), or the stimulus appearing outside the RF (*right*). This paradigm allows researchers to compare the responses of V4 neurons when the monkey is either attending toward or away from the RF stimulus (*spotlight cartoons*). *Center panel*: Many area V4 neurons are tuned for stimulus orientation, responding more when a stimulus of a preferred orientation is presented in the RF (*left*), and giving a weaker response when a stimulus of a nonpreferred orientation is presented in the RF (*right*). During attention, or before a saccade that targets the RF stimulus (*open bars*), the responses to stimuli of preferred orientations are more enhanced than are responses to nonpreferred stimuli. *Lower panel*: Similar V4 neuron response modulations occur while monkeys perform a saccade task in which they must saccade either toward or away from the stimulus presented in the RF.

facilitated at the endpoints of saccades, even when given a cue to attend elsewhere (Deubel & Schneider, 1996; Hoffman & Subramaniam, 1995; Shepherd et al., 1986). Thus, planning a saccade also affects covert attention. These results led to the proposal that a single mechanism drives both the selection of objects for perceptual processing and the information needed to produce an appropriate motor response (Schneider, 1995).

In the 1980s, Rizzolatti and colleagues proposed a "premotor theory of attention," which hypothesized that the mechanisms responsible for spatial attention and the mechanisms involved in programming saccades are the same, but that in the covert case "the eyes are blocked at a certain peripheral stage" (Rizzolatti et al., 1987, p. 37). This group later performed experiments examining the influence of covert attention on saccades (Sheliga et al., 1994). The authors reasoned that if covert attention reflects saccade commands that are programmed but not executed, directing spatial attention covertly should interfere with saccade execution. Subjects were instructed to initiate saccades to a location in one half of the VF (e.g., lower half) according to cues presented in the other half. The cues themselves could be presented in one of several locations in the cued half of the VF (e.g., left side of upper field). The major finding from this study was that saccade trajectories were systematically deviated according to the location of the covertly attended (cued) location. This and similar observations (Kowler et al., 1995; Shepherd et al., 1986) demonstrate that the deployment of covert attention perturbs saccade programming.

THE FRONTAL EYE FIELD

The fact that psychophysical studies have demonstrated both that the deployment of attention influences saccades and that saccade planning influences attention suggests that the two processes depend on common neural resources. Ferrier's early lesion studies had implicated the PFC as a possible site for the control of both gaze and attention (Ferrier, 1890). His approach in that study was subsequently refined by 20th-century scientists who found that similar deficits in attention resulted from PFC lesions that were restricted to

a small band of tissue lying anterior to the arcuate sulcus, known as the *frontal eye field* (FEF) (Welch & Stuteville, 1958; Latto & Cowey, 1971) (Figure 7.2). The FEF is located at the interface between more anterior regions of PFC and motor cortex, placing it between brain areas involved in high-level cognition and movement planning. The FEF was actually discovered by Ferrier in another series of experiments, in which he applied electrical stimulation to different regions of cortex to examine what behaviors could be elicited (Ferrier, 1876). Using this approach, he identified the FEF as a region in PFC from which contraversive movements of both eyes could be elicited with electrical stimulation. More recent work demonstrated that the majority of eye movements produced by FEF stimulation are contralateral, fixed-vector saccades that are indistinguishable from those made during natural behavior (Robinson & Fuchs, 1969, Bruce et al., 1985). In addition, subthreshold FEF stimulation (i.e., stimulation with currents below that required to evoke a saccade) does not evoke a saccade (by definition) but nonetheless increases the likelihood that an animal will subsequently make the saccade represented at the stimulation site. This latter observation indicates that even subthreshold FEF stimulation biases saccade planning (Schiller & Tehovnik, 2001).

The dynamics of spiking responses recorded during saccade tasks suggest the existence of a continuum of visual and movement functions among neurons within the FEF. Some neurons exhibit purely visual activity in response to the onset of a stimulus, and others respond exclusively before a saccade is initiated, although many FEF neurons exhibit a combination of these visual and movement response properties (Bruce & Goldberg, 1985; Sommer & Wurtz, 2000). Like the neurons in visual cortex discussed earlier, FEF neurons respond to visual stimuli appearing in, and saccades made to, a restricted region of space known as the receptive field (Bruce & Goldberg, 1985). The RF location of a particular neuron also predicts the direction and amplitude of the saccades that can be evoked by microstimulation at that site (Bruce et al., 1985).

Anatomically, the FEF is appropriately situated for a role in visually guided saccades (Figure 7.2). The FEF neurons receive projections from most

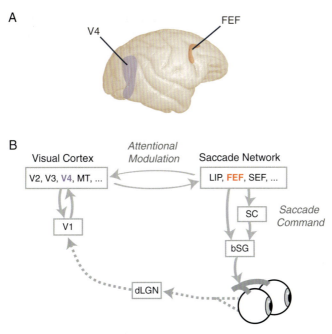

FIGURE 7.2   (**A**) Lateral view of a macaque brain showing visual area V4 (*blue*) on the prelunate gyrus in extrastriate cortex and the frontal eye field (FEF, *red*) on the anterior bank of the arcuate sulcus in prefrontal cortex. (**B**) A schematic of the pathways by which the saccade network sends commands to the eye muscles in the form of saccade commands and back to visual cortex in the form of attentional modulation. Areas such as the FEF, the lateral intraparietal area (LIP), and the superior colliculus (SC) are involved in transforming incoming visual information into saccade commands. Each of these areas is connected to each other, and to extrastriate visual cortex (*box* with sample visual areas). The SC and FEF also have projections directly to the brainstem saccade generator (bSG). Recent neurophysiological studies have uncovered a role of the FEF, LIP, and the SC in the allocation of visual spatial attention.

of the functionally defined areas within visual cortex (Schall et al., 1995; see also Chapter 9 in this volume), and FEF neurons send projections both to the brainstem saccade generator and to the SC, a midbrain structure with a known involvement in saccade production (Fries, 1984; Stanton et al., 1988; Lynch et al., 1994). However, the FEF also sends feedback projections to much of visual cortex (Schall et al., 1995; Stanton et al. 1995), suggesting a pathway by which saccade-related signals can influence visual representations (Figure 7.2). In addition, the fact that FEF neurons represent spatial locations but not stimulus features (Mohler et al., 1973, but see Peng et al., 2008) suggests that FEF activity could potentially act as a "salience map" (Koch & Ullman, 1985), representing the behavioral significance of particular visual items regardless of their visual properties

(Moore et al., 2003; Thompson & Bichot, 2005). Thus, the FEF has several properties consistent with a dual role in saccade planning and visual spatial attention.

FRONTAL EYE FIELD NEURON RESPONSE ENHANCEMENT DURING SACCADES AND ATTENTION

The visually driven responses of some classes of FEF neurons (visual and visuomovement) are enhanced when the RF stimulus is used as a saccade target compared to when no saccade is made to the stimulus (Bruce & Goldberg, 1985; Goldberg & Bushnell, 1981; Wurtz & Mohler, 1976). In addition, neural correlates of visual selection have been observed in the FEF during a search task in which monkeys were required to make a saccade to a singleton embedded among distracters (Schall, 2004). Although early studies suggested that FEF neuron response enhancement was specifically related to the execution of a saccade (Goldberg & Bushnell, 1981), a more recent study by Thompson and colleagues demonstrated that FEF visual responses are enhanced even in the absence of saccades during purely covert attention (Thompson et al., 2005). They recorded neural activity in the FEF during a visual search task that required monkeys to maintain their gaze on a central spot and respond with a manual joystick. The majority of visually responsive FEF neurons, a population including both visual and visuomovement neurons, had elevated responses to the appearance of the search target in the RF compared to the appearance of a distracter, even though no saccades were made to the target. By contrast, neurons with purely movement-related properties were not enhanced and were often inhibited, perhaps reflecting the "peripheral" motor inhibition that Rizzolatti and colleagues had suggested must occur during covert attention (1987).

SUBTHRESHOLD FRONTAL EYE FIELD MICROSTIMULATION DRIVES ATTENTION

The responses of neurons recorded during overt and covert attention tasks suggest that the FEF participates in both the allocation of covert attention and in saccade planning. Moore and Fallah tested whether the FEF has a causal role in directing spatial attention by examining the influence of subthreshold FEF microstimulation on monkeys performing a covert attention task (Moore & Fallah, 2001, 2004). They reasoned that if shifts of spatial attention occur when saccades are planned to a particular location, then it should be possible to direct attention by manipulating saccadic signals within the FEF via microstimulation. Monkeys were required to fix their gaze on a central spot and to covertly monitor a stable peripheral target while a distracter stimulus was flashed sequentially at different screen locations. The monkeys indicated a transient change in the target's luminance using a manual lever press. During a fraction of behavioral trials, the target luminance change was preceded by subthreshold microstimulation of the FEF. Moore and Fallah found that when they microstimulated sites within the FEF with currents that were too low to evoke a saccade, they improved the monkey's sensitivity at detecting luminance changes. However, this improvement only occurred when the target stimulus appeared at the endpoint of the saccade that could be evoked from the FEF microstimulation site. By contrast, when the saccade endpoint and target stimulus were non-overlapping, microstimulation did not improve the monkey's detection performance. Thus, activating networks capable of evoking saccades to a particular location appeared to also drive covert spatial attention to that location.

In subsequent studies, Moore and Armstrong examined whether FEF stimulation produces the same modulations in visual cortex that are observed during covert spatial attention (Moore & Armstrong, 2003; Armstrong et al., 2006; Armstrong & Moore, 2007). Subthreshold microstimulation was applied to the FEF while simultaneously recording the responses of neurons in visual cortex while monkeys performed a simple fixation task (Figure 7.3). The stimulation and recording sites in the FEF and area V4, respectively, could be chosen for each experiment, such that the saccade vector that could be evoked with FEF stimulation and the V4 neuron's RF were either spatially overlapping or non-overlapping. In the overlapping configuration, FEF stimulation enhanced the V4 neuron's response to visual stimuli appearing in the RF, and these enhancements mirrored the modulations observed during covert spatial attention in that more enhancement was seen for preferred than nonpreferred stimuli. By contrast, in the non-overlapping configuration, no response enhancement was produced and instead responses were suppressed. Thus, subthreshold FEF stimulation produced spatially selective modulations in visual cortical responses that were indistinguishable from known correlates of attention, providing causal evidence that neural circuits involved in planning saccades also modulate the responses of neurons in visual cortex.

Consistent with microstimulation studies in monkeys, transcranial magnetic stimulation (TMS) experiments have provided causal evidence that

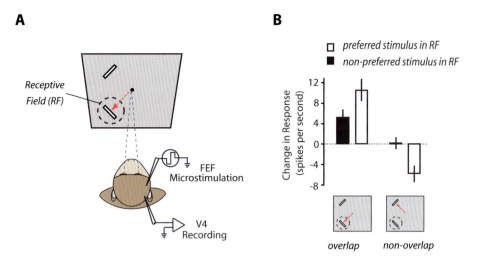

A

Receptive
Field (RF)

FEF
Microstimulation

V4
Recording

B

☐ preferred stimulus in RF
■ non-preferred stimulus in RF

Change in Response
(spikes per second)

12
8
4
0
-4
-8

overlap   non-overlap

FIGURE 7.3   Subthreshold microstimulation of the frontal eye field (FEF) produces modulations in visual responses like those seen during attention. (**A**) Subthreshold microstimulation was applied to the FEF while simultaneously recording the responses of single neurons in visual area V4. Monkeys performed a simple task in which they maintained fixation on a central point while oriented bar stimuli were presented inside the recorded V4 neuron's receptive field (RF; *dotted circle*) and at another location outside the RF. On a fraction of experimental trials, subthreshold microstimulation was applied to the FEF while the monkey continued to fixate, allowing the effect of stimulation on the V4 neuron's response to the RF stimulus to be examined. (**B**) The stimulation and recording sites in the FEF and area V4, respectively, could be chosen for each experiment, such that the FEF saccade vector (*dotted red arrow*) and the area V4 neuron's RF (*dotted circle*) were either spatially overlapping (*left*) or non-overlapping (*right*). In the overlapping configuration, FEF stimulation enhanced the V4 neuron's response to visual stimuli appearing in the RF, and these enhancements mirrored the modulations observed during covert spatial attention in that more enhancement was seen for preferred than nonpreferred stimuli (*left*). By contrast in the non-overlapping configuration no response enhancement was produced and in some cases responses were suppressed (*right*). Adapted from Moore, T., & Armstrong, K. M. (2003). Selective gating of visual signals by microstimulation of frontal cortex. *Nature, 421,* 370–373, with permission of the publisher.

saccade planning also drives spatial attention in humans (Grosbras & Paus, 2002; Grosbras & Paus, 2003; O'Shea et al., 2004; Taylor et al., 2007; Ruff et al., 2006; Silvanto et al., 2006). In addition, studies in the barn owl have found that microstimulation of gaze control circuits homologous with primate FEF produces spatially specific modulations of auditory responses (Winkowski & Knudsen, 2006). Thus, evidence from multiple experimental approaches, species, and modalities has accrued, indicating that manipulating gaze-related signals is sufficient to drive spatial attention.

The above studies indicate that FEF microstimulation not only drives saccade plans, but also covert spatial attention and its correlates in visual cortex. The apparent dual role of the FEF

in controlling both of these phenomena raises the question of how the two processes interact during visually guided behavior. Specifically, how does the brain select the target of visual attention, enhancing the perception of certain features within the visual scene, then simultaneously use information about these features to specify an appropriate saccade plan? Schafer and Moore (2007) addressed this question using a paradigm in which electrical stimulation of an FEF site pitted the potential attentional effects of stimulation against the saccadic effects. When monkeys made voluntary saccades to a sinusoidal grating drifting within a stationary aperture, the endpoints of their saccades were biased in the direction of the grating motion, consistent with an illusory shift in the perceived position of the grating. This "apparent position" illusion, and the corresponding bias of the saccades away from the center of the visual target, allowed the authors to separate the veridical position of the target in visual space from the perception of the target—and thus the endpoints of the saccades.

Low-frequency, subthreshold electrical stimulation was then delivered via a microelectrode to an FEF site corresponding to the veridical position of the center of the grating while the monkey planned and executed its targeting saccade. The authors suggested at least two possible consequences of microstimulation: First, if the saccadic and attentional roles of the FEF are largely independent, electrical stimulation could influence the monkey's saccade plan directly, without any observable effect on attention or perception. This would cause the saccade to land closer to the center of the part of space represented by the FEF stimulation site and therefore toward the center of the grating, thus eliminating the motion-induced saccade bias. Alternatively, if the attentional role of the FEF interacts with the saccadic role, microstimulation could lead to an enhancement of the apparent position illusion and a subsequent influence on the saccade plan, which would result in an increase in the motion-induced saccade bias. The authors found that when voluntary saccades were paired with low-frequency stimulation, the effect of the motion-induced illusion on saccade trajectories was enhanced, not decreased (Figure 7.4) (Schafer & Moore, 2007). Thus, the attentional effects of FEF perturbation not only interacted with, but effectively governed, the simultaneously planned saccades. More generally, the results suggested that the feedback connections from the FEF to visual cortex are integral both for appropriately

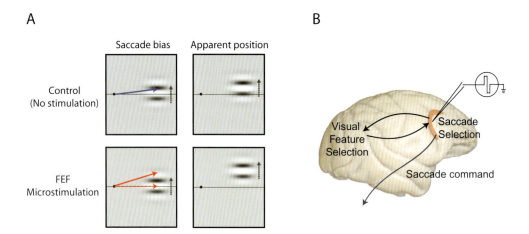

FIGURE 7.4 (**A**) Motion-induced saccade bias and the "apparent position" illusion. *Top left*: Voluntary saccades (*blue arrow*) directed toward an upward-drifting grating were biased in the direction of grating motion. Black arrow indicates direction of grating drift; black line is for horizontal reference. *Top right*: The directional saccade bias is consistent with an illusory offset in the position of the grating, as has been described by human subjects. *Bottom left*: Subthreshold, low-frequency microstimulation of a frontal eye field (FEF) site representing the center of the grating (*red dotted arrow*) caused voluntary saccades (*red solid arrow*) to be biased even further in the direction of grating motion, consistent with an enhancement of the apparent position illusion (*bottom right*). (**B**) Lateral view of a monkey brain showing the proposed route by which FEF stimulation increases the effect of target motion on the saccade plan. Rather than directly perturbing the saccade command (*gray arrow*), microstimulation strengthens a reciprocal interaction (*black arrows*) between the FEF (*orange shading*) and visual cortex. Microstimulation directs spatial attention toward the target grating, which enhances the representation of target features in visual cortex; these features concurrently select the impending saccade command.

perceiving the visual world and for preparing precise, target-guided saccades.

INACTIVATION OF THE FRONTAL EYE FIELD

The FEF microstimulation studies discussed above are complemented by experiments that employed pharmacological inactivation of sites within the FEF in monkeys performing attention and saccade tasks. Reversible unilateral inactivation of FEF neurons produces temporary impairments in contralateral saccadic eye movements, including decreases in accuracy and peak velocity and increases in latency, as well as an overall decrease in the frequency of contralateral saccades (Dias et al., 1995; Dias & Segraves, 1999; Sommer & Tehovnik, 1997). Monkeys are particularly impaired at making saccades to remembered contralateral target locations following FEF inactivation (Dias & Segraves, 1999), suggesting a role of the FEF in the short-term maintenance of spatial information required to guide impending saccades. In addition to these saccade deficits, reversible inactivation was found to impair performance of attention-demanding tasks when other distracting stimuli are present, whereas the performance of tasks with isolated stimuli was not affected (Wardak et al., 2006). Frontal eye field inactivation slowed reaction time in a covert visual search task that did not require eye movement responses, indicating a deficit in allocating attention covertly. This deficit was restricted to search targets appearing in the affected hemifield. Another study demonstrated that FEF inactivation not only disrupted performance on a search task, but also impaired monkeys' ability to use spatial cues to allocate attention (McPeek & Takahashi, 2006). Collectively, these results demonstrate that the FEF is necessary for controlling shifts of both attention and gaze.

SACCADE-RELATED REGIONS BEYOND THE FRONTAL EYE FIELD

Although many studies have perturbed the activity of FEF neurons in order to alter saccadic behavior, the FEF is only one node in a distributed network of brain regions involved in saccade planning and triggering, which includes the SC and the lateral intraparietal (LIP) area, among other areas (Johnston & Everling, 2008) (Figure 7.2). The impact of microstimulation on downstream brain regions is an area of ongoing research (Tolias et al., 2005), but it is likely that FEF microstimulation activates neurons in areas receiving projections from the FEF, including the SC and the LIP area. Like the FEF, the SC has also recently been implicated in covert spatial attention. Neuronal recordings made in the SC while monkeys performed a visual discrimination task demonstrated that both visual and visuomovement neurons were involved in covert shifts of attention, whereas, as seen in the FEF, movement-only neurons were not (Ignashchenkova et al., 2004). In addition, two studies examined whether microstimulation of the SC affected covert spatial attention. Using a change-blindness task, a paradigm known for its dependence on attention (Rensink, 2002), Cavanaugh and Wurtz showed that monkeys' ability to detect changes in a visual display across flashed presentations was improved with subthreshold stimulation of the SC (Cavanaugh & Wurtz, 2004). Monkeys were also faster at reporting changes. As in the FEF stimulation studies, this effect depended critically on the spatial correspondence of the saccade represented at the stimulation site and the location of the changing visual stimulus. Concurrently, Muller et al. carried out a different set of experiments involving microstimulation of the SC (Muller et al., 2005). In this study, the authors measured how subthreshold SC microstimulation affected monkeys' ability to discriminate the direction of randomly moving dots. They found that SC microstimulation improved visual discrimination when stimuli were presented at the VF location represented at the microstimulation site. When stimuli were positioned at other locations, SC microstimulation did not affect discrimination performance, demonstrating that, like FEF microstimulation and covert attention, SC microstimulation produces spatially specific perceptual enhancements. Finally, reversible inactivation of the SC produces deficits in target selection that cannot be attributed to a purely visual or motor impairment (McPeek & Keller, 2004) but appears to be attentional in nature (Lovejoy & Krauzlis, 2009). Reversible inactivation of the

LIP area also disrupts covert attention in the affected hemifield (Wardak et al., 2004). Thus, several brain regions known to mediate saccade programming have been causally related to shifts of visual spatial attention, indicating that these areas are involved in both saccades and attention.

THE FRONTAL EYE FIELD AND VOLUNTARY ATTENTION

Although FEF neurons tend to be inactive during spontaneous saccades made in a darkened room (Bizzi, 1967, 1969), they fire prior to purposive saccades made during learned behavioral paradigms, suggesting that the FEF has an important role in *voluntary* saccade production (Bruce & Goldberg, 1985). Past research has established distinct *goal-driven* and *stimulus-driven* routes for orienting spatial attention (Corbetta & Shulman, 2002; see Chapters 1, 2, and 5 in this volume). Indeed, in his classic treatise on attention, William James makes the distinction between "active" attention, and "passive . . . effortless" attention (James, 1890). In the case of goal-driven orienting, often referred to as *top-down* attention, attention is directed in accordance with the observer's voluntary decision about what is currently most relevant. By contrast, when specific elements in a display have a relatively high salience, be they "strange things, moving things, wild animals, bright things, pretty things, metallic things, words, blows, blood, etc.," attention can be deployed in a stimulus-driven, reflexive fashion that is often labeled *bottom-up* (James, 1890).

Two recent studies examined the responses of FEF neurons in monkeys performing *voluntary* spatial attention tasks in which the attended location did not contain any bottom-up saliency cues. One study that recorded FEF neuron activity while monkeys anticipated the appearance of a target stimulus found that both visual and movement responsive neurons encoded the attended location (Zhou & Thompson, 2009). Another study recorded neuronal activity in the FEF in monkeys trained to remember cued locations in order to detect changes in a target stimulus embedded among distracters (Armstrong et al., 2009). Monkeys maintained fixation and used a manual lever to indicate whether the target underwent a change of orientation across two flashed presentations of a stimulus array (Figure 7.5A). Similar tasks have been shown to cause "change blindness," a failure to detect localized stimulus changes when they occur simultaneously with a global visual transient, in both humans (Rensink, 2002) and monkeys (Cavanaugh & Wurtz, 2004). However, directing attention to the changing stimulus can prevent change blindness. Frontal eye field neurons persistently encoded the cued location throughout the trial, both during the delay period when no visual stimuli were present, and during visual discrimination (Figure 7.5B). Furthermore, this FEF activity reliably predicted whether monkeys would detect the target change. In addition, FEF neurons with persistent activity were better at selecting the target from among distracters than were neurons lacking persistent activity (Figure 7.5C). These results demonstrate that FEF neurons maintain spatial information that contributes to the selection of relevant visual stimuli.

These results indicate that the FEF's involvement in the short-term maintenance of spatial information is not limited to impending saccade plans, and more specifically, that FEF neurons participate in allocating attention according to remembered spatial information. Thus, when visual cues about where to attend are absent, persistently active FEF neurons may maintain an internal representation of the attended location that is relatively impervious to interference by distracting visual stimuli. Such a capability would be consistent with a theory of cognitive control that specifies prefrontal cortical regions as providing top-down signals to guide sensory processing and behavior according to internally maintained states and goals (Miller & Cohen, 2001) and with an attentional framework in which the FEF provides bias signals to retinotopically organized visual areas according to the contents of short-term memory (Knudsen, 2007).

Although recording studies cannot determine whether the persistent attention-dependent signals observed in the FEF are generated locally or are relayed from areas such as the SC and LIP or other regions of PFC, there is some evidence suggesting that the FEF may be a source of endogenous attention and saccade control signals. Results from a recent study examining both spiking responses

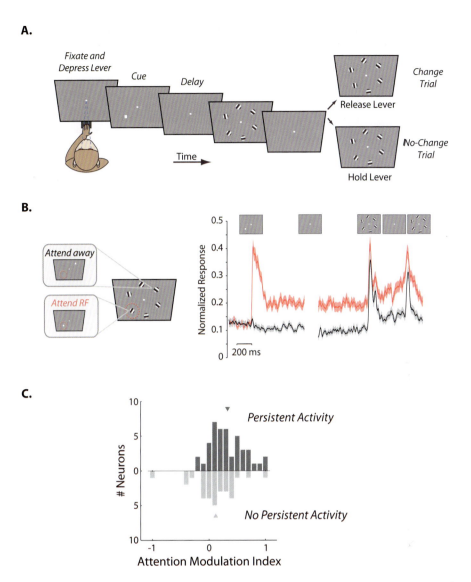

FIGURE 7.5   (A) Change detection task. The monkey maintained fixation throughout the duration of the trial. To initiate a trial, the monkey manually depressed a lever, and after a few hundred milliseconds, a peripheral cue was presented briefly, indicating the target location. Following a fixed delay period, an array of six oriented gratings was flashed twice. On trials in which the target stimulus changed orientation across flashes (change trial), the monkey was rewarded for releasing the lever. On trials where the target stimulus did not change (no-change trial), the monkey was rewarded for continuing to hold the lever for an additional 600–1000 ms. (B, *left*) Trials in which the monkey was cued to attend to the frontal eye field (FEF) receptive field (RF) are labeled "*Attend RF*," whereas trials in which the monkey was cued to attend to the opposite array location are labeled "*Attend away*." (*Right*) Histograms show the average response of the population of FEF neurons on correct trials in which the monkey was cued to attend to the RF location (*red*) and cued to attend away (*gray*). Panels along the top show a schematic diagram of the display seen by the monkey during each task epoch. (C) Attentional modulation of visual responses during change detection varies for different subgroups of FEF neurons. Attention modulation indices were computed for each neuron by taking the difference of the average visual response during the *Attend RF* and *Attend away* conditions and dividing it by the sum of the two responses. Dark and light histograms show the distribution of attention modulation indices for neurons that had persistent delay period activity and for neurons that lacked persistent activity, respectively.

and local field potentials in the FEF during an attention task implied that attention-related signals are generated locally within the FEF, rather than being conveyed from another area of the brain (Monosov et al., 2008). Another study found increases in the synchrony of neuronal firing between the FEF and visual cortex during covert attention, and these increases appeared to be initiated by the FEF (Gregoriou, 2009). In addition, studies comparing the responses of FEF neurons with those of area LIP and SC neurons during both reflexive and voluntary attention tasks have found evidence of functional segregation between these areas, with FEF neurons (and prefrontal neurons) specifically involved in initiating top-down shifts of attention (Buschman et al., 2007; McPeek & Lee, 2007). Similarly, TMS studies in humans have suggested that the FEF may play a different role in automatic and voluntary covert (Smith et al., 2005) and overt (Ro et al., 1999) orienting, and a recent TMS study provided further evidence of a functional segregation between the FEF and LIP area, suggesting that, unlike the LIP area, the FEF operates in a purely top-down fashion that is independent of activity elicited by current sensory input (Ruff et al., 2008). These results imply that neurons in the FEF might play a unique role in the voluntary control of gaze and attention, perhaps related to the ability to maintain spatial information over time.

SPATIAL WORKING MEMORY, SACCADES, AND ATTENTION IN THE FRONTAL EYE FIELD

Some models of visual selection involve attention being guided by and gating entry to working memory (Desimone & Duncan, 1995; Knudsen, 2007), suggesting that perhaps the two processes are indistinguishable at some levels (Desimone, 1996). Indeed, several psychophysical and neuroimaging studies in humans suggest that spatial working memory and spatial attention reflect a common process (Soto et al., 2008). Behaviorally, spatial working memory and attention appear to compete with one another, as extraneous shifts of spatial attention impair spatial working memory performance (Awh et al., 1998). In addition,

visual perception is enhanced at memorized locations (Awh et al., 1998), supporting the hypothesis that shifts of spatial attention underlie the maintenance of spatial information in working memory (Smyth & Scholey, 1994). However, some debate exists over the generality of this effect, as studies in which human and monkey subjects made memory-guided saccades have reported impairments, rather than enhancements, in visual discrimination at the memorized saccade target, as measured by slowed reaction times (Krishna et al., 2006; Ostendorf et al., 2004; Belopolsky & Theeuwes, 2009). Nevertheless, several studies have reported spatially localized enhancements in both evoked potentials (Awh et al., 2000; Jha, 2002) and blood oxygen level–dependent (BOLD) responses measured with functional magnetic resonance imaging (fMRI; Awh et al., 1999; Postle et al., 2004) in visual cortex at remembered locations, suggesting that enhancements of spatial attention occur by default during spatial working memory.

The involvement of FEF neurons in working memory has largely been examined in the context of memory-guided saccade tasks (Bruce & Goldberg, 1985; Funahashi et al., 1989; Sommer & Wurtz, 2000; Opris, et al., 2005; but see Sommer & Wurtz, 2001). Although this task cannot distinguish retrospective encoding of the visual stimulus from prospective encoding of a movement plan (Funashashi et al., 1993), FEF neuron responses observed during memory-guided saccade tasks are strikingly similar to the responses observed during the change detection task discussed earlier (Figure 7.5B), in which no saccades were allowed (Armstrong et al., 2009), thus suggesting a potential role of the FEF in the general maintenance of spatial information. Evidence of the FEF's involvement in saccade preparation, spatial working memory, and spatial attention raises the question of how these seemingly disparate functions are related. One possibility is that persistent FEF activity reflects saccade plans that can be maintained in the absence of visual cues, and that this activity provides a top-down influence on visual cortex (Kastner et al., 1999; Luck et al., 1997). The influence of movement preparation on movement execution has been widely studied (Rosenbaum, 1980; Wise, 1985; Churchland et al., 2006). In general, increased planning duration decreases movement reaction time (Rosenbaum, 1980) and is believed to facilitate the sensory guidance of coordinated movements (Wise, 1985). In the case of eye movements, the ability to behaviorally dissociate the preparation of saccades from their execution may also provide a convenient means of achieving both the selection of visual representations and the maintenance of spatial information. Persistent plan activity in the FEF may be best regarded as attention-related or memory-related, depending merely on whether or not a visual stimulus is present at the saccade goal.

ACKNOWLEDGMENTS

This work was supported by NIH grant EY014924, NSF grant IOB-0546891 (T.M.), NRSA grants F31MH078490 (R.J.S.), and F31NS062615 (M.H.C.), and a Walter I. Berry postdoctoral fellowship to K.M.A.

References

Armstrong, K. M., & Moore, T. (2007). Rapid enhancement of visual cortical response discriminability by microstimulation of the frontal eye field. *Proceedings of the National Academy of Sciences of the United States of America, 104,* 9499–9504.

Armstrong, K. M., Chang, M. H., & Moore, T. (2009). Selection and maintenance of spatial information by frontal eye field neurons. *Journal of Neuroscience, 29,* 15621–15629.

Armstrong, K. M., Fitzgerald, J. K., & Moore, T. (2006). Changes in visual receptive fields with microstimulation of frontal cortex. *Neuron, 50,* 791–798.

Awh, E., Anllo-Vento, L., & Hillyard, S. A. (2000). The role of spatial selective attention in working memory for locations: Evidence from event-related potentials. *Journal of Cognitive Neuroscience, 12,* 840–847.

Awh, E., Jonides, J., & Reuter-Lorenz, P. A. (1998). Rehearsal in spatial working memory. *Journal of Experimental Psychology. Human Perception and Performance, 24,* 780–790.

Awh, E., Jonides, J., Smith, E. E., Buxton, R. B., Frank, L. R., & Love, T., et al. (1999). Rehearsal in spatial working memory: Evidence from neuroimaging. *Psychological Science, 10,* 433–437.

Belopolsky, A. V., & Theeuwes, J. (2009). No functional role of attention-based rehearsal in maintenance of spatial working memory representations. *Acta Psychologica.*

Bizzi, E. (1967). Discharge of frontal eye field neurons during eye movements in unanesthetized monkeys. *Science, 157,* 1588–1590.

Bizzi, E. (1969). Discharges of frontal eye field neurons during saccadic and following eye movements in unanesthetized monkeys. *Electroencephalography and Clinical Neurophysiology, 26,* 630.

Bruce, C. J., & Goldberg, M. E. (1985). Primate frontal eye fields. I. Single neurons discharging before saccades. *Journal of Neurophysiology, 53,* 603–635.

Bruce, C. J., Goldberg, M. E., Bushnell, M. C., & Stanton, G. B. (1985). Primate frontal eye fields. II. Physiological and anatomical correlates of electrically evoked eye movements. *Journal of Neurophysiology, 54,* 714–734.

Buschman, T. J., & Miller, E. K. (2007). Top-down versus bottom-up control of attention in the prefrontal and posterior parietal cortices. *Science, 315,* 1860–1862.

Cavanaugh, J., & Wurtz, R. H. (2004). Subcortical modulation of attention counters change blindness. *Journal of Neuroscience, 24,* 11236–11243.

Chelazzi, L., Miller, E. K., Duncan, J., & Desimone, R. (1993). A neural basis for visual search in inferior temporal cortex. *Nature, 363,* 345–347.

Churchland, M. M., Yu, B. M., Ryu, S. I., Santhanam, G., & Shenoy, K. V. (2006). Neural variability in premotor cortex provides a signature of motor preparation. *Journal of Neuroscience, 26,* 3697–3712.

Corbetta, M., & Shulman, G. L. (2002). Control of goal-directed and stimulus-driven attention in the brain. *Nature Reviews. Neuroscience, 3,* 201–215.

Crovitz, H. F., & Daves, W. (1962). Tendencies to eye movement and perceptual accuracy. *Journal of Experimental Psychology, 63,* 495–498.

Desimone, R. (1996). Neural mechanisms for visual memory and their role in attention. *Proceedings of the National Academy of Sciences of the United States of America, 93,* 13494–13499.

Desimone, R., & Duncan, J. (1995). Neural mechanisms of selective visual attention. *Annual Review of Neuroscience, 18,* 193–222.

Deubel, H., & Schneider, W. X. (1996). Saccade target selection and object recognition: Evidence for a common attentional mechanism. *Vision Research, 36,* 1827–1837.

Dias, E. C., Kiesau, M., & Segraves, M. A. (1995). Acute activation and inactivation of macaque frontal eye field with GABA-related drugs. *Journal of Neurophysiology, 74,* 2744–2748.

Dias, E. C., & Segraves, M. A. (1999). Muscimol-induced inactivation of monkey frontal eye field: Effects on visually and memory-guided saccades. *Journal of Neurophysiology, 81*(5), 2191–2214.

Ferrier, D. (1876). *The functions of the brain.* London: Smith, Elder.

Ferrier, D. (1890). The Croonian lectures on cerebral localisation. *British Medical Journal, 2,* 68–75.

Fischer, B., & Boch, R. (1981). Enhanced activation of neurons in prelunate cortex before visually guided saccades of trained rhesus monkeys. *Experimental Brain Research, 44*(2), 129–137.

Fries, W. (1984). Cortical projections to the superior colliculus in the macaque monkey: A retrograde study using horseradish peroxidase. *Journal of Comparative Neurology, 230,* 55–76.

Funahashi, S., Bruce, C. J., & Goldman-Rakic, P. S. (1989). Mnemonic coding of visual space in the monkey's dorsolateral prefrontal cortex. *Journal of Neurophysiology, 61,* 331–349.

Funahashi, S., Chafee, M. V., & Goldman-Rakic, P. S. (1993). Prefrontal neuronal activity in rhesus monkeys performing a delayed anti-saccade task. *Nature, 365,* 753–756.

Goldberg, M. E., & Bushnell, M. C. (1981). Behavioral enhancement of visual responses in monkey cerebral cortex. II. Modulation in frontal eye fields specifically related to saccades. *Journal of Neurophysiology, 46,* 773–787.

Gregoriou, G. G., Gotts, S. J., Zhou, H., & Desimone, R. (2009). High-frequency, long-range coupling between prefrontal and visual cortex during attention. *Science, 29,* 1207–1210.

Grosbras, M. H., & Paus, T. (2002). Transcranial magnetic stimulation of the human frontal eye field: Effects on visual perception and attention. *Journal of Cognitive Neuroscience, 14,* 1109–1120.

Grosbras, M. H., & Paus, T. (2003). Transcranial magnetic stimulation of the human frontal eye field facilitates visual awareness. *European Journal of Neuroscience, 18,* 3121–3126.

Hoffman, J. E., & Subramaniam, B. (1995). The role of visual attention in saccadic eye movements. *Perception & Psychophysics, 57,* 787–795.

Ignashchenkova, A., Dicke, P. W., Haarmeier, T., & Thier, P. (2004). Neuron-specific contribution of the superior colliculus to overt and covert shifts of attention. *Nature Neuroscience, 7,* 56–64.

James, W. (1890). *Principles of psychology.* New York: Henry Holt.

Jha, A. P. (2002). Tracking the time-course of attentional involvement in spatial working memory: An event-related potential investigation. *Brain Research. Cognitive Brain Research, 15,* 61–69.

Koch, C., & Ullman, S. (1985). Shifts in selective visual attention: Towards the underlying neural circuitry. *Human Neurobiology, 4,* 219–227.

Johnston, K., & Everling, S. (2008). Neurophysiology and neuroanatomy of reflexive and voluntary saccades in non-human primates. *Brain and Cognition, 68,* 271–283.

Kastner, S., Pinsk, M. A., De Weerd, P., Desimone, R., & Ungerleider, L. G. (1999). Increased activity in human visual cortex during directed attention in the absence of visual stimulation. *Neuron, 22,* 751–761.

Knudsen, E. I. (2007). Fundamental components of attention. *Annual Review of Neuroscience, 30,* 57–78.

Kowler, E., Anderson, E., Dosher, B., & Blaser, E. (1995). The role of attention in the programming of saccades. *Vision Research, 35,* 1897–1916.

Krishna, B. S., Steenrod, S. C., Bisley, J. W., Sirotin, Y. B., & Goldberg, M. E. (2006). Reaction times of manual responses to a visual stimulus at the goal of a planned memory-guided saccade in the monkey. *Experimental Brain Research, 173,* 102–114.

Latto, R., & Cowey, A. (1971). Visual field defects after frontal eye-field lesions in monkeys. *Brain Research, 30,* 1–24.

Lee, D. K., Koch, C., & Braun, J. (1997). Spatial vision thresholds in the near absence of attention. *Vision Research, 37,* 2409–2418.

Lovejoy, L. P., & Krauzlis, R. J. (2009). Inactivation of primate superior colliculus impairs covert selection of signals for perceptual judgments. *Nature Neuroscience, 13,* 261–266.

Luck, S. J., Chelazzi, L., Hillyard, S. A., & Desimone, R. (1997). Neural mechanisms of spatial selective attention in areas V1, V2, and V4 of macaque visual cortex. *Journal of Neurophysiology, 77,* 24–42.

Lynch, J. C., Hoover, J. E., & Strick, P. L. (1994). Input to the primate frontal eye field from the substantia nigra, superior colliculus, and dentate nucleus demonstrated by transneuronal transport. *Experimental Brain Research, 100,* 181–186.

McAdams, C. J., & Maunsell, J. H. (1999). Effects of attention on orientation-tuning functions of single neurons in macaque cortical area V4. *Journal of Neuroscience, 19,* 431–441.

McPeek, R., & Takahashi, N. (2006). Deficits in cued and uncued shifts of attention after inactivation of frontal eye field. Program No. 606.10. In: Society for Neuroscience, 2006. Atlanta, GA: 2006 Neuroscience Meeting Planner.

McPeek, R. M., & Keller, E. L. (2004). Deficits in saccade target selection after inactivation of superior colliculus. *Nature Neuroscience, 7*, 757–763.

McPeek, R. M., & Lee, B.-T. (2007). Roles of superior colliculus and frontal eye field in reflexive and top-down attentional shifts. Program No. 717.10. In: Society for Neuroscience, 2007. San Diego, CA: 2007 Neuroscience Meeting Planner.

Miller, E. K., & Cohen, J. D. (2001). An integrative theory of prefrontal cortex function. *Annual Review of Neuroscience, 24*, 167–202.

Mohler, C. W., Goldberg, M. E., & Wurtz, R. H. (1973). Visual receptive fields of frontal eye field neurons. *Brain Research, 61*, 385–389.

Monosov, I. E., Trageser, J. C., & Thompson, K. G. (2008). Measurements of simultaneously recorded spiking activity and local field potentials suggest that spatial selection emerges in the frontal eye field. *Neuron, 57*, 614–625.

Moore, T. (1999). Shape representations and visual guidance of saccadic eye movements. *Science, 285*(5435), 1914–1917.

Moore, T., & Armstrong, K. M. (2003). Selective gating of visual signals by microstimulation of frontal cortex. *Nature, 421*, 370–373.

Moore, T., Armstrong, K. M., & Fallah, M. (2003). Visuomotor origins of covert spatial attention. *Neuron, 30*, 671–683.

Moore, T., & Chang, M. H. (2009). Presaccadic discrimination of receptive field stimuli by area V4 neurons. *Vision Research, 49*(10), 1227–1232.

Moore, T., & Fallah, M. (2001). Control of eye movements and spatial attention. *Proceedings of the National Academy of Sciences of the United States of America, 98*, 1273–1276.

Moore, T., & Fallah, M. (2004). Microstimulation of the frontal eye field and its effects on covert spatial attention. *Journal of Neurophysiology, 91*, 152–162.

Moore, T., Tolias, A. S., & Schiller, P. H. (1998). Visual representations during saccadic eye movements. *Proceedings of the National Academy of Sciences of the United States of America, 95*(15), 8981–8984.

Mountcastle, V. B., Lynch, J. C., Georgopoulos, A., Sakata, H., & Acuna, C. (1975). Posterior parietal association cortex of the monkey: Command functions for operations within extrapersonal space. *Journal of Neurophysiology, 38*, 871–908.

Muller, J. R., Philiastides, M. G., & Newsome, W. T. (2005). Microstimulation of the superior colliculus focuses attention without moving the eyes. *Proceedings of the National Academy of Sciences of the United States of America, 102*, 524–529.

Opris, I., Barborica, A., & Ferrera, V. P. (2005). Effects of electrical microstimulation in monkey frontal eye field on saccades to remembered targets. *Vision Research, 45*, 3414–3429.

O'Shea, J., Muggleton, N. G., Cowey, A., & Walsh, V. (2004). Timing of target discrimination in human frontal eye fields. *Journal of Cognitive Neuroscience, 16*, 1060–1067.

Ostendorf, F., Finke, C., & Ploner, C. J. (2004). Inhibition of visual discrimination during a memory-guided saccade task. *Journal of Neurophysiology, 92*, 660–664.

Peng, X., Sereno, M. E., Silva, A. K., Lehky, S. R. & Sereno, A. B. (2008). Shape selectivity in primate frontal eye field. *Journal of Neurophysiology, 100*, 796–814.

Posner, M. I. (1980). Orienting of attention. *Quarterly Journal of Experimental Psychology, 32*, 3–25.

Postle, B. R., Awh, E., Jonides, J., Smith, E. E., & D'Esposito, M. (2004). The where and how of attention-based rehearsal in spatial working memory. *Brain Research. Cognitive Brain Research, 20*, 194–205.

Remington, R. W. (1980). Attention and saccadic eye movements. *Journal of Experimental Psychology. Human Perception and Performance, 6*, 726–744.

Rensink, R. A. (2002). Change detection. *Annual Review of Psychology, 53*, 245–277.

Reynolds, J. H., & Chelazzi, L. (2004). Attentional modulation of visual processing. *Annual Review of Neuroscience, 27*, 611–647.

Rizzolatti, G., Riggio, L., Dascola, I., & Umilta, C. (1987). Reorienting attention across the horizontal and vertical meridians: Evidence in favor of a premotor theory of attention. *Neuropsychologia, 25*, 31–40.

Ro, T., Cheifet, S., Ingle, H., Shoup, R., & Rafal, R. (1999). Localization of the human frontal eye fields and motor hand area with transcranial magnetic stimulation and magnetic resonance imaging. *Neuropsychologia, 37*, 225–231.

Robinson, D. A., & Fuchs, A. F. (1969). Eye movements evoked by stimulation of frontal eye fields. *Journal of Neurophysiology, 32*, 637–648.

Rosenbaum, D. A. (1980). Human movement initiation: Specification of arm, direction, and extent. *Journal of Experimental Psychology, Gen, 109*, 444–474.

Ruff, C. C., Bestmann, S., Blankenburg, F., Bjoertomt, O., Josephs, O., Weiskopf, N., et al. (2008). Distinct causal influences of parietal versus frontal areas on human visual cortex: Evidence from concurrent TMS-fMRI. *Cerebral Cortex, 18*, 817–827.

Ruff, C. C., Blankenburg, F., Bjoertomt, O., Bestmann, S., Freeman, E., Haynes, J. D., et al. (2006). Concurrent TMS-fMRI and psychophysics reveal frontal influences on human retinotopic visual cortex. *Current Biology: CB, 16*, 1479–1488.

Schafer, R. J., & Moore, T. (2007). Attention governs action in the primate frontal eye field. *Neuron*, *56*(3), 541–551.

Schall, J. D. (2004). On the role of frontal eye field in guiding attention and saccades. *Vision Research*, *44* (2004), 1453–1467.

Schall, J. D., Morel, A., King, D. J., & Bullier, J. (1995). Topography of visual cortex connections with frontal eye field in macaque: convergence and segregation of processing streams. *Journal of Neuroscience*, *15*, 4464–4487.

Schiller, P. H., & Tehovnik, E. J. (2001). Look and see: How the brain moves your eyes about. *Progress in Brain Research*, *134*, 127–142.

Schneider, W. (1995). VAM: A neuro-cognitive model for visual attention control of segmentation, object recognition, and space-based motor actions. *Visual Cognition*, *2*, 331–376.

Sheliga, B. M., Riggio, L., & Rizzolatti, G. (1994). Orienting of attention and eye movements. *Experimental Brain Research*, *98*, 507–522.

Shepherd, M., Findlay, J. M., & Hockey, R. J. (1986). The relationship between eye movements and spatial attention. *Quarterly Journal of Experimental Psychology*, *A 38*, 475–491.

Silvanto, J., Lavie, N., & Walsh, V. (2006). Stimulation of the human frontal eye fields modulates sensitivity of extrastriate visual cortex. *Journal of Neurophysiology*, *96*, 941–945.

Smith, D. T., Jackson, S. R., & Rorden, C. (2005). Transcranial magnetic stimulation of the left human frontal eye fields eliminates the cost of invalid endogenous cues. *Neuropsychologia*, *43*, 1288–1296.

Smyth, M. M., & Scholey, K. A. (1994). Interference in immediate spatial memory. *Memory & Cognition*, *22*, 1–13.

Sommer, M. A., & Tehovnik, E. J. (1997). Reversible inactivation of macaque frontal eye field. *Experimental Brain Research*, *116*, 229–249.

Sommer, M. A., & Wurtz, R. H. (2000). Composition and topographic organization of signals sent from the frontal eye field to the superior colliculus. *Journal of Neurophysiology*, *83*, 1979–2001.

Sommer, M. A., & Wurtz, R. H. (2001). Frontal eye field sends delay activity related to movement, memory, and vision to the superior colliculus. *Journal of Neurophysiology*, *85*, 1673–1685.

Soto, D., Hodsoll, J., Rotshtein, P., & Humphreys, G. W. (2008). Automatic guidance of attention from working memory. *Trends in Cognitive Sciences*, *12*, 342–348.

Sperling, G. (1960). The information available in brief visual presentations. *Psychological Monographs: General and Applied*, *74*, 1–29.

Stanton, G. B., Bruce, C. J., & Goldberg, M. E. (1995). Topography of projections to posterior cortical areas from the macaque frontal eye fields. *Journal of Comparative Neurology*, *353*, 291–305.

Stanton, G. B., Goldberg, M. E., & Bruce, C. J. (1988). Frontal eye field efferents in the macaque monkey: II. Topography of terminal fields in midbrain and pons. *Journal of Comparative Neurology*, *271*, 493–506.

Taylor, P. C., Nobre, A. C., & Rushworth, M. F. (2007). FEF TMS affects visual cortical activity. *Cerebral Cortex*, *17*, 391–399.

Thompson, K. G., & Bichot, N. P. (2005). A visual salience map in the primate frontal eye field. *Progress in Brain Research*, *147*, 249–262.

Thompson, K. G., Biscoe, K. L., & Sato, T. R. (2005). Neuronal basis of covert spatial attention in the frontal eye field. *Journal of Neuroscience*, *25*, 9479–9487.

Tolias, A. S., Sultan, F., Augath, M., Oeltermann, A., Tehovnik, E. J., Schiller, P. H., & Logothetis, N. K. (2005). Mapping cortical activity elicited with electrical microstimulation using FMRI in the macaque. *Neuron*, *48*, 901–911.

Wardak, C., Ibos, G., Duhamel, J. R., & Olivier, E. (2006). Contribution of the monkey frontal eye field to covert visual attention. *Journal of Neuroscience*, *26*, 4228–4235.

Wardak, C., Olivier, E., & Duhamel, J. R. (2004). A deficit in covert attention after parietal cortex inactivation in the monkey. *Neuron*, *42*, 501–508.

Welch, K., & Stuteville, P. (1958). Experimental production of unilateral neglect in monkeys. *Brain*, *81*, 341–347.

Winkowski, D. E., & Knudsen, E. I. (2006). Top-down gain control of the auditory space map by gaze control circuitry in the barn owl. *Nature*, *439*, 336–339.

Wise, S. P. (1985). The primate premotor cortex: Past, present, and preparatory. *Annual Review of Neuroscience*, *8*, 1–19.

Wurtz, R. H., & Goldberg, M. E. (1972). Activity of superior colliculus in behaving monkey. 3. Cells discharging before eye movements. *Journal of Neurophysiology*, *35*, 575–586.

Wurtz, R. H., & Mohler, CW (1976). Enhancement of visual responses in monkey striate cortex and frontal eye fields. *Journal of Neurophysiology*, *39*, 766–772.

Zhou, H. H., Thompson, K. G. (2009). Cognitively directed spatial selection in the frontal eye field in anticipation of visual stimuli to be discriminated. *Vision Research*, *49*, 1205–1215.

8

Attention and the Parietal Lobe

MICHAEL E. GOLDBERG, ANGELA GEE, ANNA IPATA, JAMES W. BISLEY, AND
JACQUELINE GOTTLIEB

SINCE THE 19th century, it has been apparent, from neuropsychological evidence that the parietal cortex is important in spatial attention (Critchley, 1953). This comes from two deficits seen in patients with parietal defects: *neglect*, in which patients with parietal lesions behave as if the contralateral part of the visual world or an object did not exist; and *extinction* or *perceptual rivalry*, the tendency of patients with parietal lesions to choose the ipsilateral of two stimuli when both are presented simultaneously, although they have no trouble perceiving the contralateral object when it is presented alone. It is also clear that the parietal lobe is important in movement—patients with parietal lesions have *optic ataxia*, difficulty looking at or reaching contralateral targets—although this motor deficit usually parallels an attentional deficit.

The physiological role of the posterior parietal cortex in the generation of behavior in the monkey has been the subject of a rather heated debate. The earliest single-neuron studies made it clear that parietal neurons discharge before visually guided movement (Hyvarinen & Poranen, 1974; Lynch et al., 1977), but they also are active in tasks that require visual attention (Robinson et al., 1978; Bushnell et al., 1981) but in which movements were forbidden. These early studies did not fractionate the posterior parietal cortex, but much recent work has subdivided the intraparietal sulcus into a number of different areas, each of which deals with the sensory processing in specific motor workspace (Colby & Duhamel, 1991; Colby & Goldberg, 1999). The area that deals with visual space explored by the eyes is the lateral intraparietal (LIP) area, which was defined on the basis of its connections to the frontal eye fields (FEF; Andersen et al., 1990), lateral pulvinar, and the superior colliculus (SC; Andersen et al., 1985).

LIP has reciprocal connections to both the dorsal and ventral cortical visual streams (Seltzer &

Pandya, 1980; Neal et al., 1988), as well as to oculomotor areas such as the SC and the FEFs (Asanuma et al., 1985; Andersen et al., 1990; Schall et al., 1995). In keeping with these connections, both visual and saccadic activity have been described in LIP. Since Andersen and Gnadt's original demonstration that neurons in LIP respond throughout a memory-guided delayed saccade task (Gnadt & Andersen, 1988), different studies have suggested that LIP has activity correlating with saccadic intention (Barash et al., 1991a,b; Colby et al., 1996; Snyder et al., 1997) and visual attention (Colby et al., 1996; Gottlieb et al., 1998; Bisley & Goldberg, 2003; Balan & Gottlieb, 2006; Oristaglio et al., 2006; Balan et al., 2008; Balan & Gottlieb, 2009; Peck et al., 2009). LIP also has activity that seems uncorrelated with attention (Platt & Glimcher, 1997; Snyder et al., 1997).

Often the same neurons can be shown to correlate with visual attention and saccadic eye movements. Thus, in an antisaccade task in which the monkey must make a saccade to a spatial location *opposite* a visual cue, neurons in LIP respond more strongly when the stimulus it is in the receptive field (RF) than to the saccade when its spatial location is in the RF. Although the bulk of neurons respond more actively to a saccade made to a visual stimulus than to the antisaccade to the same location, some neurons show no difference in their response (Gottlieb & Goldberg, 1999; Zhang & Barash, 2000), although the response to the saccade goal occurs later than the response to the antisaccade cue. Similarly, some neurons in LIP give identical responses when a monkey makes a visually guided saccade, a learned saccade without any visual target, or performs a peripheral attention task in which the monkey must signal a luminance change in a peripheral stimulus, but not make a saccade to that stimulus (Colby et al., 1996). Furthermore, in a visual search task in which a monkey must find a target that signals a hand movement, but may not move its eyes, LIP neurons identify the spatial location of the target (Oristaglio et al., 2006), showing that overt saccades are not needed to trigger a response.

Several recent experiments illustrate the difficulty of assigning an attentional or a motor role uniquely to LIP. Some of these studies show that neural activity in LIP correlates with a monkey's

visual attention and can absolutely be separated from the planning or generation of saccades (Bisley & Goldberg, 2003; Balan & Gottlieb, 2006; Bisley & Goldberg, 2006; Oristaglio et al., 2006; Balan et al., 2008; Balan & Gottlieb, 2009; Peck et al., 2009). Other studies demonstrate that, under conditions of free visual search, neural activity in LIP predicts not only the goal of a saccade but its latency (Ipata et al., 2006a; Thomas & Pare, 2007). We resolve this seeming paradox by proposing that LIP represents a priority map that can be used by both the oculomotor system to choose a saccade goal when a saccade is appropriate, and by the visual system to determine the locus of visual attention. Thus, rather than serving a dedicated sensorimotor function, the same signal can serve as an intention or attention signal, depending on the recipient area and the behavioral context. Furthermore, the genesis of the spikes is irrelevant to their interpretation: Thus, spikes evoked by the abrupt onset of a visual stimulus can drive saccades, and spikes evoked by the plan for a memory-guided delayed saccade can drive visual attention. LIP sums all the signals that project to it to create the priority map.

ATTENTION MODULATES LATERAL INTRAPARIETAL ACTIVITY

It is clear that neurons in LIP do not respond identically to a given visual stimulus at all times. Instead, the visual response of these neurons can be modulated by the behavioral significance of the stimulus (Bushnell et al., 1981; Colby et al., 1996; Platt & Glimcher, 1999; Sugrue et al., 2004; Balan & Gottlieb, 2006; Oristaglio et al., 2006; Balan et al., 2008), and the response is enhanced when the stimulus is important to the animal. The importance of behavioral relevance was made clear in a study in which the monkey made a saccade that brought a stimulus in the RF of a neuron. For a behaviorally irrelevant, stable stimulus (e.g., a stimulus that has not recently appeared in the environment but instead, like the architectural features of the room in which the reader is reading this chapter, is stable and unchanging), the response of LIP neurons was weak (Figure 8.1). Conversely, for a behaviorally relevant stimulus,

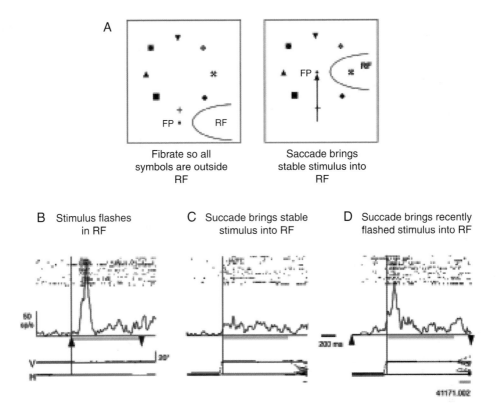

FIGURE 8.1 Attentional modulation of visual responses in the lateral intraparietal (LIP). (**A**) Stable target task. A radially symmetric array remains on the screen throughout the duration of the experiment. *Left*: The monkey fixates outside the array (FP), and no member of the array is in the receptive field (RF). *Right*: The monkey makes a saccade that brings one member of the array into the RF. (**B**) Response of the cell to the flash of the stimulus in the RF when the monkey fixates a fixation point in the center of the array. In the raster display, each dot is a unit discharge, each line a trial; successive trials are synchronized on the appearance of the stimulus in the RF. The spike density plot beneath the raster quantifies the raster. Horizontal (H) and vertical (V) eye movements are displayed beneath. Note that the monkey does not make a saccade to the stimulus. (**C**) Much weaker response when the monkey makes a saccade that brings the stable member of the array into the RF. (**D**) Much stronger response when the monkey makes a saccade that brings the stimulus into the RF when it has appeared immediately before the saccade. Reproduced from Gottlieb, J. P., Kusunoki, M., & Goldberg, M. E. (1998). The representation of visual salience in monkey parietal cortex. *Nature, 391*, 481–484, with permission of the publisher.

for example a pending saccade target, or a recently flashed stimulus, the neurons discharged more intensely (Gottlieb et al., 1998).

If LIP were primarily to have a saccade-planning function, then in a similar way neurons in LIP should filter out saccade-irrelevant stimuli even though they may be salient for other reasons, such as abrupt onset or sudden motion. Once the monkey was committed to planning a given saccade, a stimulus appearing far away from the saccade goal should evoke a weaker response than a stimulus at the saccade goal or even the stimulus that specified the saccade goal. In fact, neurons in LIP show equivalently strong responses to task-relevant stimuli that are never saccade targets (Colby et al., 1996; Balan & Gottlieb, 2006; Oristaglio et al., 2006; Balan et al., 2008; Peck et al., 2009), and to salient but saccade-irrelevant stimuli that appeared away from the goal of a planned memory-guided saccade (Powell & Goldberg, 2000).

In humans, there is an attentional advantage at the goal of a saccade (Kowler et al., 1995; Deubel

& Schneider, 1996). There is also an attentional advantage at the site of an abruptly appearing stimulus (Yantis & Jonides, 1984). One logical way of interpreting the demonstration of an enhanced response to a stimulus that appears away from the goal of a planned memory-guided saccade is that the activity represents an attentionally salient object in the visual field even though it was not a saccade target.

In the past, several methods have been used to describe the locus of attention: a post hoc method that says that if a subject responds to a stimulus it must have attended to it (Goldberg & Wurtz, 1972); a reaction time method, defining the locus of spatial attention as the area of the visual field in which the response to a discriminandum has the lowest latency (Posner, 1980; Bowman et al., 1993); and a visual perceptual method, which defines the spatial locus of attention as that area of the visual field with enhanced visual sensitivity, measured either as an improvement in contrast sensitivity (Bashinski & Bacharach, 1980) or an improved ability to find a target among clutter (De Weerd et al., 1999).

A classic experiment illustrates the pitfalls of using the post hoc method. Snyder, Batista, and Andersen (1997) trained monkeys to make simultaneous saccades and reaches to different targets. Activity in LIP decreased during the delay period, when the monkeys were planning the reach to the RF and the saccade elsewhere. Using the post hoc method of assigning attention, the authors assumed that the monkeys were attending to the reach target and to the saccade target equally throughout the delay period. The authors used the decrement in LIP activity prior to reach movements to suggest that LIP was doing saccade planning and not pinning attention. However, using psychophysical measurements of a perceptual threshold, Deubel and Schneider (2003) showed that visual attention is sustained at a saccade goal throughout the delay period, but lies at the goal of a planned reach movement only for 300 ms. In LIP, neural signals were identical for saccade and reach movements for the first 300 ms after the targets appeared, and in this early interval a decoder could not predict whether the monkey was making a saccade or a reach to the RF (Quian Quiroga et al., 2006). Therefore, the decrement of LIP

activity at the reach goal during the delay can be ascribed not to LIP's dedication to saccade planning but to the lack of maintained attention at the reach goal.

To study the relationship of parietal activity to saccade planning and distractors, Bisley and Goldberg (2003) used contrast sensitivity to measure attention explicitly, to examine how attention changed over time and under different visual conditions. This technique ruled out the possibility that any attentional advantage could be on the motor side of the response, a problem present when defining attention by changes in reaction time. The monkey had to make a perceptual decision embedded within a memory-guided saccade task (Figure 8.2A). The monkey was first presented with a visual stimulus that appeared briefly, specifying the location to which the monkey had to plana saccade. While the monkey was waiting for the signal to make the saccade (the disappearance of the fixation point), a probe stimulus appeared for a single video frame, consisting of three circles and a Landolt ring. Depending on the orientation of the ring, when the fixation point disappeared, the monkey had either to make the planned saccade or cancel it. The contrast of the probe varied to assess the monkey's visual perception. The animal's performance was better when the probe appeared at the saccade goal than when it appeared elsewhere (Figure 8.2C). The significance of this result was that it suggested that the activity in LIP that occurred during the delay period of a memory-guided delayed saccade task, although it reflected saccadic intention, might actually be a corollary discharge from the motor system, driving the attention found at the goal of the saccade and not necessarily a part of the neural mechanisms driving the movement itself. This attentional advantage lingered throughout the delay period of the memory-guided delayed saccade task. There was enhanced performance for stimulus onset asynchronies (SOAs) from the saccade target to the probe of 800, 1,300, and 1,800 ms (Figure 8.2D).

In humans (Yantis & Jonides, 1984), the abrupt onset of flashed task-irrelevant attractor draws attention away from a task goal. Similarly, in the attention task, the distractor drew the monkey's attention away from the saccade goal. The distractor

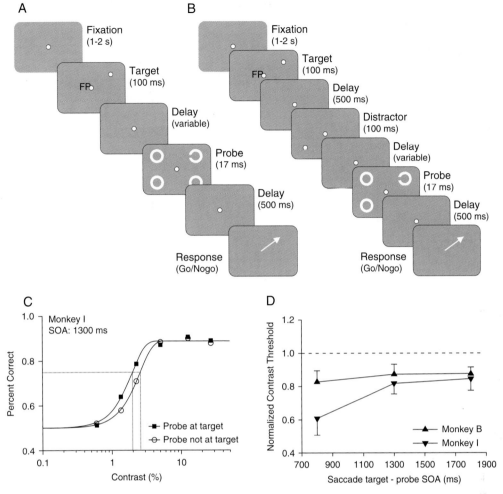

FIGURE 8.2   Effect of saccade planning on perceptual threshold. (**A**) Simple attention task. The monkeys began the trial by fixating a small spot (FP). After a short delay, a second spot (the target) appeared for 100 ms at one of four possible positions equidistant from the fovea and evenly distributed throughout the four visual quadrants. The exact target locations varied from day to day, to prevent long-term perceptual learning and to ensure that the saccade goals and/or probe would appear in the receptive field (RF) of the neuron under study. This target specified the goal for the memory-guided saccade that the monkey would have to make unless the probe told it otherwise. At some time after the target disappeared, a Landolt ring (the probe) and three complete rings of identical luminance to the probe flashed for one video frame (~17 ms) at the four possible saccade target positions; 500 ms after the probe the fixation point disappeared, and the animals had to indicate the orientation of the Landolt ring by either maintaining fixation for 1000 ms (when the gap was on the right—a NOGO trial) or making a saccade to the goal and remaining there for 1,000 ms (when the gap was on the left—a GO trial). The Landolt ring could appear at any of the flour positions. The luminance of the rings varied from trial to trial, changing the contrast between the probe and the background. (**B**) Distractor attention task. In half of the trials, a task-irrelevant distractor, identical to the target, was flashed 500 ms after the target either at or opposite the saccade goal. (**C**) Psychometric functions from Monkey I from trials with a target-probe stimulus onset asynchronies (SOA) of 1,300 ms. The solid squares are from trials in which the probe was at the location of the target; the hollow circles are from trials in which the probe was not at the saccade goal. The data are pooled results from 22 sessions (~800 trials per point). The performance from the two conditions was significantly different on the slopes of the functions (*p* <0.01, Chi-squared test at each contrast).

(*Continued on next page*)

FIGURE 8.2 (*Continued*)   The solid lines were fitted to the data with a Weibull function, weighted by the number of trials at each point, using the maximum likelihood method programmed in Matlab. (**D**) Normalized contrast thresholds for the three SOAs from the two monkeys when the probe was at the location of the saccade goal (*solid triangles*). Data for each delay were normalized by the performance at that delay when the probe was not at the saccade goal (*dashed line*). Points significantly beneath the dashed line show attentional enhancement, and all points were significant when tested with paired t-test comparing the prenormalized performance when the probe was at the saccade goal with the prenormalized performance when the probe was away from the saccade goal. No distractor appeared in any of these trials. Reproduced from Bisley, J. W., & Goldberg, M. E. (2003). Neuronal activity in the lateral intraparietal area and spatial attention. *Science, 299*, 81–86, with permission of the publisher.

appeared on half of the trials and was either presented at the saccade goal or opposite the saccade goal (Figure 8.2B). The distractor was identical to the target in size, brightness, and duration, but appeared 500 ms after the target. It remained on the screen for 100 ms.

LIP neurons responded similarly to the distractor and the saccade goal. When the saccade target appeared in the RF, the cell responded with a brisk-onset transient, then activity fell to a delay period level of less than the onset transient but greater than the background (Figure 8.3A). When the distractor appeared in the RF, the onset transient was brisk, but the activity fell closer to background (Figure 8.3B). The average across the population was similar to the single cells (Figure 8.3C and D show normalized average responses to both target and distractor for each monkey). Note that the activity evoked by the distractor was transiently greater than the delay period activity evoked by the saccade plan.

The attentional response of the monkey paralleled the neural response. When the distractor appeared in the opposite location of the target, and the probe appeared 200 ms after the distractor, and the perceptual threshold decreased at the distractor site and increased at the saccade goal (Figure 8.3C, D), suggesting that the distractor had drawn attention away from the saccade goal, just as the neural response to the distractor was greater than the response to the saccade plan. Five hundred milliseconds later, the perceptual advantage had returned to the saccade goal and had left the distractor site, and neural activity at the saccade goal was greater than activity evoked by the distractor. Thus, as in humans, the abrupt onset

of a distractor in the visual field draws attention. In the monkey, this occurs even while the animal is planning a saccade, but the attentional effect of the distractor lasts for less than 600 ms, by which time attention has returned to the saccade goal. The effect on attention was the same (in terms of perceptual threshold) both at the distractor site and the saccade goal, lowering the contrast sensitivity threshold by the same amount.

The time at which the activity evoked by the distractor fell beneath the activity evoked by the saccade plan (the "crossing point") had behavioral significance. For each monkey there was a window of 80–90 ms in which there was no significant difference between the activity (as determined by a 100 ms window that slid across the entire period in 5 ms steps) evoked by the distractor and the activity related to the saccade plan ($p > 0.05$ by Wilcoxon sign rank test). During this window of neuronal ambiguity, when activity at both sites did not differ, the monkey did not show a psychophysical attentional advantage at either site (Figure 8.3E and F). At the crossing point, there was no spatial region of enhanced sensitivity in either monkey, but within 500 ms, attention had shifted back to the site of the target in both monkeys, with normalized thresholds similar to those seen in the earlier experiment. This is in stark contrast to the effect of LIP activity on saccades: When there was equal activity in the two populations, even in the 50 ms epoch immediately before the saccade, there was no measurable effect on the latency, accuracy, or even early trajectory of the planned saccade (Powell & Goldberg, 2000).

It is possible that a period of time follows the distractor when attention is shifting, and this

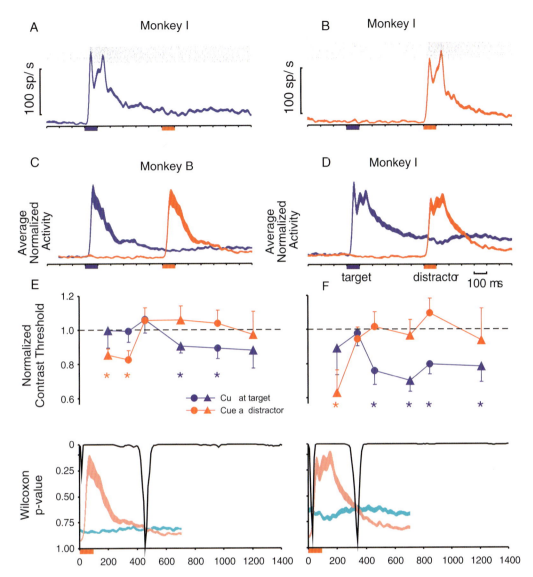

FIGURE 8.3 Behavioral and neural effects of a distractor flashed while the monkey performs the attention task. (**A**) Raster and spike density diagrams of one neuron's response to the target appearing in the receptive field (RF; *blue bar*). Subsequently, the distractor appears outside the RF (*red bar*). The thickness of the traces represents the standard error of the mean. (**B**) The same neuron's response when the distractor appeared in the RF (*red bar*) and the target appeared outside the RF were recorded while the monkey was performing the task on threshold. (**C**) Averaged normalized spike density functions from 18 cells from Monkey B. The thickness of the traces represent the standard error of the mean. (**D**) Averaged normalized spike density functions from 23 cells from Monkey I. (**E, F**) Normalized contrast threshold in the distractor task (Figure 8.2B) for monkey B (**E**) and Monkey I (**F**) plotted against stimulus onset asynchrony (SOA) between distractor and probe, for trials in which the probe appeared at the saccade goal (*blue symbols*) or at the distractor site (*red symbols*). Data for each delay were normalized by the performance at that delay when the probe was not placed at the saccade goal in trials without a distractor. In the trials shown here, the distractor appeared opposite the saccade goal. Points significantly beneath the dashed line show attentional enhancement (*: $p < 0.05$, paired t-test on prenormalized data). The circle data was recorded at the crossing point in each monkey (455 ms for monkey B, 340 ms for monkey I) and 500 ms later. Data were also collected from both animals at the crossing point recorded in the other animal. Statistical significance was confirmed with a paired t-test on the prenormalized data (*: $p < 0.05$).

(*Continued on next page*)

FIGURE 8.3 (*Continued*)   The black traces in the bottom section shows the p-values from Wilcoxon paired sign rank tests performed on the activity of all the neurons for a monkey over a 100 ms bin, measured every 5 ms. A low p-value (high on the axis) represents a significant difference in the activity from the two conditions. The gray column signifies when there is no statistical difference between the activity in both populations. The normalized spike density functions from **C** and **D** have been superimposed to show the time course of activity in lateral intraparietal following the onset of the distractor for the two monkeys. Reproduced from Bisley, J. W., & Goldberg, M. E. (2003). Neuronal activity in the lateral intraparietal area and spatial attention. *Science, 299,* 81–86, with permission of the publisher.

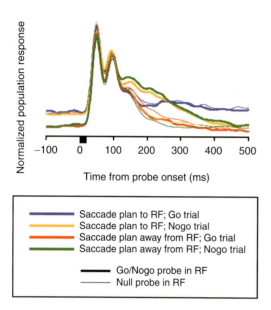

FIGURE 8.4   The response to the probe in the receptive field (RF). The normalized population responses from one monkey to the GO, NOGO, and null probes under different task conditions. The thick black bar on the abscissa shows the time of presentation of the probe. *Thick blue trace*: Saccade plan to RF, probe in RF signals GO. Note the delay period activity consistent with the saccade plan, and the rapid fall of the activity to the delay level. *Thin blue trace*: Null probe in RF, saccade plan to RF. Note that this response is not different from the response to the GO probe. *Thick orange trace*: Saccade plan to RF, probe in RF signals NOGO. Note that the response is enhanced relative to the GO probe in the RF. *Thin orange trace*: Saccade plan to RF, NOGO trial, null probe in RF. Note that although the probe elsewhere cancels the saccade, there is no enhanced response to the null probe. *Thick green trace*: Saccade plan away from RF, probe in RF signals NOGO. Note that although there was no delay period activity, the response to the NOGO probe was enhanced. *Thin green trace*: Saccade plan away from RF, null probe in RF, NOGO trial. *Thick red trace*: Saccade plan away from RF, probe signals GO. *Thin red trace*: Saccade plan away from RF, null probe in RF.

period just happens to coincide with the change in activity, although not being related to it. On the other hand, if the activity in LIP were related to attention, then the behavior should be different in the two animals, because the windows of neuronal ambiguity did not overlap between the two monkeys (see the troughs of the black traces in Figure 8.3E and F). When the probe appeared to Monkey I at the crossing point for Monkey B (455 ms), the location of the attentional advantage in Monkey I had already returned to the saccade goal. When the probe appeared to Monkey B at the crossing point for Monkey I (340 ms), the attentional advantage was still at the location of the distractor. Thus, activity in LIP predicts the monkey's measurable locus of attention on a millisecond-by-millisecond, monkey-by-monkey basis.

The absolute level of neural activity did not determine the locus of attention. Instead, the locus of attention lay at that part of the visual field associated with the greatest neural activity in LIP. Thus, the delay period activity, which determined the locus of attentional advantage when it was the greatest activity in LIP, could not sustain that advantage when the onset of the distractor transiently evoked a significantly greater response. Although at times there was only a small difference in the normalized activity of neurons representing the attentionally advantaged and disadvantaged spatial locations, this difference was extraordinarily robust across the population.

These results show that the attention to be paid to a probe flashed for one video frame is predicted by the activity present in LIP *at the time that the probe appears*. Previous studies of attentional modulation suggested that the enhanced response evoked by the attended object itself is responsible for the attention to that object (Goldberg & Wurtz, 1972). However, in this experiment, the determinant of attention was the state of priority map in LIP when the probe appeared, and not the response evoked by the attended probe. When the probe was in the RF, the initial on-responses were the same regardless of where the cue appeared or what it dictated (Figure 8.5). After 100 ms, these responses diverged. When the probe signaled GO elsewhere, the response fell rapidly. When the probe signaled GO to the RF, the response fell slightly more slowly, and resumed the preprobe delay period level. When the probe signaled NOGO, and the monkey was planning a saccade to the RF, the response fell far less rapidly, as if the stimulus requiring a cancellation of a saccade plan evoked attention longer than one confirming the saccade plan. Across the sample, the response to this cancellation of a saccade plan was significantly greater than the response to the confirmation signal both, when the monkey was planning a

saccade to the RF and even more so when the monkey was planning a saccade (and hence attending) to a location away from the RF. When the response finally fell, however, it fell to the level of the GO-elsewhere response. Incidentally, this enhanced response to a stimulus canceling a saccade to the RF clearly shows that LIP activity can be dissociated from motor intention, unless the first step in canceling a saccade is to plan it more.

The enhanced response to the NOGO probe was not a nonspecific result of arousal evoked by the change in plan. On every trial, there was either a probe (the Landolt ring) or a complete ring in the RF. However, only the actual NOGO probe evoked the enhanced cancellation response. The ring did not evoke an enhanced response when the NOGO probe appeared outside of the RF.

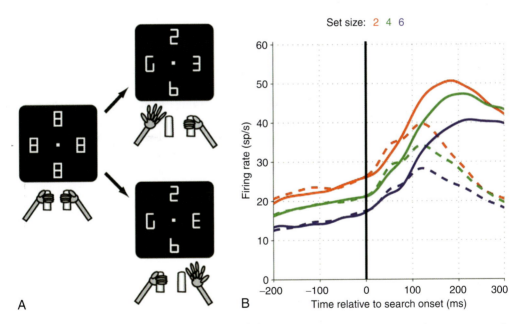

A   B

FIGURE 8.5   Set size effect in fixation search task. (**A**) Task. Throughout the experiment there is an array of objects on the screen. Ordinarily the array consists of identical placeholders (*left*). Each trial begins when the monkey presses two bars and a fixation point appears. The placeholders change into distractors and a left- or right-facing E (*right*). The monkey reports the orientation of the E by releasing on of the levers. (**B**) Neural response. Target selection in arrays with two (*red trace*), four (*green trace*), or six (*blue trace*) stimuli. After the search display appeared, the population response increased strongly when there was a target in the receptive field (RF; *solid traces*) and increased less when there was a distractor in the RF (*dotted traces*). Increasing the number of distractors decreased the neural response to both targets and distractors. Reproduced from Balan et al. (2008). Functional significance of nonspatial information in monkey lateral intraparietal area. *Journal of Neuroscience, 29*, 8166–8176, with permission of the publisher.

UNDER CONDITIONS OF VISUAL SEARCH THE LATERAL INTRAPARIETAL AREA DEMONSTRATES VISUAL, SACCADIC, COGNITIVE SIGNALS, AND TARGET SELECTION SIGNALS

The previous experiment, like the great bulk of studies using eye movements, rewarded the monkey at different times for making or not making an eye movement. In the real world, however, primates make saccades to facilitate vision, and there is no such thing as a wrong or incorrectly timed eye movement, except for the occasional social taboo. Recent experiments have dissociated LIP activity from the artifact of the rewarded saccade using a manual response task with two different approaches. In two experiments, monkeys held their gaze fixed and used covert attention to find and discriminate a peripheral target (Oristaglio et al., 2006; Balan et al., 2008), whereas in a third experiment, monkeys were free to move their eyes prior to the manual action and there was no experimenter-imposed reward contingency linked to the saccade (Ipata et al., 2006a).

Oristaglio et al. used a visual search task in which the target was not physically salient and had to be selected through covert top-down attention. Throughout a block of trials, an array of two, four, or six placeholders remained stably on the screen during the intertrial interval. After the monkey achieved fixation on each trial, the placeholders would transform, with only a small change luminance, into a target (a right- or left-facing letter "E") at an unpredictable location, surrounded by physically similar distractors (digital pseudo-letters similar to the "E"). Without shifting gaze from straight ahead, monkeys had to indicate the orientation of the E (right- or left-facing) by releasing a bar held, respectively, in the right or left hand. LIP neurons responded much more strongly if the "E" than if a distractor appeared in their RF. Thus, neurons encoded visual selection without an overt saccade prior to a nontargeting hand movement that was unrelated to the target's location. The target-selective response was present on correct but not on error trials, suggesting that errors were accompanied by a failure in target selection.

This result was consistent with a previous study by Wardak, Olivier, and Duhamel (2004) that showed that reversible inactivation of LIP using the γ-aminobutyric acid (GABA) agonist muscimol selectively impaired visual selection if the target appeared in the contralesional hemifield, a result later confirmed by Balan and Gottlieb (2009). These findings implicate LIP in visual selection independently of the nature or modality of the motor report. A hallmark of top-down attention is the set-size effect, whereby reaction times to find a target increase as a function of the number of distractors. A second study using the "E-search" task showed that target-related activity in LIP declined as a function of set size and correlated with behavioral reaction time both within and across set sizes. (Balan et al., 2008; Fig 8.5A). A similar set-size effect was shown by Churchland et al. (2008) when monkeys had to choose among two or four possibilities for a motion detection task.

The decrement in response that both Churchland et al. and Balan et al. noticed most likely arises from surround suppression in LIP, which has recently been demonstrated explicitly: Planning a saccade to the surround suppresses the response to a flashed distractor in the excitatory center of LIP RFs, and the delay activity during a memory-guided saccade can be suppressed by the appearance of a task-irrelevant distractor in the center (Falkner, 2010).

In the second set of experiments, monkeys were free to move their eyes prior to the manual response, but the reward was not contingent on a saccade location. The monkey initiated each trial by grabbing two bars, one with each hand (Figure 8.6A). Then a white fixation appeared in the center of the screen, which the monkey fixated for 1 to 1.75 ms, after which the fixation point disappeared, a search array appeared, and the monkey was free to move its eyes. The array consisted of a target and seven distractors arranged in a radially symmetric circular pattern, so that the target or a distractor appeared in the center of the RF on every trial. The position of the target among the distractors varied randomly. The target was a black, upright, or inverted capital T, and the monkeys had to signal the orientation of the target by releasing one of the two bars. The distractors were lowercase t's whose horizontal and vertical components were identical

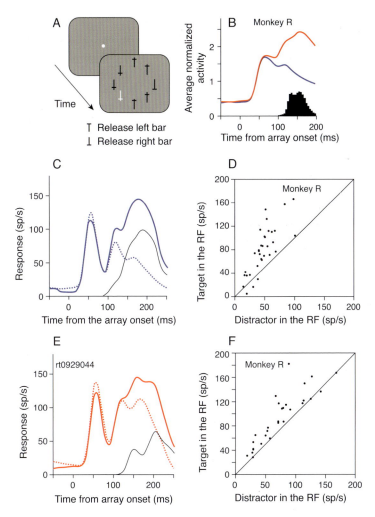

FIGURE 8.6   The free-viewing visual search task and the response of the lateral intraparietal population. (**A**) The free-viewing visual search task. After an initial fixation period (1–1.75 s), the search array appeared. One of the stimuli, either the target (an upright or inverted T) or a distractor, appeared in the center of the neuron's receptive field (RF). Monkeys had 3 seconds to indicate the orientation of the target by releasing one of two bars. During the presentation of the search array, no constraints were imposed on the monkey's eye movements, and they were not required to fixate the target before giving the response. (**B**) Average normalized activity when the monkey made a saccade to the RF (*red trace*) compared with the average activity when the monkey made a saccade away from the RF (*blue trace*). Initially, the activity in the two kinds of trials are superimposed, but begin to separate around 80 ms. The histograms shows the distribution of first saccade latencies relative to array onset. Reproduced from Ipata, A. E., Gee, A. L., Goldberg, M. E., & Bisley, J. W. (2006a). Activity in the lateral intraparietal area predicts the goal and latency of saccades in a free-viewing visual search task. *Journal of Neuroscience, 26*, 3656–3661, with permission of the publisher. (**C**) Cognitive signal when the monkey made a saccade away from the RF. *Solid blue trace*: Monkey made saccade away from target in RF. *Dotted blue trace*: Monkey made saccade away from distractor in RF. *Black trace*: The cognitive signal, the difference between the two traces. (**D**) Activity across the population. Activity for each cell in the interval 100–250 ms after the array appeared for saccades away from the target in the RF (ordinate) plotted against activity for saccades away from a distractor in the RF (abscissa). (**E**) Cognitive signal when the monkey made a saccade away to the RF. *Solid red trace*: Monkey made saccade away from target in RF. *Dotted red trace*: Monkey made saccade away from distractor in RF. *Black trace*: The cognitive signal, the difference between the two traces. (**F**) Activity across the population. Activity for each cell in the interval 100–250 ms after the array appeared for saccades to from the target (ordinate) in the RF plotted against activity for saccades to a distractor in the RF (abscissa).

to those of the target, but which intersected each other at different places on the vertical line. On some trials, one distractor was bright green but matched the shape of the other distractors. Because eye movements were neither rewarded nor punished, the animals' oculomotor behavior was completely unconstrained after the onset of the array. The monkeys had 3 seconds to respond, and the only error the monkey could make was not to make the proper hand movement. Both monkeys performed the task correctly on 95%–99% of the trials. As in the fixation experiment above, monkeys performed like humans in this task: There was a set-size effect in manual reaction time when the target resembled the distractors (slopes of 15 and 5 ms/array object) but not for trials in which the target popped out (Bisley et al., 2009)

In the free-saccade visual search task, LIP expressed three different signals: an undifferentiated visual signal, a saccadic signal, and a cognitive signal, neither purely visual nor motor, that was selective for the search target independent of the direction of the impending saccade. For the first 80 ms after the array appeared, LIP responded in an undifferentiated manner to the onset of the search array, in which a target or a distractor might appear in the RF. This undifferentiated signal did not distinguish between the target and the distractor, nor did it distinguish the direction of the impending saccade (Figure 8.6B).

Activity in LIP began to distinguish the direction of the upcoming saccade roughly 90 ms after the array appeared (Figures 8.6B). The responses diverged, so that the population was more active when the monkey was going to make a saccade to the RF than when the monkey was going to make a saccade away from the RF. Whereas in the attentional experiments described above, LIP activity could be entirely dissociated from saccade planning, in this experiment, the time at which activity in LIP reflected the selection of the saccade target predicted the time at which the monkey subsequently made the saccade (Ipata et al., 2006a). The cognitive signal appeared last. This signal distinguished between a target and a distractor in the RF independently of the upcoming saccade. The cognitive signal was computed by subtracting the response to a distractor in the RF from the response to the target in the RF in trials when the

monkey made a saccade *away* from the RF. The response to the target in the RF was significantly greater than response to a distractor in the RF, both for a single cell (Figure 8.6C) and across the entire sample of cells. (Figure 8.6D). The cognitive response was not merely a plan for the next saccade: One monkey made many three-saccade trials, and there was a similar cognitive signal for trials in which the next saccade did not go to the target. The cognitive signal is unlikely to be a pattern-specific signal describing the low-level visual properties of the object in the RF. Had it been, one would have expected to see some neurons selective for a distractor pattern, but there was never a neuron selective for the distractor.

A cognitive signal also was manifest when the monkey made a saccade to the RF (Figure 8.6E for a single neuron, Figure 8.6F for the population). The cognitive signal when the monkey made a saccade to the RF was greater than the cognitive signal when the monkey made a saccade away from the RF. However, the waveforms were strikingly similar, and the two cognitive signals were correlated (Ipata et al., 2009). The cognitive signal was more significant later, when the monkey made a saccade to the RF, than when the monkey made a saccade to the RF, becoming significant at 117 ms in the saccade-away case, and 133 ms in the saccade-to case.

THE LATERAL INTRAPARIETAL AREA COMBINES THE UNDIFFERENTIATED VISUAL, COGNITIVE, AND SACCADIC SIGNALS IN FREE VISUAL SEARCH

LIP serves as a summing junction among these disparate signals (saccadic, undifferentiated visual, top-down cognitive) to create a priority map of the visual field. In this framework, the neural activity when the monkey made a saccade away from the target was the sum of the undifferentiated visual and cognitive signals; the activity when the monkey made a saccade to the distractor was the sum of the saccadic and undifferentiated visual signals; and the activity when the monkey made a saccade to the target was the sum of all three signals, the cognitive, undifferentiated visual, and saccadic signals. In keeping with this, the waveform in trials when the monkey made a saccade to the target in the RF (i.e., that with all three components) could be predicted by adding the components calculated using waveforms from the three other trial types, each of which had only one or two of the components (Ipata et al., 2009) (Figure 8.7).

LEARNED TOP-DOWN RESPONSES AFFECT LATERAL INTRAPARIETAL ACTIVITY

Several studies show that, when monkeys learn the behavioral significance of a stimulus, LIP neurons reflect this learning in their activity, and this learning can be manifested in several ways. Neurons show suppression of responses to a popout stimulus when that stimulus is not relevant to a task (Ipata et al. 2006b), show changes in baseline activity and in their visual response depending on the current behavioral context (Balan & Gottlieb, 2006), and show modulations of visual responses by learned stimulus–reward associations (Peck et al., 2009).

In some trials of the search task used by Ipata et al. (Figure 8.7), a green popout stimulus was included in the array. Early in the experiments,

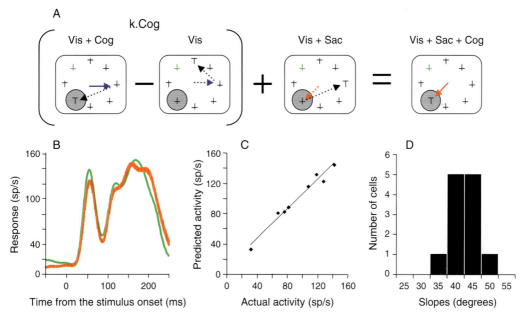

FIGURE 8.7   Summation in lateral intraparietal. (**A**) A cartoon illustration of the test of summation. The cognitive signal (*Cog*) was computed by subtracting the undifferentiated visual signal (when the monkey made a saccade away from the receptive field, RF) from the response when the monkey made a saccade away from the search target in the RF, which was the sum of the visual and cognitive signals. The cognitive signal, adjusted by a constant (k) for the effect of the saccade to the RF, was added to the response when the monkey made a saccade to the distractor in the RF (which was the sum of the visual and saccadic signals) to create the response when the monkey made a saccade to the target in the RF, the sum of the saccadic, cognitive, and visual signals. (**B**) Single-cell responses from trials in which the saccade was made to the target in the RF (*orange trace*) are compared to the calculated signal obtained by summing the three components obtained from the three other trial types (*green trace*). (**C**) The mean activity in 20 ms time intervals from 80 ms to 240 ms after array onset, measured in saccade-to-target-in-the-receptive-field trials (abscissa) against the activity in the same intervals calculated from the other three trial types (ordinate), for the same single neuron. Least-squares correlation line is shown with a dashed gray line. (**D**) Bar plot of the distribution of the slopes, in degrees, from the regression analyses for each cell. Adapted from Ipata, A. E., Gee, A. L., Bisley, J. W., & Goldberg, M. E. (2009). Neurons in the lateral intraparietal area create a priority map by the combination of disparate signals. *Experimental Brain Research*, 192, 479–488, with permission of the publisher.

this popout was often a target, in order to establish that monkey visual search was like human visual search, showing set-size effects for hard but not for popout targets (Bisley et al., 2009). When the target could be a popout, the monkeys also made relatively frequent saccades to the popout when it was a distractor.

The monkeys' response to the popout changed with experience (Ipata et al., 2006b). During the recording experiments, the experiment required trials in which the monkey made saccades away from the target. Such saccades were more likely when the target was never the popout. Under these circumstances, the monkeys learned to ignore this ordinarily salient stimulus and rarely made saccades to the popout distractor. The neural activity reflected this behavior. Although the onset transient responses were similar, after about 90 ms, there was a marked suppression of the response to the popout distractor (Figure 8.8A for one cell, 8.8B for the population).

The monkeys' ability to suppress making saccades to the popout distractor varied from day to day, as did the neuronal suppression of the response to the popout distractor. On days in which the animals were unable to suppress saccades to the popout distractor, neuronal responses to the popout distractor were equal to or stronger than the responses to the non-popout distractors. On days in which the neural response to the distractor was suppressed, the monkeys were unlikely to make saccades to the distractor (Figure 8.8C)

To examine if LIP neurons were sensitive to task context, Balan et al. (2006) used the placeholder-E task described above (Figure 8.5), but, in addition to the target, introduced a visually salient perturbation. On each trial, the appearance of the search display was preceded by a 50 ms visual perturbation: a brief movement, luminance change, size change, or color change of a placeholder, or the brief appearance of a frame around the placeholder. The significance of the perturbation was varied in randomly interleaved blocks of trials. In some blocks, the perturbation appeared at the same location as the orientation stimulus, thus validly cueing the target location. In other

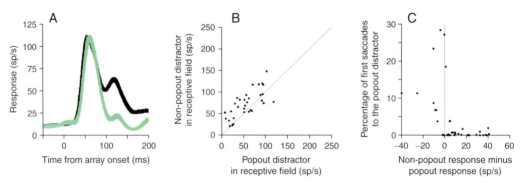

FIGURE 8.8   Suppression of response to the popout distractor. All data are from trials in which the monkey made the first saccade to the target and released the correct bar. During the experiments shown, the target was never a popout. (**A**) Responses of a single cell to the appearance of an array object in the receptive field (RF) are plotted against time from target onset. *Black trace*: Response to a non-popout distractor in the RF when the monkey made a saccade to the target elsewhere. *Green trace*: Response to the popout distractor in the RF when the monkey made a saccade to the target elsewhere. (**B**) Popout suppression across the population. Response to the non-popout distractor in the epoch 80–130 ms after the array appearance (ordinate) plotted against the response to the popout distractor in the same epoch (abscissa). (**C**) Cell-by-cell correlation of response suppression with saccade suppression. The percentage of trials in which the first saccade went to the popout distractor for each session (ordinate) is plotted against the difference in the number of spikes between the responses (80–130 ms) to the non-popout and popout distractors for the cell recorded in that session (abscissa). Reproduced from Ipata, A. E., Gee, A. L., Gottlieb, J., Bisley, J. W., & Goldberg, M. E. (2006b). LIP responses to a popout stimulus are reduced if it is overtly ignored. *Nature Neuroscience, 9*, 1071–1076, with permission of the publisher.

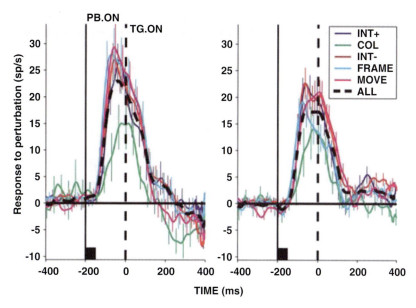

FIGURE 8.9   Top-down enhancement of perturbation transient. *Left*: Responses of a LIP neuron to different perturbations when the perturbation signaled which placeholder would become the target. The perturbations began 200 ms (PB ON, *solid black vertical line*) before the target appeared (TG ON, *dotted black vertical line*). The different perturbations were a transient increase in intensity (INT+, black trace), a transient color change (COL, green trace), a transient intensity decrement (INT-, red trace), movement of the placeholder (MOV, magenta trace), appearance of a frame around the placeholder (FRAME, blue trace). The dotted black line shows the average of all the perturbations (ALL). *Right*: Responses to the perturbations in blocks when the perturbation did not presage the appearance of the target. Reproduced from Balan, P. F., & Gottlieb, J. (2006). Integration of exogenous input into a dynamic salience map revealed by perturbing attention. *Journal of Neuroscience*, 26, 9239–9249, with permission of the publisher.

blocks, the perturbation appeared at a different, unrelated location and was irrelevant to the search task. Monkeys were sensitive to this manipulation and learned to use or ignore the perturbation as appropriate for the current context. In perturbation-relevant blocks, the monkey's reaction time was shorter than in perturbation-irrelevant blocks.

LIP neurons also showed contextual sensitivity, emitting enhanced responses to the perturbation in the relevant relative to the irrelevant context, an enhancement that correlated with the effect of the perturbation on reaction times (Figure 8.9). The increment in the visual response was accompanied by an increase in the baseline activity of the neurons even before the perturbation occurred, and the fractional increase in baseline activity was not different from the fractional increase in the visual response, suggesting that the context of the experiment affected the neural

response in all epochs in an identical multiplicative fashion.

When monkeys learn stimulus–reward associations, the activity of LIP neurons reflect this association, both in the intensity of responses to reward-associated stimuli (Sugrue et al., 2004; Platt & Glimcher, 1999) and the degree to which reward affects the intensity of surround suppression (Falkner et al., 2010). Peck et al. (2009) examined the behavioral and neural effects of reward associations for stimuli that were not saccade targets and that were trained on short and long time scales. They used a paradigm in which each trial began with presentation of a reward cue (RC), an abstract pattern that predicted whether the monkey would receive a reward (RC+) or no reward (RC−). The RC appeared in the RF or at the opposite location and was followed, after a delay period, by a saccade target that appeared randomly either at the same or at the opposite location as the RC. To complete the trial, the monkey had to make a saccade to the target. On RC+ trials a correct saccade was immediately rewarded. On RC− trials, the saccade was unrewarded but the monkey had to complete this saccade in order to proceed to the next (possibly rewarded) trial.

Even though the RC was never a saccade target, its reward associations were encoded in LIP. RC+ cues evoked a stronger visual response and sustained, excitatory delay period activity, whereas RC− cues evoked a weaker visual response and sustained suppression during the delay period. These responses were correlated with spatial biases produced by the RC. In particular, reaction time was longer and saccade accuracy worse when the saccade target fell at the same location as an RC−, suggesting that the RC− stimulus repelled attention from its location. Even though this repulsion interfered with task performance (increasing reaction times and lowering saccade accuracy), it became stronger with training. Overtrained RC− produced stronger neuronal suppression appearing earlier in the trial in LIP and a stronger interference, with saccades toward the RC− location relative to newly learned RC−(Fig 8.10).

In addition to becoming stronger, reward effects became more automatic with training. This was shown in a second paradigm in which overlearned RC biased attention even in a context in which they no longer predicted reward. In this paradigm, the authors first flashed an informative RC− or RC+ cue away from the RF, and flashed a second probe in the RF, just before the monkey's saccade. The probe stimuli had previously learned reward significance, but they were no longer predictive of reward in this context. The monkeys licking behavior, a

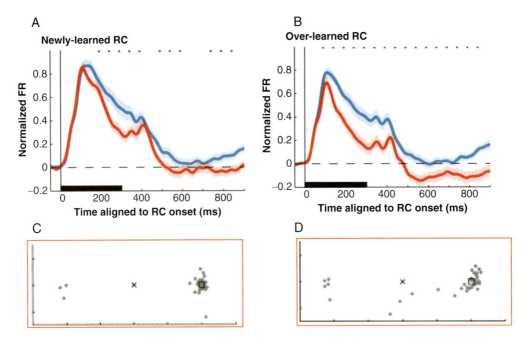

FIGURE 8.10 Newly learned and overtrained reward associations in lateral intraparietal (LIP). (A) Response to newly learned RC+ (*blue*) and RC− (*red*) probes in LIP, aligned on probe appearance. *Ordinate*: Normalized firing rate. *Abscissa*: Time from probe appearance. Black bar depicts probe duration. (B) Response to overlearned probe, same conventions as A. (C) Effect of overlearned RC+ probe on saccade accuracy (target at the site of the probe). Final eye position of each saccade represented by a dot in the Y (ordinate), X (abscissa) plane. The target is at the right. (D) Effect of RC− probe, same conventions as C. Reproduced from Peck, C. J., Jangraw, D. C., Suzuki, M., Efem, R., & Gottlieb, J. (2009). Reward modulates attention independently of action value in posterior parietal cortex. *Journal of Neuroscience, 29*, 11182–11191, with permission of the publisher.

measure of the monkey's estimate of the impending reward, was entirely determined by the informative cue, and unaffected by the probe. The recently learned probes had no effect on the neural response or the monkey's behavior, but when the overlearned RC+ probe was away from the saccade goal, LIP neural activity was increased and the monkey's saccadic reaction times were delayed. Conversely, an overlearned RC− probe away from the saccade goal evoked decreased activity and facilitated the saccade. This suggests that, after short-term training, reward effects in LIP are restricted to contexts in which the stimuli validly predict reward, but after long-term training these effects become automatic and bias attention independently of reward expectation.

CONCLUSION

How the Lateral Intraparietal Area Can Drive Both Attention and Saccades

The experiments described above are not consistent with LIP having a role exclusively dedicated to the planning of saccadic eye movements or to the placing of visual attention, but they are consistent with LIP's providing a representation of significant objects in the visual field —acting as a priority map. Of course, the goal of a saccade is usually the object of attention, and, in fact, Rizzolatti has postulated that attention in the primate is merely a readout of a possible saccade plan (Rizzolatti et al., 1987). However, in one experiment described above, where attention, as actually measured by an improvement in visual perception, and an ongoing saccade plan were effectively dissociated, LIP still predicted attention.

If, however, we consider that LIP describes a priority map of the visual field in an agnostic manner, without specifying how that map is used, the seemingly contradictory views described above can be reconciled. The priority map is constructed from a number of different and independent signals. The search experiment described above provides an example of this summation: LIP sums cognitive, visual, and saccadic signals to create map when the monkey makes a saccade to the RF.

A number of other studies have delineated other response properties of LIP neurons. Thus, LIP activity has been associated with expected value (Sugrue et al., 2004); perceptual (Shadlen & Newsome, 2001); categorical (Freedman & Assad, 2006) or economic (Platt & Glimcher, 1999; Dorris & Glimcher, 2004) decision making; perceived motion (Assad & Maunsell, 1995); time representation (Leon & Shadlen, 2003; Janssen & Shadlen, 2005); & stimulus shape (Sereno & Maunsell, 1998). All of these studies are consistent with a spatial priority map hypothesis, but also could be interpreted as indicating that LIP participates in nonspatial functions as opposed to emphasizing the spatial location relevant to a nonspatial function. To test this hypothesis, Balan et al. (2009) trained monkeys on a number of tasks, including a timing task and a value task. If LIP were involved in nonspatial decision processes, one would expected that a LIP lesion would have a general effect on the decision process and not have it limited to a particular spatial location. Transient inactivation of LIP with muscimol only had a spatial effect, not a nonspatial one. Thus, although LIP has access to nonspatial decision processes, it is unlikely that those decisions are formed in LIP.

The actual function of the priority map depends on the area to which it projects. LIP has a strong projection to two oculomotor areas, the FEF (Andersen et al., 1985) and the SC (Ferraina et al., 2002). If a saccade is appropriate, the peak of the salience map in LIP can provide targeting information. If a saccade is inappropriate, for example during the delay period of a memory-guided delayed saccade task, the oculomotor system can ignore LIP. LIP also projects to inferior temporal cortex, the ventral visual stream areas involved in pattern recognition (Baizer et al., 1991). Neurons here have large, bilateral RFs, including the fovea, and could not be useful for targeting saccades— but attention is critical for visual perception, and neurons in inferior temporal cortex show attentional modulation (Richmond & Sato, 1987). The ventral stream can use the exact same priority map for attention that the oculomotor system uses for targeting—the priority map in LIP.

The use of the priority map does not depend on the genesis of the spikes. Bottom-up spikes from abrupt-onset, top-down spikes from a saccade plan or a cognitive input about the stimulus all contribute to the priority map. LIP is agnostic to both the origin of the spikes and the use to which they will be put. Trying to determine if the spikes are "sensory" or "motor" is irrelevant. Thus, the attentional system can be driven by a saccade plan, and the saccadic system by the abrupt onset of a visual stimulus, both of which contribute to the priority map in LIP.

These experiments raise an important caveat: Introspectively, attention is both divisible and graded. Thus, human subjects can attend to multiple objects at roughly the same time (Pylyshyn & Storm, 1988), and a hallmark of parietal damage is the inability to do so (Hecaen & De Ajuriaguerra, 1954). Attention can also be graded; the more likely an object is to appear at a given location, the better the performance it evokes (Ciaramitaro et al., 2001). However, such distributed attentional processes only operate over relatively long periods of time. Over the time period in which we describe an attentional advantage—one video frame—there is evidence that attention may be indivisible and ungraded (Joseph & Optican, 1996). However, the activity in LIP is graded, and so, over a longer period of time, the multiple peaks of the priority map in LIP may contribute to the divisibility and gradation of attention that is present in psychological studies

ACKNOWLEDGMENTS

MEG was supported by grants from the Zegar, Keck and Dana Foundations, the National Eye Institute (R24EY015634, R21EY017938, R01EY017039, and R01EY014978. ALG was supported by the National Institute of Neurological Diseases and Stroke (F31 NS058059), JWB was supported by McKnight Scholar Award National Eye Institute (R01 EY019273-01).

References

Andersen, R. A., Asanuma, C., & Cowan, M. (1985). Callosal and prefrontal associational projecting cell populations in area 7a of the macaue monkey: A study using retrogradely transported fluorescent dyes. *Journal of Comparative Neurology, 232,* 443–455.

Andersen, R.A., Asanuma, C., Essick, G., & Siegel, R. M. (1990). Corticocortical connections of anatomically and physiologically defined subdivisions within the inferior parietal lobule. *Journal of Comparative Neurology, 296,* 65–113.

Asanuma, C., Andersen, R. A., & Cowan, W. M. (1985). The thalamic relations of the caudal inferior parietal lobule and the lateral prefrontal cortex in monkeys: Divergent cortical projections from cell clusters in the medial pulvinar nucleus. *Journal of Comparative Neurology, 241,* 357–381.

Assad, J. A., & Maunsell, J. H. R. (1995). Neuronal correlates of inferred motion in primate posterior parietal cortex. *Nature, 373,* 518–521.

Baizer, J. S., Ungerleider, L. G., & Desimone, R. (1991). Organization of visual inputs to the inferior temporal and posterior parietal cortex in macaques. *Journal of Neuroscience, 11,* 168–190.

Balan, P. F., & Gottlieb, J. (2006). Integration of exogenous input into a dynamic salience map revealed by perturbing attention. *Journal of Neuroscience, 26,* 9239–9249.

Balan, P. F., & Gottlieb, J. (2009). Functional significance of nonspatial information in monkey lateral intraparietal area. *Journal of Neuroscience, 29,* 8166–8176.

Balan, P. F., Oristaglio, J., Schneider, D. M., & Gottlieb, J. (2008). Neuronal correlates of the set-size effect in monkey lateral intraparietal area. *PLoS Biology, 6,* e158.

Barash, S., Bracewell, R. M., Fogassi, L., Gnadt, J. W., & Andersen, R. A. (1991a). Saccade-related activity in the lateral intraparietal area. *II. Spatial properties. Journal of Neurophysiology, 66,* 1109–1124.

Barash, S., Bracewell, R. M., Fogassi, L., Gnadt, J. W., & Andersen, R. A. (1991b). Saccade-related activity in the lateral intraparietal area. *I. Temporal properties. Journal of Neurophysiology, 66,* 1095–1108.

Bashinski, H. S., & Bacharach, V. R. (1980). Enhancement of perceptual sensitivity as the result of selectively attending to spatial locations. *Perception & Psychophysics, 28,* 241–248.

Bisley, J. W., & Goldberg, M. E. (2003). Neuronal activity in the lateral intraparietal area and spatial attention. *Science, 299,* 81–86.

Bisley, J. W., & Goldberg, M. E. (2006). Neural correlates of attention and distractibility in the lateral intraparietal area. *Journal of Neurophysiology, 95,* 1696–1717.

Bisley, J. W., Ipata, A. E., Krishna, B. S., Gee, A. L., & Goldberg, M. E. (2009). The lateral intraparietal area: A priority map in posterior parietal cortex. In M. Jenkin, & L. Harris (Eds.), Cortical mechanisms of vision (pp. 5–30). Cambridge: Cambridge University Press.

Bowman, E. M., Brown, V. J., Kertzman, C., Schwarz, U., & Robinson, D. L. (1993). Covert orienting of attention in macaques: I. Effects of behavioral context. *Journal of Neurophysiology, 70*, 431–443.

Bushnell, M. C., Goldberg, M. E., & Robinson, D. L. (1981). Behavioral enhancement of visual responses in monkey cerebral cortex: I. Modulation in posterior parietal cortex related to selective visual attention. *Journal of Neurophysiology, 46*, 755–772.

Churchland, A. K., Kiani, R., & Shadlen, M. N. (2008). Decision-making with multiple alternatives. *Nature Neuroscience, 11*, 693–702.

Ciaramitaro, V. M., Cameron, E. L., & Glimcher, P. W. (2001). Stimulus probability directs spatial attention: An enhancement of sensitivity in humans and monkeys. *Vision Research, 41*, 57–75.

Colby, C. L., & Duhamel, J.-R. (1991). Heterogeneity of extrastriate visual areas and multiple parietal areas in the macaque monkey. *Neuropsychologia, 29*, 517–537.

Colby, C. L., Duhamel, J-.R., & Goldberg, M. E. (1996). Visual, presaccadic and cognitive activation of single neurons in monkey lateral intraparietal area. *Journal of Neurophysiology, 76*, 2841–2852.

Colby, C L., & Goldberg, M. E. (1999). Space and attention in parietal cortex. *Annual Review of Neuroscience, 23*, 319–349.

Critchley, M. (1953). *The parietal lobes.* London: Edward Arnold.

De Weerd, P., Peralta, M. R., 3rd, Desimone, R., & Ungerleider, L. G. (1999). Loss of attentional stimulus selection after extrastriate cortical lesions in macaques. *Nature Neuroscience, 2*, 753–758.

Deubel, H., & Schneider, W. X. (1996). Saccade target selection and object recognition: Evidence for a common attentional mechanism. *Vision Research, 36*, 1827–1837.

Deubel, H., & Schneider, W. X. (2003). Delayed saccades, but not delayed manual aiming movements, require visual attention shifts. *Annals of the New York Academy of Sciences, 1004*, 289–296.

Dorris, M. C., & Glimcher, P. W. (2004). Activity in posterior parietal cortex is correlated with the relative subjective desirability of action. *Neuron, 44*, 365–378.

Falkner, A. L., Krishna, B.S., & Goldberg, M. E. (2010). Surround suppression sharpens the priority map in the lateral intraparietal area. *Journal of Neuroscience.* In press.

Ferraina, S., Paré, M., & Wurtz, R. H. (2002). Comparison of cortico-cortical and cortico-collicular signals for the generation of saccadic eye movements. *Journal of Neurophysiology, 87*, 845–858.

Freedman, D. J., & Assad, J. A. (2006). Experience-dependent representation of visual categories in parietal cortex. *Nature, 443*, 85–88.

Gnadt, J. W., & Andersen, R. A. (1988). Memory related motor planning activity in posterior parietal cortex of macaque. *Experimental Brain Research, 70*, 216–220.

Goldberg, M. E., & Wurtz, R. H. (1972). Activity of superior colliculus in behaving monkey. II. Effect of attention on neuronal responses. *Journal of Neurophysiology, 35*, 560–574.

Gottlieb, J., & Goldberg, M. E. (1999). Activity of neurons in the lateral intraparietal area of the monkey during an antisaccade task. *Nature Neuroscience, 2*, 906–912.

Gottlieb, J. P., Kusunoki, M., & Goldberg, M. E. (1998). The representation of visual salience in monkey parietal cortex. *Nature, 391*, 481–484.

Hecaen, H., & De Ajuriaguerra, J. (1954). Balint's syndrome (psychic paralysis of visual fixation) and its minor forms. *Brain, 77*, 373–400.

Hyvarinen, J., & Poranen, A. (1974). Function of the parietal associative area 7 as revealed from cellular discharges in alert monkeys. *Brain, 97*, 673–692.

Ipata, A. E., Gee, A. L., Bisley, J. W., & Goldberg, M. E. (2009). Neurons in the lateral intraparietal area create a priority map by the combination of disparate signals. *Experimental Brain Research, 192*, 479–488.

Ipata, A. E., Gee, A. L., Goldberg, M. E., & Bisley, J. W. (2006a). Activity in the lateral intraparietal area predicts the goal and latency of saccades in a free-viewing visual search task. *Journal of Neuroscience, 26*, 3656–3661.

Ipata, A. E., Gee, A. L., Gottlieb, J., Bisley, J. W., & Goldberg, M. E. (2006b). LIP responses to a popout stimulus are reduced if it is overtly ignored. *Nature Neuroscience, 9*, 1071–1076.

Janssen, P., & Shadlen, M. N. (2005). A representation of the hazard rate of elapsed time in macaque area LIP. *Nature Neuroscience, 8*(2), 234–241.

Joseph, J. S., & Optican, L. M. (1996). Involuntary attentional shifts due to orientation differences. *Perception & Psychophysics, 58*, 651–665.

Kowler, E., Anderson, E., Dosher, B., & Blaser, E. (1995). The role of attention in the programming of saccades. *Vision Research, 35*, 1897–1916.

Leon, M. I., & Shadlen, M. N. (2003). Representation of time by neurons in the posterior parietal cortex of the macaque. *Neuron, 38*, 317–327.

Lynch, J. C., Mountcastle, V. B., Talbot, W. H., & Yin, T. C. (1977). Parietal lobe mechanisms for directed visual attention. *Journal of Neurophysiology, 40*, 362–389.

Neal, J. W., Pearson, R. C. A., & Powell, T. P. S. (1988). The organization of the cortico-cortical connections between the walls of the lower part of the superior temporal sulcus in the inferior parietal lobule in the monkey. *Brain Research, 438,* 351–356.

Oristaglio, J., Schneider, D. M., Balan, P. F., & Gottlieb, J. (2006). Integration of visuospatial and effector information during symbolically cued limb movements in monkey lateral intraparietal area. *Journal of Neuroscience, 26,* 8310–8319.

Peck, C. J., Jangraw, D. C., Suzuki, M., Efem, R., & Gottlieb, J. (2009). Reward modulates attention independently of action value in posterior parietal cortex. *Journal of Neuroscience, 29,* 11182–11191.

Platt, M. L., & Glimcher, P. W. (1997). Responses of intraparietal neurons to saccadic targets and visual distractors. *Journal of Neurophysiology, 78,* 1574–1589.

Platt, M. L., & Glimcher, P. W. (1999). Neural correlates of decision variables in parietal cortex. *Nature, 400,* 233–238.

Posner, M. I. (1980). Orienting of attention. *Quarterly Journal of Experimental Psychology, 32,* 3–25.

Powell, K. D., & Goldberg, M. E. (2000). Response of neurons in the lateral intraparietal area to a distractor flashed during the delay period of a memory-guided saccade. *Journal of Neurophysiology, 84,* 301–310.

Pylyshyn, Z. W., & Storm, R. W. (1988). Tracking multiple independent targets: Evidence for a parallel tracking mechanism. *Spatial Vision, 3,* 179–197.

Quian Quiroga, R., Snyder, L. H., Batista, A. P., Cui, H., & Andersen, R. A. (2006). Movement intention is better predicted than attention in the posterior parietal cortex. *Journal of Neuroscience, 26,* 3615–3620.

Richmond, B. J., & Sato, T. (1987). Enhancement of inferior temporal neurons during visual discrimination. *Journal of Neurophysiology, 56,* 1292–1306.

Rizzolatti, G., Riggio, L., Dascola, I., & Umilta, C. (1987). Reorienting attention across the horizontal and vertical meridians: Evidence in favor of a premotor theory of attention. *Neuropsychologia, 25,* 31–40.

Robinson, D. L., Goldberg, M. E., & Stanton, G. B. (1978). Parietal association cortex in the primate: Sensory mechanisms and behavioral modulations. *Journal of Neurophysiology, 41,* 910–932.

Schall, J. D., Morel, A., King, D. J., & Bullier, J. (1995). Topography of visual cortex connections with frontal eye field in macaque: Convergence and segregation of processing streams. *Journal of Neuroscience, 15,* 4464–4487.

Seltzer, B., & Pandya, D. N. (1980). Converging visual and somatic sensory cortical input to the intraparietal sulcus of the rhesus monkey. *Brain Research 192,* 339–351.

Sereno, A. B., & Maunsell, J. H. (1998). Shape selectivity in primate lateral intraparietal cortex. *Nature, 395,* 500–503.

Shadlen, M. N., & Newsome, W. T. (2001). Neural basis of a perceptual decision in the parietal cortex (area LIP) of the rhesus monkey. *Journal of Neurophysiology, 86,* 1916–1936.

Snyder, L. H., Batista, A. P., & Andersen, R. A. (1997). Coding of intention in the posterior parietal cortex. *Nature, 386,* 167–170.

Sugrue, L. P., Corrado, G. S., & Newsome, W. T. (2004). Matching behavior and the representation of value in the parietal cortex. *Science, 304,* 1782–1787.

Thomas, N. W., & Pare, M. (2007). Temporal processing of saccade targets in parietal cortex area LIP during visual search. *Journal of Neurophysiology, 97,* 942–947.

Wardak, C., Olivier, E., & Duhamel, J. R. (2004). A deficit in covert attention after parietal cortex inactivation in the monkey. *Neuron, 42,* 501–508.

Yantis, S., & Jonides, J. (1984). Abrupt visual onsets and selective attention: evidence from visual search. *Journal of Experimental Psychology. Human Perception and Performance, 10,* 601–621.

Zhang, M., & Barash, S. (2000). Neuronal switching of sensorimotor transformations for antisaccades. *Nature, 408,* 971–975.

9

A Stage Theory of Attention and Action

JEFFREY D. SCHALL AND GEOFFREY F. WOODMAN

WE BELIEVE a wide range of empirical findings and theoretical views can be organized by the *stage theory of attention and action,* which holds that decisions to shift gaze to a particular location are almost entirely dependent upon two cognitive processes. The first is a selection process corresponding with the allocation of visual-spatial attention, and the second is a response process that produces movements of the eyes or other effectors. Importantly, though, attentional allocation and response preparation, although linked, are distinct process accomplished by different networks of neurons spanning multiple cortical and subcortical structures. By bringing into focus the sensory–motor transformations underlying flexible, visually guided behavior, this theory moves beyond the biased competition theory (that only addresses target selection and attention allocation) and the premotor theory of attention (that identifies target selection entirely with saccade preparation). The theory also provides a

framework for understanding rapid error correction, flexible stimulus–response mapping, and the adjustment of processing speed relative to accuracy.

It is important for us to begin with two definitions to lay the groundwork upon which this theory is built. First, we will discuss how perceptual attention influences early visual processing. We believe that one of the most difficult aspects for both producers and consumers of attention research is adequately defining what is meant by the term "attention." This is a result of the use of the term attention to describe selection mechanisms that operate during a great variety of computations that the brain performs (Luck & Vecera, 2002), as well as to characterize certain kinds of neural modulation (Reynolds & Chelazzi, 2004) in senses that are not always compatible. Indeed, much of the literature on divided attention utilizes the psychological refractory period (PRP) paradigm, and there is abundant evidence that the observation of capacity limits in this paradigm is often due to a limit in our ability to select multiple responses at the same time (e.g., Pashler, 1994). For this reason, we will use the term "perceptual attention" to refer to those selection mechanism or mechanisms that focus processing on task-relevant inputs, such that internal representations of important incoming information can be built most efficiently (see Chapters 1 and 4 of this volume). This serves to disambiguate the topic of our discussion from other selection mechanisms and states of arousal that have fallen under this catchall term (e.g., selection for storage in working memory, response selection, dual-task performance, vigilance, etc.). Making this distinction is particularly important given existing evidence that different selection mechanisms can be dissociated (Thompson et al., 1996; Woodman & Luck, 2003a; Woodman, Vogel, & Luck, 2001a). Second, throughout the presentation of the stage theory of attention and action, we will describe the cognitive and neural activity that results in an overt response (e.g., the movements of the eyes or a manual button press) as a stage of cognitive processing (see Chapter 7 in this volume). At the extreme, this is controversial, given that the operations carried out by the brainstem could hardly be described as cognitively penetrable. However, our use of this term is built on the previous work that describes the operations of deciding to make a given movement and preparing that response as an operation under cognitive control (Logan & Cowan, 1984; Luce, 1986; Ratcliff, 2006). The justification for our usage of the terms "perceptual attention" and "response stage of cognitive processing" is a primary point of the stage theory and will be developed throughout our discussion.

The stage theory of attention and action is derived from four propositions. First, the cognitive processing necessary to perform every task of interest to cognitive scientists is accomplished by dissociable processing stages. Although this is one of the oldest proposals in cognitive science, we will describe how modern neuroscientific evidence has validated and enlivened it. Second, the demands of a given task are met by transformations within specific stages (e.g., target selection and response preparation) and by transmission between stages (e.g., stimulus–response mapping,

speed–accuracy adjustment). Third, the theoretical constructs of the onset of processing of a stage, the rate of information accumulation within a stage, and the threshold level that enacts decisions are realized in the patterns of activity of specific networks of neurons that account for the variability of response time (RT). Fourth, executive control that enables correction of errors that occur before visual processing is complete, flexible stimulus–response mapping, and speed–accuracy adjustments originates in a neural network distinct from those selecting targets and producing responses. We propose that this executive control interacts with the response preparation process but not with target selection, although other executive control mechanisms can and do guide this operation of perceptual attention.

EVIDENCE FOR DISTINCT FUNCTIONS AND STAGES

Cognitive psychology has shown that human RT data cannot be explained without allowing for the existence of successive stages of processing (Donders, 1868/1969; Luce, 1986; Sternberg, 2001) even in models that identify all the interesting variability in RT and response probability with a single stage (e.g., Ratcliff & Smith, 2004). Cognitive theories have proposed that these stages may overlap in time (McClelland, 1979) or be at least partially overlapping (Miller, 1988), but essentially all such large-scale models have this characteristic. Most of these cognitive models have the commonality of describing separate stages of perception and response processing, with some also discussing the subcomponents of perceptual processing (Treisman, 1969) and many ignoring the proposal of a similarly serial flow of information through memory stages (Atkinson & Shiffrin, 1968). Signal detection theory (Green & Swets, 1966) may seem to contradict this norm, being static in nature. However, like its complementary counterpart, biased choice theory (Luce, 1963), signal detection theory adds to its sensitivity metric a bias metric that allows for the subject's willingness to respond, which is set prior to the appearance of a stimulus.

The interpretation of event-related potential (ERP) recordings presents no clear alternative to a stage-like view of information processing in the human brain. That is, the ERPs time locked to the onset of a visual search array allow us to visualize the sequence of processing as cognition unfolds (see Figure 9.1). The series of ERP components indicate that information is transformed from the sensory components most sensitive to low-level visual features (i.e., the C1, P1, and N1 components), to waveforms modulated by the deployment of attention (e.g., the N2 posterior contralateral [N2pc]), followed by components associated with categorization of the visual stimulus (e.g., the N2/P3 complex), waveforms indexing working memory updating (i.e., the P3 and contralateral delay activity), then waveforms elicited by the preparation of the response (i.e., the lateralized-readiness potential or LRP), ending with waveforms elicited during the intertrial interval related to evaluating performance on the trial that just occurred (e.g., the error-related negativity or ERN). A detailed discussion of how findings from ERP experiments support the stage theory is beyond the scope of this chapter. Instead, we refer readers to more detailed accounts of the cognitive mechanisms indexed by ERP components (Luck, 2005; Rugg & Coles, 1995) and will focus on research that integrates findings from ERP recordings with another primary neuroscientific technique, single-unit recordings (see also Chapter 1 of this volume).

Neuroanatomical observations also invite—if not demand—the concept of stages of processing. Anyone who looks at a histological section of cerebral cortex must notice the morphological diversity of neurons arranged in different layers. Given the well-known relation of structure and function in nervous systems, this anatomical diversity predicts a corresponding physiological diversity. However, the range of neuron types described in areas like the frontal eye field (FEF) hardly matches the anatomical diversity. The literature hints at a large variety of neurons in the FEF (Bruce & Goldberg, 1985; Schall, 1991), but the history of neuroscience teaches that functional diversity is proportional to morphological diversity.[1] According to the logic of labeled lines, a distinction between neural processes must correspond to distinct functional processes. For example, distinct fibers originating in different

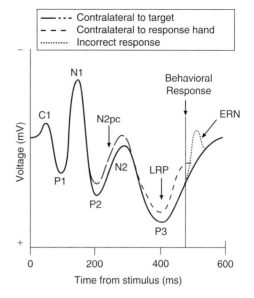

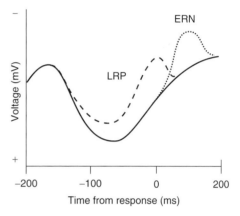

FIGURE 9.1 Idealized event-related potential (ERP) waveforms from humans elicited during a visual search task. Top panel shows the sequence of ERP components from the earliest sensory responses (i.e., the C1 component) to the performance monitoring responses (i.e., error-related negativity [ERN]). The ERP components are labeled using the conventional polarity-ordinal nomenclature. Bottom panel illustrates how ERP components time-locked to the response are related to response preparation and evaluation of task performance. Note that the lateralized components are not typically observed at the same electrode sites but are shown in the same waveform here for illustration purposes. Abbreviations: C1, Component 1; P1, 1st Positive component; N1, 1st Negative component; P2, 2nd Positive component; N2pc, 2nd Negative component; Posterior, Contralateral; N2, 2nd Negative component; LRP, Lateralized-Readiness Potential; P3, 3rd Positive component; ERN, Error-Related Negativity.

sensory receptors and terminating in different brain centers lead to distinct sensory experiences, like sight or touch. Likewise, if a neural representation of a stimulus that must be located and categorized to guide a saccade can be distinguished from a neural representation of the endpoint of a saccade, then this would be evidence for two functional kinds of selection. In fact, we have distinguished two types of visual selection neurons, one that selects the stimulus and the other that selects the endpoint of the saccade (Sato & Schall, 2003; Schall, 2004). The formulation of this theory also calls attention to obvious facts that are often not considered in functional descriptions. For example, in higher cortical areas, some neurons are anatomically closer to the retinal input whereas others are closer to the muscles. These afferent and efferent relationships are embodied by the specific distributions of cell bodies, dendrites, and afferent axon terminals in the different cortical layers. Each layer has different intrinsic and extrinsic connections, so the diversity of neurons is embedded in a diversity of circuits. Laminar differences in cell body and axon terminal location translate into differences in connectivity with excitatory and inhibitory neurons (e.g., Medalla et al., 2007) that have important functional implications. For example, local connections respect efferent targets (Vicente et al., 2008). Currently, the variety of functional hypotheses is at least an order of magnitude less than the variety of neurons distinguished by morphology, location, and connectivity. The mathematical and statistical elegance of sequential sampling models does not necessitate that a unique population of neurons instantiates each process directly. However, that is an intuitive assumption that simplifies the evaluation of such models using neuroscientific methods. On the other hand, the functions proposed by models (e.g., sequential sampling and race) may be instantiated by a multiplicity of morphologically distinct neurons. Although, if the latter were the case, then specific linking propositions would be difficult to work out. Alternatively, the functional process models may require refinement into smaller functional parts.

Recording from the neurons in visuomotor structures like the FEF also allows little room for doubt that the brain has distinct networks of neurons performing different functions that span the sensory–motor continuum. As shown in Figure 9.2, the FEF includes a type of neuron that participates in selecting targets for orienting after an array of objects appears (visual neurons) and another type of neuron that contributes to preparing to execute (planning) saccadic eye movements (movement neurons). These types of neurons are clearly distinct in the functional roles they play (as will be elaborated below). They are also probably distinct in their laminar distribution (although definitive data remain to be gathered) and, thus, in their afferent and efferent connectivity. They are also heterogeneous, ranging between shorter or longer latencies of response, more transient or sustained, selecting the location of the attended object or the endpoint of the saccade. They are also not the only types of neurons in the FEF, for it also consists of neurons active specifically during fixation, others active specifically after saccades, and a commonly encountered type referred to as visuomovement neurons. The visuomovement neurons respond to visual stimuli, have maintained discharge rates even if the stimuli disappear and finally exhibit a pronounced increase of discharge rate before saccades are initiated. This intermediate type of neuron is often interpreted as both visual- and movement-related; however, we have recently obtained evidence that visuomovement neurons are biophysically distinct from visual and movement neurons (Cohen et al., 2009c) and that they are not modulated in a manner consistent with the function of preparing saccades (Ray et al., 2009). For the purposes of this chapter, we will focus our attention on those visual neurons that select targets for orienting and the movement neurons that lead to overt responses. Ultimately, because the FEF is a prefrontal area that receives converging inputs from a multitude of other cortical areas, we believe that it can be interpreted as a microcosm of the key processes necessary for accurate visually guided saccades.

THE STAGE THEORY OF ATTENTION AND ACTION IN ACTION

To present the theory, we describe the sequence of transformations and transmissions that occur

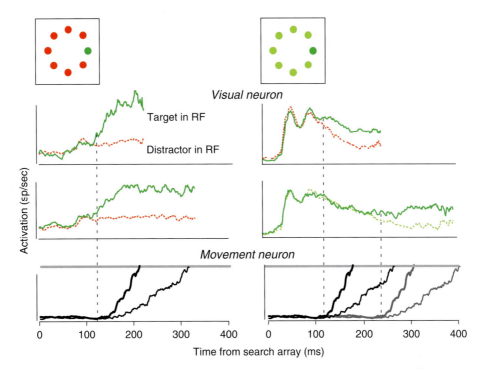

FIGURE 9.2 Two stages to direct a saccade during efficient (*left*) and inefficient (*right*) search for a color singleton recorded in the frontal eye field (FEF) of monkeys. Activity of two visual neurons (*top two panels, left and right*) and movement neuron (*bottom panels*) are illustrated. Visual neuron activity is shown for trials when the target appears in the receptive field (RF; *green*) and for trials when the distractor is easy to distinguish from the target (*red*) or the distractor is difficult to distinguish from the target (*light green*). During efficient search, visual neurons in the FEF select the target at a relatively constant interval after the array appears. Saccades are initiated when the activity of movement neurons reaches a threshold (*gray horizontal bar*). Saccades are initiated earlier (*thick*) or later (*thin*) according to variation in the rate of growth of the activity. The systematic delay of response time (RT) when search is not efficient comes about because the movement neurons do not begin accumulating activity (*gray plots on right*) until the target is selected by visual neurons, with variation in rate contributing additional variability in RT.

from visual stimulus encoding until extraocular muscle contraction in a participant performing a visual search task in which a target is embedded in a cluttered scene.

Task Set Preparation

Every trial of every task is embedded in history. Consequently, each trial begins in some state of preparatory set. For an observer who is sufficiently motivated, the outcome of the previous action can guide the participant to become more or less cautious, which will influence the ultimate RT through executive control (e.g., Rabbitt et al., 1979; Emeric et al., 2007). For example, when an observer performs a feature search task, the target is located effortlessly and is said to "pop-out." However, when the target versus distractor features in the array switch between trials, then performance is slower and more error-prone (Maljkovic & Nakayama, 1994; Maljkovic & Nakayama, 2000) in a manner that can be attributed to neural processes in the FEF (Bichot & Schall, 2002). Also, visual search performance changes with longer-term experience with search arrays (e.g., Chun & Jiang, 1998; Bichot & Schall, 1999; Chun, 2000; Johnson et al., 2007).

Such adjustments based on trial history require some kind of memory. Although it is proposed that visual search tasks have minimal memory requirements compared to other tasks (Wolfe, 1998), the observer must at least know what to search for and how to respond appropriately, and must maintain this task set to respond correctly. Similar to some of our theoretical relatives (Bundesen, 1990; Desimone & Duncan, 1995; Duncan, 1996; Bundesen et al., 2005), we propose that working memory plays a vital role in maintaining a target representation and the proper stimulus–response mapping. However, we emphasize the importance of repetition with a specific stimulus–response mapping in a way that models of visual search typically do not. Specifically, we propose that, as an observer repeatedly searches for the same target with the same response set, long-term memory representations drive selection by visual attention and not working memory representations. This hypothesis is derived from extensive research on task automaticity (Logan, 1988).

We recently tested this idea using a behavioral dual-task paradigm with human observers (Woodman et al., 2007). The observers were required to perform a visual working memory task concurrently with a visual search task in which the searched-for target was either the same across trials or changed every trial. We found that when the search target changed from trial to trial there was mutual interference between the search and working memory tasks. However, when the search target identity was the same across trials, minimal interference was observed, replicating previous findings (Woodman et al., 2001b). These findings led us to conclude that visual working memory representations of targets and attended items drive selection by perceptual attention mechanisms in conditions of variable mapping, but in consistent stimulus–response mapping conditions long-term memory representations drive selection. These behavioral findings from humans were also consistent with a study in which the prefrontal cortex of monkeys was lesioned during a similar experimental manipulation (Rossi et al., 2007).

Even a natural behavior such as visually scanning text or an image exhibits signatures of executive control. For example, fixation duration during visual scanning is adjusted strategically according to target–distractor similarity (e.g., Hooge & Erkelens, 1998; Over et al., 2007). These adjustments are based on experience with targets, responses, and consequences.

Encoding, Selection, and Attention

When a complex scene first appears, the signals sweep through the visual system, arriving at a succession of subcortical and hierarchically organized cortical areas (Felleman & Van Essen, 1991; Petroni, Panzeri, Hilgetag, Kotter, et al., 2001; Petroni, Panzeri, Hilgetag, Scannell, et al., 2001). The timing of the arrival of visual signals in different brain structures follows certain patterns. It has long been known that information is propagated through the magnocellular pathway more quickly than through the parvocellular pathway of the visual system (Van Essen et al., 1992). This appears to underlie the observation that areas like the FEF, which is near the top of the hierarchy based on neuroanatomy, can receive visual information very early in time (Schmolesky et al., 1998). Such early information, though, is not very discriminative. Thus, in response to the presentation of a visual search array, neurophysiological studies in parietal and frontal cortex, as well as the superior colliculus, have shown that the first volley of activity following the onset of a visual search array is not selective. By that we mean that the response of a neuron to the stimulus in its receptive field (RF) codes for the low-level visual features of that stimulus and not its task relevance. After this initial indiscriminate volley of activity, a transformation of representation carried by the spiking of the cells occurs, such that neurons with the target or objects similar to the target in their RF are more active and neurons with nontarget objects in their RF become less active (see Figure 9.2).

When the difference in firing rate for neurons with a target versus distractors in their RFs arises, one can say that the target has been selected. Can one say that attention is allocated? Although everybody may know what attention is (James, 1890), the description of attention in the neuroscience literature is rather confused with statements that are mutually incompatible or commit outright category errors. Attention is commonly regarded as a mechanism by which a specific aspect of the environment is selected for scrutiny. It is also said that attention can be directed to different locations or attributes. The basic observation made by many laboratories is that the activity of (certain) neurons in (diverse but not all parts of) the brain is modulated when monkeys (in which the neurons reside) are (said to be) attending. Many authors argue about attention residing in some but not other parts of the visual pathway. But how can attention be both in the visual pathway and directed to an object at a particular location? Also, many authors refer to the effects of attention; thus, for attention to have any effects, it must be causal. In fact, it is not uncommon to read about attention influencing the activity of neurons. However, this cannot be the case, because only neurons (and glia) can influence neurons. Also, if attention causes effects, how can it (at the same time) be directed (as an effect)? For this to make sense, another process must be invoked that moves attention and that causes its effects. But what is this other process? This confusion hinders progress.

It seems sensible to assert that visual-spatial attention ought to refer to the manifestation of a particular brain process or state during the performance of a task in the presence of alternative stimuli or locations. This interpretation seems necessary for the word to have meaningful reference at the behavioral or phenomenal level. Accordingly, the allocation of attention across the visual field need be no more or less than the selective differential activation of neurons in the appropriate network that includes the FEF. In other words, attention can be said to be allocated when certain neurons enter a certain state. Hence, when particular FEF neurons (as well as neurons in other parts of the network) signal differentially the location of the stimulus of interest, it can be said that attention was allocated. Thus, attention is allocated when and to the extent that the activity of particular neurons represent one as opposed to another location. We will demonstrate below that this operational definition of the allocation of attention can be distinguished in time and neural process from when, whether, and where gaze shifts.

After the initial visual response to the onset of a search array, the stage theory proposes that attention is deployed to locations at which the target is likely to appear in the present context. Of course, if attention is focused on a location in advance of the presentation of the target in a search array, the initial, typically nonselective, neural response can be selective of the location compared to the response to the same stimulus at unattended locations. In addition, preparatory deployments of attention can also be observed in the elevated neural activity of cells representing a specific location prior to the onset of an array (e.g., Woodman et al., 2009). In most circumstances outside the laboratory, the focus of covert attention corresponds to the endpoint of a subsequent saccade (Hoffman & Subramaniam, 1995; Kowler et al., 1995). We conceive of free-viewing oculomotor search tasks as equivalent to a sequence of trials beginning with the new fixation location, punctuated by saccades, in which the stimulus remains stable (Motter & Belky, 1998; Findlay & Gilchrist, 2005). That is, the array appears, initial perceptual processing is carried out, attention is deployed to a location, and an eye movement to that location is executed. Of primary importance, we propose that the modulation of visual neurons in sensorimotor structures like the FEF can be identified with the allocation of attention because the neurons modulate in conditions, at the time and to the degree that corresponds to the best psychophysical estimates of where and when attention is allocated in these conditions (Sato & Schall, 2003; Schall, 2004).

Neural correlates of visual selection have been described during a search task in which monkeys were required to make a saccade to a singleton target (e.g., a red stimulus among green distractors, see Schall & Hanes, 1993; Schall et al., 1995; Thompson et al., 1996; Sato et al., 2001). The initial activity of visually responsive neurons did not discriminate whether the target or distractors of a search array fell in the RF, but the later phase of the activity of these neurons reliably differentiated the target from the distractors. This pattern of activity was observed even when the monkeys withheld a saccade (Thompson et al., 1997; Sato & Schall, 2003; Schall, 2004; Thompson et al., 2005). These observations support the hypothesis that the representation of stimuli by visual activity in the FEF corresponds to the allocation of attention (reviewed in Thompson et al., 2001).

Visual search for a target object among distractors often takes longer when more distractors are present. To understand the neural basis of this capacity limitation, we recorded activity from visually responsive neurons in the FEF of macaque monkeys searching for a target among distractors defined by form (randomly oriented T or L) (Cohen et al., 2009a,b). To test the hypothesis that the delay of RT with increasing number of distractors originates in the delay of attentional allocation by the FEF neurons, we manipulated the number of distractors presented with the search target. When monkeys were presented with more distractors, visual target selection was delayed and neuronal activity was reduced in proportion to longer RT. These findings indicate that the time taken by visual FEF neurons to select the target is a likely source of the variation in visual search efficiency.

The findings from recordings of visual neurons in the FEF together with lesion studies indicate that they participate in, and perhaps drive, the selection of targets by a network of areas during visual search. These findings also indicate another possible avenue of inquiry that could link the neural activity in attentional control structures like the FEF to other observations made in cognitive neuroscientific studies of humans performing search. Specifically, electrophysiological recordings from human subjects performing visual search have shown that attention appears to be shifted in a serial manner between the possible target items during the perceptual stage of processing. Woodman and Luck (1999, 2003b) focused on the N2pc component of observers' ERPs to distinguish between parallel and serial models of the deployment of attention during visual search. Some of these models propose that attention is deployed to one object at a time and is rapidly shifted between items during perceptual processing (e.g., Treisman & Gelade, 1980; Wolfe, 2007), whereas other theories propose that perceptual attention is simultaneously deployed to multiple items, and the sequential aspect of processing is how they are entered into short-term or working memory (e.g., Bundesen, 1990; Duncan & Humphreys, 1989; Bundesen et al., 2005).

The N2pc is particularly useful for distinguishing between these competing models because it has been shown to index a perceptual mechanism of selective attention that operates prior to awareness and encoding into working memory (Luck & Hillyard, 1994; Woodman & Luck, 2003a). Woodman and Luck (1999, 2003b) showed that, when a visual search task required observers to process items in opposite visual hemifields, the N2pc shifted between hemispheres of the brain. These findings indicate that perceptual attention is shifted between task-relevant items during visual search, consistent with serial models of attentional deployment during search, and ruling out all but the most flexible parallel-deployment models of attention.

It should be possible to test the hypothesis that the visual neuronal activity in the FEF measures the same perceptual selection mechanism indexed by the N2pc in human ERP studies of visual search. That is, future analyses of FEF activity can determine whether or not visual neurons show evidence for serial shifts of selection between possible targets during search; one study has investigated this, but the results are ambiguous because the period of neural activity that was analyzed occurred after the saccade and so cannot contribute to guiding the saccade (Buschman & Miller, 2009). Another approach to understanding the relationship between these neurophysiological metrics of perceptual attention across species of primates (i.e., monkeys and humans) will be discussed below.

A significant thrust of the stage theory is in unifying observations and concepts from psychology and neuroscience. This tenet requires that another type of link be made for a comprehensive understanding of attentional selection during cognitive processing of complex visual information. This empirical link is between electrophysiological studies of attention with humans and with monkeys. The work described here details how electrophysiological studies of activity in the FEF supports the idea that the brain implements cognitive processing using a sequence of distinct stages. Because the FEF entertains bidirectional connections with both dorsal and ventral visual steams of processing and contains neurons that connect to structures that ultimately control the muscles that move the eyes, it is an ideal structure in which to test hypotheses regarding the general nature of information processing in the brain. Electrophysiological studies of humans have been the other main testing ground for hypotheses about the locus of behavioral effects within specific processing stages (e.g., Meyer et al., 1988; Miller & Hackley, 1992; Coles et al., 1995; Vogel et al., 1998; Luck et al., 2000; Woodman & Luck, 2003a). Thus, a central proposal of the stage theory is that findings across these methodological realms must be integrated using a common mode of experimentation.

Building on previous studies that recorded ERPs from nonhuman primates (Arthur & Starr, 1984; Van der Marel et al., 1984; Schroeder et al., 1991; Lamme et al., 1992; Schroeder et al., 1992), several recent studies have sought to directly relate the mechanisms of attentional selection used to study the processing of complex scenes in humans to the mechanisms in the FEF discussed above. Specifically, Woodman, Kang, Rossi, and Schall (2007) recorded ERPs from monkeys performing the difficult visual search task for a T among Ls, or vice versa, mentioned above. Using this task, it was found that monkeys exhibited an ERP component that selected the target item, similar to the N2pc component recorded from humans. Subsequent manipulations and analyses showed that this contralateral measure of selection recorded over extrastriate visual cortex in monkeys exhibited the same sensitivity to cognitive manipulations, had similar relative timing within the sequence of visual ERP components, and had the same distribution across the head as the human N2pc component (for details see Woodman, Kang et al., 2007). We believe the next most useful step involves simultaneously recording activity in the FEF and from the monkey ERP electrodes to directly relate the attention mechanisms measured using these different methods to each other. In doing so, this work will serve to link studies of attention in psychology and neuroscience into a more integrated framework.

Target selection has been measured using a variety of neurophysiological metrics, specifically, using the polarization of local-field potentials (LFPs) in V4 (Bichot et al., 2005) and the FEF (Monosov et al., 2008) and a surface ERP over extrastriate visual cortex in monkeys described above (Woodman, et al., 2007). Is visual selection manifest simultaneously across these different levels? Also what temporal relations measured through coherence and other measures are found between spikes and LFP in the FEF and the m-N2pc (e.g., Gregoriou et al., 2009)? Work has begun to address these questions by measuring multiple electrophysiological indices of attention allocation simultaneously. Cohen, Heitz, Schall, and Woodman (2009) recently recorded neuronal spikes, LFPs, and the m-N2pc simultaneously while monkeys performed the difficult T among L (or vice versa) visual search task. They found that the first index of attentional selection that occurred across the neural signals was that carried by the spiking activity of the FEF neurons. Approximately 50 ms later, they observed that the LFPs in the FEF selected the target location. Then, approximately 20 ms after the FEF LFPs, the m-N2pc recorded over lateral occipital-temporal cortex selected the target location. The importance of measuring multiple neural signals of attentional deployment seems self-evident for determining when we can say that attention is allocated to an item during a task. In addition, data such as these are critical to the theoretical question of whether selection is carried out by one or more mechanisms (e.g., Woodman et al., 2001a). However, the methodological details of such experiments are critical given that different neural signals could potentially have different signal-to-noise ratios (Cohen et al., 2009a) or the stimuli used in a task might not be optimal to elicit activity from one or any of the neural measures being collected (Schall et al., 2007).

In summary, we propose that covert attention is shifted between possible target items in the search array until the target for the task at hand is found. This is accomplished by variation in the level of activation of certain populations of visually responsive neurons distributed among multiple cortical and subcortical structures. A central proposition of the stage theory is that this neural state is not necessary or sufficient for the production of an overt response, such as a saccadic eye movement. It is not necessary because saccades can be produced in the absence of any visual stimulation or inattentively. It is not sufficient because attention can be allocated without producing any body movement whatsoever. This independence between stages of processing affords the flexibility of behavior that is particularly apparent in humans and other primates (e.g., Bullock, 2003). We now turn to the neural and cognitive processes responsible for producing movements that can be guided by visual-spatial attention.

RESPONSE PREPARATION

Although the idea of distinct mechanisms performing perceptual-attentional processing and response preparation will not seem controversial to many, this is where the Stage Theory differs drastically from an account of covert attention like the premotor theory of attention.

Although much progress has been made, debate continues over the mechanistic distinction between covert and overt orienting (e.g., Rizzolatti et al., 1987; Klein & Pontefract, 1994; Eimer et al., 2005; Ekstrom et al., 2008). On the one hand, visual attention can be allocated to at least some extent without moving the eyes (e.g., Posner, 1980). On the other hand, several studies have shown that visual attention is allocated to the endpoint of a saccade before initiation of the movement, and that it is difficult to direct attention to a different object even if the object is close to the endpoint of the saccade (Shepherd et al., 1986; Hoffman & Subramaniam, 1995; Kowler et al., 1995; Deubel & Schneider, 1996). Moreover, it has been shown that a shift of attention can influence the production of saccades (Sheliga et al., 1994, 1995; Kustov & Robinson, 1996).

The premotor theory proposes that the deployment of attention is due to subthreshold activity in neurons that control the movements of the eyes. However, we point to four lines of evidence for distinct mechanisms of visual attention allocation and saccade response preparation:

(1) Visual attention and saccade preparation interact but are dissociable (Shepherd et al., 1986; Hoffman & Subramaniam, 1995; Kowler et al., 1995; Sheliga et al., 1995; Deubel & Schneider, 1996; Hooge & Erkelens, 1998; Belopolsky & Theeuwes, 2009).

(2) Target selection and the allocation of perceptual attention can occur independently

of saccade preparation (Juan et al., 2004, see also Gold & Shadlen, 2003). Visual target selection in the FEF occurs even if no eye movement is produced (Thompson et al., 1997; Schall, 2004; Thompson et al., 2005) or if the saccade is directed away from a conspicuous singleton (Murthy et al., 2009; Murthy et al., 2001; Sato & Schall, 2003; see also McPeek & Keller, 2002). Thompson, Biscoe, and Sato (2005) show an extreme case of this in which monkeys perform a visual search task requiring a manual response. While perceptual processing of the search arrays is occurring, the movement-related neurons in the FEF show activity that is actually suppressed relative to baseline levels.

(3) Neurons that shift gaze can be distinguished from those that select targets (e.g., Murthy et al., 2009). Saccade-related neurons in the FEF produce signals sufficient to specify whether and when a saccade will be produced during the search-step task, but the visual neurons in the FEF that select the location of conspicuous objects do not produce signals sufficient to contribute to the control of saccade generation.

(4) The ability of movement neurons to function independently from the visual selection neurons permits flexible stimulus–response mapping (e.g., Sato & Schall, 2003) and corrective saccades with latencies of less than visual encoding and target-selection time (Murthy et al., 2007). Parallel distinctions are made between ERP components related to early visual processing, attention allocation, and motor preparation (e.g., Coles et al., 1995; Smulders et al., 1995; Woodman & Luck, 2003a).

The dissociation of target selection and saccade preparation was accomplished by training monkeys to produce a prosaccade, an antisaccade, or no saccade, cued by the shape of the color singleton in a visual search array (Sato & Schall, 2003). If the selection process exhibited by visual FEF neurons corresponds to the covert selection of the location of the singleton, then the singleton should be selected regardless of the required response. Moreover, the time of the selection should be the same across the three response conditions. On the other hand, if the process of selection by visually responsive FEF neurons corresponds only to preparation of a saccade, then only the endpoint of the saccade should be selected, and the time of the selection should be affected by the stimulus–response compatibility. Recently, evidence has been produced for both types of neurons in the FEF (Sato & Schall, 2003). Furthermore, when no saccade is produced, many FEF neurons still exhibit selection of the singleton and, later in the trial, many neurons select the endpoint of the unexecuted antisaccade. This modulation for unexecuted saccades cannot be due to bottom-up visual processing and thus must be the product of an endogenous process that can be usefully identified with the allocation of attention coordinated with preparation of the saccade. It is likely that this sequence of attention selection of one object and then another is analogous to the process of attentional shifting that occurs during inefficient visual search tasks (e.g., Woodman & Luck, 1999, 2003b).

This task creates at least a momentary dissociation between the focus of attention and the endpoint of a saccade. In another experiment, saccade preparation was probed by measuring the direction of saccades evoked by intracortical microstimulation of the frontal eye field at different times following the search array (Juan et al., 2004). Saccades evoked in one direction when monkeys are preparing a saccade to a stimulus in another direction exhibit a systematic deviation in the direction of the partially prepared saccade (Sparks & Mays, 1983). This property has been used to probe the preparation of saccades during various tasks (Kustov & Robinson, 1996; Barborica & Ferrera, 2004; Gold & Shadlen, 2003; Opris, Barborica, & Ferrera, 2005). If the premotor theory of attention is correct, then the deviation of saccades evoked at different times in this task should correspond to the level of activation signaling the location of the singleton as compared to the saccade endpoint. Eye movements evoked on prosaccade trials deviated progressively toward the singleton that was the endpoint of the saccade. However, eye movements evoked on antisaccade trials deviated not toward the singleton but only toward the saccade endpoint opposite the singleton. Thus, the visual system can covertly orient attention without preparing a saccade to the locus of attention.

Few would argue that covert orienting of attention and overt orienting of gaze are not guided by

common selection mechanisms and coordinated in time (Klein, 1980; Shepherd et al., 1986; Henderson, 1993; Sheliga et al., 1994, 1995; Hoffman & Subramaniam, 1995; Kowler et al., 1995; Deubel & Schneider, 1996; Hunt & Kingstone, 2003; Doré-Mazars et al., 2004; Peterson et al., 2004). The oculomotor readiness or premotor theory of attention has been suggested as an explanation for this relationship. As discussed earlier, one impediment to testing hypotheses generated by this theory has been a lack of precision in specifying the hypotheses. On the one hand, if "mechanisms" and "circuits" refer to particular populations of neurons instantiating a single process, then the results of the Juan et al. (2004) experiment contradict this claim. This conclusion is based on three premises: (1) if an attention shift is just a covert saccade plan and (2) if the monkeys shifted attention to the singleton even in antisaccade trials and (3) if a covert saccade plan is revealed by deviations of evoked saccades, then saccades evoked after the singleton was selected, but before the endpoint was selected, must deviate toward the singleton. We found no such deviation. Therefore, one of the antecedent premises must be incorrect. A literature has been based on the observation that deviations of evoked saccades measure growing saccade plans, and we believe the stimulus properties and task demands offer little room to doubt that the monkeys shifted attention to the singleton. Therefore, by a process of elimination, we can reject the premise that an attention shift is simply a covert saccade plan. On the other hand, if "mechanisms" refer to entire brain structures or circuits comprised of heterogeneous populations of neurons performing different functions (like shifting attention by selecting stimuli and preparing saccades), then our results cannot challenge the theory. However, if the theory is formulated too generally to map onto specific neural populations, then it loses the relevance of mechanism and the force of falsifiability. Thus, these results suggest abandonment or refinement of the premotor theory of attention. We believe that the premotor theory can be regarded as correct insofar as it posits a relationship between saccades and attention that occurs through some overlap between the brain circuits responsible for both. However, it seems clear that a premotor theory based on an identity of saccade planning and attention shifting, such that attention is simply an unexecuted saccade, cannot be correct.

These results and conclusions are important for understanding an important recent observation concerning the role of the FEF in attention allocation. Weak electrical stimulation of the FEF in macaques improves the allocation of attention at the location corresponding to the endpoint of the saccade that would be evoked with stronger stimulation, and this occurs through an influence on the activity of neurons in extrastriate visual area V4 (Moore & Armstrong, 2003; Moore & Fallah, 2004; Armstrong et al., 2006). This result has been interpreted as strong evidence in support of the premotor theory of attention, but the evaluation of this claim must be framed by the anatomical connectivity between the FEF and V4. Specifically, is the influence on V4 exerted by the population of neurons in the FEF that also delivers saccade command signals to subcortical structures? We recently addressed this question anatomically by analyzing the pattern of neurons labeled by retrograde tracers placed in V4 and the superior colliculus (SC; Pouget et al., 2009). The strongest evidence for the premotor theory of attention would be finding individual neurons in the FEF projecting to both the SC and V4. However, we found no neurons in the FEF projecting both to SC and V4. In the FEF, all neurons innervating SC are located in layer 5, whereas the large majority of neurons innervating extrastriate visual cortex are located in supragranular layers (see also Barone et al., 2000). The conjunction of physiological and anatomical findings suggests that the signal conveyed from the FEF to extrastriate visual cortex does not correspond to saccade preparation but instead can be identified with the allocation of visual spatial attention. The functional insights afforded by these anatomical results illustrate the utility of the stage theory of attention and action in organizing diverse kinds of data.

Further evidence for the stage theory was obtained by examining the timing and pattern of visual target selection and saccade preparation in a task that required observers to respond to random changes of target location on some trials. The search-step task combines a standard visual search task with the classic double-step saccade task. On most trials (referred to as no-step trials) observers were rewarded for making a saccade to a color oddball target among distractors. On the remaining trials (step-trials), the target and one distractor unexpectedly swapped positions after presentation of the array. When the target stepped from its original position to a new position, observers were rewarded for directing gaze to the new target location (compensated trials). However, observers often fail to compensate for the target step and made a saccade to the original target location (noncompensated trials). In other words, they shift gaze to a location different from that occupied by the target. This behavior is not rewarded. We have shown that performance of macaque monkeys and humans is qualitatively indistinguishable and can be understood as the outcome of a race between a process that produces the first saccade, a process that interrupts the first one, and a process that produces the second saccade (Becker & Jürgens, 1979; Camalier et al., 2007).

Noncompensated saccade trials provided data to test the dissociation of visual target selection from saccade preparation. Even when gaze shifted away from the popout oddball of the search array, visual neurons in the FEF represented the current location of the target (Murthy et al., 2009). Further evidence for a functional dissociation of visual selection and response preparation was obtained in the trials in which the target stepped out of the receptive or movement field, and monkeys canceled the initial saccade to redirect gaze to the final target location. Whereas the visual neurons continued to discharge as if no stimulus change had occurred, the movement neurons were strongly modulated early enough to control the initiation of the saccade (Murthy et al., 2009).

The search-step task provides still further evidence that saccade preparation and production can be accomplished without or in spite of visual processing. During target-step trials, after generating the error saccade to the original target location, humans and monkeys commonly produce corrective saccades to the final target location. Many of these corrective saccades are initiated with latencies that are so short (<100 ms) relative to the error saccade that they could not be guided by the outcome of visual processing. Nevertheless, the latency of these corrective saccades is predicted by the timing of movement-related activity in the FEF. Preceding rapid corrective saccades, the movement-related activity of neurons began before visual feedback of the error could be registered. Moreover, the movement-related activity of a few neurons began even before the error saccade was completed (Murthy et al., 2007).

Although perceptual and response processes can be dissociated, the ultimate RT of saccades is partially determined by the duration of processing at the perceptual stage. The contribution of target selection time during perceptual processing to the variability of saccadic response latency varies with target discriminability and task demands (Thompson et al., 1996; Bichot et al., 2001; Sato et al., 2001; McPeek & Keller, 2002; Sato & Schall, 2003; Ipata et al., 2006; Shen & Paré, 2007; Thomas & Paré, 2007; Balan et al., 2008; Cohen, Heitz et al., 2009). For example, during feature-search tasks for a red target among green distractors (or vice versa), the time that elapses between the initial volley of visual activity and when the visual cells in the FEF select the feature target accounts for a small proportion of the ultimate trial-to-trial variability in reaction time (RT; Sato et al., 2001). However, when macaques search for a complex form-defined visual target (e.g., a rotated T among randomly rotated Ls), a much larger proportion of the RT variability is accounted for by the variance in the measure of perceptual processing by visual cells in the FEF (Cohen, Heitz et al., 2009). Next, we turn to the issue of how information is transmitted from the network of neurons that carry out perceptual processing to those that perform response-level processing.

The issue of interstage information transmission has received a significant amount of study by cognitive psychologists using electrophysiological methods but often is absent from the neuroscience literature. One critical and contentious issue regarding the flow of information through different stages of information processing is whether processing at one stage is completed before information is transmitted to the next stage. The competing cognitive architectures that have been proposed are often referred to as *discrete versus continuous*

models of information processing (Miller, 1982; Meyer et al., 1984; Meyer et al., 1988). Guided by Donders' ideas, Sternberg (1969b) proposed that information was transmitted in a discrete manner between the stage of perceptual processing and subsequent stages, such as the stage of response selection. This framework was extremely effective in accounting for RT effects in different paradigms and has provided an effective way to interpret results from a variety of cognitive tasks (Sternberg, 1984). However, subsequent cognitive models have shown that the same findings from RT experiments can be accounted for with overlapping stages of processing (McClelland, 1979). Because both types of models can account for behavioral data with similar success it is not possible to distinguish between these categories of models with RT data alone.

In fact, it was recognized that partitioning RT into constituent stages could not be done conclusively without some way of measuring the termination or initiation of covert stages. Research over the last 30 years or so—and especially in the last 10 years—has demonstrated how to solve this measurement problem. The approach uses physiological measures that are believed to correspond to or index the timing of particular cognitive processes. This was addressed first with ERPs, but single-unit recordings from monkeys performing tasks like visual search have provided equally useful information. Typically, studies focused on distinguishing between discrete or continuous flow models have measured the timing of the P3 component, to index the end of perceptual processing (also called *stimulus evaluation time*; for a review see Coles et al., 1995) or the LRP, which indexes response preparation (Coles et al., 1988; Miller & Hackley, 1992; Osman et al., 1992; Miller & Schroter, 2002; Rinkenauer et al., 2004). The results of these experiments have indicated that it is possible for information to flow continuously between stages of perceptual and response processing. However, as Miller and colleagues have pointed out, the evidence is also consistent with a model in which information about individual features of a stimulus can be processed independently with different time courses, and when one feature is processed it is transmitted to the response stage (Miller, 1988; Miller &

Hackley, 1992). We have found this model of interstage information transmission to be effective in accounting for findings from unit recordings from the FEF during visual search and other tasks.

A series of studies have sought to understand the nature of interstage information transmission by recording from neurons in the FEF of monkeys performing attention-demanding tasks (Sato et al., 2001; Woodman et al., 2008). The findings from these studies are consistent with the view that response processing does not begin until perceptual processing is completed (e.g., Woodman et al., 2008), but these conclusions are tentative (see Bichot et al., 2001) and appear to be sensitive to the number of features defining the target. The studies performed thus far used neuronal recording techniques in which activity from a single neuron or a small number of similar neurons was recorded at the same time (see also Mouret & Hasbroucq, 2000). This means that neurons instantiating covert target selection and those instantiating saccade response processes were recorded at different times. Firm conclusions about the flow of information between computational stages will require future studies to record the neural activity indexing processing in different stages simultaneously. The stage theory points to this empirical gap in our knowledge as critical for describing how cognitive subsystems work together.

After information is transmitted to the network of neurons that controls the physical movement of the eyes, the appropriate saccade must be prepared and initiated. When saccade preparation is carried out, movement cells in the FEF exhibit a build-up of activity preceding the saccade that results in an eye movement fixating the target location (Hanes & Schall, 1996). During free-viewing search, the process of saccade preparation would occur after each item receives the benefit of a covert shift of attention (Hoffman & Subramaniam, 1995; Kowler et al., 1995).

In a recent study, we showed how measuring different aspects of the activity in these saccadic response cells in the FEF could be used to quantify different constructs described in many cognitive models of attention, categorization, and decision. Woodman et al. (2008) analyzed the spiking activity recorded from movement-related neurons in the FEF during a variety of visual search tasks (color and motion feature-search tasks and search for form-defined targets) and related these different neural metrics to the RT effects that were observed. We measured four different characteristics of the neural activity. First, we measured the baseline-firing rate of these cells prior to the presentation of the visual search array. This metric provides an estimate of the degree to which neurons coding for a specific response (i.e., a saccade into the movement field of the neuron) are biased prior to the beginning of the trial. Because responses in any direction were equally likely, we expected not to find any systematic biases in response direction prior to the response. Next, we measured the time of the onset of the build-up of activity preceding the saccadic response. This served as a measure of the beginning of the response stage of processing that prepares the ultimate behavioral response to the search array. Third, we measured the slope of the build-up of activity in these saccadic response-related neurons. This served as a concrete measure of the rate at which information accrued at the response stage. Finally, we measured the activity level in the interval immediately preceding the saccadic response (i.e., the 20 ms before the saccade into the movement field). This provides a measure of the threshold for neural activity in these movement-related cells, the crossing of which causes the saccade to be triggered (Hanes & Schall, 1996). We found that saccadic-response variability during visual search was best accounted for by delays in the onset of the response stage. This finding is consistent with models of visual attention that propose that search tasks heavily tax perceptual attention mechanisms but not response or memory subsystems (Wolfe, 1998). This study provides an example of linking components of cognitive models to specific neural markers in order to provide definitive tests of models of processing.

Performance Monitoring

At the moment when the saccadic response is made, the trial is over, but cognitive processing is not. The response was either correct, in that the target was fixated, or an error was made. In experiments with monkeys, this means that reward is delivered when the behavior was correct and withheld when the response was wrong, which provides explicit feedback regarding task performance. However, in many experiments with human observers, no feedback about task performance is explicitly provided. Does the brain know if the task was performed correctly? If so, how does this information about the outcome of performance change how information is processed on the next trial?

There is now abundant evidence that the brain has an extensive performance-monitoring network. In humans, electrophysiological studies have shown that, if an observer makes an error, the brain registers this incorrect performance immediately after the response. Response-locked ERPs indicate that when an error is made, a medial-frontal negativity is recorded and often followed by a positivity with a more parietal distribution (Gehring et al., 1993; Falkenstein et al., 2000; Gehring & Willoughby, 2002). The error-related negativity (or ERN) has been interpreted to index error detection (Gehring et al., 1993), response conflict (Botvinick et al., 2001), or dopamine-regulated learning signals (Holroyd & Coles, 2002; Brown & Braver, 2005). It has been proposed that this error signal may arise from the anterior cingulate cortex (ACC) and is used to modify how information is processed on the subsequent trial. However, it remains an open question whether such adjustments in how information is processed are focused on perceptual processing, the response stage, or both. In other words, which stage(s) does the executive control? And how?

Unit recording studies suggest that neurons in the performance-monitoring network may reside in more areas than just ACC. Specifically, neural activity recorded in the supplementary eye field (SEF) consistently shows evidence for error- and reward-related modulations following the response in a task (Stuphorn et al., 2000). The causal influence of the SEF on performance of oculomotor control tasks has been demonstrated using microstimulation in macaque monkeys. Stuphorn and Schall (2006) examined the behavioral performance of monkeys during the ocular–motor countermanding paradigm immediately following the delivery of microstimulation of the SEF. They found that this stimulation caused the

monkeys to behave more conservatively compared to baseline performance trials without microstimulation. In particular, the monkeys' saccadic RT was increased, so that error rates were reduced following weak microstimulation of the SEF. This shows that the SEF is part of the network that monitors performance and controls the visual and motor subsystems that perform perceptual and response processing. At this point, it is unclear whether the performance monitoring and control network only includes medial and dorsal cortical structures (such as ACC and SEF), or whether the network of areas implementing these functions is more widespread. For example, intracranial recordings of electrical potentials in human patients (Halgren et al., 2002; Wang et al., 2005) have suggested that regions of the parietal lobe also produce error-related activity and may be a part of a broad network that evaluates the outcome of behavioral responses and influences future processing. Similarly, imaging studies of normal human observers have implicated regions of the inferior frontal cortex in performance monitoring and control functions (Aron et al., 2004). Clearly, the research examining the localization versus distribution of cognitive monitoring and control functions is ongoing.

In summary, even after the trial is over, cognitive processing continues. This could be thought of as the most recently discovered stage of processing, as it has become the focus of cognitive models only in the last decade (e.g., Botvinick et al., 2001; Holroyd & Coles, 2002; Brown & Braver, 2005). Based on the density of connections of medial frontal areas with motor areas (such as the FEF) and the paucity of connections with extrastriate visual areas, we hypothesize that the product of this stage is attenuation or facilitation of the response preparation process. By changing the willingness to respond, by speeding or slowing the response preparation process, the executive control network can enable speed at the cost of accuracy or vice versa.

RELATIONSHIP TO OTHER THEORIES

In its attempt to be comprehensive, the stage theory of attention and action relates to and expands on other major theoretical approaches in cognitive psychology. Certainly, the proposition that selective processing can occur according to stimulus and task demands within any of a sequence of processing stages is similar to proposals that have shaped debates for some time and remain vibrant avenues of research (Luce 1986; Meyer et al., 1988; Luck & Hillyard, 2000; Sternberg, 1969a, 2001). Some models gain specificity at the cost of scope. For example, stochastic models of RT in target discrimination tasks explain the systematic variability of RT and choice entirely in terms of sequential sampling of perceptual evidence. Errors produced by the response stage are not accounted for in these models. However, the FEF visual neurons select the target correctly even when monkeys make errors with the eyes (Murthy et al., 2001; Murthy et al., 2009) or hands (Trageser et al., 2008). Meanwhile, stochastic models of RT and choice in stimulus perturbation tasks (like stop signal or double-step) explain the systematic variability of RT and choice effectively in terms of a race between alternative response channels (Logan & Cowan, 1984; Camalier et al., 2007). Independent race models can be implemented in neural networks with the proper temporal pattern of interaction (Boucher et al., 2007; Lo et al., 2009). However, the input to these models is unspecified.

Current stochastic accumulator models implement speed-accuracy adjustments through strategic changes of the threshold of the accumulation process (Smith & Ratcliff, 2004; Gold & Shadlen, 2007). The evidence for distinct stages of processing suggests that speed–accuracy adjustments can be accomplished through changes of the visual selection stage or the saccade preparation stage, or both. The neural mechanism(s) of speed–accuracy adjustments is not understood. Signal detection theory (Green & Swets, 1966) and biased choice theory (Luce, 1986) both distinguish sensitivity, which is limited by the sensory apparatus, from response bias, which is the willingness to respond. The statement "willingness to respond" seems to point very clearly to the mechanism of speed–accuracy adjustment.

How can sequential sampling models of perceptual evidence (target vs. distractor) and race models of response production (saccade here vs.

there) be integrated? Are they different descriptions of one process? Or, are they descriptions of different processes that operate in succession? In general, numerous models of visual search have been developed, but the models have fundamentally different architectures (e.g., Bundesen, 1998; Hamker, 2004; Wolfe, 2007). It is difficult or impossible to decide between alternative models based only on behavioral data (e.g., Van Zandt et al., 2000). We advocate the proposition that appropriate neurophysiological data can discriminate between alternative mechanisms if proper linking propositions are established (Schall, 2004; Teller, 1984).

CONCLUSION

The stage theory of attention and action is proposed with the aim of organizing and integrating a diverse and often bewildering collection of observations, hypotheses, and suppositions. Beyond the possible unification of disparate views, it is hoped that the stage theory identifies important questions to answer with investigative techniques that provide greater anatomical, conceptual, and temporal resolution. We are optimistic that such research will reveal the cognitive and associated neural processes responsible for selecting targets on which to allocate attention and to which to shift gaze.

ACKNOWLEDGMENTS

The original research reviewed has been supported by R01-EY08890, R01-MH55806, F32-EY015043, NSF BCS0218507, AFOSR, a McKnight Investigator Award, P30-EY08126, P30-HD015052, and by Robin and Richard Patton through the E. Bronson Ingram Chair in Neuroscience.

References

Armstrong, K. M., Fitzgerald, J. K., & Moore, T. (2006). Changes in visual receptive fields with microstimulation of frontal cortex. *Neuron. 50*, 791–798.

Aron, A. R., Robbins, T. W., & Poldrack, R. A. (2004). Inhibition and the right inferior frontal cortex. *Trends in Cognitive Sciences, 8*, 170–177.

Arthur, D. L., & Starr, A. (1984). Task-relevant late positive component of the auditory event-related potential in monkeys resembles P300 in humans. *Science, 223*, 186–188.

Atkinson, R. C., & Shiffrin, R. M. (1968). Human memory: A proposed system and its control processes. In K. W. Spence (Ed.), *The psychology of learning and motivation: Advances in research and theory* (Vol. 2, pp. 89–195). New York: Academic Press.

Balan, P. F., Oristaglio, J., Schneider, D. M., & Gottlieb, J. (2008). Neuronal correlates of the set-size effect in monkey lateral intraparietal area. *PLOS Biology, 6*, e158. doi:10.1371/journal.pbio.0060158

Barborica, A., & Ferrera, V. P. (2004). Modification of saccades evoked by stimulation of frontal eye field during invisible target tracking. *Journal of Neuroscience, 24*, 3260–3267.

Barone, P., Batardiere, A., Knoblauch, K., & Kennedy, H. (2000). Laminar distribution of neurons in extrastriate areas projecting to visual areas V1 and V4 correlates with the hierarchical rank and indicates the operation of a distance rule. *Journal of Neuroscience 20*, 3263–3281.

Becker, W., & Jürgens, R. (1979). An analysis of the saccadic system by means of double step stimuli. *Vision Research, 19*, 967–983.

Belopolsky, A. V., & Theeuwes, J. (2009). When are attention and saccade preparation dissociated? *Psychological Science, 20*, 1340–1347.

Bichot, N. P., Rao, S. C., & Schall, J. D. (2001). Continuous processing in macaque frontal cortex during visual search. *Neuropsychologia, 39*, 972–982.

Bichot, N. P., Rossi, A. F., & Desimone, R. (2005). Parallel and serial neural mechanisms for visual search in macaque area V4. *Science, 308*, 529–534.

Bichot, N. P., & Schall, J. D. (1999). Effects of similarity and history on neural mechanisms of visual selection. *Nature Neuroscience, 2*(6), 549–554.

Bichot, N. P., & Schall, J. D. (2002). Priming in macaque frontal cortex during popout visual search: Feature-based facilitation and location-based inhibition of return. *Journal of Neuroscience, 22*, 4675–4685.

Botvinick, M. M., Braver, T. S., Barch, D. M., Carter, C. S., & Cohen, J. D. (2001). Conflict monitoring and cognitive control. *Psychological Review, 108*(3), 624–652.

Boucher, L., Stuphorn, V., Logan, G. D., Schall, J. D., & Palmeri, T. J. (2007). Inhibitory control in mind and brain: An interactive race model of countermanding saccades. *Psychological Review, 114*, 376–397.

Brown, J. W., & Braver, T. S. (2005). Learned predictions of error likelihood in the anterior cingulate cortex. *Science, 307*, 1118–1121.

Bruce, C. J., & Goldberg, M. E. (1985). Primate frontal eye fields I Single neurons discharging before saccades. *Journal of Neurophysiology, 53*, 603–635.

Bullock, T. H. (2003). Have brain dynamics evolved? Should we look for unique dynamics in the sapient species? *Neural Computation, 15*, 2013–2027.

Bundesen, C. (1990). A theory of visual attention. *Psychological Review, 97*, 523–547.

Bundesen, C. (1998). A computational theory of visual attention. *Philosophical Transactions of the Royal Society of London. Series B, Biological Sciences, 353*, 1271–1281.

Bundesen, C., Habekost, T., & Kyllingsbaek, S. (2005). A neural theory of visual attention: Bridging cognition and neurophysiology. *Psychological Review, 112*, 291–328.

Buschman, T. J., & Miller, E. K. (2009). Serial, covert shifts of attention during visual search are reflected by the frontal eye fields and correlated with population oscillations. *Neuron, 63*, 386–389.

Camalier, C. R., Gotler, A., Murthy, A., Thompson, K. G., Logan, G. D., Palmeri, T. J., et al. (2007). Dynamics of saccade target selection: Race model analysis of double step and search step saccade production in human and macaque. *Vision Research, 47*, 2187–2211.

Casagrande, V. A. (1994). A third parallel visual pathway to primate area V1. *Trends in Neurosciences, 17*, 305–310.

Chun, M. M. (2000). Contextual cueing of visual attention. *Trends in Cognitive Science, 4*(5), 170–178.

Chun, M. M., & Jiang, Y. (1998). Contextual cueing: Implicit learning and memory of visual context guides spatial attention. *Cognitive Psychology, 36*(1), 28–71.

Cohen, J. Y., Heitz, R. P., Schall, J. D., & Woodman, G. F. (2009a). On the origin of event-related potentials indexing covert attentional selection during visual search. *Journal of Neurophysiology. 102*, 2375–2386.

Cohen, J. Y., Heitz, R. P., Woodman, G. F., & Schall, J. D. (2009b). Neural basis of the set-size effect in frontal eye field: Timing of attention during visual search. *Journal of Neurophysiology, 101*, 2485–2506.

Cohen, J. Y., Pouget, P., Heitz, R. P., Woodman, G. F., & Schall, J. D. (2009c). Biophysical support for functionally distinct cell types in the frontal eye field. *Journal of Neurophysiology, 101*, 912–916.

Coles, M. G. H., Gratton, G., & Donchin, E. (1988). Detecting early communication: Using measures of movement-related potentials to illuminate human information processing. *Biological Psychology, 26,* 69–89.

Coles, M. G. H., Smid, H. G. O. M., Scheffers, M. K., & Otten, L. J. (1995). Mental chronometry and the study of human information processing. In M. D. Rugg, & M. G. H. Coles (Eds.), *Electrophysiology of mind: Event-related brain potentials and cognition* (pp. 86–131). Oxford, UK: Oxford University Press.

Desimone, R., & Duncan, J. (1995). Neural mechanisms of selective visual attention. Annual Review of Neuroscience, 18, 193–222.

Deubel, H., & Schneider, W. X. (1996). Saccade target selection and object recognition: Evidence for a common attentional mechanism. *Vision Research, 36,* 1827–1837.

Donders, F. C. (1868/1969). On the speed to mental processes (W. G. Koster, Trans.). In W. G. Koster (Ed.), *Attention and performance* (Vol. II, pp. 412–431). Amsterdam: North-Holland Publishing Co.

Doré-Mazars, K., Pouget, P., & Beauvillain, C. (2004). Attentional selection during preparation of eye movements. *Psychological Research, 69,* 67–76.

Duncan, J. (1996). Cooperating brain systems in selective perception and action. In T. Inui, & J. L. McClelland (Eds.), *Attention and performance: Information integration in perception and communication.* (Vol. XVI, pp. 549–78). Cambridge, MA: MIT Press.

Duncan, J., & Humphreys, G. W. (1989). Visual search and stimulus similarity. *Psychological Review, 96*(3), 433–458.

Eimer, M., Forster, B., van Velzen, J., & Prabhu, G. (2005). Covert manual response preparation triggers attentional shifts: ERP evidence for the premotor theory of attention. *Neuropsychologia, 43,* 957–966.

Ekstrom, L. B., Roelfsema, P. R., Arsenault, J. T., Bonmossar, G., & Vanduffel, W. (2008). Bottom-up dependent gating of frontal signals in early visual cortex. *Science, 321,* 414–417.

Elston, G. N. (2003). Cortex, cognition and the cell: New insights into the pyramidal neuron and prefrontal function. *Cerebral Cortex, 13*(11), 1124–1138.

Emeric, E. E., Brown, J. W., Boucher, L., Carpenter, R. H., Hanes, D. P., Harris, R., et al. (2007). Influence of history on saccade countermanding performance in humans and macaque monkeys. *Vision Research, 47,* 35–49.

Falkenstein, M., Hoormann, J., Christ, S., & Hohnsbein, J. (2000). ERP components of reaction errors and their functional significance: A tutorial. *Biological Psychology, 51,* 87–107.

Felleman, D. J., & Van Essen, D. C. (1991). Distributed hierarchical processing in the primate cerebral cortex. *Cerebral Cortex, 1,* 1–47.

Findlay, J. M., & Gilchrist, I. D. (2005). Eye guidance and visual search. In G. Underwood (Ed.), *Cognitive Processes in Eye Guidance* (pp. 259–281). Oxford, UK: Oxford University Press.

Gehring, W. J., Gross, B., Coles, M. G. H., Meyer, D. E., & Donchin, E. (1993). A neural system for error detection and compensation. *Psychological Science, 4,* 385–390.

Gehring, W. J., & Willoughby, A. R. (2002). The medial frontal cortex and the rapid processing of monetary gains and losses. *Science, 295,* 2279–2282.

Gold, J. I., & Shadlen, M. N. (2003). The influence of behavioral context on the representation of a perceptual decision in developing oculomotor commands. *Journal of Neuroscience, 23,* 632–651.

Gold, J. I., & Shadlen, M. N. (2007). The neural basis of decision making. *Annual Review of Neuroscience, 30,* 535–574.

Green, D., & Swets, J. (1966). *Signal detection theory and psychophysics.* New York: Wiley.

Gregoriou, G. G., Gotts, S. J., Zhou, H., & Desimone, R. (2009). High-frequency, long-range coupling between prefrontal and visual cortex during attention. *Science, 324,* 1207–1210.

Group, P. I. N., Ascoli, G. A., Alonso-Nanclares, L., Anderson, S. A., Barrionuevo, G., Benavides-Piccione, R., et al. (2008 July). Petilla terminology: Nomenclature of features of GABAergic interneurons of the cerebral cortex. *Nature Reviews. Neuroscience, 9*(7), 557–568.

Halgren, E., Boujon, C., Clarke, J., Wang, C., & Chauvel, P. (2002). Rapid distributed fronto-parieto-occipital processing stages during working memory in humans. *Cerebral Cortex, 12*(7), 710–728.

Hamker, F. H. (2004). A dynamic model of how feature cues guide spatial attention. *Vision Research, 44,* 501–521.

Hanes, D. P., & Schall, J. D. (1996). Neural control of voluntary movement initiation. *Science, 274*(5286), 427–430.

Henderson, J. M. (1993). Visual attention and saccadic eye movements. In G. d'Ydewalle, & J. Van Rensbergen (Eds.), *Perception and cognition: Advances in eye movement research* (pp. 37–50). Amsterdam: North-Holland.

Hendry, S. H., & Reid, R. C. (2000). The koniocellular pathway in primate vision. *Annual Review of Neuroscience, 23,* 127–153.

Hoffman, J. E., & Subramaniam, B. (1995). The role of visual attention in saccadic eye movements. *Perception & Psychophysics, 57,* 787–795.

Holroyd, C. B., & Coles, M. G. H. (2002). The neural basis of human error processing: Reinforcement learning, dopamine, and the error-related negativity. *Psychological Review, 109*, 679–709.

Hooge, I. T., & Erkelens, C. J. (1998). Adjustment of fixation duration in visual search. *Vision Research, 38*, 1295–1302.

Hunt, A. R., & Kingstone, A. (2003). Covert and overt voluntary attention: Linked or independent? *Cognitive Brain Research, 18*, 102–105.

Ipata, A. E., Gee, A. L., Goldberg, M. E., & Bisley, J. W. (2006). Activity in the lateral intraparietal area predicts the goal and latency of saccades in a free-viewing visual search task. *Journal of Neuroscience, 26*, 3656–3661.

James, W. (1890). *The principles of psychology*. New York: Holt.

Johnson, J. S., Woodman, G. F., Braun, E., & Luck, S. J. (2007). Implicit memory influences the allocation of attention in visual cortex. *Psychonomic Bulletin & Review, 14*, 834–839.

Juan, C. H., Shorter-Jacobi, S. M., & Schall, J. D. (2004). Dissociation of spatial attention and saccade preparation. *Proceedings of the National Academy of Sciences of the United States of America, 104*, 15111–15116.

Klein, R. M. (1980). Does oculomotor readiness mediate cognitive control of visual attention? In R. Nickerson (Ed.), *Attention and Performance* (Vol. VIII, pp. 259–276). Hillsdale, NJ: Erlbaum.

Klein, R. M., & Pontefract, A. (1994). Does oculomotor readiness mediate cognitive control of visual attention? Revisited! In C. Umilta, & M. Moscovitch (Eds.), *Attention and Performance: Conscious and Nonconscious Information Processing* (Vol. XV, pp. 333–350). Cambridge, MA: MIT Press.

Kowler, E., Anderson, E., Dosher, B., & Blaser, E. (1995). The role of attention in the programming of saccades. *Vision Research, 35*, 1897–1916.

Kustov, A. A., & Robinson, D. L. (1996). Shared neural control of attentional shifts and eye movements. *Nature, 384*, 74–77.

Lamme, V. A., Van Dijk, B. W., & Spekreijse, H. (1992). Texture segregation is pressed by primary visual cortex in man and monkey. Evidence from VEP experiments. *Vision Research, 32*(5), 797–807.

Lo, C. C., Boucher, L., Paré, M., Schall, J. D., & Wang, X.-J. (2009). Proactive inhibitory control and attractor dynamics in countermanding action: A spiking neural circuit model. *Journal of Neuroscience, 29*, 9059–9071.

Logan, G. D. (1988). Toward an instance theory of automatization. *Psychological Review, 95*, 492–527.

Logan, G. D., & Cowan, W. B. (1984). On the ability to inhibit thought and action: A theory of an act of control. *Psychological Review, 91*, 295–327.

Luce, R. D. (1963). Detection and recognition. In R. D. Luce, R. R. Bush, & E. Galanter (Eds.), *Handbook of mathematical psychology* (pp. 103–189). New York: Wiley.

Luce, R. D. (1986). *Response times: Their role in inferring elementary mental organization*. New York: Oxford University Press.

Luck, S. J. (2005). *An introduction to the event-related potential technique*. Cambridge, MA: MIT Press.

Luck, S. J., & Hillyard, S. A. (1994). Electrophysiological correlates of feature analysis during visual search. *Psychophysiology, 31*, 291–308.

Luck, S. J., & Hillyard, S. A. (2000). The operation of selective attention at multiple stages of processing: Evidence from human and monkey electrophysiology. In M. S. Gazzaniga (Ed.), *The new cognitive neurosciences*. Cambridge, MA: MIT Press.

Luck, S. J., & Vecera, S. P. (2002). Attention. In S. Yantis (Ed.), *Stevens' handbook of experimental psychology: Vol. 1: Sensation and perception* (3rd ed.). New York: Wiley.

Luck, S. J., Woodman, G. F., & Vogel, E. K. (2000). Event-related potential studies of attention. *Trends in Cognitive Sciences, 4*, 432–440.

Maljkovic, V., & Nakayama, K. (1994). Priming of pop-out: I. Role of features. *Memory & Cognition, 22*(6), 657–672.

Maljkovic, V., & Nakayama, K. (2000). Priming of pop-out: III. A short-term implicit memory system beneficial for rapid target selection. *Visual Cognition, 7*(5), 571–595.

Masland, R. H. (2001). The fundamental plan of the retina. *Nature Neuroscience, 4*(9), 877–886.

McClelland, J. L. (1979). On the time relations of mental processes: An examination of systems of processes in cascade. *Psychological Review, 86*(4), 287–330.

McPeek, R. M., & Keller, E. L. (2002). Saccade target selection in the superior colliculus during a visual search task. *Journal of Neurophysiology, 88*, 2019–2034.

Medalla, M., Lera, P., Feinberg, M., & Barbas, H. (2007). Specificity in inhibitory systems associated with prefrontal pathways to temporal cortex in primates. *Cerebral Cortex, 17*(Suppl. 1), i136–150.

Meyer, D. E., Osman, A. M., Irwin, D. A., & Yantis, S. (1988). Modern mental chronometry. *Biological Psychology, 26*, 3–67.

Meyer, D. E., Yantis, S., Osman, A., & Smith, J. E. K. (1984). Discrete vs. continuous models of response preparation: A reaction time analysis. In S. Kornblum, & J. Requin (Eds.), *Preparatory states and processes* (pp. 69–94). Hillsdale, NJ: Erlbaum.

Miller, E. K., & Cohen, J. D. (2001). An integrative theory of prefrontal cortex function. *Annual Review of Neuroscience, 24,* 167–202.

Miller, J. (1988). Discrete and continuous models of human information processing: Theoretical distinctions and empirical results. *Acta Psychologica, 67,* 191–257.

Miller, J. O. (1982). Discrete versus continuous stage models of human information processing: In search of partial output. *Journal of Experimental Psychology.: Human Perception and Performance, 8,* 273–296.

Miller, J. O., & Hackley, S. A. (1992). Electrophysiological evidence for temporal overlap among contingent mental processes. *Journal of Experimental Psychology: General, 121,* 195–209.

Miller, J. O., & Schroter, H. (2002). Online response preparation in a rapid serial visual search task. *Journal of Experimental Psychology. Human Perception and Performance, 28,* 1364–1390.

Monosov, I. E., Trageser, J. C., & Thompson, K. G. (2008). Measurements of simultaneously recorded spiking activity and local field potentials suggest that spatial selection emerges in the frontal eye field. *Neuron, 57,* 614–625.

Moore, T., & Armstrong, K.M. (2003). Selective gating of visual signals by microstimulation of frontal cortex. *Nature. 421,* 370–373.

Moore, T., & Fallah, M. (2004). Microstimulation of the frontal eye field and its effects on covert spatial attention. *Journal of Neurophysiology 91,* 152–162.

Motter, B. C., & Belky, E. J. (1998). The zone of focal attention during active visual search. *Vision Research, 38,* 1007–1022.

Mouret, I., & Hasbroucq, T. (2000). The chronometry of single neuron activity: Testing discrete and continuous models of information processing. *Journal of Experimental Psychology. Human Perception and Performance, 26,* 1622–1638.

Murthy, A., Ray, S., Shorter, S. M., Priddy, E. G., Schall, J. D., & Thompson, K. G. (2007). Frontal eye field contributions to rapid corrective saccades. *Journal of Neurophysiology, 97,* 1457–1469.

Murthy, A., Ray, S., Shorter, S. M., Schall, J. D., & Thompson, K. G. (2009). Neural control of visual search by frontal eye field: Effects of unexpected target displacement on visual selection and saccade preparation. *Journal of Neurophysiology, 101,* 2485–2506.

Murthy, A., Thompson, K. G., & Schall, J. D. (2001). Dynamic dissociation of visual selection from saccade programming in frontal eye field. *Journal of Neurophysiology, 86,* 2634–2637.

Nassi, J. J., & Callaway, E. M. (2009). Parallel processing strategies of the primate visual system. *Nature Reviews. Neuroscience, 10*(5), 360–372.

Opris, I., Barborica, A., & Ferrera, V. P. (2005). Effects of electrical microstimulation in monkey frontal eye field on saccades to remembered locations. *Vision Research, 45,* 3414–3429.

Osman, A., Bashore, T. R., Coles, M., Donchin, E., & Meyer, D. (1992). On the transmission of partial information: Inferences from movement-related brain potentials. *Journal of Experimental Psychology. Human Perception and Performance, 18,* 217–232.

Over, E. A., Hooge, I. T., Vlaskamp, B. N., & Erkelens, C. J. (2007). Coarse-to-fine eye movement strategy in visual search. *Vision Research, 47,* 2272–2280.

Pashler, H. (1994). Dual-task interference in simple tasks: Data and theory. *Psychological Bulletin, 116,* 220–44.

Peterson, M. S., Kramer, A. F., & Irwin, D. E. (2004). Covert shifts of attention precede involuntary eye movements. *Attention, Perception & Psychophysics, 66,* 398–405.

Petroni, F., Panzeri, S., Hilgetag, C. C., Kotter, R., & Young, M. P. (2001). Simultaneity of responses in a hierarchical visual network. *Neuroreport, 12,* 2753–2759.

Petroni, F., Panzeri, S., Hilgetag, C. C., Scannell, J. W., Kotter, R., & Young, M. P. (2001). Hierarchical organization and neuronal response latencies in the primate visual system. *NeuroComputing, 38–40,* 1519–1523.

Posner, M. I. (1980). Orienting of attention. *Quarterly Journal of Experimental Psychology, 32,* 3–25.

Rabbitt, P., Cumming, G., & Vyas, S. (1979). Improvement, learning, and retention of skill at visual search. *Quarterly Journal of Experimental Psychology, 31,* 441–459.

Ratcliff, R. (2006). Modeling response signal and response time data. *Cognitive Psychology, 53,* 195–237.

Ratcliff, R., & Smith, P. L. (2004). A comparison of sequential-sampling models of two choice reaction time. *Psychological Review, 111,* 333–367.

Ray, S., Pouget, P., & Schall, J. D. (2009). Functional distinction between visuomovement and movement neurons in macaque frontal eye field during saccade countermanding. *Journal of Neurophysiology 102,* 3091–3100.

Reynolds, J. H., & Chelazzi, L. (2004). Attentional modulation of visual processing. *Annual Review of Neuroscience, 27,* 611–647.

Rinkenauer, G., Osman, A., Ulrich, R., Mueller-Gethmann, H., & Mattes, S. (2004). On the locus of speed-accuracy trade-off in reaction time: Inferences from the lateralized readiness potential.

Journal of Experimental Psychology: General, 133, 261–282.

Rizzolatti, G., Riggio, L., Dascola, I., & Umilta, C. (1987). Reorienting attention across the horizontal and vertical meridians: Evidence in favor of a premotor theory of attention. *Neuropsychologia, 25,* 31–40.

Rossi, A. F., Bichot, N. P., Desimone, R., & Ungerleider, L. G. (2007). Top down attentional deficits in macaques with lesions of lateral prefrontal cortex. *Journal of Neuroscience, 27,* 11306–11314.

Rugg, M. D., & Coles, M. G. H. (Eds.). (1995). *Electrophysiology of mind.* New York: Oxford University Press.

Sato, T., Murthy, A., Thompson, K. G., & Schall, J. D. (2001). Search efficiency but not response interference affects visual selection in frontal eye field. *Neuron, 30,* 583–591.

Sato, T. R., & Schall, J. D. (2003). Effects of stimulus-response compatibility on neural selection in frontal eye field. *Neuron, 38,* 637–648.

Schall, J. D. (1991). Neural basis of saccadic eye movements in primates. In A. G. Leventhal (Ed.), *The neural basis of visual function* (Vol. 4, pp. 388–442). London: Macmillan.

Schall, J. D. (2004). On building a bridge between brain and behaviour. *Annual Review of Psychology, 55,* 23–50.

Schall, J. D., & Hanes, D. P. (1993). Neural basis of saccade target selection in frontal eye field during visual search. *Nature, 366,* 467–469.

Schall, J. D., Hanes, D. P., Thompson, K. G., & King, D. J. (1995). Saccade target selection in frontal eye field of macaque. I. Visual and premovement activation. *Journal of Neuroscience, 15*(10), 6905–6918.

Schall, J. D., Paré, M., & Woodman, G. F. (2007). Comment on "Top-down versus bottom-up control of attention in the prefrontal and posterior parietal cortices". *Science, 318,* 44b.

Schmolesky, M. T., Wang, Y.-C., Hanes, D. P., Thompson, K. G., Leutgeb, S., Schall, J. D., et al. (1998). Signal timing across the macaque visual system. *Journal of Neurophysiology, 79,* 3272–3278.

Schroeder, C. E., Tenke, C. E., & Givre, S. J. (1992). Subcortical contributions to the surface-recorded flash-VEP in the awake macaque. *Electroencephalography & Clinical Neurophysiology, 84,* 219–231.

Schroeder, C. E., Tenke, C. E., Givre, S. J., Arezzo, J. C., & Vaughan, H. G. J. (1991). Striate cortical contribution to the surface-recorded pattern-reversal VEP in the alert monkey. *Vision Research, 31,* 1143–1157.

Sheliga, B. M., Riggio, L., & Rizzolatti, G. (1994). Orienting of attention and eye movements. *Experimental Brain Research, 98,* 507–522.

Sheliga, B. M., Riggio, L., & Rizzolatti, G. (1995). Spatial attention and eye movements. *Experimental Brain Research, 105,* 261–275.

Shen, K., & Paré, M. (2007). Neuronal activity in superior colliculus signals both stimulus identity and saccade goals during visual conjunction search. *Journal of Vision, 7,* 15.11–15.13.

Shepherd, M., Findlay, J. M., & Hockey, R. J. (1986). The relationship between eye movements and spatial attention. *Quarterly Journal of Experimental Psychology. A, Human Experimental Psychology, 38,* 475–491.

Smith, P. L., & Ratcliff, R. (2004). Psychology and neurobiology of simple decisions. *Trends in Neurosciences, 27,* 161–168.

Smulders, F. T. Y., Kok, A., Kenemans, J. L., & Bashore, T. R. (1995). The temporal selectivity of additive factor effects on the reaction process revealed in ERP component latencies. *Acta Psychologica, 90,* 97–109.

Sparks, D. L., & Mays, L. E. (1983). Spatial localization of saccade targets: I. Compensation for stimulation-induced perturbations in eye position. *Journal of Neurophysiology, 49,* 45–63.

Sternberg, S. (1969a). Memory scanning: Mental processes revealed by reaction time experiments. *American Scientist, 57,* 421–457.

Sternberg, S. (1969b). The discovery of processing stages: Extensions of Donder's method. In W. G. Koster (Ed.), *Attention and performance* (Vol. II, pp. 276–315). Amsterdam: North Holland.

Sternberg, S. (1984). Stage models of mental processing and the additive-factor method. *Behavioral and Brain Sciences, 7,* 82–84.

Sternberg, S. (2001). Separate modifiability, mental modules, and the use of pure and composite measures to reveal them. *Acta Psychologica, 106,* 147–246.

Stuphorn, V., & Schall, J. D. (2006). Executive control of countermanding saccades by the supplementary eye field. *Nature Neuroscience, 9,* 925–931.

Stuphorn, V., Taylor, T. L., & Schall, J. D. (2000). Performance monitoring by supplementary eye field. *Nature, 408,* 857–860.

Teller, D. Y. (1984). Linking propositions. *Vision Research, 24,* 1233–1246.

Thomas, N. W. D., & Paré, M. (2007). Temporal processing of saccade targets in parietal cortex area LIP during visual search. *Journal of Neurophysiology, 97,* 942–947.

Thompson, K. G., Bichot, N. P., & Schall, J. D. (1997). Dissociation of visual discrimination from saccade programming in macaque frontal eye field. *Journal of Neurophysiology, 77*(2), 1046–1050.

Thompson, K. G., Bichot, N. P., & Schall, J. D. (2001). From attention to action in frontal cortex. In J. Braun, C. Koch, & J. Davis (Eds.), *Visual attention and cortical circuits* (pp. 137–157). Cambridge, MA: MIT Press.

Thompson, K. G., Biscoe, K. L., & Sato, T. R. (2005). Neuronal basis of covert spatial attention in the frontal eye field. *Journal of Neuroscience, 12,* 9479–9487.

Thompson, K. G., Hanes, D. P., Bichot, N. P., & Schall, J. D. (1996). Perceptual and motor processing stages identified in the activity of macaque frontal eye field neurons during visual search. *Journal of Neurophysiology, 76*(6), 4040–4055.

Trageser, J. C., Monosov, I. E., Ilya, R., Zhou, Y., & Thompson, K. G. (2008). A perceptual representation in the frontal eye field during covert visual search that is more reliable than the behavioral report. *European Journal of Neuroscience, 28,* 2542–2549.

Treisman, A. M. (1969). Strategies and models of selective attention. *Psychological Review, 76,* 282–299.

Treisman, A. M., & Gelade, G. (1980). A feature-integration theory of attention. *Cognitive Psychology, 12,* 97–136.

Van der Marel, H., Dagnelie, G., & Spekreijse, H. (1984). Subdurally recorded pattern and luminance EPs in the alert rhesus monkey. *Electroencephalography & Clinical Neurophysiology, 57,* 354–368.

Van Essen, D. C., Anderson, C. H., & Felleman, D. J. (1992). Information processing in the primate visual system: An integrated systems perspective. *Science, 255,* 419–423.

Van Zandt, T., Colonius, H., & Proctor, R. W. (2000). A comparison of two reaction-time models applied to perceptual matching. *Psychonomic Bulletin & Review, 7,* 208–256.

Vicente, R., Gollo, L. L., Mirasso, C. R., Fischer, I., & Pipa, G. (2008). Dynamical relaying can yield zero time lag neuronal synchrony despite long conduction delays. *Proceedings of the National Academy of Sciences of the United States of America, 105,* 17157–17162.

Vogel, E. K., Luck, S. J., & Shapiro, K. L. (1998). Electrophysiological evidence for a postperceptual locus of suppression during the attentional blink. *Journal of Experimental Psychology. Human Perception and Performance, 24,* 1656–1674.

Wang, C., Ulbert, I., Schomer, D. L., Marinkovic, K., & Halgren, E. (2005). Responses of human anterior cingulate cortex microdomains to error detection, conflict monitoring, stimulus-response mapping, familiarity, and orienting. *Journal of Neuroscience, 25,* 604–613.

Wolfe, J. M. (1998). Visual search. In H. Pashler (Ed.), *Attention* (pp. 13–73). Hove, UK: Psychology Press/Erlbaum.

Wolfe, J. M. (2007). Guided Search 4.0: Current progress with a model of visual search. In W. Gray (Ed.), *Integrated models of cognitive systems* (pp. 99–119). New York: Oxford Press.

Woodman, G. F., Arita, J. T., & Luck, S. J. (2009). A cuing study of the N2pc component: An index of attentional deployment to objects rather than spatial locations. *Brain Research, 1297,* 101–111.

Woodman, G. F., Kang, M.-K., Rossi, A. F., & Schall, J. D. (2007). Nonhuman primate event-related potentials indexing covert shifts of attention. *Proceedings of the National Academy of Sciences of the United States of America, 104,* 15111–15116.

Woodman, G. F., Kang, M.-K., Thompson, K. G., & Schall, J. D. (2008). The effect of visual search efficiency on response preparation: Neurophysiological evidence for discrete flow. *Psychological Science, 19,* 128–136.

Woodman, G. F., & Luck, S. J. (1999). Electrophysiological measurement of rapid shifts of attention during visual search. *Nature, 400,* 867–869.

Woodman, G. F., & Luck, S. J. (2003a). Dissociations among attention, perception, and awareness during object-substitution masking. *Psychological Science, 14,* 605–611.

Woodman, G. F., & Luck, S. J. (2003b). Serial deployment of attention during visual search. *Journal of Experimental Psychology. Human Perception and Performance, 29,* 121–138.

Woodman, G. F., Luck, S. J., & Schall, J. D. (2007). The role of working memory representations in the control of attention. *Cerebral Cortex, 17,* i118–124.

Woodman, G. F., Vogel, E. K., & Luck, S. J. (2001a). Attention is not unitary [commentary]. *Behavioral and Brain Sciences, 24,* 153–154.

Woodman, G. F., Vogel, E. K., & Luck, S. J. (2001b). Visual search remains efficient when visual working memory is full. *Psychological Science, 12,* 219–224.

10

Top-down Biases in Visual Short-term Memory

MARK G. STOKES AND ANNA C. NOBRE

THE ABILITY to hold visual information in mind beyond the duration of the initial sensory stimulation critically underpins many higher-level cognitive functions. In particular, visual short-term memory (VSTM) provides the perceptual continuity that is necessary for visual information to guide behavior across short temporal delays. In this chapter, we explore how the mechanisms of attention optimize VSTM. First, we consider how top-down attention biases VSTM encoding to favor information that is most likely to be relevant to behavior. Next, we consider more recent evidence that top-down attention can also bias representations already stored within VSTM. Flexible allocation of attention within VSTM enables the visual system to prioritize and update stored representations to accommodate changing task demands.

ICONIC BEGINNINGS

Half a century ago, researchers began to explore the basis of immediate visual memory using briefly presented letter stimuli (e.g., Sperling, 1960; Averbach & Coriell, 1961). In a classic series of experiments, Sperling (1960) asked participants to report as many letters as possible from very briefly presented (50 ms) visual displays. On some trials, up to nine letters were presented, yet participants were rarely able to report more than four. This apparent limit contrasted with the subjective experience: Participants remarked that they could "see" many more letters than they could report. Further experiments revealed that this subjective impression was no illusion. Although participants could not report more than four or five letters, they could select which four or five letters to report from the larger array. Immediately after the offset of the test array, participants were provided an instructional cue to report only letters from a specific, but randomly selected, row of the letter array. Remarkably, performance for the reduced set was almost perfect, implying that almost all letters were available for some time after the offset of the memory array.

Following these results, and related findings by Averbach and Coriell (1961), the relatively rich sensory impression described by participants was attributed to a fragile high-resolution visual store, later denoted *iconic memory* (Neisser & Sperling, 1967). Although rich in detail, this snapshot of the visual scene decays very rapidly. Information that was not transferred to a more durable store before the decay of iconic memory would be lost.

BEYOND ICONIC MEMORY: EARLY STUDIES OF VSTM

In the early 1970s, researchers began to probe visual memory beyond the temporal limits of the immediate iconic trace using specially designed tests of visual memory that did not rely on verbal encoding (Cermak, 1971; Phillips, 1974). For example, in a change detection task developed by Phillips (1974), participants were sequentially presented with two checkerboard stimuli at various interstimulus intervals (ISIs), and the task was to detect any change between the two patterns. On 50% of trials, the two stimuli were identical (i.e., no change trials); however, on the remaining trials, one element in the checkerboard matrix changed from white to black, or vice versa (i.e., change trials; see Figure 10.1A). Change detection between patterns presented at very short ISIs (~20 ms) was almost perfect, even for very complex patterns. Presumably, at very short delays, participants could still use the high-resolution iconic trace of the first array to compare against the second array for any change. However, the critical finding was that participants could still detect some changes between the two patterns even when the test stimulus was presented long after the expected duration of iconic memory (i.e., >1 s; see Figure 10.1B). Because this change detection task did not require, or even easily permit, verbal encoding (cf. Sperling, 1960; Averbach & Coriell, 1961), accurate performance at these long delays was attributed a purely visual form of memory that dramatically outlasts the expected duration of iconic memory. This new form of short-term memory was coined *visual short-term memory* (Phillips & Baddeley, 1971).

Phillips (1974) further demonstrated that VSTM is qualitatively different from the previously described iconic memory. In particular, the capacity of VSTM was more limited than that of iconic memory: Performance from 1 s onward

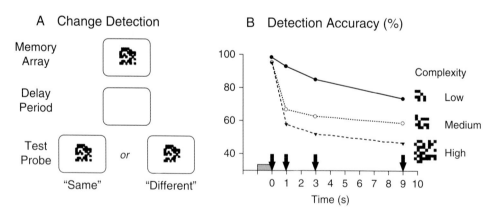

FIGURE 10.1   Change-detection paradigm used to probe the contents of visual short-term memory (VSTM). (**A**) In the task developed by Phillips (1974), each experimental trial begins with a memory stimulus, presented for 1 s. Memory stimuli are randomly arranged patterns of varying complexity. A test probe is then presented after a variable (0.02, 1, 3, or 9 s) delay period. Participants indicate whether the probe stimulus is the same as or different from the memory stimulus. (**B**) Change-detection accuracy is very high if the probe is presented while the iconic trace of the memory array is still available, in this case 20 ms after the offset of the memory stimulus. At longer delays, however, performance rapidly declines, especially for more complex stimuli, revealing a more durable, but capacity-limited, memory store.

critically depended on the visual complexity of the memoranda. Also, in contrast to the rapid decay function characterizing iconic memory, change detection based on VSTM was relatively constant over increasing delays (from 1 to 9 s). Finally, Phillips also found that VSTM representations are position invariant and resistant to interference from pattern masking, unlike the equivalent iconic representations probed at shorter intervals.

Since these seminal studies, VSTM has remained a core topic for cognitive psychology and neuroscience. Although often used synonymously with working memory (WM), it is important to differentiate the two concepts. Originally, VSTM was used to denote relatively stable visual memories that persist after the decay of iconic memory (Phillips, 1974), whereas the concept of WM was developed to encompass short-term memory stores and the executive mechanisms that operate upon these (Baddeley & Hitch, 1974). These definitions clearly overlap and, correspondingly, the terms are often used interchangeably, with WM sometimes further narrowed to visual WM (VWM). However, for clarity, we will respect and maintain the conceptual distinction between VSTM and WM. We use VSTM to denote stable visual representations that persist beyond the original visual input and its associated iconic trace, whereas we treat as distinct the mechanisms, such as attention, that operate upon VSTM representations.

NEURAL BASIS OF VSTM: PREFRONTAL AND PARIETAL DELAY ACTIVITY

The lateral prefrontal cortex has long been associated with short-term memory function (e.g., Goldman-Rakic, 1995). Early studies in the monkey demonstrated that the structural (Butters & Pandya, 1969) and functional (Stamm, 1969) integrity of the prefrontal cortex is necessary for successful maintenance of information over short delays. Subsequently, neurophysiological recordings around the principal sulcus in dorsolateral prefrontal cortex (dlPFC) of the awake, behaving monkey identified an electrophysiological correlate of short-term memory, termed the "memory cell" (Fuster & Alexander, 1971; Kubota &

Niki, 1971). The response profiles of these cells closely matched short-term memory demands of a delayed reaching task, presumably reflecting maintenance of the appropriate motor command throughout an experimentally imposed delay period.

Subsequent studies developed variants of the change detection task to explore the cellular basis of short-term maintenance of *visual* information. For example, Miller and colleagues (1996) identified neurons within the prefrontal cortex that responded selectively to visual memoranda with an elevated firing rate that persists throughout a memory delay period. Moreover, stimulus-specific delay activity in prefrontal cortex is durable against distraction; presenting additional nontarget visual stimuli during the delay period did not disrupt prefrontal delay activity (Miller et al., 1996). Similarly, in the human prefrontal cortex delay activity corresponds closely to VSTM demands (for reviews, see Curtis & D'Esposito, 2003; Passingham & Sakai, 2004).

Prefrontal delay activity thus provides a plausible neural substrate for a short-term memory system that is not only durable across time, but also across distraction (Miller et al., 1996; Sakai et al., 2002). Some subregions of prefrontal cortex may be specialized for specific types of memoranda. For example, the frontal eye field (FEF) appears to be especially important for encoding spatial coordinates of remembered items (Kastner et al., 2007). However, functional specialization is less clear within the dlPFC. Neural populations distributed in and around the principal sulcus of the monkey that encode the critical information during the maintenance period do not necessarily represent the intrinsic physical characteristics of the stimulus (Freedman et al., 2001, 2002). Rather, delay activity in dlPFC appears to encode the task-relevant information across a flexibly assigned subpopulation of prefrontal neurons (Duncan, 2001).

Neurons with strikingly similar delay-response properties have also been identified in the parietal cortex. To compare parietal and prefrontal contributions to short-term memory directly, Chafee and Goldman-Rakic (1998) recorded from neurons in the lateral bank of the intraparietal sulcus and principal sulcus during the delay period of a memory-guided saccade task. Remarkably, they found that the response properties of parietal neurons were almost indistinguishable from prefrontal neurons: in both cases, delay activity was consistent with mnemonic maintenance of remembered spatial locations (Chafee & Goldman-Rakic, 1998). In human parietal cortex, delay activity also appears to reflect capacity limits associated with VSTM. For example, a sustained electrophysiological signature of VSTM maintenance, whose source is thought to include parietal cortex, increases with increasing number of items stored in VSTM (variously referred to as contralateral delay activity [CDA; Vogel & Machizawa, 2004] or sustained posterior contralateral negativity [Jolicoeur et al., 2008]). Similarly, studies using functional magnetic-resonance imaging (fMRI) have identified neural activity in parietal cortex that also scales with the number of items that can be successfully maintained (e.g., Todd & Marois, 2004). Finally, similar to prefrontal cortex, mnemonic coding in parietal cortex is also flexibly tuned to the task demands. Recording from the monkey intraparietal sulcus, Freedman and Assad (2006, 2009) found that activity during the delay period represents memoranda according to task-relevant feature space, rather than stimulus-driven visual attributes.

NEURAL BASIS OF VSTM: PERSISTENT VISUAL ACTIVITY

Memory-related delay activity is also observed in visual cortex (for review, see Pasternak & Greenlee, 2005). However, in contrast to mnemonic coding in higher-level prefrontal and parietal cortex, delay activity in visual cortex engages content-specific visual representations, thus furnishing the perceptual contents of VSTM.

The earliest evidence for VSTM encoding in visual cortex was observed in the inferior temporal cortex of the monkey (Fuster & Jervey, 1981; Miyashita & Chang, 1988). Initially, Fuster and Jervey (1981) identified persistent activity corresponding to the color of an item that was being maintained in VSTM. Subsequently, Miyashita and Chang (1988) used more complex visual stimuli to identify delay activity in inferior temporal cortex that also codes the shape of items

maintained in VSTM. Unlike delay activity in dlPFC, however, maintenance in temporal cortex is susceptible to interference (Miller et al., 1993). Intervening stimuli disrupt persistent activation in temporal cortex, suggesting that higher-level brain areas, such as prefrontal cortex, constitute a crucial store for distractor-resistant VSTM. Moreover, mnemonic coding in ventral visual cortex also corresponds more closely to the perceptual features of the memoranda than the equivalent prefrontal (Freedman et al., 2001, 2002, 2003; Meyers et al., 2008) or parietal codes (Freedman et al., 2006; Freedman & Assad, 2009).

Persistent perceptual activity is also observed in human visual cortex (e.g., Awh et al., 1999; Pessoa et al., 2002; Xu & Chun, 2006; Sligte et al., 2009). In V4, for example, persistent activity is observed within patches of visual cortex that represent the spatial location of items that are maintained within VSTM (Sligte et al., 2009). Persistent activity has also been observed in visual areas as early as V1 (Awh et al., 1999; Pessoa et al., 2002; Postle et al., 2004). Using multivoxel pattern analysis, Harrison and Tong (2009) found that the pattern of neural activity significantly resembled the neural patterns elicited by direct sensory stimulation (see also Ester et al., 2009; Serences et al., 2009). In some cases, stimulus-specific delay activity could reflect attentional preparation for the probe stimulus (Desimone & Duncan, 1995; Offen et al., 2009; Lepsien et al., 2011; Stokes, 2011). It is now well established that top-down mechanisms preactivate retinotopically specific visual areas during preparatory spatial attention (Luck et al., 1997; Kastner et al., 1999; Ress et al., 2000), and nonspatial attention also activates perceptual representations in preparation for an attention-demanding target stimulus (Chelazzi et al., 1998; Stokes et al., 2009b). However, very similar effects are also observed during visual imagery (e.g., Slotnick et al., 2005; Stokes et al., 2009a), demonstrating that, under some circumstances at least, top-down mechanisms can activate perceptual templates in early visual cortex, even in the absence of any subsequent attention-demanding perceptual task.

In addition to sustained firing rates, oscillatory brain activity is also modulated during short-term memory delays (Duzel et al., 2010). For example, oscillations in the high-frequency γ-band increase with increasing memory load (Howard et al., 2003). Interestingly, recent findings also suggest that memory-related γ oscillations are phase-locked to low-frequency θ oscillations (Lee et al., 2005; Sauseng et al., 2009; Siegel et al., 2009). Computationally, phase-encoding could help differentiate distinct items in VSTM (Lisman & Idiart, 1995) and, in general, widespread entrainment to the θ rhythm could facilitate communication across a distributed cortical network (Canolty et al., 2006), which would be particularly important for robust maintenance of coherent, feature-integrated, representations in VSTM (Duzel et al., 2010).

RELATIONSHIP BETWEEN VSTM AND PERCEPTION

Evidence for persistent activation of perceptual representations has contributed to the idea that VSTM can be thought of as a special case of perception without direct, or continuing, sensory stimulation (e.g., Harrison & Tong, 2009). However, considering the subjective phenomenology of VSTM, there is clearly no confusion between perceptual and mnemonic representations, presumably owing to important neural differences.

At first glance, it may seem intuitive to suppose that quantitative differences in visual activity differentiate perception and VSTM. According to this argument, relatively weak, or subthreshold, activation of a perceptual template could maintain visual information without eliciting the usual experience that accompanies visual perception during direct sensory stimulation of the same neural population. Recent empirical work provides some support for this view. Harrison and Tong (2009) found that the neural patterns associated with VSTM maintenance closely match the patterns of activity that were elicited by a corresponding stimulus presented at low contrast and outside the focus of attention.

Although intuitive, a subthreshold perceptual account is likely to be oversimplified. At a functional level, weak activation of a perceptual template may not be sufficient for robust maintenance of task-relevant perceptual information. Instead, stable

VSTM might be stored more reliably if maintained by strong activity, but distributed across a subset of the neuronal population that codes the corresponding percept. When observed at the macro scale of fMRI, such a sparse representation might resemble a weak form of perception, despite qualitative differences at the level of individual coding units. Supporting evidence for a sparsified perceptual code associated with VSTM maintenance, a recent neurophysiological study found that only a subset of neurons encoding a specific item during direct stimulation remained active during a memory delay (Woloszyn & Sheinberg, 2009). Moreover, examining the population-coding properties of individually recorded visual neurons, Meyers and colleagues found that VSTM representation in inferior temporal cortex becomes gradually sparser throughout the delay period (Meyers et al., 2008).

Although the precise instantiation of VSTM in visual cortex is likely to differ from perception, important similarities imply that similar mechanisms may operate on both types of representation. In particular, the mechanisms of attention that shape perceptual processing also strongly influence VSTM representations in visual cortex. Below, we consider how the principles of competition and top-down bias influence VSTM representations.

COMPETITIVE INTERACTIONS AND CAPACITY LIMITS

Perceptual processing is inherently competitive. As sensory stimulation triggers activity along the processing pathway, preferential activation of neurons that are tuned to the specific attributes of the driving stimulus inhibits neighboring neurons that are tuned to other sensory attributes. Consequently, when more than one attribute is presented simultaneously, the balance between excitation and inhibition generates a competitive environment in which only the most active neuronal ensembles survive. Winner-take-all dynamics exert an important selective pressure, which may account for most, if not all, stimulus-driven mechanisms of attentional control (Itti & Koch, 2001). Insofar as VSTM also depends on activity in visual cortex, similar competitive mechanisms are likely to operate between items stored in

VSTM, effectively limiting the amount of visual information that can be stored simultaneously (Edin et al., 2009).

Capacity limitation is one of the defining features of VSTM: Even from the earliest studies of VSTM, it was evident that people can only maintain a limited amount of visual information (Phillips, 1974). Initially, these capacity limits were considered with respect to complexity (Phillips, 1974) or precision (Palmer, 1990); however more recent research has focused on the *number* of individual items that can be maintained in VSTM (Cowan, 2001). For example, testing VSTM for simple features, such as color or shape, indicates that change detection accuracy decreases rapidly when more than about four items are presented (e.g., Luck & Vogel, 1997; Vogel et al., 2001). Although this limit might represent an upper bound for VSTM capacity measured using change detection paradigms for simple, and highly discriminable, visual features, the effective storage capacity of VSTM can be much lower depending on the precision (Palmer, 1990; Bays & Husain, 2008), similarity (Olsson & Poom, 2005), and/or complexity (Phillips, 1974; Alvarez & Cavanagh, 2004) of the memory items. Whether VSTM capacity can exceed a fixed upper limit remains a matter of debate (Bays & Husain, 2008, 2009; Cowan & Rouder, 2009), but again the absolute number of items that can be recalled probably also depends on how VSTM is measured.

Interestingly, behavioral evidence suggests that VSTM capacity limits may be specific to feature dimensions (Magnussen et al., 1996; Luck & Vogel, 1997; Vogel et al., 2001; Xu, 2002). Feature-specific limits could reflect local competitive dynamics that determine the representational capacity of feature-specialized functional modules of the visual system. Increasing the number of features within a specific physical dimension (e.g., color) reduces the number of coding units available for each representation, thereby reducing the overall precision with which each feature can be stored (Palmer, 1990; Wilken & Ma, 2004; Bays & Husain, 2008). However, by the same token, it would seem inefficient to continue subdividing the neural allocation ad infinitum. Presumably, at some point, the representations would become too coarse to guide behavior effectively. The balance

between number and resolution of items in VSTM could be determined by similar competitive dynamics that shape perception. For example, suppressive interactions between competing items could reduce the overall number of items stored in VSTM, with the benefit of increasing the potential coding resource available to each surviving item (Edin et al., 2009).

TOP-DOWN CONTROL OVER ACCESS TO VSTM

As a direct consequence of capacity limitation in VSTM, access to VSTM must be selective. So far, we have discussed the competitive mechanisms that influence the amount of information that can be stored in VSTM. In this section, we consider how mechanisms of attention bias competition for VSTM to favor the selective maintenance of the most behaviourally relevant visual input.

Clues From Partial Report

In the classic partial-report experiments described above (Sperling, 1960; see also Averbach & Coriell, 1961), recall performance was almost perfect when participants were explicitly cued to report only four letters at a specific spatial location. This partial-report advantage implies that participants could flexibly select a subset of information from the high-resolution visual iconic trace to encode into VSTM. In these original partial-report studies, the selection cue was presented after the offset of the memory array. Consequently, the instruction needs to be processed, and the selection rule implemented, before iconic memory has decayed. The rapid decay function of iconic memory, therefore, effectively limits the flexibility of cued selection during iconic memory to relatively simple perceptual features (Coltheart, 1980).

In subsequent partial-report experiments (e.g., Duncan, 1983; Bundesen et al., 1984), the instruction for selection was established at the beginning of an experimental block, and therefore, the selection rule could be applied before or during perceptual analysis of the memory array. Under these less restrictive cueing conditions, participants could flexibly select items to encode into VSTM according to a broad range of features, including location, brightness, color, shape, and alphanumeric class (Bundesen et al., 1984). Importantly, the partial-report experiments conducted by Duncan (1980, 1983) and Bundesen, Pedersen, and Larsen (1984) also varied the number of target and nontarget stimuli to disentangle the relative contribution of selection and storage capacity to overall recall performance. Essentially, recall in the absence of distractors (full report) reflects storage capacity, whereas performance as a function of the number of distractors (partial report) reflects the efficiency of selection (Bundesen, 1990; Duncan et al., 1999; Peers et al., 2005). Combining these two parameters captures the real-world challenge of selection for a limited-capacity system, as task-relevant information almost always occurs within the broader context of task-irrelevant sensory input. The hypothesis that effective capacity is limited as much by efficient selection as underlying storage capacity is further supported by evidence from individual-differences studies that demonstrate a close relationship between efficiency of selective attention and measures of short-term memory (Kane et al., 2001; Engle, 2002).

Despite important differences between verbal partial-report experiments (e.g., Duncan, 1983; Bundesen et al., 1984) and more typical VSTM paradigms (e.g., Phillips, 1974; Vogel et al., 2001), the recall limit they measured was still probably determined by VSTM capacity (Bundesen et al., 1984; Bundesen, 1990). Moreover, subsequent studies have confirmed that similar capacity limits, and top-down attentional influences, apply to short-term memory paradigms using nonletter stimuli. For example, Palmer (1988, 1990) used a change-detection paradigm to measure VSTM independently of verbal encoding contributions. A partial-report cue presented before the memory array (or immediately afterward, i.e., during iconic memory in Palmer, 1988) dramatically increased discrimination sensitivity for cued items. These results are consistent with the evidence from previous partial-report experiments that top-down control mechanisms can bias access to VSTM. Similar results have also been observed for probabilistic precueing, in which attentional cues indicate which item is most likely to be probed (Palmer, 1990; Schmidt et al., 2002; Griffin & Nobre, 2003).

The extant evidence from brain imaging suggests that attentional mechanisms that bias access to VSTM share a similar neural substrate to the processes of attention that optimize visual analysis. Preparatory attention is associated with top-down feedback from prefrontal and parietal brain areas (Kastner & Ungerleider, 2000; Nobre, 2001) to preactivate task-relevant representations in visual cortex (Desimone & Duncan, 1995), which in turn bias competition in favor of behaviourally relevant visual input. Similarly, VSTM encoding cues also trigger mechanisms of preparatory attention (Nobre et al., 2004; Ruff et al., 2007). For example, evidence from fMRI demonstrates that spatially specific partial-report cues activate a similar network of frontal and parietal brain areas that is typically engaged during top-down control of spatial attention for perception (Nobre et al., 2004), including intraparietal sulcus and FEF (see also Ruff et al., 2007). Similarly, neural indices of attentional preparation predict the efficiency of selective VSTM encoding (Murray, Nobre & Stokes, 2011; McNab & Klingberg, 2008). Finally, attentional modulation of the neural response to cued vs. uncued memory items also predicts memory performance (Rutman, Clapp, Chadick & Gazzaley, 2010; Zanto, Rubens, Thangavel & Gazzaley, 2011; for a review, see Gazzaley, 2011).

TOP-DOWN CONTROL WITHIN VSTM

As reviewed above, selection cues presented either before (precue), or just after (iconic-cue) a memory array bias access to VSTM. Adopting a winner(s)-take-all competitive framework (e.g., Bundesen, 1990), attention may be viewed as a mechanism that determines the subset of perceptual information that will be represented within capacity-limited VSTM. These representations can then be used directly to guide behaviour (Bundesen, 1990; Desimone & Duncan, 1995) or maintained in VSTM for use at a later time period. In the latter case, in which the behavioral response can only be made after a delay period, competitive dynamics are likely to persist, and to continue to influence the nature of the representations in VSTM. For example, continued suppression of items with relative low competitive strength could reduce the overall number of distinct items in VSTM (Zhang & Luck, 2009) and/or the quality of their representation (Bays et al., 2009). Attention, therefore, could provide an important mechanism for biasing these continued competitive mechanisms in favor of a specific item represented in VSTM (reviewed in Lepsien & Nobre, 2006).

Partial Report Revisited

To examine attentional dynamics within VSTM, Griffin and Nobre (2003) developed a cueing paradigm that directly compares spatial orienting to perceptual and VSTM representations (see Figure 10.2A). On one half of trials, a spatial precue was presented prior to the memory array.

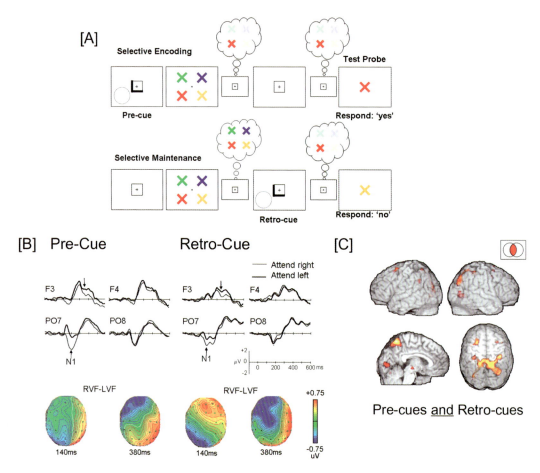

FIGURE 10.2   Retrocueing paradigm used to manipulate attentional selection during visual short-term memory (VSTM) maintenance. (**A**) As in a typical VSTM paradigm, participants are presented with a memory array, then a test probe after a delay period. In Griffin and Nobre (2003), participants then decide whether the probe matches the cued item. Selective attention was manipulated either prior to the presentation of the memory array (precue condition, *upper panel*), or during the delay period (retrocue condition, *lower panel*). (**B**) Both cue types elicited similar event-related potentials. These included spatially specific responses in posterior (early: 120–160 ms) and anterior (late: 360–400 ms) electrodes. (**C**) Results from functional magnetic-resonance imaging (fMRI) also demonstrated similar activations across retrocueing and precueing in prefrontal and parietal cortex. [Adapted from Griffin, I. C., & Nobre, A. C. (2003). Orienting attention to locations in internal representations. *Journal of Cognitive Neuroscience, 15,* 1176–1194; and Nobre, A. C., Coull, J. T., Maquet, P., Frith, C. D., Vandenberghe, R., & Mesulam, M. M. (2004). Orienting attention to locations in perceptual versus mental representations. *Journal of Cognitive Neuroscience, 16,* 363–373, with permission of the publishers].

As in many previous partial-report experiments (e.g., Bundesen et al., 1984), these precues could be used to select which items to encode from the subsequent memory array. In line with the well-established influences of attention for VSTM access reviewed above, the predictive information carried by these precues facilitated recall for cued relative to uncued items. Critically, on the other half of trials an equivalent spatial cue was presented seconds after the offset of memory array. Again, as for precue trials, these cues could be used to predict which item from the memory array would be probed at the end of the trial, but this predictive information was only available *after* the presentation of the memory array and after dissipation of the accompanying iconic trace. At this delay, spatial predictions cannot be used to bias initial processing of the visual stimulus for selective access to VSTM (as in Rutman, Clapp, Chadick & Gazzaley, 2010), but rather retrodictive cues (retrocues) can only influence information that is already being maintained in VSTM.

Despite the profound differences in the demands associated with pre- and retrocueing, the pattern of performance observed by Griffin and Nobre (2003) was almost identical for both types of spatial cue. Behavioral responses were faster and more accurate when memory was probed for cued relative to uncued items, irrespective of whether the predictive information was made available before or after the memory array (for related results, see Landman et al., 2003). Moreover, comparison to neutral trials further confirmed that the observed validity effect was due to a relative enhancement for cued items (validity benefit), as well as a performance decrement for the noncued items (invalidity cost).

Griffin and Nobre (2003) also recorded event-related potentials associated with precues and retrocues. Both cue types elicited a similar pattern of spatially specific potentials, initially over posterior electrodes (between 120 and 160 ms) and later over anterior electrodes (between 360 and 400 ms; see Figure 10.2B). These similar activation profiles accord with the striking behavioral overlap observed between attentional control for external events and internal representations maintained within VSTM. However, in addition to these similarities, retrocues also triggered an enhanced early response distributed across frontal scalp regions. Therefore, along with common mechanisms, additional neural processes may be required to generate attentional biases when predictive information is provided only after the offset of the initial memory array (i.e., during VSTM maintenance).

In a follow-up fMRI experiment, Nobre et al. (2004) also compared the neural systems underlying attentional control for perception and internal representations maintained within VSTM. Both precues and retrocues engaged a large network of brain areas, spanning prefrontal and parietal cortices. In particular, parietal activity that was common to spatial orienting for perceptual and VSTM representations included precuneus, superior parietal lobule, and intraparietal sulcus (Figure 10.2C). In the frontal cortex, activation in the FEF and more inferiorly in the lateral premotor cortex was also common to both predictive and retrodictive orienting. These areas of common activation correspond closely with similar patterns of brain activity observed in previous studies of visual spatial orienting (Kastner & Ungerleider, 2000; Nobre, 2001), consistent with the overlap in behavioral consequences and electroencephalogram (EEG) activity associated with pre- and retrocueing (Griffin & Nobre, 2003). Lepsien, Griffin, Devlin, and Nobre (2005) extended these results to show that the activation of this attentional network via retrocueing depends on the number of items held within VSTM. Moreover, Lepsien and Nobre (2007) further demonstrated that nonspatial retrocues also activate key nodes of the prefrontal and parietal network implicated in spatial retrocueing, including the interparietal sulcus, superior parietal lobule, precuneus, inferior frontal sulcus, and cingulate (Lepsien & Nobre, 2007; see also Lepsien, Thornton and Nobre, 2011).

In summary, EEG and fMRI studies demonstrate a striking overlap between activation profiles associated with pre- and retrocues. The extensive neuroanatomical overlap complements highly comparable behavioral effects, and is consistent with the general hypothesis that spatial orienting in both the perceptual and VSTM share common neural structures.

Facilitating Memory Retrieval

Initial retrocueing experiments demonstrate that predictive spatial information directed to VSTM representations facilitates retrieval for task-relevant information (Griffin & Nobre, 2003; Landman et al., 2003; Nobre et al., 2004). Moreover, brain-imaging studies provide strong evidence for a common control mechanism mediating attention to perception and VSTM representations: both precues and retrocues activate frontal and parietal brain regions that have been extensively implicated in spatial orienting of attention (Kastner & Ungerleider, 2000; Nobre, 2001; Corbetta & Shulman, 2002). To explore more directly the locus of this retrocueing advantage, Nobre, Griffin, and Rao (2007) specifically measured the neural consequences of retrocueing. Again, participants were directed to attend to a specific item long (>1 s) after the offset of the memory array (Figure 10.3A); however, in this experiment, Nobre et al. (2007) focused on activity associated with retrieval from VSTM. Moreover, by manipulating set size (one, two, or four items) as well as retrocue validity (valid vs. neutral), they were also able to tease apart the relationship between retrocueing dynamics and memory demands.

Considering behaviour on neutral trials first, performance varied with set size: Response times increased and accuracy decreased systematically with increasing set sizes (Figure 10.3B). Reduced recall accuracy is consistent with the well-established capacity limit of VSTM (e.g., Luck & Vogel, 1997). On the other hand, increasing response latencies for larger set sizes demonstrates that the efficiency of retrieval depends on the number of items being maintained, consistent with an exhaustive serial search through the contents of VSTM (Sternberg, 1966). Moreover, analysis of the evoked neural response to probe stimuli on neutral trials revealed an electrophysiological marker of retroactive search, termed the $N3_{RS}$ (RS: retro-search; Figure 10.3C). As with behaviour, this negativity scales with demand during retro-search, increasing in magnitude with increasing set sizes (see also Kuo et al., 2009). The $N3_{RS}$ further demonstrates that the efficiency of retroactive search depends on the number of items stored within VSTM. Importantly, retrocues

dramatically reduced the search cost associated with increasing number of items in VSTM. Behaviourally, retrocues reduced the reaction-time and accuracy costs associated with memory load (see also Lepsien et al., 2005) and, neurally, retrodictive cueing effectively abolished the neurophysiological marker of retro-search, $N3_{RS}$. These results demonstrate that retrieval from VSTM does not necessarily proceed in an automatic serial search, but can be influenced flexibly according top-down attentional guidance.

Biasing Mnemonic Representations

As reviewed above, convergent evidence suggests that persistent activation of perceptual representations in visual cortex may provide the perceptual characteristics of VSTM (Pasternak & Greenlee, 2005). If similar principles of competition apply to visual activity underlying perception and VSTM, perhaps competitive dynamics within VSTM can be biased via top-down control mechanisms according to similar principles that govern attentional modulation of perceptual representations. According to this hypothesis, attentional cues presented during the maintenance period (i.e., retrocues) modulate VSTM representations, granting a competitive advantage for task-relevant information and ultimately increasing the probability that a stable representation will last until the memory probe.

Lepsien and Nobre (2007) directly tested this prediction. They used fMRI to determine how retrospectively directed attention influences the delay activity in posterior fusiform gyrus (FG) and parahippocampal gyrus (PHG) involved in VSTM maintenance for faces and scenes, respectively. Each experimental trial commenced with two memory items, one face and one scene sequentially presented in a randomized order. After a 4–9.5 second delay, an initial retrocue directed participants to attend to either the face or scene stimulus, then almost 5 seconds later another retrocue directed participants either to reorient to the previously uncued item (switch trials), or to keep attention focused on the initially cued item (stay trials; see Figure 10.4A).

After the presentation of the first retrocue, activity increased within the PHG when attention

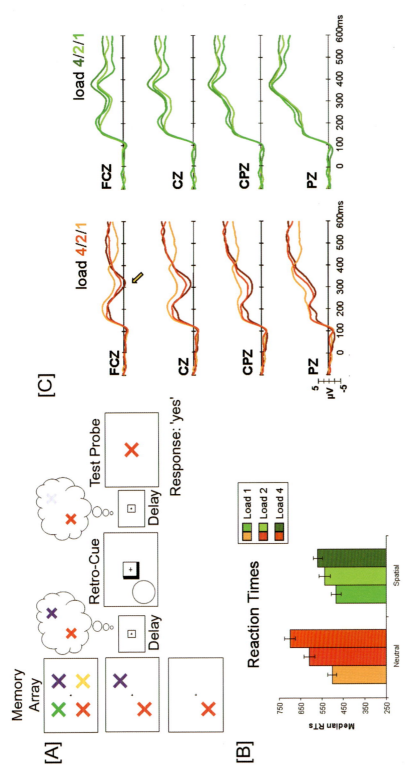

FIGURE 10.3   Retrocueing facilitates retrieval of information from visual short-term memory (VSTM). (**A**) In Nobre et al. (2008), participants were cued retrospectively to attend to the location of an item in VSTM, and memory load was manipulated (one, two, or four items). (**B**) First, in the absence of a retrocue (neutral condition), increasing memory load was associated with a performance decrement. Retrocueing significantly reduced this behavioral cost. (**C**) Increasing search demands were also reflected in an electrophysiological marker of retroactive search, termed N3$_{RS}$ (RS: retro-search), which was abolished by retrocueing. [Adapted from Nobre et al., 2008]

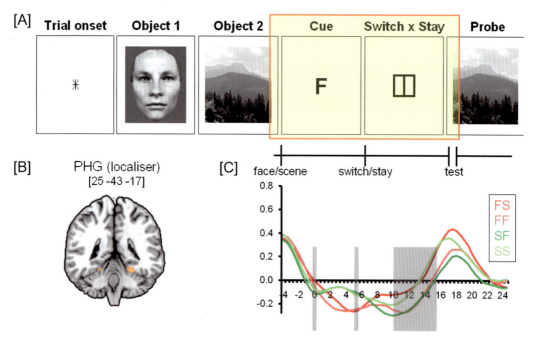

FIGURE 10.4 Retrocueing modulates maintenance activity in visual cortex. (**A**) In Lepsien and Nobre (2007), each trial commenced with a pair of memory items, comprising one image of a face and one image of a scene. After a long and variable delay, participants were then cued to attend to either the face or scene. After another delay, participants were then further cued to switch the focus of attention to the other item or to stay focused on the initially cued item. Finally, a test stimulus was presented to probe the contents of visual short-term memory (VSTM) at the end of the trial. (**B**) Localizer tasks were used to identify visual areas that responded preferentially to scene (parahippocampal gyrus, shown) or face (posterior fusiform gyrus) stimuli. (**C**) Results from functional magnetic resonance imaging (fMRI) showed attention-specific modulation of maintenance-related activity in these specialized areas. Time course of activation is shown for the parahippocampal region. [Adapted from Lepsien, J., & Nobre, A. C. (2007). Attentional modulation of object representations in working memory. *Cerebral Cortex, 17*, 2072–2083, with permission of the publisher].

was directed to the scene item held in VSTM, and conversely, right FG activity increased when the first retrocue directed attention to the face item being maintained (see Figure 10.4B, C). Interestingly, Lepsien and Nobre (2007) also found that reorienting could reverse the effect of the first retrocue. Irrespective of the instruction provided by the initial retrocue, the second retrocue also elicited content-specific activation: When attention was re-directed from scene (or face) to face (or scene) memoranda, activation biases also switched from PHG (or FG) to FG (or to PHG).

These results suggest that attentional cueing during VSTM maintenance directly modulates the delay activity that underlies the mnemonic code (see also Kuo, Stokes and Nobre, 2011). Moreover, the double-cue manipulation further highlights the flexibility of attentional orienting in VSTM: Attention can be reoriented to previously uncued items. The neural and behavioral evidence for reorienting within VSTM implies that the attentional bias established by the initial retrocue in Lepsien and Nobre (2007) did not completely suppress the persistent activity relating to the uncued item. Similarly, Landman et al. (2003) found that participants could use double retrocues to reorient spatially to previously uncued items, again highlighting the flexibility of top-down control within VSTM.[1]

As in sensory analysis, therefore, the principles of biased competition seem to apply to representations in VSTM. Accordingly, retrocueing provides top-down feedback to bias competition within VSTM, thereby establishing a competitive advantage for the most behaviourally relevant mnemonic information. Retrocueing evidence also demonstrates that representations in VSTM are not all-or-none, as implied by winner(s)-take-all models of VSTM (e.g., Bundesen, 1990). So, the question arises: Are all "winners" equally likely to remain in a stable activation state until the end of the delay period? Evidence from retrocueing indicates that top-down biases exerted during VSTM maintenance strongly influence whether neural ensembles coding for a particular item in VSTM will remain active until the end of a delay period. Adopting a more dynamic approach to competition within VSTM, therefore, winners can only be declared at the endpoint, that is, when VSTM is finally used to guide behaviour. Until then, competitive dynamics continue to influence VSTM representations, and top-down mechanisms remain important for biasing competition in favor of task relevant information.

Going Beyond Traditional Estimates of VSTM Capacity

Retrocueing studies demonstrate that attention can selectively modulate delay activity, biasing VSTM representation in favor of task-relevant information (Lepsien & Nobre, 2007). Strikingly, retrocueing can also increase the probability of recall beyond the traditional estimates of the capacity limits of VSTM (Landman et al., 2003; Sligte et al., 2008, 2009). For example, Sligte et al. (2008) found that even when participants are presented with 32 memory items, the probability of accurate recall after retrocueing is still remarkably high, at around 50%. Using the standard logic of partial report, 50% probability of recall implies a memory capacity of 16, well beyond traditional estimates of approximately four items (e.g., Cowan, 2001). The exceptional performance observed by Sligte et al. (2008) could not be attributed to residual high-capacity iconic memory. As in previous retrocueing experiments, the retrodictive spatial information was presented long after the decay of iconic memory. Moreover, Sligte et al. (2008) also functionally dissociated this high-capacity

VSTM from iconic memory. They found that iconic memory depends on visual after images, whereas performance after retrocueing did not vary with the strength of afterimages.

Functional characteristics may also differentiate memory representations underlying retrocued recall from performance normally associated with VSTM test probes. High-capacity recall associated with retrocueing is sensitive to interference from visual pattern masking (Makovski et al., 2006; Sligte et al., 2008), as well as the overall duration of the retention interval (Sligte et al., 2008). However, in the absence of a retrocue, memory performance, although much lower, is more robust to delay (Sligte et al., 2008) and visual interference (Makovski et al., 2006; Sligte et al., 2008).

To account for these results, Lamme, Sligte, and colleagues (Landman et al., 2003; Sligte et al., 2008, 2009) differentiate two forms of VSTM: weak and strong. Weak and strong VSTM representations are directly associated with corresponding gradations of neural activation levels in visual cortex (see also Sligte et al., 2009). According to their analysis, strong VSTM can only encode about four items, but within this capacity limit, representations are relatively stable across long delays and robust to interference from subsequent visual input. Weak VSTM, on the other hand, can encode many more items than strong VSTM, but is vulnerable to decay (~4 s) and interference. Importantly, this vulnerability presents a practical challenge for experimental measurement. Somewhat analogously to the observer effect that motivated Heisenburg's uncertainly principle, the probe used to measure VSTM necessarily interferes with weak VSTM, thereby changing the very nature of the representation before it can be observed. Consequently, standard change-detection tasks (e.g., Luck & Vogel, 1997) can only measure strong VSTM. Retrocueing, however, provides a practical solution to an apparent catch-22. Directing attention to a specific item *prior* to the presentation of the probe can selectively bias unstable representations in weak VSTM, leading to a more robust neural representation that can resist probe-related interference (i.e., strong VSTM).

In this chapter, we have reviewed evidence that VSTM is shaped by attentional principles of competition and top-down bias. Elsewhere, others have argued that VSTM is maintained by focusing attention on specific perceptual representations (e.g., Awh et al., 1999; Cowan, 2001). Although the evidence reviewed here clearly demonstrates that attention is important for optimizing VSTM, the data do not necessarily imply that without top-down attention, nothing is maintained. Indeed, evidence from retrocueing suggests that even unattended stimuli can be maintained within VSTM, albeit in a less stable form. When a retrocue directs attention to a specific item in VSTM, the underlying neural representation is enhanced, resulting in a more robust memory trace that is more durable across time and distraction. Within this framework, attention increases the likelihood that a specific stimulus will be maintained for long enough to guide behaviour.

FURTHER ISSUES

Neural activity observed during the delay period of a VSTM task is typically interpreted as evidence for mnemonic maintenance. However, in many respects, delay activity also closely resembles prestimulus activity associated with *preparatory* attention. Similar to VSTM delay activity, preparatory attention activates specific neurons in visual cortex that encode the relevant spatial (Luck et al., 1997; Kastner et al., 1999) or nonspatial visual features (Chelazzi et al., 1998; Stokes et al., 2009b). Generally, preparatory attention is associated with difficult perceptual tasks, whereas probe items used in VSTM tasks are not usually perceptually demanding. Nevertheless, in many short-term memory tasks, probe stimuli are presented in the context of task-irrelevant distractor items (e.g., Chelazzi et al., 1998; Vogel & Machizawa, 2004; Sauseng et al., 2009) that may compete with the probe item. In these cases, preparatory biases toward the target attribute would benefit performance (Desimone & Duncan, 1995). Moreover, simply expecting a task-relevant probe item might also elicit preparatory attention, even if not strictly necessary for processing the probe stimulus (Lepsien, Thornton, & Nobre, 2011). These considerations raise the possibility that some of the neural indices that have been

attributed to VSTM maintenance are instead measures of preparatory attention in anticipation of the probe item (reviewed in Stokes, 2011).

In one recent attempt to disentangle maintenance from attentional preparation in early visual cortex, Offen et al. (2009) found that delay activity increased as the perceptual demands of the probe stimulus increased but not memory demands. However, this study only examined mean increases in visual activity relative to baseline, whereas previous evidence for VSTM maintenance in early visual cortex indicate that the activation *pattern* is more likely to reflect the mnemonic content than the overall mean (Ester et al., 2009; Harrison & Tong, 2009; Serences et al., 2009).

Maintenance and attention can also be disentangled by presenting the memory probe at a different spatial location than the original to-be-remembered stimulus. In this case, mnemonic activity would be expected at the location of the initial stimulus, whereas preparatory activity would emerge at the expected location of the subsequent probe. Recently, Freedman and Assad (2009) used a similar paradigm to explore the spatial specificity of task-dependent category representation in parietal cortex. Although they addressed a conceptually distinct question, their experimental paradigm included a delay period during which information regarding the visual category of a sample stimulus is maintained, and therefore their results were directly relevant to VSTM maintenance. Recording from neurons in monkey parietal cortex during the delay period between a sample stimulus and an exemplar in a delayed category matching task, they found that the majority of cells encoded the remembered perceptual category at the location of the initial stimulation rather than the expected location of the exemplar probe.

In a related study, Lebedev and colleagues (2004) developed a task to disentangle the relative contribution of attention and maintenance in prefrontal cortex. While a specific spatial location was retained in short-term memory, attention was simultaneously directed to another spatial location. Recording from monkey dlPFC, they found that the majority of neurons coded the attended location, whereas only a smaller subset of neurons coded the location stored in memory (Lebedev et al., 2004). These results provide strong evidence that dlPFC encodes task-relevant stimuli in the absence of any memory demand. However, more generally, their results also accord with accumulating evidence that the dlPFC constitutes a flexible coding space that is able to represent diverse aspects of the current behavioral task, including the location of task-relevant stimuli, present or remembered, but also more abstract task-parameters such as the task rules (Wallis et al., 2001) and discrete steps of a mental program (Sigala et al., 2008; Duncan, 2010).

Importantly, information processing in the dlPFC and parietal cortex is relatively protected from the sensory input that constantly bombards lower cortical areas, such as striate and extrastriate visual cortex. Functional insulation from the constant inflow of sensory information is critical for stable representations that can span the length of a trial, and more broadly, behavioral context in general. Context-dependent coding within such a processing environment could guide behaviour according to overall task goals, and/or rules. Stable representations in high-level brain areas that feedback onto neural populations in visual cortex would be ideal for orchestrating brain activity for memory, as well as preparatory states that optimize perception, according to the behavioral context.

In the case of visual attention, top-down feedback modulates baseline firing patterns in visual cortex to optimize activation states to favor sensory input that is relevant to behaviour. Depending on the task, the optimized state could closely match the pattern of neural activity associated with direct stimulation by the attended feature (e.g., Chelazzi et al., 1998), or maximize the difference between the target and distractor items (Navalpakkam & Itti, 2007; Scolari & Serences, 2009). In the case of VSTM, flexible codes in prefrontal and parietal cortex could represent the attended subset of to-be-remembered stimuli, and feedback to perceptual cortex could enhance the corresponding neural code, thereby increasing the likelihood that the most relevant information will be maintained for long enough to guide behaviour. If the behavioral context changes (e.g., retrocueing), coding flexibility in prefrontal and parietal cortex (Duncan, 2001; Miller & Cohen, 2001) would

enable the coding space to update rapidly, and, consequently, a new pattern of feedback connectivity with visual cortex could be established. Within this general framework, the mechanisms for maintaining preparatory attentional states share a fundamental relationship to the neural basis of VSTM maintenance.

Similar principles may also account for some aspects of visual imagery. Visual imagery is self-generative; in the absence of corresponding sensory input, the configuration of visual activity is modulated to resemble activation patterns associated with veridical perception (Kosslyn et al., 2001; see Stokes et al., 2009; 2011). Internal generation of precise patterns of visual activity presents a similar computational problem to establishing a specific attentional state according to an abstract cue, which presumably relies on associative connections that are established by high-level instruction and/or learned during the course of past experience (Summerfield et al., 2006). *Maintaining* a self-generated mental image, however, presents a very similar challenge to maintaining visual information during a VSTM task, and/or maintaining an attentional state in preparation for a difficult perceptual task. Indeed, there may be very little difference between the neural principles underlying maintenance of visual information in general, although the precise instantiation is likely to depend on the specific demands of the task.

CONCLUSION

The evidence to date demonstrates that task goals strongly influence how visual information is encoded and maintained in VSTM. In the first instance, top-down attention shapes the visual information that will be represented in VSTM. In particular, attentional precues bias which stimuli will be encoded in VSTM and subsequently guide behaviour. More recent evidence from retrocueing studies further demonstrates how changing task goals can also be accommodated: Attentional cues presented during VSTM maintenance also bias representations in VSTM to optimize behaviour. The new perspective offered by retrocueing experiments illustrates the dynamic interplay between high-level task goals and the activation states in visual cortex that shape our perception. According to the framework outlined in this chapter (see also Nobre & Stokes, 2011), VSTM does not constitute a fixed perceptual representation that gradually fades over time; rather, VSTM representations can be dynamically modified to accommodate changing behavioral contexts. This degree of flexibility provides an important impetus to reconceptualize VSTM as an integrated neural system that maintains visual information for a variety of purposes, including perceptual comparisons between temporally asynchronous visual inputs, as well as specific patterns of visual activity that underlie sustained preparatory attention or visual imagery.

References

Alvarez, G. A., & Cavanagh, P. (2004). The capacity of visual short-term memory is set both by visual information load and by number of objects. *Psychological Science, 15,* 106–111.

Averbach, E., & Coriell, A. S. (1961). Short-term memory in vision. *Bell System Technical Journal, 40,* 309–328.

Awh, E., Jonides, J., Smith, E. E., Buxton, R. B., Frank, L. R., Love, T., et al. (1999). Rehearsal in spatial working memory: Evidence from neuroimaging. *Psychological Science, 10,* 433–437.

Baddeley, A. D., & Hitch, G. J. (1974). Working memory. *The Psychology of Learning and Motivation, 8,* 47–90.

Bays, P. M., & Husain, M. (2008). Dynamic shifts of limited working memory resources in human vision. *Science, 321,* 851–854.

Bays, P. M, & Husain, M. (2009). Response to comment on "Dynamic shifts of limited working memory resources in human vision." *Science, 323,* 877.

Bays, P. M., Catalao, R. F. G., & Husain, M. (2009). The precision of visual working memory is set by allocation of a shared resource. *Journal of Vision, 9,* 1–11.

Bundesen, C. (1990). A theory of visual attention. *Psychological Review, 97,* 523–547.

Bundesen, C., Pedersen, L. F., & Larsen, A. (1984). Measuring efficiency of selection from briefly exposed visual displays: A model for partial report. *Journal of Experimental Psychology. Human Perception and Performance, 10,* 329–339.

Butters, N., & Pandya, D. (1969). Retention of delayed-alternation: Effect of selective lesions of sulcus principalis. *Science, 165,* 1271–1273.

Canolty, R. T., Edwards, E., Dalal, S. S., Soltani, M., Nagarajan, S. S., Kirsch, H. E., et al. (2006). High gamma power is phase-locked to theta oscillations in human neocortex. *Science, 313,* 1626–1628.

Cermak, G. W. (1971). Short-term recognition memory for complex free-form figures. *Psychonomic Science, 25,* 209–211.

Chafee, M. V., & Goldman-Rakic, P. S. (1998). Matching patterns of activity in primate prefrontal area 8a and parietal area 7ip neurons during a spatial working memory task. *Journal of Neurophysiology, 79,* 2919–2940.

Chelazzi, L., Duncan, J., Miller, E. K., & Desimone, R. (1998). Responses of neurons in inferior temporal cortex during memory-guided visual search. *Journal of Neurophysiology, 80,* 2918–2940.

Coltheart, M. (1980). Iconic memory and visible persistence. *Perception & Psychophysics, 27,* 183–228.

Corbetta, M., & Shulman, G. L. (2002). Control of goal-directed and stimulus-driven attention in the brain. *Nature Reviews. Neuroscience, 3,* 201–215.

Cowan, N. (2001). The magical number 4 in short-term memory: A reconsideration of mental storage capacity. *Behavioral and Brain Sciences, 24,* 87–114.

Cowan, N., & Rouder, J. N. (2009). Comment on "Dynamic shifts of limited working memory resources in human vision." *Science, 323,* 877.

Curtis, C. E., & D'Esposito, M. (2003). Persistent activity in the prefrontal cortex during working memory. *Trends in Cognitive Sciences, 7,* 415–423.

Desimone, R., & Duncan, J. (1995). Neural mechanisms of selective visual attention. *Annual Review of Neuroscience, 18,* 193–222.

Duncan, J. (1983). Perceptual selection based on alphanumeric class: Evidence from partial reports. *Perception & Psychophysics, 33,* 533–547.

Duncan, J. (2001). An adaptive coding model of neural function in prefrontal cortex. *Nature Reviews. Neuroscience, 2,* 820–829.

Duncan, J. (2010). The multiple-demand (MD) system of the primate brain: Mental programs for intelligent behaviour. *Trends in Cognitive Sciences, 14,* 172–179.

Duncan, J., Olson, A., Humphreys, G., Bundesen, C., Chavda, S., & Shibuya, H. (1999). Systematic analysis of deficits in visual attention. *Journal of Experimental Psychology: General, 128,* 450–478.

Duzel, E., Penny, W. D., & Burgess, N. (2010). Brain oscillations and memory. *Current Opinion in Neurobiology, 20,* 143–149.

Edin, F., Klingberg, T., Johansson, P., McNab, F., Tegnér, J., & Compte, A. (2009). Mechanism for top-down control of working memory capacity. *Proceedings of the National Academy of Sciences of the United States of America, 106*, 6802–6807.

Engle, R. W. (2002). Working memory capacity as executive attention. *Current Directions in Psychological Science, 11*, 19–23.

Ester, E. F., Serences, J. T., & Awh, E. (2009). Spatially global representations in human primary visual cortex during working memory maintenance. *Journal of Neuroscience, 29*, 15258–15265.

Freedman, D. J., & Assad, J. A. (2009). Distinct encoding of spatial and nonspatial visual information in parietal cortex. *Journal of Neuroscience, 29*, 5671–5680.

Freedman, D. J., Riesenhuber, M., Poggio, T., & Miller, E. K. (2001). Categorical representation of visual stimuli in the primate prefrontal cortex. *Science, 291*, 312–316.

Freedman, D. J., Riesenhuber, M., Poggio, T., & Miller, E. K. (2002). Visual categorization and the primate prefrontal cortex: Neurophysiology and behavior. *Journal of Neurophysiology, 88*, 929–941.

Freedman, D. J., Riesenhuber, M., Poggio, T., & Miller, E. K. (2003). A comparison of primate prefrontal and inferior temporal cortices during visual categorization. *Journal of Neuroscience, 23*, 5235–5246.

Freedman, D. J., Riesenhuber, M., Poggio, T., & Miller, E. K. (2006). Experience-dependent sharpening of visual shape selectivity in inferior temporal cortex. *Cerebral Cortex, 16*, 1631–1644.

Fuster, J. M., & Alexander, G. E. (1971). Neuron activity related to short-term memory. *Science, 173*, 652–654.

Fuster, J. M., & Jervey, J. P. (1981). Inferotemporal neurons distinguish and retain behaviorally relevant features of visual stimuli. *Science, 212*, 952–955.

Gazzaley, A. (2011). Influence of early attentional modulation on working memory. *Neuropsychologia, 49*(6), 1410–1424. doi: S0028-3932(10)00555-5 [pii]10.1016/j.neuropsychologia.2010.12.022

Goldman-Rakic, P. S. (1995). Cellular basis of working memory. *Neuron, 14*, 477–485.

Griffin, I. C., & Nobre, A. C. (2003). Orienting attention to locations in internal representations. *Journal of Cognitive Neuroscience, 15*, 1176–1194.

Harrison, S. A., & Tong, F. (2009). Decoding reveals the contents of visual working memory in early visual areas. *Nature, 458*, 632–635.

Howard, M. W., Rizzuto, D. S., Caplan, J. B., Madsen, J. R., Lisman, J., Aschenbrenner-Scheibe, R., et al. (2003). Gamma oscillations correlate with working memory load in humans. *Cerebral Cortex, 13*, 1369–1374.

Itti, L., Koch, C. (2001). Computational modelling of visual attention. *Nature Reviews. Neuroscience, 2*, 194–203.

Jolicoeur, P., Brisson, B., & Robitaille, N. (2008). Dissociation of the N2pc and sustained posterior contralateral negativity in a choice response task. *Brain Research, 1215*, 160–172.

Kane, M. J., Conway, A. R. A., Bleckley, M. K., & Engle, R. W. (2001). A controlled-attention view of working-memory capacity. *Journal of Experimental Psychology: General, 130*, 169–183.

Kastner, S., & Ungerleider, L. G. (2000). Mechanisms of visual attention in the human cortex. In *Annual Review of Neuroscience* (pp. 315–341).

Kastner, S., Pinsk, M. A., De Weerd, P., Desimone, R., & Ungerleider, L. G. (1999). Increased activity in human visual cortex during directed attention in the absence of visual stimulation. *Neuron, 22*, 751–761.

Kastner, S., DeSimone, K., Konen, C. S., Szczepanski, S. M., Weiner, K. S., & Schneider, K. A. (2007). Topographic maps in human frontal cortex revealed in memory-guided saccade and spatial working-memory tasks. *Journal of Neurophysiology, 97*, 3494–3507.

Kosslyn, S. M., Ganis, G., & Thompson, W. L. (2001). Neural foundations of imagery. *Nature Reviews. Neuroscience, 2*, 635–642.

Kubota, K., & Niki, H. (1971). Prefrontal cortical unit activity and delayed alternation performance in monkeys. *Journal of Neurophysiology, 34*, 337–347.

Kuo, B. C., Rao, A., Lepsien, J., & Nobre, A. C. (2009). Searching for targets within the spatial layout of visual short-term memory. *Journal of Neuroscience, 29*, 8032–8038.

Kuo, B. -C., Stokes, M., & Nobre, A. C. (in press). Attention modulates maintenance of representations in visual short-term memory. *Journal of Cognitive Neuroscience.*

Landman, R., Spekreijse, H., & Lamme, V. A. F. (2003). Large capacity storage of integrated objects before change blindness. *Vision Research, 43*, 149–164.

Lebedev, M. A., Messinger, A., Kralik, J. D., & Wise, S. P. (2004). Representation of attended versus remembered locations in prefrontal cortex. *PLoS Biology, 2*, 1919–1935.

Lee, H., Simpson, G. V., Logothetis, N. K., & Rainer, G. (2005). Phase locking of single neuron activity to theta oscillations during working memory in monkey extrastriate visual cortex. *Neuron, 45*, 147–156.

Lepsien, J., & Nobre, A. C. (2006). Cognitive control of attention in the human brain: Insights from orienting attention to mental representations. *Brain Research, 1105*, 20–31.

Lepsien, J., & Nobre, A. C. (2007). Attentional modulation of object representations in working memory. *Cerebral Cortex, 17*, 2072–2083.

Lepsien, J., Griffin, I. C., Devlin, J. T., & Nobre. A. C. (2005). Directing spatial attention in mental representations: Interactions between attentional orienting and working-memory load. *NeuroImage, 26*, 733–743.

Lepsien, J., Thornton, I., & Nobre, A. C. (2011). Modulation of working-memory maintenance by directed attention. *Neuropsychologia, 49*(6), 1569–1577. Doi: S0028-3932(11)00143-6 [pii] 10.1016/j.neuropsychologia.2011.03.011

Lisman, J. E., & Idiart, M. A. P. (1995). Storage of 7 +/− 2 short-term memories in oscillatory subcycles. *Science, 267*, 1512–1515.

Luck, S. J., & Vogel, E. K. (1997). The capacity of visual working memory for features and conjunctions. *Nature, 390*, 279–284.

Luck, S. J., Chelazzi, L., Hillyard, S. A., & Desimone, R. (1997). Neural mechanisms of spatial selective attention in areas V1, V2, and V4 of macaque visual cortex. *Journal of Neurophysiology, 77*, 24–42.

Magnussen, S., Greenlee, M. W., & Thomas, J. P. (1996). Parallel processing in visual short-term memory. *Journal of Experimental Psychology. Human Perception and Performance, 22*, 202–212.

Makovski, T., Shim, W. M., & Jiang, Y. V. (2006). Interference from filled delays on visual change detection. *Journal of Vision, 6*, 1459–1470.

McNab, F., & Klingberg, T. (2008). Prefrontal cortex and basal ganglia control access to working memory. *Nature Neuroscience, 11*(1), 103–107. doi: nn2024 [pii] 10.1038/nn2024

Meyers, E. M., Freedman, D. J., Kreiman, G., Miller, E. K., & Poggio, T. (2008). Dynamic population coding of category information in inferior temporal and prefrontal cortex. *Journal of Neurophysiology, 100*, 1407–1419.

Miller, E. K., & Cohen, J. D. (2001). An integrative theory of prefrontal cortex function. *Annual Review of Neuroscience, 24*, 167–202.

Miller, E. K., Li, L., & Desimone, R. (1993). Activity of neurons in anterior inferior temporal cortex during a short-term memory task. *Journal of Neuroscience, 13*, 1460–1478.

Miller, E. K., Erickson, C. A., & Desimone, R. (1996). Neural mechanisms of visual working memory in prefrontal cortex of the macaque. *Journal of Neuroscience, 16*, 5154–5167.

Miyashita, Y., & Chang, H. S. (1988). Neuronal correlate of pictorial short-term memory in the primate temporal cortex. *Nature, 331*, 68–70.

Murray, A. M., Nobre, A. C., & Stokes, M. G. (2011). Markers of preparatory attention predict visual short-term memory performance. *Neuropsychologia, 49*(6), 1458–1465.

Navalpakkam, V., & Itti, L. (2007). Search goal tunes visual features optimally. *Neuron, 53*, 605–617.

Neisser, U., & Sperling, G. (1967). The information available in brief visual presentations. *Cognitive Psychology, 74*, 1–29.

Nobre, A. C. (2001). The attentive homunculus: Now you see it, now you don't. *Neuroscience and Biobehavioral Reviews, 25*, 477–496.

Nobre, A. C., Coull, J. T., Maquet, P., Frith, C. D., Vandenberghe, R., & Mesulam, M. M. (2004). Orienting attention to locations in perceptual versus mental representations. *Journal of Cognitive Neuroscience, 16*, 363–373.

Nobre, A. C., & Stokes, M. G. (2011). Attention and short-term memory: Crossroads. *Neuropsychologia, 49*(6), 1391–1392.

Offen, S., Schluppeck, D., & Heeger, D. J. (2009). The role of early visual cortex in visual short-term memory and visual attention. *Vision Research, 49*, 1352–1362.

Olsson, H., & Poom, L. (2005). Visual memory needs categories. *Proceedings of the National Academy of Sciences of the United States of America, 102*, 8776–8780.

Palmer, J. (1990). Attentional limits on the perception and memory of visual information. *Journal of Experimental Psychology. Human Perception and Performance, 16*, 332–350.

Palmer, J. (1988). Very short-term visual memory for size and shape. *Perception & Psychophysics, 43*(3), 278–286.

Passingham, D., & Sakai, K. (2004). The prefrontal cortex and working memory: Physiology and brain imaging. *Current Opinion in Neurobiology, 14*, 163–168.

Pasternak, T., & Greenlee, M. W. (2005). Working memory in primate sensory systems. *Nature Reviews. Neuroscience, 6*, 97–107.

Paus, T. (1996). Location and function of the human frontal eye-field: A selective review. *Neuropsychologia, 34*, 475–483.

Peers, P. V., Ludwig, C. J. H., Rorden, C., Cusack, R., Bonfiglioli, C., Bundesen, C., et al. (2005). Attentional functions of parietal and frontal cortex. *Cerebral Cortex, 15*, 1469–1484.

Pessoa, L., Gutierrez, E., Bandettini, P., & Ungerleider, L. (2002). Neural correlates of visual working memory: FMRI amplitude predicts task performance. *Neuron, 35,* 975–987.

Phillips, W. A. (1974). On the distinction between sensory storage and short term visual memory. *Perception & Psychophysics, 16,* 283–290.

Phillips, W. A., & Baddeley, A. D. (1971). Reaction time and short-term visual memory. *Psychonomic Science, 22,* 73–74.

Postle, B. R., Awh, E., Jonides, J., Smith, E. E., & D'Esposito, M. (2004). The where and how of attention-based rehearsal in spatial working memory. *Cognitive Brain Research, 20,* 194–205.

Ress, D., Backus, B. T., & Heeger, D. J. (2000). Activity in primary visual cortex predicts performance in a visual detection task. *Nature Neuroscience, 3,* 940–945.

Ruff, C. C., Kristjánsson, A., & Driver, J. (2007). Readout from iconic memory and selective spatial attention involve similar neural processes. *Psychological Science, 18,* 901–909.

Rutman, A. M., Clapp, W. C., Chadick, J. Z., & Gazzaley, A. (2010). Early top-down control of visual processing predicts working memory performance. *Journal of Cognitive Neuroscience, 22*(6), 1224–1234.

Sakai, K., Rowe, J. B., & Passingham, R. E. (2002). Active maintenance in prefrontal area 46 creates distractor-resistant memory. *Nature Neuroscience, 5,* 479–484.

Sauseng, P., Klimesch, W., Heise, K. F., Gruber, W. R., Holz, E., Karim, A. A., et al. (2009). Brain oscillatory substrates of visual short-term memory capacity. *Current Biology, 19,* 1846–1852.

Schmidt, B. K., Vogel, E. K., Woodman, G. F., & Luck, S. J. (2002). Voluntary and automatic attentional control of visual working memory. *Perception & Psychophysics, 64,* 754–763.

Scolari, M., & Serences, J. T. (2009). Adaptive allocation of attentional gain. *Journal of Neuroscience, 29,* 11933–11942.

Serences, J. T., Ester, E. F., Vogel, E. K., & Awh, E. (2009). Stimulus-specific delay activity in human primary visual cortex. *Psychological Science, 20,* 207–214.

Siegel, M., Warden, M. R., & Miller, E. K. (2009). Phase-dependent neuronal coding of objects in short-term memory. *Proceedings of the National Academy of Sciences of the United States of America, 106,* 21341–21346.

Sigala, N., Kusunoki, M., Nimmo-Smith, I., Gaffan, D., & Duncan, J. (2008). Hierarchical coding for sequential task events in the monkey prefrontal cortex. *Proceedings of the National Academy of Sciences of the United States of America, 105,* 11969–11974.

Sligte, I. G., Scholte, H. S., & Lamme, V. A. F. (2008). Are there multiple visual short-term memory stores? *PLoS One, 3,* 1–9.

Sligte, I. G., Scholte, H. S., & Lamme, V. A. F. (2009). V4 activity predicts the strength of visual short-term memory representations. *Journal of Neuroscience, 29,* 7432–7438.

Slotnick, S. D., Thompson, W. L., & Kosslyn, S. M. (2005). Visual mental imagery induces retinotopically organized activation of early visual areas. *Cerebral Cortex, 15,* 1570–1583.

Sperling, G. (1960). The information available in brief visual presentations. *Psychological Monographs, 74,* 1–29.

Stamm, J. S. (1969). Electrical stimulation of monkeys' prefrontal cortex during delayed-response performance. *Journal of Comparative and Physiological Psychology, 67,* 535–546.

Sternberg, S. (1966). High-speed scanning in human memory. *Science, 153,* 652–654.

Stokes, M. (2011). Top-down visual activity underlying VSTM and preparatory attention. *Neuropsychologia, 49*(6):1425–1427.

Stokes, M., Thompson, R., Cusack, R., & Duncan, J. (2009a). Top-down activation of shape-specific population codes in visual cortex during mental imagery. *Journal of Neuroscience, 29,* 1565–1572.

Stokes, M., Thompson, R., Nobre, A. C., & Duncan, J. (2009b). Shape-specific preparatory activity mediates attention to targets in human visual cortex. *Proceedings of the National Academy of Sciences of the United States of America, 106,* 19569–19574.

Stokes, M., Saraiva, A., Rohenkohl, G., & Nobre, A. C. (2011). Imagery for shapes activates position-invariant representations in human visual cortex. *Neuroimage, 56*(3), 1540–1545.

Summerfield, J. J., Lepsien, J., Gitelman, D. R., Mesulam, M. M., & Nobre, A. C. (2006). Orienting attention based on long-term memory experience. *Neuron, 49,* 905–916.

Todd, J. J., & Marois, R. (2004). Capacity limit of visual short-term memory in human posterior parietal cortex. *Nature, 428,* 751–754.

Vogel, E. K., & Machizawa, M. G. (2004). Neural activity predicts individual differences in visual working memory capacity. *Nature, 428,* 748–751.

Vogel, E. K., Woodman, G. F., & Luck, S. J. (2001). Storage of features, conjunctions, and objects in visual working memory. *Journal of Experimental Psychology. Human Perception and Performance, 27,* 92–114.

Wallis, J. D., Anderson, K. C., & Miller, E. K. (2001). Single neurons in prefrontal cortex encode abstract rules. *Nature, 411,* 953–956.

Wilken, P., & Ma, W. J. (2004). A detection theory account of change detection. *Journal of Vision, 4,* 1120–1135.

Woloszyn, L., & Sheinberg, D. L. (2009). Neural dynamics in inferior temporal cortex during a visual working memory task. *Journal of Neuroscience, 29,* 5494–5507.

Xu, Y. (2002). Encoding color and shape from different parts of an object in visual short-term memory. *Perception & Psychophysics, 64,* 1260–1280.

Xu, Y., & Chun, M. M. (2006). Dissociable neural mechanisms supporting visual short-term memory for objects. *Nature, 440,* 91–95.

Zanto, T. P., Rubens, M. T., Thangavel, A., & Gazzaley, A. (2011). Causal role of the prefrontal cortex in top-down modulation of visual processing and working memory. *Nature Neuroscience, 14*(5), 656–661.

Zhang, W., & Luck, S. J. (2009). Sudden death and gradual decay in visual working memory: Research report. *Psychological Science, 20,* 423–428.

11

Conflict Control Loop Theory of Cognitive Control

MARIE K. KRUG AND CAMERON S. CARTER

THROUGHOUT A typical day, we perform many complex goal-related behaviors. Actions must be monitored, adjusted, and redirected in order to obtain the desired end result. For example, a seemingly simple task is driving to work, with the goal of a safe and punctual arrival at the correct destination. While driving, attention must be directed to relevant stimuli such as road signs, nearby passing and merging traffic, and the speedometer, so that speed can be maintained or adjusted. The focus of attention must be controlled despite numerous distractions. For example, one could be distracted by irrelevant yet similar road signs, flashy billboards, and distant cars and traffic that present no immediate danger (see Chapter 2 in this volume). Distractions with negative and positive affective valence are particularly powerful (see Chapter 12), and driving could be compromised while passing by a horrific car crash (negative) or a car with an attractive passenger (positive). Progress has been made in recent years

in elucidating the cognitive mechanisms and the underlying neural system(s) that allow us to adjust our attention dynamically in the face of varying perceptual and cognitive demands and distractions. This system includes brain regions that detect when too much interference or conflict from distracting stimuli has occurred, and which then recruit top-down control to assure that attention is directed to the appropriate stimulus, in line with our current goals.

In this chapter, we will explore the *conflict control loop theory* of cognitive control, a mechanistic framework that helps explain the behavioral and neural mechanisms that are engaged due to conflict from distracters and the subsequent control and recovery these mechanisms enable. In the first section, we illustrate the conflict control loop theory by describing the typical behavioral effects in response conflict tasks; these tasks provide well-studied paradigms in which conflict and cognitive control reliably occur. This is followed by a review of extensive neuroimaging evidence regarding the neural circuitry involved in these behavioral manifestations of conflict and subsequent cognitive control. Next, we investigate how conflict control loop theory can account for distraction from emotionally laden stimuli. Last, we relate conflict control loop theory to complementary theories of decision making and cognitive control strategy, demonstrating the robustness and generalizability of this theory.

CONFLICT CONTROL LOOP THEORY

Behavioral Evidence for Conflict and Subsequent Control

In 1935, J.R. Stroop discovered a behavioral phenomenon that is now termed the *Stroop effect* (Stroop, 1935). In his first experiment, he had subjects read lists of color words printed in black ink, and then read lists of color words printed in nonmatching ink colors (Example: the word "red" written in blue ink, correct response being "red"). He found that reading words printed in a conflicting ink color did not take longer than reading words printed in black ink. In a second experiment, he asked subjects to name the color ink and ignore the meaning of the words. He found that subjects were, on average, 74% slower at naming the ink color in which a color word is printed (Example: the word "red" written in blue ink, correct response being "blue") in comparison to naming the color ink of a nonword symbol, suggesting that word reading interferes significantly with color naming when both processes produce conflicting responses.

Since this initial study nearly 75 years ago, countless experiments have implemented different variants of the Stroop task (MacLeod, 1991). Current studies, including those involving neuroimaging, typically use a single-trial presentation of the Stroop task (as opposed to reading an entire list of words) first developed by Tecce and Dimartino (1965). Incongruent trials (those in which ink color naming and word reading elicit different responses) are often mixed, on a trial-by-trial basis, with congruent trials (trials in which the color naming and the word reading produce

the same response) and/or some form of neutral trials (Example: a series of XXXX's or a noncolor word such as "chair" printed in blue ink, correct answer "blue"). Congruent trials often produce a facilitation effect, whereby reaction time (RT) to congruent trials is faster than RT to neutral trials, although this is highly dependent on the type of neutral trials used and is generally quantitatively much smaller than the interference effect (MacLeod, 1991). In most studies, the interference effect is calculated by subtracting the mean RT on congruent trials from the mean RT on incongruent trials.

In addition to the interference effect, response conflict tasks such as the Stroop also produce other measurable behaviors. In a Flanker task, for example, it was shown that behavior on the current trial is influenced by the congruency of the preceding trial (Gratton, Coles, & Donchin, 1992). Subjects were presented with a five-letter array, and asked to respond whether the central letter was an "S" or "H." Flanker letters could be either response congruent ("SSSSS" or "HHHHH") or response incongruent ("SSHSS," "HHSHH"). Gratton et al. found that, as expected, incongruent trials were significantly slower than congruent trials. However, they noticed that incongruent trials preceded by another incongruent trial (iI trials) were faster than incongruent trials preceded by a congruent trial (cI trials). They concluded that trial history strategically induces a change in performance. One interpretation is that following a congruent trial, subjects allow the task-irrelevant dimension to influence responding, whereas following an incongruent trial, the influence of the task-irrelevant dimension is reduced. This suggests that interference on response conflict tasks can be reduced through control processes that are engaged by conflicting responses.

A third and similar behavioral effect found in Stroop and Flanker tasks is a trial-type frequency effect (Gratton et al., 1992; Tzelgov, Henik, & Berger, 1992). In blocks with a high proportion of incongruent trials, the interference effect in RT is significantly reduced compared to blocks in which incongruent trials are infrequent. When incongruent trials are reasonably anticipated, an adjustment in cognitive control reduces the interference of the task-irrelevant response. However, when incongruent trials rarely occur, the task-irrelevant response has a much greater effect on performance.

To begin to provide a more computationally explicit and neurally plausible account for these behavior effects of dynamic adjustments in control, Botvinick, Braver, Barch, Carter, and Cohen (2001) present a computational model with a key component—a conflict monitor that recruits cognitive control—to account for the above behavioral effects (as well as others not addressed in detail in this chapter). In this model of the Stroop task, the task stimulus presented on each trial activates input units for the ink color and the word. As these units become activated, they feed into a response unit. A response is made once a particular response (either the color naming or word reading response) is activated enough that it reaches the response threshold. A conflict monitoring module detects energy at the response unit. This energy increases if two different responses are simultaneously activated, as would occur on an incongruent trial, and increases as the magnitude of activation of the two different responses increases. The conflict monitor converts this response level energy into a cognitive control signal, which adjusts levels of attention diverted to the color naming or word reading task demand, thus increasing or decreasing the processing of the associated inputs, and the subsequent weighting of those associated responses on the next trial (see Figure 11.1).

On cI trials, the conflict measurement is high, as both potential responses are highly activated. This recruits high amounts of cognitive control, resulting in enhanced attention to the color naming task demand. Thus, on the next incongruent trial (iI), attention is more strongly allocated to the ink color (or, in the Flanker task, the central letter), activating the appropriate response more strongly than the incorrect response and resulting in less conflict and faster responding on that trial. Likewise, in tasks in which there are several incongruent trials in a row, control is continually recruited, resulting in a decrease in conflict and improved behavioral performance on incongruent trials. When incongruent trials are infrequent,

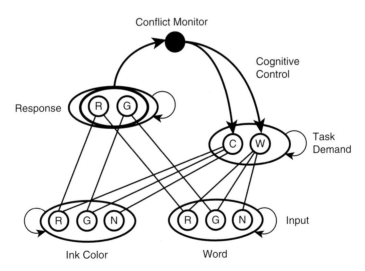

FIGURE 11.1   A model of the color–word Stroop task that accounts for behavioral adjustments in performance as a result of conflict detection and subsequent cognitive control. Processing of a color–word Stroop stimulus activates ink color and word reading input modules, which feed into the associated responses. If two different responses are simultaneously activated at the response module, the conflict monitor is activated. The conflict monitor converts this activation into a cognitive control signal, which in the case of the color–word Stroop task, enhances attention to the color naming task demand. R, red; G, green; C, color naming; W, word reading; N, neutral Adapted with permission from Botvinick, M.M., Braver, T.S., Barch, D.M., Carter, C.S., & Cohen, J.D. (2001). Conflict monitoring and cognitive control. *Psychological Review, 108*(3), 641, with permission of the publisher, the American Psychological Association.

a conflict signal is rare, so control is not implemented. Thus, when an incongruent trial does occur, processing of the word reading response is high. The two responses are highly activated at the response level, resulting in high levels of conflict and a stronger interference effect (Botvinick et al., 2001). Functional neuroimaging studies have been able to directly test this model and pinpoint specific brain regions in conflict monitoring and cognitive control, as well as posterior processing regions targeted by cognitive control.

Neural Regions Mediating Conflict Monitoring and Cognitive Control

Pardo J.V., Pardo P.J., Janer, and Raichle (1990) were the first to investigate neural activity during the color–word Stroop task. Stroop trials were presented in a blocked design; subjects first received a series of congruent trials, followed by a series of incongruent trials while undergoing positron emission tomography (PET) scanning. They were instructed to name the color ink in which the words were printed, without reading the word. The incongruent–congruent contrast revealed strong activity in dorsal anterior cingulate cortex (dACC). Although few definitive conclusions regarding the specific role of the dACC during incongruent trials could be made, these authors concluded, "Differences between the incongruent and congruent conditions must, therefore, be related directly to the attentionally mediated selection of cognitive processing between color naming and reading" (Pardo et al., 1990).

Carter, Mintun, and Cohen (1995), in another blocked-design PET study of the color–word Stroop task, also reported activity in dACC for an incongruent–congruent contrast. In their task, incongruent and congruent blocks were mixed with neutral trials (Example: the word "dog" written in red ink, correct response "red"). Subjects also were given a block of neutral trials only, allowing for incongruent–neutral and congruent–neutral contrasts. Dorsal ACC activity was also found for the incongruent–neutral contrast and, notably, the congruent–neutral contrast. They concluded that dACC is involved in general attentional control processes. For the incongruent blocks, attentional demands are high, as color naming must be

selected despite the automatic and conflicting word reading response. For the congruent blocks, dACC-mediated attentional control is required due to the demands of switching between a strategy of word reading, which is facilitative on congruent trials, and color naming, which is necessary on the neutral trials presented in the congruent blocks.

These simple blocked-design Stroop tasks could not distinguish between a role for the dACC in conflict monitoring or implementation of cognitive control. However, electroencephalogram (EEG) data suggested a more specific role for the dACC. In several studies, a negativity immediately following errors (termed the *error-related negativity*, or ERN) was modeled as having an ACC source, suggesting that the role of the dACC was to monitor and compensate for errors (Hohnsbein et al., 1989; Gehring et al., 1990; Gehring et al., 1993; Dehaene et al., 1994). This was difficult to reconcile with dACC activity found on Stroop tasks in which relatively few errors were made (for example, in Carter et al. (1995), the mean error rate on incongruent trials was only 1.9%).

Using an event-related design in concert with fMRI, Carter et al. (1998) were able to look at the neural activity of both correct trials and error trials during performance of the AX Continuous Performance Task (AX-CPT). During this task, letters are presented as cue–target pairs. Subjects are required to make a target response to an A-X sequence, and a nontarget response to any other cue–target pairs. Because A-X pairs occur at a high frequency, B-X (an "X" preceded by a "non-A" letter) and A-Y (an "A" followed by a "non-X" letter) trials evoke high levels of response conflict. They found that both high-conflict trials and errors activated the same region of dACC, suggesting that dACC is not solely involved in error-related control processes (Figure 11.2). Instead, Carter et al. (1998) argued that conflict loop theory accounts for dACC activity in both correct, high-conflict trials and errors. They suggested that the dACC is the conflict monitor, and, as described above, activates when there is competition between conflicting responses, which occurs both during error trials and also during high-conflict correct trials. In the AX-CPT task, for

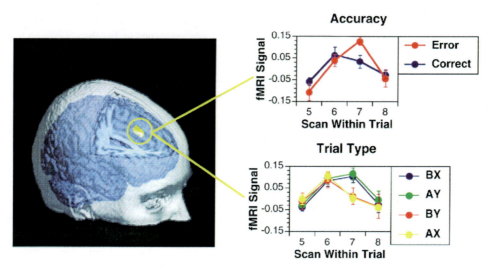

FIGURE 11.2   Dorsal anterior cingulate cortex (dACC) activates to both error trials and high-conflict correct trials. During performance of the AX Continuous Performance Task (AX-CPT) task, dACC activates more to error trials than to correct trials. For correct trials only, the same dACC area activated more for high response conflict BX and AY trials in comparison to low response conflict BY and AX trials. The graphs show the time course of activation, plotted as % signal change with error bars indicating the standard error of the mean. From Carter, C.S., Braver, T.S., Barch, D.M., Botvinick, M.M., Noll, D., & Cohen, J.D. (1998). Anterior cingulate cortex, error detection, and the online monitoring of performance. *Science*, *280*(5364), 748, with permission from the publisher, AAAS.

example, dACC is active on AY trials because the automatic and incorrect "target" response is prompted, as well as the correct "nontarget" response.

Event-related potential (ERP) data in support of this conflict detection theory soon followed. Gehring and Fencsik (2001) had subjects perform a color–word Stroop task. For each of the four possible color responses, subjects were required to respond using a specified hand (right or left) or foot (right or left). If the ERN is involved in error-detection, the ERN should be greater in magnitude following a "dissimilar" incorrect response (Example: An error committed by responding with the wrong limb, on the opposite side of the body). If the ERN is involved in conflict detection, it should be greater following an error committed by making a similar response (Example: An error committed by responding on the correct side of the body but with the wrong limb). They found that the ERN was indeed greater following an error committed by making an incorrect motor response that was similar to the correct response.

Botvinick et al.'s (2001) theory of conflict and cognitive control had differential predictions regarding the time course of conflict (and dACC activity) on correct high-conflict trials and errors that could be directly addressed with ERP experiments. During incongruent trials in the Stroop task, the automatic word naming response is activated quickly. The correct color naming response slowly gains more activation, until both the incorrect and correct responses are simultaneously highly activated. Eventually, the color naming response reaches a particular response threshold, and a correct response is made. During errors, both responses are also activated. However, most likely due to random noise in the system, the incorrect response prematurely surpasses the response threshold, resulting in an error. After the incorrect response is made, the correct response continues to activate, leading to a simultaneous activation of both responses, and activation of the conflict monitor after the error has been committed. Thus, the highest levels of response conflict for correct trials would occur *prior* to responding, when both responses are activated and the correct response has not yet reached threshold, whereas for errors, response conflict would be greatest *following* error commission as the correct response continues to activate (Botvinick et al., 2001).

Van Veen and Carter (2002) provided ERP data in support of this model. During performance of the Erikson Flanker Task, subjects showed a postresponse ERN, and a preresponse negativity during high-conflict correct trials (called the N2). Dipole modeling predicted dACC sources for both the N2 and ERN, confirming that a conflict monitoring theory of dACC function can account for both the presence and timing of dACC activity on incorrect and correct trials.

Several fMRI experiments solidified the dACC as having a role in conflict detection, as opposed to direct implementation of control. Botvinick, Nystrom, Fissell, Carter, and Cohen (1999) separated incongruent trials based on whether they were high in conflict (incongruent trial preceded by a congruent trial, "cI") or high in control (incongruent trial preceded by an incongruent trial, "iI"). They found that dACC was more active on cI trials in comparison to iI trials, confirming the role of the dACC in conflict detection as opposed to selection for action. Additionally, differences in RT between cI and iI trials was positively correlated with dACC activity, suggesting that dACC activates more in subjects who show greater amounts of response conflict behaviorally.

Instead of looking at cI and iI trials to determine if dACC is involved in conflict monitoring or control, Carter et al. (2000) tested another prediction of conflict theory by manipulating expectancy for incongruent trials. In high-expectancy incongruent blocks, 80% of trials were incongruent. Because subjects learn that incongruent trials occur frequently, control processes are highly engaged, and response conflict on incongruent trials would be low. In high-expectancy congruent blocks, only 20% of trials were incongruent. Because incongruent trials occur rarely, in these blocks, control would be lowered as subjects would benefit from relying on the facilitative word reading response. When an incongruent trial does occur, response conflict would be very high. Behaviorally, as expected, interference effects

(incongruent RT- congruent RT) were much greater in the high-expectancy congruent blocks than in the high-expectancy incongruent blocks, indicating higher amounts of response conflict for unexpected incongruent trials. Imaging results showed the dACC was highly activated during incongruent trials, but only in the high-expectancy congruent blocks, providing further evidence that dACC is associated with greater interference effects, and that dACC is activated particularly when control processes are not yet implemented (Figure 11.3). Incongruent trials that occur in situations of high control are not characterized by dACC activation.

Last, MacDonald, Cohen, Stenger, and Carter (2000) used a task-switching version of the color–word Stroop paradigm. Subjects were given an instruction prior to each trial to either respond according to ink color or word reading. The following trial could be congruent or incongruent. Functional MRI results showed that dACC was active on incongruent trials following color naming instructions, replicating the result that dACC is involved in conflict monitoring. On the other hand, left dorsolateral prefrontal cortex (DLPFC) was active following the color naming instruction, and activity in left DLPFC during color naming instructions was correlated with a reduced Stroop interference effect. They concluded that DLPFC plays a preparatory role in cognitive control, reducing response conflict and interference when an incongruent trial is encountered.

If dACC is monitoring or detecting conflict, it must then recruit cognitive control centers to produce the characteristic improvements in task performance that occur on successive incongruent trials (Gratton et al., 1992). Botvinick et al. (2001) modeled a control system that receives the conflict reading from the conflict detector and then enacts control by enhancing attention to the task-relevant stimulus or stimulus dimension. This occurs on a trial-by-trial basis, with control greatest following a high-conflict stimulus. Results from MacDonald et al. (2000) suggested that DLPFC is this control region, although more conclusive evidence of a link between dACC, and DLPFC and behavioral adjustments was necessary and was provided by Kerns et al. (2004).

Kerns et al. (2004) provided the most conclusive evidence in support of the conflict control

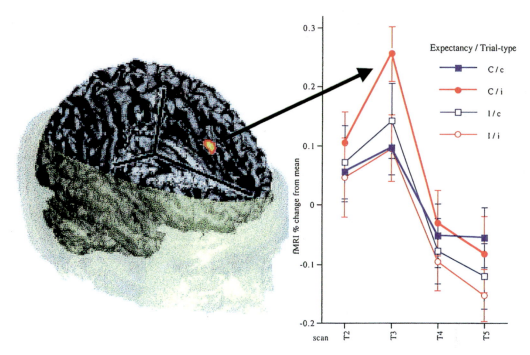

FIGURE 11.3   Dorsal anterior cingulate cortex (dACC) activates more to incongruent trials in high expectancy congruent blocks than to incongruent trials in high expectancy incongruent blocks. The graphs show the time course of activation, plotted as % signal change with error bars indicating the standard error of the mean. C/c, congruent trial, high expectancy congruent condition; C/i, incongruent trial, high expectancy congruent condition; I/c, congruent trial, high expectancy incongruent condition; I/i, incongruent trial, high expectancy incongruent condition. From Carter, C.S., Macdonald, A.M., Botvinick, M.M., Ross, L.L., Stenger, V.A., Noll, D., & Cohen, J.D. (2000). Parsing executive processes: Strategic vs. evaluative functions of the anterior cingulate cortex. *Proceedings of the National Academy of Sciences of the United States of America*, 97(4), 1946, with permission of the publisher.

loop theory as laid out in Botvinick et al. (2001) by clearly showing how both dACC and DLPFC interact to monitor for conflict and implement control. As in Botvinick et al. (1999), incongruent trials were separated based on the congruency of the preceding trial. As expected, high-conflict cI trials were slower than high-control iI trials. Once again, dACC was active on high-conflict cI trials, and dACC activity was greater on cI trials in comparison to iI trials. Dorsal ACC activity on cI trials was related to behavior on the next incongruent (iI) trial. Kerns et al. (2004) showed that iI trials characterized by a speeded RT (showing a control-related adjustment) were preceded by cI trials with higher amounts of dACC activity than were iI trials characterized by a slower RT. Last, and most importantly, DLPFC was related to these adjustments in control. Right DLPFC was

more active during fast iI trials than slow iI trials. Additionally, dACC activity on cI trials was significantly and positively correlated with DLPFC activity on the subsequent incongruent trial. This study showed that conflict detection in the dACC recruits another region, the DLPFC, and recruitment of this brain region is associated with characteristic adjustments in behavior as a result of cognitive control. Several other studies have replicated this result using a range of conflict tasks (Egner & Hirsch, 2005; Kerns, 2006; Egner et al., 2008)

Mechanism of DLPFC-mediated Cognitive Control

If dACC is detecting conflict and signaling DLPFC-mediated control, the next question to answer is *how* DLPFC implements cognitive control. In the PET study of the color–word Stroop described above, Carter et al. (1995) compared incongruent and congruent trials. They found, as expected, greater activity in dACC and PFC on incongruent trials. However, incongruent trials were also characterized by increased activity in the left lingual gyrus and decreased activity in left extrastriate cortex. They suggested that during difficult incongruent trials, due to the conflicting nature of the color and word aspects of the stimulus, color processing is enhanced, leading to increased activity in the left lingual gyrus, and word reading processing is decreased, leading to decreased activity in the left extrastriate cortex. Likewise, during congruent trials, subjects can be facilitated by the automatic word reading response (since it will always provide the correct response), so processing of ink color is not needed and word reading processing is more favored.

Polk, Drake, Jonides, Smith, and Smith (2008) provided a more sophisticated test of this theory. In addition to performing the color–word Stroop task, all subjects participated in color viewing and word viewing blocks during fMRI scanning to localize color and word processing areas in each individual subject. In comparison to a neutral task, incongruent Stroop trials were characterized by increased activity in color processing areas and deactivation in word processing areas, confirming the results of Carter et al. (1995).

Weissman, Warner, and Woldorff (2009) investigated posterior processing of task-relevant and task-irrelevant stimuli during lapses of attention (when cognitive control is not engaged). They used a cross-modal Stroop task in which subjects had to respond to a visually presented "X" or "O" stimulus, while ignoring a simultaneously presented "X" or "O" auditory stimulus that could be response congruent or response incongruent. They defined a reduction in attention as increased RT on a particular trial type. For both congruent and incongruent trials, an increase in RT was associated with increased activation in auditory processing regions and a decrease in activation in visual processing regions. Additionally, increases in RT were associated with increased activity in dACC, particularly on incongruent trials, suggesting that lapses of attention, when

they occur during incongruent trials, produce response conflict. This study provided evidence that behavioral impairment, as indexed by RT slowing, is associated with *both* decreased processing of the task-relevant stimulus and enhanced processing of the task-irrelevant stimulus, even when the two stimuli are from two different sensory modalities.

Last, Egner and Hirsch (2005) looked at cognitive control mechanisms enacted specifically during high-control iI trials. They used a facial Stroop task, in which faces of famous actors and politicians were presented along with a superimposed name of another actor or politician. According to task instructions, subjects had to either judge whether the face was that of an actor or politician (face–target condition) or whether the word was the name of an actor or politician (face–distracter condition). On each trial the simultaneously presented face and word could be categorically congruent or incongruent (Figure 11.4A). Subjects also viewed a succession of faces during a face processing localizer scan, and a subject-specific fusiform face area (FFA) region of interest (ROI) was extracted. Typical behavioral conflict adaptation effects were observed in RT in both the face–target condition and the face–distracter condition (Figure 11.4B, *top*). In the face–target condition, high-control iI trials were associated with an increase in FFA activity in comparison to cI trials, suggesting that behavioral conflict adaptation effects are mediated by enhanced processing of the task-relevant face (Figure 11.4B, *bottom left*). Functional connectivity analyses showed that in the face–target condition iI trials are associated with enhanced DLPFC–FFA coupling, suggesting that DLPFC is mediating the increase in task-relevant face processing. In the face–distracter condition, high control iI were not characterized by decreased processing in FFA, suggesting that behavioral conflict adaptation effects are *not* mediated by inhibition of distracting or task-irrelevant stimuli (Figure 11.4B, *bottom right*).

The results of Egner and Hirsch (2005) show that cognitive control is mediated by enhanced posterior processing of task-relevant information, whereas Carter et al. (1995) and Polk et al. (2008) provide results showing that both enhanced processing of task-relevant information and decreased

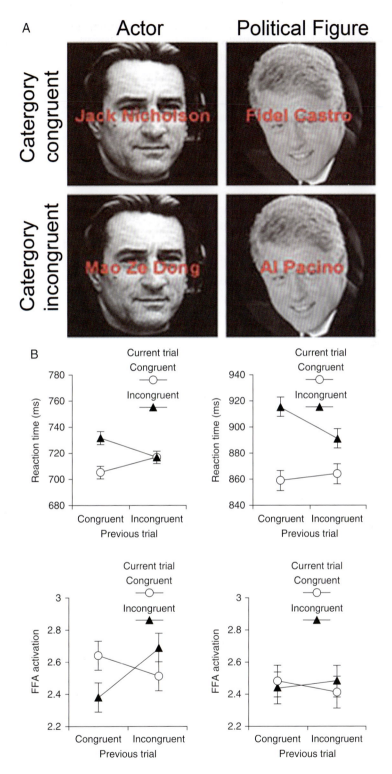

FIGURE 11.4 Implementation of cognitive control is mediated by enhanced attention to task-relevant stimuli. (**A**) For the facial Stroop task, subjects were required to categorize the face target or word target (depending on task instruction) as a politician or actor. Word and face could be either category/response congruent (*top*) or category/response incongruent (*bottom*). For example, the face of Bill Clinton (politician) with the name Fidel

(*Continued on next page*)

FIGURE 11.4 (*Continued*)   Castro (politician) would be a congruent trial, whereas the face of Bill Clinton (politician) presented with the name Al Pacino (actor) would be an incongruent trial. (**B**) Reliable trial-to-trial adjustments were observed in both the face–target condition (*upper left*) and the word–target condition (*upper right*). In both conditions, iI trials were faster than cI trials. In the face–target condition, high control iI trials were associated with greater activity in fusiform face area (FFA) (*bottom left*) than cI trials. In the word–target condition, cI and iI trials had equivalent amounts of FFA activity (*bottom right*). Figure adapted from Egner, T., & Hirsch, J. (2005). Cognitive control mechanisms resolve conflict through cortical amplification of task-relevant information. *Nature Neuroscience*, 8(12), 1785–1786, with permission of the publisher, Macmillan.

processing/inhibition of task-irrelevant information are characteristic of control during Stroop tasks. In a similar vein, Weissman et al. (2009) argued that lapses in attention (or lack of control) are also mediated both by decreased processing of the task-relevant information and increased processing of the task-irrelevant information. Polk et al. provided a nice discussion of why Egner and Hirsch had different results, suggesting that the use of two objects (face and word) versus one object with two features (word, with color and word-meaning features) could have elicited different forms of control. However, Weissman et al. showed similar results to Polk et al., and they used stimuli presented in two entirely different sensory modalities (visual and auditory). To determine how control is implemented on iI trials, future studies will need to reconcile these disparate findings by combining the strengths of each of these studies, including using a design that allows for analysis of trial-to-trial effects (Egner & Hirsch, 2005), extraction of ROIs for both the attended and unattended stimulus dimensions (Polk et al., 2008; Weissman et al., 2009), and perhaps task(s) that allow for a comparison of cognitive control mechanisms based on whether the response conflict arises from two features of the same object or two separate objects.

CONFLICT CONTROL LOOP THEORY AND EMOTION

Although the dACC has been implicated in conflict monitoring across a wide variety of cognitive tasks, a more rostral and anterior region of the ACC appears to play a role in emotion processing. Rostral ACC (rACC), or the affective subdivision of ACC, includes the rostral portions of BA 24 and 32, as well as subgenual regions BA 33 and

25, and is characterized by extensive anatomical connections to limbic regions such as the amygdala, orbitofrontal cortex, periaqueductal gray, and autonomic brainstem nuclei (Vogt et al., 1992; Devinsky et al., 1995; Bush et al., 2000). Several meta-analyses of neuroimaging studies have found that although the dACC is activated by cognitively demanding tasks such as the Stroop, the rACC is typically activated in tasks with emotional content (Drevets & Raichle, 1998; Bush et al., 2000; Steele & Lawrie, 2004)

Many studies have attempted to discern the exact role of the rACC in tasks with emotional stimuli. Bush et al. (1998) had subjects perform a cognitive counting Stroop task. Subjects had to report how many words were presented on the screen while ignoring the word reading response, which was also numerical and could be response-congruent or response-incongruent (Example: the word "three" written four times, with the correct answer being "four"). In another study, the same subjects performed a comparable emotional counting Stroop paradigm (Whalen et al., 1998). They were asked to report how many words were presented on the screen while ignoring the word meaning, which could be neutral or negative in valence (Example: the word "murder" written four times, with the correct answer being "four"). Subjects activated the dACC on incongruent trials in comparison to congruent trials in the cognitive counting Stroop paradigm. For the emotional counting Stroop task, the same subjects activated the rACC on negative word trials in comparison to neutral word trials (Figure 11.5). However, there were no behavioral interference effects in the emotional counting Stroop paradigm, so it was impossible to determine whether rACC was processing the distracting emotional content, inhibiting processing of the emotional

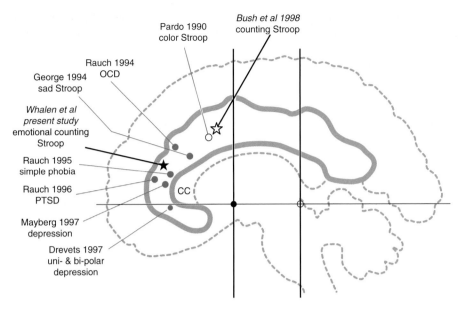

FIGURE 11.5   A cognitive counting Stroop task activates dorsal anterior cingulate cortex (dACC) while an emotional counting Stroop task activates rostral ACC. The same subjects performed both the cognitive and emotional counting Stroop tasks. The black star indicates the ACC activation found in the emotional counting Stroop, and the white star indicates the ACC activation found for the cognitive counting Stroop. The activated region of ACC in the emotional counting Stroop is more rostral than the region of ACC activated in the cognitive counting Stroop and other cognitive interference tasks, and is typically activated in other emotional paradigms. CC, corpus callosum. Reprinted from Whalen, P.J., Bush, G., McNally, R.J., Wilhelm, S., McInerney, S.C., Jenike, M.A., & Rauch, S.L. (1998). The emotional counting Stroop paradigm: A functional magnetic resonance imaging probe of the anterior cingulate affective division. *Biological Psychiatry, 44*(12), 1225, copyright (1998), with permission from Elsevier.

content, or signaling processing conflict due to the presence of the emotional content in an attempt to recruit other prefrontal control regions.

Bishop, Duncan, Brett, and Lawrence (2004) more specifically addressed the question of whether the rACC signals processing conflict from emotional distracters, comparable to the role of the dACC in signaling response conflict from nonemotional distracters. In their task, subjects had to decide whether two houses were identical or different while ignoring simultaneously presented face pairs that could be either neutral or fearful in expression. They manipulated the frequency of threat-related, task-irrelevant distracters by block, reasoning that when distracters are infrequent, control is low, resulting in greater behavioral interference and conflict-related activity (see Carter et al., 2000). They found that rACC activity was greater in response to infrequent threat-related distracters, much as

dACC was more highly activated in response to infrequent incongruent trials in Carter et al. (2000). In a control task in which the faces were the attended stimuli, they did not see an increase in rACC activity in response to infrequent threatening faces. They concluded that rACC signals emotional processing conflict and recruits lateral PFC control. However, analyses such as those laid out in Kerns et al. (2004) were not possible due to ceiling performance on the task and the lack of behavioral interference from the fearful face distracters. Although this study suggested that rACC is involved in detecting processing conflict from emotional distracters, rACC activity could not be directly correlated with RT slowing or subsequent improvement in performance and recruitment of lateral PFC.

Although the emotional stimuli used in Whalen et al. (1998) and Bishop et al. (2004) did not produce conflict at the response level, Haas,

Omura, Constable, and Canli (2006) used an emotional facial Stroop paradigm to determine which regions of ACC are activated when emotional stimuli produce conflicting responses. In their task, subjects were presented with a word and a face, and had to judge whether the word was positive or negative in valence, while ignoring a simultaneously presented face of response-congruent or response-incongruent valence. Incongruent trials compared to congruent trials activated dACC, suggesting that dACC detects response conflict regardless of whether it arises from emotional or nonemotional stimuli.

An auditory emotional Stroop paradigm revealed similar results. Wittfoth et al. (2010) had subjects listen to sentences that were either congruent or incongruent in the emotional valence of semantic content and prosody. They were required to judge whether the prosody was neutral, positive (happy), or negative (angry). The incongruent–congruent contrast showed activation in dACC, suggesting that the role of the dACC as a conflict monitor extends to emotional conflict present in the auditory domain. Unlike the previous emotional conflict studies described above, these two studies did not find any evidence of rACC activation.

Etkin, Egner, Peraza, Kandel, and Hirsch (2006) implemented an emotional facial Stroop task that was optimally designed to assess trial-to-trial conflict adaptation effects, with the goal of separating conflict-related and control-related neural activity. In this task, subjects had to judge whether a face was happy or fearful in emotion while ignoring the superimposed word "fear" or "happy," which could be either response-congruent or response-incongruent (Figure 11.6A). They saw typical RT conflict adaptation effects. Not only were incongruent trials slower than congruent trials, but iI trials were faster than cI trials, allowing them to clearly separate conflict and control related activity with cI - iI and iI - cI contrasts. For high-conflict cI trials, they found activity in the amygdala, dorsomedial PFC, and bilateral DLPFC, whereas high-control iI trials activated rACC. Activity in amygdala, dorsomedial PFC, and right DLPFC during cI trials was significantly correlated with rACC activity on iI trials. Follow-up functional connectivity analyses showed that on iI trials only, rACC activity was negatively correlated with amygdala activity, and

that previous trial incongruency modulated an inhibitory pathway from rACC to amygdala. They concluded that the rACC is not involved in emotional conflict detection, but rather resolves emotional conflict, signaled by the amygdala, dorsomedial PFC, and DLPFC, via inhibition of the amygdala.

In a follow-up study, Egner, Etkin, Gale, and Hirsch (2008) had subjects perform the same emotional facial Stroop task as in Etkin et al. (2006), as well as a nonemotional facial Stroop task in which subjects had to judge whether faces were male and female in gender while ignoring the superimposed words "male" and "female" (Figure 11.6A). Conflict and control contrasts for each of the two tasks could then be directly

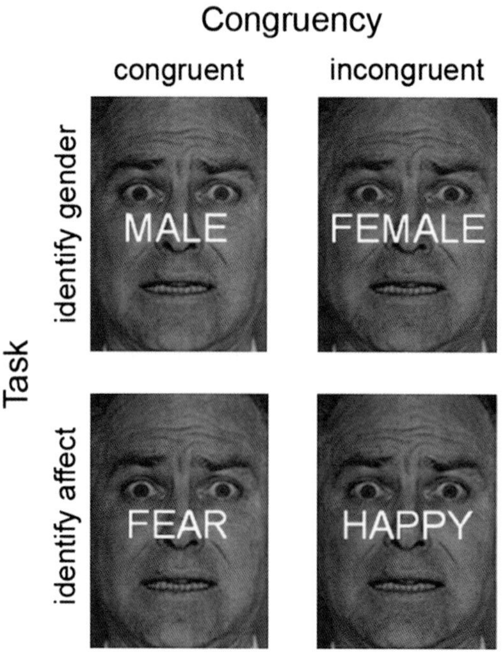

FIGURE 11.6 Emotional and nonemotional conflict recruit distinct cognitive control mechanisms. (**A**) In a nonemotional facial Stroop task, subjects judged whether a face was male or female in gender while ignoring the word "male" or "female." In an emotional facial Stroop task, used in both Etkin et al. (2006) and Egner et al. (2008), subjects judged whether a face was happy or fearful in emotion while ignoring the word "fear" or "happy." Word meaning could be congruent or incongruent to the face category.

(*Continued on next page*)

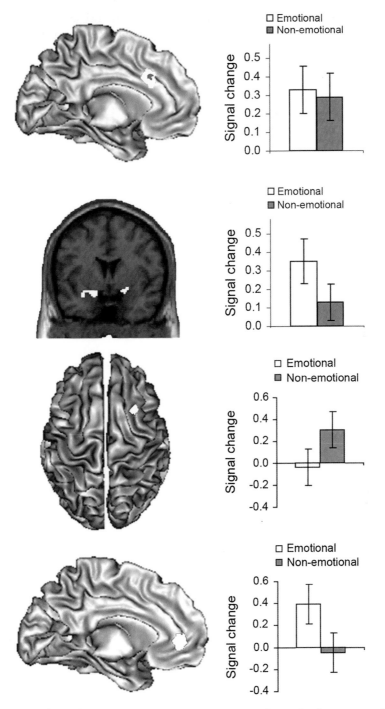

FIGURE 11.6 (*Continued*)   (**B**) A cI–iI contrast indicated that in both tasks, conflict detection was characterized by activity in both dorsal anterior cingulate cortex (dACC) (*top*) and the amygdala (*bottom*). Mean β values are displayed in the bar graphs, with error bars indicating the standard error of the mean. (**C**) An iI–cI contrast indicated that control trials activated LPFC in the nonemotional task (*top*) and rostral ACC (rACC) in the emotional task (*bottom*). Mean β values are displayed in the bar graphs, with error bars indicating the standard error of the mean. From Egner, T., Etkin, A., Gale, S., & Hirsch, J. (2008). Dissociable neural systems resolve conflict from emotional versus nonemotional distracters. *Cerebral Cortex, 18*(6), 1476, 1479, and 1480, with permission of the publisher, Oxford University Press.

compared to see if similar or different conflict and control networks are recruited. They found that while cI trials in both tasks activated dACC, conflict resolution on iI trials was mediated by rACC in the emotional task and right DLPFC in the nonemotional task (Figure 11.6B, C). Connectivity analyses showed that in the nonemotional task, DLPFC activity on iI trials predicted enhanced activity in fusiform face processing areas, whereas in the emotional task, rACC activity was associated with decreased amygdalar activity during iI trials. Although this experiment did not support their previous conclusions that the amygdala detects conflicts from emotional stimuli, they did replicate their result that the rACC is involved in emotional conflict resolution, most likely through inhibitory control over the amygdala.

In a similar study, Krug and Carter (2010) also had subjects perform emotional and nonemotional versions of a facial Stroop task. The nonemotional task was similar to Egner et al. (2008), whereas in the emotional task, subjects were required to judge whether a face was neutral or fearful in emotion while ignoring the word "fearful" or "neutral." Incongruent trials in both tasks activated nearly identical networks of brain regions, including dACC, DLPFC, and VLPFC, with no evidence of rACC activity in the emotional task. However, analyses of individual differences in trait anxiety revealed an interesting result. Subjects high in trait anxiety were particularly slow on cI trials, but only for the neutral face–fearful word combination. High-anxious subjects activated the dACC more on these trials in comparison to low-anxious subjects. High-anxious subjects may have difficulty diverting attention away from emotional stimuli (Koster et al., 2004; Salemink et al., 2007), which may have resulted in increased response conflict on incongruent trials with a distracting "fearful" word. Low-anxious subjects, on the other hand, had significant rACC activity on cI neutral face–fearful word trials. Low-anxious subjects may avoid distraction from the fearful word via rACC-mediated control.

It is not surprising that recruitment of rACC-mediated control processes are related to individual differences in anxiety. Bishop et al. (2004) found that subjects high in state anxiety showed

less rACC activity overall, a hypoactive rACC is characteristic of post-traumatic stress disorder (Shin et al., 2001) and depression (Pizzagalli et al., 2006), and greater rACC activity is predictive of recovery from generalized anxiety disorder and major depression (Pizzagalli et al., 2001; Whalen et al., 2008; Nitschke et al., 2009; Salvadore et al., 2009).

Finally, Ochsner, Hughes, Robertson, Cooper, and Gabrieli (2009) also compared conflict detection and resolution in emotional and nonemotional tasks. However, they used a verbal flanker task instead a facial Stroop task, reasoning that use of a word–face stimulus could introduce additional conflicts due to the presence of two different stimulus representations. Additionally, the word and face stimuli could differentially activate certain brain regions. In their nonemotional task, subjects were asked to categorize a centrally presented target word as a fruit or metal. They had to ignore two distracting words, placed above and below the target word, which could be categorically congruent or incongruent. In the emotional task, subjects had to indicate whether a target word was positive or negative in valence while ignoring distracting flanker words that could be either congruent or incongruent in valence. They found that dACC, DLPFC, and posterior medial PFC (including BA 6 and 8) were commonly activated in both tasks. Left VLPFC and left parietal cortex were activated more for the incongruent–congruent contrast in the nonemotional task than in the same contrast for the emotional task. When they relaxed their threshold for statistical significance, rACC was activated more for the incongruent–congruent contrast in the emotional task. Next, they correlated behavioral RT interference (incongruent–congruent) with activity in the incongruent–congruent contrast. For the nonemotional task, behavioral interference correlated with activity in VLPFC, whereas in the emotional task behavioral interference correlated with activity in rACC/subgenual cortex. They concluded that emotional and nonemotional conflict tasks recruit both common (dACC, DLPFC, and posterior medial PFC) and distinct (VLPFC, rACC) brain regions. Greater interference effects in the nonemotional and emotional task lead to enhanced activity in VLPFC and rACC, respectively, most likely because these areas are involved in semantic category selection processes specific to these tasks. Because this study was not designed to look at trial-to-trial effects, they could not determine whether the rACC is involved in conflict detection or control-related processes.

In conclusion, although the rACC is often recruited during tasks involving emotion processing, comparable dACC and DLPFC networks appear to be recruited for the monitoring and resolution of response conflict from both emotional and nonemotional stimuli. However, there is substantial evidence that the rACC plays an important role in emotional tasks, most likely through top-down control over the amygdala. Future studies will need to confirm and expand upon the role of the rACC in control over emotional response conflict, as well as the role of the rACC when emotional stimuli produce processing conflict. There has been some inconsistency in finding rACC activity, most likely because recruitment of rACC is dependent upon stimulus set characteristics and individual differences in anxiety and task performance.

EXTENSION OF CONFLICT CONTROL LOOP THEORY

Over the years, the conflict control loop theory of cognitive control has been extended beyond response conflict tasks to account for a wider range of behaviors. The dACC in particular is consistently activated across many different tasks and experimental manipulations. Many of these theories are complementary to or can be reconciled with conflict control loop theory. We briefly review Botvinick (2007), which presents a unifying theory to explain dACC activity in both conflict tasks and in decision making and learning, and Braver, Gray, and Burgess' (2007) dual mechanisms of control (DMC) theory, which accounts for between and within subject differences in implementation of cognitive control and adequately explains many conflict control loop theory phenomena.

Decision Making

The role of the dACC in conflict monitoring can be fairly easily reconciled with the role of the dACC in decision making (Botvinick, 2007). In decision-making models, the dACC is often active during negative outcome events. It is thought that this dACC signal serves as a learning signal to guide behavior away from that which caused the aversive experience and toward behaviors that have more advantageous outcomes (Gehring & Willoughby, 2002; Holroyd & Coles, 2002; Johansen & Fields, 2004; Botvinick, 2007). Botvinick suggests that the occurrence of conflict is an aversive event. Consequently, in addition to recruiting cognitive control to improve performance, dACC may also bias decisions such as task selection and/or task strategy to minimize the risk that conflict will occur in the future. These two functions of the dACC may be acting in parallel. In the color–word Stroop task, for example, dACC activity on a cI trial signals response conflict and an aversive event. As described above, the dACC recruits cognitive control, which enhances task-relevant processing and improves behavioral performance on a trial-by-trial basis. However, the dACC could also bias task selection and/or task strategy to minimize risk of conflict in the future (Figure 11.7). On trials following dACC activity a "word reading" strategy would be less likely.

Botvinick (2007) provides a computational model for the role of the dACC in both conflict detection and decision making that is based on behavioral performance during a demand selection task. In this task, subjects are allowed to freely select task trials represented in two separate decks of cards. Unbeknownst to the subjects, one deck contains more difficult trials than the other. Over time, after several choices from both decks are made, subjects learn to choose from the "easy deck" and avoid choosing from the "hard deck." Botvinick models this behavior based on a dACC-mediated learning signal. As a subject encounters a difficult trial in the hard deck, response conflict activates the dACC. Greater and more frequent dACC activation during trials from the hard deck eventually biases the subject toward choosing from the easy deck instead (Botvinick, 2007).

Future neuroimaging studies will determine if dACC-mediated learning signals are both guiding behavior and indexing response conflict in the demand selection task. Additionally, some

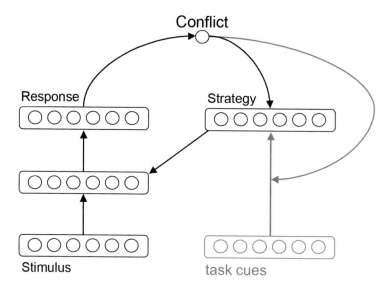

FIGURE 11.7   Dorsal anterior cingulate cortex (dACC) could play a dual role in both conflict monitoring and decision making. The portion of the diagram in black shows how the dACC detects conflict and then implements top-down control by adjusting attention to task-relevant stimuli at the strategy level on a trial-by-trial basis, as described in Botvinick et al. (2001). The portion in gray shows how conflict could also serve as a bias or learning signal, influencing which strategy is selected on future trials. From Botvinick, M.M. (2007). Conflict monitoring and decision making: Reconciling two perspectives on anterior cingulate function. *Cognitive, Affective, and Behavioral Neuroscience, 7*(4), 361, with permission of the publisher.

predictions of conflict theory would have to be reconciled with theories of decision making. For example, according to conflict theory, previous trial history is continuously being updated and influencing adjustments in cognitive control in a dynamic and trial-by-trial manner. Even after cognitive control has been implemented, if incongruent trials are not presented for some time, cognitive control relaxes, and a word reading strategy is adopted, allowing response conflict (and dACC) activity to occur once again (Botvinick et al., 2001). A learning signal, on the other hand, seems to induce more long-lasting changes. Although Botvinick's new model accounts for occasional switches back to the hard deck (after a rare encounter with a difficult trial in the easy deck) and does give preferential weighting to more recent trials, the use of the term "learning" seems to imply a more long-term strategy shift than that described by conflict control loop theory. Future studies will need to tease apart these two mechanisms and also determine how they interact.

Dual Mechanisms of Control: Proactive Versus Reactive Control Strategy

Braver et al. (2007) present the DMC theory to help elucidate differences in working memory task performance and neural activity both between and within individuals. They lay out two different cognitive control strategies: proactive control and reactive control. *Proactive control* is considered preparatory and goal-oriented and is characterized by sustained activity, usually in lateral PFC. Although proactive control heavily utilizes cognitive and metabolic resources, it is the optimal strategy for fast and accurate task performance in most situations. A proactive control strategy keeps relevant task or goal-related information on hand, so that when a future event occurs, this information is ready when needed. *Reactive control*, on the other hand, occurs "just in time." It happens at the last moment and is associated with a transient activation usually involving the ACC during the response, or a transient response in lateral PFC that occurs during or immediately following the event in which it is needed. Reactive control is susceptible to interference, resulting in RT slowing and errors. It uses less cognitive and metabolic resources than proactive control and allows for greater processing of task-irrelevant stimuli or environmental changes.

Although their theory is formulated mainly to answer questions regarding cognitive control during working memory tasks, they explicitly acknowledge that DMC is well aligned with conflict control loop theory: "the conflict signal in ACC might be used to increase the tendency to use proactive control on subsequent trials . . . it might also be the case that ACC serves as a core component of reactive control processing, by rapidly signaling the need for increased control on the current trial, to resolve interference, increase response strength, or correct an impending error" (Braver et al., 2007). Implementation of proactive versus reactive control strategies can explain differences in task performance and neural activity within the same individuals, between individuals with high and low fluid intelligence, older and younger adults, and individuals with different affective states and traits.

One study describes how DMC theory accounts for changes in behavior and neural activity as a result of interference expectancy. Subjects performed two versions of a recent-negative Sternberg working memory task. In the low interference expectancy task, only 20% of the trials were difficult interference trials. In the high interference expectancy task, 80% of the trials were interference trials. Behavioral results showed that subjects high in general fluid intelligence (high-gF) showed less interference, particularly in the high interference expectancy task, than did subjects low in general fluid intelligence (low-gF). Neuroimaging results indicated that the high-gF subjects had sustained delay-related activity in left VLPFC in the high interference expectancy task whereas the low-gF showed more transient probe-related PFC activity, similar to that demonstrated by both high- and low-gF subjects in the low interference expectancy task. Braver et al. conclude that high-gF subjects reduce interference through the use of a proactive control strategy

during conditions in which interference is expected. Low-gF subjects show behavioral interference due to their reliance on a reactive control strategy, which is more susceptible to interference, even in situations where interference is expected.

This experiment is strikingly similar in design, results, and interpretation to Carter et al. (2000), discussed in detail above. In the color–word Stroop task, greater interference (and dACC activation) in the low expectancy incongruent blocks could be attributed to a reactive control strategy, which would be favored when interference is less likely. Lack of dACC activation and less interference in the high expectancy incongruent block could likewise be attributed to a proactive strategy of control. Braver et al. interestingly show that individual differences in intelligence can determine how well the proactive strategy is implemented in situations in which it is advantageous, and similar results would be expected if low- and high-gF individuals were tested in the paradigm used in Carter et al. (2000).

Last, Braver et al. (2007) discuss how differences in affect relate to implementation of proactive versus reactive control. They predict that individuals high in behavioral approach sensitivity (BAS) are more attuned to goals and rewards, and are thus more likely to adopt a proactive strategy of control. Individuals high in behavioral inhibition sensitivity (BIS) are more attuned to punishment and threats, and would favor a more reactive strategy of control to better monitor the environment. They cite some evidence in support of this distinction. For example, high BAS score was negatively correlated with event-related dACC activity in a working memory task (Gray et al., 2005), and high-anxious subjects showed increased transient and reduced sustained activation in cognitive control regions during a working memory task (Fales et al., 2008). As described above, we found that high-anxious subjects (compared to low-anxious subjects) showed increased behavioral interference and dACC activity during performance of an emotional facial Stroop task, particularly when the task-irrelevant word was emotional (Krug & Carter, 2010). The DMC theory can easily account for this result.

High-anxious subjects may be more likely to use a reactive control strategy to constantly monitor the environment for threatening stimuli. Thus, when a cI trial occurs, a reactive strategy of cognitive control is implemented after the trial has been presented, in an attempt to resolve interference caused by the incongruent word. Activity in dACC is the neural marker of this reactive control. Reactive control may be particularly ineffective when the conflicting word is "fearful" (because high-anxious subjects may have difficulty disengaging from threatening stimuli), resulting in increased dACC activity and slowed RT. Another possibility is that high-anxious subjects could have equivalent amounts of proactive control in comparison to low-anxious subjects. However, due to enhanced attention to the fearful word on cI neutral face–fearful word trials, proactive control may not be adequate and reactive control could be engaged in a compensatory manner.

The DMC and conflict loop theories are in no way mutually exclusive. However, a perfectly efficient proactive strategy of control would most likely abolish the need for the conflict and cognitive control loop entirely. Behaviorally, this would be characterized by a lack of interference effects and trial-to-trial adjustments, and sustained PFC activity. In most cases, this is not achieved and interference effects, trial-to-trial adjustments in behavior, and activity in associated conflict and control regions are apparent and can be accounted for according to conflict loop theory. The DMC theory will be most useful in explaining individual differences, not only in relation to intelligence and trait anxiety, but also in differences in performance between subjects in general. For example, it is often the case that some subjects do not show trial-to-trials adjustments at all (Botvinick et al., 1999). Modeling of both sustained and event-related activity could determine if these subjects are simply utilizing a proactive control strategy, or if their lack of control-related adjustments is caused by a faulty or ineffective reactive control system.

CONCLUSION

In conclusion, we have summarized behavioral and neural evidence in support of conflict control loop theory. When two conflicting responses are activated, as would occur on an incongruent trial of the color–word Stroop task, the dACC activates, recruiting DLPFC-mediated cognitive control, ultimately resulting in an improvement in performance on subsequent incongruent trials. This control is most likely accomplished through enhanced processing of task-relevant information and decreased processing task-irrelevant information.

Emotional response conflict tasks produce similar behavioral effects and also activate the same dACC/DLPFC network. There is some evidence that rACC plays an important role as well, most likely through inhibition of the amygdala. Rostral ACC results are not as consistent, most likely because rACC activity is greatly influenced by individual differences, particularly in anxiety.

Conflict loop theory is readily reconciled with other theories that extend beyond the dynamic adjustments in control that are seen during the performance of forced-choice RT tasks. For example, during decision making, it has been hypothesized that dACC signaling associated with response conflict may represent an aversive event that may serve as a learning signal that biases future decision making. The conflict-monitoring and cognitive control loop could also be an important component of a reactive control strategy, and individual differences in trial-to-trial effects could be due to utilization of this strategy.

References

Bishop, S., Duncan, J., Brett, M., & Lawrence, A. D. (2004). Prefrontal cortical function and anxiety: Controlling attention to threat-related stimuli. *Nature Neuroscience, 7*(2), 184–188.

Botvinick, M., Nystrom, L. E., Fissell, K., Carter, C. S., & Cohen, J. D. (1999). Conflict monitoring versus selection-for-action in anterior cingulate cortex. *Nature, 402*(6758), 179–181.

Botvinick, M. M. (2007). Conflict monitoring and decision making: Reconciling two perspectives on anterior cingulate function. *Cognitive, Affective, and Behavioral Neuroscience, 7*(4), 356–366.

Botvinick, M. M., Braver, T. S., Barch, D. M., Carter, C. S., & Cohen, J. D. (2001). Conflict monitoring and cognitive control. *Psychological Review, 108*(3), 624–652.

Braver, T. S., Gray, J. R., & Burgess, G. C. (2007). Explaining the many varieties of working memory variation: Dual mechanisms of cognitive control. In A. R. A. Conway, C. Jarrold, M. J. Kane, A. Miyake, & J. N. Towse (Eds.), *Variation in working memory* (pp. 76–106). Oxford, UK: Oxford University Press.

Bush, G., Luu, P., & Posner, M. I. (2000). Cognitive and emotional influences in anterior cingulate cortex. *Trends in Cognitive Sciences, 4*(6), 215–222.

Bush, G., Whalen, P. J., Rosen, B. R., Jenike, M. A., McInerney, S. C., & Rauch, S. L. (1998). The counting Stroop: An interference task specialized for functional neuroimaging—Validation study with functional MRI. *Human Brain Mapping, 6*(4), 270–282.

Carter, C. S., Braver, T. S., Barch, D. M., Botvinick, M. M., Noll, D., & Cohen, J. D. (1998). Anterior cingulate cortex, error detection, and the online monitoring of performance. *Science, 280*(5364), 747–749.

Carter, C. S., Macdonald, A. M., Botvinick, M., Ross, L. L., Stenger, V. A., Noll, D., & Cohen, J. D. (2000). Parsing executive processes: Strategic vs. evaluative functions of the anterior cingulate cortex. *Proceedings of the National Academy of Sciences of the United States of America, 97*(4), 1944–1948.

Carter, C. S., Mintun, M., & Cohen, J. D. (1995). Interference and facilitation effects during selective attention: An h215o pet study of Stroop task performance. *Neuroimage, 2*(4), 264–272.

Dehaene, S., Posner, M. I., & Tucker, D. M. (1994). Localization of a neural system for error detection and compensation. *Psychological Science, 5*(5), 303–305.

Devinsky, O., Morrell, M. J., & Vogt, B. A. (1995). Contributions of anterior cingulate cortex to behaviour. *Brain, 118*(Pt 1), 279–306.

Drevets, W. C., & Raichle, M. E. (1998). Reciprocal suppression of regional cerebral blood flow during emotional versus higher cognitive processes: Implications for interactions between emotion and cognition. *Cognition and Emotion, 12*(3), 353–385.

Egner, T., Etkin, A., Gale, S., & Hirsch, J. (2008). Dissociable neural systems resolve conflict from emotional versus nonemotional distracters. *Cerebral Cortex, 18*(6), 1475–1484.

Egner, T., & Hirsch, J. (2005). Cognitive control mechanisms resolve conflict through cortical amplification of task-relevant information. *Nature Neuroscience, 8*(12), 1784–1790.

Etkin, A., Egner, T., Peraza, D. M., Kandel, E. R., & Hirsch, J. (2006). Resolving emotional conflict: A role for the rostral anterior cingulate cortex in modulating activity in the amygdala. *Neuron, 51*(6), 871–882.

Fales, C. L., Barch, D. M., Burgess, G. C., Schaefer, A., Mennin, D. S., Gray, J. R., & Braver, T. S. (2008). Anxiety and cognitive efficiency: Differential modulation of transient and sustained neural activity during a working memory task. *Cognitive, Affective, and Behavioral Neuroscience, 8*(3), 239–253.

Gehring, W. J., Coles, M. G., Meyer, D. E., & Donchin, E. (1990). The error-related negativity: An event-related potential accompanying errors. *Psychophysiology, 27*, S34.

Gehring, W. J., & Fencsik, D. E. (2001). Functions of the medial frontal cortex in the processing of conflict and errors. *Journal of Neuroscience, 21*(23), 9430–9437.

Gehring, W. J., Goss, B., Coles, M. G., Meyer, D. E., & Donchin, E. (1993). A neural system for error detection and compensation. *Psychological Science, 4*, 385–390.

Gehring, W. J., & Willoughby, A. R. (2002). The medial frontal cortex and the rapid processing of monetary gains and losses. *Science, 295*(5563), 2279–2282.

Gratton, G., Coles, M. G., & Donchin, E. (1992). Optimizing the use of information: Strategic control of activation of responses. *Journal of Experimental Psychology: General, 121*(4), 480–506.

Gray, J. R., Burgess, G. C., Schaefer, A., Yarkoni, T., Larsen, R. J., & Braver, T. S. (2005). Affective personality differences in neural processing efficiency confirmed using fMRI. *Cognitive, Affective, and Behavioral Neuroscience, 5*(2), 182–190.

Haas, B. W., Omura, K., Constable, R. T., & Canli, T. (2006). Interference produced by emotional conflict associated with anterior cingulate activation. *Cognitive, Affective, and Behavioral Neuroscience, 6*(2), 152–156.

Hohnsbein, J., Falkenstein, M., & Hoormann, J. (1989). Error processing in visual and auditory choice reaction tasks. *Journal of Psychophysiology, 3*, 320.

Holroyd, C. B., & Coles, M. G. (2002). The neural basis of human error processing: Reinforcement learning, dopamine, and the error-related negativity. *Psychological Review, 109*(4), 679–709.

Johansen, J. P., & Fields, H. L. (2004). Glutamatergic activation of anterior cingulate cortex produces an aversive teaching signal. *Nature Neuroscience, 7*(4), 398–403.

Kerns, J. G. (2006). Anterior cingulate and prefrontal cortex activity in an fMRI study of trial-to-trial adjustments on the Simon task. *Neuroimage, 33*(1), 399–405.

Kerns, J. G., Cohen, J. D., MacDonald, A. W., 3rd, Cho, R. Y., Stenger, V. A., & Carter, C. S. (2004). Anterior cingulate conflict monitoring and adjustments in control. *Science, 303*(5660), 1023–1026.

Koster, E. H., Crombez, G., Verschuere, B., & De Houwer, J. (2004). Selective attention to threat in the dot probe paradigm: Differentiating vigilance and difficulty to disengage. *Behaviour Research and Therapy, 42*(10), 1183–1192.

Krug, M. K., & Carter, C. S. (2010). Adding fear to conflict: A general purpose cognitive control network is modulated by trait anxiety. *Cognitive, Affective, and Behavioral Neuroscience, 10*(3), 357–371.

MacDonald, A. W., 3rd, Cohen, J. D., Stenger, V. A., & Carter, C. S. (2000). Dissociating the role of the dorsolateral prefrontal and anterior cingulate cortex in cognitive control. *Science, 288*(5472), 1835–1838.

MacLeod, C. M. (1991). Half a century of research on the Stroop effect: An integrative review. *Psychological Bulletin, 109*(2), 163–203.

Nitschke, J. B., Sarinopoulos, I., Oathes, D. J., Johnstone, T., Whalen, P. J., Davidson, R. J., & Kalin, N. H. (2009). Anticipatory activation in the amygdala and anterior cingulate in generalized anxiety disorder and prediction of treatment response. *The American Journal of Psychiatry, 166*(3), 302–310.

Ochsner, K. N., Hughes, B., Robertson, E. R., Cooper, J. C., & Gabrieli, J. D. (2009). Neural systems supporting the control of affective and cognitive conflicts. *Journal of Cognitive Neuroscience, 21*(9), 1842–1855.

Pardo, J. V., Pardo, P. J., Janer, K. W., & Raichle, M. E. (1990). The anterior cingulate cortex mediates processing selection in the Stroop attentional conflict paradigm. *Proceedings of the National Academy of Sciences of the United States of America, 87*(1), 256–259.

Pizzagalli, D., Pascual-Marqui, R. D., Nitschke, J. B., Oakes, T. R., Larson, C. L., Abercrombie, H. C., et al. (2001). Anterior cingulate activity as a predictor of degree of treatment response in major depression: Evidence from brain electrical tomography analysis. *The American Journal of Psychiatry, 158*(3), 405–415.

Pizzagalli, D. A., Peccoralo, L. A., Davidson, R. J., & Cohen, J. D. (2006). Resting anterior cingulate activity and abnormal responses to errors in subjects with elevated depressive symptoms: A 128-channel EEG study. *Human Brain Mapping, 27*(3), 185–201.

Polk, T. A., Drake, R. M., Jonides, J. J., Smith, M. R., & Smith, E. E. (2008). Attention enhances the neural processing of relevant features and suppresses the processing of irrelevant features in humans: A functional magnetic resonance imaging study of the Stroop task. *Journal of Neuroscience, 28*(51), 13786–13792.

Salemink, E., van den Hout, M. A., & Kindt, M. (2007). Selective attention and threat: Quick orienting versus slow disengagement and two versions of the dot probe task. *Behaviour Research and Therapy, 45*(3), 607–615.

Salvadore, G., Cornwell, B. R., Colon-Rosario, V., Coppola, R., Grillon, C., Zarate, C. A., Jr., & Manji, H. K. (2009). Increased anterior cingulate cortical activity in response to fearful faces: A neurophysiological biomarker that predicts rapid antidepressant response to ketamine. *Biological Psychiatry, 65*(4), 289–295.

Shin, L. M., Whalen, P. J., Pitman, R. K., Bush, G., Macklin, M. L., Lasko, N. B., et al. (2001). An fMRI study of anterior cingulate function in posttraumatic stress disorder. *Biological Psychiatry, 50*(12), 932–942.

Steele, J. D., & Lawrie, S. M. (2004). Segregation of cognitive and emotional function in the prefrontal cortex: A stereotactic meta-analysis. *NeuroImage, 21*(3), 868–875.

Stroop, J. R. (1935). Studies of interference in serial verbal reactions. *Journal of Experimental Psychology, 18*, 643–662.

Tecce, J. J., & Dimartino, M. (1965). Effects of heightened drive (shock) on performance in a tachistoscopic color-word interference task. *Psychological Reports, 16*, 93–94.

Tzelgov, J., Henik, A., & Berger, J. (1992). Controlling Stroop effects by manipulating expectations for color words. *Memory and Cognition, 20*(6), 727–735.

Van Veen, V., & Carter, C. S. (2002). The timing of action-monitoring processes in the anterior cingulate cortex. *Journal of Cognitive Neuroscience, 14*(4), 593–602.

Vogt, B. A., Finch, D. M., & Olson, C. R. (1992). Functional heterogeneity in cingulate cortex: The anterior executive and posterior evaluative regions. *Cerebral Cortex, 2*(6), 435–443.

Weissman, D. H., Warner, L. M., & Woldorff, M. G. (2009). Momentary reductions of attention permit greater processing of irrelevant stimuli. *NeuroImage, 48*(3), 609–615.

Whalen, P. J., Bush, G., McNally, R. J., Wilhelm, S., McInerney, S. C., Jenike, M. A., & Rauch, S. L. (1998). The emotional counting Stroop paradigm: A functional magnetic resonance imaging probe of the anterior cingulate affective division. *Biological Psychiatry, 44*(12), 1219–1228.

Whalen, P. J., Johnstone, T., Somerville, L. H., Nitschke, J. B., Polis, S., Alexander, A. L., et al. (2008). A functional magnetic resonance imaging predictor of treatment response to venlafaxine in generalized anxiety disorder. *Biological Psychiatry, 63*(9), 858–863.

Wittfoth, M., Schroder, C., Schardt, D. M., Dengler, R., Heinze, H. J., & Kotz, S. A. (2010). On emotional conflict: Interference resolution of happy and angry prosody reveals valence-specific effects. *Cerebral Cortex, 20*(2), 383–392.

12

Emotional Influences on Visuospatial Attention

HARLAN M. FICHTENHOLTZ AND KEVIN S. LABAR

A MAJOR function of attentional control systems is to allocate processing resources to environmental stimuli that are relevant for goal-directed behavior. From an evolutionary perspective, goal-directed behavior has been shaped by pressures related to survival, reproduction, and adaptations to environmental change. These selective pressures inherently entail motivational and emotional faculties that tune sensory representations, sharpen attentional control capabilities, and initiate appropriate actions. For instance, imagine the complex challenges faced in a predator–prey encounter. Although attentional systems can facilitate the detection of a predator's movement and direct eye movements toward possible escape routes, the mobilization of bodily resources from the viscera to the skeletomuscular system requires engagement of emotional systems that regulate autonomic functions. Autonomic and skeletomuscular feedback signals, in turn, recruit additional mechanisms to redirect visuospatial processing and

maintain vigilance, in order to update action readiness and motor execution once a change in emotional meaning of the situation has been detected. Thus, the relationship between attention and emotion is deeply intertwined, and these systems often cooperate to integrate mental and physical resources to adaptively interact with other agents in the environment. Attention to affective communicative cues such as facial expression, gesture, and vocalization is critical for effective social bonding and management of interpersonal relationships.

At times, however, attentional and emotional goals conflict, which requires higher-order executive processes to balance the biases of these systems and prioritize action hierarchies. These behavioral control mechanisms are particularly taxed in individuals who suffer from anxiety disorders (Matthews & Wells, 2000). Although such instances of system conflict are informative, it is important to keep in mind that attentional and emotional functions are typically synergistic and provide complementary information to form salience maps of the environment and to instigate appropriate action repertoires for particular interpersonal contexts. For this reason, we do not ascribe to the dualistic idea of diametrically opposed "hot" and "cold" systems that compete for behavioral expression (Metcalfe & Mischel, 1999; Deutsch & Strack, 2006). Instead, our view is that the implementation of attentional and emotional control is carried out by parallel processing streams in the brain that interact at multiple stages of information processing (Johnson & Weisz, 1994; Pessoa, 2008), are mediated by cortical–subcortical feedback loops, and converge on common sensory and motor targets to guide behavior. This chapter focuses specifically on how emotional processing in the amygdala and related limbic regions interact with frontoparietal attentional control systems and the visual processing stream, as these interactions are the best understood to date. Such effects have been elucidated by studying neurologic patients with brain damage, as well as by functional brain imaging methods in healthy individuals. A systematic treatment of attentional biases in affective disorders is beyond the scope of this chapter, although we will mention some studies that investigate how anxiety as a trait marker moderates emotion–attention interactions. We will also consider the time course of emotional influences on visual processing that have been revealed by event-related potential (ERP) studies in humans.

THEORETICAL BACKGROUND

Theoretical models of attention have largely neglected specifying the role of emotion, despite the fact that these processing domains share some common objectives, such as understanding the construct of arousal and determining how conscious awareness affects stimulus processing. Hence, unlike many facets of attention discussed throughout this volume, studies of emotional influences have limited grounds for detailed hypothesis testing. Nonetheless, one of the earliest ideas put forth by Easterbrook (1959) was that high emotional arousal narrowed the focus of attention, so that fewer cues in the environment

could be used for task-relevant processing, particularly in the context of negative affective states like fear. The *Easterbrook hypothesis* has been expanded more recently by Fredrickson (2001), who has argued that, in contrast to these narrowing effects of negative emotional arousal, positive emotions broaden attentional focus in order to build social relationships (the *broaden-and-build hypothesis*) (see also Isen, 1987). Unfortunately, most research conducted to date has focused on negative emotions, so direct tests of these valence-specific hypotheses are difficult to assess.

Other researchers have linked emotion and attention by appealing to basic motivational constructs such as approach and avoidance. For instance, Bradley (2009) has postulated that attending to novel events and processing emotionally significant events both involve orienting processes that engage defensive and appetitive motivational systems to mobilize bodily resources, enhance perception, and prepare for action. Derryberry and Tucker (1994) further propose that phasic and tonic motivational states adaptively regulate the direction and breadth of attention to focus processing resources on stimuli that are most relevant to the organism's current needs. For the present purposes, we will include only empirical studies that directly manipulate the emotional properties of stimuli presented during attention-demanding tasks rather than those that manipulate emotions indirectly through motivational state inductions (e.g., reward or frustration paradigms).

ANATOMICAL CONSIDERATIONS: PARALLEL PROCESSING STREAMS AND EMOTION–ATTENTION HUBS

Mesulam (1981, 1998) has long argued that broad mental faculties are organized into parallel-distributed, large-scale neurocognitive networks. Relevant for the present discussion, the limbic forebrain is particularly well-positioned anatomically to integrate the exteroceptive and interoceptive processing necessary to coordinate affective and motivational behaviors. Although the concept of a monolithic limbic system for the processing of all aspects of emotion has received much criticism (LeDoux, 1990), it is clear that some limbic and paralimbic structures play key roles in social, affective, and motivational behaviors. The amygdala, in particular, has emerged as a critical structure for initiating reactions to emotionally significant stimuli in the environment through its extensive and sometimes privileged connections with sensory processing regions, autonomic and motoric effectors, and heteromodal association cortices. Anatomical studies that have estimated numbers of synaptic connections have placed the amygdala at the top of the primate forebrain hierarchy in terms of its overall connectivity (Young, 1993); consequently, it can exert a powerful influence across a broad swath of cortex to prioritize processing resources. Affective neuroscience studies have shown that the amygdala is especially sensitive to the arousal dimension of emotion, responding maximally to stimuli that are emotionally intense or particularly salient to the organism's current state or situational context (Cahill & McGaugh, 1998; Sander et al., 2003; LaBar, 2007).

In contrast, as described elsewhere in this volume, large-scale theories of attentional control have emphasized the regulatory functions of the dorsal fronto-cingulo-parietal system(s) over sensory processing (Mesulam, 1981; Corbetta & Shulman, 2002; see also Chapters 1 and 5 in this volume). Curiously, the amygdala has minimal monosynaptic connections to the components of this network, save for the rostral and ventral portions of the anterior cingulate gyrus. For this reason, Mesulam (1981) has termed the cingulate the "motivational" interface of the dorsal attentional control system. One can only speculate as to why a degree of separation evolved between these processing streams. Presumably, this anatomical arrangement permits more flexible use of resources in the environment and mitigates against stereotyped action repertoires in response to salient events. Nonetheless, emotional processing in the amygdala interfaces with attentional control circuitry through several anatomical "hubs" as well as more diffuse neuromodulatory actions (see Figure 12.1). In addition to the anterior cingulate, emotion–attention hubs include paralimbic zones in the insula, inferior frontal gyrus, and orbitofrontal cortex, which link the amygdala with dorsal frontoparietal sectors. Evidence for an integrative role of these hubs comes from neuroimaging studies that indicate an additive effect of attentional and emotional manipulations in the strength of the hemodynamic signal (e.g., Fichtenholtz et al., 2004). Moreover, neurobiological models of clinical depression have emphasized that activity in these hubs maintains a balance between dorsal attentional and ventral somatic streams of processing in order to regulate mood (Mayberg, 1997).

Emotional processing can also impact attentional systems indirectly through feedback effects on sensory processing targets. The extensive feedback projections from the amygdala throughout the ventral visual processing stream, including V1 in the primate, have received considerable interest as a putative mechanism for enhancing sensory representations of emotionally significant events (Amaral et al., 1992; Vuilleumier & Driver, 2007). Moreover, the amygdala has direct outputs to other brain regions that release a variety of neuromodulators, including the hypothalamus for release of stress hormones via the hypothalamic-pituitary-adrenal axis and the nucleus basalis of Meynert for the release of acetylcholine. These agents have a broad impact on cortical targets, including those mediating attentional functions, through both direct actions and indirect feedback mechanisms. For instance, acetylcholine enhances synaptic plasticity in the cortex by reducing thresholds for action potential firing, which enhances readiness for information processing during high arousal states. Amygdala damage in rodents leads to failures in this cholinergic regulation of attentional responses to conditioned cues (Gallagher & Holland, 1994). Enhanced sensory feedback and neuromodulatory influences may even redirect attentional control systems to alter emotional processing directly through mechanisms of emotion regulation, whereby limbic system structures are themselves the target of attentional control (see Ochsner & Gross, 2005, for a review).

The diversity of synaptic effects, multiple levels of system interfaces, and breadth of behavioral constructs make the study of attention-emotion interactions a complex undertaking. Whereas both the dorsal fronto-cingulo-parietal attentional

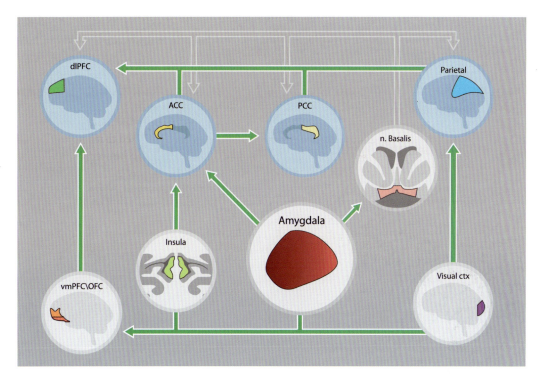

FIGURE 12.1   Simplified model of large-scale attention–emotion interactions in the brain. Amygdala-based emotional evaluation interacts with dorsal frontoparietal attentional control regions via "hubs" in the insula, anterior cingulate, and frontal lobes. Additional interactions occur via feedback projections from the amygdala to the visual stream (not shown), and neuromodulatory actions such as cholinergic effects mediated by the nucleus basalis of Meynert. From LaBar, K. S. (2010). Emotion-cognition interactions. In G. F. Koob, M, LeMoal, & and R. F. Thompson (Eds.), *Encyclopedia of behavioral neuroscience, Vol. 1* (Vol. 1, pp. 469–476). New York: Elsevier Science, with permission of the publisher.

control system(s) and an amygdala-based emotional arousal system exert top-down control over sensory processing streams, these effects may be temporally dissociated even if they are anatomically convergent. Not surprisingly, initial cognitive neuroscience efforts in this area have led to some contradictory findings. Below, we review the progress made to date in the domains of overt orienting, covert attention, and gaze-directed cueing, and make recommendations for future work.

NATURAL SELECTIVE ATTENTION: ORIENTING TO EMOTIONAL STIMULI

Overt Orienting

When engaging the complex world, individuals will preferentially attend to emotional information.

Eye tracking studies have examined emotional modulation of both attentional orienting and sustained attention processes. During novel competitive visual presentations, initial eye fixation is more likely to be attracted to emotional than neutral information. Such emotional biases in initial attentional orienting have been reported using emotional images (LaBar et al., 2000; Mogg et al., 2000; Numenmaa et al., 2006; Calvo et al., 2007; Kwak et al., 2007; Mogg et al., 2007; Alpers, 2008) or emotional elements of a complex image (Lykins et al., 2006). These effects occur even when subjects are explicitly instructed not to direct gaze to emotional targets (Numenmaa et al., 2006), and they can override the prepotent left-to-right visual scanning patterns when emotional information is presented in the right visual field (LaBar et al., 2000) (Figure 12.2). Given that initial fixations occur within 200–250 ms of stimulus onset, there

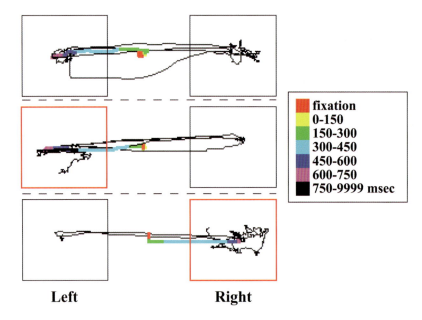

Left   **Right**

FIGURE 12.2   Emotional modulation of overt orienting and sustained attention. Oculographic patterns on three paired-stimulus viewing trials. *Top row*: Neutral–neutral stimulus pair; *middle row*: negative–neutral stimulus pair; *bottom row*: neutral–negative stimulus pair. Red box, negative scene; black box, neutral scene. Subjects began each trial by fixating on a central crosshair. Colored line segment indicates the initial saccade direction away from fixation in 150 ms time bins. Black line segment indicates the eye position for the remainder of the trial. The presence of emotionally negative scenes modulates both initial orienting responses away from fixation and sustained attention over a 10 s free viewing period relative to neutral–neutral control trials. From LaBar, K. S., Mesulam, M.-M., Gitelman, D. R., & Weintraub, S. (2000). Emotional curiosity: Modulation of visuospatial attention by arousal is preserved in aging and early-stage Alzheimer's disease. *Neuropsychologia, 38,* 1734–1740. New York: Elsevier Science, with permission of the publisher.

are covert mechanisms that reflexively guide attention toward emotional targets prior to active visual exploration. Eye tracking studies have further shown that sustained attention responses (after initial orienting) are also prolonged by the emotional features of stimuli, even when the stimuli are aversive, and these effects can last for several seconds (LaBar et al., 2000; Lykins et al., 2006; Alpers, 2008). One downstream consequence of this prolonged attentional engagement is enhanced perception of sensory details and memory formation for emotional compared to neutral stimuli (Calvo et al., 2007; Murty et al., 2010), although tradeoff effects can occur such that enhanced memory for central emotionally negative information comes at the expense of impaired memory for peripheral neutral details (Heuer & Reisberg, 1990).

These biases in attentional orienting are also modulated by anxiety and motivational significance.

As anxiety increases, so does the magnitude of the bias toward emotional stimuli, particularly negative stimuli (Mogg et al., 2000, 2007). Consistent with these findings in general anxiety, post-traumatic stress disorder patients demonstrate greater orienting toward emotional words (Bryant et al., 1995). Phobic disorders are also associated with attentional orienting biases toward the object of the phobia, but in contrast to the sustained attentional biases in healthy participants, the length of attentional engagement is shorter (Rinck et al., 2006). Motivationally important images, such as cigarettes to smokers, also demonstrate an initial orienting bias (e.g., Kwak et al., 2007).

Further studies have investigated emotional influences on attentional behavior during pro- and antisaccade tasks. Kissler and Keil (2008) demonstrated that participants are more likely to make errors in an antisaccade task toward an irrelevant emotional stimulus. In prosaccade tasks, faster reaction times (Nummenmaa et al., 2006, 2009; Kissler & Keil, 2008; Bannermann et al., 2009, 2010) and more accurate responses (Bannermann et al., 2009, 2010) are made toward emotional stimuli. The path of eye movements between separated neutral stimuli also deviates by the presence of an emotional distractor, indicating that extraneous emotional information also influences the online trajectory of goal-directed oculomotor behavior (Nummenmaa et al., 2009).

Studies of Spatial Neglect Patients

Additional evidence of socioemotional prioritization in information processing comes from studies of patients with spatial neglect. These patients provide an important model system for understanding the functions of the dorsal frontoparietal network, and they are particularly interesting for evaluating the relative independence of emotional and attentional control functions (see Figure 12.1). In these patients, socially relevant stimuli (images of schematic neutral faces) presented to the contralesional visual field are more easily detected than similarly constructed geometric shapes,

suggesting that there may be an attentional advantage for more meaningful stimuli (Vuilleumier, 2000). Vuilleumier and Schwartz (2001a,b) further demonstrated that schematic images of emotional expressions (positive and negative) and fear-relevant stimuli (spiders) engage the limited attentional mechanisms available in neglect patients (Figure 12.3). These studies have used geometric shapes and schematic images of flowers that are composed of identical structural elements to rule out differences in lower-level visual features. Interestingly, the rate of extinction for neutral stimuli in the contralesional visual field did not differ with respect to the emotional stimulus presented to the ipsilesional visual field. This finding suggests that, although the emotional nature of the stimulus was able to elicit attentional orienting toward the contralesional visual field, it did not show a similar effect in directing attention away from the contralesional field. Fox (2002) conducted a similar study using photographs of emotional facial expressions (fearful, happy, and neutral) as stimuli. Consistent with Vuilleumier and Schwartz (2001a,b), less extinction was seen for both fearful and happy expressions than neutral expressions. The emotion presented to the

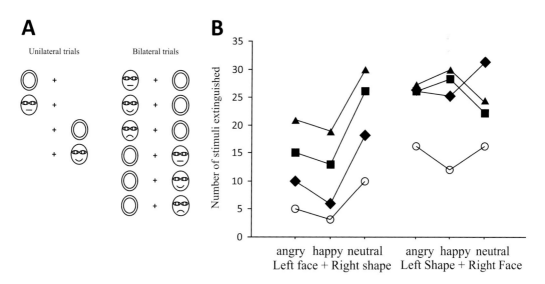

FIGURE 12.3   Emotional expression enhances contralesional face detection in hemispatial neglect patients. (**A**) Example of unilateral stimulus trials and all possible bilateral stimulus trials. (**B**) The total number of stimuli missed in the contralesional hemifield on bilateral trials as a function of stimulus condition. Reproduced from Vuilleumier, P., & and Schwartz, S. (2001a). Emotional facial expressions capture attention. *Neurology, 56,* 153–158, with permission of the publisher. Data represents individual patients.

contralesional visual field can even prime affective judgments of succeeding foveally presented faces, even when the lateral primes were not consciously perceived (Williams & Mattingly, 2004). Extending this work into the auditory domain, Grandjean and colleagues (2008) presented patients with neglect with two independent auditory streams containing vocal stimuli with positive, negative, and neutral prosody. As with the visual studies, vocal stimuli with emotional prosody showed less extinction than those with neutral prosody. These findings are fairly consistent in revealing preserved emotional prioritization in patients with neglect syndrome with frontoparietal damage, suggesting a partially independent pathway for mediating the behavioral effects.

A functional magnetic resonance imaging (fMRI) study of the extinction of facial expressions in a patient with spatial neglect (Vuilleumier et al., 2002) demonstrated activations in left amygdala, fusiform gyrus, orbitofrontal cortex, and right intraparietal sulcus in response to fearful faces, regardless of conscious perception; faces that were perceived activated left fusiform gyrus, parietal, and frontal cortex, regardless of expression. The interaction effect, reflected by regions that vary in their response based upon both the expression on the face and whether or not attention is directed toward the face (i.e., more activation to the fearful faces when reported than extinguished), revealed engagement of left fusiform gyrus, bilateral anterior parietal and frontal regions, and right anterior temporal pole.

These results suggest that the response in the amygdala is invariant to the amount of attention paid to the stimulus, at least for moderate ranges of attentional load (see also Fichtenholtz et al., 2004; for a contrary view that encompasses high-load manipulations, see Pessoa, 2008). The direct comparison of unseen fearful and neutral faces in bilateral trials yielded left amygdala responses along with visual areas, suggesting increased processing of unseen emotion. The response in the amygdala to neutral faces was greater when the faces were extinguished than when consciously perceived, indicating that the emotional specificity of the amygdala response might decrease during periods of inattention to allow for the

accurate detection of a possible threat (see also Anderson et al., 2003). Activation of the amygdala by extinguished faces suggests that it could be receiving input through a subcortical pathway, including the pulvinar, as seen by Morris and colleagues (2001), but does not preclude the possibility that the response of the intact primary visual pathway was sufficient to produce the activation.

In sum, these findings imply the existence of an emotional processing system that operates preattentively, allowing for fast orienting toward a potential threat in the environment. This preattentive emotional processing system, especially the amygdala, may receive input from a fast subcortical pathway from the retina through the superior colliculus and thalamus bypassing visual cortex (Vuilleumier et al., 2003). However, the existing studies do not prove that an extrageniculate pathway is involved. Preattentive processing of emotional salience may also bias visual processing either through direct amygdalar feedback connections onto visual cortex or via emotion–attention hubs that interface with dorsolateral prefrontal and parietal cortices (see Figure 12.1). It is also possible that the emotional information is biasing attention and entering awareness through residual integrity of dorsal frontoparietal cortex that was spared by the lesions associated with spatial neglect, as suggested by the interaction between emotional processing and attention in Vuilleumier et al. (2002). Further research is warranted to disentangle these alternative explanations.

Covert Orienting

Consistent with the notion of a preattentive emotional processing system, emotional stimuli presented in the periphery are associated with specific event-related magnetic fields as early as 80 ms after stimulus onset (Bayle et al., 2009). These early responses have been localized to frontal and temporal regions including the amygdala, consistent with a rapid response system that would produce the type of overt eye movement results discussed above. The question that remains is how are the succeeding stimuli processed when they appear at the same or different locations as the cue? Variations of reflexive attentional cueing tasks, such as those designed by Posner and colleagues (Posner, 1980; Posner et al., 1982), have been developed using emotional stimuli as directional cues. The stimulus used as the cue has varied across studies; some have used conditioned stimuli (e.g., Stormark & Hugdahl, 1996; Armony & Dolan, 2002), whereas others have used faces with emotional expressions (Pourtios et al., 2004) or emotionally valent words (Stormark et al., 1995). Although the majority of studies have presented visual stimuli, auditory stimuli were used by Pauli and Roder (2008), who presented neutral sounds at locations that had been aversively conditioned. By assessing the interaction between the cue validity and emotional conditions, it is possible to determine if the emotional content of the cue and cue validity affect attentional orienting either independently or in concert.

EVENT-RELATED POTENTIAL STUDIES

Due to their high temporal resolution, ERPs provide a straightforward way to compare how emotional and neutral attentional cues affect subsequent target processing, even at short stimulus onset asynchronies (SOAs) (see Chapter 2 for a discussion of ERP studies of reflexive attention). Across three studies (Stormark et al., 1995, 1999; Stormark & Hugdahl, 1996), both inherently emotional stimuli and emotionally conditioned stimuli were used, with different effects found in each study. Their first study, Stormark et al. (1995) implemented emotional or neutral words as attention directing cues. Participants showed a benefit in reaction time (RT) for validly cued trials with emotional words and a RT cost for invalidly cued trials with emotional words. No effect of validity was seen on RT for the neutral cue trials. Following the target presentation, there was a significant emotion by validity interaction for the occipital P1 component. Responses to validly cued targets following emotional words were smaller than responses to validly cued targets following neutral words, and there was no difference between the responses to invalidly cued targets. These results suggest that emotional words capture and hold attention more strongly than do than neutral words, but the decreased response to the emotionally cued targets suggests that the priming of visual processing areas usually seen in response to

a cue (Mangun & Hillyard, 1991) may not be occurring when the cue is emotional. This pattern of response is more consistent with inhibition of return (IOR) (Hopfinger & Mangun, 1998; McDonald et al., 1999; Hopfinger & Mangun, 2001), which has been demonstrated following irrelevant negative, but not positive cues (Chao, 2010). In contrast, subsequent reflexive cueing studies by the same group (Stormark & Hugdhal, 1996; Stormark et al., 1999) used more traditional cues (highlighting the outline of a box or highlighting the entire box) that were subject to aversive conditioning. Trials with neutral stimuli demonstrated a validity effect on RT, but no effect was seen for the aversively conditioned stimuli, and no ERP effects were seen for attentional targets.

More recently, several studies have demonstrated enhanced target processing following emotional cues (Pourtois et al., 2004; Brosch et al., 2008; Pauli & Roder, 2008; Santesso et al., 2008). In contrast to the verbal and conditioned stimuli used by Stormark and colleagues, the majority of these studies used facial expressions (Pourtois et al., 2004; Brosch et al., 2008; Santesso et al., 2008), whereas another study had no explicit attention-directing cue but instead presented targets at locations that had been previously aversively conditioned (Pauli & Roder, 2008). In all four studies, targets presented at a location cued by a negative emotion showed an enhanced P1 response compared to targets presented at a neutral location. The effect of positive emotional cues was less consistent. This negativity bias, if supported by additional research, may indicate differences in how cues in the environment are utilized as a function of emotional valence, as predicted by theoretical models (see the section "Theoretical Background"). Thus, at least in the presence of negative affect, there is facilitated attentional orienting in a spatial location where a target is expected to appear. It is not as well established whether concomitant attentional costs occur at invalidly cued locations.

FUNCTIONAL MAGNETIC RESONANCE IMAGING STUDIES

Functional MRI studies of emotion–attention tasks have demonstrated two consistent findings: ventral visual and emotional processing regions (including fusiform gyrus, amygdala, and insula) activate more in response to emotional compared to neutral cues, and dorsal attentional control regions (including intraparietal sulcus, dorsolateral prefrontal cortex, and anterior cingulate) activate in response to attention directing cues (Armony & Dolan, 2002; Pourtios et al., 2006; Carlson et al., 2009) (Figure 12.4). These findings are consistent across multiple cues, including aversively conditioned stimuli (Armony & Dolan, 2002), emotional faces (Pourtios et al., 2006), and masked emotional faces (Carlson et al., 2009). Carlson and colleagues (2009) have demonstrated enhanced left amygdala activation when a masked fearful face was directing attention. Attentional targets

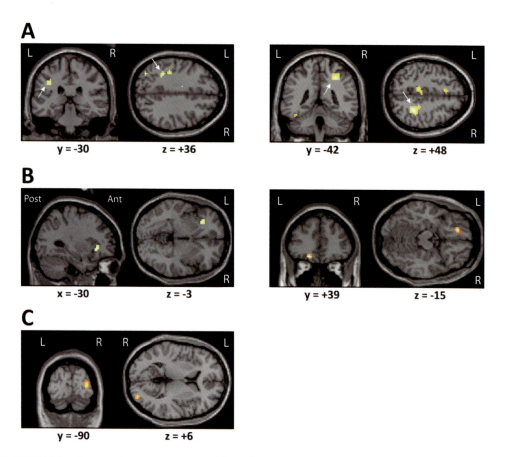

FIGURE 12.4 Patterns of activation in parietal, frontal, and occipital regions by targets following fearful face cues. (**A**) *Left panel*: Intraparietal sulcus (IPS) activation (*P* <0.001, uncorrected) obtained in the fear valid > fear invalid contrast for left visual field (LVF) targets. *Right panel*: Right IPS activation (*P* <0.001, uncorrected) obtained in the fear valid > fear invalid contrast for RVF targets. IPS activity is reduced when peripheral targets appear in the ipsilateral visual field following an invalid face on the contralateral side, indicating that threat-related cues not only draw attention but also produce higher disengage costs. (**B**) Lateral orbitofrontal cortex (OFC) activation (*P* <0.001, uncorrected) obtained in the fear invalid > fear valid contrast. *Left panel*: LVF Targets. *Right panel*: RVF Targets. This region is engaged when attention needs to be reoriented following a fearful face. (**C**) Right extrastriate cortex activation (*P* <0.005, uncorrected) obtained in the fear valid > fear invalid contrast, irrespective of the spatial location of targets. Visual processing of the target is enhanced in the location cued by the face. All of these effects were selective for fearful cues relative to happy cues, and were greater on cue–target trials than cue-only trials. From Pourtois, G., Schwartz, S., Seghier, M. L., Lazeyras, F., & and Vuilleumier, P. (2006). Neural systems for orienting attention to the location of threat signals: An event-related fMRI study. *NeuroImage, 31,* 920–3393, with permission of the publisher.

activated brain regions consistent with nonemotional spatial attention tasks (e.g., Woldorff et al., 2004), including supplementary motor area, anterior cingulate gyrus, intraparietal sulcus, and extrastriate visual cortex (Pourtois et al., 2006). Increased activation in parietal cortex ipsilateral to fearful faces suggests that the fearful face is acting as a reflexive attentional cue (Pourtios et al., 2006). Although these initial findings support parallel processing of emotional and attentional functions across ventral, emotional, and dorsal, attentional, streams, respectively (see Figure 12.1), greater specificity in characterizing functional localization along these pathways is needed in future research.

GENETIC FACTORS

Recently, a number of studies have investigated the role of serotonin transporter-linked promoter region (5-HTTLPR) polymorphisms in attentional orienting to emotional stimuli. Individuals with low expression polymorphisms of the 5-HTTLPR gene (S and L[G]) demonstrated enhanced orienting to (Osinsky el al., 2008) and difficulties disengaging from emotional or fear-relevant stimuli (Bevers et al., 2009, 2010). A more detailed genotyping (Perez-Edgar et al., 2010), including all possible combinations of the S, L(G), and L(A) polymorphisms, suggests that there may be a linear relationship between expected 5-HTTLPR expression and attentional orienting to emotional stimuli. Increasing 5-HTTLPR expression was correlated with increases in attentional bias toward negative emotion and decreasing bias toward positive emotion. Because this nascent field is rapidly evolving, undoubtedly other single nucleotide polymorphisms will also be found to contribute to emotional influences on attention. Neurogenomics studies will be useful for linking these serotonergic actions to activity in the relevant processing networks.

MULTICHANNEL SOCIAL ORIENTING: GAZE–EXPRESSION INTERACTIONS

The face contains a rich source of information used during human social interaction. Although much research has elucidated the neural substrates of components of facial processing, how the brain integrates the variety of signals conveyed by the face during dyadic exchanges remains an important goal in social neuroscience. Developmental research on joint attention has long shown that infants acquire information about the utility of environmental stimuli by following nonverbal cues from caregivers, including facial expression, gaze, gesture, and prosody (Klinnert et al., 1983). Learning how to interpret subtle changes in these cues and integrating information across multiple nonverbal channels remains important for maintaining healthy social relationships throughout the lifespan. Although several studies have begun to explore how brain regions such as the amygdala respond to both gaze and expression (Adams et al., 2003), few neuroscientific studies have incorporated multiple nonverbal cues to investigate social attentional orienting.

An experimental paradigm that can facilitate this research objective is an adaptation of the Posner cueing paradigm, which uses facial expressions with averted gaze as attention-directing cues. Such gaze-cueing studies have reliably demonstrated that individuals automatically shift their attention to gazed-at locations, even if they are told that gaze direction does not predict where the target will appear (e.g., Friesen & Kingstone, 1998; see Frischen, Bayliss, & Tipper, 2007, for a review). Additionally, ERP studies have shown that peripheral targets presented at the gazed-at location (valid) elicit enhanced P1 responses and decreased P3 responses compared to targets presented in the opposite (invalid) visual field (Schuller & Rossion, 2001, 2004, 2005).

Behavioral studies extending this paradigm to investigate the effect of facial expression on reflexive orienting, however, have yielded mixed results. In a series of experiments, Hietanen and Leppänen (2003) examined the effects of facial expression (happy, angry, fearful and neutral) and gaze direction on target detection. Although participants were consistently faster at detecting targets that appeared in a gazed-at location (the cueing effect), there was no evidence that the cueing effect was modulated by facial expression. Using happy, angry and neutral faces, Hori and colleagues (2005) found that the cueing effect of gaze was not consistently affected by facial expression, being larger for happy female faces only. Using the participants' eye movements as the dependent measure, Bonifacci and colleagues (2008) showed that participants made more errors locating invalidly compared to validly cued targets and took longer to locate targets following angry faces. Bayliss and colleagues (2007) did not observe any differences in orienting to targets cued by disgusted and happy faces, but the expression of the face cue affected participants' evaluations of the targets—objects cued by happy faces were liked more than those cued by disgusted faces. Taken together, these studies indicate that facial expression does not consistently modulate reflexive orienting to gaze. Such discrepant findings suggest that the interaction of expression and gaze on attentional orienting depends on the parameters of the task. Graham and colleagues (2010) directly investigated this question and found cue–target SOA to play an important role in the impact of expression on the gaze validity effect. At short SOAs (<250 ms), the effects of expression and gaze were independent, with emotional expressions speeding up reaction times across all gaze conditions, but at long SOAs (>500 ms), trials with emotional expressions demonstrated enhanced validity effects. This temporal dissociation implicates relatively parallel processing of affect and gaze in faces early on during stimulus processing, with integration of these multiple channels of social communication emerging somewhat later in time (see also Graham & LaBar, 2007), between 300 and 500 ms poststimulus (see Klucharev & Sams, 2004; Pourtois et al., 2004; Graham et al., 2010).

Other studies have reported modulation of the cueing effect by facial expression, but only after individual differences are taken into account. Mathews, Fox, Yiend and Calder (2003) found that the cueing effect did not differ in magnitude for neutral and fearful face cues in nonanxious participants, but it was significantly larger for fearful faces in anxious individuals. Enhanced orienting to fearful faces and attenuated orienting to angry faces in highly anxious individuals were also observed in a subsequent study (Fox et al., 2007). Thus, gaze in fearful faces is a more powerful trigger for reflexive orienting for highly anxious individuals.

Tipples (2006) examined whether emotional (fearful and happy) faces enhanced orienting to gaze in a target identification task, as well as the role of individual differences on the cueing effect. This study found evidence for an enhanced cueing effect when the face cue was fearful but not neutral or happy. There was also a positive correlation between trait fearfulness and the cueing effect, especially for fearful faces. Putman, Hermans, and van Honk (2006) reported similar findings in which the cueing effect for fearful expressions was larger than that for happy expressions, and the magnitude of this effect was correlated with state anxiety. Holmes, Richards, and Green (2006, Experiment 3) found that the cueing effect was larger for fearful and angry faces relative to happy and neutral face cues; however, this was only true for high state-anxious participants.

In sum, the behavioral studies investigating gaze–expression interactions on attentional orienting are inconclusive. In addition to differences in experimental design across studies, one possibility is that emotional expression and gaze influences do not converge onto the same stage of target processing, which may increase the variability in behavioral effects. By varying the task (target detection, location, or discrimination) and timing (cue–target SOA, target duration), previous studies may be engaging somewhat different neural mechanisms.

Event-related potential studies have shed some light on these issues by comparing how facial expressions in gaze-directional cues impact waveform components elicited to subsequent attentional targets. Across two studies, early visual responses to the targets (occipital P1 component) were modulated by the expression of the cueing face, with larger P1 responses following fearful faces compared to neutral (Fichtenholtz et al., 2009) (Figure 12.5), and happy faces compared to fearful faces (Fichtenholtz et al., 2007). Consistent with previous studies using neutral face cues, long-latency P3 responses were reduced for valid compared to invalid targets (except for trials with happy cues) (Fichtenholtz et al., 2007, 2009). This separation of expression and gaze effects

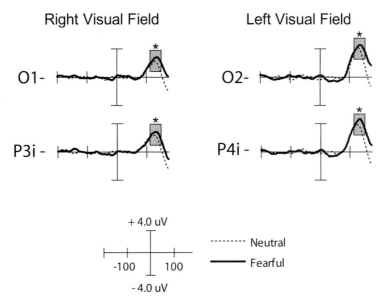

FIGURE 12.5 Negative emotional expression enhances target processing during gaze-directed cueing. Event-related potential (ERP) waveforms of the P1 component comparing targets preceded by fearful and neutral expressions. The left column is the response to right visual field targets from left (contralateral) occipital electrode sites. The right column is the response to left visual field targets from right (contralateral) occipital electrode sites. Responses are time-locked to the onset of the target. From Fichtenholtz, H. M., Hopfinger, J. B., Graham, R., Detwiler, J. M., & LaBar, K. S. (2009). Event-related potentials reveal temporal staging of dynamic emotional expression and gaze shift effects on attentional orienting. *Social Neuroscience, 4*, 317–331, with permission of the publisher.

is consistent with the behavioral results using short SOAs (Graham et al., 2010). Additionally, De Jong and colleagues (2008) found that, using a long SOA, participants exhibit enhanced P1 and N1 responses following trials with increasingly fearful faces, but not following trials with reductions in fear. Interestingly, participants with autism (De Jong et al., 2008) and Asperger's syndrome (Uono et al., 2009) show no difference between fearful and neutral cues in their effects on ERP responses to subsequent attentional targets.

One limitation of most of the existing expression-gaze cueing studies to date is that the targets following the gaze cues have been emotionally neutral. However, it is possible that, for the meaning of the facial expression to be optimally processed, the presence of a facial expression should predict an impending affective stimulus that requires some valenced appraisal. Consistent with this idea, when participants are explicitly evaluating the emotional valence of verbal targets, there are greater behavioral attentional orienting effects following negative expressions relative to neutral or happy expressions (Pecchinenda et al., 2008). The emotion manipulation in this report had no effect when participants were engaged in a neutral task in response to the verbal targets (identifying whether the words were in upper- or lowercase). Fichtenholtz and colleagues (2007) further showed robust ERP effects on valenced targets following expression-gaze cues. Early processing benefits (P1 amplitude enhancement over contralateral occipital sites) were found following happy expressions, and positively valenced targets elicited faster P3 responses. These positivity effects were not spatially directed, supporting the idea that positive states broaden attentional focus and initiate approach responses. Fearful expression reduced P3 amplitude for gazed-at targets, providing evidence of enhanced spatially directed attention following negative cues, as predicted by the

Easterbrook hypothesis. These studies highlight the utility of conducting ecologically valid experiments in which affective cues predict affective outcomes, which will help to bridge laboratory studies of attention with real-world applications, in order to understand how attention is directed and used during socioemotional exchanges.

CONCLUSION

The presence of an emotional target in a complex environment biases initial attentional orienting and subsequent sustained attention responses to visual stimuli. These effects occur across both overt and covert attentional paradigms, and in some cases appear to be obligatory. Patients who suffer from hemispatial neglect may exhibit benefits in detecting stimuli in the contralesional field when they are affectively salient, indicating parallel pathways for attentional control and emotional evaluation. Cognitive neuroscience research is beginning to reveal how ventral limbic regions specialized for emotional signaling, such as the amygdala, interact with dorsal frontoparietal networks to bias sensory processing and initiate actions. Several emotion–attention hubs exist in the ventral and medial prefrontal cortex, insula, and anterior cingulate to link the affective and emotional control of behavior. In the presence of negative affect and anxiety, spatially directed attention is enhanced, which may be related in part to individual differences in serotonergic function. Gaze and expression are processed in partially independent systems up to approximately 300 ms after stimulus onset, at which point interaction effects emerge across these facial communication channels. Spatially directed attention effects are generally stronger for negative than positive stimuli, which supports theories positing that negative affect restricts the use of cues in the environment (thereby directing attention to select locations), whereas positive affect broadens attentional focus and approach behaviors toward other agents (irrespective of their spatial locus). Future studies should use ecologically valid paradigms to assay emotional influences on social attention and include a variety of emotions in the same research design to more directly test valence-based hypotheses of emotion–attention interactions.

ACKNOWLEDGMENTS

This work was supported in part by NIH grant 2 P01 NS041328.

References

Adams, R. B., Gordon, H. L., Baird, A. A., Ambady, N., & Kleck, R. E. (2003). Effects of gaze on amygdala sensitivity to anger and fear faces. *Science, 300,* 1536–1537.

Alpers, G. W. (2008). Eye-catching: Right hemisphere attentional bias for emotional pictures. *Laterality, 13,* 158–178.

Amaral, D. G., Price, J. L., Pitkanen, A., & Carmichael, S. T. (1992). Anatomical organization of the primate amygdaloid complex. In J. P. Aggleton (Ed.), *The amygdala: Neurobiological aspects of emotion, memory, and mental dysfunction* (pp. 1–66). New York: Wiley-Liss.

Anderson, A. K., Christoff, K., Panitz, D., De Rosa, E., & Gabrieli, J. D. (2003). Neural correlates of the automatic processing of threat facial signals. *Journal of Neuroscience, 23,* 5627–5633.

Armony, J. L., & Dolan, R. J. (2002). Modulation of spatial attention by fear conditioned stimuli: An event related fMRI study. *Neuropsychologia, 40,* 817–826.

Bannermann, R. L., Milders, M., de Gelder, B., & Sahraie, A. (2009). Orienting to threat: Faster localization of fearful facial expressions and body postures revealed by saccadic eye movements. *Proceedings of the Royal Society of London. Series B, Biological Sciences, 276,* 1635–1641.

Bannerman, R. L., Milders, M., & Sahraie, A. (2010). Attentional cueing: Fearful body postures capture attention with saccades. *Journal of Vision, 10,* 1–14.

Bayle, D. J., Henaff, M. A., & Krolak-Salmon, P. (2009). Unconsciously perceived fear in peripheral vision alerts the limbic system: a MEG study. *PLoS One, 4,* e8207, http://www.plosone.org/article/info:doi%2F10.1371%2Fjournal.pone.0008207

Bayliss, A. P., Frischen, A., Fenske, M. J., & Tipper, S. P. (2007). Affective evaluations of objects are influenced by observed gaze direction and emotional expression. *Cognition, 104*(3), 644–653.

Beevers, C. G., Pacheco, J., Clasen, P., McGeary, J. E., & Schnyer, D. (2010). Prefrontal morphology, 5-HTTLPR polymorphism and biased attention for emotional stimuli. *Genes, Brain, & Behavior, 9,* 224–233.

Beevers, C. G., Wells, T. T., Ellis, A. J., & McGeary, J. E. (2009). Association of the serotonin transporter gene promoter region (5-HTTLPR) polymorphism with biased attention for emotional stimuli. *Journal of Abnormal Psychology, 118*, 670–681.

Bonifacci, P., Ricciardelli, P., Lugli, L., & Pellicano, A. (2008). Emotional attention: Effects of emotion and gaze direction on overt orienting of visual attention. *Cognitive Processing, 9*, 127–135.

Bryant, R. A., Harvey, A. G., Gordon, E., & Barry, R. J. (1995). Eye movement and electrodermal responses to threat stimuli in post-traumatic stress disorder. *International Journal of Psychophysiology, 20*, 209–213.

Brosch, T., Sander, D., Pourtois, G., & Scherer, K. R. (2008). Beyond fear: Rapid spatial orienting toward positive emotional stimuli. *Psychological Science, 19*, 362–370.

Cahill, L., & McGaugh, J. L. (1998). Mechanisms of emotional arousal and lasting declarative memory. *Trends in Neurosciences, 21*, 294–299.

Calvo, M. G., Nummenmaa, L., & Hoyona, J. (2007). Emotional and neutral scenes in competition: Orienting, efficiency, and identification. *Quarterly Journal of Experimental Psychology, 60*, 1585–1593.

Carlson, J. M., Reinke, K. S., & Habib, R. (2009). A left amygdala mediated network for rapid orienting to masked fearful faces. *Neuropsychologia, 47*, 1386–1389.

Chao, H. F. (2010). Inhibition of return to negative emotion: Evidence from an emotional expression detection task. *Emotion, 10*, 272–277.

Corbetta, M., & Shulman, G. L. (2002). Control of goal-directed and stimulus-driven attention in the brain. *Nature Reviews. Neuroscience, 3*, 201–215.

Derryberry, D., & Tucker, D. M. (1994). Motivating the focus of attention. In P. M. Niedenthal & S. Kitayama (Eds.), *The heart's eye: Emotional influences in perception and attention* (pp. 170–197). San Diego: Academic Press.

Deutsch, R., & Strack, F. (2006). Duality models in social psychology: From dual processes to interacting systems. *Psychological Inquiry, 17*, 166–172.

De Jong, M. C., van Engeland, H., & Kemner, C. (2008). Attentional effects of gaze shifts are influenced by emotion and spatial frequency, but not in autism. *Journal of the American Academy of Child & Adolescent Psychiatry, 47*, 444–455.

Easterbrook, J. A. (1959). The effect of emotion on cue utilization and the organization of behavior. *Psychological Review, 66*, 183–201.

Fichtenholtz, H. M., Dean, H. L., Dillon, D. G., Yamasaki, H., McCarthy, G., & LaBar, K. S. (2004). Emotion-attention network interactions during a visual oddball task. *Brain Research. Cognitive Brain Research, 20*, 67–80.

Fichtenholtz, H. M., Hopfinger, J. B., Graham, R., Detwiler, J. M., & LaBar, K. S. (2007). Facial expressions and emotional targets produce separable ERP effects in a gaze directed attention study. *Social, Cognitive, and Affective Neuroscience, 2*, 323–333.

Fichtenholtz, H. M., Hopfinger, J. B., Graham, R., Detwiler, J. M., & LaBar, K. S. (2009). Event-related potentials reveal temporal staging of dynamic emotional expression and gaze shift effects on attentional orienting. *Social Neuroscience, 4*, 317–331.

Friesen, C. K., & Kingstone, A. (1998). The eyes have it! Reflexive orienting is triggered by nonpredictive gaze. *Psychonomic Bulletin and Review, 5*, 490–495.

Frischen, A., Bayliss, A. P., & Tipper, S. P. (2007). Gaze cueing of attention: Visual attention, social cognition, and individual differences. *Psychological Bulletin, 133*, 694–724.

Fox, E. (2002). Processing emotional facial expressions: The role of anxiety and awareness. *Cognitive, Affective & Behavioral Neuroscience, 2*, 52–63.

Fox, E., Mathews, A., Calder A., & Yiend, J. (2007). Anxiety and sensitivity to gaze direction in emotionally expressive faces. *Emotion, 7*(3), 478–486.

Friedrickson, B. L. (2001). The role of positive emotions in positive psychology: The broaden and build theory of positive emotions. *American Psychologist, 56*, 218–226.

Gallagher, M., & Holland, P. C. (1994). The amygdala complex: Multiple roles in associative learning and attention. *Proceedings of the National Academy of Sciences of the United States of America, 91*, 11771–11776.

Graham, R., Friesen, C. K., Fichtenholtz, H. M., & LaBar, K. S. (2010). Modulation of reflexive orienting to gaze direction by facial expressions. *Visual Cognition, 18*, 331–368.

Graham, R., & LaBar, K. S. (2007). Garner interference reveals dependencies between emotional expression and gaze in face perception. *Emotion, 7*, 296–313.

Grandjean, D., Sander, D., Lucas, N., Scherer, K. R., & Vuilleumier, P. (2008). Effects of emotional prosody on auditory extinction for voices in patients with spatial neglect. *Neuropsychologia, 46*, 487–496.

Heuer, F., & Reisberg, D. (1990). Vivid memories of emotional events: The accuracy of remembered minutiae. *Memory & Cognition, 18*, 496–506.

Hietanen, J. K., & Leppänen, J. M. (2003). Does facial expression affect attention orienting by gaze direction cues? *Journal of Experimental Psychology.*

Human Perception and Performance, 29(6), 1228–1243.

Holmes, A., Richards, A., & Green, S. (2006). Anxiety and sensitivity to eye gaze in emotional faces. *Brain and Cognition, 60*, 282–294.

Hopfinger, J. B., & Mangun, G. R. (1998). Reflexive attention modulates processing of visual stimuli in human extrastriate cortex. *Psychological Science, 9*, 441–447.

Hopfinger, J. B., & Mangun, G. R. (2001). Tracking the influence of reflexive attention on sensory and cognitive processing. *Cognitive, Affective, & Behavioral Neuroscience, 1*, 56–65.

Hori, E., Tazumi, T., Umeno, K., Kamachi, M., Kobayashi, T., Ono, T., & Nishijo, H. (2005). Effects of facial expression on shared attention mechanisms. *Physiology & Behavior, 84*(3), 397–405.

Isen, A. M. (1987). Positive affect, cognitive processes, and social behavior. In L. Berkowitz (Ed.), *Advances in experimental social psychology* (Vol. 20, pp. 203–253). New York: Academic Press.

Johnson, M. K., & Weisz, C. (1994). Comments on unconscious processing: Finding emotion in the cognitive stream. In P. M. Niedenthal, & S. Kitayama (eds.), *The heart's eye: Emotional influences in perception and attention* (pp. 146–169). San Diego: Academic Press.

Kissler, J., & Keil, A. (2008). Look-don't look! How emotional pictures affect pro- and anti-saccades. *Experimental Brain Research, 188*, 215–222.

Klinnert, M. D., Campos, J. J., Sorce, J. F., Emde, R. N., & Svejda, M. (1983). The development of social referencing in infancy. In R. Plutchik, & H. Kellerman (Eds.), *Emotion: Theory, research, and experience: Vol. 2. Emotion in early development* (pp. 57–86). New York: Academic Press.

Klucharev, V., & Sams, M. (2004). Interaction of gaze direction and facial expression processing: An ERP study. *Neuroreport, 15*, 621–626.

Kwak, S. M., Na, D. L., Kim, G., Kim, G. S., & Lee, J. H. (2007). Use of eye movement to measure smokers' attentional bias to smoking-related cues. *Cyberpsychology & Behavior, 10*, 299–304.

LaBar, K. S. (2007). Beyond fear: Emotional memory mechanisms in the human brain. *Current Directions in Psychological Science, 16*, 173–177.

LaBar, K. S. (2010). Emotion-cognition interactions. In G. F. Koob, M, LeMoal, & R. F. Thompson (Eds.), *Encyclopedia of behavioral neuroscience* (Vol. 1, pp. 469–476). New York: Elsevier Science.

LaBar, K. S., Mesulam, M.-M., Gitelman, D. R., & Weintraub, S. (2000). Emotional curiosity: Modulation of visuospatial attention by arousal is preserved in aging and early-stage Alzheimer's disease. *Neuropsychologia, 38*, 1734–1740.

LeDoux, J. E. (1990). The limbic system concept. *Concepts in Neuroscience, 2*, 169–199.

Lykins, A. D., Meana, M., & Kambe, G. (2006). Detection of differential viewing patterns to erotic and non-erotic stimuli using eye-tracking methodology. *Archives of Sexual Behavior, 35*, 569–575.

Mangun, G. R., & Hillyard, S. A. (1991). Modulations of sensory-evoked brain potentials indicate changes in perceptual processing during visual-spatial priming. *Journal of Experimental Psychology. Human Perception & Performance, 17*, 1057–1074.

Mathews, A., Fox, E., Yeind, J., & Calder, A. (2003). The face of fear: Effects of eye gaze and emotion on visual attention. *Visual Cognition, 10*, 823–835.

Matthews, G., & Wells, A. (2000). Attention, automaticity, and affective disorder. *Behavior Modification, 24*, 69–93.

Mayberg, H. (1997). Limbic-cortical dysregulation: A proposed model of depression. *Journal of Neuropsychiatry and Clinical Neuroscience, 9*, 471–481.

McDonald, J. J., Ward, L. M., & Kiehl, K. A. (1999). An event-related brain potential study of inhibition of return. *Perception & Psychophysics, 61*, 1411–1423.

Mesulam, M. M. (1998). From sensation to cognition. *Brain, 121*, 1013–1052.

Mesulam, M. M. (1981). A cortical network for directed attention and unilateral neglect syndrome. *Annals of Neurology, 10*, 309–325.

Metcalfe, J., & Mischel, W. (1999). A hot/cool-system analysis of delay of gratification: Dynamics of willpower. *Psychological Review, 106*, 3–19.

Mogg, K., Garner, M., & Bradley, B. P. (2007). Anxiety and orienting of gaze to angry and fearful faces. *Biological Psychology, 76*, 163–169.

Mogg, K., Millar, N., & Bradley, B. P. (2000). Biases in eye movements to threatening facial expressions in generalized anxiety disorder and depressive disorder. *Journal of Abnormal Psychology, 109*, 695–704.

Morris, J. S., DeGelder, B., Weiskrantz, L., & Dolan, R. J. (2001). Differential extrageniculostriate and amygdala responses to presentation of emotional faces in a cortically blind field. *Brain, 124*, 1241–1252.

Murty, V. P., Ritchey, M., Adcock, R. A., & LaBar, K. S. (2010). FMRI studies of emotional memory encoding: A quantitative meta-analysis. *Neuropsychologia.* In press.

Nummenmaa, L., Hyona, J., & Calvo, M. G. (2006). Eye movement assessment of selective attentional capture by emotional pictures. *Emotion, 6,* 257–268.

Nummenmaa, L., Hyona, J., & Calvo, M. G. (2009). Emotional scene content drives the saccade generation system reflexively. *Journal of Experimental Psychology. Human Perception & Performance, 35,* 305–323.

Ochsner, K. N., & Gross, J. J. (2005). The cognitive control of emotion. *Trends in Cognitive Sciences, 9,* 242–249.

Osinsky, R., Reuter, M., Kupper, Y., Schmitz, A., Kozyra, E., Alexander, N., & Henning, J. (2008). Variation in the serotonin transporter gene modulates selective attention to threat. *Emotion, 8,* 584–588.

Pauli, W. M., & Roder, B. (2008). Emotional salience changes the focus of spatial attention. *Brain Research, 1214,* 94–104,

Pecchinenda, A., Pes, M., Ferlazzo, F., & Zoccolotti, P. (2008). The combined effect of gaze direction and facial expression on cueing spatial attention. *Emotion, 8,* 628–634.

Perez-Edgar, K., Bar-Haim, Y., McDermott, J. M., Gorodetsky, E., Hodgkinson, C. A., Goldman, D., et al. (2010). Variations in the serotonin-transporter gene are associated with attention bias patterns to positive and negative emotion faces. *Biological Psychology, 83,* 269–271.

Pessoa, L. (2008). On the relationship between emotion and cognition. *Nature Reviews. Neuroscience, 9,* 128–158.

Posner, M. I. (1980). Orienting of Attention, *Quarterly Journal of Experimental Psychology, 32,* 3–25.

Posner, M. I., Cohen, Y., & Rafal, R. D. (1982). Neural systems control over spatial orienting. *Philosophical Transactions of the Royal Society of London. Series B, Biological Sciences, 2908,* 187–198.

Pourtois, G., Grandjean, D., Sander, D., & Vuilleumier, P. (2004). Electrophysiological correlates of rapid spatial orienting towards fearful faces. *Cerebral Cortex, 14,* 619–633.

Pourtois, G., Schwartz, S., Seghier, M. L., Lazeyras, F., & Vuilleumier, P. (2006). Neural systems for orienting attention to the location of threat signals: An event-related fMRI study. *NeuroImage, 31,* 920–93.

Putman, P., Hermans, E., & van Honk, J. (2006). Anxiety meets fear in perception of dynamic expressive gaze. *Emotion, 6,* 94–102.

Rinck, M., & Becker, E. S. (2006). Spider fearful individuals attend to threat, then quickly avoid it: Evidence from eye movements. *Journal of Abnormal Psychology, 115,* 231–238.

Sander, D., Grafman, J., & Zalla, T. (2003). The human amygdala: An evolved system for relevance detection. *Reviews in the Neurosciences, 14,* 303–316.

Santesso, D. L., Meuret, A. E., Hofmann, S. G., Meuller, E. M., Ratner, K. G., Roesch, E. B., & Pizzagalli, D. A. (2008). Electrophysiological correlates of spatial orienting towards angry faces: A source localization study. *Neuropsychologia, 46,* 1338–1348.

Schuller, A.-M., & Rossion, B. (2001). Spatial attention triggered by eye gaze increases and speeds up early visual activity. *Neuroreport, 12,* 1–7.

Schuller, A.-M., & Rossion, B. (2004). Perception of static eye gaze direction facilitates subsequent early visual processing. *Clinical Neurophysiology, 115,* 1161–1168.

Schuller, A.-M., & Rossion, B. (2005). Spatial attention triggered by eye gaze enhances and speeds up visual processing in upper and lower fields beyond early striate visual processing. *Clinical Neurophysiology, 116,* 2565–2576.

Stormark, K. M., & Hugdahl, K. (1996). Peripheral cueing of covert spatial attention before and after emotional conditioning of the cue. *International Journal of Neuroscience, 86,* 225–240.

Stormark, K. M., Hugdahl, K., & Posner, M. I. (1999). Emotional modulation of attention orienting: A classical conditioning study. *Scandinavian Journal of Psychology, 40,* 91–99.

Stormark, K. M., Norby, H., & Hugdahl, K. (1995). Attentional shifts to emotionally charged cues: Behavioural and ERP data. *Cognition and Emotion, 9,* 507–523.

Tipples, J. (2006). Fear and fearfulness potentiate automatic orienting to eye gaze. *Cognition and Emotion, 20,* 309–320.

Uono, S., Sato, W., & Toichi, M. (2009). Dynamic fearful gaze does not enhance attention orienting in individuals with Asperger's disorder. *Brain & Cognition, 71,* 229–233.

Vuilleumier, P. (2000). Faces call for attention: Evidence from patients with visual extinction. *Neuropsychologia, 38,* 692–700.

Vuilleumier, P., Armony, J. L., Clarke, K., Husain, M., Driver, J., & Dolan, R. J. (2002). Neural response to emotional faces with and without awareness: Event-related fMRI in a parietal patient with visual extinction and spatial neglect. *Neuropsychologia, 40,* 2156–2166.

Vuilleumier, P., Armony, J. L., Driver, J., & Dolan, R. J. (2003). Distinct spatial frequency sensitivities for processing faces and emotional expressions. *Nature Neuroscience, 6,* 624–631.

Vuilleumier, P., & Driver, J. (2007). Modulation of visual processing by attention and emotion: Windows on causal interactions between human brain regions. *Philosophical Transactions of the Royal Society London. Series B, Biological Sciences, 362*, 837–855.

Vuilleumier, P., & Schwartz, S. (2001a). Emotional facial expressions capture attention. *Neurology, 56*, 153–158.

Vuilleumier, P., & Schwartz, S. (2001b). Beware and be aware: Capture of spatial attention by fear-related stimuli in neglect. *Neuroreport, 12*, 1119–1122.

Williams, M. A., & Mattingley, J. B. (2004). Unconscious perception of non-threatening facial emotion in parietal extinction. *Experimental Brain Research, 154*, 403–406.

Woldorff, M. G., Hazlett, C. J., Fichtenholtz, H. M., Weissman, D. H., Dale, A. M., & Song, A. W. (2004). Functional parcellation of attentional control regions of the brain. *Journal of Cognitive Neuroscience, 16*, 149–165.

Young, M. P. (1993). The organization of neural systems in the primate cerebral cortex. *Proceedings of the Royal Society London. Series B, Biological Sciences, 252*, 13–18.

Endnotes

Chapter 2

1. An important detail of the analysis is that we used the adjacent response (ADJAR) filter method (Woldorff, 1993) to separate the cue processing from the target processing. Without a method to separate these processes, data from the short cue–target interval condition would have been contaminated by overlap between cues and targets. This method iteratively estimates and subtracts the cue processing from the target processing to isolate the target processing; importantly, it allows the effects of involuntary attention to be examined.

Chapter 4

1. Computational complexity is a theoretical area of computer science whose main concern is to provide a formal mathematical means to understanding the difficulty of computational problems. Of interest are the resources required to run algorithms and the overall cost of solutions, and the inherent difficulty in providing algorithms that are efficient for both general and specific computational problems. It is relevant in this context because it provides a way to address the memory and time processing requirements for vision problems in a general manner that is independent of the realization of solution; that is, independent of whether one is considering the brain or a computer.

2. There have been many formulations of winner-take-all processes (see Yuille & Geiger, 1995, for an overview). The one used by ST is unique and allows for proofs of convergence and convergence time. Of interest is the fact that its time to convergence is dependent only on the relative strength of the stimuli (or rather, neural responses to stimuli). It has been described in detail in Tsotsos et al. (1995).

Chapter 9

1. Consider the alternative that morphological diversity in visuomotor areas exists without corresponding functional diversity. Such an outcome has never been found in the visual pathway beginning in the retina (Masland, 2001), dorsal lateral geniculate nucleus (Casagrande, 1994; Hendry & Reid, 2000), or primary visual cortex (e.g., Group et al., 2008 July). In fact,

microcircuits of bewildering complexity have been described in visual cortex (Nassi & Callaway, 2009). And morphological complexity only increases in the frontal lobe (Elston, 2003).

Chapter 10

1. Note that Matsukura, Luck, and Vecera (2007) found that participants could not reorient attention to initially uncued items according to a second spatial retrocue. However, the ability to reorient to previously unattended items in VSTM is likely to depend on the overall demands of the task. In both Lepsien and Nobre (2007) and Landman et al. (2003), the initial retrocue was only directed to one item, whereas the cues used in Matsukura et al. (2007) retrospectively cued attention to all items in one or other hemifield. Multiple cued locations might have increased the cognitive demands (Makovski & Jiang, 2007) thereby limiting the flexibility of attentional control.

Index

Stimulus-response mapping, working memory, 192
Stimulus-reward associations, monkeys learning, 181–183
Stimulus selection
    circuitry for, in midbrain system, 140, 142–144
    forebrain salience map for bottom-up, 138–139
    midbrain network for birds, 142*f*
    midbrain salience map for bottom-up, 139–140
Stochastic accumulator models, 202
Stochastic models, reaction time, 202
Strategies, visual attention, 83–84
Stroop effect, 230
Stroop tasks. *See also* Cognitive control loop theory
    auditory emotional, 240
    blocked-design, 232
    cognitive counting, 238
    color-word, 231*f*, 232, 234, 243, 246
    conflict control loop theory, 230–232
    cross-modal, 236
    emotional counting, 238–239
    emotional facial, 240, 242
    facial, 236, 237*f*
Subthreshold microstimulation, frontal eye field (FEF) driving
        attention, 156–159
Summing junction, lateral intraparietal (LIP), 178–179
Superior colliculus
    covert spatial attention, 159
    gaze shift in mammals, 134
    inactivation effect on target selection for gaze in monkey, 145*f*
    midbrain gaze control, 136–138
    reflexive and voluntary attention, 162
    sensory responses, 139–140
    switch-like response suppression, 140, 141*f*
    visual cortex, 152
Superior parietal lobule (SPL), dorsal attention network, 101–102
Superior temporal gyrus (STG), 113
Superior temporal sulcus (STS), 113
Supplementary eye field (SEF)
    dorsal attention network, 101–102
    oculomotor control tasks, 201
Suppression
    mechanisms, 84–92
    visual attention, 84
Supramarginal gyrus (SMG), temporoparietal jucntion (TPJ), 113
Surround suppression
    attentional beam after, 94*f*, 96*f*
    selective tuning, 91, 94–95
Switchboard function, thalamic reticular nucleus (TRN), 64–65

Target selection
    lateral intraparietal (LIP) area, 176–178
    neurophysiological metrics, 195
Task relevance, ventral attention network, 115
Task set preparation, stage theory of attention and action, 191–192
Temporoparietal junction (TPJ). *See also* Ventral frontoparietal
        attention network (VAN)
    distraction, 47–49
    involuntary attention, 37
    right TPJ during theory of mind (ToM), 115, 117
    ventral attention network (VAN), 103*f*
    ventral region, 116*f*
Thalamic reticular nucleus (TRN)
    attentional modulation in macaque, 65–67
    modulatory influences on lateral geniculate nucleus (LGN),
        63–65
    thalamus, 55
Thalamus. *See also* Lateral geniculate nucleus (LGN); Pulvinar
    functional magnetic resonance imaging (fMRI), 54–55
    lateral geniculate nucleus (LGN), 55–56

nuclei of visual, 55
    perception and cognition, 54
    pulvinar, 55, 73, 74
    sensory impulses, 54
Theory. *See* Conflict control loop theory; Stage theory of attention
        and action
Theory of mind (ToM), right temporoparietal junction (TPJ)
        activity during, 115, 117
Timing, interactions between ventral and dorsal attention networks,
        118
Top-down attention. *See also* Visual short-term memory (VSTM)
    lateral intraparietal (LIP) activity, 179–183
    set size effect, 176
    term, 160
Top-down control
    access to visual short-term memory (VSTM), 214–215
    facilitating memory retrieval, 218, 219*f*
    partial-report experiments, 216–217
    within VSTM, 215–222
Top-down localization, attentional beam after, 94*f*, 96*f*
Top-down mechanisms, processing during capture of attention, 43
Top-down selection, focus of attention, 11–14
Top-down sensitivity control, attention, 132*f*, 133
Topographic organization, dorsal attention network (DAN),
        105, 107
Transcranial magnetic stimulation (TMS), monkeys, 156–158
Trial-by-trial cuing, 7
Trial sequence, involuntary attention cuing paradigm, 32*f*

Uncued location
    long cue-target interval, 38*f*
    short cue-target interval, 36*f*

Ventral frontal cortex (VFC), ventral attention network, 113, 114
Ventral frontoparietal attention network (VAN). *See also* Dorsal
        frontoparietal attention network (DAN)
    beyond spatial reorienting, 114–115
    definition, 113–114
    filtering hypothesis, 115, 116*f*
    filtering irrelevant sensory information, 115
    functions, 114–118
    interaction with dorsal attention network (DAN), 118–119
    rapid serial visual presentation (RSVP), 115, 116*f*
    reorienting, 101
    stimulus-driven control of attention, 114
    stimulus-driven reorienting, 113, 115
    task relevance, 115
    temporoparietal junction (TPJ), 113
    theory of mind (ToM), 115, 117
    TPJ activity during theory of mind, 115, 117
    VAN and locus coeruleus/noradrenergic (LC–NE) system, 116*f*,
        117–118
    visual search paradigm, 115, 116*f*
    voxelwise statistical map, 103*f*
Visual attention
    basic selective tuning (ST) model, 85–87
    computational problems, 81–83
    feature based, 15
    mechanisms, 84–92
    object based, 19
    premotor theory, 196
    selective, 3
    spatial, 4, 7
    strategies, 83–84
    thalamus, 54–55
Visual cortex. *See also* Frontal eye field (FEF)
    attentional response modulation, 60*f*
    attention and neuronal correlates in, 151–152